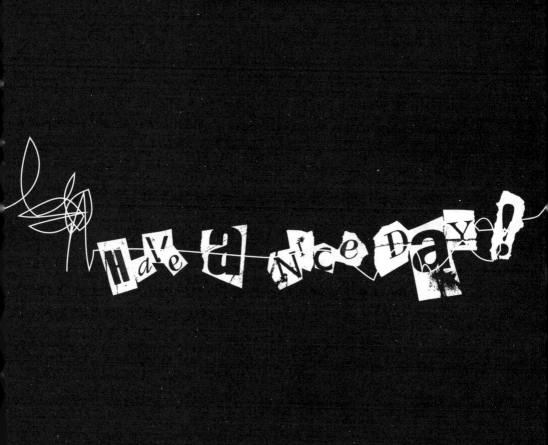

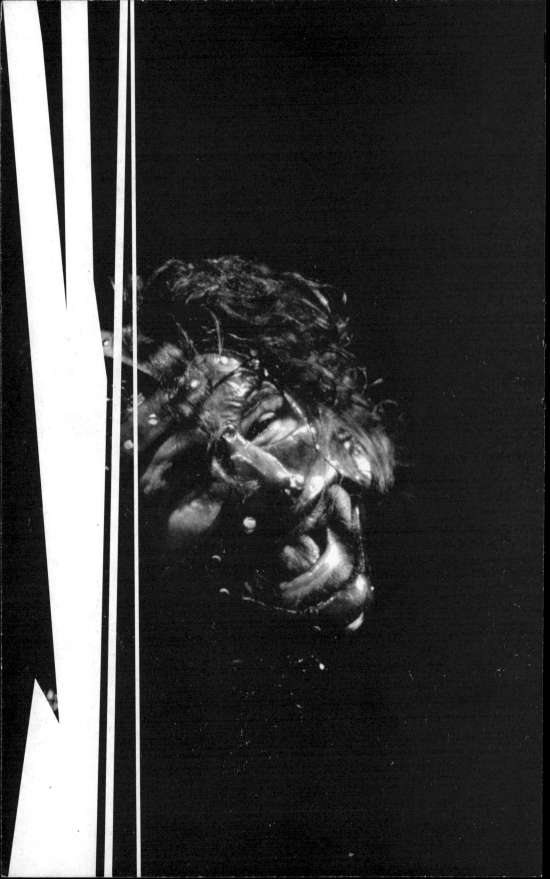

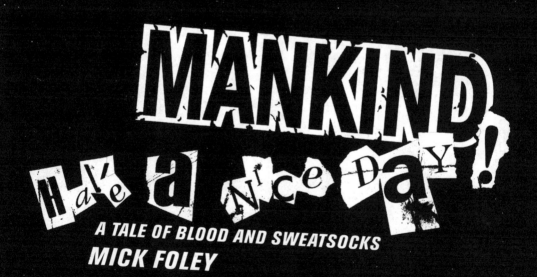

MANKIND

Have a Nice Day!

A TALE OF BLOOD AND SWEATSOCKS

MICK FOLEY

ReganBooks

An Imprint of HarperCollinsPublishers

MANKIN

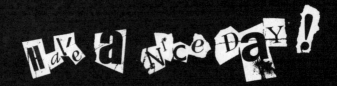

Designed by
P.R. Brown & Kyle Kushner @ bau-da design lab, inc.

ISBN 0-06-039299-1

99 00 01 02 03 ❖/qwv 20 19 18 17 16 15 14 13 12

For Owen and Brian

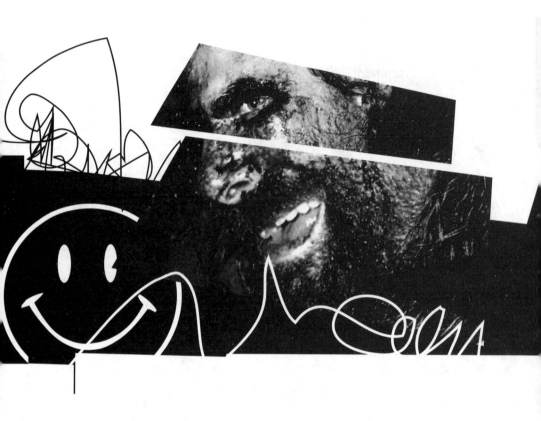

1

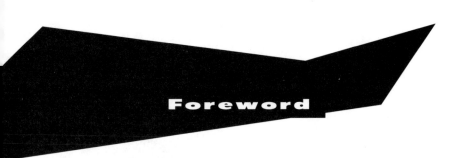

Foreword

In the three decades that I have had the privilege of broadcasting the unique product that is professional wrestling, I have never met anyone like Mick Foley. Wrestlers are often described as intimidating, insensitive, and illiterate, but these words do not accurately or fairly describe Mrs. Foley's baby boy. Mick Foley is a passionate man who loves his family and his chosen profession, in that order. This is the story of a man who as a child dreamed of entertaining the masses inside a wrestling ring and, in the face of overwhelming odds, succeeded.

This story speaks of sacrifice . . . of paying the retail price for success. What price? Try multiple concussions, a nose broken twice, a dislocated jaw, numerous knocked-out teeth, a broken wrist, a broken thumb, broken ribs, a broken toe, bone chips in his elbow, two herniated discs, more than 300 stitches, a torn abdominal muscle, a surgically repaired knee, and, oh yes, a partially amputated right ear! Indeed, Mick Foley has paid a helluva price to become one of the top stars in the sports-entertainment game.

This book traces the steps a semi-normal kid from Long Island took through a childhood cooked in normalcy, but spiced with Mick's own unique seasonings. You will read of the genuine sincerity with which Mick approaches everyday life, his love for performing, and his special bond with fans all over the world.

You will feel the experience that Mick has had in the most unique and, sometimes, controversial business in the world. It's a behind-the-scenes look through the eyes of one of the most honest men I've ever known in any walk of life.

Some of these stories, much like my own personal experience with Mick over the years, will make you laugh. Some will make you cry. And some will have you shaking your head in disbelief.

I guess in some ways this is a love story. The story of one man's love of his life. A life worth living.

—Jim Ross, September 1999

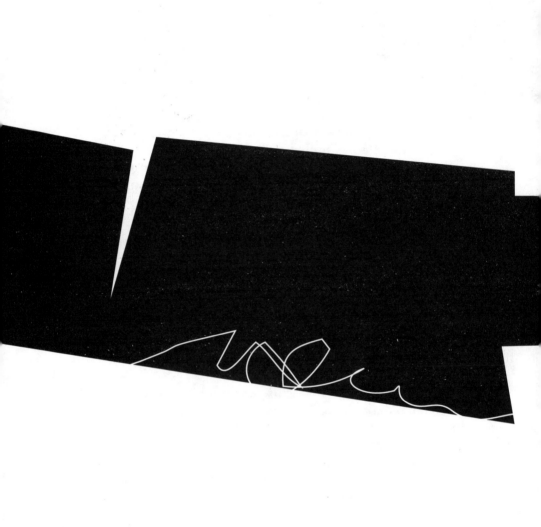

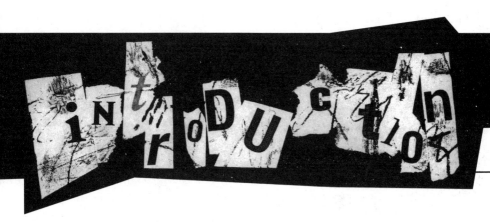

introduction

I came bounding in the door
of my house in the Florida Panhandle on May 17, 1999, with an almost unbelievable amount of energy. After a trip that had consisted of an hour's drive from my hotel in London to Heathrow Airport, a two-hour layover, an eight-and-a-half-hour flight to New York's JFK airport, a two-hour layover, a two-hour flight to Atlanta, another hour-and-a-half layover, a one-hour flight to Pensacola, and an hour drive home, I should have been exhausted. But I wasn't. My wife, Colette, saw how upbeat I was and assumed that I'd gotten a lot of sleep on the flight. "No, not really," I said. "Actually I didn't sleep at all." She suddenly got concerned and asked me if I'd done drugs while on the plane. "Of course not," I answered, but Colette looked worried. After all, what could account for this great rush of energy her normally exhausted husband had? "What have you been doing then," she asked, to which I answered, "Writing."

I had written the entire length of the trip back to Pensacola, as well as the whole way to England. Really, I'd been writing for almost the entire time since May 7, when I convinced the World Wrestling Federation's head of marketing that I could write my own autobiography. I hate to spoil this for a lot of people, but most autobiographies are not actually written by the supposed authors, but by biographers and ghostwriters. Talking into a tape recorder and having someone else make a book out of it didn't bother me, but the idea of "creative license" did. I just wasn't comfortable with the idea of a writer putting words in my mouth. If the book was boring, it wouldn't be the writer taking the rap, it would be me, and I wasn't willing to put that much faith in someone else's hands. Hey, if this book stinks, I want it to stink because of me. At least I want you as the reader to have the comfort of knowing that if the words stink, they are my own words, and if the stories stink, they are my stories as well.

My mom used to try to convince me to write a book when I was younger, because she thought I had a gift for it, but I lost interest when she told me that I couldn't write bad words in it. When I started wrestling, my dad told me I should keep a journal, so that one day I could write my memoirs. I kept saying that I would, and he kept telling me that I should do it soon, before I forgot everything. As it turned out, my memory is outstanding, which is a little scary considering all the shots I have taken to the head over the years. My main problem in writing this book is that my trusty old Sears electric typewriter, which I used to type out my school reports with one finger, had bitten the dust five years earlier, and being computer illiterate, I had no realistic way to put my story on paper. Except the old-fashioned way. So I hope you can appreciate that what you are about to read was written by hand on 760 pages of notebook paper in the seven weeks spanning May 7 to July 1, 1999.

There are a few different subjects I'd like to touch on before you embark on this daring literary journey into the world of sports-entertainment.

Hardcore Legend—I will occasionally refer to myself by this name throughout the pages of the book. Please don't take it seriously. I just get a kick out of referring to myself by that name.

Al Snow—Al Snow's name appears often, and what I say about him is not usually meant to be taken seriously. Al and I have had a long-standing insult contest, which had to be stopped a few months ago when feelings started getting hurt. It is my hope that the cheap shots and digs I get in at a defenseless Al will jump-start our contest, because causing Al Snow pain and embarrassment is one of the simple joys in my life. In truth, Al is a great guy and an excellent wrestler, and if he gets the chance to write a book, I would consider it an honor to be insulted by him in it. Then, after buying Al's book, I will buy some rock salt to sprinkle on all the places where hell just froze over.

Ric Flair—Hey, I know Ric Flair is a legend, and I enjoy him as a performer, but as a boss, I didn't think too much of him, and would be less than honest if I told it any other way.

I really hope that some of the people who read this are not wrestling fans. Professional wrestling is truly an amazing world, and I think that fan and nonfan alike will be intrigued by what goes on behind the scenes. I refer occasionally in the book to what I consider the three best things I have ever done in the wrestling business. Writing this book has been a joy and privilege, and I honestly feel that if I were to hang up the tights (or in my case the sweats) tomorrow, my career will have been made complete because of writing it. I now truly consider it among the four best things that I have ever done.

Enjoy the book, and if you do, recommend it to a friend because I would really consider it a triumph to see my name on the bestseller list. From then on, I could appear on talk shows as Mick Foley—Wrestler/Bestselling Author, and that, I know would make my parents proud. If you don't enjoy it, well, let's just keep that our little secret.

Read on, prosper, and oh, HAVE A NICE DAY.

Sincerely,

Mick Foley

July 1, 1999, in a trailer in Los Angeles on the set of the USA television series *GvsE*

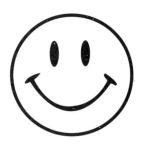

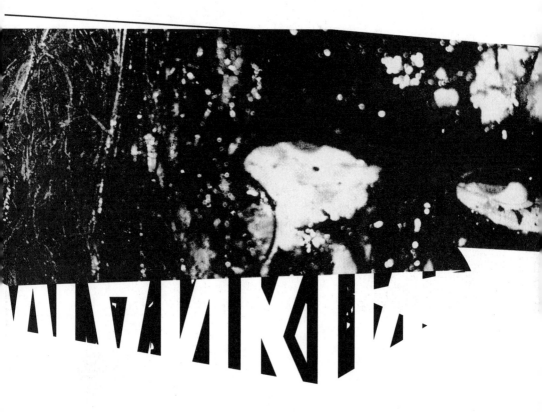

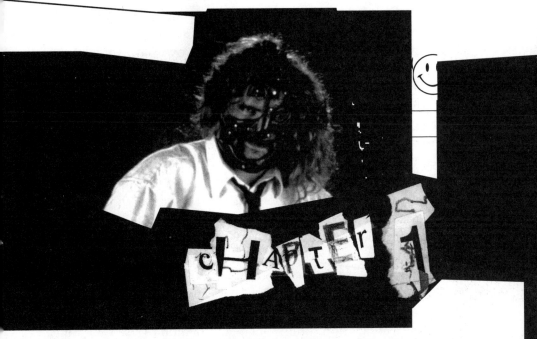

March 17, 1994, Munich, Germany

"I can't believe I lost my fucking ear; bang bang!" Now, I'm not a big proponent of the "F" word—in fact, I went from age six to age twenty-one without saying it once—but this was a special occasion and it cried out for a strong expletive. In fact, without the "F" word, that statement just isn't as impressive, is it? Bang bang? Well, for those who know, no explanation is necessary, and for those who don't, well, we'll get to "Bang bang" soon enough.

March 17, 1994, wasn't shaping up to be a real great day anyway, even before the F'ing ear in question was torn off the side of my head. I was not all that happy with my current place of employment. World Championship Wrestling was owned by Ted Turner, but even with Ted's deep pockets behind it, WCW had never really seemed to be on the right path. Part of the reason—a huge part of the reason, actually—was a blatant misuse of talent, a category that I, as Cactus Jack, certainly fell into. In this case we were on a two-week tour of Germany, and I was the only guy on the tour who spoke German. Good German. So it would seem like a natural to have Cactus Jack leading the promotional charge, right? Well, not exactly. In the first week of the tour, I did a few local radio spots while the other guys appeared on national television shows, print work, and promos.

On the first day of the tour Ric Flair, our booker (wrestling vernacular for the guy who makes or breaks you), admitted he wasn't familiar with my work as a babyface (good guy). Now, Flair was a legendary performer in the ring—great charisma, conditioning, and promos that could raise goose bumps on your arm. But apparently, preparation wasn't the Nature Boy's forte. Not familiar with my work? What the hell does that mean? It's his job to be familiar. I'd been a babyface for all of his fourteen months back with the company. I'd main-evented Pay-Per-Views that he wrestled on. Not being familiar with the talent he was in charge of meant that, in my book (and hey, this is my book), he was every bit as bad on the booking side of things as he was great on the wrestling side of it.

About an hour before the match, Flair had talked to me for a long time about changing the course of my career. Naitch, short for Nature Boy, felt that I needed to be a heel (bad guy). His rationale was simple. "You and Vader had the most brutal bouts I've ever witnessed," began Flair in his trademark voice, a strange combination of lisping and perfect enunciation. "But your rematch didn't raise the ratings at all. Nobody cares about you as a babyface."

Even before the Monday night *Raw/Nitro* wars, WCW had always lived and died by its television ratings. At that time, its flagship show was *WCW Saturday Night*. Also at that time, there were no quarter-hour breakdowns to more accurately determine just who was responsible for viewing patterns. In other words, Flair was holding my fifteen minutes on air responsible for the ratings of the entire two-hour show. He also failed to realize that ratings increases are more a result of trends and ongoing story lines than just one match. In my book (and once again, this is my book) Flair was wrong about the ratings. But he sure as hell was right about the brutality of my matches with Vader.

Vader, the real life Leon White, was in 1994 the greatest monster in the business. Guys were terrified of him. His style was the stiffest in all of wrestling. Some guys have a style that looks like they're hurting guys when they're not, which is good. Some guys' stuff looks like crap, but it hurts like hell, which is bad. Vader left no room for error; his stuff looked like it hurt, and believe me, it did.

Some of the newer guys used to actually leave the arena if they saw their name on the board opposite Vader. Other guys would hide until that evening's card had been drawn up, and then come out of hiding if Vader wasn't their opponent. Really, underneath it all, Vader was a nice, sensitive guy. I even saw him cry in the dressing room after he paralyzed a young kid named Joe Thurman (Joe recovered the feeling below his waist a few hours later). Still, when that red light turned on, the '94 Vader's sensitive side seemed to turn off.

Strangely, I enjoyed my battles with Vader. I'd pump myself up for days before a big match and would usually hurt for a few days after. The two matches that Flair had mentioned had indeed been brutal. During the first match, at my suggestion, Vader did a number on my face, even though it seemed that my interpretation of "try to raise a little swelling around my eyes" varied dramatically from his. The toll after match number one was impressive: broken nose, dislocated jaw, fourteen stitches in my eyebrow and seven underneath my eye. The second match almost put me out of wrestling for good.

Now, we should probably get something straight. I know you didn't pay $25 (unless your cheap ass waited for the paperback) to have your intelligence insulted. I will not try to portray professional wrestling as being a "real, competitive sport." I will readily admit to occasionally stomping my foot on the mat, and always placing a greater emphasis on entertainment value than on winning. I have, however, over the course of fifteen years of blood, sweat, and tears, compiled a list of injuries that I would compare to that of any "legitimate" athlete. So unless otherwise noted, please consider all injuries to be legit. In our strange little world of sports-entertainment, I hope you will see that life can often be both "real" and "competitive."

Anyway, back to March 17, 1994. My opponent for that night: you guessed it, Vader. Except that this was an injured Vader, who was having trouble with the feeling in his fingers. He even asked for the night off, but Flair said no. "It's no problem, Ric," I said, "I'll work around it." As a matter of fact, I looked forward to the challenge of coming up with a good match with an opponent who was injured—it was the one of the signs of a good worker (wrestler). As a matter of fact, for a guy with all the natural athletic ability of a giant three-toed sloth, I had a pretty damn good bag of tricks up my sleeve. One of these "tricks" would send me home from Europe without my ear.

After about ten minutes of back-and-forth action, I charged at Vader, who was standing against the ropes. Earlier in the match, I had successfully caught Vader with the patented Cactus clothesline. In this move, I clothesline my opponent and let my momentum carry me over, as well. It was a pretty impressive sight, especially when you consider that in this case, over 750 pounds of humanity were tumbling to the floor. This time, however, Vader moved out of the way. I launched myself into the ropes and prepared to catch my head and

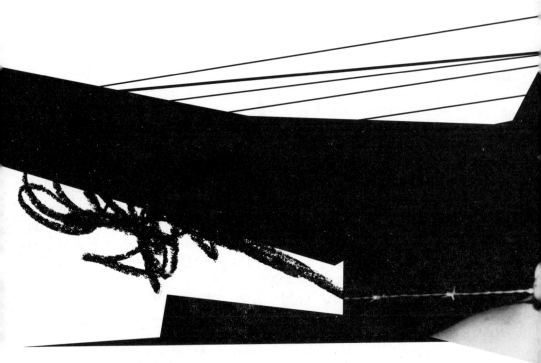

neck between the second and third ropes, sail my body over, and, using precise timing and my own body's momentum, twist the second rope over the third. This is a move known as the hangman because the end result is the illusion of a man being hanged by his neck while his body kicks and writhes in an attempt to get out. In fact, although it is a planned maneuver, it is no illusion, as the man actually *is* hanging by his neck and the body really *does* kick and writhe in an attempt to get out.

I was probably the sport's foremost practitioner of the move, and I had the scars to prove it—about fifty of them behind both ears. It's funny, as many times as my ears were stitched, and as many times as I would watch them turn from black to purple to blue to slight shades of green and yellow, I never did have a problem with cauliflower ears the way some guys do. As a matter of fact, unless you looked closely behind my ears, at the zippers that decorated my auditory landscape, you wouldn't know that I'd been a veteran of so many late-night emergency room visits.

There was no doubt about it; the hangman was a difficult move, but even more so in World Championship Wrestling. WCW didn't

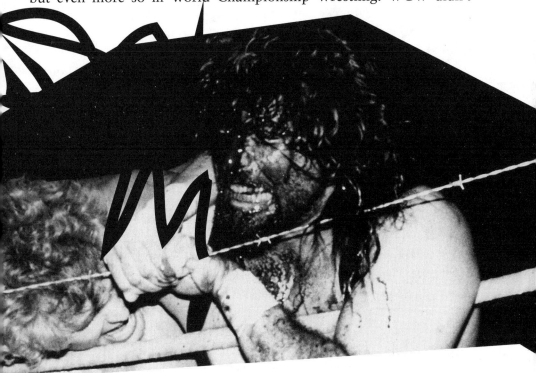

actually use ring ropes—it used elevator cable covered with a rubber casing, and when the cables were entwined, they were almost impossible to pull apart. Now, throw a human head into the equation, and we're talking about considerable pain. This night in Munich would turn out to be even more pain. Too Cold Scorpio, a brilliant high flyer (aerial wrestler), had wrestled in the evening's first match and had complained that the ropes were too loose. Unbeknownst to me, the German roadies had tightened the cables to the maximum; there was no give on the ropes at all.

With my head caught in the ropes, I could immediately feel the difference. Instead of the normal pain that I had long ago accepted as a consequence for this exciting move, I felt as if my neck was in a vise. I literally felt like I was going to die right there in the Sporthalle in

Munich. I'm usually known as a pretty good ring general, and I had kept a calm head in some pretty bizarre conditions, but in this case I was panicking big time. I began to do what no tough-guy, big-cheese, blood-and-guts wrestler would ever, under normal conditions, even think of—I began screaming—and I do mean SCREAMING—for help. Vader later took the credit for getting me out, thereby saving my life, but video evidence showed the big SOB with his back to me, yelling at the crowd and doing his "who's the man?" gorilla-grunting routine.

Even with the panic setting in, I knew enough about the human anatomy to know I was in trouble. I knew that if the pressure continued on my carotid arteries, which run along both sides of the neck, I would soon pass out, and then, without exaggeration, could suffer brain damage and even death. With that grisly knowledge in mind, I made one last effort to get myself free and wrenched my head from between the ropes. I later likened it to a fox that chews off its paw to escape a trap.

I lay on the floor momentarily, and then got to my knees. Blood was literally pouring out of my right ear. I could actually hear the pitter-patter of drop after drop of bright red blood hitting the blue protective mats that surround the ring. This struck me as strange—I mean, as many times as the backs of my ears had been laid wide open, they had never really bled. They are made up mostly of cartilage, after all. But this was different. It was gushing. For some strange reason, I didn't initially touch that right ear; instead I felt behind my left. To my disgust, there was a split I could damn near fit my finger in. "If this one feels like this, the other one must be real bad," I remember thinking. I climbed into the ring and the match continued. "Nice juice, huh?" I said to Vader as he set me up for a monstrous forearm to the head. Loosely translated, that means "I'm bleeding pretty bad." At this point, my ear was still hanging on . . . barely. I blocked Vader's third forearm and threw a blow of my own. When this happened, a fan's videotape clearly shows something fall off the side of my head. Also at this point, in any other event, a ripped-off ear would probably be cause for a time-out. I mean, if Mark McGwire were beaned out at the plate, he probably wouldn't jog to first base with a missing body part. If Shaquille O'Neal drove the lane and came up an ear short of a pair, he probably wouldn't go to the foul line with "juice" running down his tank top. But in our sport, the *fake* sport, we have a single rule—"The show must go on." And I went on as best I could.

The events that happened next are almost too ridiculous to be real. Almost. Because two of our referees had been injured on the tour and had been sent home, a referee from France had been flown in. Because he spoke no English, he was unable to tell me that he had picked up part of my body and was holding it in his hand. He handed the ear to ring announcer Gary Michael Cappetta. With his face turning white, Gary tiptoed the ear back to the dressing room, where he informed Ric Flair, "I have Cactus's ear; where should I put it?" Flair, being the thoughtful guy he was, arranged to have it put in a bag of ice for me. I later asked Cappetta what the ear looked like, and he told me in his perfect announcer's voice, "Well, it looked like a piece of uncooked chicken, with tape on it."

I have often imagined how this entire scene would play out on film, with Martin Scorsese directing, in black and white if possible. Dramatic music in the background. Vivid close-ups of the ear as it pirouetted in the air before dropping gracefully to the canvas, old-fashioned flashbulbs going off all the while. The referee screaming in French with tears streaming down his face. Cappetta sprinting to the back, trying not to lose his lunch. Flair, played perhaps by Buddy Ebsen, crying at the fate of Cactus Jack. Except in the movie version, I'll be damned if I'm going to scream for help. No, I'm going to take it like a man on the big screen.

Anyway, back in the ring, the match continued for about another two minutes. Yeah, I know, it would be great to say that I won the match and was carried away victoriously on the fans' shoulders. But even though I'm writing about a sport that some feel is not "real," this is a real story, and the real truth is I did the job that night (lost the match). With the match won, Vader went back into his "who's the man?" when Doug Dillinger, the head of security, rushed in and told him to get the hell out of the ring. I reached for my right ear, and, well, there wasn't a whole lot there to feel. I got a sick feeling in my stomach, and then sucked it up and headed back to the dressing room.

Believe it or not, I was actually in high spirits when I got there. I have often been referred to by doctors and nurses as "the most cheerful patient they've ever treated." I like that. It may not be as badass as "the toughest SOB in the World Wrestling Federation," or as colorful as "the most electrifying man in sports-entertainment," but it's something I'm proud of nonetheless. Can't you just hear Howard Finkel at *WrestleMania XVII* as he announces: "Ladies and gentlemen, making his way to the ring, he weighs in at 287 pounds and is known around the world as the most cheerful emergency room patient in the world . . . Mick Foley!"

Vader, once again showing his sensitive side—the big softy—was pretty upset about the whole thing. He even wanted to ride to the hospital with me. Of course, being shaken up about it would not prevent him from claiming for years that he had been the man who tore Cactus Jack's ear off. Too Cold Scorpio offered to show me my ear in the plastic bag. I declined. Emergency medical technicians prepared to take me to the hospital. But, wait . . . something was missing . . . I couldn't leave yet. This event needed to be recorded for posterity—we needed a camera. I grabbed an English photographer named Colin, and he snapped about a dozen photos of the gruesome injury. If you look closely at the photos you can detect a gleam in my eye and just the slightest hint of a smile.

I hopped into the *Krankenwagen*, or ambulance, and we headed for the *Krankenhaus*, or hospital. Amazingly, we were denied access to the first hospital. Luckily, there was room at the second, and I hopped out, but not before uttering a German sentence that probably had never been used before, and possibly will never be used again: "*Vergessen Sie nicht, bitte, mein ohr in der Plastik Tasche zu bringen,*" or "Please don't forget to bring my ear in the plastic bag."

A plastic surgeon was called in and he gave me some unfortunate news. I should mention at this point that I had the utmost confidence that the wonders of medical science would enable him to sew my ear on in no time. After all, John Wayne Bobbitt had been sewed up, right? Oh, but I guess that wasn't an ear. Anyway, the surgeon explained to me that unlike an ear that had been cut off and would be relatively easy to repair, mine had more or less been pushed off my head and had been too badly destroyed to salvage. There was hope, however. I underwent a four-hour operation during which all the cartilage from the missing ear was removed and placed in a man-made pocket an inch above my remaining lobe. By doing this, the cartilage would remain vital for a reconstructive operation somewhere down the road. And yes, I am at this very moment feeling that lump of stored cartilage, like a play toy that I'll never misplace.

After the operation, one of the *Krankenschwesters*, or nurses,

showed me the remains of my ear, except by now, without my cartilage, it looked like a giant skin flap, kind of like the cheese on a pizza
that's been sitting at room temperature. I asked her if I could have it—
"*Ich mochte mein ohr zu haben?*" She looked at me as if I'd just farted
in church, pinched her nose with her fingers, and replied that the ear
would become *schmutzig*, or dirty and smelly. Now that's a hell of a
thing to say about something as near and dear as my ear, but as I
searched in vain for the German word for formaldehyde, the
Krankenschwester did something, the image of which would haunt me
for months. She calmly stepped on the foot pedal that lifted the lid of
the medical waste basket, and with a flick of her wrist, disposed of my
former ear forevermore. She then turned to me and with the inquiring
eyes of a child said, "*Der catch ist alles schauspiel, ya?*" or "Isn't
wrestling all fake?"

Welcome to my world, the world of professional wrestling, where
fact is often stranger than fiction, and the line between the two keeps
getting tougher and tougher to distinguish.

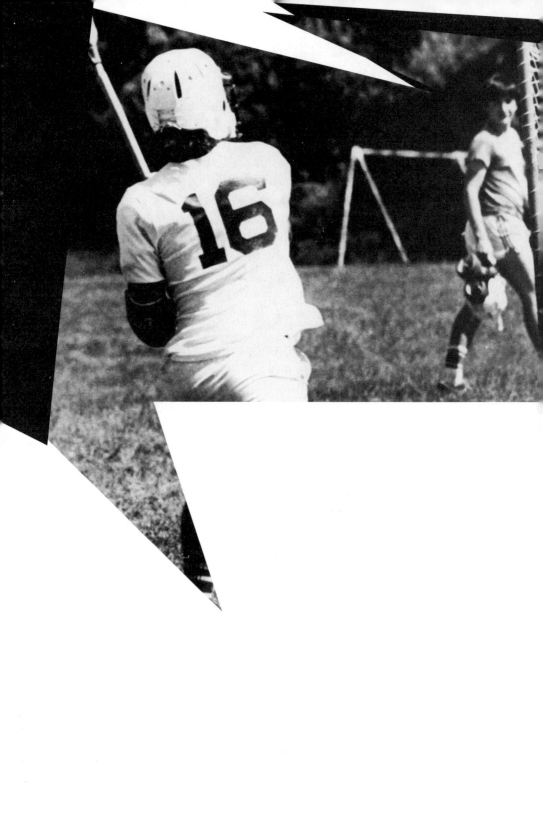

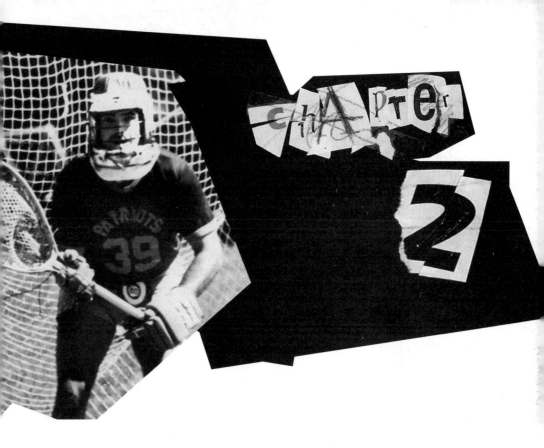

I was eighteen in the fall of 1983.

Upon graduation from Ward Melville High School in East Setauket, New York, that June, I had spent the summer lifeguarding at the Stony Brook Racquet Club, and daydreaming about professional wrestling. Up on the stand for continuous eight-hour shifts, I had plenty of time to envision suplexes and dives off the top rope like my idol, Jimmy "Superfly" Snuka, while I watched over the well-being of a bunch of spoiled rich kids. My brother, John, on the other hand, was in his third year as a prestigious "Town of Brookhaven" lifeguard, which meant that, unlike me, he guarded at an actual beach that actual good-looking women frequented. In addition, he was given an hour off for every hour worked, during which, rumor had it, the town guards would pump up with a pair of dumbbells before taking the stand.

But, hey, my job had its benefits too, such as free tennis privileges at the club, which I used liberally—until my racket-throwing, yelling, and court-diving ways led to the termination of my court privileges. Looking back, I think I may have actually thrown the town lifeguarding test to avoid the indignity of wearing the official bikini bathing suit that the town guards were required to wear. Even at a lean, mean

200 pounds, Mrs. Foley's little boy was never cut out for Speedos. So as a result, I grudgingly accepted my responsibility to watch out for children.

Hell, it wasn't so bad. I was actually something of an institution at the club; I had not only guarded the summer before, but worked at Arthur's Take Out in the winter. Arthur's Take Out was the brainchild of club owner Arthur Grower, who paid me and my buddy Rob Betcher minimum wage to cook and deliver broasted (a combination of broiling and roasting—but it looked like fried) chicken out of the freezing snack bar. There was no heat in the place, so we would have to throw water on the stove and do calisthenics to keep warm while we waited for the phone that seemed to never ring.

As a result, we had lots of free time in the snack bar, and I had taken to whittling objects out of potatoes and then broasting them. One night, Danny Zucker, who would later go on to manage me in the Dude Love movies, called in an order, and I set out whittling my best potato penis complete with two potato testicles that we attached to the starchy shaft through the miracle of toothpicks.

I set out with two orders in my car, and after dropping off the first, headed over to the Zucker residence to unveil my unique sculpture. "You're going to love this, Zuck," I promised, as Danny opened the box to reveal a normal order of fries. Oops. I never did find out if Mrs. Smith on lower Sheep Pasture Lane enjoyed her meal.

I had been on several recruiting trips with Rob Betcher during the winter and spring, as we were prized players on the Ward Melville High School lacrosse team, which were perennial county champions. I was a goalie and Betch played attack. It didn't matter that the two of us hardly played as juniors—the important thing was that we played for Joe Couzzo's Patriots and had been seen in summer camp action by college scouts. It was actually at Couzzo's Suffolk Lacrosse Camp that I had honed the skills necessary to promote a big wrestling match.

The situation started innocently enough—I was taunting one of the counselors, a Ward Melville graduate named Dave McCulloch. Dave had been my idol when I was a sophomore, and I felt such a bond to him that I even fell for his girlfriend, Crystal Kost, in a crush that only lasted for two years. I eventually went to the prom with Crystal—at her request—but left prom night without even so much as a kiss on the cheek or a dance. Back then, even as a popular if somewhat strange kid, I would have had trouble scoring even if she had pulled the goalie.

Dave and I were good friends, but there was a small resentment that he'd felt for me ever since I had sung a song I wrote about him and Crystal over the school intercom. Feel free to sing along to the tune of "The Wreck of the Edmund Fitzgerald," by Canadian legend Gordon Lightfoot.

```
"The Ballad of Dave and Crystal" by M. Foley
His day was a loss, he was playing lacrosse, he had
nothing else better to do.
But he came to his home to answer the phone, and the
voice of Bob Whehman came though.
He said "I've got a notion, let's go to the ocean,
we can ride those big waves.
We'll have some fun, we're leaving at one, what do
you say to it, Dave?"
And if it's all right with you, there is someone else
too, to go on this trip we are plannin'
It isn't just Sean, who will bore you till dawn, but
a pretty female companion
She looked so good on the beach that Dave could not
speak—she was wearing a nice white bikini
And the look of that suit on her body so smooth, sent
a tingle right down his big weenie.
```

Oh, there was more, much more, but because the song was fictional and I was using creative license, it got a little graphic and unfortunately ended in one of the three ways that my songs always did—pregnancy, venereal disease, or the cutting off of the penis. Actually, it was the latter subject that had won the high school talent show for me and my buddies, John Imbriani, John McNulty, Scott Darragh, and Zucker—collectively known as the B.P.'s (The Brothers Penis). However, the next day we were called into the principal's office and told that we were disqualified for "inappropriate song material," and that we would therefore have to forfeit the grand prize of $40 worth of Chinese food. "Man, I sure could go for an egg roll right now," I mumbled as Mr. Marschack continued to admonish us.

"You really think this is funny, don't you, Mickey?" Marschack asked me. "I mean, this is humorous to you, isn't it?"

"No, Mr. Marschack," I politely answered. "I don't think it's funny. We were judged to be the winners by a team of judges, and now you are stripping us of our rightful prize."

Marschack laughed, because as my seventh grade English teacher who had remained friendly with me over the years, he knew that I was dead serious. I wanted the food. "Mickey, I cannot in good conscience give the grand prize to a bunch of guys who sing about a penis."

Now he had me mad. "Mr. Marschack, there's a lot more to it than just a penis. It's about the guy who is attached to the penis, who can't cope with his guilt and therefore has no other alternative than to get rid of the part of his body that's causing him so much pain. It's actually a pretty touching song." I then recited the sensitive song and waited for Marschack's ruling, which came about a second later. "No food for you guys" was the final word.

After all these years, I still feel that we were wronged, and now you can be the judge. Sung to the tune of the Kinks' "Lola," and with sincere apologies to Ray Davies, here is the award-winning "Boner" by Mickey Foley.

```
Well I don't acquaint with girls I don't know, and
I don't go to parties, I stay at home—I'm a loner
L-O-N-E-R Loner.
But I saw her out there alone on the street, her
body was built, I looked at my meat—I had a boner
B-O-N-E-R boner, bo bo bo bo boner.
She said, "Hey boy won't you come inside, and when
I walked inside, I felt my penis rise into a boner.
Bo bo bo bo boner.
We sat at the bar and I bought her a drink, and she
glanced at my pants, and she said, "I think you've
got a boner." Bo bo bo bo boner. Bo bo bo bo boner.
Well I could feel the blood flow though my sack and
I could feel the cloth stretch in my slacks.
```

Actually, I forget the rest, but it had something to do with becoming oversexed, and cutting off the penis as a cure. Probably not much of a cure. Just as important as the lyrics was our show-stopping finale, in which I did a horrible front handspring into a flat-backed landing, and sat up just in time for Danny Zucker to smash me over the head with a plastic "Village People" guitar. Sure the guitar was fake, as were all the B.P.'s instruments (we had a real band behind the curtain), but it was still a pretty impressive sight, and a sign of things to come.

Let's get back to Joe Couzzo's camp. The tension between Dave and me was growing to the point that it would have to be settled in a "bout," which was the name given to camp boxing matches in the cabins, with lacrosse helmet and gloves on for protection. Actually the lacrosse helmet is a lot lighter than a football helmet, and its shock-absorbing usefulness was arguable. I began promoting this bout to the best of my abilities. I wrote humiliating facts about Dave in Magic Marker on my chest. I did pushups during lunch with a plate of beans beneath my face and scoffed down a bite between each poorly exe-cuted push. I even wore a bull's-eye over my balls for the camper–staff game, of which Dave was a part.

By the time the bout rolled around, it was the hottest issue at the camp. For some reason, all of the younger kids looked up to me, and my entrance was met with great enthusiasm from the campers. McCulloch, however, was booed relentlessly. There was no bell, so someone blew on a horn, and the bout was on. I came out fast and furi-ous and threw everything I had at the college sophomore. Lefts, rights, hooks, uppercuts—you name it, and I threw it—for about thirty sec-onds. At the half-minute mark, my arms felt like lead, my legs felt even worse, and my entire respiratory system felt like it was failing me.

I looked at Dave, and he was smiling. He knew I had nothing left, and he began throwing punches with bad intentions. Dave was damn near a man, and I was just a boy, and he was hammering me relentless-ly. I got through the round, but tasted the stale iron of my own blood. His punches had split my lip, and I was, to quote many a wrestling show, "busted wide open." The coaches stepped in, and seeing that I was getting the crap beaten out of me, stopped the fight. I believe it was the last "bout" ever held at the Suffolk lacrosse camp. When they stopped me, I went ballistic. "Don't stop it, Coach, I'm okay," I argued.

"Mick, it's over," Coach Ray Weeks told me. "Now go clean your-self up."

"This isn't right," I yelled for the whole camp to hear, "I was just getting started."

Slowly, I walked outside to the bathroom building. I stepped inside and shut the door. I looked into the mirror at my bloody face and had to admit that I liked it. I envisioned a big wrestling match, with Vince

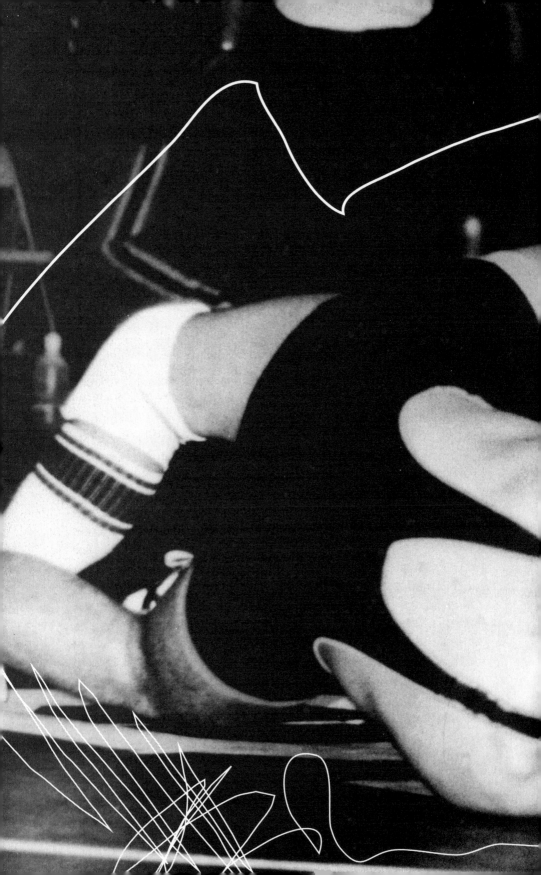

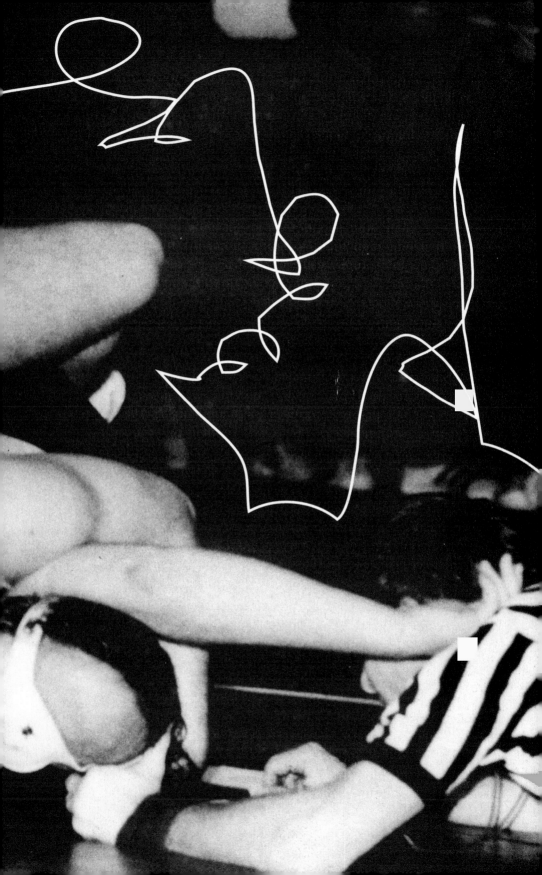

McMahon screaming, "Look at Foley, my goodness, he's busted wide open!" I smiled at the thought and then another thought hit me. "Thank God they stopped that damn fight."

Lacrosse had been my passion for several years. At my father's request, I had also played football and basketball as a sophomore, but I had sucked at both of them. I think I had one tackle and one basket for the entire season on each of those teams. It wasn't that I wasn't a good athlete—I just seemed to be an underachiever when it came to team sports. In football, I would actually bend down to tie my shoes when it came time to pick sides for practice. In basketball, I liked to stand outside and wait for long-range jumpers.

Contact wasn't the issue. In a game of one-on-one, or even up to three-on-three, I was impassioned when it came to boxing out, or playing defense, or driving the lane. When the game turned to five-on-five, or eleven-on-eleven, I just kind of disappeared and figured my teammates would take care of it. To this day, I've kept a little bit of that inside me, which is why I've always preferred wrestling as a single. As a single, I get caught up in the match easily—as part of a team, I really have to fight the tendency to rely on my partner.

I guess that's why I enjoyed playing goalie in lacrosse. Even though I was part of a team, the responsibility was all mine. I loved the challenge of stopping shots without a chest protector or cup. It was my propensity for playing without a cup that led to the much-publicized "testicle the size of a grapefruit" story on *Raw Is War* fourteen years later. Actually the whole story is slightly misleading, as I didn't make a habit of playing without a cup, I just oftentimes forgot to wear one. My ball wasn't exactly the size of a grapefruit either—more like a medium-size tangerine.

Lacrosse was so important to me that as a senior, I went out for the winter track team strictly to shape up for the spring season, during which I would grace the goal for the Patriots. The fact that I was no runner was soon discovered, and I began taking to bailing out on the far side of the track and hiding in the woods for a couple of laps. I threw the shot-put and discus too, but one look at my shoulder development should tell you how I fared at that endeavor.

One day before practice, I was talking to fellow B.P. John McNulty, who was nicknamed McNugget in honor of the McDonald's food of questionable origin. "Track, huh, slick guy," he said, before adding, "You might be the slowest guy in the school."

"I know," I agreed, "but I just want to get in shape for lacrosse."

John thought it over before saying the words that would have a profound effect on my life: "Why don't you go out for wrestling," he wondered. "Even if you never have a match, it will get you in better shape than track will."

Wrestling, now there was an idea. With my father as the school district's athletic director, I had grown up watching amateur wrestling in addition to the fake stuff on TV. I knew Coach Jim McGonigle well, as he had coached my brother for two years and also had been my instructor for driver's education. Hell, I'd even covered the team for the local newspaper and baby-sat the coach's children on a couple of occasions. In addition, my living room matches with my brother, John, had taught me techniques that would prove invaluable on the mat. In gym class, I had even dominated a school bully so bad that he begged me not to pin him and ruin his reputation. After that, Rob Pilla and I always had a special bond, even though if I had to do it all over again, I would have pinned his ass. "What the hell," I said, laughing, to McNulty, "I'll do it."

I went out for the team and had the time of my life. I loved it. I loved the competition and the pressure, and the knowledge that whatever I did was done on my own. I highly advise any kid to wrestle, as I learned more about being a man during one season on the mats than I had in the seventeen previous years put together. A lot of athletes won't go out for wrestling because of the potential ego and image damage it can do. Who wants to lose or, worse yet, be pinned in front of his friends, especially if he just ran for touchdowns a month earlier on the football team?

I was moderately successful right from the start, as I defeated and pinned bigger and more experienced opponents with my unorthodox style I had learned in the Foley living room. One match in particular sticks out in my mind during my time in the green Melville singlet. I was sick as hell one night and was not even scheduled to wrestle, but the meet was close and it would be decided by the final match. Coach McGonigle looked at me, and I looked back, and without saying a word, I started warming up. I looked across the mat at Artie Mimms, who was a big muscular black guy with an imposing Mohawk that made him look like Mr. T. Remember this was back in early 1983, before Mr. T ended up in the "where are they now" file. Mimms was ranked second in the county. I put on my headgear, and I walked over to Coach McGonigle, who patted me on the back and said, "We need a pin to win, Mick, a pin to win." I nodded and went out to get the job done.

Actually this is one of those "good news/bad news" stories. The good news was, there definitely was a pin. The bad news was, I wasn't the one doing the pinning. I put up a hell of a fight, but my "double underhook into a body scissors" backfired, and I ended up throwing myself on my back at the very start of the third period. After nearly two minutes of fighting the inevitable, I tried to breathe, and no air entered my lungs. A moment later, I heard a slap on the mat and I was done.

I looked up at the crowd and saw a few of my friends with sadness in their eyes. I spotted a few girls whom I had actually lusted over, and guessed that they weren't lusting over me. I got up slowly and shook Mimms's hand. I then walked over and shook his coach's hand. I then walked over and shook Coach McGonigle's hand, as he put his arm around me. "It's all right, Mick, ya know why?" he said, as I smiled a disappointed smile. "It's all right because that's the best I've ever seen you wrestle. I was laughing to myself, because I couldn't believe how well you were doing against that guy." I walked away disappointed but proud. I continued walking down two flights of stairs to the wrestling room where we practiced under hot conditions. Only during meets did we venture upstairs to the gym. I sat down in the empty room and I cried my eyes out.

I hadn't cried in almost three years—when I found out that Renee Virga was going to the junior high prom with Chris Lenz instead of me. It would take seven more years, after the death of my brother's cat Snowy, until I shed tears again. Nowadays, forget it, I cry during the Christmas episode of *Happy Days*—the one where Richie spots Fonzie heating up a can of ravioli by himself on Christmas Eve. Yeah, and I cry at the end of *Old Yeller* also.

John McNulty came into the room as I was about all tapped out, and he made me laugh at some of his weak humor. I got dressed and drove my brother's old Mustang II home. My parents were visiting my brother in Indiana, and so a few friends came over to cheer me up. I actually had a good time, and I remember that night with friends warmly. Conspicuous by his absence, however, was John Imbelliosio, who skipped out on his distraught buddy to see *Taboo II* at the Rocky Point cinema with the Renee Virga–stealing Chris Lenz. What a guy. The sequel to my all-time favorite Kay Parker film, and he leaves me hanging.

I finally did get to kiss Renee Virga at Imbelliosio's wedding in 1989. I saw her recently and told her she was going to be in my book. I also asked her if she'd seen the Chris Lenz issue of *TV Guide*.

I really only had one problem with wrestling. I simply liked it so much that I lost my desire to play lacrosse. I had been a big pro wrestling fan for a long time, but I never considered it as a career option. Now, however, with a little bit of amateur background behind me, I began to see the possibilities. I began studying tapes of my favorite wrestlers. I became obsessed with the sport/art form, and began to believe I could actually do it. In June 1983, I attended my first match at Madison Square Garden to see Jimmy Snuka battle Don Muraco in a bloody double disqualification. I was hooked. I didn't need lacrosse anymore—I had pro wrestling.

The absence of lacrosse as a factor brought about a problem of its own. I had applied to colleges with the intention of playing goalie, and now that intention was gone. I really had no desire to go to the schools that had recruited me: Salisbury State, in Maryland, or Western Maryland in, well, Western Maryland. Instead, I settled on Cortland State University, which was located in between Syracuse and Binghamton in upstate New York.

Upon enrollment, I immediately began a quest with Scott Darragh, my old B.P. buddy, to be an amazingly average student. And in that quest, I was successful. I was on course to achieving straight C's across the board when I went home for fall break. Fall break presented a tricky schedule problem. I was supposed to return to school on Sunday, October sixteenth, in order to be at classes on Monday. This would be in direct conflict to the highly anticipated rematch between the Superfly and Muraco, which was scheduled for October seventeenth. I considered my options. On one hand, I had sociology class with John Alt. On the other, I had my favorite wrestler and his bitter rival at the most famous arena in the world—inside a steel cage, no less. I thought about John Alt, who had lost me the moment he said, "Let's talk about narcissism, or more simply, narcissistic self-proliferation." Then I thought about Snuka and his dive off the top of the cage a year ago in a matchup with Bob Backlund. It was no contest. John Alt and his vocabulary that was so ridiculous we were required to carry a dictionary with us to tests had lost out to the man who Vince McMahon had declared was "no less than phenomenal."

Yes, I was going to the matches, but that was still a problem. My dad would never buy a cage match as an excuse to miss college. No way. He was going to drive us to the Greyhound bus station twenty minutes from our house, drop me and Scott off, and continue with my mom on to Indiana for a visit with my brother. I saw an opening and devised my plan. It was pure genius. I would go with my mom and dad to the bus station and be dropped off as scheduled. After all the good-byes, we would wait until my parents drove away and then hide in the woods and await the arrival of John Ambrionio, who was attending a local college. The three of us would take the train to New York City the following day, and then feast on the buffet of bloodshed that the Superfly and the Magnificent One would surely serve up.

The plan was taking effect. We were in the car on the way to the station, and my parents were chatting amiably to us. I got the slightest twinge of guilt in my throat as I thought about the people I was planning to lie to and deceive.

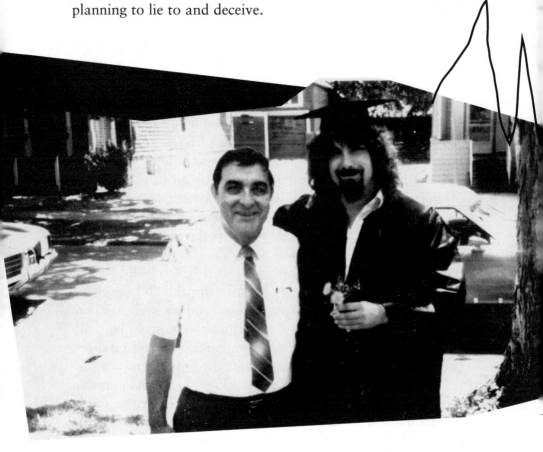

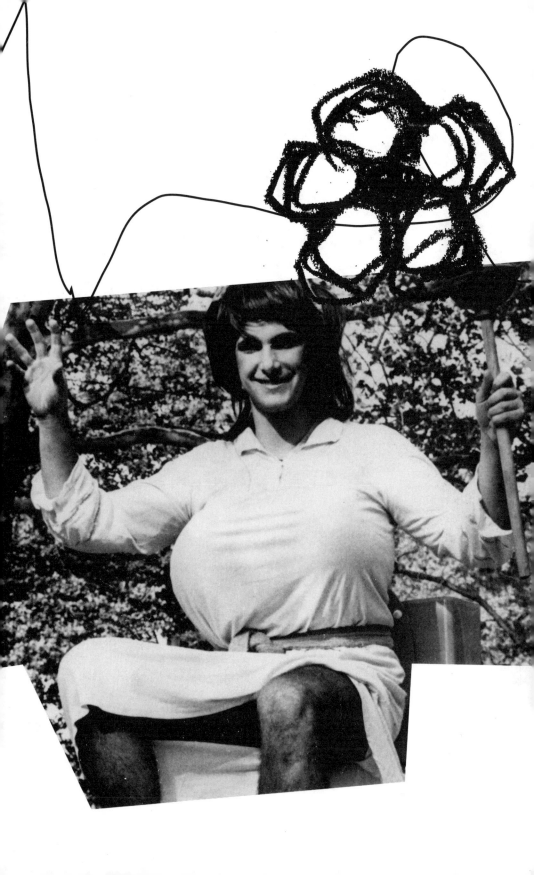

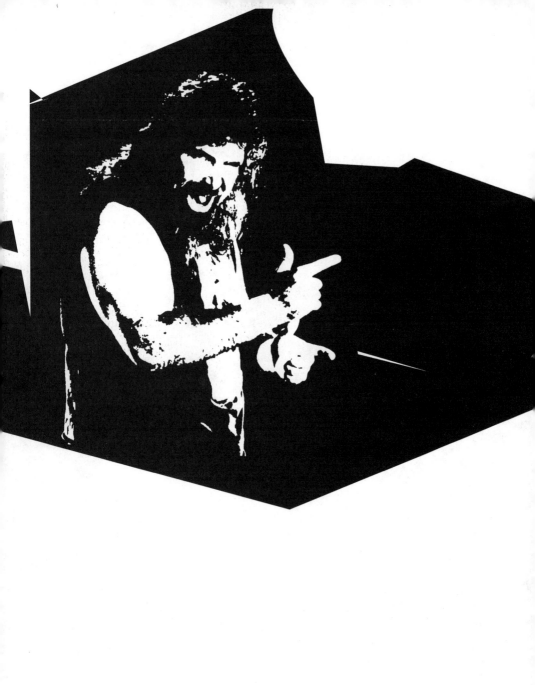

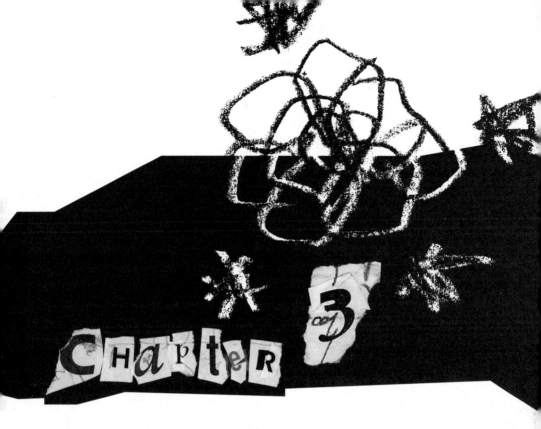

My father, Jack Foley—the original

Cactus Jack—was a true legend in the field of athletic administration. After starting out at the Setauket High School, which is now an elementary school, my dad went on to become the director of health, physical education, and recreation for a school system that was made up of five elementary schools, two junior high schools, and Ward Melville High School, a place so nice that it could pass for a college campus.

In addition, he was the chairman of basketball and lacrosse in our county, was host to the yearly county wrestling championships and the Special Olympics, and was a member of so many groups and organizations that I can't count them all. For his efforts, he was selected as the athletic director of the year for the entire nation in 1988—which is kind of like a World Wrestling Federation title belt for ADs. Upon his retirement, the ultimate honor was bestowed upon him, when the Ward Melville Gymnasium was officially renamed the Jack Foley Gymnasium.

I recently asked my dad if he'd been by the gym to see the plaque honoring him as the gym's namesake. He replied that he had, but that he'd had to move a soda machine in order to see it.

My mom was the first member of her family to attend college, earning a degree in physical education from Brockport State in upstate New York and later a master's from Stony Brook. She became a phys-ed teacher at the Setauket school, and it was there that she fell for the vaunted Foley charm. After giving birth in 1964 to my brother, John, she gave up teaching to become a full-time mom. It's funny, my dad has the doctorate, but any time I had a question, I always went to my mother. She had a thirst for knowledge that made her almost like an encyclopedia—or a *Jeopardy!* contestant. My mom would take college courses just for the hell of it—if she wanted to learn more about a certain subject, she'd just sign up. She'd then come home from class with her notebook and proceed to copy her notes directly into another notebook—again, not to pursue a degree—just to pursue knowledge. That is something I always found admirable . . . or a little sick—I'm not sure which. Even to this day, my mom will still polish off at least two good-size novels a week.

My dad also liked to read, but his reading had a dark side to it. No, I'm not talking about stacks of porno magazines at the Foley house—I'm talking about newspapers. Lots and lots of newspapers. I'm convinced that somewhere in his childhood, my dad must have had a traumatic episode involving a newspaper, because he had an obsession with the damn things. Two papers every day. Two local papers every week, and four—count them—four newspapers every Sunday: *Long Island Newsday*, the *New York Times*, the *Daily News*, and the *Long Island Press*. Sometimes he'd bring home a *New York Post* just for the hell of it.

Most of the time my dad was so busy that he would leave for work before we woke up, and he'd return when it was just about bedtime. I would go downstairs to get him a Schmidt's of Philadelphia and he'd knock off a few pages of *Newsday* while swigging down what many would consider the worst-tasting brew of all time.

Now Sundays were a different story. That was paper day. With the accompaniment of either a Yankee, college basketball, or pro football game in the background, depending on the season, my dad would launch into a day-long quest to devour the news. It didn't matter that much of the news was damn near a week old, he'd read it anyway. Not just read it, but underline the important parts—I'm not kidding. A small correction here—if the Sunday reading sessions fell between November 25 and December 24, the audio of the ball game would be turned off and would be replaced by the soothing sounds of classic Christmas music, cracking and popping on our antique turntable. I still to this day carry at least one Christmas CD with me on the road at all times. There's nothing like "White Christmas" on a hot July afternoon, even if old Bing did beat the crap out of his kids.

Unfortunately for my dad, he would usually run out of time before he'd run out of papers. But he couldn't bear to part with them. Instead of throwing them out, he would stack them in the garage, where over the course of time they resembled many pulpy, musty leaning towers of Pisa. By the time my mother gave him an ultimatum last year, my dad had papers dating back to the early seventies, swearing up to that horrible day the commercial Dumpster arrived that he would one day find the time to read them all. My brother said it was quite a sight to watch my dad getting rid of over twenty-five years of treasures. He couldn't just throw them out, he had to look through them first—a fighter till the end.

The reason I dwell on the papers so much is that, other than that one particular peculiarity, my dad was the straightest guy you could ever meet. I mean, he has looked basically the same for the last forty years: crewcut with sport coat and tie—or when he's relaxing, golf shirt and shorts with green or black socks pulled up as high as they'd go, and a pair of loafers to complete the ensemble. That's my dad. No photos of embarrassing pork chop sideburns to hide, no leisure suits or medallions hanging on a bare chest to try to explain to my kids. No, times may change, but my father never will. Come to think of it, my own look hasn't changed a whole lot since I was eighteen, give or take a tooth or an ear.

I probably attended more sporting events than any other kid in Three Village history. As athletic director, my dad was always checking out the various teams, and he would bring me and my brother with him. In addition to the big ones—football, basketball, and baseball—we caught everything from bowling to wrestling to women's field hockey to volleyball. But of all the sports, baseball, or more accurately its little cousin wiffleball, was the one I liked best.

Wiffleball was practically a religion to the neighborhood kids on Parsonage Road. Our backyard was the original stamping grounds for the Parsonage Pirates: Tom and Matt Dawe, Joe Moose Miller, Brett Davis, Marc Forte, and the Foley Boys.

My dad was more than happy to feed our baseball hunger. We

were frequent spectators at the old Yankee Stadium—the house that Ruth built. He'd even pick us up from school early so we could stand outside the lot where the Yankees parked and wait for autographs. Remember, this was the early seventies when ballplayers still did that type of thing. I'll never forget the day that I received my hero Thurman Munson's autograph. It was my birthday, which also happened to be Munson's, and he must have felt the cosmic connection, because he passed by all the kids but me and jotted down his John Hancock.

What I liked about Thurman most was the little things he did that often went unnoticed. People who really know baseball are the only ones who really know how good he was. Now, as a wrestler, I like to compare myself to Munson in that way—by doing all the things that only other wrestlers notice. Thurman Munson died tragically in a plane crash when I was thirteen. I don't think I've watched a dozen baseball games since. But I'll always fondly recall my days at Yankee Stadium.

Those road trips were also educational, because it was in the car on the way to and from the stadium that I became aware of curse words. There is a line in the movie *A Christmas Story* where Ralphie recalls, "My dad worked in swear words like some artists work in oils or watercolors." Well, my dad was an artist as well. Like a lot of men from that era, my dad would refuse to ask directions, no matter how lost we were or how many innings we missed. Seeing as how my dad liked to leave the game at the end of the seventh inning to "beat the traffic," we needed to get as much game time in as we could. So when we got lost, he reached his boiling point, and he'd let it rip. "Welcome to New York City—the fun capital of the world," he'd usually begin. And then the bad words would appear. Lots of Ss and GDs, but never any Fs. In all my life, I only heard him say the "F" word once, and that was when he was quoting somebody—so that doesn't even really count.

But the "S" word was a different story. Old Jack could weave such a rich tapestry of "S" words as to leave a kid in awe. One night, when my cousin Doug was visiting, the Yankees were on the road, so my dad made a rare Shea Stadium appearance to see the Mets play. After the game, which was attended by only about 8,000 fans (this was back when the Mets sucked), my dad in a rare moment of weakness asked a police officer for directions. Needless to say, we wound up lost. My dad started with a few innocent observations about the men in blue. "You can always tell a New York City cop—a fat mick with a beer belly." He then helpfully pointed out the attendance woes the Mets had been having. "And they wonder why they only draw 8,000 fans? Eight thousand assholes. Only an asshole would go to Shea!" I'm not sure if my dad was including us in that group of assholes. And then it happened. At first it was just a rumbling way down in his chest and then it gathered momentum until it became an unstoppable force just waiting to release its wrath on the three innocent kids cowering in the 1972 white Mustang. Seven "S" words in a row. Almost like a vulgar haiku: "Shit! Shit! Shit! Shit! Shit! Shit! Shit!"

My poor dad also did a lot of cursing every summer. That is when he would work on his dissertation to complete his doctorate. I don't know if it was a real rule, or just my dad's rule, but the papers had to be typed perfectly—no white-outs, no typos, no erasers. As a result, the sounds of summer in our house went something like this: "Click, click, click, click, click, click, click—oh shit, oh dammit to hell, god-dammit." For me and my brother, this was our cue to run behind the house and laugh. When we did so, my mom would admonish us. "You're father is working very hard, you'd better not let him catch you laughing like this." I don't know why my dad didn't just pay somebody to type the damn thing—I guess he would have considered that cheating. If he'd only had a word processor or computer he would have saved a couple of years of his life.

Strangely, even though I was exposed to a great deal of swearing as a kid, and even though half the guys in the dressing room can't go a full sentence without an "F" word—"I shot him in the fuckin' ropes, I caught him with the big fuckin' elbow, and then, fuck, I made a big fuckin' comeback"—I have escaped almost F free. One time when I was waiting on the drive-through line at McDonald's, my son Dewey calmly asked if he could "get some fuckin' fish." I didn't get mad, but just gently told him that we didn't use that word at the house, and nei-ther should he. I haven't heard it used since.

My daughter Noelle is especially cute when she hears bad words. I took the family to see *There's Something About Mary* without realiz-ing all the bad language. Every time she heard a bad word, and there were plenty of them, she would turn to her mother, Colette, and give her the patented DX sign (crotch chop). Last week I mentioned that I was going to water the plants with the hose. She gasped and said, "You said the bad word." I guess in her mind she envisioned the Godfather's girls (the hoes) coming over to help me with the yardwork.

Maybe my poor dad should be entitled to his papers without the ridicule from his family. After all, this was a man who worked monumental hours, but still found ways to spend quality time with the family, even if it meant taking the family on business trips and turning them into little vacations. For some reason it seems that he was never

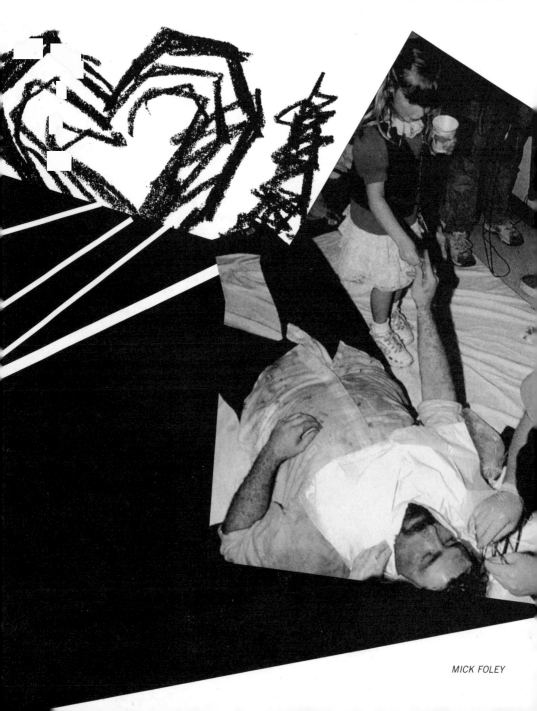

around, but on closer examination, I realize just how far out of his way he went to spend time with us. Yankee games, Mets games, school sports, camping in Nova Scotia, NCAA basketball tournaments, Santa's Village, Playland, Amish country, a rare trip to the movies so I could see *Rocky* for the seventeenth time, and too many others to list. Any time I think I had a rough childhood—please, somebody slap me.

*   *   *

Apparently all of those fond memories didn't mean quite as much as the thought of Snuka in a cage. My parents dropped us off, and I quickly said my good-byes. Too quickly, as it turned out. Before their car was even out of sight, we hightailed it into a thinly wooded area along the back fence, where we lay waiting against a slight embankment for the car that would take us home. To this day, I have no idea why we hid instead of just waiting. After several minutes, Scott peeked his head up to look for Imbrianio's car. I heard him gasp, and he dropped down quickly.

"What is it?" I asked as I looked at Scott, who had suddenly turned pale.

"It's your parents!" he exclaimed.

"That's impossible," I stated, before taking a look for myself. I too dropped down and got pale. "Oh my God, you're right," I gasped. "What are we going to do?" I had seen them only for a moment, but I'll remember the image of them on their manhunt forever. My mom searching for evidence as if she were Angela Lansbury on *Murder She Wrote*. My dad was on the lookout as well—he was looking for us. "We're done for, Nom," I said, using Scott's nickname derived from the heavy-drinking Mr. Peterson on *Cheers*. "My dad's giving us 'the look.'"

Nom knew all too well what "the look" was all about—every kid who had ever attended a Ward Melville basketball game knew it too. "The look" had many uses, but it was mainly a way to keep control at basketball games. Sportsmanship was highly valued by my dad, and the common practice of stomping feet and yelling during an opposing team's foul shot was strictly taboo. (No, not the Kay Parker movie.) From his spot ten feet to the right of the basket, my dad would ready himself for the noise, and when it began, he'd give "the look," and the noise would magically subside. It never failed. I'd seen plenty a tough high school punk try to withstand its force, but they all eventually went down. That look had caused me considerable discomfort when I was a kid trying to rid myself of the stigma of being "Dr. Foley's son," but never as much discomfort as it caused me right then. I had not been hit by my parents since the Parsonage Road spanking incident back in '68 that had left handprints on my little ass comparable to the handprints I leave on Al Snow's ass now. But, hey, there was always a first, and this blatant slap in the face of education just might set it off.

Don't get me wrong, my dad liked wrestling, and the sport had actually done a lot to make us closer. It wasn't easy growing up with a man like Jack Foley for a father, and for a few years things had been a little tense between us. Wrestling, however, gave us a common bond. My dad used to look up from his papers, and be amazed at some of the things he saw. "Hey, Mick, these guys are pretty good athletes," I once heard him say, and from then on, his glances up from his paper became more frequent. Eventually, it reached a point where he wouldn't look at the paper at all, and we'd watch the hot World Wrestling Federation action as father and son.

Yes, my dad was a wrestling fan, and under different conditions, he might have been up for seeing a little double juice inside a cage. But not where school was concerned. Yeah, if my dad found me, the guy getting juice might be me.

Minutes later, I saw them leaving, and sighed a deep sigh of relief. Scott and I decided to wait for the next bus, which was four hours later, and go back to school. John Ambrionio showed up minutes later, and the three of us sat back and reminisced about things we hadn't done yet.

When I got back to school, I had the terrible feeling that I had let myself, the World Wrestling Federation, and, most importantly, Snuka himself down. If he truly was going to dive off the cage, as I believed he would, than certainly I should make the extra effort to be there. Where there is a will, there is certainly a way. Now, as a wrestler, I pride myself in making my dates, no matter what. Several times I have driven all night and switched flights to make personal appearances that others would have canceled. When I give my word, I want it to mean something—and in a strange way, I felt as if I'd given Snuka my word.

I tried the easy way first. As I ran up and down the third floor of Fitzgerald Hall I yelled desperately, "Hey, does anyone want to go to New York City?" No takers. I guess I should point out now that I didn't have a car until a year later. Finally, I did get someone to give me a ride—to the Greyhound station.

At Greyhound, I left the driving to them—for forty miles to Binghamton. From there, I walked to the highway, stuck out my thumb, and waited . . . and waited, while visions of Superfly Splashes danced through my head. About three rides and eleven hours later, I showed up at Madison Square Garden, where, to my dismay, the marquee read "Sold Out." Fortunately for me, the institution of scalping was alive and well in New York City, and because I was by myself, was able to procure a third-row seat for only $40—only ten hours of lifeguarding.

Most of the card was forgettable, or maybe I was just exhausted, but when Howard Finkel announced an intermission, and I saw the chain link fence come out, I felt my senses tingle. I actually was nervous. This was the culmination of the bloody Snuka–Muraco wars, and I knew that at Madison Square Garden, inside a steel cage, they would let it all hang out. Back in 1983, and for decades before that, MSG was the place to be. Before Pay-Per-View and huge Monday night telecasts, the Garden was actually the biggest show in all of wrestling. Even today, there is just something about the place that makes you want to give just a little more. I remember clips of Vince McMahon Sr.'s posthumous induction into the Madison Square Garden Hall of Fame were shown on World Wrestling Federation programming, and Vince Jr. saying, "Before he died, my father said to me—Vinnie, the Garden will always be the Garden."

I later must have watched a video of that Snuka–Muraco cage match a dozen times, and in truth, it was just an average cage match—a little on the short side as well. But the magic in the air was unmistakable. I wasn't the only one anticipating something special. Within minutes, both combatants were busted wide open. Because this was before the day of 20/20 exposés and The Secrets of Pro Wrestling on national TV, I knew nothing about the blood, but of course assumed it was fake. I would find out the hard way that it wasn't. So, as a result, I kept looking for a blood capsule, or that other ridiculous theory—the bottle of ketchup underneath the ring.

Just as Snuka had things going his way, the match was over. He sprang off the ropes and delivered a flying headbutt that sent Muraco through the ropes and out the door. "That's it," I said out loud, "a twelve-hour trip for that?" Sure it had been a good match, but it wasn't what I paid to see. Suddenly, I saw Snuka's unmistakable display of rage inside the ring. When it came to displays of rage, no one was more animated than Snuka. Really, it's pretty much the Ken Shamrock "snapping" routine—to put things into a modern perspective. I felt my heart rate pick up a little as the Fly went after his prey outside the ring. A moment later, both men were back in ring, and a Snuka suplex had the Magnificent One lying prone in the middle.

Immediately, Snuka climbed to the top rope, and the Garden stood in unison. We were about to see the famed Superfly leap. This was back in 1983—before the day of moonsaults, saltos, planchas, and a lot of other foreign words that faceless Mexicans perform to little or no response. For my money, the impact has always been more important than the flips, and I would later learn just how much impact that splash had. That's one of the "secrets" of professional wrestling—make it hurt for real. Then, with nothing but a glance, I realized my vision was about to come true.

All it took was that one glance upward, at the steel mesh that surrounded him, and the Garden started to buzz. A loud buzz that grew with each upward step that Snuka made. After all these years, it's still the most impressive sight I've ever seen—the muscular Snuka standing barefoot on top of the cage, his face a mask of crimson, while flashbulbs bathed him in light. In a moment it was over, but the memory will live with me forever. It was a defining moment in my life—it was the day I knew without a doubt what I wanted to do with my life. I wanted to be a wrestler, but even more, I wanted to make people feel the way I had just felt.

I got back to school at 10 A.M.—twenty-eight hours after my departure. A week later, I talked to my parents. "How was the match?" my dad wanted to know.

I started to lie, but realized it wasn't worth it. "It was great, Dad, but how did you know?"

My dad laughed and said, "Because your Mother and I watched the tape, and saw our son sitting in the third row with his red flannel shirt." He had caught me red-handed, and now he wanted to play Columbo and figure out the events of the crime. "You seemed to be in an awfully big hurry for us to leave, so we felt like you must have hid somewhere and had a friend come get you. Were we right?"

I proceeded to tell what might generously be called a half-truth. "No, Dad, I definitely caught a bus to Cortland, and then I hitchhiked the next day."

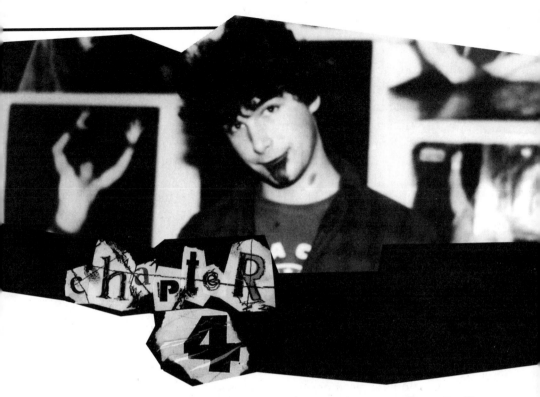

December 1983 I knew what I

wanted to do with my life—I just didn't know how to go about doing it. A snowy winter night shortly before Christmas break would serve as a strange catalyst for my professional wrestling career.

I was in a bar called Toody & Muldoon's on a Saturday night, courtesy of the fake ID I had purchased in New York City during my first Snuka–Muraco encounter back in June. The bar had two levels—one that played rock and roll, and one that played dance music. Somehow, against my better taste and judgment, I always ended up in the basement listening to "It's Raining Men," and trying to look cool. Probably failing at it, too. I was hanging with my buddies, John Hennessey and Steve McKiernan, who was now my roommate.

Steve had started out as Scott Darragh's roommate, but Nom had never quite been happy at C-State, and had let his grades fall to nearly unchartable levels. At one point, a mutual friend named Dan Hegerty (a.k.a. "Hags") had shown up, and the two of them were miserable together for about a week. "I swear," Steve had told me during that time, as we walked back from class, "if I walk into my room and see Hags and Scottie D. looking through their yearbook and listening to Bonnie Tyler, I'm going to scream." Moments later, he opened the door and I heard a husky female voice singing "your love is like a shadow on me all of the time," followed by screams.

Nom really bottomed out when a combination of girlfriend problems and not making the baseball team sent him into a tailspin. Many was the time that I had heard a knock on the door, followed by a disheveled Nom simply saying "three." I felt for Scott, and would immediately hand him side three of Pink Floyd's *The Wall*, which was our standard album side for depression and misery.

I was having fun at school, however, and this night was shaping up to be a good one. The World Wrestling Federation was on the television above the bar, and a rare title match was taking place. In the present-day wrestling scene, hot matches take place all the time on television—but back in '83, the World Wrestling Federation, like most shows, featured a series of one-sided matchups. So it was with great excitement that I witnessed Tony Atlas and Rocky Johnson, whose then eleven-year-old son Duane would go on to become the most electrifying man in sports-entertainment, defeat the Wild Samoans for the World Wrestling Federation tag team championship.

I would have been perfectly content to just bask in the glow of that glorious title change, but my night suddenly went from great to history making when I saw Kathy walk down the stairs. Man, I liked Kathy. She was beautiful, she was funny, but more important, she made me feel great just to be around her.

At this point in time, I could probably be described as a shy, insecure, poorly dressed, weird guy, who also happened to be polite, kind, funny, and borderline not too bad-looking. I was like a diamond in the rough, but man, you had to look pretty hard to find me. My failure with women was legendary. It wasn't that they didn't like me, but I had a tendency to be too ambitious with my choices, and had a terrible lack of finesse in closing the deal. In other words, I had no killer instinct, and a knack for not saying or doing the right thing.

I had flubbed a major one during my first week in school only about a foot from where I stood on that December evening. A hot chick walked up to me and started talking to me, while breathing dangerously close to my ear, which guaranteed instant wood. My ears were always real sensitive; it's a shame that one of them is missing, and that the wax content keeps my wife miles away from the other one. I swear, my mom used to irrigate my ear, and things the size of marbles used to fall out of there. Anyway, after a few minutes, this hot-blooded woodmaker leaned in a little closer and informed me, "I've been looking at you since you were a freshman." I thought her comment over, and somewhere in the resources of my mind came back at her with "But I'm a freshman now." In a moment it was gone—all of it. The hot breath, the arm around the shoulder, the girl, and the wood. Gone, gone, all gone!

A girl named Amy probably represented the pinnacle of my ineptitude. This was also during the first week of school, on the second day actually, when a group of us third-floor Fitzgerald people were invited to the room of Battling Bill Esterly and John Heneberry, whom we would affectionately call Dingle. Bill and John were sophomores from Baldwinsville, New York, and wanted to hold a little social function in their room to help the new people get to know one another better. Within minutes, I was getting to know Amy better, as the vaunted Foley charm was striking in a big way.

Amy was beautiful, and had a figure that was impossible for me to take my eyes off of. Usually, I don't like people when they're smoking, but she had a look about her when she took a drag of her cigarette that put a twinkle in my eye and a bulge in my trousers. That rare combination of sexy voice, gorgeous face, swinging sweater puppets, and a somewhat morally casual attitude had my heart racing when we found ourselves somehow alone in Sue Kootz's room. I believe she could sense my innocence as she began questioning me in a very suggestive way.

"Have you ever had sex before?" she purred.

"No," I quickly gulped, "have you?"

She smiled as she sexily replied, "Lots of times." Her questioning wasn't over yet. "How about oral sex—has a woman ever done that to you?"

She was smiling seductively as I squirmed on Sue's bed. I'd heard my friends talk about it, and I'd seen Kay Parker perform it, and from all indications, I felt it was something that I wanted to be a part of. "No," I replied, "how about you, have you ever done it to a man?"

"Oh yeah," came her sex kitten answer.

I pressed further, sensing what she was interested in. Yeah, I could smell what this chick was cooking. "Do you like it?" I had the nerve to say, with my right eye squinted like the Clint Eastwood poster I had hanging on my dormitory wall.

"Love it," she simply said, as she snuggled up next to me, with a hand on my thigh and her blouse dropping down at the neck so that

I was afforded a view of what looked to be paradise. Her next words were ones that I'd thought I'd never hear—"Can I kiss you?"

Man, this was too good to be true. I really felt that this could be my one way ticket out of the "V-Club" which, along with Chris Walker and John Imbriani, I'd been a card-carrying member of for all my life. No doubt about it, this was the moment of truth. I leaned in and proceeded to give her the worst kiss in the history of Cortland, maybe even in all of the seven valley region. It was a kiss all right, but a kiss with no parted lips, no probing tongue—not

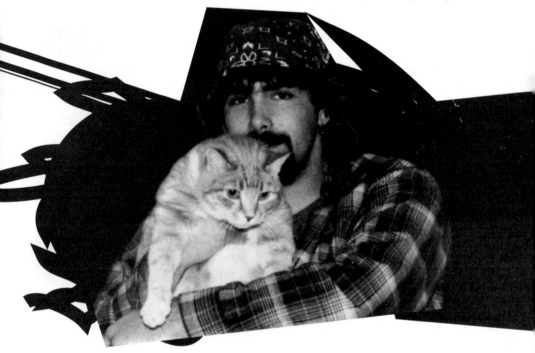

even any real pressure behind it. Foreign soccer players kissed each other with more passion after scoring a goal. I'd blown it—underneath all the amusing anecdotes and leftover summer tan and (at that time) perfect smile, I was really just a dork, and she'd seen right through me. In a matter of moments, she too was gone, gone, all gone.

Actually, Amy would go on to be responsible for some of my finest passionate moments—it's too bad that she wasn't present while they were happening.

Kathy was different, though. I didn't judge her by the stretching in my slacks, but rather how much fun I had talking to her. Her eyes would light up, and she would literally beam when I talked to her. It didn't matter to me that she was my friend Kevin's former girlfriend, and that he'd dropped her like a bad habit—I would be there to pick her up. She was too good for Kevin anyway. I could talk to her for hours, and I did so on that fateful evening. It also didn't matter that she was slightly intoxicated and that the intoxication made walking quite difficult for her. I was there for that too. "Lean on me," I told her, "when you're not strong, I'll be your friend, I'll help you carry on. Just call on me, Kathy, and I'll lend a hand." Well, maybe those

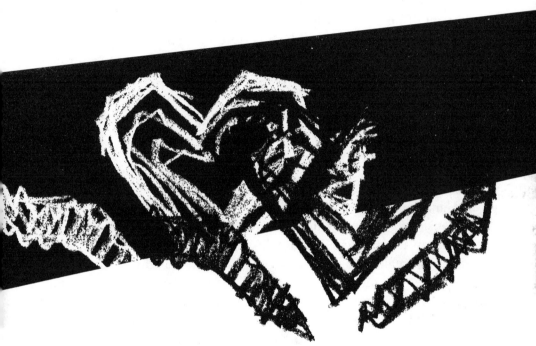

weren't my words exactly, but I'm sure they were pretty damn romantic.

The downtown area in Cortland was at the bottom of a hill that led to the campus. Kathy's dorm was directly at the top of the hill, and I accompanied her on the walk home, while flurries of snow fell softly around us. Without warning, her cold little hand was in mine, and despite the winter chill, I started to sweat, because, believe it or not, I'd never been that far before. But Kathy's presence calmed me down, because, after all, this wasn't some girl I was clumsily going to grope at the end of our stroll—she was my Kathy, and she was all I'd ever wanted in a girl.

When we got to her dorm, we talked for a few more minutes. I wasn't about to weasel my way into her room, as I was confident that there would be plenty of time for that type of thing in our future. I thought of my Amy failure, and decided to show romantic fortitude for once. "Can I kiss you goodnight, Kathy?" I politely asked the Irish beauty with the glowing smile. Man, she looked incredible, even in a slightly drunken haze. She didn't answer me verbally, but instead responded by reaching up and pulling my head down to her softly. I was ecstatic to be the recipient of a genuinely tender kiss that included neither parted lips nor probing tongue, but consisted of just the right amount of lip-to-lip pressure. I didn't have a lot of experience to draw from, but it seemed to me like a perfect kiss.

Up to that point, it was certainly the most romantic moment in my life, and even now rates up in the top ten. I looked into her eyes, and they were smiling, as I gently rubbed her chilled cheek with my thumb. "Good night, Kathy," I said softly. "I had a great time with you."

She responded with the words that buried my heart, but launched my career, "Good night . . . *Frank*."

My whole life felt like a record needle being scratched across an album as I struggled to gain my bearings. Frank? There had to be an explanation. Maybe she was thinking of my middle name, Francis, and just figured she'd call me Frank for short. Yeah, that was logical. Yeah, my ass it was logical. Reality had bit me, and it was holding on hard, and reality was that this girl I thought so highly of didn't know my name. My mind and heart were hurting bad as I bounded home, which was another half-mile away. I looked at my shadow on the wall of the Fine Arts Building, and I could see that my hair was getting long. After a lifetime of short hair, including unstylish ridiculed crew cuts, and a Mohawk that nearly got me thrown out of my house, I wanted to have long hair. Hair that would bounce when I dove off a top rope or cage—hair like the Superfly.

Like Superfly, I too was going to fly tonight. Physical pain always somehow seemed to relieve mental pain for me, and I was in need of some relief. And how did I spell relief? S-U-P-E-R-F-L-Y. I had a ritual that was a big hit with a few friends. They would fill the room with clouds of baby powder (our version of dry ice) to the opening chords of "Diary of a Workingman" by Blackfoot. By the time the tempo picked up, I would be pumped for my move, and the dive off my bed would take place just as Ricky Medlocke hit the high-pitched scream in the song. I felt like this ritual would make me forget about the whole Kathy incident, even if just for a little while.

I walked into the room, and Steve McKiernan was already there. "How's it going, Mitch," he cheerily said. He always called me by the wrong name on purpose, in honor of a guy named Bruce Schenkel, who never could get my name straight. I don't get it—is Mick really that tough to remember? Anyway, I didn't feel like getting into details, and I simply told Steve to get the baby powder and the Blackfoot album ready because I was ready to take flight. After the dive, which knocked the wind out of me, hurt my ribs, and drew praise from a couple of drunks who were hanging out in Bill and Dingle's room, I was ready to talk.

I relayed the tragic story to Steve, who didn't really know what it was like to be a flop with chicks. Steve was king of the bar room rap, and once he talked a girl into coming to his room, the deal was sealed. He had a surefire method for action known as a . . . guitar. He kept the damn thing in such an obvious place that girls would always ask about it, and once he started strumming, it wouldn't be long before they started humming. Whenever I heard the guitar, I knew to look elsewhere for my beauty sleep.

"What are you going to do about it, Mitch?" he asked, without any real feel for the pain I was going through. I decided to handle this problem the way I handled the all-important events in my life. "Get the camera, Steve, let's document this thing." I had been given a Cannon AE1 for Christmas a year earlier, and I had been wearing it out ever since. In much the same way I would react when my ear was torn off in Germany, I wanted visual proof of the important events of my life.

So there I was, looking forlorn in my red flannel shirt that I'd had since eighth grade. The shirt had been huge on me back then, and I remember vividly pulling a feather out of it and blowing it in the air during social studies class. While the rest of the thirteen-year-olds tried to address the Boche case, I was doing a heck of job keeping that feather in the air. Finally, the feather got away from me, and as I reached for one last blow, I fell out of my chair and tumbled to the cold, hard concrete as my classmates laughed at me. They had been watching my act for the past several blows.

The red flannel was also my shirt of choice during my infamous barbed wire match with Eddie Gilbert in 1991. It was also the reason that one girl had dropped her crush on me earlier in the year. "He's nice," she'd told Lisa Cerone, a fellow Ward Melville graduate, "but doesn't he ever change that shirt?" The answer was, "Not often." It wasn't just my shirt, it was my jacket, my security blanket, and my friend. I finally had to stop wearing it in 1996, when I brought it out of storage for an ECW (Extreme Championship Wrestling) barbed match, because I had finally outgrown it. That shirt had seen me through good times and bad—it had been in MSG to see Snuka go off the top of the cage, and it had been on hand to see me get my feelings crushed. There will never be another shirt like it.

"Steve, I have an idea—let's make a story."

Steve seemed perplexed. "About what, ya weirdo," he wanted to know.

"About tonight," I answered. The dive had done me good, and I didn't want to dwell on my problems, I wanted to capitalize on them. "It will be great, Steve, we'll take pictures of my heartbreak, suicide attempt, rescue, and rehabilitation. What do you think?"

"I think you're a weirdo," Steve answered back.

Shot one was simple—the forlorn Foley walking into the room. The caption read, "Mick walks into his room after Kathy called him Frank. It is clearly the worst moment of his young life."

Shot two shows me attempting to jump out the window, with the caption, "Steve McKiernan, Mick's roommate and close friend, tries to console him, but it is to no avail, and Mick makes an attempt to jump out the window."

Shot three reads, "Foley disappears into the brisk January air, leaving McKiernan speechless and holding on to one of the big guy's boots."

Shot four is fairly self-explanatory, with a caption reading, "A battered Foley lies at the bottom of the hill—a mere shell of his former self. To add to his problems, it's cold out, and he's only wearing one boot."

Shot five shows me being carried into the room. With nothing else to use, we smeared grape jelly on my face for the "busted wide open effect." The caption reads, "McKiernan enlists the aid of 'Battling' Bill Esterly, who, with biceps bulging, carries Mick up the stairs."

The final shot is completely ridiculous as I lie in a comatose state, with Steve holding my hand, and a shirtless Esterly giving me Last Rites with Rosary beads in hand. Around me hang my posters—

Jimmy Snuka, Candy Loving (the Twenty-Fifth Anniversary *Playboy* Playmate), and the American flag. The caption is equally ridiculous, reading, "Not knowing whether he will ever regain consciousness, his friends gather close in a touching display of brotherhood and faith."

The pictures were an immediate hit among my tiny circle of friends. "Photos were good, but this story needs to be put on film." I thought, and we began to put *The Legend of Frank Foley* onto eight-millimeter film. I guess I'm dating myself when I talk about eight-millimeter film, but videocassette recorders were fairly new in 1983, and video cameras were practically nonexistent. So we borrowed an eight-millimeter projector, and in January 1984, decided to record the events of December 1983 for posterity.

The ancient camera required a huge spotlight for lighting, and the glow attracted an overflow crowd to the doorway of room 317 to see what was going on. They were treated to a cloud of baby powder, a high-pitched Ricky Medlocke scream, and a now-220-pound weirdo in an old red flannel, diving off his bed onto a teddy bear. Unbeknownst to the spectators, I had put a mouthful of red food coloring into my mouth as I climbed up the bed, and upon impact, "Wiffpt," I spit the whole thing out. Again my wind was knocked out, but even in my pain I heard a female voice cry out, "Ooh, that's the most disgusting thing I've ever seen." I vividly remember thinking, "I've got to get some more of that response."

Unfortunately, the filming was a flop, as the ancient camera broke, and I was left with a room of splattered red to clean up, a spool of useless eight-millimeter film, and a desire to disgust as many people as I could. "Hey, if they won't love me, maybe they'll at least hate me," was the way I felt about it. Man, that sounds kind of serial killerish, doesn't it? As the months rolled by I couldn't get my story out of my mind. I never did recapture the magic of that snowy night with Kathy, but I at least got her to semi-admit a "kind of" attraction a year later. To this day, I'm not sure if she realizes what a big influence she had on my career. Also, I wonder if she has the special "Kevin" cover of *TV Guide* hanging on her wall.

I got home from school that summer and immediately made *The Legend of Frank Foley* a priority. In a few short days, we rented a video camera and proceeded to put together thirty minutes of horrible acting, bad jokes, and even worse wrestling. Many people are familiar

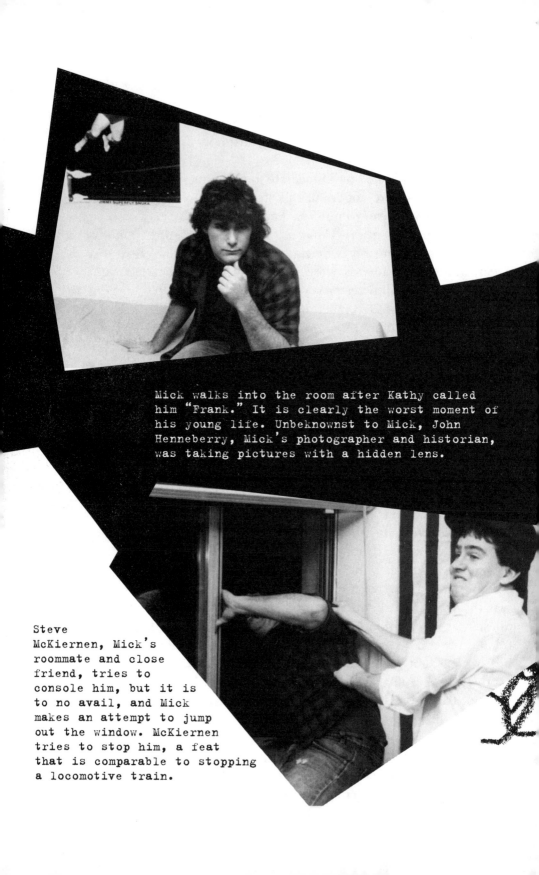

Mick walks into the room after Kathy called him "Frank." It is clearly the worst moment of his young life. Unbeknownst to Mick, John Henneberry, Mick's photographer and historian, was taking pictures with a hidden lens.

Steve McKiernen, Mick's roommate and close friend, tries to console him, but it is to no avail, and Mick makes an attempt to jump out the window. McKiernen tries to stop him, a feat that is comparable to stopping a locomotive train.

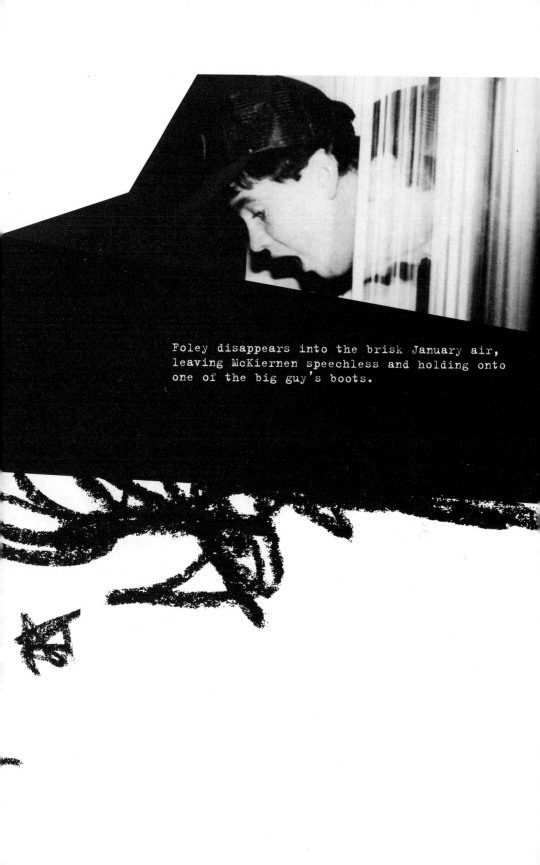

Foley disappears into the brisk January air,
leaving McKiernen speechless and holding onto
one of the big guy's boots.

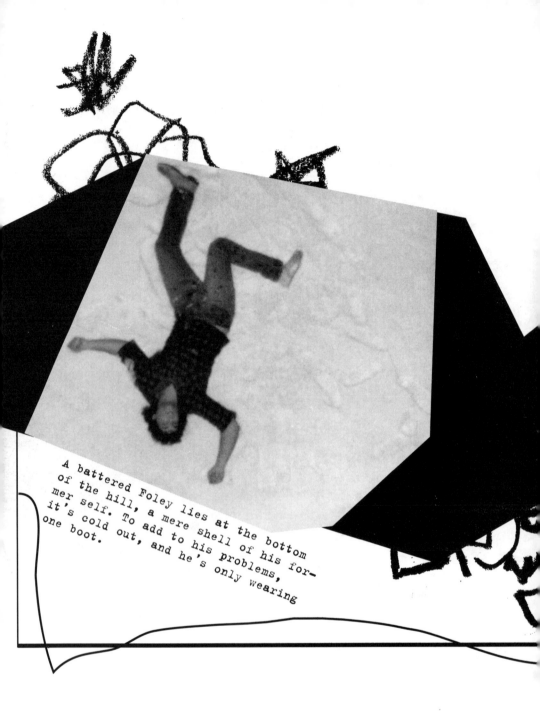

A battered Foley lies at the bottom of the hill, a mere shell of his former self. To add to his problems, it's cold out, and he's only wearing one boot.

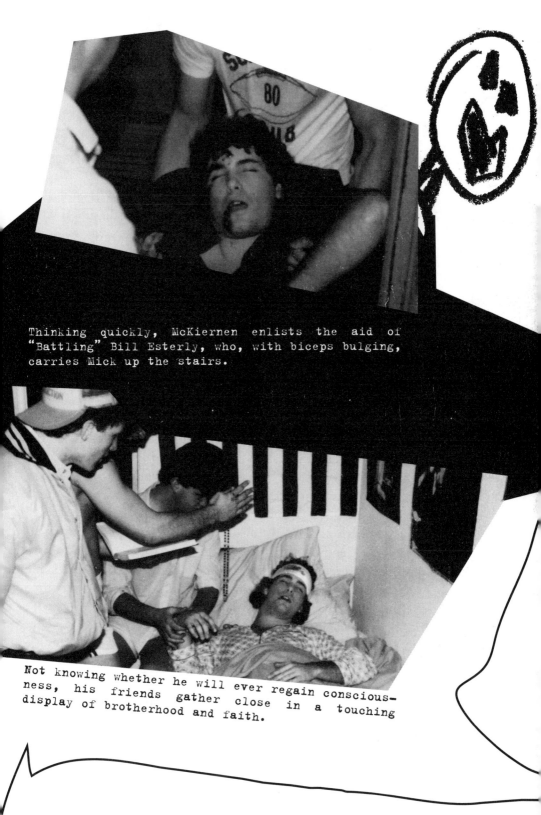

Thinking quickly, McKiernen enlists the aid of "Battling" Bill Esterly, who, with biceps bulging, carries Mick up the stairs.

Not knowing whether he will ever regain consciousness, his friends gather close in a touching display of brotherhood and faith.

with the second movie we made, called *The Loved One*, but it is a little-known fact that Dude Love actually made his first appearance in this fiasco. I'll bet the Internet fans would clamor for a look at this piece of history, where the Dude actually does a three-minute posing demonstration while wearing a tinfoil-covered weight-lifting belt with "WWF" written on the front. Believe it or not, at 220 the Dude didn't look all that bad.

Dude Love was my fantasy creation of what a man was supposed to be. I never envisioned a freak like Mankind or a weirdo like Cactus Jack to be in the cards for me. No way. As the Dude, I was going to be all the things that Mick Foley never was—rich, successful, and the recipient of more ass than a toilet seat.

The June 1984 Dude was quite a bit different from the Dude who finally entered the World Wrestling Federation in 1997. He wasn't a shucker and jiver—he was more of a laid-back cat. Actually, his interviews were pretty impressive, as he talked about his spinning sidewinder suplex and hawked his "Love Potion" protein drink. I actually felt like a different guy when I put on the Dude's ensemble of long brown wig, orange headband, mirrored shades, and pajama top. For some reason, to me, nothing said "cool" like a pajama top. Many nights, I would actually go out with my friends while dressed as the Dude. The results were impressive as the girls actually flocked to the cool antics of the Dude. I was also much more prone to cutting a rug when I was parading as the champ, simply because, as the Dude, I knew the secret of being a good dancer—do nothing on the floor. I would get out there and barely move a muscle, except for an occasional nod of the head or a snap of the fingers, and I actually looked cool doing it. Unfortunately, underneath it all, I was still the same Mick Foley who'd laid that pitiful lip lock on Amy, and when it came to closing the deal, I was far from shagadelic.

More than anything, *The Legend of Frank Foley* was about wrestling. After being called Frank by Kathy, who was played by my friend Diane Bentley, I used creative license to drive away, instead of walking, and drove up to my house instead of a dormitory. Waiting for me was an open driveway with two mattresses and some cardboard boxes in the middle, upon which was placed my opponent, Chris P. Lettuce. I think because of Chris P., I've always hated punny names in wrestling, like the evil dentist Isaac Yankem, D.D.S., from *Decay*-tur, Illinois. To add to the drama, Danny Zucker was calling the action, as

I suplexed, pile drove, body slammed, and elbow dropped the lifeless doll on the cold concrete driveway.

I set Chris P. down on the mattresses and pulled up the garage door as Danny speculated on what I was doing. "Oh, he's cleaning house, the Dude's cleaning house," my skinny Jewish buddy yelled, as I emerged with a vacuum cleaner. Then I pulled out a ladder, and set it up against the basketball backboard where I had spent so many hours practicing my shot and proving the theory that "white men can't jump." With all the grace of an African bull elephant, I navigated the steel ladder, taking only a brief time-out to swig red food coloring out of a vial. Finally, I was there. "Look at Foley, he must be twenty, thirty feet in the air," yelled Zucker, as I stood perched atop the ten-foot rim. I wonder if that same technique would work if I hired Zuck to announce my sex life—"Look at that penis on Foley, it must be thirteen, fifteen inches in length and just as big in diameter."

Taking a deep breath, I surveyed the situation, flipped the Snuka "I love you" sign, and took to the sky. A second later, Chris P. was history as I rolled triumphantly off the landing pad. With "blood" running down my chin, I approached the camera and prophetically stated, "Do you know who you're looking at? You're looking at fat Mick Foley. You remember that, Vince McMahon, you remember that!" Following the match, "fat Mick Foley" decides his life isn't worth living and tries to end it all with a plunge out the window. He is nursed back to health by his buddies and reemerges as the cool and talented Dude Love.

Six months went by, and still I was obsessed with being Dude Love. Even though I went to a school where girls had about as much resistance to sex as the Swiss army has to a military invasion, I was still unable to turn on a light switch. I did kiss a pretty senior (who went on to be my first love), but found out later that she was prone to blackouts and didn't remember it. I was real close to receiving oral sex once when my back went out on me. What the hell?

I was completely consumed with wrestling at this point in my life, and no longer saw everyday things for what they were, but instead saw them in terms of how they could be used in a wrestling match. I was living in a place called the Towers now, which consisted of two-bedroom suites that I shared with Steve, John Hennessey, and a guy named Mac who hasn't crossed my mind in fourteen years. One night, Mac had a drunk girl in his room, and as I walked in I saw not an easy target for sexual fulfillment, but instead an easy target for an elbow drop off a desk. (No, I didn't drop it, but it wasn't for the lack of wanting.)

One night I was at a party halfway between the Towers and downtown. I wasn't a very regular drinker, but when I did, I did it right. I probably drank only twenty times during my few years in Cortland, which has got to be some kind of a record, but when I did—look out. Out of those twenty nights, I probably got sick on fifteen occasions. I was on fire that night, and was actually "catching raps" left and right, when I suddenly bailed out of the house. Twenty minutes later, Bob Spaeth, who was like a hero to John, Steve, and me because of his exciting sexual adventures and even greater verbal embellishments of them, saw me standing on the front lawn, looking up at the roof. I heard, "What are you doing, Mick?" and it shook me out of my spell. I answered, "Oh nothing, Spaethie, I'm just thinking."

"What are you thinking of?" he asked, with real concern in his usually jolly voice.

"Oh, nothing really," I lied, which he picked up on immediately.

"Come on, Mick," he urged me, "you look like you were in a trance out here."

"Well," I slowly started, because even though I was drunk, I had enough sense to know the oddness of my thought, "I was just wondering, if I dove off that roof [which had to be a legitimate fifteen feet], do you think that garbage can would break my fall?"

He looked at me in a strange, but appreciative way, and said, "Let me get you another beer."

I haven't seen or heard from Bob, who used to refer to sex as "jukes," in over twelve years, but I heard from my old roommate Steve that Bob wanted me to speak to his class at school. If I did, I would have to serenade him with an old song I wrote, which is sung to the tune of the New York Yankees jingle. Sing along if you like.

The song is meant as a joke, but I had to watch myself when I drank, or else my sensitive side would sneak out. I was entertaining as hell, especially when I ran into Kathy after inhaling six shots of Jack Daniel's in an hour, while she stood with (believe it or not) Kevin on her arm. (This was about nine months after the original "Frank incident.") Yeah, they were back together again, at least for a few days, but that didn't stop me from telling her about *The Legend of Frank Foley* and Dude Love, and how her heartbreaking name negligence was going to one day make me a star. She was still beautiful, and was still beaming, but in truth, it seemed to be more of a scared beam—as if she thought if she didn't give me the beam of old that I might come off the bar with a big elbow. I wouldn't, but hell, even if

```
"Spaethie" by M. Foley
Spaethie, everyone knows and loves Bob—Spaethie,
a god with lacrosse gloves, he is Spaethie
Ya spell it S-P-A-E-T-H hey
Spaethie, all of the things he taught us—Bob—
Spaethie all of the drinks he bought us
he's after J-U-K-E-S Hey—Spaethie I'll remember
you to the end. For drinks, jukes, jokes and
laughs, but most of all—as a friend.
Spaethie.
Now, that's Spaethie
```

I did, I'd make sure in true Foley fashion that I absorbed most of the punishment.

I remember feeling funny when I saw them walking up the hill. Not really sad anymore, but just at a loss to explain human emotions. What the hell did Kevin have that I didn't? I was the storyteller, I was the jovial drunk, I was the guy she beamed at—even if it was a scared beam—I was the basketball rim diver, wasn't I? For crying out loud, she had a chance to shag Dude Love, didn't she, and she let it slip away for what? Kevin?

Later that night, despite my best effort, I let sensitive, drunk Mick Foley rear his wimpy head. I reached for my wallet, and though I tried to fight it, I pulled it out. No, not a condom, even though I had one packed away just in case. Eventually, when I tried to use it, in the summer of 1988 on the Caribbean island of Dominica, the damn thing was so old that it literally crumbled in my fingers. I never knew latex could crumble. What I pulled out were the lyrics to a Kinks song called "The Way Love Used to Be," and when I showed it to my friend Joanne Adams, I could literally see her respect for me disappear. As far as chicks go, some sensitivity is a good thing, but "The Way Love Used to Be" is probably a little much. In six days from this writing, on my way from Hershey Park in Pennsylvania to Santa's Village in New Hampshire, I'll be stopping by Joanne Adams's house with my wife and kids. I wonder if she'll be able to look past the missing teeth, missing ear, barbed-wire scars, and seventy-three-pound weight gain and see the lovestruck loser who showed her the sappy song.

As Christmas of 1984 rolled around, I was well aware that Mick Foley had dropped the ball. It was high time that the Dude picked up the damn thing and ran with it for a while.

The Loved One was taped in the three days spanning January 11–13, 1985. In addition to being historic for giving birth to the "roof" dive that was later seen by millions on World Wrestling Federation programming, it was one of the best times I can remember. It was like a great party for me and a bunch of my friends. My friends didn't know their lines, so they had them taped to wrestling magazines, and even with the verbiage right in front of them, their performances were so poor that they made Pete Gas look like Sir Laurence Olivier by comparison.

My parents were away for a few days, which meant I had room to let my creativity run rampant, which I did in a highly inebriated state. Like I said, I'm not a very regular drinker, but if anyone wants to get a look at Mick Foley when he's drunk, *The Loved One* is your chance. With the exception of the famed "backyard match," I'm hammered in every scene.

The Loved One was essentially a retelling of the Frank Foley movie, but with several added plot twists, and much greater technical expertise. It was still so bad that I have never allowed my wife to see it, and when the World Wrestling Federation years later wanted to put the Dude tape on the tube, I gave them access only to the wrestling scenes. Actually, the entire movie was recently screened at Danny Zucker's house in Seattle, and was a great hit, but when it comes to *The Loved One*, I like to think it has a limited audience of about the five people who were in it and their immediate families.

The film starts out as Danny Zucker walks hand in hand with my friend Felice, sits down at a picnic table where Felice's lines are taped to firewood, and asks her to marry him. Danny is disguised with the classic Groucho glasses with the big nose, furry eyebrows, and mustache, but even the getup can't hide his pain as she tells him, "No, Danny, I can't marry you because I feel like you're hiding something from me."

"All right, Felice, I'll tell you," Zuck said, "I guess we'll start at the beginning." With that, the scene—complete with gentle love music in the background—fades out, and the strange saga of Dude Love unfolds.

Mick Foley is my character in the beginning, a tortured soul who is still trying to put the embarrassment of his suicide attempt behind him. Like many survivors of suicide and incorrect name calling from the woman of his dreams, Mick is without ambition, as he sits munching salty snacks amid his concerned friends. "Why don't you go back to wrestling?" John McNulty helpfully suggests.

For a moment Mick's face lights up as he says, "Do you really think so?"

"Sure," John fires back, "you were winning almost fifty percent of your matches, and the fans really liked your clean-cut ways and sportsmanship."

Mick is interested, but has a few reservations, as he states, "But everyone knows I tried to kill myself, if I show up to wrestle, I'll be laughed right out of the ring."

"Why don't you wear a mask?" Cortland dropout Scott Darragh chimes in.

"Yeah," Mick is quick to answer, "but what will I call myself? I'll need a cool name."

At that point, a bunch of names are fired at Mick, which he quickly shoots down. Finally, Scott, who in real life seemed to live to argue about everything and anything, stepped in by firmly stating, "Come on, Mick, stop arguing, all you ever do is debate."

With that word, a light bulb seems to go on in Mick's head. "Debate, debate, that's it!" he yells triumphantly. "I'll call myself the Masked Debator."

Pretty cool, huh? Actually, don't be surprised to see a "Masked Debator" making his way to World Wrestling Federation rings soon, as the gimmick has money written all over it.

Unfortunately, things do not go well for the Debator, who is dressed in a blue polo shirt, a Baltimore Orioles ski cap (to hide my hair) and a sparkling mask that looks like Julie Newmar's Catwoman disguise in the *Batman* series. I wonder if Julie watches wrestling, because man, I'd like to . . . Never mind—I don't know if we need to get into my fixation on seventies sitcom stars, and my theory that I might be able to nail some of them now that they're sixtyish and I'm on TV. I've actually got permission from my wife to nail Barbara Eden if I ever get the chance.

The Debator gets a little down when an anti-drug talk he's giving leads to disrespect. "Dammit, Scott, nothing's really changed, I still don't get any respect," Mick sneers angrily, before adding, "I'm sick and tired of being treated like a dog—get me something to eat."

"How about a Milk-Bone, Mick?" Scott replies, and then proceeds to make the poor Debator beg, roll over, play dead, and drink water out of a bowl on the ground, before finally giving him the crunchy canine treat.

"There's only one person who can help me," the distraught Debator declares, and opens the yellow pages to the Grand Lizard of Wrestling.

In the next scene, the Debator shows up at the Lizard's door, which oddly is just to the side of the Foley living room, with pictures of Mick and John Foley hanging in the background. The Debator throws himself at the mercy of the Lizard, who after lambasting him both verbally and physically, admits that he sees that "eye of the tiger" in Mick and agrees to take him under his wing. First the Lizard (who is actually Dan Zucker without the Groucho glasses) tears off the Debator's "preppy piss rag" and says, "Here, wear this, it's your first pajama top."

The action picks up as Mick's swinging friends are sitting on a couch reading wrestling magazines, wondering where their buddy has gone, and mentioning they haven't "seen that rat Zuck around either." All of a sudden, the Dude appears. He has entered the building alongside his manager, the Grand Lizard of Wrestling. The Dude is looking good with his long hair wig, pajama top with matching headband, long underwear with shorts over them, and work boots. He also is now wearing a goatee. (In a display of cinematic genius, the Dude scenes were filmed first, and then a clean-shaven Foley and Debator did the rest.) The Lizard looks resplendent in a New Year's Eve party hat and bedspread wrapped around him.

Together, the deadly duo insult the swinging wrestling magazine readers, prompting a "Who are you?" from Tim Goldstein.

After a bunch of incoherent drunken slurs, I was able to spit out "Dude Love."

"You're Dude Love?" Tim suddenly gasps. "The master of the spinning sidewinder suplex, the man who's been terrorizing the midwest for the past four months?" (Remember, back then professional wrestling still had many regional territories, instead of two national powers.)

The Dude then launches a verbal diatribe, which ends with "We're here for one reason, and one reason only: fame, honor, glory, and fortune; to destruct, to destroy, and to take the World Wrestling Federation belt—the ten pounds of gold—from around the fat waist of Ishmala the Puerto Rican Giant"(our version of Kamala the Ugandan Giant).

With that, the movie segues into a music video that is actually a good piece of storytelling, chronicling the Dude's rise to glory in the World Wrestling Federation. Combining interviews, locker room pull-aparts, and wrestling matches that took place in the snow in my front yard next to our big pine tree, the segment ends with a "busted open" Dude taking the gold from Ishmala. I think *The Loved One*'s greatest achievement is that we were able to get the real-life, five-foot-eight, two-hundred-and-eighty-pound Ishmael Lozada to wrestle in his underwear in seventeen-degree weather. I also should point out that unlike today's backyard wrestlers, who foolishly maim each other, no one was hurt during our wrestling sequences. Plenty of fake punches, though, and the Dude's ever-present "palm to the forehead thrust."

Unfortunately, success seems to have gone to the Dude's head as he shows up at a party in the Foley living room, where the swinging party animals are still sitting on the couch flipping through their wrestling periodicals. The Dude is now smoking stogies and throwing down brews, as he sports the same tinfoil belt around his waist that the original Dude wore in *Frank Foley*. The Dude is rude and crude, but seems to be especially intent on ruining the life of John Imbriani, once he's informed that "Imbro's engaged to a nice Irish girl."

"Oh, really?" asks the Dude.

"No, O'Riley" comes the answer. The Lizard then offers the Dude a hundred spot if he can steal poor Imbro's girl.

"How can you do that to him," a peeved McNugget yells, even managing to get up off the couch for a moment, but still holding an open wrestling magazine. "Ya never liked John anyway."

The Lizard hears this and is perturbed. "Yes, I do," he states. "And I even wrote a piece of poetry about him." With that, Zuck then proceeds to read a piece of poetry that I had actually written two years earlier. I guess you could say that John was kind of like my Al Snow back then, and I'm sure he's going to love seeing this in print.

With that, Imbro, who was five feet four and 200 pounds, jumped off the couch. As a running back in junior high school, he had once rushed for 350 yards in a single game and had a compact, muscular body somewhat like former wrestler Ivan Putski. Like Putski, Imbro attempted to level the Lizard with a "Polish hammer," but the 130-pounds-soaking-wet Lizard was able to avoid the horrible-looking hammer, and sent Imbro to the ground with a flurry of elbows to the head. As he worked over a stunned Imbro, the Dude made his move, and with a simple "Play your cards right, and with the Dude you'll spend the night," walked away with the poor little Italian guy's girl.

Tragically, Imbro, who in real life was a junk food junkie, was found in his bed (the Foley couch) amid a plethora of Ding-Dongs, Fritos, and candy bars, that had been handed to him in a dream by the Dude, who was brandishing a guitar and singing a touching ballad entitled, "Hey Imbro."

"Hey Imbro" by M. Foley
Hey Imbro, give this chocolate fudge cake a try.
Hey Imbro, you know I want you to have a piece of this
apple pie.
Forget that you're a short little guido, have another
bag of these Fritos
Have another soda, because nutrition is a dirty word
Oh yeah, hey Imbro, Oh yeah, hey Imbro
Hey Imbro, I think that you've been acting awful rude.
Hey Imbro, don't be disturbed, because you lost your
girl to the Dude
Sit here and have another soda. [At this point, I for-
get the words and ad lib a line that was beyond bad.]
Your dad's as old as Minnie Minosa,
Have another Ho-Ho, 'cause nutrition is a dirty word.
Oh yeah, hey Imbro, oh yeah, hey Imbro

With that, Imbro is handed the dreaded snacks that lead to tragedy. Scott Darragh was the first to find him, and immediately spotted lines of a white substance on a mirror on the ground. A simple test revealed his deepest fears. "Oh no, Imbro's back on the sugar," he cries. "I'd better call an ambulance."

The next short shows a haggard Dude, presumably after a night of erotic pleasure, still dressed in his Dude wear and mirrored shades. He turns on his radio and immediately hears a news flash about his deceased little buddy. The touching scene fades out as a guilt-ridden Dude weeps openly into his hands.

A press conference is called, and Dude (who is now clean-shaven, due to the fact that the climatic wrestling scene was filmed last) admits the error of his ways, and dedicates his big "backyard match" to the memory of Imbro. In a tribute to Jimmy Snuka's legendary nonsensical interviews, I used an exact Superfly quote in admitting that "I can break a bone out there, and I'm talking about any part of a bone."

It was time for the fateful match, set in the Zucker backyard, as passing cars whizzed by us on that cold January morning. The Grand Lizard was calling the action along with Steve Zangre, and the Lizard had a list of thirty wrestling clichés on a piece of paper to refer to liberally throughout the match. My opponent for the big match was Danny's younger brother, Teddy, who was using the name Big Dick Zuck and who used wrestling's most devastating maneuver—sodomy. "Welcome to the backyard match," beer-toting referee Scott Darragh began, "rules, are there are no rules." With that, the match began, and Dude fought off a Big Dick slap to the face with a flurry of really fake offense, culminating in the deadly palm thrust. Things were really going the Dude's way until a big "Dude Love, you suck" echoed in the chilly East Setauket air. "Uh-oh, it's taunting by Ishmala," Zangre informed the audience. It was true, the former champion had

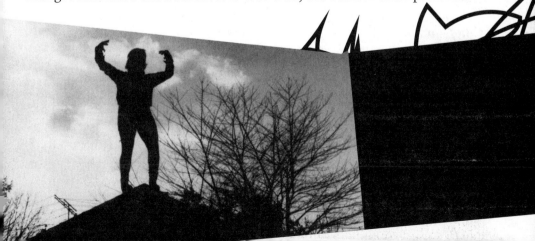

made his way to the Zucker backyard, and as Dude turns his attention to the fat bastard, Big Dick seized the opportunity and leveled me with a wiffle ball bat to the head. A hell of a swing, too. For the Dude to get out his blood supply, which was in a Jif peanut butter jar, Ted was supposed to parade around with the bat, so that the camera could get off the Dude, who needed his privacy. But he forgot, so the Lizard's commentary was a little suspicious as he said, "Look at Zuck, he's parading around with the bat. Teddy, Teddy, parade around with the bat. Ted, you need to parade around with the bat. He's parading around with the bat. He's showing the fans he's number one."

When the camera goes back to the Dude he is "busted wide open." With the Loved One in trouble, Big Dick proceeded to grab him in what the Lizard described as "the big ball grab." "He's really got a handful there," Zangre expertly added. Even with his testicles in turmoil, the Dude had the presence of mind to feel the warm flow of blood streaming down his face, and when he touched the juice and saw the red residue, his scrotal suffering seemed to disappear. With that, I wound up a punch that missed by about six inches, and began a comeback that was Ricky Steamboat–like in its intensity.

Using his hidden resources of strength, the badly bleeding Dude was able to counter with a backbreaker that left Big Dick twitching. Off camera, someone snapped a twig on cue, leading Zangre to speculate, "I think he broke his back on that one." Even with the taste of red food coloring and corn syrup dripping into his mouth, the Dude was able to continue on, and carried the wounded Zuck to his landing pad of mattresses and cardboard boxes in the middle of the Zucker driveway.

"Look at this," the Lizard yelled. "A lot of guts, pride, and intestinal fortitude." Then the Dude pulled the ladder from the side of the house, and began climbing slowly as the camera showed Big Dick on the landing pad. "Look at Zucker, he's busted wide open. This is a . . . vendetta," the Lizard screamed, as he searched for a cliché that hadn't been used yet. Also, Big Dick was definitely not busted wide open, even though the Dude was about to be . . . again.

"Look at Foley, he must be fifty, sixty, seventy feet in the air," Liz dramatically stated, in what had to be one of the greatest exaggerations in sports-entertainment history. "He will die tonight!" With that, the Dude took off from the roof of the circa 1878 Zucker house, which was probably a legitimate thirteen feet in the air. The dive was completely inspired, and was actually performed without a whole lot of fear. The fact the Big Dick rolled out of the way and avoided certain injury did nothing to taint the beautiful leap.

With Dude in a daze, Big Dick covered the champ, and referee Scott Darragh put down his beer in time to make the three count. There was a new champion, but he wasn't done with the Loved One just yet. In a flash, he bent Dude over, pulled down his shorts, and appeared to violate the former champ with one quick thrust. "Oh, it's the sodomize. Dude Love has been sodomized," a frantic Lizard yelled, as his man rolled around in agony, having been "busted wide open" in a sense never meant for pro wrestling. Thanks to the magic of clumsy editing and my trusty Jif jar, it appeared as if blood was soaking through the Dude's long gray underwear and shorts ensemble.

Like most people who are the victim of an uninvited anal intrusion, the pain the Loved One was feeling was at least fifty percent mental, and in his shame, he takes off through the woods, while the Lizard follows, shouting "Dude, Dude, come back Dude," as my friends laugh hysterically.

As the camera faded out, you could hear the faint voice of cameraman Ed Fuchs saying, "That sucked."

"What do you mean?" I asked Ed. "I thought that went great."

"Yeah," Fuchs admitted, "but you jumped too soon, I didn't get it."

"Too soon?" I whined. "I told you to zoom out as soon as I flashed the Snuka sign."

"Hey I'm sorry," Ed apologized, and then added, "Do you want to see it?" Sure enough, the Dude's awesome leap was but a blur, and a few minutes later, I found myself on the Zucker roof again, but this time suffering from a severe case of testicular nonfortitude.

Yeah, it's true, the Dude was chickening out big time. The roof looked a lot higher, the landing pad looked smaller, and I really didn't foresee a happy ending to this take. In truth, the boxes that had helped break my fall were now crumpled and almost useless. Finally I got the nerve and jumped, but it was far from the dynamic leap of minutes earlier. No height at all. But at least we had our dive on tape. It's just too bad that the World Wrestling Federation didn't see the first dive, and it's also unfortunate that many Internet people incorrectly assumed that the stain on the Dude's shorts was a big poop stain from the impact of the fall, instead of a bloodstain from the impact of a weenie.

The next scene is a tearjerker, as Dan and Felice are shown at their picnic table after sharing the whole sordid story. "There's one thing that I don't understand," Felice asks. "From what you've told me, you and Mick Foley weren't even good friends, and when Dude Love was around, I thought you were in Ethiopia, teaching women how to give blowjobs. Why are you so upset?"

"Because, Felice," Dan answered while taking off his Groucho glasses, "I am the Grand Lizard of Wrestling."

Felice is shocked at this astounding revelation, and responds by announcing, "Yes, Danny, now I understand, and yes, I will marry you, but there's one thing I need to know. Whatever happened to Dude Love?"

Dan gets a little misty when he thinks of his bunghole-busted buddy, and sadly states, "I don't know whatever happened to him, but wherever he is I'm sure he's too psychologically scarred to ever wrestle again. Come on, Felice, let's go."

With that the happy couple shuffles away, while the love theme from *Officer and a Gentleman* plays. No, not "Up Where We Belong," which was a big radio hit, but the slow violin music that played while the camera afforded us a nice view of Debra Winger's tiny boobs as she lovingly rode Richard Gere. While that music plays, the camera slowly pans up a giant evergreen tree to find a shirtless, drooling Dude about twenty-five feet in the air. The camera goes to black and a video montage airs to the music of Jethro Tull's "Elegy," which is about as nice a piece of music as I've ever heard.

The movie was odd in that despite the bad jokes, bad wrestling, and horrible acting, it was actually pretty touching, and I have seen people (no joke here) fight back tears as they watch it. I have also heard that someone had offered $2,000 on the Internet for a tape of the entire movie, as only clips have been shown on TV. I sincerely hope it doesn't get out to the public, as it's kind of special to watch it every several years with friends knowing that it is a completely private showing. If *The Loved One* surfaces, I'll hunt down the Grand Lizard and make him suffer, as he and I are the only ones with a copy of the landmark film.

When we were nineteen and drunk in my parents' house, none of us ever dreamed that our little movie, or at least portions of it, would be seen by millions across the world. I also had no idea that *The Loved One* would allow me to get my foot in the door to the world of sports-entertainment.

* * *

In March 1985, my dad called me with exciting news—professional wrestling was coming to Ward Melville High School. "I talked to the promoter," my dad told me, "and he said that if you come to the show, he would talk to you about becoming a wrestler." Man, I couldn't wait. It was going to be a loaded-up card, and I was going to be there.

I drove the five hours from Cortland, New York, in nervous anticipation of what the evening would have in store for me. I even got a speeding ticket by the Johnson dairy stand, where we used to stop for ice cream on the way to my grandmother's house in Wayland. Even a ticket from a state trooper couldn't ruin my mood, as I thought about suplexes and pile drivers, and getting to meet some of the guys.

I arrived at the Melville gym (now, as I mentioned, the Jack Foley gym) at around three o'clock, as the ring was just arriving. My dad introduced me to promoter Tommy Dee, a man with all the flash and sizzle of a UPS truck. I asked Dee about becoming a wrestler, but he didn't offer any encouragement. "You have to find somebody to train you" is all he said. He then asked me if I had any wrestling videos, as the wrestlers might like to watch them in the dressing room.

"Yes sir, I've got a great collection of MSG matches," I informed the unsmiling Mr. Dee. "I'll go get them." I hurried home, picked out half a dozen videos, and started to walk out of my tiny room, when I stopped and turned around. I looked at my desk and saw *The Loved One* sitting there with Dude Love on the front of the box, and the words, "a journey into greatness starring the B.P." Without thinking why, I grabbed the tape and headed out the door.

When I got back to the gym, a television monitor and VCR were waiting for me. Lacrosse practice was just letting out, and the guys who were sophomores when I was a senior were very happy to see me. Like I mentioned earlier during the Dave McCulloch fight scene, for some reason kids looked up to me, and many of these people in the Ward Melville gym were the same kids who had looked up to me three years earlier.

"Hey Mick," one of them said. "Do you have that movie you guys made?"

"Well yeah, I do," I had to admit.

"Can you put it in?" he asked me next.

I started to stutter and stammer, but was soon overcome by shouts of encouragement that convinced me to have an impromptu screening.

But I wasn't about to lose these impressionable young Foley fans with bad dialogue and acting, so I wisely fast-forwarded to the Dude's first entrance, knowing that our music video would provide quality entertainment.

When the Dude appeared on the screen, the high school kids actually cheered. The sound was up loud so that the room of students could all hear, and I guess the noise must have attracted more kids, because a stream of them started flocking over to the television set. By the time the music video began there were, without exaggeration, a hundred high school athletes around me, and to every one of them I was the man. At least at that moment I was. It may be the Jack Foley Gymnasium now, but in March 1985, I owned the place.

The Dude was on the screen throwing fake-looking chops. They were cheering. The Dude was in a living room brawl with Ishmala—more cheers. And when the Dude opened up a can of whoop-ass and took the World Wrestling Federation gold—forget about it—the place went crazy. I looked around, and I saw these high school kids, most of whom I didn't even know, cheering for a guy with a wig and long underwear. Then, out of the corner of my eye, I spotted Tommy Dee, and he had a smile from ear to ear. All of a sudden, I wasn't just a college punk with a pipe dream of being a wrestler. I'm pretty good about reading people's faces, and his was an easy one—I read, "I've just discovered a star."

Next, I fast-forwarded to the wrestling scene, and the partisan Ward Melville crowd shouted their approval. They cheered when the Dude was on the attack, exploded when he flew off the roof, and howled with laughter as the violated Dude ran off through the woods. I looked at Tommy Dee, and his huge smile told me that he had really dug the backyard match. Either that, or he just thought the idea of me being bent over and banged in the butt was funny. Regardless, Tommy approached me a little while later and asked if I would like to start working on his ring crew. "I run about four shows a month," he said in his thick New York accent. "If we get the ring set up in time, I'll get one of the veterans to work with ya in the ring."

I was overjoyed. I met and had photos taken with many of the stars, including Sergeant Slaughter, Larry Zbyszko, Bob Backlund, and Rick Martel. In the background of my Backlund photo, there is a gawky nineteen-year-old who would turn out to be Paul E. Dangerously. My dad and I had a great dinner at Mario's in East Setauket after the show. We talked about the show, which had sold out the 2,500-seat Ward Melville gym, and about the chance that I might one day step inside the squared circle. I was foolish enough to believe that every Tommy Dee show would draw a sellout, and that every crowd I worked for would cheer my every move. The world of pro wrestling was about to teach me some hard lessons.

It was September before Tommy Dee ran shows again, as he never ran during the summer. For years, Tommy had promoted shows for the World Wrestling Federation, but struck out on his own when the Federation's national expansion made small Federation shows in the New York area pretty much a thing of the past. So now Tommy booked whoever he could, and sometimes it drew, and . . . sometimes it didn't.

My first Tommy Dee show was a memorable experience. I began the day by leaving Cortland at 4 A.M. and driving to "the big yellow storage building" in the middle of Brooklyn—a horrible yellow landmark in a horrible part of the city. I guess I should point out that even though I grew up on Long Island, and watched shows in Madison Square Garden, I actually can't stand the city. Especially Brooklyn—except for the pizza. I met Tommy at Big Yellow and was told my assignment for the day. I had to go up to the eighth floor of the building, take the ring out of storage, load it into a truck, drive the truck to a high school in Staten Island, set up the ring, tear it down when the night was over, drive it back to Big Yellow, unload it, load it into the freight elevator, unload it at the top, and load it into storage. I then drove the five hours back to school. I had left Cortland at 4 A.M. and returned twenty-six hours later and $25 richer, before expenses. I will always be grateful for that day, however, because it was the day I met Dominic DeNucci.

I hadn't had a chance to train with DeNucci, who was the "veteran" that Tommy had lined up for me, because the ring hadn't been set up in time. But a week later, in a church in Brooklyn, with the ring set up, my mind longing for sleep, and my body weary, I stepped inside the ring for the first time. I had seen Dominic wrestle as a kid and had seen him defend the tag titles on two different occasions. He spoke on TV with a heavy Italian accent, and I soon learned that the accent, like much of wrestling itself, was no act.

"So, you wanna be a wrestler?" DeNucci sarcastically asked. That turned out to be a common question as he tested my will many times in the coming months. "I tella you what," he offered. "I'lla step into the corner, and I wanta you to givea me a forearm."

Wow, this was going to be easy. I had seen forearms thrown a thousand times, and I knew just what to do. "Are you ready?" I asked.

"Come on kid, show me whata you got," came the reply.

"Okay," I warned him, and reared back with my right arm, while simultaneously lifting my left foot. Stomp! My foot came down in perfect synchronization with my forearm, and made a huge noise. It was good, and I knew it. There were a couple of other wrestlers watching this training session, and I knew that they knew it was good.

Apparently DeNucci didn't know that I knew that they knew it was good, and told me a piece of advice that I will never forget. Actually, he told me quite a few things that I would never forget. "Kid, don't think that this is alla bullshit like you see on TV." This was a definite downer. I really thought that this whole thing would be easy after the Ward Melville show, and now I was about to find out differently. "This is how you throw a forearm," he declared, and then reared back with his massive arm and thrunk, delivered a huge blow across my upper chest. I felt like my breastbone was going to cave in. "So you wanna be a wrestler," he sneered, as he proceeded to pummel me with five more consecutive smashes that left me longing for John Alt's lectures.

"If only I could be back there taking tests with my dictionary," I thought, as I tried to recover from my lesson in respect. I heard a lot of things going on in that ring in those few moments. I heard DeNucci laughing, I heard myself gasping, and I heard the sickening thud of a fifty-year-old man's bare forearm across my T-shirted flesh. I did not, however, hear one foot stomping.

"That, my boy," said a proud DeNucci, "is howa ya throw a forearm."

I knew right then that I had learned a valuable lesson. I looked at DeNucci, and I knew that he knew that I knew I had learned a valuable lesson. I looked up at the small group of wrestlers and I knew that they knew that Dominic knew that I knew I had just learned a valuable lesson.

Looking back at the Brooklyn forearm incident, I really wish that I had made my blow count a little more. It was the last offensive move I would get in for four months.

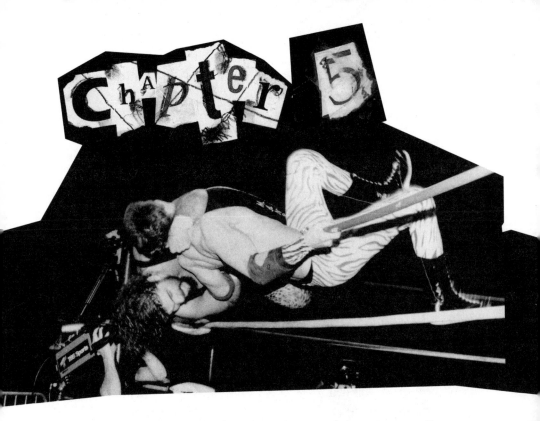

By the middle of December, I had set

up the ring for Tommy Dee about a dozen times, earned $300, but unfortunately had been in the ring only four times. It wasn't DeNucci's fault—he was more than willing to throw me around and twist my body in ways that nature never intended. I just wasn't physically able to set up the ring in time to fit in our training. In those four sessions, however, I had begun to learn one thing—how to bump. Or as armchair wrestling experts around the country would say—"I knew how to land."

Bumping is, without a doubt, the most valuable thing a wrestler can learn. Without it, a career would be awfully short, as the injuries would pile up in a hurry. I guess it's no secret that the trick in landing is to try to disperse the fall over as great an area of the body as possible. I've heard for years that I don't feel pain, which is ridiculous, but I do believe that I was blessed with a perfect body for bumping—wide back, wide hips, and a wide flat ass. As a result, I don't look all that good in a tight pair of jeans, but I can absorb unbelievable punishment. I also believe that the human body can adapt to the physical grind we go through. In the same way that a body isn't made to run a marathon, but instead is trained to do it, I believe that my body has been trained to take punishment. François Petit, a master in shiatsu massage, who has performed over 50,000 shiatsu massages, swears that my body is the strangest that he's ever worked. "Meek, Meek," he always says in his French pronunciation of Mick, "your spine is like that of a crock-o-dile—it's unbelievable, Meek!"

Dominic was not an easy guy to impress, and when he was impressed, he wasn't real big on compliments. I guess that's why it meant so much to me when he finally started praising me. Don't get me wrong, it wasn't like he was cold-hearted, he was just more likely to say, "It wasa not bad" about something that had gone well. I did find out, however, that he'd been impressed with my ability to get back up after taking a backdrop. "I give that kid from New York ten backdrop, and he musta have a ball this big [his hands showing the size of a grapefruit] because he kept getting up," I later heard he had said about our first training sessions.

After the marathon backdrop session, Dominic talked to me alone in the dressing room, and I guess for the first time realized not only how much this wrestling thing meant to me, but also that I may have possessed the testicular fortitude to see it through. "I traina some boys in Pittsburgh," he informed me, adding, "If you really wanna to learn maybe you should come there."

I was flattered, but thought that DeNucci's "school" might pose a problem. "I appreciate that, Dominic," I replied, "but I really don't have much money to pay you."

DeNucci nodded in understanding and quickly told me, "You come to Pittsburgh, and we can work something out." He then gave me the single best piece of advice I ever received in wrestling, and maybe in life in general. "Don't think you gonna make a living doing this bullshit." I nodded blankly and listened intently as he offered up his only stipulation: "You a college boy, you stay in school or else I don't train you." Over the years, I have passed this along to every hopeful wrestler I have ever encountered. The chances for success in this strange business are so slim that a college education is absolutely essential.

So, in the beginning of 1986, I headed to the Pittsburgh suburbs of Freedom, Pennsylvania, for the first of about seventy trips. If I'd known that Pittsburgh was 400 miles from Cortland, I might very well have declined Dominic's offer. However, by the time my dad handed me the Triple-A Trip-Tik, I had already committed. I will freely admit to being scared as hell about my first trip to Freedom. I had driven down the day before and stayed at the $16-a-night Admiral Perry Motor Lodge, which is now a Toyota dealership, at the point where Interstate 80 intersects with Interstate 79. I had absolutely no offensive moves in my repertoire (unlike the list of four I have been using for the last three years), no confidence, and $100 to my name. As I said earlier, however, I had learned how to bump. And as with most things, I learned by practice, practice, and more practice.

I might have had only four training sessions under my belt, but I'd been doing my homework in a very strange way. Every night, I would drive my car, which by this point was the '78 Ford Fairmont that I'd inherited from my mother, to a park about a mile away and commence to bumping. It might not have been a cold concrete floor, but it sure as hell was a hard grass floor, which tended to get real hard in the Cortland winter, which stretched from November into April. I would set up an obstacle of some sort, usually a garbage can, and would practice diving over it and landing on my back over and over, until my wind was gone and my flat ass was sore. Then I'd catch my breath and bump some more, until landing on my back became second nature. To this day, I defy anyone to find footage of me putting an elbow or a hand out to break my fall. I really don't think such footage exists.

One night, I heard voices coming from the bushes. It was John (from now on called Jake) and Steve, and they were somewhat baffled by what they'd seen. "What the hell are ya doing, you weirdo," Steve interrogated me.

"I'm just working on my falls," I said, somewhat embarrassed, as I didn't really want my new endeavor to be publicized.

"You," Steve flatly stated, "are a weirdo." Steve had taken to calling me a "weirdo" more often, ever since I showed up at his parents' house too tired to drive after a Tommy Dee show and asked his poor mother if I could rest there for a couple of hours.

Steve and Jake were great guys, but I didn't sense a great deal of support from them on the subject of wrestling, so from that point on, for the next eight months, I didn't talk about wrestling anymore. I didn't even tell them about DeNucci's school, and I instead explained my weekend absences with a weak story about a girlfriend in Pittsburgh.

I walked into DeNucci's school in Freedom and meekly met the other trainees. The school was actually in the gym of the old Freedom elementary school, which had been abandoned. It had no heat in the winter, and as I would find out, no air conditioning in the summer. What it did have, however, was Dominic DeNucci and four hungry students who wanted to learn. It was with great interest and great trepidation (believe it or not, one of Steve Austin's favorite words) that I met my fellow trainees—Dave Klebanski, Kurt Kaufman, Troy Martin, and John Pamphilles.

Klebanski was a mountain of a man about six feet tall and 320 pounds, with a huge chest, a huge head, and a horribly bushy hairstyle to cover it. Deep down, he was like a big kid, whose voice would get real high when he complained, and whose business choices would ground what should have been a promising career. Not the least of his problems was his friendship with David Sammartino, whose own odd business choices grounded his own promising career.

Kurt Kaufman was a late starter—about thirty at the time, and the owner of a good physique, which unfortunately didn't stand up well to the constant barrage of punishment in the Freedom gym. He was a hell of a nice guy, though, who put me up in his home several times. I will always remember Kurt for his rapid adoption of the "grizzled old veteran" demeanor, in which he talked softly, called everybody kid, and talked about his short career as if he were Terry Funk. "I'll tell you, kid," Kurt once confided in me, "those West Virginia fans may be tough, but they're some of the best people I've ever worked in front of." I think he'd had three matches at the time. It was almost as if he'd channeled both the spirit and look of DeNucci, as Kurt began wearing a weight belt outside his clothes, smoking small stogies, and walking DeNucci style, even if he didn't have Dominic's twenty-five years' experience to account for it. Kurt Kaufman will also go down in the record books for holding a victory over Cactus Jack in the Hardcore Legend's first outing.

Troy Martin would go on to greater fame as Shane Douglas, the Franchise of ECW fame and the Dean of World Wrestling Federation nonfame. He was intelligent, athletic, and handsome, and if anyone from DeNucci's school looked like a surefire prospect, it was him. Shane has been his own worst enemy sometimes, has burned bridges that he shouldn't have even bothered looking back at, and has had more retirements than both Funk brothers put together. Without him, though, I wouldn't be where I am today, and might not have graduated from DeNucci's gym.

John Pamphilles was a talented guy, but he was small, kind of plain, and moved away soon after my training began.

After my hellos, DeNucci brought me into the ring. "This isa Mickey, he's froma New York. He's green, but he takea decent bump." That last part of the quote did me in—the part about "takea decent bump." He might as well have put meat loaf underwear on me and walked me past a pack of wild dogs. The four of them proceeded to bump me without mercy for most of the next three hours. I was slammed, hip tossed, suplexed, and back body dropped so many times that I couldn't even afford to guess how many. To make matters worse, I didn't have experience hitting the ropes, and as a result, took the force of the cable on my liver instead of my latissimus muscle. By the next morning, I was peeing blood, but I went through it all again the next day. I was so banged up that I could hardly move.

Dinner following my first session in Freedom stands out as a particularly memorable occasion. There was a Bonanza steakhouse about seventy-five yards from the Admiral Perry, and despite the sure eight dollars I would have to spend, I decided I deserved it and headed out the door. I was so weak that I could hardly hold the heavy oak door, and nearly tripped and fell onto the marble-tiled floor. Actually, it was a cheap pressboard door and a dirty rug, but it was difficult nonetheless. Without exaggeration, the seventy-five-yard walk took me at least ten minutes, as every fiber in my being throbbed with pain. The porterhouse on my plate did nothing to soothe me, as "What the hell am I doing here?" became my question of the day. Actually, I would ask myself that same question every day for the next several weeks, whenever I wrestled in Western Pennsylvania.

I was both physically and mentally exhausted when Dominic asked to speak to me after my Sunday workout. "Kid, we need to talk about money," he said flatly. "How much ya think you should pay?" This was uncomfortable to me, especially the part about me suggesting a price. Even today, I hate to be asked how much money I want. I would rather shoot down an offer and make a counter offer for much more than flat-out request the same amount. I had heard that DeNucci's school was $100 a day. I didn't even have $100 period, let alone per day, so I decided to shoot low with the veteran and said, "How about fifty?"

He thought it over and shook his head. "No," he said, "I can't do that." My heart sank, before he continued his dismissal. "It's too

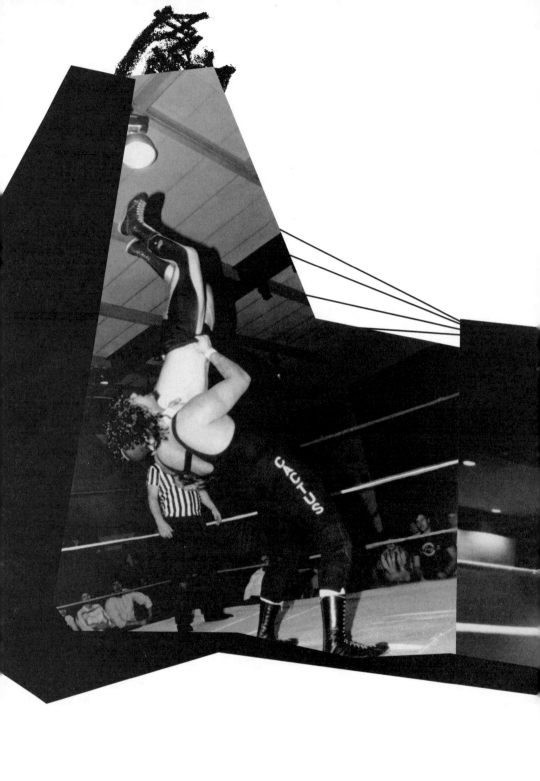

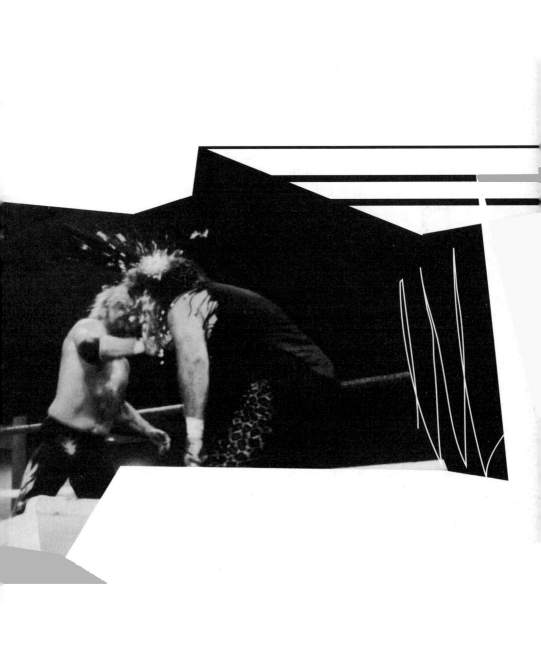

high—how about $25?" I couldn't believe it. Next he said, "You gonna need some boots, these are brand-new—you want them, give me $25, okay?"

"Yes sir," I quickly answered, as even in my wrestling infancy, I knew a bargain when I saw one. Those $25 boots would go on to see ceiling (lose matches) in some of the finest arenas in the country—as well as some of the emptiest armories and parking lots.

Even at the discounted rate I had so shrewdly bargained for, I knew that I couldn't continue to throw money around like I had. So I began skimping on certain things like food and lodging. The Bonanza was out, as was just about any place that charged for food. The era of the jar of peanut butter and the loaf of bread was ushered in. Even at $16 a night, I knew I couldn't afford both Friday and Saturday night in a motel, so Fridays officially became car night. I threw two sleeping bags into the backseat of my Fairmont, where they stayed for the next year and a half. I would leave Cortland at 10 P.M. every Friday night for the eight-hour trip to Freedom—giving myself six extra hours to rest. If I made it all the way, I would park at the gym and sleep in front of it. If I got tired along the way, I would simply pull over at a hotel and park in the lot, curl up, and catch a nap.

Sometimes the guys would get to the school and have to wake me up. Often the car would be covered in snow, and I would emerge like a bear from hibernation, ready to rumble. I actually enjoyed my backseat bed, as I was very aware that this was part of my paying my dues, and as I kept reminding myself in ten-degree weather, it was building character. It seems to have worked, and I can honestly say that one of the great comforts in my life is that I feel completely deserving of all the good things that have come my way in the last few years. I know for a fact that I earned them.

Not all my car memories are happy ones. About a year after starting at DeNucci's school, I set out for another weekend of training. I would alternate driving the New York State Thruway west to Erie, Pennsylvania, where I would turn south to Pittsburgh. At that point, I'd never heard of a lake effect storm or snow squall. It had been snowing for some time, but as a road veteran, I was having no problems. Suddenly, just as I was coming to an exit, the wind was blowing and the snow was flying to the point that driving became almost impossible. For some reason, I went on, thinking it would suddenly clear. I was wrong. An hour later, I had traveled only a few miles, and

I pulled over for the night and checked into my Fairmont Hotel, where I slept soundly inside my two sleeping bags.

I was awakened by the tapping of a motorist on my windshield. "Are you okay?" he yelled.

I was still half asleep, and responded with a ridiculous "Sure, yeah, go ahead," that I later regretted deeply. I climbed into the front seat and attempted to fire the mother up. Needless to say, the mother didn't fire. Neither did it flicker or even spark. It was one dead mother. I got out of the car and my initial reaction was, "I'm going to die." It was so cold and so windy that the wind was whipping right through my trusty red flannel and freezing me to the bone. In an act of self-preservation, I began to run, and with luck on my side, found a trooper station less than a mile up the road. A day later, the Interstate opened up and I drove the five hours back to Cortland just in time to catch the Super Bowl.

I had some other driving mishaps, but these were sometimes mental lapses on my part. One time, I drove to Freedom to find Dominic on an independent trip that I had forgotten about, as had Tony Nardo, another aspiring student. We drove to Dominic's house, where we were given the bad news by his wife Jeneane. Jeneane was nice enough to give us the key to the gym, and Tony and I rolled around for an hour, returned the key, and went home. Total training time, one hour—total driving time, sixteen hours.

I did that trip one better shortly after college graduation when I was living with my parents in East Setauket. East Setauket was almost 500 miles away, instead of the 400 that Cortland was, and so it was with great sadness that I showed up in Freedom, only to find out that training was canceled. After a few minutes of somber soul-searching as to what the hell I was doing in the wrestling business, I did an about-face and drove home. Total training time, zero minutes—total driving time, twenty hours. I chalked up all these situations to paying my dues.

After about four trips to Dominic's, I found I really had only two problems. One, I sucked at pro wrestling, and two, I hated it. After my big Ward Melville Dude Love debut, everything had been downhill. Now, at Dominic's, I was finally getting to try some offensive moves, and couldn't cut the mustard. Even the simplest things were confusing to me. Doing a hip toss was like doing algebra—I didn't have a clue. A schoolboy rollup might as well have been nuclear physics, and a drop toe hold, brain surgery. I have several witnesses who can attest that I was the worst natural wrestler they ever saw. So when in the ring with me, the other students concentrated instead on what I was capable of—namely, taking an ass kicking—and proceeded to help me hone my skills in that specific area. I was really so bad that I wanted to quit, and the only thing that was stopping me was my pride. I had talked so much about wrestling for so many years that, if I quit, I would have felt like a huge failure.

Thankfully, after a long time, the fog began to lift, and I began to learn, and in turn began to enjoy myself. I credit my turnaround to hard work and perseverance, but above all else, the dedication of that old "som un a bitch," Dominic DeNucci. Too many times, I've heard horror stories of wrestlers' "training" guys just as a way to rip them off. The Undertaker recently told me that he paid Buzz Sawyer to train him and basically learned how to lock up (begin a match) in Buzz's backyard before showing up and finding that Buzz had skipped town. On the contrary, I think Dominic saw me as his special project—as if he wanted to see if combining my thimbleful of talent and my "ball thisa big" could somehow turn out a decent pro.

On several occasions, he would arrange for me to come back later in the evening for one-on-one training, during which I did things I never thought possible. One night he wanted me to learn a sunset flip, and I flat out told him that it was impossible. He persisted, and after several embarrassing attempts, I managed to pull one off. I was elated to the point of jumping up and down. It was like the first time I was able to climb the rope in gym class, except without the half woody. "How was that, Dominic, how was that?" I excitedly asked my mentor.

"It wasa notta bad," he replied, in typical DeNucci fashion.

He was a vivid storyteller who spoke in parables to illustrate his point. When one new wrestler asked about learning fancy moves, his reply sounded like it came straight from one of the Gospels. "My boy," be began, "thisa business is likea the alphabet. Ya can not spell big words without learning all the letters. First, you heara the letters, next you spell out a little word. Then next you using big college words likea Mickey and Troy."

"Gee, Dominic," offered Dave Klebanski, "you're kind of smart for a guy who can't speak English."

Well, maybe Dominic never has mastered the English language,

MICK FOLEY

even after forty years in this country. Then again, maybe he goes home and drops the Italian accent completely, like a pizza shop owner I know who uses it only as a business gimmick. I do know, however, that my view of Dominic changed when we began traveling overseas, where I stood with my college-educated thumb up my butt, while Dominic rattled off fluent French, Spanish, and of course Italian in all the different countries we went to.

I wrote a little earlier about Dominic testing my will, which he did, but I have to explain how healthy a thing that is. Throughout much of the history of the business, wrestling trainers have often had two schools of thought about aspiring wrestlers. The first school is to take anybody who has the money, teach him the very bare essentials, and throw him to the wolves. Unfortunately, with so many "trained" wrestlers out there, and so few shows being run, most of the guys' "careers" consist of only a few very small matches. The wrestling landscape is literally littered with thousands of wannabe wrestlers who don't know a wristlock from a wristwatch.

The other school of thought is the "let's show them wrestling is real" school. The concept is drummed into these poor unsuspecting kids in different ways, the most popular of which is to exercise them until they puke, and then get them in the ring and eat them alive. I'm guessing most of these trainers didn't get enough love as children. Some would intentionally injure a prospective student, so as to send him back to the real world with a different outlook on wrestling. A common ploy was to goad an unsuspecting student into the hands-and-knees amateur wrestling "referee position," under the impression of learning some technical skills. Once the student was in the position, the trainer would abruptly drop a knee on the back of the poor kid's ankle, immediately breaking it, and therefore putting him in a cast so he could tell all his friends that wrestling was "real."

If a prospective wrestler came from an athletic background, he was often singled out as an example. I knew a guy who helped train wrestlers in the Midwest who told me he was encouraged to "stretch" legitimate athletes to show them just how real wrestling was. Never mind that this guy was one of the worst pros to ever lace up the boots—he was a skilled amateur who knew all the dirty tricks, and he sent many a pro football player packing. So instead of having a quality lineup of great athletes, this one promoter scared off all the good talent and ended up showcasing some of the worst abortions the business has ever seen.

Bar fighting was another way to show how real wrestling was. Sometimes inflicting injury was not enough to prove a point—permanent injury was the answer. For a while in an era that I thankfully was not a part of, the art of taking out another man's eye was a noble effort in the quest to legitimize pro wrestling in people's minds. When I broke in, I heard stories that made me sick, including one where an eye was not only torn out of its socket, but was also purposely stepped on and crushed as the victim tried to retrieve it.

I wonder how these people live with themselves now as senior citizens, knowing that there are people their age walking around with hollow sockets because of a stupid, cruel, and senseless code of manhood that they lived by decades earlier. An old episode of *Hawaii Five-O* that has stuck in my mind for almost thirty years makes me think of these pathetic wrestlers. In the episode, a tough military man admits to raping a girl, even though his sexual impotence makes the admission impossible to believe. McGarrett asks the man why he would be willing to risk a twenty-year sentence for a crime he didn't commit. "I'd risk my whole life," the tough guy boldly states, "to keep the rest of the guys from finding out I wasn't a man."

"A man?" a flabbergasted McGarrett shouts. "Do you know what it really means to be a man! You haven't a clue, you haven't a CLUE! Danno, get him out of here!" When it comes to being a man, sadly, a lot of wrestlers, both past and present, haven't a clue either.

Thankfully, DeNucci subscribed to neither theory. He neither took my money selfishly nor tried to make an example of me. Yes, he made me respect the business, and yes, he put me in some holds that were sheer torture, but he never tried to prove himself by abusing me or anyone else. I once heard it said that "there is no such thing as a bad student, only a bad teacher." I'm not sure if that's always the case, but I do know that it was Dominic's patience and skill as a teacher that turned me into such a good student.

In addition to my wrestling studies, I was also turning into quite a scholar at Cortland. Wrestling seemed to give me a focus, and this focus helped me achieve more scholastically than I ever thought possible. My projects in radio and television production, which I had decided to major in, were class favorites, and upon graduation, I was even awarded the Anne Allen Award for the outstanding student in my major. So what if there were only ten students in my major, and the rest of the school were gym teachers—the award was mine, mine, all mine.

One of these school projects nearly cost me one of my most valued friendships. I was doing my documentary project along with a girl named Debbie James, who I'd been friends with since my freshman year. Debbie agreed to accompany me to Pittsburgh for a weekend so that we could do our documentary on DeNucci's school. Now, I feel that my Freedom travels taught me a lot of lessons about life, but unfortunately, these lessons did not include how to treat a woman on the road. Don't get me wrong, I wasn't mean or abusive, but when it came time to sleep on Friday night, she was more than a little surprised to find that a motel didn't fit into my plans. Grudgingly, she went along with my routine (it was spring, so the weather was no problem) but it was several days before she spoke to me again. "Mickey, you made me sleep in a car," was her simple rationale for the silent treatment, when she finally did decide to speak. Somehow, we were able to turn out a great documentary that looked close to professional quality, and she was able to turn out a few kids who are now big Mankind fans. I can't wait until they get old enough to learn what a cheap bastard their hero was.

After three months at DeNucci's, I arrived back in Cortland on a Sunday night to a rude welcoming from Jake and Steve. "We need to talk to you" they said.

"What is it?" I innocently wanted to know.

"You say you have a girlfriend," Steve said, as the interrogation got under way.

"Yeah, so what," I was quick to say.

"Well," Jake interjected, "you never call her and she never calls you. You leave every Friday and you come home every Sunday. You smell like shit, and your hair is all plastered to your head. You have sleeping bags in your car, and there are food wrappers everywhere. You have about ten jars of peanut butter in your car, and you have a black eye every other week."

"So what," I countered, "what are you trying to say?"

Steve jumped in and came right out with the wicked accusation: "We think you're wrestling."

"No, I wish I was, but I'm not," I lied as I headed up the stairs.

"This isn't over, Rich [he'd been calling me that ever since the "Frank" incident], not by a long shot. I know you're wrestling, Rich, I know you're wrestling!"

I hated to lie, especially to guys that I spent so much time with. But

I honestly felt that wrestling was something I wanted to keep just to myself—at least until I reached my goal. And my goal at that time was simple. It wasn't to be the World Wrestling Federation champ, or to be the King of the Death Match, or to be the tag champs, or even to be a sports-entertainer. I simply wanted to have a pro match and then I would consider myself a success. As school came to an end in May I was getting close to reaching my goal.

In the second week of June 1996, I left a summer school session in Cortland, where I caught up on all my credits and then officially moved to Pittsburgh for the summer. I really didn't know if the Fairmont could withstand those 1,000-mile round trips. Seventy thousand miles later, when the car finally died, I realized that I was wrong. I got into Emsworth, Pennsylvania, where Rob Betcher had set up a place for me to live with his grandmother, a relationship that almost immediately went sour.

Mrs. Betcher lived in a tiny house on a tiny street. Pittsburgh was in the middle of a heat wave, and the little Betcher house didn't have air conditioning. And I didn't have a room, so I slept on the pullout couch in the living room. As a result, Mrs. Betcher, who like many elderly people was an early riser, was treated to a regular morning view of my hot, sweaty, twenty-year-old body sprawled in her living room, attired in only my Fruit of the Looms. I guess even at 210 pounds (which I was down to due to a lack of food in my budget), I had a body that spanned all generations in its ability to turn off the female gender.

A few days later, a professional football player died of a drug overdose, which, combined with the oil spill the size of a nickel I left on her driveway, spelled trouble. I guess one of her friends got into her ear and convinced her that the football OD meant all athletes, including me, were drug users. Apparently, she felt strong enough about it to wake me up out of a near-naked sleep to request my immediate departure from her humble abode. "Ricky [yes, even older women forgot my name], you've got to go right now," she yelled, as she shook a feather duster for emphasis. Sadly, I left the little house, and went to the University of Pittsburgh, where for $25 a week I sublet a room in a house with two college students that I got along fine with. When I got to Clarksburg, West Virginia, on June 24, for my first battle royal (where all the guys are in the ring at the same time), I was ready.

I was feeling cool and confident when I got to Clarksburg. After all, how difficult could a battle royal be? I had seen them as a fan and also sat ringside at Tommy Dee's shows, so I knew that there wasn't a whole lot to them. This, I felt, would be a great way to get my feet wet, without actually having to dive all the way in. Suddenly, Dominic appeared, and in one quick sentence, shot down my cool and confidence and my whole "feet wet" strategy. I was going to wrestle in a singles match. "Mickey, you a gonna wrestle Kurtains [Kurt Kaufman] in the second match tonight," he informed me. "And I want to see some wrestling, no punch-kick."

Man, this was nerve-wracking. To be in the prestigious Clarksburg Armory alongside such wrestling luminaries as Jerry "the Wanderer" Macintyre, Bill Berger, Lord Zolton, Buddy Donovan, and Irish Mike McGhee was all I could have ever hoped for. I sought out ring announcer Hank Hudson to give him my statistics. "You're one of DeNucci's students, aren't you?" the velvet-tongued Hudson asked.

"Yes, Mr. Hudson, I am," I replied.

"Okay, what's your name?" Hudson inquired.

That was a tough one. I wanted to be Dude Love, but I knew that I didn't have the experience or the talent to be the Dude just yet. Maybe in another six months. In the meantime, I needed another name while I developed the poise to be the Dude. I thought back to a fantasy wrestling game that I had ordered a few years earlier, in which I had been Mick "Big Train" Foley, and my dad had been Cactus Jack.

The Cactus Jack name had come up as a joke when I asked Danny Zucker why everyone seemed to be nervous when they came over to my house. "Well," Zuck had said, "we're afraid to do anything wrong when your dad's around."

"Zuck, don't be ridiculous," I informed the former Grand Lizard, "my dad is nothing like that when he's home. As a matter of fact, he doesn't even want to be called Dr. Foley at home—he wants to be called Cactus Jack." This was a complete lie that was told in the hope of Danny coming over and saying, "What's up, Cactus Jack?" to my unsuspecting father, who would no doubt have put his papers down long enough to give Zuck a look as if he'd just farted in church.

So when Hank asked me my name, "Cactus Jack" was the answer that came out. "Where are you from, Cactus Jack?" the veteran ring announcer/postal worker asked next.

"Um, um, Bloomington, Indiana," came my weak reply.

Hudson quickly showed why he earned the big bucks by responding, "I don't think there's any cactuses in Indiana, what about Arizona?"

"Okay," I agreed, "is Tucson, Arizona, good?"

Now Tucson would have been just fine, but not to a man like Hank

Hudson, whose postal training had exposed him to every hometown under the sun. "Isn't there a Truth or Consequences in Arizona?" Hank asked my blank face. "Oh no," he corrected himself, "that's Truth or Consequences, New Mexico."

The hometown fit like the pants of a man with five penises—like a glove. I liked the hometown so much that I kept it for the next twelve years. I kept the Cactus Jack thing longer than expected, too.

I had a name and a hometown—now I just needed to wrestle. I was lucky enough to be wrestling against the grizzled two-match veteran Kaufman, whose "Don't worry kid, I'll lead you through it" did little to soothe my nerves. Fortunately, I remembered a series of moves that we had done at DeNucci's gym earlier, and asked him if we could try the "leapfrog dropkick thing" we were working on earlier.

"Sure, kid," said the battle-tested Kaufman with a Backwoods stogie clenched between his teeth. "No problem."

Despite Kurt's reassurances, there was indeed a problem. A leapfrog, you see, can be done two different ways. In one way the man in the middle of the ring leapfrogs over a charging opponent. In the other, the man in the middle bends down for a backdrop and the charging opponent does the leapfrog over him. Can you see where this is headed? Midway through the match, I shot Kurt into the ropes and bent over for the backdrop, expecting a leapfrog. For his part, Kurt came charging off the ropes with his head down, expecting my jumping skills to carry me over him. Klong! We smacked our heads together like two rams performing a mating ritual. The force of the collision sent both of us on our asses, as the audience both gasped and laughed at the sick sound of our skulls cracking together. I saw stars, but also saw red. "Come on Kurt," I pleaded. "Let's do the leapfrog." Another whip, two more heads going down, and klong, an exact repeat of our previous debacle. Luckily, I don't remember the rest of the match, although whether it was due to the injury or selective memory I'm not certain. I do know that I lost the match, and that the show in Clarksburg was the first day that I met Brian Hildebrand.

Brian was a manager that night, although of whom, I can't recollect. At one time or another, Brian managed everybody in the West Virginia-Ohio-Western Pennsylvania area. I believe the show in Clarkburg was his final one as Heimi Schwartz, as he has spent the last thirteen years as Marc Curtis. When he came to DeNucci's the next day, it was obvious that he was far more than just a manager—at 140 pounds, he was one of the most well-rounded wrestlers I had ever seen. Brian had the ability to work any style, from brawling to technical to high flying. He was studying Japanese tapes and attempting their moves long before I knew such things existed. If he'd been fifty pounds heavier, he would have been a big star in the business, but his rapid metabolism never allowed him to put on weight. As a result, he went into managing as a second choice, and as a result, became my second manager, after the Grand Lizard.

I often wondered why Brian came to DeNucci's at all, as after the Clarksburg show, he became a regular for the rest of the gym's existence. "How much better does he need to be," I thought, "especially when he's a manager!" The truth is, Brian was simply out there because he loved this business more than anyone I have ever met, and he would do anything to be around it. His presence at Dominic's was like having another teacher there, and because he was my manager for the next two years, I was privy to an expert's analysis of my match immediately. I have since had the benefit of being managed by some very good people, many of whom have been national stars, and I can honestly say that none of them knew or loved wrestling like Brian did. His knowledge and presence helped me greatly and his friendship and support have been among the most prized possessions in my life.

Over the summer of 1986, I also began developing a strong friendship with Troy Martin. DeNucci now had several students, and many of them seemed to think that they would learn by proxy—as if all that was required was their presence in the gym to improve. Getting in the ring, it sometimes seemed, was not a prerequisite for success. For some of them, DeNucci's became a place to joke around. For me and Troy, who had made something of a pact that summer, the gym became a place to make our dreams come true. By the time the summer ended, I not only had a partner to develop moves and matches with, I also had a place to stay every Saturday. Friday was still car night, because I could never guarantee my arrival, but Troy and his mom proceeded to house me almost every Saturday after that. As the summer came to a close, I was actually starting to show some potential, and was elated to get a mid-August call from DeNucci.

"Vince needs some boys to do the TV," DeNucci's unmistakable voice informed me. "Do you want to do?" I was dumbfounded. On one hand, I knew that being an extra, or a "job guy" (body to be thrown around), for the World Wrestling Federation was great exposure. On the other hand, I knew that performers were easily typecast in their role of loser, and once in it might be unable to get out. I know that I remember perennial World Wrestling Federation losers like Israel Matia, Gino Corabella, Ken Jugan, Mike Shape, Mac Rivera, S. D. Jones, and Steve Lombardi every bit as well as the guys who defeated them. Still, the World Wrestling Federation was on a roll, and I, along with Troy, Tony Nardo, Kurt Kaufman, and trainee Ray Miller, shuffled off to Providence and Hartford for a chance in the big leagues. It turned out to be a rude awakening.

*   *   *

I ran into Vince McMahon in the gym in Providence and we spotted each other on the bench. I helped him squeeze out a couple of extra reps by yelling, "Feel that pump, Vince, feel it burn!" Afterward, he thanked me and told me he'd been following me on the independent scene for a long time.

Actually, he just said a quick hello in a two-second encounter that he forgot as soon as it was over. For some reason, I just like the sound of the first story better.

When I got to the Civic Center in Providence, I basically stood around and stared at all the stars I had been watching on television and in the arenas for years. I wish I had possessed the Dude's confidence and charisma, but instead I just sat in the room like a 235-pound slug (weight training and emergency food relief from my parents had plumped me up). Some time later, Pat Patterson (of current stooge fame) asked to speak to me. Pat informed me that along with my partner for the night, Les Thornton, I would be taking on the British Bulldogs—Davey Boy Smith and Dynamite Kid—who were the current tag team champions.

"What's your name?" Patterson asked me.

"Cactus Jack" came my reply.

"Well, we can't let you use a gimmick name," Pat told me. "We'll have to use your real name. Also, kid, you'll have to get rid of the bandanna."

Patterson then asked me how many matches I'd had, and I made the mistake of telling him the truth. "Just one," I quickly answered, while Pat shook his head in disbelief.

"Well, what can you do out there?" he wanted to know.

"I can take a lot of bumps," I was glad to inform him.

By this time, the Bulldogs had walked over to get a look at this guy they would be facing. "Hey Dynamite, it's nice to meet you," I said to the man who pound for pound may have been the top wrestler in the world.

In addition to his World Wrestling Federation matches, I had seen tapes of many classic encounters in Japan that, for my money, were among the best matches of all time. I felt privileged to share the same ring with him, and I wanted him to know that I was going to be doing my best for him. "You can give me that snap suplex if you want," I offered the man who had been responsible for bringing high risk into the Federation, and who would also be responsible for my inability to eat solid food for the next month.

"Thanks, mate," he said with a smile, as he turned and winked at Davey.

Hey, I didn't want to forget about Davey—I had something special lined up for him too. "Hey Davey," I offered. "I throw this really great elbow, and I was going to try to work that in. Is that okay?"

I saw Davey and Dynamite laugh, but didn't think anything of it, as Davey said in his thick British accent, "Yeah, sure, I think we'll do a lot of great stuff out there."

I went out to the ring and started yelling at the fans. There was a whole world of difference between the 300 who were scattered about the armory in Clarksburg and the 18,000 who jammed the Civic Center in Providence, so I actually had a little bit of a rush going through my body when the fans responded to my verbal taunting. At this point in my career, with Dude Love still off in the future, I figured I would concentrate on making Cactus Jack kind of a rebel with an attitude. Really, for a beginner, a lot of finding a gimmick is simply throwing as much crap at the wall as possible and seeing what sticks. And what usually ends up sticking is not all that much different from the guy who is throwing it, although I was too green to see that at the time. In Providence, Rhode Island, in 1986, I thought I was doing just fine.

The Bulldogs came to the ring accompanied by Captain Lou Albano and their royal English entrance theme. I began to feel slightly out of my element. When the match started, I knew instantly that I was in trouble. Les Thornton was, like the Bulldogs, an English wrestler, and a technical expert. For two minutes, he and Davey did some fine technical wrestling, and then Davey tagged the Dynamite Kid, and Les tagged the scared twenty-year-old *kid*. An announcement might as well have been made, saying, "Ladies and gentlemen, the scientific part of the match has just concluded, but please stay tuned for a major ass whipping." It was devastating. I tied up (began the match), and right off the bat, in accordance with my previous wishes, I was snap suplexed nearly out of my boots.

The suplex offered me my first chance to experience the Federation ring, and although stiff, my body seemed just fine, at least for the time being. A snapmare came next, followed by a diving head butt so painful that I could see my eyes crossing on the video replay. As I struggled to get to my feet, Davey Boy was tagged in to resume the fun.

A big horizontal suplex and a powerslam followed, but hey, these were both moves I'd endured countless times at DeNucci's gym, and when Smith hooked me in a loose front facelock, I figured it was my time to have some fun. I immediately began firing weak-looking elbows at his midsection, in a quest to get in my big elbow on national television. Davey could have no doubt clamped down on the hold and shut me down completely, but instead he let go. Knowing Davey as I do now, I think he was probably just getting a kick out of my youthful exuberance and wanted to see where it would take us. It took us right to the ropes, where I fired off my amused opponent, and caught him coming off the opposite strands with my big flying elbow. I'd done it—I'd landed my big move on Federation television. Sadly, instead of the "ooh" or "aah" that I felt such a devastating move would merit, I heard laughter, and looked up to see Smith smiling. One headbutt later, which thankfully didn't hurt, Davey tagged out, and a fired-up Dynamite Kid came in with bad intentions in his mind.

Dynamite had broken into wrestling as a skinny fifteen-year-old in England, where for years he'd been told he was too small to make the big time. As a result, he had worked harder and became more vicious in the ring than anyone I've ever seen. I also believe he had a genuine mean streak in him. With 225 pounds of muscle packed onto a frame that was probably never meant to hold more than 180, he was a devastating mental and physical presence. Looking back at it, I honestly think that he saw my weak attempt at offense as a slap in the face, and his body started physically shaking on the ring apron as he begged for the tag. When he tagged in, there is no doubt in my mind now, as I believe there was none in his then, that he planned to hurt me. He shot me into the ropes and followed me a half step behind the whole way. When I came off the ropes, he clubbed me across the jaw with his biceps, in what I guess was technically a clothesline. I never saw it coming, and the effect was devastating. Pain shot from the tip of my jaw through my ears. Then, with my ears still ringing and my head was pounding, I was suplexed backward off the top rope, and I fell in an awkward way onto my shoulders and the back of my head. As future Minnesota governor

MICK FOLEY

Jesse Ventura called the slow-motion replay, I could see Dynamite looking back at me with a combined look of concern/satisfaction.

I was helped to the back by one of the referees, and when I got there, saw a look on veteran wrestlers' faces that was comparable to that of an observer of a car wreck. Even Greg Valentine, whose career had not exactly been characterized by touching displays of affection, gave me a concerned, "Are you okay, brother?"

"Do you know where the Bulldogs are?" was my only reply.

"They went in there, brother." Valentine smiled, and I could see others raising their eyebrows in surprise at what they probably viewed as the beginning of some stupid retaliatory locker room attempt. I have since seen many a locker room incident over wrestlers "taking liberties" on their opponents, and if anyone ever had just cause to be a little bit peeved, it would be me.

I opened the door and saw them standing together, looking like the cumulative cat who swallowed the canary. I didn't hesitate a bit in telling them what was on my mind. "Thank you very much," I said, while shaking hands with both men. "I really appreciate it." They smiled with a touch of disbelief, and let me know that they too had enjoyed themselves.

Wrestling is strange in that way. Respect for the veterans is a necessity, although, in my mind, so too is respect for your opponent's body. I learned a long time ago that in the wrestling business, as well as in life in general, you run into the same people on the way down that you did on the way up. It is my hope that through kindness and respect, these people will see fit to let me down gently instead of dropping me. Unfortunately, it seems that the Dynamite Kid has been dropped, and his ex-wife told me he lives, unable to walk, in his native England. Although I don't agree with what he did to me in my second match, he was extremely nice to me when I toured Japan with him in 1991, and I recently spoke to his ex-wife about organizing a benefit that may one day help him walk. After seeing how much he gave to his sport, and how little it left him in return, I would consider it an honor to try to help him.

I traveled to Hartford for the second set of World Wrestling Federation tapings. It was several hours before the show, but my parents were standing out in front of the building nonetheless. They had been in attendance, and wanted to tell me how much they enjoyed my match. "Great job out there," my dad informed me. "Your mother was so impressed that she even put her book down when you went out."

I gave them a "Thank you," but I guess my dazed eyes gave me away, and my concerned mother asked me if I was all right. "Well, my jaw is really hurting, and I can't close my mouth or eat food, but other than that, I guess I'm all right."

My mom seemed stunned and offered the same sentiment that I'd heard so many times before—"But I thought it was all fake?"

Even in my clouded state, I offered up words that were a pretty good synopsis of the previous night—"Mom, nothing has ever felt so real in my life." I don't think my mother has enjoyed a match since then. Even to this day, she will tape my matches, and then only watch them when she finds out I'm all right.

In the dressing room, I sat down and minded my own business, but I felt like I had somehow become slightly accepted because of my previous night's mugging. Both Bulldogs asked how I was, and King Kong Bundy extended his hand in friendship, even though he immediately rescinded after seeing me adjusting my balls with my shaking hand. A couple of guys talked about possibly seeing the Jeff Goldblum movie *The Fly*, and they wondered if anyone had seen it. When I raised my hand, and offered my Siskel-like thumbs-up, Les Thornton chimed in, "You looked like a fly yourself last night, mate." The laughter of the boys made me somehow feel like one of the guys. Unfortunately, my efforts on this night made me feel like the greenhorn I truly was.

I was scheduled to team with veteran Terry Gibbs against the Killer Bees, Jim Brunzell and B. Brian Blair. I saw Blair just a couple of weeks ago, and he remembered me only as the guy who kept pulling his pants up and bleeding from the mouth. That basically sums up the match. I was shot in early in the match for a back bodydrop and landed fine. Unfortunately, the injury from the night before caused my jaw to swell, and my bite to become misaligned. As a result, when I landed, instead of my mouth closing as normal, my teeth smashed together, and the two front ones were knocked in. Now anyone who has seen me wrestle for the past ten years knows that my front teeth are gone anyway, but back then, all I could think of was that my perfect smile was gone. Blood was coming out of my mouth, I was still out of it from the Bulldog beating, but for some reason I pulled up my pants after every move. It was miserable. We were the second-to-last match of the night, which meant that no one made a peep after four hours of tedious wrestling, and I was at my absolute worst.

I left the dressing room despondent and got into my Fairmont to head up to school. These two shows had actually taken place on the first two days of school, and I needed to make some time on the 300-mile trip back so as not to miss another day. As I pulled out of the back lot, I saw some familiar figures at the gate. Danny Zucker, John Imbriani, John McNulty, Dan Hegerty, and Ed Fuchs were there waving me down, and when I stopped they were all sporting the biggest smiles I'd seen since we all used to pile into a car with our fake IDs and a fistful of ones for Pepper Night at Centerfolds. It didn't matter to them that I'd stunk up the place—I was their buddy, and they thought that my just being in the sold-out Hartford Civic Center was good enough. We went out to eat, and their spirits brightened mine. I left the diner with a different outlook—an outlook that said, "I have made it. I accomplished my dream!" With that in mind, it seems that the past thirteen years have just been a constant readjusting of my dreams—with my current one being to retire in one year with my health intact.

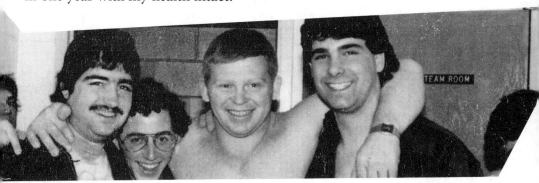

I rolled into Cortland about four in the morning, and was awakened early by Jake and Steve, who had seen my trusty Fairmont outside in the drive. "We know you're wrestling," yelled Steve, "and your name is Catfish Jake."

I smiled as I thought of my vow not to share my wrestling with them until I'd had my one match. "You're right," I admitted, while the two teeth that would require root canals to save them throbbed in my mouth. "I've been wrestling this whole time."

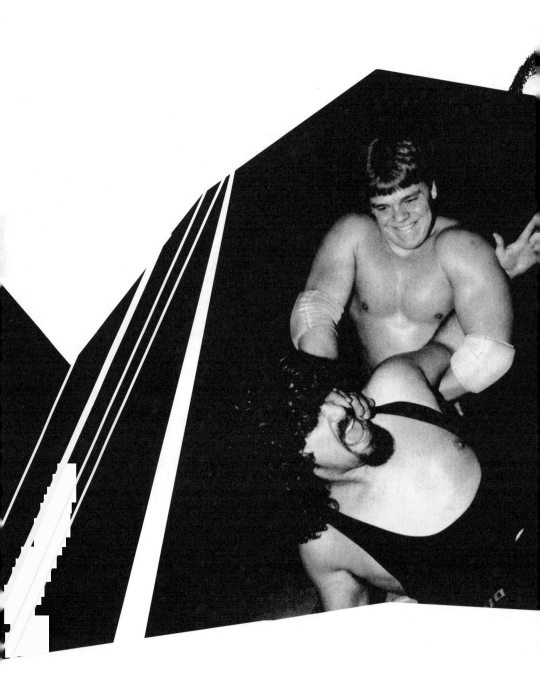

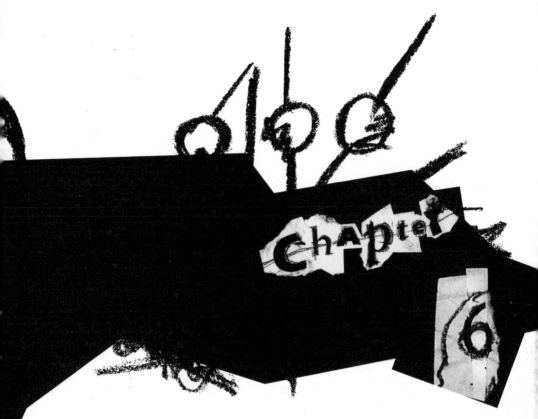

I took a couple of weeks off from the wrestling wars while my jaw shrunk back to normal size, and I enjoyed being a college senior. I had actually had a short-term girlfriend (the "first love" I mentioned earlier) at the end of my sophomore year, but she had made seeing other guys look like an Olympic sport that she was extremely dedicated to. As a result, I came out of the relationship wounded, more insecure than ever, and determined not to let the same thing happen again. So I shut off my romantic feelings almost completely and threw all of my emotions into wrestling. To be quite honest, I enjoyed thinking about wrestling nonstop during my eight-hour commutes, and I became a great visualizer of future triumphs. My mind has always been my best asset in the ring, and I certainly developed my propensity to "think wrestling" during my first year in the business. Sometimes I would have to force myself to calm down when the images got too strong, especially when my favorite road song, "The Ride" by David Allen Coe, was playing.

With the airing of my World Wrestling Federation matches, things began to change socially for me also. Suddenly, I was on TV and girls were coming out of the woodwork to talk to me when I went out. After a few minutes of small talk, the conversation would inevitably end up the same, with the girl saying, "I hear you wrestle," and me saying, "How did you know?" Every last time, the answer would be the same—"Because my boyfriend told me," and then she'd point to some fraternity guy standing behind a wooden beam, giving me a big thumbs-up. I can honestly say that no girl I ever met in college was attracted to me because I was a wrestler. Or if they were, maybe they were just doing a good job of hiding it from me. Actually, there was not a whole lot of time for socializing anyway, because in my senior year, a time that most college guys are having the time of their lives, I spent twenty-eight out of thirty-two weekends in Freedom, Pennsylvania, or whatever small town I happened to be wrestling in. And believe me, I wrestled in some small ones.

Maybe the low point of my career was our big event in Polka, West Virginia, at the Polka High School, home of the Polka Dots. Yes, the team's name was the Dots. Now that must have sent a shiver down the spines of countless opponents. The trip started out in fine form, with me, Troy, Brian, and Dominic all in the same car, having a jolly good time. Actually, a lot of the times were good ones back then, despite the fact that I was beaten up, financially destitute, and couldn't get laid if I was in a women's prison with a fistful of weekend passes. There was just an innocence to it then, because my motives were so pure. I loved wrestling, plain and simple. Now, with wrestling being hotter than it's ever been, I tend to look at it as a business and don't want to risk too much on any given night—whereas back in those days, I'd put it all on the line no matter what the attendance was. Polka, however, was pushing it.

We got to the building, and there were only two cars and a ring truck there. "Maybe we're early," I cheerfully said to Brian, who, with several years under his belt, knew better. "Cactus, think of this as a practice session that you will make $10 for." In Polka, West Virginia, in front of exactly twenty-six people (I know because I counted them when I was out there), Troy and I had a full dress rehearsal and gave the people who were dumb/lucky enough to be there a match that was probably better than half the stuff that's currently on WCW Pay-Per-View. At that time, I was just starting to be a high-impact risk taker, and I took risks on that empty gym floor that I won't take on *Raw* tapings these days.

We drove back 200 miles to Freedom, elated from the match instead of deflated from the bomb scare (poorly attended match) in

Polka. I spent my $10 payoff at a RAX restaurant, and there wasn't a sour face at the table. Even Dominic was happy, looking at "his boys."

Somewhere around this time, Dominic pulled me aside at the gym in Freedom. "How long you been coming here?" he wanted to know.

"I don't know," I began before adding, "I guess about nine months."

"And all this time you been paying me, right?" he added in what seemed like a strange tone of voice. I didn't know where he was coming from, and I wasn't sure I liked it. Dominic then eased my mind. "I tella you what—from nowa on, you don't pay me. What you have done take a ball about this big [basketball size] and you don't need to pay me anymore." So for the next year, I went to Dominic's free of charge. I learned and improved a great deal that year.

I did a few more Federation shows in the next few months, but stopped as soon as I sensed the slightest recognition from the fans. I didn't want to be the next Israel Matia, and so I politely declined the next invitation I received. A month later, I was given the chance to indirectly work for Bill Watts, whose Mid-South territory was now attempting to expand nationally. Watts was known in the industry as one of the founding fathers of exciting television. While Vince McMahon's Federation had expanded nationally by virtue of great marketing and the image of sports-entertainment, Watts had depended on a more physical style and an episodic TV format. Unfortunately, Watts's territory of Louisiana, Oklahoma, and parts of various Mid-South states had felt the financial sting of the oil business drying up, and as a result, he was looking elsewhere to run his territory. He already had TV syndication in Pittsburgh, Ohio, and West Virginia, and he was using Dominic's shows as a litmus test for future expansion.

The four shows would feature UWF (Watts had changed to Universal Wrestling Federation so as not to be stigmatized as a Southern group) stars Terry Taylor, Buddy Roberts, Eddie Gilbert, Missy Hyatt, Chris Adams, Dark Journey, and the Missing Link, and talent from DeNucci's school. I drove with Troy along 150 miles of back roads to get to Hundred, West Virginia. The roads were so desolate that we envisioned another Polka on our hands as we weaved in and out of dense mountains. When we got to Hundred, we were shocked. The tiny high school gym was packed with 1,000 screaming fans, and we were on first, so I headed for the dressing room to take a quick Snow and get dressed for my match.

Apparently, Hundred, West Virginia didn't believe in pooping in peace, as the toilets were unsheltered in what seemed to be the middle of the dressing room. It was on this rather revealing bowl that I met Eddie Gilbert, who would go on to be one of my best opponents, and his wife, Missy Hyatt, who at that time I thought was the most beautiful woman in the world. I quickly wiped my Sarven (Al's real name) and once dressed, proceeded to tear the house down with Troy, who by this time was wrestling as Troy Orndorff, supposedly the nephew of World Wrestling Federation superstar Paul Orndorff.

The next day, several of the UWF wrestlers were raving about the show. Terry Taylor told me that I would make a great "middle heel" in the UWF, and Buddy Roberts, in his own inimitable way, rasped, "You might have a future in this business." Of all the comments, though, Dominic's praise meant the most. After ridiculing Tony Nardo and Crusher Klebanski for having a match that was "the absolute drizzling shit," he pointed to me and said, "Now Mickey and Troy can take that match and go anywhere in the world with it." It was the biggest compliment I had ever received from that som un a bitch Dominic, and it meant a lot to me.

The next few nights with Troy were so impressive that I was matched up with Chris Adams, one of the UWF's top stars, on the final night. Apparently, this matchup had come at the request of Watts himself, to further verify all the positive things he'd been hearing. The Adams match in Ohio was the highlight of my career until that point. The high school gym was packed with 1,500 rabid fans and their support for the English Gentleman was strong. So strong that their cheering and stomping actually made my legs weak as I held Adams from behind in a rear chinlock. The Adams match was my first real hands-on lesson in ring psychology, and I analyzed it in my head for days to learn just why the crowd was so tuned in. I had been told several times, but I had no real way of understanding that in pro wrestling, it's not just what you do that matters, but when you do it and why. From then on, when "The Ride" boomed over my "top of the line" speakers in my "bottom of the line" car, I visualized not just what great moves I would do, but also when and why.

If January in Ohio had made me high, March in Johnstown, Pennsylvania, brought me as low as I've ever felt in my career, as I saw my big chance practically blow up in my face. My emotions were already jumpy when I found out that Bill Watts had sold the UWF to

Jim Crockett, who owned the NWA (National Wrestling Alliance), the company that would later be sold to Ted Turner to create WCW. I was convinced by DeNucci, however, that Crockett was intent on keeping the two companies as entirely different entities in order to do a Super Bowl of Wrestling–type supercard. As it turned out, Crockett took all the top stars for his own NWA, and pretty much killed off the UWF, but all of that was unknown to us on that dreary March 1987 evening. What was known was that Troy was on his way to the UWF as Shane Douglas and that the company was high on me for a good spot once I graduated college two months later. I really felt like this show in Johnstown was a final tryout for me, and my opponent for the night was Sam Houston.

Sam was the half-brother of Jake Roberts, and the son of former wrestler Grizzly Smith, and a hell of a young talent. He was skinny as a rail, but the chicks seemed to dig his youthful good looks. I knew I was in a separate locker room from Sam and couldn't even say hello, which was the way Bill Watts always wanted it, so I asked Michael Hayes for a little information on Sam. "What does he like to do?" I asked the leader of the Freebirds, who informed me "since Sam is small, he likes to fight from underneath—maybe out of a bear hug." I thanked Hayes for his opinion and imagined all the sympathy that would be pouring down on Sam when I wrapped my seventeen-inch pythons around his tiny waist.

The crowd wasn't exactly what Dominic had been hoping for, but they were enthusiastic and were getting quite into my contest with Sam, which was going very well. Sam was a natural and we had good chemistry, right until I shot him into the ropes for my dreaded bear hug, and I saw my career fall apart two seconds later.

As I was shooting him off, he said three words that baffle me even to this day—"Watch the elbow." I am as confused about it today as I was twelve years ago. "Watch the elbow"? What does that mean? Watch it do what? Do I duck it? Do I take it? I really didn't know, but any answer would have been better than the one I came up with. Sam came bounding off the ropes full speed, and I saw him in the opening stages of what certainly looked to be a flying elbow off the ropes. I had every intention of taking it, and making Sam look like a million bucks in the process. Sam certainly did come at me with a big elbow, and I went down like I'd been shot, but immediately knew that I had screwed up worse than I'd ever messed up before. The elbow had missed me by at least two feet, and I had gone down—not just gone down but flown off my feet. I wanted to crawl in a hole—I hadn't been so embarrassed since my mother walked in on me when I was fourteen and caught me playing Coleco electronic football nude. At least then, I'd had an alibi. Barbara Mandrell's "If Loving You is Wrong (I Don't Want to Be Right)" was on the radio, and I'd quickly slipped off my gray corduroys. Barbara's wholesome sexiness always turned me on, but before I could get to know my body a little better, I'd seen the game, which was the hottest thing in school, sitting on my desk. My competitive spirit had won out over my primal urges, and I was in the middle of a hell of a game—the door opened and . . . I took a huge bump off of Sam Houston's invisible elbow.

At least there had only been one witness to the unique Coleco game. Two thousand people had witnessed my Johnstown blunder, and their laughter had let me know that I wasn't going to get a free pass on this one. I knew enough to get up immediately and proceeded to get some good heat on Sam. We finished our match, but I knew I'd lost my prospective job. Sometimes, all it takes is one big mistake for a hot prospect to be written off completely, and I'd just made it. Shane Douglas was going to the UWF, but his buddy Cactus Jack was going back to the drawing board.

That night, I sat almost comatose at a booth in the lounge of the Plaza Hotel in Pittsburgh. The other guys from Dominic's school tried to cheer me up, but it was no use. Brian Hildebrand did come close with one story, however. "There was a guy in a battle royal in the seventies who was one of the last three left," Brian began. "After he eliminated the third guy, he turned to the crowd with his arms in the air. A fan threw a box of popcorn at him which hit him in the head. This guy thought it was his opponent, and he took a huge bump over the top rope to end the match. You see, Mick, what you did tonight wasn't so bad."

"Well, yeah, that was pretty bad," I had to admit, "but let me ask you this—was the guy's career riding on that match?" Brian had to admit that it wasn't. "Mine was," I said sadly. "And I blew it."

Yes, I had blown it, but life went on, and I found myself faced with a heck of an opportunity as graduation closed in. Dominic had a spot open on a trip to West Africa one week after I graduated. Burkina Faso was a third-world country that had previously been known as

Upper Volta of Upper and Lower Volta fame, and it was trying to change its image. The tour was actually booked through a friend of the country's president, Thomas Sankora, who had already done quite a bit to improve his impoverished country. Professional wrestling was one of many things that summer, including a concert by Kool and the Gang and an appearance by Muhammad Ali, that were to be provided to entertain the citizens of Burkina. Because the tour was guaranteed by the government, we were to be paid $1,500 a week each for the two-week trip. I was overjoyed. While it may not have been the UWF, three grand was a lot of money for someone just out of college—in actuality, it was more money than I'd made in my two years in the business.

We touched down in the Ivory Coast, and I was immediately stunned by the poverty. On the outskirts of the city of Abidjan, most people didn't even live in houses—they lived in huts made of earth and twigs. As we walked along the streets, foul smelling human waste ran through the streets in a sewage system that was more primitive than I could have imagined. The next day, we flew to the swinging city of Ouagadougou, the capital of Burkina Faso, where conditions were even worse. President Sankora had attempted to cut down on the amount of panhandling in the country by teaching the locals various crafts. As a result, Burkina crafts were everywhere as we made our way by bus to the hotel that we were told was the best the country had to offer, but that looked suspiciously like a Days Inn in Cleveland. Actually, it wasn't too bad, and it even had a nice pool where we spent several hours a day swimming during the three days leading up to our first big show at the national soccer stadium.

It was at this pool that we spied Dave Klebanski, slathering on baby oil while sitting in his chair in the oppressive 110-degree weather. "Dave, what are you doing," I tried to warn him, "don't you know that baby oil will make you burn?"

I was backed up by several other members of the tour, but Dave would have none of it. "You guys treat me like a baby," he whined in a 320-pound high-pitched Three Stooges voice. "Leave me alone, I know what I'm doing." We left him alone.

By nightfall, we were all still at poolside, as there was only French television in the former French colony. As the sky turned darker, we could see flying objects darting into the huge tree to the side of the pool, until the tree literally chattered with the sound of thousands of bats. We were, as midget wrestler Butch Cassidy decided, "in a suburb of hell." For the record, Butch Cassidy was the first pro wrestler I ever met back when Tommy Dee had brought wrestling to Ward Melville.

Later that night, we went out to a restaurant to eat. The restaurant became our source for all meals over the next three days. The restaurant will go down in my personal history as being the first place I regularly drank beer, and the place with the worst chicken I had ever tasted and the meanest owner I had ever seen in my life. The guy was so nasty that I heard he was thrown in jail after we left for his mistreatment of the wrestlers.

The beer issue was a tough one for me to resolve in my mind, having been a nondrinker for so long. I prided myself on being an easy drunk, and I didn't need Burkina Faso screwing up my tolerance level. Sadly, it was the only logical choice I could make. I had been strictly warned against any water that was not bottled, so tap water was out. We were only allowed one drink with dinner, and our choice was between a ten-ounce bottle of soda, or a twenty-four-ounce bottle of beer. I went with quantity over quality.

The chicken was the sorriest thing I have ever seen, not including the Al Snow–Tiger Ali match from England. My mouth was literally watering when I ordered the chicken, as did everyone else on the tour. We forgot, however, that these weren't the farm-raised, grain-fed chickens that Frank Perdue turns out; these were West African chickens, which were a bit more anorexic than what I'd been used to. Needless to say, the chicken didn't exactly hit the spot—I don't think it even grazed it. I went to bed my first night in Africa with a rumbling in my stomach, and a "What the hell am I doing here?" right on the tip of my tongue. The next day would do little to satiate my hunger or answer my question.

Only a very small percentage of all Burkina citizens had access to television, so to advertise the matches, it was decided that we would provide the city access to us. All the wrestlers were loaded onto the back of a flatbed truck, where we were put on display for the next eight hours, while a recorded message blared over the loudspeakers. On that truck, for damn near all the city to see, stood one of the worst collections of pro wrestlers ever assembled. Besides DeNucci and five of his trainees, including me, stood Power Uti, the Nigerian champ, who was as rude and untalented as he was muscular; Mr. Haiti, a co-promoter of the trip; Butch Cassidy and his midget opponent, the Haiti Kid;

George Espada, a grizzled Puerto Rican, whose claims to being a great wrestler turned out to be a figment of his imagination; and a few other lost souls who, odds are, will never have their own action figures.

There we were, like gypsies on parade, as we rolled along past tiny huts filled with families and peddlers offering everything from eggs to water. Among our group, Dave Klebanski was still oiling up in his tank top, despite signs of blistering on his shoulders. At about the four-hour mark, a craving for water overcame our better judgment, and several plastic bags filled with questionable H_2O were ingested readily by our ragtag little group of thirsty future dysentery sufferers.

By the time we got to the national soccer stadium at the end of the third day, stomachs were rumbling and spirits were low. There were almost no cars in the parking lot, but a few thousand bikes were lined up as we made our way to the dressing rooms. I wrestled Dominic that night in front of 10,000 Burkina fans, which is an impressive number for a regular show, but not for a stadium that held 60,000. "Not to worry," we were assured by Belozzi Harvey, our chief promoter, a man so close to Sankora that he'd named his son after the president. "This is a political trip, and President Sankora is personally guaranteeing that all of you will be paid."

I felt a hell of a lot better with that knowledge as I took to the ring after a fifty-yard walk filled with the deafening silence of 10,000 people who had no idea what professional wrestling was supposed to be. I tried everything I could, including a backdrop on the grass, but got no reaction. Then Dominic snapmared me, and with a clap of his hands applied a rear chinlock, which caused the 10,000 to cheer in unison. "You see, my boy," Dominic said, laughing, "sometimes punchkick is no good, then you gotta do the wrestling." So for the rest of the match, we went through all the holds and reversals that I could remember, while the crowd clapped along.

The tour went downhill fast after that. Every day brought about an eight-hour bus ride over roads that Lewis and Clark probably would have had second thoughts about crossing. Our first stop was at a small soccer stadium with about 300 spectators. I remember it specifically for the classic contest between Crusher Klebanski, whose chest and shoulders were now blistering, and the masked veteran George Espada, whose tights were so tight that the seam pressed mightily against the middle of his testicles, and gave the impression that he had an awfully big vagina. Besides a low dropkick, George's offense consisted mostly of chops to the chest, which is probably not a good idea when your opponent is blistering. Within minutes, Dave's chest was no longer blistering but bleeding, and he was sent home as a very sunburned malaria victim a few days later when a mosquito apparently dined on his chest wound and infected him.

The next day drew approximately sixty fans to a small courtyard-like annex inside a large building. I remember the scene vividly: as a small family of bats congregated in a corner of the dressing room, we changed and pondered the possibility of our payoff. Again, Belozzi Harvey was there to reassure us that all of this was no problem—the tour was guaranteed by the president, and we would all be paid after the tour.

The sky looked threatening as the first match went into the ring, and literally opened up pouring rain a few minutes after the bell rang. Both wrestlers hightailed it to the dressing room, followed by the fans—yes, the fans. There we stood—the wrestlers, the sixty fans, and the family of bats, for the next forty-five minutes. When the sky cleared, the fans took their seats, and the show went on.

By this time, most of the crew was sick as hell, and on a few occasions, the wrestlers didn't even make it back from the ring before vomiting. Maybe it all looked like part of the show to the fans. For my part, I wrestled well every night, even though smells were starting to drift out of my butthole that I didn't think were legal. I even dragged a good match out of Power Uti, whose "Bring me butter, bring me bread" breakfast commands had shocked me with their crassness. I later found out that he bossed everyone in Nigeria around in the same way and, because he was something of a national hero in his homeland, he could.

By the time my two weeks were up, I couldn't wait to get home. When I got home, I wasn't the same for a long time. I suffered stabbing pains in my stomach and diarrhea for well over a month, but at least I had three grand to show for it, right? Well, not so fast.

About a week after I got home, I was watching television on the same couch where Dude Love had stolen John Imbriani's fiancée. Since I had been home, I had been checking every day for my government check from Belozzi. My dad was, as usual, reading the paper, and I'm sure there was some kind of game on television. "Hey Mick," I heard my dad say in a voice that sounded like it bore bad news. "What was the name of that country you just wrestled in?"

"Burkina Faso, why?" was my quick answer to the quiz.

"Well, I think you better look at this," my dad answered back, and then actually made a special trip over to deliver the bad news. He handed me the paper and pointed to a heading in the Sunday "World" section. There in black and white was the end of my $3,000 dream. "Government Overthrown, President Assassinated." I never did call Belozzi about the status of my payoff, but I went under the assumption that the new government wasn't going to pick up the old administration's sports-entertainment debts. I guess in retrospect, I had picked the wrong week to quit sniffing glue. (*Airplane* joke.)

*   *   *

My brother was married in July 1987. He had asked me to be his best man, but I had declined, thinking that I had another African trip lined up. As it was, the tour was postponed a few weeks, but by the time I found out, my position of honor had already been filled. I did opt, however, to work an independent date 500 miles from home, in West Virginia, the night before the nuptials. My payoff for the 1,000-mile round trip was an impressive $40. Taking into consideration gas money, tolls, and one night's lodging, I stood to lose about $100 on this show. Sure, I could have been eating a nice wedding rehearsal dinner and catching up on old times with relatives, but there was an independent wrestling show, dammit, and I didn't miss shows. Period.

I look back now and think of how ridiculous the whole thing seems, but at the time, there was no shaking me from my beliefs. I can fully understand when the Jamestown people in Guyana all drank the deadly Kool-Aid back in the late seventies. Sure it seemed stupid to anyone with any sense, but these people were believers in their cause, just like I was a believer in mine. My parents had looked at me like I was crazy when I told them my plan. "What do you mean, you're going to wrestle the night before?" my dad had asked me in an attempt to talk some sense into his son. "You'll miss your brother's wedding, for crying out loud."

"No, I won't," I reasoned with conviction in my words. "The show's only 500 miles away. That's an eight-hour drive if I make good time and don't stop. I'll make it home by six—with four hours to spare." My dad pleaded with me, but to no avail. My final words sent him away probably wondering where he went wrong as a parent. "Dad, I can't miss a show."

"Was it the doctorate in the summer?"

"Dad, I can't miss a show."

"Was it the nonstop Christmas music?"

"Dad, I can't miss a show."

Actually, it wasn't bad parenting, it was simply a firm belief that no show was complete unless I was in it, and the thought that maybe my big break would elude me if I slowed down for any reason. Then again, I'm not sure all those "S" words were that healthy, either.

As it turned out, the show would have been just fine, and the 200 people at the ramshackle race track probably would have understood if a wrestler they never heard of had stayed home for his brother's wedding, instead of driving 1,000 miles to get beat up and lose a Ben Franklin. To my credit, I tore up the pavement, and with the accompaniment of Steve Earle's "Guitar Town" and Lone Justice's "Shelter," won world titles numerous times in my mind, and dove off steel cages more times than I can remember by the time I turned into our driveway at 6 A.M. on the nose.

My brother woke me up three hours later. Was it to tell me what a good younger brother I'd been, and how he knew I'd make an even better uncle one day? Hell no! Instead, it was an attempt to appeal to my better fashion senses. "Mick, you can't wear jeans to my wedding," he said in disbelief as I pulled the blankets over my head and lovingly yelled, "Leave me alone," on the biggest day of his life.

Again, he insisted, "Mick, you need another pair of pants." In response, I muttered something so unintelligible that it didn't even have a vowel in it and went back to sleep.

I woke up with a start half an hour later, like Alistair Sim in *A Christmas Carol*, when he believes he's missed Christmas Day. I looked at my poor unloved jeans folded neatly over the chair. I knew this was my brother's big day, but wasn't he being a little stuffy about this thing? I had a jacket, after all, and the jeans were brand-new. Besides, I never did look good in any clothes, even before I approached the three bills (hundred pounds) mark. I didn't want to start a family feud, though, and time was running short, so I jumped into my battle-worn Fairmont, which now in the summer was down to one sleeping bag in the back, and headed off to Swezey's department store, which was on the way to the church. I grabbed a pair of chinos off the rack, changed in the dressing room, and took off the tag after paying cash for my purchase.

I was now racing against the clock. I knew I was late when I pulled into the church parking lot, but I thought that with entrances and Bible readings, I could make the meat and potatoes of the ceremony. Hey, I'd had to kill time in the ring while waiting for a main event performer to show up—surely they could hold up the proceedings for the master of the backyard match! I heard voices as I got out of my car. I was all set to rush in when I looked at my tie. It wasn't tied. Uh-oh, this posed a problem. These days, I can tie a tie as Mankind no problem. But back then, I was drawing on very limited experience that hadn't been exercised in several years. Still, I couldn't just rush in. If my brother had nixed the jeans, then he certainly wasn't going to go for the untied look. I thought for a moment about undoing a couple of buttons and going in with the leisure suit look that Lee Majors had used so well on the *Six Million Dollar Man*. "No," I thought, "that looked tacky even when it was in style." Instead I fumbled for what seemed like minutes while the voices mumbled inside the church. There—done. I walked inside to hear the clergyman say, "Let them see you now as Mr. and Mrs. John Foley."

I had officially missed the wedding. My plan was to play it off as if I'd been there the whole time, even though I knew that I hadn't. Out of the corner of my eye, I could see my dad giving me "the look." He knew that I had missed my brother's wedding, and "the look" showed me that he knew I knew he knew I had missed it. I saw the disappointment in my mom's face and I knew that she knew my dad knew that I knew he knew I had missed the wedding. Fortunately, my brother was too busy being happily married to worry about his little brother's blue jean blues. At least until this book comes out, and then he too will know that my mom knows that my dad knows that I know he knows I missed my bother's wedding. If he asks me about it, I guess I could sum it up by using a Hulk Hogan–like promo. "Well, brother, let me tell you something, brother. The reason I missed my brother's wedding, brother, is because my brother didn't like his brother's clothes, brother. Brother, maybe he wished he'd had another brother, brother. Oh, brother."

A few weeks later, I went on another African trip—this time to Nigeria. As a matter of fact, I went on two fourteen-day trips over the course of the next several months. These trips would mark my first two experiences with bloodletting of any consequence. I had experienced bloody lips and noses, abrasions and contusions, but Nigeria was the first place that I was ever "busted wide open." At least it was the first time I pulled off the trick without the aid of a Jif peanut butter jar. I arrived in Nigeria without the benefit of a tour group—indeed, I was the only American on the cards, which were to be held in the capital city of Lagos, and Power Uti's hometown of Benin. Lagos, as many travelers may recall, is the only city that is regularly listed at all airports as failing to meet international security codes. After my arrival, I could see why. I was whisked through the airport with the aid of a policeman, without going through customs or immigration. I also made the rather naive mistake of letting the promoter hold my return ticket.

I went through my match in Lagos with promoter Mr. Haiti, and then began promoting my big Nigerian championship match with Power Uti. On the trip from Lagos to Benin, I learned just how unlawful the Nigerian police were and also just how much influence Uti wielded in his homeland. I was scared half to death as our driver sped along at what felt like 100 mph on two-lane streets whose terrain was dotted with accident victims. It was not uncommon to see a tractor trailer truck full of poor manual laborers tipped over, with injured bodies strewn across the side of the road. With no exaggeration, I saw at least three such incidents during my time there. Oddly enough, the accidents didn't cause rubbernecking delays, as no one slowed down to view the accident. They just didn't care.

About halfway through our trip, I saw a roadblock up ahead, and could sense the tension in the car. "What's wrong?" I nervously asked.

"It's a roadblock," Mr. Haiti informed me. I really didn't see what the big deal was and told him so. "You don't understand," Mr. Haiti nervously said. "If they check our car, they can take whatever they want." I'm not ashamed to say that I got real scared when I heard that information. I didn't own a lot in the world, but most of my valued possessions were in my bag in the trunk.

Suddenly, a flashlight beamed through the window—temporarily blinding me. A police officer banged on the glass, and the driver opened it up. "What do you have in the car?" the crooked officer demanded.

"Nothing," Uti was quick to reply.

The officer was not impressed. "Open the trunk." My heart was pounding. I really felt like my bag was the least of my problems. Deep inside, I was hoping that this officer hadn't seen *Deliverance*.

Then Uti spoke up in a booming voice and yelled, "I'm Power Uti.

I'm on my way to Bendel State for a match. Don't waste my time!" Amazingly, the police officer let us go, and even wished the champ well in the match. One thing was very clear to me at that time—there was no way that I was going to win that match. They could not have paid me enough money to beat Power Uti in his hometown.

I'll be damned—my wish came true. I lost the match, but not before I witnessed several strange events. The match was scheduled to start at 8 P.M., but at 8:15, the place was empty. "I don't get it," I uttered with a shake of my head, "I thought Uti was popular here."

"Oh no, you don't understand," came a kind voice. It was Nigerian veteran Flash Mask Udor, who was a mountain of a man, but who possessed a truly gentle spirit. "This is Nigerian time. If it says eight Nigerians know to come at nine or nine-thirty. Don't worry, they will be coming very soon."

I was confused and let him know. "Does everybody know this?" I politely asked.

"Oh yes, Mr. Jack, everyone knows."

Sure enough, by nine-thirty the place was almost full, and at that time, the ring announcer went out to the ring. At ten-fifteen, he was still talking. Apparently, his job was not just to do the announcing, but also to entertain the crowd with a standup comedy routine. Finally, he announced the next ring luminary, who made his way to the ring. Was he a wrestler? No, silly, he was the witch doctor, who did a rain dance to ward off the rain spirits who might threaten the outdoor show. I swear I'm not making this up. Finally, with Mother Nature held in check by the nifty moves of the doctor, the show was under way.

Honestly, I can't remember a thing about my big match except being split open, losing to the champion, and the aftermath that almost did me in.

Uti was in command of his comeback when he took me toward the steel ring post. I wanted it to look good, but at the same time, I was counting on Uti's respect for me to keep me safe. Apparently, that respect thing didn't mean a whole lot to him as he sent me headfirst to the steel with all the power in his massive physique. With a sickening thud, I heard my head split like a ripe melon, and temporarily saw stars. When I regained my senses, I felt something hot and wet running down my face. I would be lying if said I didn't like it just a little.

Within seconds the match was over, courtesy of a sunset flip, of all things. I knew the match hadn't exactly been a classic, but it had been nothing to be ashamed of either, and as the crowd went crazy, I lay back for just a moment to bask in the glory of the job moderately well done. My basking didn't last too long, because as I hopped out of the ring, I felt as if I was smack dab in the middle of the running of the bulls in Pamplona. Fans were everywhere, and they were dead set on rushing the ring, whether I was in the way or not. I saw a few faces, and they looked as if they were drunk on national pride, or something equally as intoxicating. I had just about two seconds left before I would surely be flattened like Leslie Nielsen in *The Poseidon Adventure*.

Luckily, the warm sensation of my own blood had sparked an adrenaline rush, and I decided to go on the offensive. I was thinking of Lou Ferrigno as the Incredible Hulk as I let out my best scream and charged the rushing crowd. Chuck Heston would have been proud of me as I parted the Benin fans like the Red Sea, even though the only guns in my possession were the seventeen-inch ones that threw wild haymakers at whoever stood in my path.

As I got halfway through the mob scene, several of the Nigerian wrestlers, including Flash Mask Udor, came to my aid. When I got to the back, I was dripping both blood and confidence as one by one the Nigerian boys voiced their concern. "Sorry" seemed to be the popular word for the boys, who by this time had grown quite fond of their American friend. Eventually I got cleaned up, strapped an ice pack to my wound, and waited more than three hours to be paid for the tour. Like most guys who have just been opened up, I had walked around for a great length of time with dried blood clinging to my face.

While waiting for the money to be counted, a religious discussion began, and I was more than happy to share my viewpoints. At one point in my life (actually about the age of nineteen) I'd briefly considered being a man of the cloth. I guess I must have gotten impassioned about something religious in that dressing room, because the wrestlers started looking at me as if I was a holy presence. One of them actually got down before me and said, "You are very close to the Kingdome."

"Not really," I replied naively. "I'm actually a long ways away." This astonished the wrestlers, who collectively agreed that I was very close to the Kingdome. Apparently, they didn't know their geography. "Look," I tried to point out, "I live in New York—the Kingdome is all the way on the other side of the country in Seattle." Their faces showed nothing but confusion. I was midway through explaining the

Seahawks and the Mariners to them, when one stood up and said, "Mr. Jack, we are talking about the Kingdom of God—you are very close to that." Suddenly, I understood—I was close to the Kingdom, not the King Dome.

Shortly after my discussion, I was handed my payoff. Three hundred dollars for the two-week tour. Wow! Maybe I should have been a man of the cloth, because although the vow of celibacy may have proved difficult, pro wrestling was doing a damn good job of preparing me for a vow of poverty.

My dad was at JFK to greet me when the plane touched down. Halfway through the trip home, he asked me about my financial compensation. "I got three hundred," I sadly replied and waited for a lecture about throwing away my college education. Instead, I got a vote of confidence.

"Hey, it's a great experience—how many people can say they've been to Nigeria?"

"Good point, Dad, but why would they want to?"

Upon returning from Africa, I embarked on a memorable trip through the Dakotas, Montana, Idaho, and Wyoming. I headed out of Columbus, Ohio, by Winnebago and had a blast, as it was the last time that I remember the DeNucci school together as a whole. On the downside, we performed in front of miniscule crowds and received about $20 a day. But I prefer to think of it as a free vacation with some of my best friends through beautiful scenery, Yellowstone Park, and the site of Custer's Last Stand at the Battle of the Little Big Horn.

I was also developing rapidly as a wrestler. With only a little over two years' experience to my credit, I was actually touring and performing like a veteran, even though I never did start smoking stogies and calling everybody "kid." My timing was getting to be real good, my psychology was coming along, and my chemistry with Brian at ringside was resulting in some classic stuff.

My most vivid memory of the trip was almost the last memory of my life as our RV lost its brakes on the way down a mountain in Yosemite. I was listening to a tape and feeling fine with the world when I became aware that our lives were in danger. For some reason, I didn't feel even the slightest twinge of panic. I saw my buddies holding on to each other and crossing themselves, but it all seemed like a dream and I had no doubt that I'd be fine. Not even the impact of our vehicle crashing into the mountain to slow our momentum could ruin the moment for me, although everyone else seemed pretty upset about the whole situation. I saw Dominic nonchalantly head down a hill into a meadow with a stream, where rumor has it he removed his underwear, which were no long suitable for wearing. After a day of repairing the Winnebago, we continued our tour.

After the western disaster, I headed back to Nigeria—where I was scheduled to perform as a manager and referee and wrestler on three different cards that would take ten days to complete.

I showed up in the country and was almost immediately taken to a house for breakfast. I was informed that many of the Nigerian wrestlers were at the house, so I packed a dozen or so T-shirts that I had brought them. These were not wrestling shirts even, for at the time the concept of a Cactus Jack shirt selling to anyone outside my immediate family was unreasonable. Instead, these were shirts that I had either outgrown or didn't wear. I handed them to the boys as I walked in and excused myself to use the restroom. When I came back less than a minute later, every last one of the wrestlers was wearing the hand-me-down gift they'd been given. The smiles on their faces were unbelievable.

For reasons that I never could quite figure out, I was sent to the ring as a manager with a generic black mask. Tony Nardo, who was usually Moondog, but for this trip was "Eric the Red, Jr.," was my wrestler. Eric the Red had been a big name in Nigeria for years, and the exploitation of Nardo was supposed to pack the crowds in for another Uti title defense. It didn't. Something to do with running the show at the end of the month when no one had any money left, or so I was told.

Power Uti entered the ring to the thunderous applause of about 8,000 people in a 30,000-seat soccer stadium, and the match was on. At the right moment, I handed Nardo his special prop—an eighteen-inch cow's thigh bone that he used as part of his ring persona. Nardo hit Uti with the bone as I distracted the referee, and then handed it back when the referee went to check on Power Uti. I really didn't think too much about it—after all, without outside interference, wrestling might start resembling a real sport, and I don't want any part of that boring stuff. To the fans in attendance, however, it was a very big deal.

I sensed a rumbling and turned just in time to be clubbed with what felt like a chair, although I'm not certain. Whatever it was, it was delivered with a great deal of force, as it put me down with one shot, which, as people who watch *Raw* will attest, is no simple feat. When I gained some semblance of rationality, I realized that I was being stomped, being punched, and getting my ass kicked in general, by what had to be at least a dozen people. I would like to be able to say that I jumped up and fought them all off, but the truth is I got up and rolled into the general calm of the ring. This is generally the best place to fight off a fan attack, as you can see them coming, and can usually knock their dick stiff the moment they stick their head through the ropes. I could see that the mob was mad, but I didn't have any further trouble.

I felt my head, and even through my stupid black mask I could feel a large divot in my hairline. Mr. Haiti was refereeing, and didn't seem to have a whole lot of sympathy for my plight. "Get out of the ring, get out," he yelled, in his heavily accented English.

"I'm hurt, I'm hurt," I yelled, in an attempt to reason with him. No dice. He again ordered me out, as I looked at police officers armed with machine guns who were much more intent on watching the match than they were on helping a bloody white guy with a cheap black mask. Finally, the cavalry of Nigerian wrestlers came, lead by Flash Mask Udor, and escorted me to safety.

I took off my mask and was sickened by the heavy blood loss. Unlike the incident during my previous trip to Nigeria, I had not enjoyed this feeling at all. To make things worse, my black mask had hid all the precious juice, so no one even knew I was busted wide open.

Also unlike my last cut, which I had patched up myself, this one definitely needed stitches. "Flash, how do I get to the hospital?" I asked the grizzled Udor. His response both worried and surprised me. "Mr. Jack, the hospital is no good—we will take you to a chemist's office. They will take care of you."

"A chemist's office?" I asked with slight dismay in my voice. "Are you sure?"

"Yes, Mr. Jack," my friend assured me, "it will be okay."

An hour later, without the benefit of anesthesia, I received seven stitches in a chemist's office with a dirt floor. Back at the hotel, where we were no longer allowed to eat in the Chinese restaurant because "it will cost the promotion too much," I had a revelation that I shared with Tony Nardo—"I need to write a book."

The next day, Nardo flew home, and I spent the next five days as the only Caucasian I saw. Fortunately, I had two things to keep me company—*Fatal Vision*, an excellent book by Joe McGinniss, and the Nigerian wrestlers, who almost considered me one of them. I even had a chance to go out to a club, and noticed two things that appeared rather strange to a tough guy like myself. Guys danced with each other, instead of with women, and they also held hands when they walked. I had seen some of the wrestlers holding hands on the way to meals and asked what it meant. "Holding hands is a gesture of respect and friendship," a wrestler named Sunday had told me. I liked the name so much that I suggested it for our firstborn, but my wife shot it down immediately.

With only a few days left on the tour, I was walking to breakfast with a few of the guys when I felt it. A man's hand. In mine. Flash Mask Udor was not just holding my hand, he was swinging it as he walked. I didn't know what to do. At that moment, I felt like every kid in America who gets a physical and has to turn his head and cough while the doctor feels his nads. Our sports physical guy in high school, Dr. Eihacker, had felt so many teenage testes in his life that he actually had the nickname "Happy Hands." Every kid in school was terrified of Happy Hands, because the last thing he wanted was an overabundance of blood in the region when Eihacker went to squeezing, lest he appear as if he enjoyed it. Jay Johnson had suffered the misfortune of giggling while in the office, and the poor guy's reputation was shot from then on. With that in mind, I was really hoping that my blood would be in short supply, as I tried to figure out what to do or say. Wisely using the hand that wasn't being held by a 260-pound man, I discreetly felt for my little buddy, and was relieved to find him in his normal unaroused state. With irrefutable physical proof that I was indeed a true man, I decided to speak up and end this romantic stroll. I did decide, however, to do it gently.

"Uh, Flash, can I tell you something?" I politely asked my too close friend.

"Yes, Mr. Jack, what is it?" his kind voice wanted to know.

"Well, I know over here in Nigeria, you guys hold hands with each other, but where I come from, we usually just hold hands with girls."

Flash immediately saw where I was coming from and let me loose. "I'm sorry, Mr. Jack," he politely said. "I didn't mean to make you feel bad."

We walked the rest of the way and talked amiably, and as I

MICK FOLEY

walked, I began to see his gesture in a different light. Here was a huge Nigerian man in his mid-forties, reaching out to accept an American man in his early twenties. I felt foolish for having been so troubled about it, and immediately saw his gesture as the ultimate sign of acceptance. It was a true compliment, given from a true gentleman.

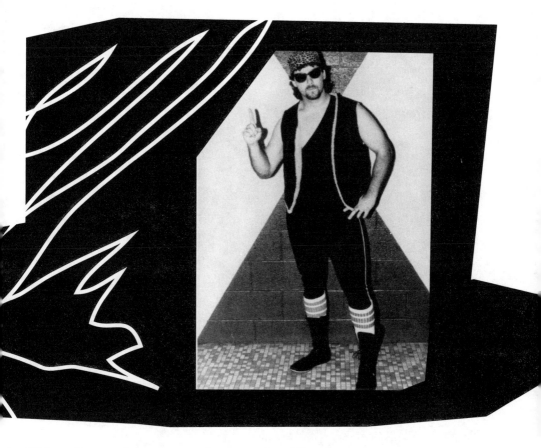

Either that or the guy secretly wanted to hammer me.

At the end of the tour, I was handed my money, which consisted of eighteen crisp U.S. bills. Too bad they were all tens. I had spent a total of six weeks in Africa on three different tours, and had brought home a cool $480 total. The guy at the 7–Eleven was making more dispensing Slurpees than I was for my overseas bludgeonings. I had to face the fact that some things in my life had to change.

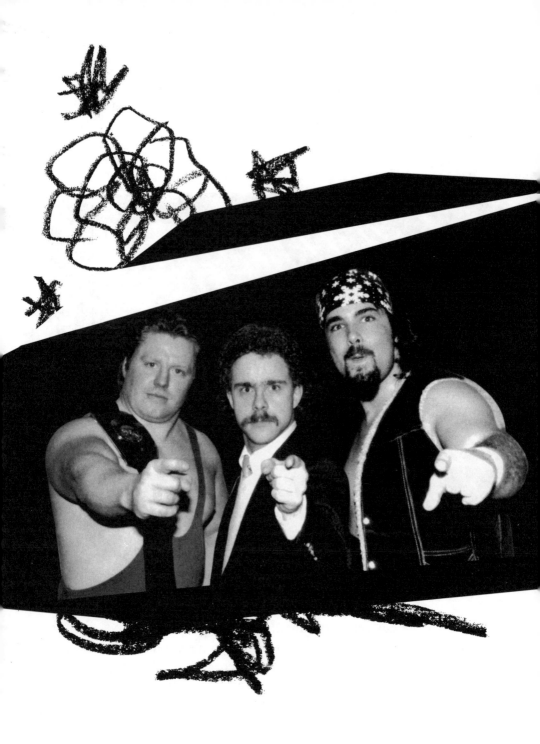

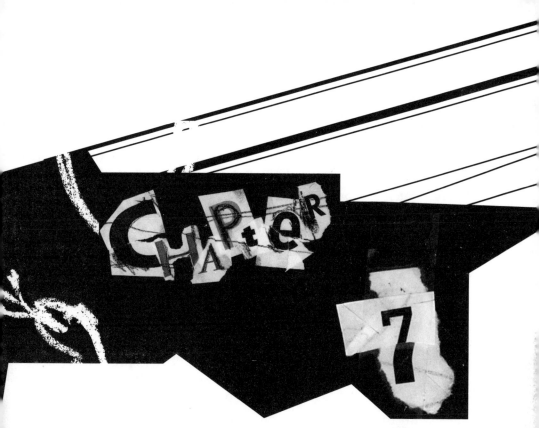

I was at a stalemate as I entered
1988. I had been going to DeNucci's school in Freedom for two straight years, and had benefited enormously from his training, but I had to accept the fact that I just couldn't improve enough in an empty gym 500 miles from home to justify going there. I will always consider myself a DeNucci student, but at this point, I effectively stopped my whole routine. I still forayed out that way occasionally, but only when I was booked on shows. Fortunately, I was starting to get some recognition in New York, mainly based on shows I did for a friend of Dominic's named Mark Tendler. Back in 1988, if you had looked up the word "character" in the dictionary, you probably would have seen a picture of Mark Tendler's smiling face. Mark was a big loud man who wore loud clothes with big loud jewelry. He also made big loud noises when he ate. He wore a huge "Mark" nameplate across his chest, which we referred to as the "Tendler license plate." He wore one of the world's worst wigs, which for some reason had dandruff in it. I guess to make it look more natural. He was also a genuinely warm, nice guy, who made his home on Long Island our house and who invited me to train in his new wrestling school free of charge.

Mark's promoting style was comical, to put it mildly. With the exception of one or two stars he booked per card, Mark filled his shows with unknown wrestlers. But if you didn't look closely, a casual fan might believe that a Super Bowl of Wrestling had just come to his town.

Fellow Long Islander Lou Fabiano, with whom I became fast friends, became the Magnificent LaRocca. A long-haired blond guy became Buck Hogan. A fat, bald guy became Ding Dong Bundy. He had a tag team of Tom Brandi and Bill Woods called, the Rock n' Roll Connection, whose opponents, King Kaluha and I, were the South Sea Islanders, which was either a tribute to or a ripoff of the World Wrestling Federation team, the Islanders. I had no issue with Kaluha, whose Philippine/Hawaiian ancestry made him a passable Islander. But me? I had to question it. "Mark, I appreciate the spot on the card," I said, "but I really don't want to change my name to do the Islander thing."

"Hey, no problem," the gregarious Tendler replied with a huge lump of hero sandwich in his mouth, "you can still be Cactus Jack, we'll just announce you from the Fiji Islands." Hey, who could disagree with that logic? On second thought, coming from a promoter who had taught two twelve-year-olds to walk bowlegged so they could pass as midget wrestlers, and who got a black guy to be his "Russian," the South Sea Cactus Jack wasn't so bad. It also helped that, as "Islanders," Kaluha and I were stealing the show.

As spring rolled around I even got a real job—three of them, actually. I worked full-time as a landscaper by day, went to Mark's for a few hours a few times a week, and bounced/tended bar at a local institution called the Check Mate Inn. I was putting in about sixty hours a week, plus wrestling most weekends, and was bringing home almost $400 a week. During this time, I got a call from Shane Douglas, whom Eddie Gilbert had brought with him to Alabama in the Continental Wrestling Federation. As would be the case for much of Shane's career, he wasn't too happy there. "Cactus, if you're making $400 a week at home," Shane said, "there's no reason to move here to make the same thing."

"Shane, I'm not sure you understand," I shot back. "This isn't exactly what I want to do for the rest of my life—I want to wrestle."

I would have jumped at any chance to wrestle full-time. Sadly, most of the full-time regional territories had dried up, and the openings that were available were often taken by local boys who were already known entities even if their presence was stale and unmarketable. I never did quite understand why Eddie didn't bring me in—I could have contributed to his CWF (Continental Wrestling Federation), and his guidance would have benefited me greatly. As for Shane, thankfully, I'd already learned that although he was an exceptionally bright guy, career guidance was not a strong point for him. I can honestly say that if I had ever listened to Shane's advice, including his later World Wrestling Federation warnings, I would be out of wrestling and probably cutting grass instead of kicking ass.

When I first showed up at the Tendler house, I almost immediately made the transition from trainee to trainer. Mark Tendler was a lot of things, but a polished wrestling technician was not one of them. Once I stepped inside the Tendler ring, which was really just amateur mats on the floor and jerryrigged ropes running along three sides of his basement walls, I was pretty much the teacher. For two hours I would show holds and reversals, while Mark answered the phone and ate sandwiches of astonishing size.

I will admit to being fairly rough on the new guys, but I never took liberties with them. They might have left with a couple of bruises, but at least they were still walking and they still had both eyes. Training the guys also had the added benefit of helping me, as the repetition of teaching reinforced many of the scientific skills I had stopped using. Now, I know a lot of people are probably saying, "What scientific skills?" and I will freely admit to not presently displaying a wide array of holds and picture-perfect pinning predicaments. But you've got to understand one thing—I noticed a direct correlation between how many nice moves I did and how many peanut butter sandwiches I had to eat. More skills—more peanut butter. Punching, kicking, and throwing chairs—less peanut butter. So, I more or less decided to dance with the one that brought me, and scientific wrestling became a thing of the past. Still, it's comforting to know that I have it, and unlike the petrified prophylactic I pulled out in the Caribbean, I'm hoping my old skills will still work when I need them.

Guess what, I even got a girlfriend at Mark's house—an older veteran of the ladies' circuit. I'll leave it up to you fans to figure out who it was, but I'll give you a hint—Adrian Street wrote a song about her called "Mighty Big Girl." Unfortunately, when we weren't throwing each other around Tendler's basement, we didn't have a whole lot to say, which made me pretty miserable in the relationship, and the whole thing fizzled out about as quickly as an Al Snow entrance pop.

Tragically, Mark Tendler's life would end less than two years later. I had kept in touch with Mark, and had even been to see him at the small nightclub he had just bought. On that night he had told me, "You know, Cactus, it's impossible to open up a club around here without the right connections." A week later, my dad told me that Mark had been gunned down outside his club in what appeared to be a professional hit. Whenever I stop to remember Mark, I am always reminded of those last words he said to me.

I was at Brian Hildebrand's in the early summer of '88, when I saw him reading a strange publication called the *Wrestling Observer*. I had heard about these "dirtsheets" (inside newsletters) that "exposed" wrestling to its readers, but had never actually seen one. At the time, these sheets were probably read by fewer than a thousand people, but nonetheless carried a lot of weight in the business. Men as important as Bill Watts were known to change the company's direction if the sheets didn't like what was going on, while many others swore they'd kill the guy who wrote it if they ever found him. In 1990, the guy, Dave Meltzer, introduced himself to me in Greensboro, North Carolina, and I was shocked that he actually appeared in public. I thought he was like Salman Rushdie of *The Satanic Verses* fame.

"Hey, Brian," I said, "could I take a look at that thing when you're done?"

"Sure," he replied, "you're in it."

"I am?" I asked in disbelief. "For what?" Before he could answer, I changed my mind. "Never mind, I'll read it myself." When Brian handed me the sheet, I took it to a place where I could concentrate, and it was there, on the bowl of the Hildebrand house in Pittsburgh while squeezing out a solid Snow, that I read the biggest compliment of my young career. "Cactus Jack, who many consider to be the best no-name independent in the country."

I couldn't believe it—as much as the *Observer* was maligned by people in the business, a wrestler getting a favorable write-up was like an actor getting a good review in the *New York Times*. Whether it was coincidence or not, I'll never know, but interest in Cactus Jack picked up immediately.

A phone call came in minutes later, which Brian answered. I could tell right away he was excited. "Yes, yes sir. I sure would, Tommy. Thank you very much." Brian then smiled at me, and continued talking briefly. "Yes, Tommy, as a matter of a fact he's right here. Would you like to talk to him?"

He handed me the phone, and without a clue as to what was going on, I said, "Hello."

"Cactus, this is Tommy Gilbert," the voice informed me. Tommy was Eddie's dad—a former wrestler himself, and also the referee for my big blunder match with Sam Houston. I didn't know what to expect.

"Hi, Tommy, how are you?" I asked.

Tommy got right to the point. "Look, I'm going to open up a small territory in Kansas City, and I'd like you and Brian to come. I can't promise you a lot of money, but you'll be working full-time. What do you think?" I didn't need any time to think it over or discuss it with Brian. We both knew the answer. We were going to Kansas City! I hung up the phone, and we jumped around Brian's living room with our fists pumping in the air.

A few days later, I received a call from Capital Sports in Puerto Rico, also offering me a full-time job. My blood ran cold. A short time earlier, Bruiser Brody had been stabbed to death by a fellow wrestler in the locker room. Apparently Brody, who was one of my heroes, and whose tapes from Japan I had studied for hours, had been stabbed in the stomach by booker José Gonzalez. Brody died on the locker room floor an hour later, poisoned by the bile from his own wounded kidney, while waiting for an ambulance that never arrived.

Gonzalez was not only cleared of all charges in a trial because it was ruled to be self-defense, but he was also received as a hero by the Puerto Rican fans, who believed that Gonzalez was like a heroic David slaying the bully Brody.

I vowed never to work for Capital Sports, but ended up spending a weekend there in 1994 at the request of Eddie Gilbert. I will never forget the feeling in my gut when I shook hands with the man who killed Brody. It was a feeling of shame.

I was glad to be able to inform Puerto Rico in 1988 that I wasn't interested in coming to their island.

Two weeks went by and I hadn't heard anything from Tommy Gilbert, so when I answered the phone and I was given a starting date in Memphis by booker Randy Hales, I jumped at the opportunity. I never did hear anything else about Kansas City.

The Championship Wrestling Association, or CWA, was better

known simply as Memphis. Memphis was the city the entire territory worked around, with the Mid-South Coliseum being the site of weekly Monday night cards for a few decades. In addition, the Channel 5 TV studio hosted a Saturday morning wrestling TV show that was a local institution. The show aired live every Saturday in Memphis, and then played a week later in the rest of the towns. The territory was run completely off the angles and story lines on television, and shows were run on a weekly basis in Nashville, Louisville, and Evansville. Other shows, called spot shows, were run on off days in various locations throughout Mississippi, Kentucky, Tennessee, and parts of Arkansas.

At one time, Memphis had been a hotbed of wrestling, with the alumni reading like a *Who's Who* of the mat game. Many were the times that a green wrestler came into the territory with nothing to offer but potential, and left as a polished performer. The rapid pace of the television show—made necessary by the weekly shows in the towns—enabled a young wrestler to become immersed in angles and interviews, and most of the time, a wrestler couldn't help but improve.

For years, the territory was also a great place to make money, as the Mid-South Coliseum was a sellout much of the time, but fate hadn't been kind to the company in the past few years. Gone were the days of $1,500 paychecks, and it was common knowledge that most of the young guys had to get by on $300 a week or less. Many of the guys established a network of girls to feed them, house them, and physically take care of them just to make ends meet. Still, even with all the drawbacks, landing a full-time job in Memphis was a matter of prestige for a young wrestler, and I was filled with excitement on my 1,000-mile trip.

I pulled into the Channel 5 studio with five hours to spare, so I curled up in the back of the Fairmont for a typical night's sleep. Unfortunately, the oppressive August heat made it hell to sleep, so I ended up lying in the parking lot until the studio was opening. When I walked into that studio, I might well have been walking into a whole new world, as much of what I had learned was no longer needed and much of what I didn't know would quickly become exploited.

The show began and aired a replay of Robert Fuller, the leader of the Stud's Stable, firing Brickhouse Brown. I had never seen anything quite like Robert Fuller (later known as Colonel Parker and Tennessee Lee) and come to think of it, I still haven't. He was an unbelievable talker, an animated wrestler, and the most avid crazy eights player I have ever seen. During that show I was brought out as the newest member of the "Stable" with very little hoopla.

Later in the show, I was brought back out for my first TV match, against Surfer Ray Odyssey. I ran into a big problem that day because in all my training at DeNucci's and all my matches around the globe, I had never once been put in a position of having to make myself look good. It had always been about helping the other guy. With Ray Odyssey, this weakness was so obvious that I later learned they were going to let me go because of it. Don't get me wrong, it wasn't a bad match, it's just that they didn't want the Surfer laying a beating on a Stud's Stable guy, especially when it was my debut. I learned immediately in Memphis that sometimes selfishness is a necessity.

That night I drove the 200 miles to Nashville for my first house (non-televised) show, which was held at the Nashville Fairgrounds. I teamed with Jimmy Golden against a young Jeff Jarrett, which in case you didn't know, is spelled J–A–ha ha–double R–ha ha–E–double T–ha ha, and a returning Bill Dundee. Dundee was a fixture in the territory and Jarrett was the boss's son (who also happened to be a very good talent), so I thought I knew my role in the match. Ironically, the things that had made me look so bad in the office's eyes earlier that morning suddenly made me look pretty good, as I flew through the air and staggered through the crowd. With that one match, I was given a new lease on life in the CWA.

The next night, Randy Hales got a hold of me at the Motel 6 in Murphreesboro, Tennessee, and gave me a better idea of my job description. "Cactus, we have a pecking order here," Hales began in his high-pitched, cracking voice, which seemed perfectly suited for his six-foot-five, 190-pound frame. "When you mess up that order, you mess up our plans. We can't have you taking the same bumps for Ray Odyssey that you do for Jeff Jarrett." I began to see the light. Then Hales ran by the Memphis philosophy of "getting heat," which I didn't agree with then and still don't today. "A heel has got to cheat to get his heat," Randy stated emphatically. "If he doesn't cheat, he's not a heel." They more or less didn't want a heel to do anything that might look remotely gutsy or skillful. That would make the heel a babyface.

I don't completely disagree with Hales but I think making all the guys fit into one mold takes away from part of what makes a wrestler great—the individuality. A quick look throughout history shows that the great heels weren't always cowards. Goliath of David and Goliath sure wasn't a coward; he was a great heel because he was so damn big. Apollo Creed in *Rocky* wasn't a coward either—he was a heel because he was the best and he knew it. The shark in *Jaws* wasn't a coward; he got his heat by eating people. The mother with the black veil hated the shark because it ate her son, not because it attacked while Chief Brody's back was turned. Benedict Arnold, on the other hand, probably would have been pushed to the top by Hales, despite his poor physique and weak interview skills.

In general, my time in Memphis was every bit as miserable as it was valuable. No matter what I did, I never could please anyone. I really wasn't comfortable being a cowardly heel, but still I begged off when the good guy was on the attack, just like everyone else there. When I did play the coward, it was hard to be something else. Frank Morell was a veteran wrestler turned referee, who seemingly made it his goal to torment every college graduate about his decision to wrestle. "What are you doing in this business," Frank yelled during my first week. "You've got a college education, why don't you use it instead of being in this Godforsaken business?" I guess Frank didn't realize it but I already had enough things to hate about the company without adding him to the list. Aside from his questionable guidance skills, Frank may also have been the worst referee that I ever worked with. Actually, "worked against" would be more accurate, as he truly seemed like my enemy when I was out there. I had come to Tennessee with a pinched nerve in my right shoulder. Brickhouse Brown had a dropkick that came in high on my face with lots of force—resulting several times in my head being snapped back violently. This would bring about what is commonly known as a stringer, a very innocent-sounding word for such a sickeningly painful injury. When Brickhouse planted me with the dropkick, my right arm would literally feel like it was on fire and I would roll out of the ring to try to get my bearings. My physical pain seemed to have no bearing on Frank's count. However, as he would fire out those numbers. "One, two, three . . ."

"Frank, I'm hurt, I'm hurt."

"Four, five, six . . ." with a gleam in his eye.

"Frank, help me, I'm hurt."

"Seven, eight, nine . . ." Finally I'd roll in and try to get Brick to help me recover.

At one point, the pinched nerve was so bad that I seriously questioned whether I was physically cut out for wrestling. We were in the main event of the TV show and the "Stable" was beating up on somebody when the babyface cavalry of Brick, Jarrett, and Dundee stormed the ring. With a succession of quick moves, including a Brickhouse dropkick, the ring was quickly cleared of all the dastardly bad guys, who all hightailed it to the back. All except one, that is. The pinched nerve was so excruciating that I had simply rolled onto the floor and stayed there. I wouldn't feel quite this helpless again until Chyna slammed the cage door on my head at the 1997 *Summerslam*.

At least the cold tile floor of the Channel 5 studio was of slight comfort, and my goal was to simply lie there until I stopped suffering, which would take about two hours. The triumphant babyfaces were already on their way to the back when a fan stooged off my position. "Someone get this piece of garbage out of here," the prick yelled, loud enough for the boys to hear too. A moment later, I was back in the ring and being triple teamed, until I finally rolled out and headed for softer ground.

I had tears in my eyes as I cradled my right arm with my left so that it wouldn't dangle. I really felt as if I'd been shot. Apparently, Randy Hales didn't think much of my plight, as I later found out from his heartless comment of "Cactus Jack has got to be the biggest pussy I've ever seen." I'm proud to say that in my absence, Jeff Jarrett stuck up for me by saying, "Fuck you, Randy, you've never even been in the ring." I think that was very nice of Jeff, but hey, I'm not a twenty-three-year-old kid frightened for my job anymore—I'm Man F'ing Kind, and I can speak for myself. So here goes. "Yeah, fuck you, Randy Hales, you've never even been in the ring."

Actually, only one guy seemed to have faith in me and that was Robert Fuller. I used to ride to many of the towns with Rob, and it was kind of like sitting under the learning tree, because Rob had as good a head for the business as anyone. I learned a lot about what to do in the ring from Rob, but sadly learned just as much about what not to do outside it.

Rob and his brother Ron had both grown up in the business as second-generation stars, both had booked, both worked, and, for a time, co-owned Continental Wrestling. In actuality, Robert was the better performer and better talker. But somehow, at a similar age, Ron was a multimillionaire and poor Rob lived week to week. I genuinely liked Rob, but his situation depressed me and I made myself a promise that I wouldn't make the same financial mistakes he had. I believe

Robert Fuller was the only guy I ever simultaneously looked up to and looked down on, but I can honestly say that without Rob's respect and support—and the confidence they gave me—life may have not turned out quite the same for me. One night in late September, I was riding to Memphis with Rob and Jimmy Golden, and Rob was having a hard time thinking of a way out of his match. After hearing him worry out loud for an hour and a half, I kind of sheepishly belted in, "Uh, Rob, I have an idea."

"Well hell, Jack," Rob responded enthusiastically, "let's hear it."

When I finished, Rob thought about it for two seconds and then replied, "Jack, that's good—it's damn good, and I'm going to use it tonight." With that analysis, Rob helped restore faith in myself—I was getting so used to people calling me stupid that I was starting to believe it.

That night in Memphis, the idea I shared with Rob went exactly as I had envisioned. Other guys might have been getting the pops, but I felt like the proud producer waiting in the wings. Actually, I was lying on the cold concrete floor with a puddle of blood around my head, in what was described as one of the sickest scenes ever witnessed. Jeff Jarrett had gotten hold of Robert's "loaded boot" and had begun to use it on him. With the Tennessee Stud in trouble, fellow stablemates Gary Young, Phil Hickerson, and Cactus Jack hit the ring. One by one, we all took a shot with the boot, and one by one, we went down. When I got up from my fall, on the outside of the ring apron, Jeff was waiting and laced me one more time with the boot. The impact sent me flying backward off the apron and in what might best be described as the 1970s Nestea Plunge. I landed on the concrete with my back, shoulders, and, to a lesser extent, my neck and head absorbing the blow. I landed with a thud and lay there for several minutes curled up in a fetal position and pushing with my diaphragm so as to squeeze out as much blood as possible from my busted-wide-open head.

When I got to the back, wrestlers were going crazy over what they had just seen. A few veterans, including Robert, said it was the damnedest thing they'd ever seen. Even Randy Hales loved it. "Geez, Cactus, that was great," he gushed, "we'll just do it around the loop (in every town)."

Oohh! This was not good news. Once was hard enough, twice was pushing it, and three times was looking for trouble. But four? No way.

Even at twenty-three, with only three-and-a-half years in the business, I had a decent grasp on my limitations—and this, I knew, was exceeding it. Still, as a recent college graduate—a fact that Frank had been nice enough to remind me of on several occasions—I was going to give it the old college try.

We started out in Nashville on a Saturday night. Boot to the head, off I flew with a sickening thud, fetal position, puddle of blood. Louisville on Tuesday, ditto. By the time I got to Evansville on Wednesday, I was shot. My back was swollen and discolored to the point that there was actually a hump on my lower back. Truly hideous and, I'll be honest, it scared me because I really didn't know what to do about it. It certainly didn't look like a human back.

That night, I ran into a problem that has become commonplace in my career. It seems that then, as now, people see me do so many things that look inhuman, that they start to believe that I'm not human. Well, I may have a high tolerance for pain and I may have a body that has been conditioned to accept punishment, but my body is just like everybody else's—just a little less pleasing to look at.

I was sitting against the wall in the Evansville dressing room, and Robert walked by with a cheerful "Same thing tonight, Jackeroo?" I told him that I needed to talk to him and then sadly relayed the tragic news. "Rob, I just don't think I can do it tonight."

Rob thought about it for a minute and then spoke some words of wisdom. "You know, Jack, that's probably a good idea. There's not a whole lot of people there and you're not going to make a whole lot of money tonight. You might want to save that bump for a time when you can actually make some money doing it." Like most of what Robert told me, I listened, learned, and did what I'd been advised to. It was the last time I would take the Nestea Plunge in the CWA.

The territory had a tendency to be quite a bit redundant—if only on a weekly basis. It was a great place to learn because the weekly nature of the shows meant constantly creating new matches. Many times, locker rooms would be on separate sides of the building and the boys would be forced to come up with matches on the fly. Even with a few moves planned, you'd be forced to start from scratch the very next week. This did create one major drawback from a creative and business standpoint, in that shows in Memphis, Louisville, Evansville, and Nashville all tended to look alike. A lot alike.

In late October I, along with my partner, Gorgeous Gary Young, won the tag team titles in Evansville. That night, as I often did, I stayed with the DePriest family, whose daughter, Terri, was a close friend and a huge fan. Terri had spent most of her life in a wheelchair suffering from muscular dystrophy, but, amazingly, I never saw it get her down. She was eighteen and although she was unable to enjoy many of the activities that others her age did, her dad had made it a point to take her to Evansville every Wednesday for the matches. It wasn't hard to spot them in the crowd. Terri in her wheelchair and her huge father, Mike, stood out among the usual crowd of 107. That night, we were watching TV and I asked her if she had been surprised to see me and Gary win the gold, or in this case, the stainless steel. "Not really," she peppily replied. "I knew that you'd won them the last three nights also." I really didn't know what to say. Memphis had always been so adamant about "protecting the business," to the point that the bad guys weren't even supposed to talk to girls—lest they seem like real people. I'd been admonished on just such an occasion by Randy Hales, who said, "Cactus, what we're trying to do here is build a territory and we can't do that if you're exposing the business by talking to girls." Now, I may be a college graduate (right, Frank?) and granted, a degree from Cortland doesn't automatically make me Einstein, but don't you think running four consecutive title victories in towns that are 200 miles apart might be more detrimental to the business than my conversation with a girl?

I'll make no bones about it—I was miserable in that territory. A wrestler named Tommy Lane once asked me if I was scared about getting hurt during one of my high-impact falls. My answer caught him slightly off-guard. "You know, Tommy, sometimes I really do hope that I am hurt bad enough so I don't have to wrestle anymore." As far as I was concerned, if this was all wrestling had to offer—bad pay, no benefits, repetitive road trips, backstabbing, no appreciation—I really didn't need it or want it.

Thankfully, things started to look up a week later. As I mentioned earlier, the pressure of weekly television and weekly tours was enormous. To keep things interesting, talent turnover was high, and character "turns" were inevitable. Even though I didn't have a lick of heat, apparently my heel card had been played out. For the first time in my career, I was about to become a good guy.

The Stud's Stable was called out for a interview on the Channel 5 studio show. Robert started in with typical Fuller gusto about how the

World Class (Texas) Champions, the Samoans, were coming into town and that as new champions, he and Jimmy Golden would be taking them on.

"Wait a second, Rob," Gary interjected, "Jack and I won the belts—we get the shot."

"Okay, okay," Rob replied, "I was going to talk to you two guys about that in a minute. Now as I was saying, we're going to be taking on these Samoans and . . ."

Again Gary butted in, "Now just a second there, Rob, we won those damn belts and we'll be the ones taking on those damn guys."

I don't remember exactly what was said but I do remember Rob getting a great look of anger in his eye, Gary saying he quit, and me saying, "Yeah," and storming away. With our backs turned, Fuller and Golden turned on us and manager Downtown Bruno as well, and left us lying. I especially looked impressive dripping a puddle of blood the circumference of a basketball onto the white tile floor. Knowing that this was an important angle, Robert had been considerate enough to slice me with a small implement of destruction. Although it seems barbaric to say, back in the eighties, being a "willing bleeder" was a benefit to a new guy trying to make the grade.

Back in the dressing room, Gary played pattycake with the blood that was running down my chest and applied it to a gauze bandage he had wrapped around his head. I myself required several layers of gauze to stop the blood flow and minutes later, during a Fuller-Golden tag match, came out in "the Spirit of '76" comeback, to a surprisingly loud reaction from the studio audience. Apparently I wasn't just a babyface, I was a fiery white meat babyface! Yeah!

Gary and I tore down the house with the Stable at the show in Memphis two nights later. When we got back to TV, we needed a fired-up interview to continue the ball rolling and I knew I wouldn't be the one to give it. Talking was a no-no for Cactus Jack—simply because the office was afraid I'd give away my non–Truth or Consequences background. Even Rob had been blunt about my verbal future by warning me, "Jack, when you open up your mouth and they hear New York, these fans down here will turn on you in a heartbeat. I hate to say it, but I don't see you as a promo guy in the business." Thankfully for me, Gorgeous Gary nearly drowned on live TV and I was there to throw him a line.

Gary was in the middle of a decent interview when he started having trouble. He was stumbling over words. Like many people who are starting to drown, he panicked. All of a sudden he was calling Fuller and Golden "Tennessee rednecks." "Hmm," I thought, "that's not good—these people *are* Tennessee rednecks and we're supposed to be the good guys." Lance Russell was the man doing the interviews, and having been around forever, he knew how to spot a drowning man when he saw one." Lance tried to cover our butts by saying something wise and ended with "What do you think about that, Jack?"

Lance's question put me in a tough position. On one hand, I had been told never to talk on the air. On the other hand, I'd just been asked a question on live TV by Lance Russell (one of the best in the industry). I couldn't just say nothing to Lance, and also, dammit, Gary was drowning. Which meant, since he was my partner, I was drowning too. I decided to act and immediately launched into brutal diatribe against the Stud's Stable that sounded a hell of a lot more like a seasoned veteran than a goofy kid who'd been ordered to keep his mouth shut.

As we walked to the back Gary turned to me and said, "Well, I guess we can forget about not letting you talk," in a voice that sounded both complimentary and hurt.

Even Rob, one of the premier promo guys in the business, was impressed. "Damn Jack," he gushed, "that's what's known as a money interview."

I was actually given a scheduled interview the next week at the studio and turned in another quality speech promoting a "Tennessee football classic," that became known as the "Kentucky football classic" when we went to Louisville ten days later. See if you can follow me here because the setup is a little tricky. Gary and I had lost a loser leaves town match at the Mid-South Coliseum in Memphis on Monday. Of course, because Memphis was a week ahead and 200 miles away from the other towns, the fans were not supposed to know about the match. On the previous Monday, we had engaged in the football classic match in Memphis. Now, with the week-old Memphis studio show airing in all the other markets, we were set to do the football shows in all of them.

The entire scenario for the football classic is a little tough to explain as well. I'll do the best I can. Earlier on the card, Downtown Bruno had engaged in a match with Robert Fuller's wife, Sylvia. The two combatants, each armed with a Kendo stick, would later be placed in separate four-foot by six-foot wire mesh boxes. To add to the drama, if Sylvia lost, she would be dressed in a negligee for her appearance in the box. If Bruno lost, he would have to wear a diaper in his. Well, Bruno lost, so our fearless manager stepped into the box wielding a Kendo stick and sporting a diaper. A football was also added to the mix with a colored key secured to each side. The red key opened Bruno's door, and the blue opened Sylvia's. The idea was for each team to attempt to unlock their manager, so that the Kendo stick would be used to their advantage. During the course of the match, the ball would be kicked, thrown, punted, and passed from team to fans to team to fans, in what had turned out in Memphis to be a fun, fan-inclusive cross between keep away, monkey in the middle, and kill the guy with the ball.

The Louisville match had the added pressure of the Japanese media presence at the ringside. For small time, monetarily challenged grapplers like me, Japan offered a much higher-paying alternative. Even one tour in Japan could pay me as much as I could make in six months in Tennessee. Which I desperately needed as I'd seen my checks go from $370 to $395 to $530 (I thought I was rich) before dipping for good under the $300 mark and occasionally the $200 mark. Before the show, Wally Yamaguchi, who in addition to being a photographer also booked talent for one of the organizations, had approached me. "The fans really like the way you bleed," he informed me, and for some reason I said I would try to supply some more of the stuff the fans 10,000 miles away had enjoyed so much.

As it turned out, I was in luck. The loser-leaves-town, barbed-wire match with the Stud's Stable had left me with a serious gash that I felt could easily be reopened. It was so bad that I had needed to apply constant pressure with my blood-soaked towel throughout the 200-mile trip home, all the way to Edwin Street in Nashville where I rented a room for $50 a week from an eighty-five-year-old lady. I went to Robert as if I were a neighbor borrowing a hammer and asked him for a favor. "Rob, I just found out that the Japanese fans really like the way I bleed. Their photographers are out there and if it's all right with you, I'd really like you to lay me out with that Kendo stick tonight."

Rob nodded his head. "Is this really important to you, Jack?" he asked. I nodded that it was. "Well then, Jack, let me see that cut." I tore off the bandage and pulled the cut open for Rob to see. "Dear God," he screamed, "the damn thing looks like a pussy sitting up on top of your head." Robert looked like he was getting queasy. "Good

Lord, Jack-o, I don't want to open that up any further."

"Rob, you have to," I pleaded. "There's a lot of money riding on it."

"Are you sure?" he asked.

"Yeah Rob, I am," I replied.

"God, I don't want to but I will," Rob finally conceded. Doesn't it remind you somewhat of a Hallmark card? "A true friend is one who will split you open when you ask him to."

Rob turned out to be a man of his word and then some. Actually, Jimmy Golden had quit the company and Sid Vicious was his replacement. We had a wild, rollicking good time in our football match, which ended when I unlocked the diapered, caged Bruno, who showed me his gratitude by cracking me with the stick, looking like a deranged baby New Year. The treacherous Bruno then handed the stick to Rob, who, true to his word, began wearing me out with it. I felt the warm flow start to come and I squeezed and grimaced so the Japanese photographers could snap away.

Yes sir, things were working out just fine, especially when Rob caught me in the back of the head with the stick and I did the "hangman" in the ropes. I could see the photographers shooting away as Fuller cracked down time and again with his Western martial arts training weapon. "All right," I remember thinking, "that's enough of that." Unfortunately, I wasn't able to convey my message to Rob, who was desperately trying to break the stick over my head—which he finally did.

The ropes, meanwhile, were awful tight on my neck, and as I would in Munich, I began to panic. Also as in Munich, I pulled my head out as my only way to safety, and again as in Munich, my ears paid the price. I felt behind my right ear and it was split. The first of many splits behind the ears, as it would turn out. At least it's over, I thought. Not so fast. *Whack!* came another shot with the stick, which by this point was a more like a club. Man, Fuller was turning out to be a friend indeed. Several shots later, the massacre was over, and I was free to collect myself and go back to the dressing room.

Fuller was there waiting for me. "Goddamn, Jack, I'm sorry," he said with exasperation, "but I saw all that juice and all them Japs, and I remember what you had told me about Japan, and I didn't want to let you down and damn, Jack-o, I just got carried away. Ol' Jack-o had that good color tonight though. Damn, son, I'm proud of you."

"Thanks, Rob" was all I could say, as I took the Norman Bates shower and ran upstairs to see what Yamaguchi had thought. He was gone and I didn't see him again for months. I hope they enjoyed their photographs. I wonder—in the case of the bloody photos, should I get a credit for doing my own makeup?

My Memphis tenure ended a night later in Evansville, which for the first time in years was packed to the rafters with about a thousand fans. I actually got $50 for Evansville instead of the big two five that was customary for that town. I stayed overnight and, after sharing Thanksgiving dinner with the DePriest family, headed back for Texas.

Sadly, Terri died three years later, after suffering for almost her entire life. I'm sure she's resting in a better place now. To help deal with his loss, Mike began painting Christmas ceramics, and over the years has sent me many. I have four of his Old World Santas on my mantel year round and a nativity set that stays in a bookcase all year, as well. Aside from my talks with Robert, Mike's artwork is about the only pleasant reminder I have of my time in Memphis.

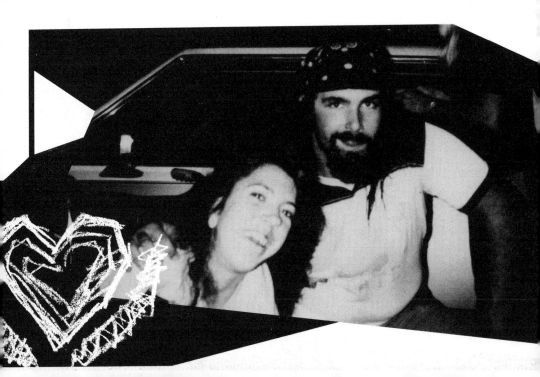

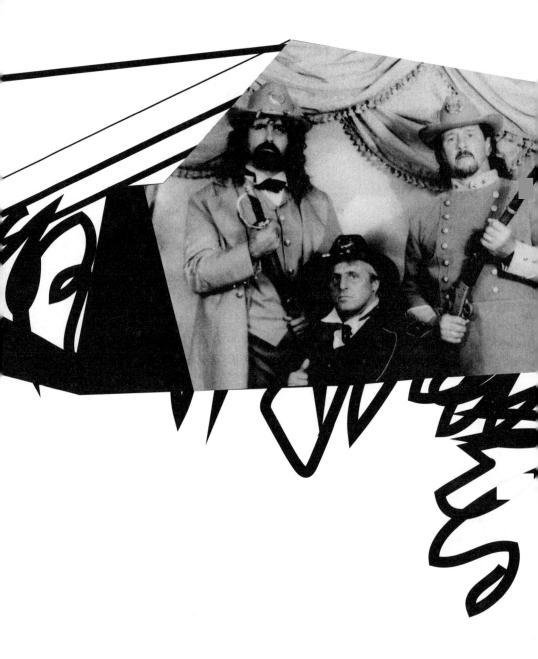

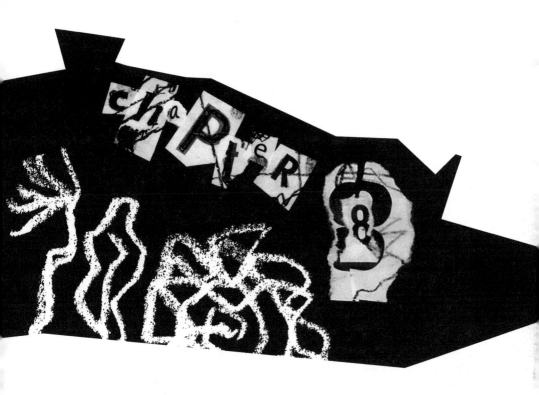

I enjoyed Texas every bit as much as I'd hated Tennessee. From the moment I limped into Dallas in the 1980 Plymouth Arrow that veteran wrestler Mike Davis had sold me when the Fairmont died, I seemed to take a liking to the state and its people. Maybe it was the barbecue or the catfish. Maybe it was the creative freedom I was given. Or maybe it was the forty-year-old Australian lady who worked at the desk at the motel I stayed in during my first week in town. Whatever the case, Texas reaffirmed my faith in the wrestling business, and I grew by leaps and bounds while I was there.

At one point in the mid-eighties, World Class Championship Wrestling (WCCW) had been the hottest promotion in the country. Fritz Von Erich owned the territory, and using his three boys, David, Kevin, and Kerry, as his top stars, he had built a hugely successful wrestling empire. The boys were seen as legitimate heroes in their native state and, to a lesser extent, the country as well, because World Class had a tremendous syndication package. Even after David died in Japan from an apparent drug overdose, the territory thrived, peaking in 1984 for the David Von Erich Memorial card in Texas Stadium, where a crowd of 42,000 saw Kerry defeat Ric Flair for the NWA title.

Eventually, World Class separated from the NWA and formed its own world championship, and business stayed strong for a few years. When the bottom dropped out, however, it dropped out completely, to the point that the weekly Friday shows at the Dallas Sportatorium, which at this point were automatic sellouts of 3,000 people, fell to around a hundred.

With business down drastically, Jerry Jarrett stepped in and purchased the company. Jarrett, also spelled J–A–ha ha–double R–ha ha–E–double T–ha ha, was the co-owner of the CWA, from which I'd just come, and was as famous for his keen mind as he was infamous for his stingy payoffs. Fortunately, Texas had a starting $75 minimum per day that Jerry kept in place, probably in fear of a wrestlers' mutiny. This was great news, as we averaged eighteen shows a month, not including Saturday morning TV tapings, which were a freebie. I would go on to average slightly under $350 a week during my ten months with the company. Those ten months were actually very good ones for the company, with houses picking up tremendously in the Sportatorium especially but in the rest of the towns as well. Oddly, with only two exceptions, my payoffs never rose above the $75 minimum, and even more oddly, I never questioned a single payoff. I was just so happy to be out of Memphis that I guess I didn't stop to ponder the economics of the company.

World Class was also different in that it offered nightly draws (loans) that would be taken out of our paychecks. I didn't even know that such a practice existed, so I didn't know quite what to think when Bronco Lubich approached me on my first night with the company. Bronco was a former star wrestler who had retired and became an icon in World Class as the world's least mobile referee. Bronco's ultra slow counts and his unwillingness to let the heels get ahead even a little bit tended to take away from the aura of a match, but his kindness and great road stories made it impossible not to like him. He was also the man responsible for handing out the draws, but seeing as that concept was foreign to me, I looked at Bronco a little strangely when he walked up with clipboard and pen, asking, "Wanna draw?" I really thought that this old guy wanted me to sit down and color with him or something, and I was just about to take him up on his kind offer and create a puppy or a choo-choo when Gary Young interrupted me.

"Jack, he wants to know if you want any money," Young yelled. I politely declined. To this day I still don't take draws unless entirely necessary.

Gary and I went to a twenty-minute draw (stalemate) on our first night in with Steve Casey and the returning Cowboy, Tony Falk. That's right—Cactus Jack couldn't defeat Tony Falk from Paducah, Kentucky. Not too promising. Usually hot newcomers will run roughshod over everyone. So apparently we weren't going to be pushed as hot newcomers. Fortunately, Jarrett had seen our match and was impressed with our teamwork to the point that we became top heels for most of our World Class stay. We were even given General Skandor Akbar as our manager and became the heart and soul of the general's Devastation Incorporated. Actually, for a while we were the only heels in the company and must have been pretty good at it, as together we fought a babyface roster consisting of Kerry Von Erich, Eric Embry, Jeff Jarrett, Brickhouse Brown, Chris Adams, Jimmy Jack Funk, Matt Borne, Billy Travis, and Steve and Shaun Simpson. Despite the ridiculous odds, we somehow managed to stay a threat during our entire run.

My first night in Dallas also heralded a change in the Cactus Jack character. Even before my forced heel cowardice in Memphis, I had always seemed more mischievous than insane. During my first interview in Dallas, I somehow went in the insane direction and the style was encouraged immediately by Jarrett, Young, and Akbar. Unfortunately, this new "wild" Cactus Jack didn't get to talk much as Young and Akbar carried out most of the verbiage. I took to the role quickly, however, and in my mind, at least, became the best weirdo in wrestling— probably because like most successful wrestling gimmicks, it wasn't much of a stretch.

"Crazy" guys usually bothered me in wrestling simply because they were trying so damn hard to be "crazy." They'd sit there and shake and make faces while their manager talked, and to me it all seemed so contrived and unbelievable.

Take college kids, for example. A guy has too much to drink, headbutts the wall, makes crude remarks to women, gets in a fight, throws up, and passes out. The next day, everyone talks about how "crazy" the guy is. I'm sorry, that's not crazy—that's stupid. On the other hand, I once accidentally walked in on a college buddy and was shocked to see him sitting Indian-style on the wooden floor, completely naked, eating brownies. He wasn't trying to be a "sick college fuck"—he was just relaxing. And that's the point that scared me. Given the choice, I'd rather fight ten drunk headbutters than one naked brownie eater because I wouldn't know what to do against the brownie guy. As Cactus Jack, that's the effect I was after. Moderation was the key, and it wasn't long before all the fans bought into Cactus Jack as a madman.

I was a nice madman, however, somewhat naive and simpleminded, to tell the truth. Much as I'd done in Tennessee with my non–New York accent practice at local honky-tonks, I began practicing my new Cactus Jack at the local Dallas nightspots. It was as Cactus Jack that I met a pretty, divorced mother of two named Valerie. She had been to the Sportatorium for the first time that night with a friend, and when her friend approached me, Valerie became intrigued with me to the point that she invited me for dinner a few nights later.

I only had one problem—I had met her as the nervous, paranoid, simple Cactus Jack and didn't really know how to tell her that I wasn't really like that guy she had met. It was a hell of a predicament. Do I go as Mick Foley, explain the strange situation, and hope for the best? Or do I continue my lie and go as Cactus Jack? I pondered it awhile as I dressed in my typical attire of cowboy boots with pointed metal toes, jeans, snakeskin belt with alligator claw buckle, rattlesnake tail earring, and (surprise) red flannel shirt. It was an ensemble that one girl called the "sleaze cowboy look." Now as I write this, clothed in blue sweats, two-day-old undies, a green Oscar the Grouch shirt, the same sneakers I wear in the ring, and (surprise) a red flannel shirt, I feel a little foolish about my Texas attire, but hey, come to think of it, there were a lot worse looks than mine in the eighties. Suddenly a realization hit me—Valerie had not invited Mick Foley over, she had invited Cactus Jack. Like most chicks, she would not dig poor Mick, while Cactus had a reasonable shot at nailing that shit (sorry, I know that is crude, but when I thought of it, it made me laugh out loud so I thought I'd include it). So rather than come clean, I continued my lie as it would continue for the next several months. I would "get up" for my Cactus Jack performances and would need time to unwind when it was over. Hey, it's not easy being "on" for hours at a time. Valerie was my first long-term relationship, but unlike other guys who claim, "She never really knew me," I was correct—she never really knew me.

Eventually, Valerie dropped me, claiming, among other things, substandard sexual techniques. But I showed her. After having a taste, I was like a kid in a candy store and I went on a short run of rampant promiscuousness that proved one of two things. Either Valerie was wrong about me, or she had quite a few people who would agree with her.

Eric Embry was our booker in Texas and also doubled as a top good guy. The guy had to be a genius because as a pudgy, sneaky heel, he was the last guy you'd think the fans would love, but over time, they went crazy over the guy. Actually, he was very bright, wrote good television, and could wrestle his ass off. He had one trait that bothered me a little, though: Eric liked to be naked.

I had been told that Eric belonged to a nudist colony in Florida, and I believed it as he turned the Sportatorium dressing room into his own personal colony. He would walk around giving instructions with his Johnson blowing in the wind, and I'd have to pretend not to see it. It reminded me of talking to a girl with huge hooters, as I would have to keep my eyes glued on his so as not to look at his menacing member. Actually, if my shorts housed a hose like Embry's, maybe I too would be prone to presenting my penis in public. But alas, the "Irish curse" had struck me hard and I know that I would be forever destined to walk to the shower with my towel around my waist.

Sadly for Eric, he was never quite the same after Robert Fuller came to Texas and showed how he'd earned the nickname Tennessee Stud.

I can say this about Eric, he gave me a chance to do my best at a time when I was almost out of choices. I was never held back, never lectured about college, and never told to "beg off" from my opponent. He gave me the freedom to be myself and I prospered with that gift. He also will go down as one of my favorite opponents, even if my favorite memory of him shows him in a somewhat embarrassing light.

We were wrestling in a Thunderdome ten-man cage match in Fort Worth, Texas, in March 1989 that Embry was a part of. A Thunderdome match is a cage in which each pinned man is handcuffed to the cage. The last man left is then handed a key with which he unlocks his teammates to unleash five minutes of destruction on their helpless foes.

The match was about ten minutes gone with about half the gang already cuffed when Embry, whom I had been beating on, began a comeback. To his credit, the little pudgy bastard had a lot of fire and when he kicked me in the balls, I heard the crowd erupt. Embry began hitting me, and the reaction got even louder. Embry was feeding off the frenzy now, and he slapped his hands on the mat and came up shaking his fists in the classic "Come on, you son of a bitch" babyface stance. The reaction was deafening. I couldn't help thinking, however, that something was wrong. The reaction was too loud, the frenzy was too heated, and despite the fact that he was the number one guy in town, Eric's response was too big. Something wasn't quite right, all right, and from my vantage point, from the corner of my cage, I saw what it was.

Terry Garvin, who was doing a gay routine as the Beauty, had been handcuffed for a few minutes. As Eric stood clenching his fists and calling me a son of a bitch, Jimmy Jack Funk and Chris Adams had spread the Beauty's legs, and Beauty was selling it big time. Funk (no relation to Terry, although at one point the World Wrestling Federation had claimed there was) and Adams threatened to maul Garvin's marbles, it seemed to coincide with Embry's posing, and in Eric's mind, the reaction was his. In truth, I don't think anyone was even looking at us, but I didn't know how to break it to him. He was my boss, after all. If he wanted to believe that he was electrifying the crowd, who was I to burst his bubble? I would rather tell my son that there is no Easter Bunny. I felt so bad for the poor guy that I even broke tradition and began begging for mercy while he popped his eyes and puffed out his cheeks like Dizzy Gillespie on a hot trumpet solo. Sadly, by the time Eric let me have it, the Beauty had already "passed out" from the fear. Eric's flurry of punches, which now had the crowd's full attention, were met with only moderate enthusiasm.

Even though my star was on the rise in Texas, I lived as if it had fallen and had been buried. I would call the place I lived in a dump, but it would be an insult to people who actually live in dumps. The house was in the middle of Arlington, about five miles from Six Flags Over Texas. Oddly, I never made the trip to it, even though today I practically live to go to amusement parks. As in Nashville, I paid $50 a week for my room, but unlike Nashville, this $50 also covered food, laundry, and auto repairs. Also unlike Nashville, my $50 a week included sharing the house with the biggest variety of losers ever assembled under one roof. Compared to these guys, I was like the Fonz or something.

Wilson was the older guy who rented out the house. He was a nice guy, but his life was ruined by the fact that he drank literally from the time he got up in the morning until the time he passed out at night. In between, he would clean clothes, sit in the backyard, and prepare dinner—usually something extremely fried. Minutes after being served,

Kyle and Roger, two Marine reservists about my age, would track Wilson down, sometimes blocks from the house, and force him to eat. "I don't want to eat," Wilson would yell as they dragged him in. Left to his own accord, Wilson would have much rather lived solely on hops and barley.

Kyle and Roger seemed like decent enough guys initially, but I eventually realized that if these guys were protecting our country, we were all in a whole lot of trouble. The two of them became hooked on an amphetamine called crank that was a huge deal in Texas, and they proceeded to throw their lives away. Roger inherited nineteen grand during this time, which seemed like a fortune to me, and it was gone literally in five days. He threw a huge party for himself in the most expensive restaurant in Dallas, bought a motorcycle for cash that he promptly crashed, and spent the rest on medical bills. When it was over, he didn't even have enough money to buy crank.

Roger's former girlfriend was a horribly messed-up seventeen-year-old girl named Allison whose mother, Susan, was engaged to another guy in our house named Dennis. Dennis liked me enough to even invite me to be his best man at his forthcoming wedding, but after he moved into Susan's place, I loaned him fifty bucks and never heard from him again. Susan's messed-up daughter had once come on to Dennis, who defended his decision to nail her by saying, "Dammit, I'm a man, and she was turning me on." I felt bad for poor Roger, who truly loved that nympho chick, until I found out that he and Kyle had once double-teamed Susan while she was engaged to Dennis.

Allison once came on to me to by exposing herself to me while I was sitting on her mom's couch, and even though, "Dammit, I'm a man," she was underage and my friend's former girlfriend, and dammit, I didn't need the hassle.

One day I came home to see small drops of blood on the hallway carpet. It turned out that Dennis, who by this time had moved out, had returned, and had been beaten up by another guy in the house named Thomas, apparently for borrowing money from Wilson. I didn't see Thomas, who was an ex-convict, all that much, and when I did, he always seemed real mellow. I understood his mellow demeanor when Susan's boyfriend-banging bimbo of a daughter informed me that "Thomas is a heroin-shooting motherfucker." When I asked her how she knew this she cheerily replied, "Because I was just thirteen the first time I got high with that motherfucker." Come to think of it,

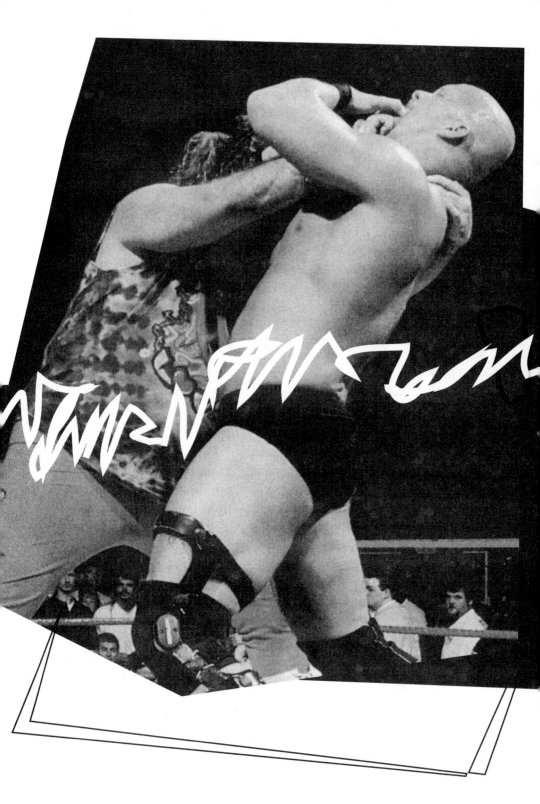

if she had called Kyle or Roger "motherfuckers," technically she'd have been correct.

Eventually I got tired of my surroundings, especially when my bike was stolen out of my room and I couldn't use the bathroom because one of Thomas's friends had passed out in there. Oh yeah, there was also a married couple in one room with a newborn. When the husband went to jail, the wife informed me that she was a lonely woman and that I could feel free to visit her room anytime I wanted to keep her company. I declined, partly because I didn't need an angry ex-con looking for me, partly because I wouldn't feel right about doing the nasty with a newborn in the room.

I left the house in Arlington and moved into an apartment in Irving with a woman named Joanne who made tights for all the boys. Despite rumors to the contrary, I never had a sexual relationship with that woman, Ms. Harriss.

I returned to the house in Arlington a year later and found things to be even worse than when I'd left. Wilson had died from alcoholism; Thomas had gotten married and moved out. Dennis hadn't been heard from, and Kyle and Roger were living in a van in front of the house. Saddest of all, Tippy, the dog I had gotten from the pound for Wilson when his dog died, had been put to sleep after Wilson's death. I remember the dog tied up to its house and starving for attention and I regretted every time I came in late from a show and didn't pay her enough attention. For ten years I have regretted that, especially because my new dog, Delilah, looks so much like her.

Back on the wrestling front I asked for some time off as we headed into April, as I hadn't been home for almost a year. I was given five days off at the beginning of May during which I would meet up with my old buddies for a return to Cortland for two days, and a visit with my parents for three. As I planned my escape, two mistakes were made—one by me and one by the office. I paid for both of them.

My first mistake was in not checking my schedule more carefully. If I had, I would have seen that we had only one show scheduled for the week before my trip. By simply checking ahead, I could have skipped the Lawton, Oklahoma show and had a twelve-day break, instead of the five I got. I'm not sure, but it's a pretty safe bet that the people of Lawton wouldn't have missed me enough to cost seven days fewer at home. It's also a safe bet that my bank account wouldn't have missed the extra $75 all that much.

The second mistake was the office forgetting about my time off and booking me and Gary in the main event at the Sportatorium against Embry and Mexican Legend (and I use that term real lightly) Mil Mascaras. The show was to fall on Cinco de Mayo (the fifth of May), and Mascaras was being brought in to capitalize on Dallas's huge Mexican population. A month earlier, Gary had used a baseball bat to injure Embry internally and now, with Embry hell-bent on revenge, the match was to be a "ball bat on a pole" match. There was only one problem. I wasn't going to be there.

I went to Eric and expressed my problem. Embry assured me it would be all right. "How are we going to cover it?" I asked.

"We'll hurt you" was Embry's immediate reply. I wanted to know how. Eric thought it over. "We'll do it with a chair," he said. Even ten years ago, I didn't feel like a chair was enough to keep Cactus Jack down and told him as much. "What do you suggest then, baby," Embry asked, using his frequent term of endearment for me.

I looked him straight in the eye so as to avoid looking at his penis and said, "I'll think of something."

That "something" turned out to be something pretty wild as Embry cracked me with the bat and I went sailing off the ring apron with the same Nestea Plunge that had almost done me in at Memphis. I hit the ancient wood floor of the Sportatorium and immediately began spitting up loogies of blood. A stretcher came and got me as the action continued in the ring. Akbar went into a verbal tirade. He was being interviewed as I was being carried away and when asked about my welfare, quickly changed the subject. "Never mind that," the incensed Akbar yelled, "he ripped this expensive shirt!"

I was a little lightheaded and my throat was hoarse from hacking up blood, but other than that, I felt all right to walk and drive. Unfortunately, I was not able to, as the show had just ended and fans were streaming into the parking lot. Unlike other crowds, the Dallas fans were treated to two wrestling shows a weekend, and as a result, knew not only the wrestlers but each other quite well. After a show, they tended to congregate for hours in the parking lot, throwing small parties complete with barbecues and beverages. I really couldn't afford to have them see my face, as the fall was supposed to keep me out all week. Instead, I climbed up the stairs into the "crow's nest," a fenced-in area where the wrestlers, their families, and their friends could watch the matches in peace. After the Sportatorium had emptied, Gentleman

Chris Adams was having his inaugural class for his wrestling school, and I sat down to have a few laughs at the beginners' expense.

My first laugh came when Adams talked about the cost of the school. "Three thousand dollars might seem like a lot of money," the Gentleman began in his perfect Stratford-on-Avon accent, "but not when you realize that I make that in one day." Oh man, that was a good one. Next, Adams arranged his dozen or so students into groups and began doing drills with them. "Man, these guys suck," I thought. "Some of these guys are even worse than I was."

All except one guy, that is, who actually seemed to be doing quite well. He was a big muscular kid with long blond hair and he stood out in the crowd like a sore thumb. The more I watched him, the more impressed I was. "Man," I thought in a slight reconsideration of my earlier harsh appraisal of talent, "that blond kid looks like he's got potential." That was the first time I ever saw Steve Austin, who would go on to become the biggest star in the history of the business.

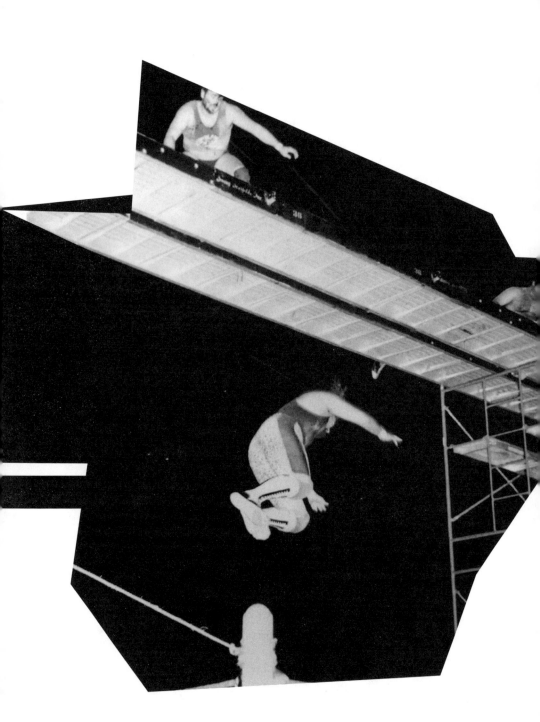

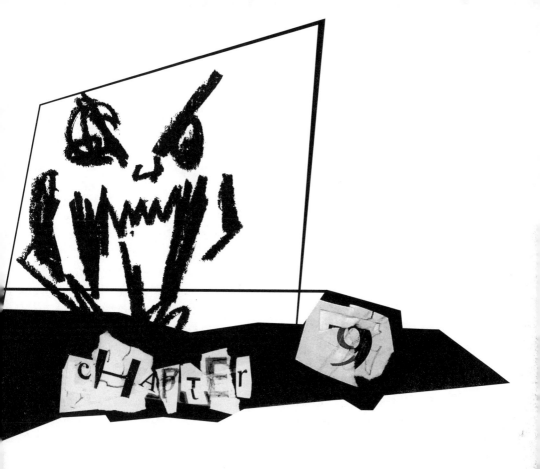

CHAPTER 9

I returned to Texas to hear some

strange news—I was booked for the following Saturday night in Fort
Worth in a scaffold match. A scaffold match is a wonder of stupidity
that some genius thought up in Memphis and that had since made the
rounds in Texas and Jim Crockett's old NWA. The object of the match
was simple—knock your opponent off the scaffold. World Class
bragged that they had the highest scaffold in the wrestling world. It
had to be more than twenty, maybe even twenty-five feet high. I
thought back to an offhand comment Embry had made months earlier.
"Would you be willing to do a scaffold match?" he had nonchalantly
asked, to which I had nonchalantly said, "Sure." Now, however, it
didn't seem like such a good idea.

A day before the match, I got a surprise phone call. The voice was
frantic. "Jack, please don't do this match," it yelled. It was Valerie,
the girl who had dumped me, and I paused for a few moments to get
myself in Cactus Jack mode.

"Why?" I asked, waiting for more of this outpouring of emotion.

"Because you're going to get hurt and I don't want you to get hurt," was her reply.

Not bad, a lot of anguish in her voice, but I was going to make her pay for daring to suggest a sexual inadequacy on my part. "I'm sorry, it's too late," I replied. "It's already been booked, there's nothing I can do about it."

"Yes there is," Valerie cried. "Tell them that you can't do it."

Oh, this was great, and now, it seemed, was the perfect time for a little sarcasm. "What do you want me to do, Valerie," I asked, "tell them that I can't do it because me ex-girlfriend won't let me?"

"Yes," she yelled, "tell them anything, just don't go up there!"

"I'm sorry," I replied in much sadness before adding, "and, Valerie, in case anything happens to me up there, I want to say good luck." She was crying when she hung up the phone. I showed her. No one, and I mean no one, makes fun of my "little buddy" and gets away with it.

I knew two things about scaffold matches before having this one. First, for the most part, they suck, with very little action being supplied by guys who are usually scared out of their wits. There had been a few exceptions, thanks to guys like Bobby Eaton, who would actually put on a show up there, but by and large most of them were stinkers.

I also knew that scaffolds were dangerous. Even though common sense and the slightest respect for the human body tells us that no one is actually going to be "thrown" off the scaffold, even a hanging drop was dangerous—especially to the knees. A few wrestlers, with Jim Cornette being the most notable example, had blown out their knees and had never been quite the same. I hoped that I would not suffer the same fate.

The scaffold match was actually my second match of the evening, as I had already wrestled in the second match of the night. Killer Tim Brooks had quit the company a month earlier and instead of hiring another heel, Joanne Harriss had sewed together a black and red outfit and a hood. Yours truly became "Super Zodiac Number II," never mind the fact that my hair stuck through the mask and that my distinctive walk and even more distinctive ass (or lack of ass) left absolutely no one fooled. I came back from my match in Fort Worth and asked Eric about the wisdom of me losing in the second match only to come out ready to kick some ass in the main event. Embry looked at me like I had two heads. "Baby," he said, before adding the words that would forever make me doubt his judgment and sanity, "no one will know—you're under a hood."

I walked out for the scaffold match with General Akbar by my side. At the last moment, Akbar had been added to the festivities as my partner, while Embry had chosen a partner as well—Percy Pringle, who would later become known as Paul Bearer. When I climbed up the scaffold, I immediately felt a rush of adrenaline, partially because I knew that potential for injury was high. I can only compare it to standing atop the Hell in a Cell in June 1998, and unfortunately the results would be comparable as well. Embry and Percy climbed up and the match was under way. Immediately, Akbar and Percy dropped to their bellies and stayed there for the duration of the match. Together, they spent more time on their bellies than most snakes do. I think any fool could tell you that neither of the two would take the tumble.

Eric and I, however, were eager to duke it out. I really can't remember a damn thing about it except being pile driven on the scaffold and rolling over on my belly to prepare for the drop. "Are you ready, baby," Embry asked as he delivered a boot to the head that eased me halfway off the structure.

"Yeah," I said weakly, as the ring below me appeared very far away. I may have said "yeah," but in reality I had no idea what to do. I knew what I was supposed to do—hang until ready, then drop, and crumple upon impact so as not to ruin my knees. Sadly, I sensed that my goal would be unobtainable because as I supported myself with one elbow, I could see that I had nothing to grab on to with which to hang. Everything I saw was much longer than my hand and impossible to grip. I really didn't see how I could hang. Twenty feet in the air was not the best place to be for a kid who could never do pull-ups in gym class.

I was swinging my legs when Embry kicked me and my elbow hold gave way. I must have been on a backward swing because when I dropped, I began to free-fall face-first—picking up speed and heading for disaster. As I was about to land, I put my hand down to block the fall, and then landed in a heap. It was a good minute before I moved because when I realized where I was, Akbar was already on the mat. I tried to stand quickly and fell down. Two more wrestlers came from the back and together helped me make my way to the dressing room. The other wrestlers wore expressions of concern as I stumbled in. "Are you all right?" they all wanted to know. I assured them I was, but in reality I was far from okay. After sitting for a half hour, I tried to change but found it very hard to do so. Untying my shoes was extremely painful to attempt. Finally, Cowboy Tony came in and helped me untie my boots. A good hour after the match had ended, I walked out to my Plymouth Arrow with the dented, unusable door, and saw a small congregation of well-wishers gathered there. Among them were Valerie and her two kids.

It was obvious that all three had been crying. "I'm sorry, Jack," she cried, "can you forgive me?"

"Sure," I said, and then in a true example of class, I treated her and the kids to Jack in the Box, where against my wishes, the kids ordered sodas instead of free tap water.

In retrospect, that match at the Will Rogers Coliseum in Fort Worth was the beginning of the end for me in World Class. I had my wrist X-rayed and, sure enough, there was a small crack in a bone in my wrist. The doctor gave me a brace and told me to wear it for two weeks. Sixteen weeks later, my arm was taken out of a cast that extended all the way to my elbow. The doctor, who, I later learned, had a less than sterling reputation, had failed to correctly diagnose my cracked bone as being the vernicular bone, which, due to poor blood supply, is one of the most difficult bones in the body to heal.

I wrestled for three months with the cast and had some good matches. The announcers never even acknowledged the cast. Apparently, they felt it might make me look sympathetic and therefore declined to comment. I was able to have matches for three months without throwing a single punch, which was beneficial in the long run, but I began to lose matches on television with increasing regularity and I began to think of other options in my life.

I had been quite friendly with Video Bob, our director and producer of the World Class show. Given the restraints on time and money that he worked under, Bob did a tremendous job on the show, and with his help, I put together an impressive music video for me and Gary set to the tune of "Born to Be Wild." We actually turned the video into a rib on Gary, who himself was known as quite a ribber. After completing the video, Bob and I spent an extra four hours making another special video in which all of Gary's great moves were edited out and replaced by boneheaded mishaps. Together, Bob and I laughed our ball off (right, Dominic?) and waited in anticipation for Gary to arrive to check out the finished product. When Gary showed up, his reaction was classic, as his face inched closer to the screen with every indignity he suffered, while I, as his partner, came across like Bruiser Brody. "What do you think," I asked him, and then waited while he fumbled for a reply. Finally, my own lack of body control gave me away and Gary caught on when he saw my stomach rapidly shaking in an attempt to withhold my laughter. "That was a good rib," Gary had to admit, "that was a good rib." We then played the real video, which was met with a huge reaction.

Bob used to always confer with me before a TV show to learn just what move I might come up with and how we could best shoot it. It was in Texas that I began using the flying elbow off the ring apron and within a few weeks, Bob had mastered how to shoot it. Back in those days, I used to get some serious distance on those leaps and Bob would make sure that the camera was right to the offside of my opponent's head while I prepared to leap. When I took off, it would look like I was diving into the fans' living rooms, and the cameraman would occasionally shake the camera upon impact for added emphasis.

My appreciation for Bob's work, along with my growing concern that I might leave wrestling both financially broke and physically broken down, led me to travel to the World Class studios in Las Calinas three days a week. In the editing suite, I would brush up on the latest technology as well as do occasional voice-overs using my "professional voice." So for any of you fans who have old World Class tapes from 1989, listen closely for the Hardcore Legend as he says, "Let's look back once again at the latest misfortune suffered by Eric Embry." In addition to learning quite a bit, I also had fun in that studio, although I'm glad to say I have never needed to use my technical skills.

About this time, I received word from my friend "Flamboyant" Freddie Fargo that Jim Ross was interested in bringing me into Ted Turner's World Championship Wrestling. I was thrilled. This, I felt, was the answer to my dreams. I got the number from Freddie and anxiously called Ross, who was the head of the WCW booking committee. Ross informed me that the company was going to be looking for new talent after the summer and that I was high on their list. It was the greatest news of my young career. Yes, yes, yes!

Two weeks later, I received bad news in the form of a wrestling newsletter, whose headline read, "Ross Resigns from Booking Committee." My heart sank past my stomach into my testicular region. No, no, nooo!

With my spirits totally down, it was with great amusement that I read a fan letter sent to me at the Sportatorium. I had received a few nice letters during my stay in Dallas, but this one took the cake. It was five pages of glowing tributes to me, including, "Your eyes are as blue as the clear Texas sky," which they aren't—they're hazel, and something about having the strength of ten men. She concluded her love letter by writing, "If you want me to write again, play with your hair when you get into the ring." Needless to say, I was flipping my flowing locks for the Sportatorium faithful—and for that one girl in particular. I wanted more of those compliments.

As it turned out, playing with the hair was probably a mistake, as when I returned to Dallas the next week, there were five more letters waiting for me—each more ridiculous than the next. Someone pointed her out to me in the crowd, as she had written in the past to other guys as well, but not to the extent that she had written me. She looked so sad and pathetic that I didn't quite know what to say when I saw her standing by my car. "Are you the girl who's been writing to me," I gently said.

"Yes," she replied with a sad smile. "Is it okay if I continue?"

I was really a little bit concerned, but I didn't want to hurt her feelings so I said, "Sure, that would be fine."

When I came back to Dallas a week later, there were ten letters in my box from her, each signed "Mary Ann Manson" in the return address area. During my time in Dallas, I had been renamed Cactus Jack Manson by Eric Embry, and the implication was very clear—she thought we were married. The contents of the letters proved as much as she wrote about our relationship and our marriage. Uh-oh, this wasn't good—I had my own personal stalker.

I decided that enough was enough and when I saw her by my Arrow with a white rose in her hand, I told her in no uncertain terms that she was not my wife and that I didn't want to hear from her or receive letters from her anymore. That, I thought, was that.

When I first got to the Sportatorium on Friday night, I was relieved to find not a single letter in my box. "Hey, I showed her who's boss," I thought, just as something caught my eye. It was her handwriting on a letter addressed to World Class announcer Marc Laurence. The return address strangely still read "Mary Ann Manson."

I asked Laurence if I could open his letter and he obliged. The contents shocked me. "By the time you read this," it read, "I will be dead. I was married to Cactus Jack but something went terribly wrong."

There was more, a lot more, but the gist of the thing is that I had killed her. When I got home that night, I called the police station in her hometown and inquired about any recent deaths in the area. They reported none.

The next week I saw her in the parking lot. I knew she was a sick lady, but I decided to be firm anyway. It was a judgment call. I told her in no uncertain terms that she was not to write to any wrestlers ever again and that if she did I would make sure that she was banned from the Sportatorium forever. I guess the threat of never setting foot in the decrepit, rat-infested, freezing in winter, hotter than hell in the summer Sportatorium was enough to cure her pen-pal-itis, as I never saw her handwriting again. I did see her at the matches, but I made sure never to play with my hair.

Toward the middle of the summer I started to get the gut feeling that it was time to leave. Part of World Class's appeal was also its drawback, as its wide syndication ensured good visibility but also ensured a large viewing audience for my recent losing efforts. I really felt like these losses were going to hurt me long-term, and I certainly wasn't being paid enough to compensate for throwing my career away. Besides, the constant pounding was making it impossible for my wrist to heal. With a heavy heart I approached Embry and told him I thought it was time to leave. I thanked him for his faith in me, and in return he offered me a place to work wherever he happened to be—a promise he actually backed up by calling me a year later when he took over the booking in Puerto Rico. For some reason, even though I was hurt, I offered to work out a six-week notice during which time he assured me of a great buildup to my departure.

I saw Frank Dusek, our color commentator and one of our town promoters, a week later when news of my imminent exit from Texas became known. Frank was concerned and called me upstairs to his office to express his feelings. "Why do you want to leave?" Dusek inquired. "Don't you like it here?"

"Hey Frank, I love it here," I was quick to reply. "It's just that my wrist doesn't seem to be healing and I'm losing a lot of matches lately." Dusek nodded his head and then asked when I would be coming back. "I'm not coming back, Frank," I answered. "I'm going to Alabama to work for Robert Fuller when I get better."

Dusek's expression looked pained as he asked, "Are you sure you want to do that?"

Now all of a sudden I wasn't sure—after all, I was just a kid with four years' experience compared with the forty-year-old Dusek, who had literally grown up in the sport. "Why?" was all I said.

"Cactus, the people like you here," he reasoned. "You would be welcome back any time. Why go someplace and start over?"

His next words chilled me to the bone and would continue to haunt me for years as I struggled to climb wrestling's ladder of success. The words were not meant in anger; he was telling it like he saw it, which made them hurt even worse, "You're never going to be a top guy in this business," he stated simply. "You will always be the bottom of the top or the top of the bottom, but you will never draw big money." I thanked him for his honesty but told him that I intended to prove him wrong. He smiled and said that he hoped so too.

I saw Frank Dusek in Greensboro, North Carolina, in early 1998. It was the first time I had seen him since my Texas departure. I was wrestling the World Wrestling Federation champion. He shook my hand, and I asked him if he remembered what he said to me a decade earlier. "Oh God," he said, laughing, "what was it?" I repeated his "bottom of the top, top of the bottom" speech and saw him wince as if he were John Winger taking a Sergeant "Big Toe" Hulka uppercut to the solar plexus. He then literally got down on his knees and jokingly bowed down to me. "Cactus," he exclaimed, "I have never been so glad to be wrong in my life."

I had envisioned great things for my sendoff at the Sportatorium. I had performed in that building over seventy times in my nine months and had engaged in some tremendous matches. I wanted to give the fans a great match to remember me by and had my head loaded with ideas as I drove to Valerie's for what would prove to be the last time I saw her. The match had been booked as a loser leaves town match and I intended to leave right from the Sportatorium and drive through the night. Over dinner I speculated about the match and saw her become slightly angry as she yelled, "Jack, I know you're going to lose tonight."

This surprised me as I had always tried to "protect the business" around her and had steadfastly denied knowing the outcomes to my matches. I decided to call her bluff. "What makes you say that?" I inquired, using the poker face I had honed to perfection years earlier at late-night card games in childhood friend Scott Biasetti's basement.

Her reply was simple and her rationale was hard to argue with. "Jack, I'm not stupid, Embry's the boss, not you." Then came the

MICK FOLEY

kicker. "Besides, I'm looking out the window at your car and you've got everything you own in it, I know you're going to lose." She then asked if I was going to come back for her and I had to admit that it probably would never happen.

My classic farewell match never happened either, as I lost to Embry in nine seconds with a simple backslide, then walked up the aisle as the fans sang "hit the road, Jack, and don't you come back no more." I actually had tears in my eyes as I pulled out of the parking lot and didn't stop for rest until I was in my old bed in East Setauket twenty-seven hours later.

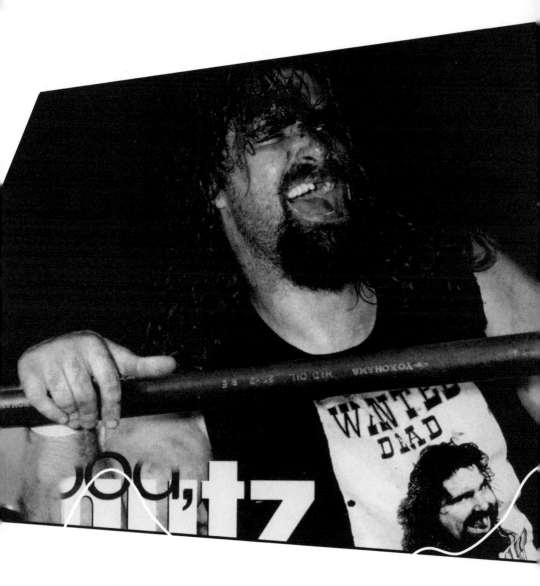

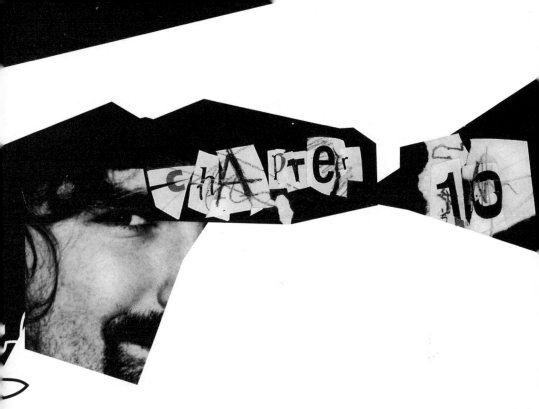

I headed into Continental country
with high hopes for the future. Robert had spoken of this territory as
being like heaven, and I couldn't wait to get started. When I got there,
Rob was his normal gregarious self and greeted me with a big hug.
"Goddamn, Jack-o, it's good to see you, boy," Rob exclaimed, and
then asked if I could give him a ride to the post office. "Some arsehole
came and repossessed my car, poo poo [this was one of Rob's favorite
terms of endearment], and I need to go and get your videotape," he
told me.

This wasn't a good sign, and I told him so. I had sent the video
that Video Bob had helped me come up with over a month ago. This
tape was of me as a single wrestler, was set to the ominous tune of
"Helter Skelter," and was a good piece of business. The Continental
area had been a part of the country not exposed to the World Class
product, and the video would have been a good way to introduce me
to the fans for a full month before I got there. Rob didn't seem so concerned. "Don't worry, poo poo," he said. "We'll just play it this week
instead."

I felt like he was missing the point. "Rob, don't you think the tape would have helped get me over?" I asked him. "Now we have to start from square one." It was damn hard to stay mad at the Stud, though—he was just so damn likable.

"Damn, Jack-o," he said, "I'm sorry—I just got so damn busy that it skipped my mind."

My first night in Montgomery was a TV taping at the Montgomery Civic Center. I decided to make up for lost time by kicking ass right out of the gate. I clotheslined my opponent over the ropes and slammed him on the cold, concrete floor, a good twelve feet from the ring. Quickly, I hopped up onto the ring apron and with a two-step approach, came sailing off the apron with a perfect elbow. When I got to the back, I asked Scott and Steve Armstrong how the elbow had looked. "What elbow?" Scott asked.

"The big one off the apron," I replied.

"No, brother, I'm sorry, but I didn't see an elbow," Stevie let me know.

I headed for the TV truck to see what was the matter. I was more than a little bit pissed—after all, the elbow is a painful thing to drop on concrete; it needs to be captured on film. Maybe I'd become spoiled by Video Bob at World Class and would have to point out the error of this veteran director's way. I opened the door and was shocked by what I saw—a bunch of scared kids looking at an angry wrestler. I immediately opted for the gentle approach. "Why didn't you guys tape my elbow?" I asked a pimply-faced teenager.

Without a trace of sarcasm but with a whole lot of trepidation, he looked at me and said, "I don't really know how to tape elbows, sir."

I thought I sensed what the poor bastard was thinking so I gently explained a little bit about the wrestling business. "No, I'm not talking about physically taping my elbow for an injury," I said, "I'm asking you why you didn't videotape me when I was getting set to leap off the ring apron?"

"I'm sorry sir," pimple face explained, "but this is only my first semester of television production."

College kids? I went to Rob and got the lowdown. It turned out that multimillionaire David Woods, who owned the company, had been losing money on the wrestling business and decided to cut costs. One of the costs he cut was the production crew, who at one point helped make Continental a thriving territory. As a big believer in close-ups and camera angles, I was not high on our company's chances for success without a decent production crew, and felt that Woods' money saving methods were unwise. I also didn't care for his decision to cut our payoffs.

Forty dollars was the minimum payoff for a show. Often I could wrestle in a single, come back in a tag, and end the night in a battle royal. For my extra efforts, I would be given an extra twenty a night, which averaged out to a cool $220 for my three-month stint in Alabama. Fortunately, we had the perk of a free two-bedroom apartment that in true starving-wrestler fashion, we jammed six guys into. The fact that I temporarily had to share a room with Downtown Bruno tended to put a damper on the joyousness of the free roof over my head.

Bruno was a true classic. A sniveling runt of a man, Bruno was the willing target of several funny but cruel practical jokes that seemed just a little too realistic for my tastes. One night in the dressing room, Bruno was reading off a list of African-American jokes that he consistently laughed the loudest at. *Click.* Suddenly, there was a gun to Bruno's head, held there by a shaking Brickhouse Brown, who claimed he'd "had enough of your jokes, you white son of a bitch. Now I'm going to show you what a black man can do!" Immediately, Bruno's knees buckled and he burst into tears and begged for his life. Brickhouse and all the boys broke out laughing. "Bruno, don't you know I wouldn't waste a perfectly good bullet on your worthless ass," Brickhouse explained.

For a little guy, Bruno could throw down brews with the best of them, and his legendary drunken escapades became the butt of many jokes, the cruelest of which actually happened months later when I was with WCW. Sid Vicious had brought Bruno to the TV taping in some far corner of Alabama, where, per Sid's request, booker Ric Flair began marveling at Bruno's managerial splendor. "Brother, I've seen you work," Flair lied to Bruno. "And may I say, you are the finest young manager I have seen in a long time." Bruno was beaming, and lit up even more when Flair informed him, "I think you'll have a new home right here in WCW."

Suddenly, Flair began sniffing the air, and asked Bruno if he'd been drinking. "Yes sir, Mr. Flair," a petrified Bruno replied, but defended himself by saying, "but only one." Flair looked repulsed as he chastised poor Bruno.

"Look, I don't know what kind of organization you come from," the Nature Boy lectured, "but we do not want drunks working here." Bruno was crushed. When I went out to wrestle, all of the fans were on one side of the small gym, in an attempt to make the place look full. All except Bruno, who sat in solitude with tears running down his sorry-ass cheeks. After Sid let him in on the joke, Bruno instantly forgave him and joined him on the ride back home. To Sid's credit, he actually did bring Bruno to the World Wrestling Federation with him a few years later, which in reality was the only place Bruno really wanted to work. He remains there in some capacity to this day. Hell, he even had an action figure made of him.

Unfortunately, laundry was not something that Bruno was real good about, as I watched his dirty clothes pile up in a corner. One day I caught him digging into his dirty clothes pile for something to wear. "What the hell are you doing," I asked.

Bruno turned around and in all seriousness replied, "Well, they've been in the pile so long, I figured they wouldn't be dirty anymore."

Despite the financial woes, which were compounded by the fact that the territory was dying, and our somewhat cramped living conditions, I had a decent time in Continental. All the wrestlers lived in the same apartment complex in Montgomery, including Brian Lee, who was married, and my old buddy Lou Fabiano, and the complex often resembled a big family. We'd have cookouts and play Wiffleball in the afternoon and sit around the pool all day on our off days, playing crazy eights with Rob.

Rob was addicted to eights, and never ceased to entertain with his running commentary during the games. "Come on, poo poo, come to old Rob," he'd say while always threatening to "drop a hoss on you," which meant throw a joker down. Rob provided commentary on more than just crazy eights, as I discovered at a motel after a late-night visit to Shoney's for "all you can eat" shrimp night. Rob, Jimmy Golden, and I had done a pretty respectable job of costing Shoney's some money that night, and we each headed back to the Days Inn with full bellies as we called it a night.

A few minutes later, I got up to get a soda and heard the unmistakable sound of Rob's voice. "Oh God, oh God, here it comes," he moaned. I didn't know what the hell to think. Here what comes? Was Rob enjoying a private moment of climactic ecstasy, and if so, why didn't he sound all that ecstatic about it? A splashing in the toilet cleared up the mystery. Unless Rob was an unbelievably virile man, the splash I had just heard was vomit and Rob was doing play-by-play on all the gastrointestinal action. "Oh, that's not good, that's not good," he bellowed, followed by a "mmphh" and a splash. "Oh, I think it was my heart that time."

I was a frequent dinner guest at Rob's apartment and was treated often to the great Southern cooking of his wife, Sylvia. I learned the pleasures of cornbread and its many versatile uses, which included being crumbled into beef stew and being crumbled into milk. I also became close with Rob's two youngest daughters, Katey and Charlotte, who I believe were seven and five at the time. I often took them to school, rode the rides with them at the Alabama State Fair, and have especially fond memories of reading to Charlotte every time I was over to their place. The little girl loved to be read to, and she'd curl up on my lap like it was the most comfortable seat in the world.

One day I picked up Rob in the trusty Arrow for a trip to the next town, and he had a huge gleam in his eye and a story he couldn't wait to tell me. "Jack-o, guess what I did last night," he asked, and then continued without waiting for my response. "I asked Charlotte if she wanted me to read to her, and she curled right up on my lap. I'm going to read to her every chance I get." I was genuinely glad that I could help Rob rediscover a simple joy in life that I treasure every chance I get with my own kids now.

Yes, I had a good time in Alabama, but I couldn't completely ignore the fact that business sucked. The crowds were bad to the point that I was starting to get buzzed regularly on a couple beers in the backseat of my car, following anemic attendance figures at our shows. I even resorted to drinking a thirty-two-ounce Colt 45 malt liquor out of a paper bag on one trip. Continental was, however, the place where Cactus Jack learned how to brawl.

Rotten Ron Starr was a veteran wrestler with a forehead that looked like pink taffy from all the years of bloodshed he had endured. He had come to the territory even though Fuller and Golden accidentally injured his neck years earlier.

I had my first match with Rotten Ron in Meridian, Mississippi, and we clicked right away. Rob had cut a great promo about Starr, saying he was hot at Cactus Jack because Cactus had done a number on Starr's "love child that he'd had with a little senorita down around El Paso." It may have been a ridiculous premise, but Starr played it up big, to the point that he came across like one mad SOB when he tore into me in Meridian. It was a true give-and-take match, with Starr giving out punishment and me taking it. We fought in the ring and outside it, up the bleachers and back down, and when I stumbled off into my dressing room, Starr returned to the ring to a huge ovation.

The next day, Ron was putting me over big time and concluded by saying, "Do you know who you remind me of, kid?" My mind started racing. Who? Harley Race? Terry Funk? Ray Stevens? His answer was a bit of a letdown. "Mike Boyette," he said, beaming. I only knew Boyette as the guy who had run off over 100 straight losses in Bill Watts's Mid-South group, and I guess Starr could see my confusion as he let me in on the fact that at his peak, Boyette, the California Hippie, was the premier bump man in the sport.

We took our match around the loop, always ad-libbing and always creating new twists along the way. Our run peaked with a memorable and bloody TV brawl at the Montgomery Civic Center that left Starr as the unlikely biggest babyface in the company. Our feud was short-lived, however, as we received word that the company would be shutting down right after Thanksgiving. After a year and a half of steady, if somewhat poorly compensated, work I now found myself with the unsavory task of looking for a job. It was during this trying time that I heard the phone ring in our apartment and when I picked it up, the voice of Shane Douglas say, "Hello, could I speak to Cactus, please?"

Shane had recently caught on with Turner's World Championship Wrestling (WCW), and even though pegged with a ludicrous tag team gimmick called the Dynamic Dudes, seemed blissfully happy in his new role. Maybe the hundred grand contract he had signed made him blind to the fact that he had to wear pink trunks and carry a skateboard to the ring with him. I'm sorry, Shane, but when you have a skateboard and don't use it, the fans will in fact know that you don't know how, just as they caught on to the fact that I couldn't crack my bullwhip in Memphis—because I never did.

Shane asked how I was and I told him of the imminent closing down of the company. "Why don't you come to a TV taping in Atlanta," Shane suggested. "Hell, it's only three hours away. This way, you can at least get your face seen." I quickly agreed and a week later, drove to the Center Stage theater in Georgia.

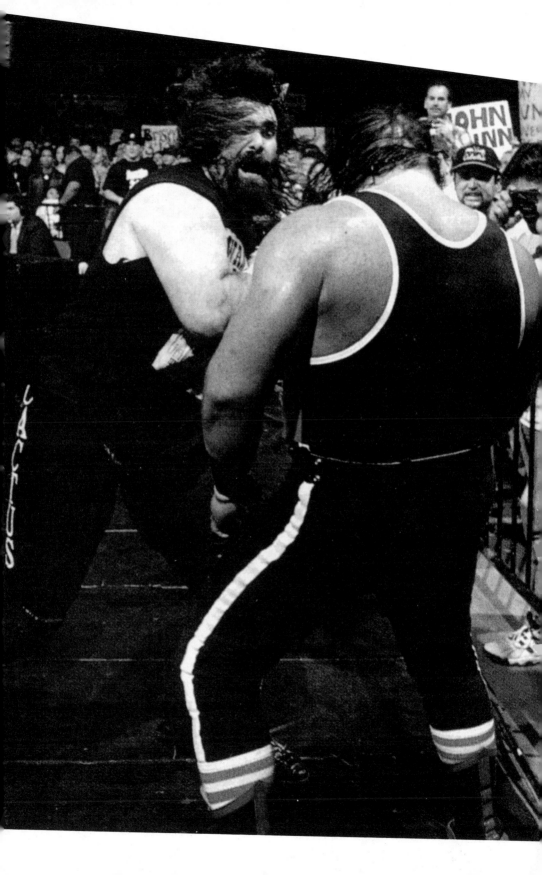

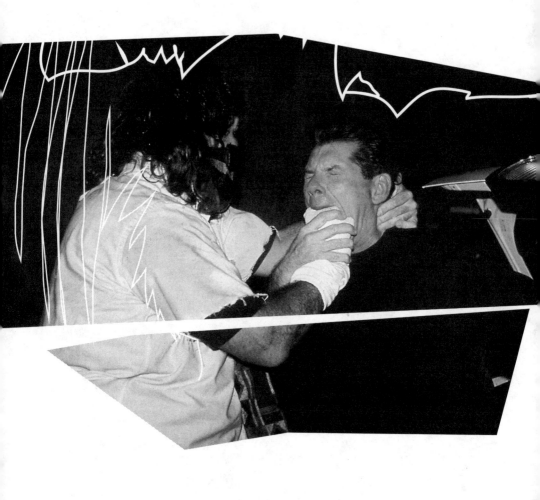

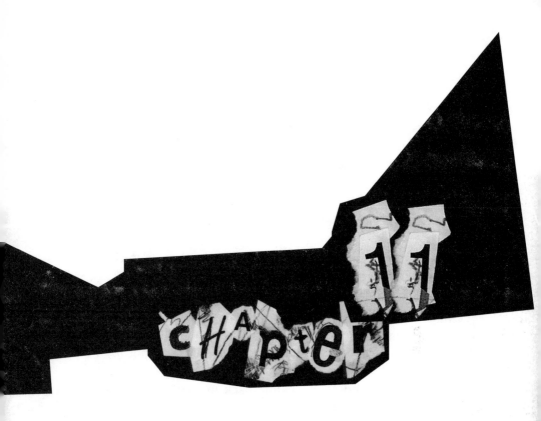

Center Stage was like a whole new
world when I walked in. I felt strangely like I had during my first day
in the World Wrestling Federation dressing room back in 1986, as I
watched all the big stars walk by. This time, however, some of the
people actually knew who I was. "Love your finish, mate," came a
deep voice with a strong New Zealand accent. It was Rip Morgon,
who expressed his admiration for the flying elbow off the apron.

A moment later, I spotted Jim Cornette, whose eyes lit up when he
saw me. Brian Hildebrand was a mutual friend of ours and as a result,
Corny came over and hugged me like he had known me all his life.
"Goddamn, Cactus, it's good to meet you, you crazy son of a gun,"
Corny exclaimed in his machine gun vocal style. "Hey, I've been trying
to throw your name around as part of a tag team with Tony Anthony,
who's a hell of a talker. We'd dress you up with weird stuff sticking
everywhere, make Brian your manager, and call you The Wild Things."
Just then, Jim Ross came into view. Although no longer part of the
booking committee, Ross was still WCW's play-by-play man, and he
was taking a break between two tapings. He spotted me, walked over,
and with less than full enthusiasm, gave me a quick "Cactus Jack, are

you still alive?" before heading into the dressing room. Needless to say, it was not quite the greeting I had been hoping for.

A minute later, however, Ross reappeared with booker and five-time (at the time) world champ Ric Flair. He said, "Hello, how are you, sir," for the first time (I should point out now that Flair had two separate stints as booker—one in 1989–90, and one in '94). Suddenly, Ross, who I thought had just blown me off, was singing my praises to the Nature Boy. "Ric, this is Cactus Jack," he said. "He's a hell of a worker, a hell of a talker [which was debatable] and takes some great bumps."

Cornette was next to give a glowing testimonial. "Ric, you've got to see this guy—you'll love him. Maybe you can put him under a hood just for one match, and take a look at how he bumps for one of our top guys."

Flair took it all in before asking, "What are you doing in two weeks?" I was tongue-tied for a moment before using my much-heralded mike skills to say, "Um, nothing."

Flair nodded and said, "Come back in two weeks, when we have TV again, and I'll take a look at you."

During those two weeks, I read the Bible and watched the G-rated movie *The Bear* twice—I wanted to get on God's good side. I visualized my tryout match a thousand times. I was going to come out with all guns blazing and was definitely going to showcase my flying elbow. I even visualized my big promo, just in case. I hadn't been given a chance to talk in months, but I knew in my heart that when called upon, I could deliver the goods.

When I arrived at Center Stage, I looked at the lineup sheet and felt all of my visualization become devisualized. There in black and white, for all the world to see, were the following words: "R. Fargo and Cactus Jack vs. The Steiners." This wasn't going to be a tryout—it was going to be a slaughter. The Steiners weren't just wrestlers, they punished you. Rick threw the hardest clothesline in the business and Scott seemed to make up suplexes as he went along. The fact that I had known Scott in Memphis did little to comfort me as I envisioned myself spending more time in the air then Kay Parker's legs in the *Taboo* trilogy. Was this really all they thought of me? I felt suddenly as if all my suffering had been for nothing, and was even contemplating packing up and leaving, when Jim Cornette and Kevin Sullivan approached me.

"Hey brotha, nice to meet you," Sullivan said in his native Boston accent. "What's your finish?"

I had no idea what he was talking about, but gave a confused answer: "I drop an elbow."

"An elbow," Sullivan groaned. "What kind of a finish is that?"

Luckily for me, Corny jumped to my defense. "Kevin, you've got to see it—it's the damnedest thing you've ever seen. He comes running down the apron and drops the elbow right on the concrete."

Sullivan seemed impressed. "You drop an elbow on the concrete, brotha?" he asked. "I'll tell you what," he offered, "After your match with the Steiners, I want you to drop that elbow on your pahtnah. Got it, brotha? No matter what Ricky or Scott do to you I want you to get up and drop that fuckin' elbow on your pahtnah."

As it turned out, the Steiners did quite a lot to me. I was slapped so hard that my jaw swelled, was clotheslined damn near out of my shoes, and was taken down to the canvas by my old buddy Scott. I was hyperventilating badly—due mainly to nerves, as I hadn't been in the ring long enough to qualify for such an exhausted state. As I lay there panting, I wondered briefly if maybe I wasn't cut out for the big time. Maybe I belonged back in Tennessee or in Texas where I could continue to play Bleeding for Dollars.

Unbeknownst to me, however, Sullivan was making me out to be a star on color commentary. "Look at that, Jim," Sullivan marvelled, "I've seen every wrestler take the Steinerline [clothesline], but this Cactus Jack just got right back up. There's something that's not quite right about this guy." I always felt like Sullivan was very underrated color guy in that he constantly put over the wrestlers and the angles, as opposed to pushing himself. I actually benefited greatly from his wisdom and perception on color, as I would from Jim Ross on play-by-play over the next decade.

When I tagged in Fargo, the Steiners put him through a quick series of torturous tumbles and ended the match. I waited until they left for my big chance to shine. Here I go. I helped Fargo to his feet, in an act of mock consideration. Once the poor guy was erect (no, not that way), I let him have it. A series of forearms to the head were followed by a toss out of the ring, where I continued to pursue him on the floor. I picked up Fargo, carried him a few steps, executed a backbreaker, and deposited him suddenly on the cold, concrete floor. Eagerly, I hopped back up on the ring apron, turned around, and got ready to pounce. "Oh my God," I thought in panic, "I'll never reach him." Without exaggeration, Fargo was at least seventeen feet from the ring. Bob Beamon or Carl Lewis would have had trouble reaching him, let alone Mick Foley, who at a height of six-foot-four had barely grazed the rim of a basketball hoop a single time. What else could I do? I thought about an alternative but quickly realized that I couldn't possibly jump down, pull him in closer, jump up on the apron, and do it again.

Instead, I took a deep breath, took my two-step approach, and pushed off with as much force as my legs could provide. I came up about one foot short and landed hard on my hip with a huge thud but caught Fargo with my outstretched arm. All in all, it was a pretty impressive debut, and my adrenaline surged when I felt the reaction of the crowd. "You were the star of that match," wrestling personality Joe Pedicino told me as I walked into the backstage area.

"You think so?" I asked, to which he replied, "Hey, it was your replay they showed—not the Steiners."

Many of the guys who had never seen me wrestle were impressed with both my big elbow and my character, and they were patting me on the back and giving me encouragement. Arn Anderson, who on that very day was making his return to WCW after a year with the World Wrestling Federation, walked by with a strange look at this strange kid who had just dove seventeen feet onto a concrete floor. "Cactus Jack," he began in his distinctive north Georgia drawl, "you just don't have any sense."

I thought about what he'd said and gave him an honest appraisal of the situation by replying, "No, but I don't have any dollars either."

"Point well taken," replied Arn. Arn was the king of the put-down, and I quickly learned that it was a compliment and not an insult to be put down by Arn.

When the taping was over, I was approached by Sullivan and Flair. Sullivan was not shy about his high ambitions for me and Flair seemed impressed, if slightly stoic. "We're going to put you on the road in about a month," Flair informed me. "In the meantime, we'd like you to make our next TV tapings in the Carolinas. I'm not sure what you will be making, but it will probably be in the neighborhood of a grand a week. I can't guarantee that, but I can guarantee that you'll be making a comfortable living." Comfortable—my ass! At a grand a week, I would be rich.

I know I've written some things about Flair that could be construed as unflattering and believe me, before I'm through, I'll write a lot more. But, personal feelings aside, Ric Flair is one of the very best to ever walk that aisle—and I will always be proud of the fact that it was the Nature Boy who hired me.

When I returned to Montgomery, I worked my last few shows for Continental and then loaded up the Plymouth for my venture into the Carolinas, which would be more or less halfway to East Setauket. With a friend's wedding coming up, to be followed by Christmas, I would be able to relax, rest up, and bask in the glory of $1,000 every week. First, however, I had shows in Greensboro and Raleigh, North Carolina, to finish.

Greensboro had been a longtime hot bed for the NWA but had fallen on hard times in the previous few years. The building was less than a third full, but as usual, WCW shifted the crowd to one side to give the illusion of a full mass. Even with a lot of empty seats, 5,000 fans were more than I'd seen in my last month of shows in Continental combined.

I was scheduled to tag with Nasty Ned Brady, who was one of my all-time favorite "underneath" wrestlers against the team of Wild Fire Tommy Rich and Ranger Ross. Rich was a former NWA world champ who went on to manage in ECW, and Ross was a former Army Ranger with a colorful background. The match, as Jim Cornette so elegantly put it, "sucked a dick." But as Nasty Ned tagged in, I waited in nervous anticipation for my chance to follow Sullivan's instructions to "Drop the elbow on Nasty Ned, brotha."

Sure enough, Ned fell to the might of Rich and Ross, and even though Ned and I had not worked well as a team, I came in to lend a hand. "Look at that," Gordon Solie, "the Dean" of wrestling announcers, pointed out. "There's Cactus Jack helping his partner up. Oh no, he's not." As soon as Ned had gotten to his feet, I had put my arm around him just long enough to slip my left leg around his and deliver a quick Russian leg sweep that sent us both down backward to the canvas. From there, I proceeded to put the boots to poor Ned and set him up against the ropes for the Cactus clothesline that sent us both tumbling over the top. Ned hit the floor and rolled into such a perfect position that I didn't even need to move him or slam him, and I sailed off onto the boards covering the Greensboro hockey ice with a perfect ten-foot elbow. When I looked up the camera was pointing right in my face. For some reason, the B-52's song "Love Shack" came into my head. For a reason still unknown to me, I looked up at the camera and with my fingers pointed like pistols, recited the "Bang, bang, bang—On the door, baby" part of the song. A catchphrase was born.

The next night, we worked at the Dorton Arena in Raleigh, where I had my first singles match with a talented young wrestler on the rise named Flyin' Brian Pillman. I went a full-tilt eight minutes with Brian, and we turned out a match that was excellent in quality and intensity. Terry Funk was doing the color commentary on the show and if you listen closely, you can hear the Funker's admiration shining through. I lost the contest but refused to leave the ring and was still there when Sting came out for his match. Being the hero to "the little stingers" that he was, Sting didn't take kindly to my poor show of sportsmanship and proceeded to beat me up all around ringside, including a backdrop over the guard rail that had the Dorton Arena fans oohing in unison. Despite the fact that I had been both beaten and beaten up, I was on cloud nine when I got back to the dressing room because I knew that I'd done well. Minutes later, Sullivan, Funk, and even Buzz Sawyer were congratulating me on the match. Unfortunately, it was probably the only time that Buzz was ever nice to me, but, hey, that was one more time than most of the young guys got.

Kevin walked up to me as I was dressing and sat down to talk. "Brotha," he said, "I am going to make it my goal to come up with as much weird shit as possible for you to do." He would prove to be true to his word in that regard.

That night, I got into the Arrow and headed for home, stopping only at my old friend Meg Morris's house in Richmond, Virginia, long enough to rest for a few hours and then drive the 400 miles home with Van Morrison on the radio and big plans on my mind. I made it home in time to go out with my buddies at night, a decision that almost derailed my wrestling plans permanently.

A friend of mine, Jean Nagle, was getting married the following day and was having a small prewedding party in a bar named Billie's in Port Jefferson. Hearing of the prenuptial plans, I hopped into the backseat of a car driven by my second grade buddy Dan Hegerty. Along with Dan Welisher riding shotgun, we took off from the Park Bench in Stony Brook, just four miles away. I was really enjoying myself that night and was in the middle of reminiscing about our mutual landscaping experiences when wham, our car was destroyed. I had been in mid-sentence with my last word being "sprinkler" when a car without its lights clipped us almost head-on when the driver, who, as it turned out, was a guy I had known since I was ten, attempted to turn into his street.

Immediately I realized that my front teeth were gone. Yeah, sorry to kill my hardcore reputation, but the missing teeth were not the result of Sting kicking them out in Raleigh as I have claimed for the past ten years. Also, since then, I've had other teeth knocked out, so I don't feel all that bad about deceiving wrestling fans around the world. Aside from the teeth, I had terrible pain in my right shoulder, which made it almost impossible to move. "Are you all right?" I called out, to which there was no reply. "Are you guys all right?" I repeated, but again, no answer was forthcoming. I looked up front and saw both Dans slumped over, unconscious. My heart sank as I feared the worst, but I managed to roll out of the car through the back door, which had been opened upon impact.

I tried Welisher's door, but it wouldn't open—I can't honestly explain why I didn't try Hegerty's. Instead, I walked into the road to wave down help but was dismayed to see the first few cars whizzing by the accident scene. I wondered out loud, "What kind of prick would bypass two totaled cars and an injured man?" But then I realized that I was in New York and that the number of potential pricks capable of doing such a thing would probably make Santa Claus's "Good Kid, Bad Kid" list look like the Cliff Notes version of *Famous Jewish Sports Stars* by comparison. Finally, the third car stopped and took me to downtown Port Jefferson, where I limped into a restaurant and dialed 911. On the way back, I realized that I could stick my tongue through a gash underneath the left side of my lower lip. By the time I got to the accident scene, two ambulances were already there and I hopped out of the car, thanked the driver for his help, and attempted to climb into the back of the ambulance.

"I think I belong in here," I said to an EMT, who questioned my move, and then I heard an urgent "We've got a bleeder!" I looked down and saw blood oozing through my black jeans and down onto the cheap snakeskin boots I had bought at a discount tack store in Nashville. The EMTs quickly cut my pants up to the knee and took off my boot, and in the three or so seconds it took for them to press a heap of gauze into the wound, I saw blood squirting out from my shin area in about ten-inch surges.

I still didn't know about my buddies' fate until I heard yelling in the emergency room. "No way, no way, you're not going to do that," the voice yelled.

"Who is that?" I asked.

"That's one of your friends," the nurse replied. "He's not too happy with the catheter we're trying to insert into his urethra." I really can't say I blamed him. Geez, right off the top of my head I can think of half a dozen things I would rather have done to my penis than that. A moment later, I heard yelling from another part of the emergency room, and it seemed that Hegerty too was resisting the unwelcome intrusion of the catheter. For some reason, I was spared the pain and humiliation of that procedure. Maybe I just didn't need it, or maybe, being a woman, the nurse had just chosen not to check out that part of my body for any reason. Poor little guy. Why didn't anybody love him?

A few minutes later, the stitching began, and a doctor worked on my leg as he waited for a plastic surgeon to arrive to work on the gash under my lip. Somewhere between the time of the final shin stitches and the arrival of the plastic surgeon, my parents showed up and were deeply concerned about their little boy. I assured them that I was all right despite the fact that in addition to my major wounds, I had about ten minor gashes on my face. When the surgeon showed up, my parents were asked to leave, but before their departure, I had two favors to ask of them. "Mom, could you search in the front pocket of my jeans and get the front tooth I put there." There, that was one. "Also, tomorrow when you come to see me, could you bring a camera?"

I left the hospital three days later, hardy able to walk and depressed about the loss of my teeth. Maybe not depressed, but definitely concerned. Friends who came to visit me all echoed the same sentiment—"Hey, that's going to look good for wrestling," to which I would give a lecture about it being almost 1990, and the day of toothless wrestlers was over. Ten days later, when I showed up at Center Stage, Jim Ross was the first person I saw. "Hey, you look great without your teeth," he said. "It gives you a whole added dimension." As it turned out, in 1990 I was the "guy without the teeth." In 1994 I became "the guy without the ear." In 1996 I became "the guy with the leather mask." And in 1998 I became "the guy with the sock."

The accident slowed me down for a little while, but I was able to suck it up on TV matches and continue with my terrible treatment of tag team associates. In addition, all the announcing teams—Ross and Sullivan on *Saturday Night,* Lance Russell and Michael Hayes on *WCW Pro*, and Chris Cruise and Terry Funk on *Worldwide* seemed to be getting into Cactus Jack, and their enthusiasm was contagious. Fans started responding well to my matches and even though I was a heel, I was being cheered heavily in many of our towns. Sullivan, whose abusive manager gimmick had always worked well, saw great potential in our pairing and stepped down from announcing to become an active wrestler and manager. Kevin had gotten really into the Cactus Jack character and came up with an idea that I loved then and still do. "Brotha," he instructed me, "when you go home, I want you to find a book, and then I want you to bring it to the ring and read it before your matches."

I nodded my head in approval, but needed more specifics. "What kind of book should I bring?" I asked.

Kevin was quick to respond. "A thick book, brotha, like an encyclopedia."

When I came back, I had a book in hand but was not sure if it would meet the former Games-master's standards. "It's not exactly an encyclopedia," I warned him as I handed over the book.

Kevin took one look at the title, *I Am in Urgent Need of Advice,* and began to smile. "That's the book, brotha," he said, laughing. "That's the book."

Thus began our strange chemistry, with me trying to sneak a look at the book during matches, and Kevin berating me for doing it. Kevin would slap my face and I would smile, and the fans were eating it up. I found out years later that even more emphasis would have been put on me except that the idea was shot down. Flair had thought over the request for my bigger role in the company, but had responded by asking the booking committee, "Do you really ever see Cactus Jack wrestling for the world's heavyweight championship?" When no one stood up to herald me as the heir apparent, the Cactus Jack discussion was over.

Two days after the clash, Sullivan's Slaughterhouse was born. The group consisted of Buzz Sawyer, Cactus Jack, and Kevin in a butcher's smock. The smock would have probably looked more imposing if TBS had allowed it to look bloody, but coming from a group so politically correct that they refer to foreign objects as "international objects," blood on a smock was unacceptable. As was something that might be interpreted as blood. As was dirt, which might be interpreted as something that could be interpreted as something that looks like blood. As a result, Kevin went to ringside looking like an anal-retentive butcher clad in laundered white.

The original plan for the Slaughterhouse was for Sullivan and Sawyer to form a tag team in cahoots with me as a single. Occasionally, we would all team. That plan ended at the February 1990 Pay-Per-View *Wild Thing*, when Buzz suffered a compound fracture of the wrist, and never returned to WCW rings. As a result, Kevin and I held down the fort in a somewhat odd feud against Captain Mike Rotunda, Norman the Lunatic, and Abdullah the Butcher.

Rotunda was an excellent wrestler who had been a part of Sullivan's Varsity Club, an excellent and successful gimmick that was disbanded as soon as it became too popular. As a result, Rotunda had languished in wrestler's purgatory until I tagged with him against the aforementioned Dynamic Dudes, and did a number on him after our loss. The dastardly attack turned Rotunda into a good guy, and somehow changed him from the captain of the team to the captain of the ship, complete with sailor's cap and nautical windbreaker. Despite the ludicrous gimmick, Mike and I had good matches around the country, until Sawyer's injury turned me into a tag team wrestler.

The February Pay-Per-View was also memorable in that it was Ric Flair's birthday, and I somehow was offered an invite from Sullivan to attend. I was thrilled to be in attendance, even after a less than stellar match against Norman the Lunatic. The Funker was there, and he came over to give me his opinion of my match in his own unique style.

For several minutes, Terry rambled on with a story about the devil who was facedown in the gutter, having his life saved by the angel. The story was making absolutely no sense until the last sentence, at which point the story, and its relation to me, became apparent. When the lovely angel was asked why she would save someone as despicable as the devil, the angel fluttered its wings, strummed its harp, and replied, "Don't you understand, without him there is no me."

Terry than looked at me and said in his soft, West Texas mumble, "Cactus Jack, Norman tried to be an angel out there, but you wouldn't let him, because you were not the devil. People can talk about your bumps all they want, but until you learn to be the devil in the ring, you will never fully be all that you can." I nodded in agreement with Terry, who seemed pleased to have had me sit for a spell underneath his learning tree.

Dennis Brent was a friend of mine from Dallas, who was currently the WCW magazine editor. He had witnessed the entire angel/devil parable and couldn't help but notice the Funker's interest in me. "Terry," Brent began, "it seems that you like Cactus because you see a little bit of yourself in him." It was a very astute observation on Dennis's part, and deserved an equally astute response, which Terry quickly provided. "I don't see shit in him," the Funker claimed, but said it in such a way that I know he agreed with Dennis.

Since that time, Terry and I have inflicted punishment on each other that might well carry jailtime if it was done on the street. But as K. C. and the Sunshine Band once put it so well, "That's the way, uh huh, uh huh, I like it."

As much as I wish it weren't true, my first stint in WCW, spanning late November 1989 to mid-June 1990, will best be remembered for my match at the February 10 *Clash of the Champions*. Unfortunately, I hated the match and considered it one of the biggest letdowns in my career. For years, however, it was the most frequently talked about subject of my career, so I'll at least try to touch on it.

The horrible chain of events started some two weeks earlier when

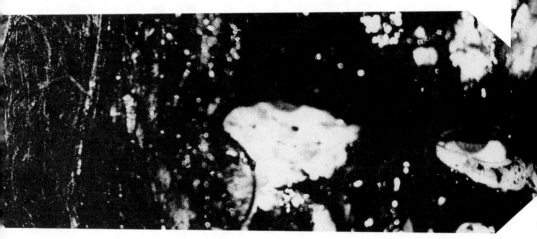

Jim Cornette approached me with what he thought was great news. "Guess who they've got you working at the *Clash* against?" Corny beamed and then shot down my first few guesses. "Nope, you're going to work with Mil Mascaras," he gushed and awaited my enthusiastic response, which never came. Jimmy was confused. "What's wrong with that?" he wanted to know.

I decided to cut around all the fat and get right to the meat of the subject. "Mascaras sucks," I stated, "and the match is going to suck." Jimmy nodded, but I wasn't done with my honest assessment of the man who had been a legitimate legend, sports hero, and film star in his native Mexico for over a quarter of a century. This may have been true, but in my dealings with Mascaras in Texas, I had found him to be selfish, redundant, and lousy. "Jimmy, why is he coming in?" I asked, and Corny quickly let me know, "It's just for a couple of shows in the Texas border towns."

This didn't make a whole lot of sense to me. If they wanted Mascaras to draw fans in towns with heavy Mexican populations, why couldn't they put him on before the televised matches started, instead of both stinking up a nationally televised *Clash,* which was TBS's most heavily hyped wrestling show, and sinking my career, which had been going so well. "Jimmy, I'll do it," I said, "but I can't promise that it won't be a stinker." Cornette seemed to understand my feelings and said that, as color commentator, he would try to make me look good on the show.

I arrived in Corpus Christi, Texas, several hours early for the show, and was delighted to hear that Mascaras had missed his flight into town. Immediately, plans were changed, and all of a sudden I was set to wrestle my old partner Rick Fargo instead. This was great—not only would I not be in the ring with the ungiving Mascaras, I was actually going to win a match in the *Clash.* So I guess I don't have to explain how dejected I was when I saw the Mexican legend show up a half-hour before the match. As it turned out, he hadn't missed the flight; he just hadn't wanted to sit around the arena for a few hours, so the prima donna booked a later departure. Obviously, the visions of grandeur I had set in my mind for Fargo were not going to apply with Mascaras, so I quickly went back to the drawing board.

I knew that it was useless to try to talk to Mascaras, so instead I talked to Cornette quickly before he went out for the show, and alerted him to a big move I was going to do, and he told me that he was going to do his best to make me look like the star of the match. He didn't let me down.

Much as I had predicted, the match, to use a Cornette term, "sucked a dick," but when the time was right, I made most of the young audience forget that Mascaras even existed. I briefly took over on the used-up loser and threw him to the outside where he gingerly landed. I then picked him up and gave him a weak backbreaker that he was so frightened to take, he actually put his hands and ass down on the ground, so that he finished the move in a sitting position. "Come on, Mil," I thought, "show a little bit of pride in your work." At that moment, I wondered if having the ability to suck in your stomach and walk on your tiptoes for twenty-five years was really all it took to become a legend in the business. Then again, bell bottoms were big in the seventies also, so there may have been a lack of sense all the way around.

With Mascaras looking about as pained on the floor as a Swedish massage recipient, I hopped up to the ring apron for the big elbow. Actually the timing of this was excellent, because as I faced the crowd with my arm in the air, signaling the imminent arrival of the flying elbow, Mascaras was rolling back into the ring. When I took my two-step approach and got ready to fly, Mascaras was nowhere to be seen. When I turned around in confusion, Mascaras was there with a dropkick, or "dropkiss," as he called it. When he hit me, I went sailing backward several feet, and as I came smacking down with what was then my 265 pounds, cameraman Jackie Crockett caught the impact perfectly, with a low-angle shot that made it look like I was crashing right into living rooms around the country.

In reality it was the same Nestea Plunge that I'd done previously in Memphis and Dallas, but this was a nationally televised live event, and fans around the country and the world had never seen anything like it. "Oh no," Cornette screamed. "Cactus Jack is dead!" It was one of the greatest calls I've ever heard. As I lay there stunned, two replays showed the sickening bump, while Ross and Corny both agreed that the match, if not my career, was over. When the camera came back to me, I was on my knees struggling to get back in the ring. Cornette went back into the action and dramatically yelled, "No human being could get up after that, but Cactus Jack is doing it."

All I wanted to do was be able to kick out of one pinning attempt, which would have made me look like Superman, but when I earlier had told Flair of this plan, he told me in no uncertain terms, "This match is not about you. No kickouts." So instead Mascaras pinned me and walked to the back as I waited for indignity number two to transpire.

The *Clash* in Corpus Christi featured a live band that played during the commercial breaks to entertain the crowd, and when they came back from commercial, I was still at ringside and was being enraged by the lead guitarist, who, I guess, was supposed to mock me. As a result, I tried to go after the skinny guitarist, only to be confronted by their buff drummer, Wolfe Wilde, who was really New Jersey independent wrestler J. T. Southern. Southern and I got into it, but the fans were not supposed to know he was a wrestler, so it looked to most of the viewing population like I was getting my ass kicked by a musician. After the show, Joe Blanchard, an old-time wrestler and promoter, who was currently in charge of the Texas ring crew, offered to take me on as well. "Well, you already put over a wrestler and a drummer," Blanchard said, laughing. "I figure you might be willing to put me over, too."

In retrospect, my WCW run would have been better served if I had stayed a single wrestler, but we certainly provided some excitement as a tag team. Eventually Bam Bam Bigelow was added as a third partner in our group, and we went around the country with a combination of tag team matches and six-man events that were met with great response.

One day, I opened my check and thought that a mistake must have been made. I was paid too much. As Flair had said, I was averaging a grand a week at that point—with five shows a week for $200 a shot. Suddenly I had a check for $3,000, and I commenced to reading the numbers to find out where I'd gone wrong. I looked at the ten individual payoffs, which were all $200. Then, at the bottom of the page, I saw a statement that confused me: "Per agreement—$1,000"— which totaled the mysterious three grand payout. I called up the office to find out what was wrong, and my worries were put to rest immediately by Jim Barnett, an old promoter turned front office person whom I had heard incredible stories about from both Dominic and Fuller. "My boy," Barnette said in a voice that couldn't be considered gruff, "We are very happy with your efforts here, and we decided that we're going to start paying you $1,500 a week."

I didn't know what to say except "Thank you Mr. Barnett," to which he quickly responded, "No, thank you, my boy." When he hung up, I danced around my room and thought of all the ways I would spend my newfound wealth. Then I got a better idea. I wouldn't spend any of it.

Sure enough, for the first time in my life, my bank account started to grow. Aside from my road expenses, which were around a hundred a day, I had few bills to pay, because I lived with my parents and was regularly putting away a grand a week. I was wrestling hard, having fun, and in my mind at least, I was one wealthy SOB. Actually, after five years in the business, I had pulled in a grand total of $30,000 before my WCW stint, so I probably had several $1,500 weeks to go before I could even qualify as destitute.

I was regularly traveling with Jim Cornette and his Midnight Express, which consisted of Sweet Stan Lane and Beautiful Bobby Eaton. Stan was like the ultimate bachelor, and even traveling with me didn't seem to tarnish his image with the ladies. One night I saw Stan opening his door carrying about ten jumbo-size bottles of baby oil, and I didn't have to wrack my brain to figure out what was going on in Stan's room that night. Actually, I never had to use my mind to figure it out—a drinking glass pressed to my ear and held against the wall usually told the tale rather explicitly.

Beautiful Bobby was one of the true greats in the sport. Aside from being perhaps the most underrated superstar in the business, he was also its nicest, and stories of Bobby's generosity were commonly recited in the dressing room. It was damn near impossible to pay for anything when Bobby was around, although I'll confess to not trying all that hard.

One night when we stopped for gas, a bum approached us as we got out of the car. I didn't say too much to him except "Hi Mr. Snow" (just kidding, Al) as I pumped the gas. A few minutes later, I was in the car with Corny and Stan, and Bobby was nowhere to be seen. Another few minutes—no Bobby. Just as Stan was about to get out to find him, we saw Bobby coming out of the store with his arm around the old bum. The old guy was now holding a new bottle of wine in his hand, and had on a new shirt as well. When they got to the car, Bobby handed the guy $10, shook his hand, and got back in the car. That was just the way he was.

My fortunes started taking a turn for the worse in mid-April in Columbus, Ohio. I was teaming with Kevin against Rick Ryder and someone else whose name escapes me at the moment. We had what I thought was a very enjoyable match, concluding with an elbow on Ryder, who was as far away, if not farther, than Rick Fargo had been four and a half months earlier. "Rick Ryder has just had his pancreas punished," Cornette yelled in response to the big elbow, which was honestly just a wrist and four fingers making contact, because he had been so far away.

I was happy about the match, but my positive feeling soon turned to shock when I ran into Ric Flair, who had been waiting for me. Flair had just resigned as booker, and I guess he decided to take his frustration and anger out on me. "What the hell are you doing out there?" Flair demanded. I didn't know what to say. Hell, I didn't even know what that question meant, and I told Flair so. "I mean you do all that shit, and just because those two [pointing to Ross and Cornette on the TV monitor] put you over, you think you're over. Don't you understand no one cares about you?" I was floored. All I could do was stare blindly as the Nature Boy continued his condemnation. "You'll be in a wheelchair by the time you're thirty," he scoffed, and followed it up with another bit of sentiment, "and nobody's going to care."

I have thought about that night in Columbus at least a thousand times since it happened. For several years, I thought about it every day, and as I approached my thirtieth birthday four years ago, I became obsessed with it. I felt strongly enough about it to do an interview on the subject on the eve of my thirtieth birthday, which the *Wrestling Observer* called "one of the greatest ever" in wrestling.

A short while ago I ran into Flair, who congratulated me on how well I'd done, and then said, "Geez, Cactus, you need to slow down so you don't get hurt. Do you remember when I told you that you were going to be in a wheelchair by the time you were thirty?" I told him that I remembered very well.

For a few weeks, WCW went ahead without a lead booker. When I found out who the new booker was, I was wishing Flair had never left, Columbus dressing room incident or not. Ole Anderson was a wrestling traditionalist who hadn't shown a whole lot of enthusiasm for my character or my style since I met him. Ole had just retired in February and had been around in some capacity since then, I think as a road agent. He had continuously teased me—usually about my ass, and even compared it to the McGuire twins, which was a little ridiculous, because the twins weighed over six hundred pounds each. Now that I think of it, for such a tough guy, Ole sure did spend a lot of time talking about my ass. Hmm.

I felt like I knew that my days were numbered, so I decided to have a talk with Ole. To his credit, Ole talked to me for a long time and did have some noteworthy points. Among them was an analogy to war atrocities, which I have since learned is one of his favorites.

"Goddamn," Ole began, "there's a guy walking around a war-torn

MICK FOLEY

country, and he comes across a girl who's been killed by a bomb. The guy drops to his knees and goddamn, he cries that it's the worst thing he's ever seen. 'Oh my God, it's terrible. Look at that poor little girl. I can't go on.' When the guy gets up, he walks a few steps and sees five kids who have also been killed and burned by a bomb. Oh God, this is really bad, he thinks, but gets up and walks until he sees ten girls who have been killed and says, 'What a shame,' as he walks by. By the time he gets to a hundred children who have been bombed and killed, he doesn't even slow down to look. He just doesn't care anymore."

I understood Ole's point, but he wasn't quite through yet. "You see, kid, the marquee says wrestling," he grumbled. "That's what we're going to give them. If people wanted to see your goddamn trampoline act, they would buy a ticket to see Cathy Rigby." He also said a bunch of things that started with, "Back in my day," and by the end of our talk, I could pretty much see the writing on the wall. Still, I hung around for a little while, simply because of the money.

A few weeks later, I had talks with Kevin Sullivan, Jim Cornette, and Jim Ross, and then gave Ole my one month's notice. He didn't exactly beg me to reconsider.

I finished up on June 10 in Hollywood, Florida, and flew home the next day feeling like I could take on the world. My name had gotten around to several independent promoters, and I already had several bookings lined up. I was ready to enter into the next phase of my career.

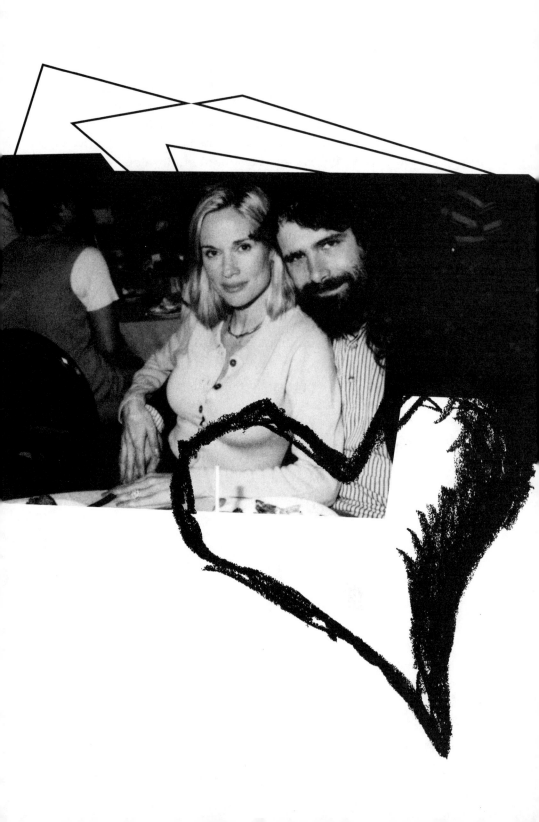

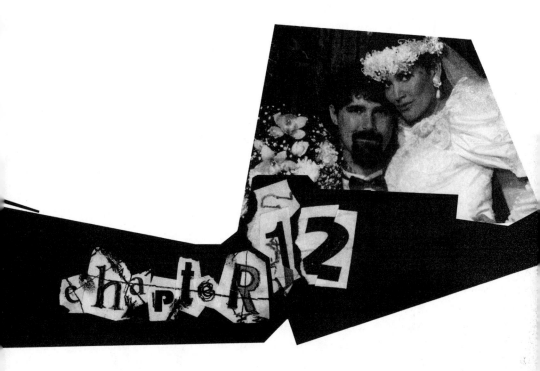

Chapter 12

One of my first independent matches after my WCW exit was for my first wrestling boss, Tommy Dee. I would go on to work quite a bit for Tommy over the next thirteen months, and always worked half price in appreciation for the help he had given me years earlier. I had set a somewhat ambitious price for myself of $250 but would work for Tommy for a cool $125. Obviously it would be impossible to match the $1,500 a week I had been pulling down in WCW, but I looked at my independent dates as a long-term investment in myself. The show was to be held on July 7 at the Riverhead Raceway in eastern Long Island, about thirty miles from my house. Because of my close proximity to the venue, I agreed to hand out flyers at the races on the previous Saturday afternoon, to help build up the matches that were set for six days later.

It was a beautiful summer afternoon at the races, and the smell of burning rubber brought back memories of when my parents used to take me to the Commack Motor Speedway when I was a kid. I was strolling about the grounds handing out flyers and was pleasantly surprised at the recognition I was receiving, when all of a sudden I saw it. A beautiful, thin waist, with a shirt that revealed just an inch or two of skin. Around the waist there was a distinctive, if somewhat S&M-ish–looking belt that I couldn't take my eyes off. I couldn't even see her face, but nonetheless felt like I had to meet her. She later would say she could feel me watching her, even though she could not see me.

I thought over my options. I could simply walk up and introduce myself, but that would take a certain amount of guts, and I knew that it was out of the question. Instead, I saw a husband/wife team of truckdrivers who had said hello earlier, and asked if they knew who she was. "No," one replied, "but would you like me to find out?" A minute later, they came back with good news. "Her name is Colette and she said she'd be happy to meet you."

Now I had a little more confidence, and I walked over and said, "Hello."

"Hello, I'm Colette Christie. How did you get the name Captain Jack?" Uh oh, an incorrect name right off the bat. For a moment, I had flashbacks to Cortland State, but then realized that this was actually a good thing. She didn't know who the hell I was, so there was no way that she could be digging me for my very small amount of fame. Then again, I wasn't so sure she was digging me anyway.

"Actually, it's Cactus Jack," I corrected her, "and it's a wrestling name."

"Oh, that sounds like fun," she said, smiling. "I went to wrestling matches at Madison Square Garden about five years ago. Have you ever wrestled there?"

"No," I had to admit, "I haven't yet."

Her next question was kind of a buzz killer. "Where do you wrestle?"

"Well, next week, I'm wrestling here at the Raceway. Would you like to go?" She laughed a little bit at the thought of wrestling in such a place, and I tried to cover myself by blurting out, "I usually wrestle in nice places."

She smiled and told me what seemed to be a sure blow-off. "Look, I'm just visiting my aunt and uncle here. I don't have a car and I could only go if they come with me."

Then I saw Tommy Dee out of the corner of my eye pointing to his watch, and I knew that it was time for my big racecar angle. I felt like I had ruined my chances already, but I decided to throw out my best line anyway. "Can I have your phone number?" I asked with about zero confidence in my voice.

"I don't like to give out my number," she replied. "Especially because I'm at my aunt and uncle's house. You can give me yours if you like." I wrote down the number and headed off to the racetrack, doubting that I would ever see her again.

When I got to the racetrack, about ten drivers were letting their engines softly idle to prepare for the next race. The public address announcer put his arm around me and said, "Ladies and gentleman, we have a special guest here today—Cactus Jack from the world of professional wrestling." Mild applause. "Cactus, we would all just like to know how you're enjoying the great town of Riverhead and the great sport of auto racing."

I tried to forget about my flop with the S&M chick and got ready to rip off the Funker. "Thank you very much for your support," I began. "You know, I'm really enjoying my time here in Riverhead. It's a beautiful town, and the people have been so nice to me since I've been here." Respectful applause. "But please, don't insult my intelligence by calling this stuff you do out here a sport, or by calling these guys athletes."

All of a sudden, the engines started revving in response to my cheap shot at their sport. One of the drivers, a big 230-ish kid named Eddie Dembrowski actually got out of his car and approached me. As his name might imply, Eddie was Polish, as was most of the town. The place was crawling with people who had "ski" at the ends of their names. "Hey," Dembrowski yelled, "we go out here and risk our lives every week. How can you come out here and say that we're not athletes?"

I really felt that this was going really well, and had especially high hopes for my next words, which were straight from Terry Funk in the horrible wrestling movie *I Like to Hurt People*. "Look," I snarled at Eddie, "I'm going to say this once, and because I know you're Polish, I'm going to say it real slow." This was great. The engines were revving and people were booing, and Eddie looked so nervous I thought he was going to pass out. "In ancient times, there were only three real sports. Ancient man either ran for his life, swam for his life, or did what I do, and fought for his life. One thing that I can guarantee you that primitive man did not do is get in his car and drive away."

With that, Eddie gave me a shove and I shoved him back. Racing security jumped in and held Eddie back, and when they did, I jumped him from behind, slammed his head into the hood, and then rolled him up onto his own hood, at which point I piledrove him. Fans were actually trying to climb over the fence to get to the infield, and other drivers, who had no idea that I was just trying to promote the show, tried to get at me. It really was a wild scene that ended with me being taken off in a wire mesh paddy wagon, as the fans yelled at the dastardly Cactus Jack. As I was being taken away, I thought about the girl I had met, and wondered if she did anything with that belt besides wear it. (Hey, I need to be honest, don't I?)

Three nights later, I heard the phone ring and picked it up to hear a voice saying, "Hello, is Jack there?"

"Which Jack are you looking for," I inquired, as, after all, my dad was the only real Jack in the house. "Cactus Jack," the female voice answered.

"This is Cactus."

"Hi, I'm Colette Christie," she said, "the girl you met at the racetrack." Moments later, I was securing my first real date in a very long time.

On Thursday, the night before my big match at the raceway, I was spiffing myself up for my big night out, and my mother walked in, slightly confused by the sight of her son applying cologne for the first time in recent memory. "Where are you going tonight, Mick," she questioned, "out with your friends?"

"Mom," I shot back with enthusiasm, "I have a date tonight with the most beautiful girl I've ever seen."

My mom looked at me and quickly asked, "No, really, Mick, where are you going?" When I left the house five minutes later, I still don't think she was convinced that I even knew a beautiful girl, let alone was going out with one.

Colette's aunt lived an hour away, so I had plenty of time to think of all the cool things I was going to say. When I got there, I realized almost instantly that I wasn't going to need any help in saying anything, because we connected right away.

Being boring, or, more accurately, having nothing to say, had been a longtime fear of mine—a compulsion almost, which unfortunately led to avoiding conversation with strangers whenever possible. I even feared one-on-one conversation with all but my closest friends. With them, I could be myself—with everyone else, in a one-on-one situation, I was always petrified. As a result, I remember wearing headphones and keeping my head down when I walked back from classes at Cortland, just hoping that I wouldn't run into someone I knew only moderately well.

I solved that problem with Colette by instantly becoming friends with her. As soon as she hopped into my black 1984 Chrysler LeBaron convertible, which had replaced the Arrow I had abandoned on the side of the road in Pennsylvania, I was not shy about hitting her with my stupid puns and dorky jokes. She responded by actually laughing, even though once in a while, she'd have to stop and ask, "Is that a joke?" As we drove to an unknown location, she fumbled with the radio, and when she started singing along with a country song, I felt like I might be falling in love. After all, a girl who was born in Queens, and who had grown up in Manhattan, actually singing country music was something I had never even considered. I remembered back to a time when I was eighteen and had two tickets to the Willie Nelson picnic at Giants Stadium, and had to give them to my parents because I could not find one person, male or female, who wanted to go with me. Then again, maybe it wasn't the country music that was the turnoff—maybe it was me.

We finally ended up in a small bar in Rockville Center, right across from the office building where the Apter wrestling magazines are published. I fed the jukebox with quarters and got to know Colette a little bit while "Tweeter and the Monkeyman" by the Traveling Wilburys played. Colette explained that she had been a model for a long time, but that at twenty-nine, she was now too old for the business. Her father, with whom she'd been very close, had died a few months earlier, and Colette had been so distraught that she'd been unable to work. As a result, she was planning on going to live with her mother in Florida. She was staying with her aunt and uncle just long enough to get her things, and then she would be Sunshine State–bound. We decided that we could at least have some fun until she left, and that maybe I could stop by and visit her in Florida sometime if I was in town for a match.

I think, however, that I may have been too charming for my own good, especially singing all the words to "Forever in Blue Jeans" by Neil Diamond. I firmly believe that when you find a girl that you feel strong enough to sing Neil Diamond in front of—especially on the first date—well, man, you've got to hold on to that girl. By the way, do you know who else who knows all the words to "Forever in Blue Jeans"? The tattooed tough-guy wrestler Mideon.

By the time I got back to Colette's aunt's house, I had already confessed to actually being named Mick and not Jack. After all, I didn't want to have to put on my act around this girl—I wanted the freedom and honestly of being my own dorky self. She invited me in for tea, and I accepted, being the tea-loving son of a bitch that I am. It was there that I met Confusion, Colette's Shetland sheepdog of ten years, and spotted a book with Colette's picture on it that I asked if I could see. It turned out to be Colette's modeling portfolio.

Now, I feel like I need to admit right here that I had certain doubts about the validity of Colette's alleged modeling career. Sure, I thought she was beautiful, but I'd met a lot of girls who said they modeled, and at most it turned out to be a few head shots and a local underwear ad. Hell, even the Godfather's Hoes consider what they do to be modeling. Instead, I was blown away by what I saw. Real pictures, real ads. Revlon, Avon, Tropical Blond, Maidenform, book covers. This was impressive. This wasn't someone claiming to be a Guess Jeans model—this was a real model. Next I turned the page and saw a two-page layout that nearly knocked me for a loop. "I know that ad," I yelled, "but what is it?"

"That's a campaign I did for Burlington Leggs," she replied, either being completely modest, or trying to sound modest, like I do when I tell stories about my matches in Japan.

"But where have I seen it?" I begged. "I know that ad from somewhere."

"It used to be on the New York City buses," she informed me. "In fact, the ad took up the whole bus."

"That's it," I gushed. "I loved that picture. My friends loved that picture. We used to talk about that picture." This was great. I had just had a date with a supermodel, and had swept her off her feet with an '84 LeBaron, a Neil Diamond song, and very little else. I even got a kiss goodnight, and was called the correct name to boot. As I drove the hour back to Setauket, I couldn't help feeling that I was going to be letting the perfect woman go when she took off for Florida, and I comforted myself with the hope that I'd maybe get to nail her (my wife and I get a personal kick out of this word, which is why I use it here) before she left.

As it turns out, all my fears were for naught, as she came to the matches to see me on Friday, went to the movies to see *Ghost* on Saturday, took a day off from Foley on Sunday, and moved across the street from me (into the room my neighbors were renting out) on Monday. The Foley charm had simply been too much to resist. For the rest of the summer, we were inseparable, except for my shows, during which time she and my mother hung out anyway. We spent a lot of time at the beach, went on road trips, and in a situation that was a little bit awkward, made many strange noises upstairs directly over Joe and Martha Forte's bedroom, so that my neighbors of twenty-four years never looked at little Mickey the same way again.

After a few weeks of fun in the summer sun, I offered to show Colette a tape of me wrestling. I just knew she was going to be impressed. She wasn't. I was a little hurt, and asked why. She got real serious and said, "I don't like the way you allow yourself to be slapped around out there—you're better than that." I had often talked to Colette about my desire to go back to one of the big two, and she saw this somewhat goofy act as being a stumbling block in front of something good. "You're better than that, Mickey," she kept saying. "You're better than that." Without any real knowledge of wrestling, she had more or less surmised what Frank Dusek had said a year earlier. "You're a goof, and goofs will never be top guys."

Maybe she had a point. Bruiser Brody didn't look like an imbecile when he was alive. Stan Hansen didn't make his name doing a Keystone Cops routine. I decided at that point to veer away from so much comedy, and concentrate on getting vicious. For the next year, I tried my best to scare fans when I went to the ring, and many times, especially in front of a small crowd, I would leave a high school gym or armory looking like a tornado had gone through it. I became fond of swinging chairs, and had the best match on almost every card I was on, and ended up turning in very solid performances with a variety of different wrestlers in a variety of different states and countries.

Around this time, I met a man named Herb Abrams at a wrestling convention in New York. It was there that Herb held a press conference and announced the formation of his new Universal Wrestling Federation, or UWF. In addition, he announced Cactus Jack as a signee with the company, which was a handshake deal that we had just agreed to. Herb really felt that his new group would instantly join the big two and felt confident that in time, it would become number one. When someone at the conference asked how he could feel so sure without having a background in wrestling, Herb replied, "What they're looking for, I have, and that's the Hollywood glitz." Herb also announced Bruno Sammartino as his color commentator and himself as play-by-play man, an idea that would prove to be entertaining, if not exactly wise.

To know Herb Abrams was to like him, or at least be amused by him, as he was a true cartoon character. About five-foot-four-ish, with a small frame, Herb realized that he would never make it in the wrestling business he loved so much, unless he bought his own company. I don't know where he got his money, but man, did he spend it, as he brought in a crew of guys that actually had more talent than the rosters of either of the big two. The guys he brought in had legitimately been huge names and had drawn big money around the globe. The list reads like a *Who's Who* of wrestling with Paul Orndorff, Dr. Death (Steve Williams), Don Muraco, Bob Orton, B. Brian Blair, Danny Spivey, Billy Jack Haynes, Sid Vicious, Ken Patera, Colonel DeBeers, David Sammartino, Jimmy Snuka, and even Andre the Giant being only some of the guys he brought in.

Even with all these guys, Herb Abrams was the star. At least that's what he thought. I remember watching his show, which was a pretty difficult thing to do. Despite his prediction, the "Hollywood glitz" was nowhere to be seen, as we toiled away in a dingy nightclub that seated, at most, 300 people, and believe me, there were not usually 300 butts in those seats. Even with all the top names, I was the crowd favorite at the nightclub, even though I was technically a bad guy. Maybe it was the "Welcome to the Jungle" music that Herb had made my entrance theme, or maybe it was the "Unpredictable" moniker that Herb had placed before Cactus Jack—the same one that had worked so well for Johny Rodz.

Anyway, during the show, there was an advertisement for wrestling cookies, which I guess Herb felt was the natural snack food choice of all wrestling fans. Herb's grating voice was doing the talking, as he hailed the benefits of "Mr. Wonderful Paul Orndorff cookies, Wild Thing Steve Ray cookies, and, coming soon, Herbie cookies."

He did the same thing with merchandise. Herb somehow landed a deal for his *Blackjack Brawl*, not only to be held at the prestigious MGM Hotel and Casino in Las Vegas, but also to be carried live around the country on SportsChannel. What a sight it was to see 200 fans in a 22,000-seat building. But hey, Herb was ready and no one could say that Vince McMahon had anything over Herb in the "marketing genius" category. After all, he did air ten commercials for UWF merchandise during the Blackjack Brawl, even if all of them did push only one product—the Mr. Electricity, Herb Abrams T-shirt. I asked his girlfriend after the show how he got the Mr. Electricity nickname, and she put her hands over her head, shook her hips, and gave a very animated, "Because when he plugs it in he really turns me on."

I think that it was at the MGM show that Herb's announcing skills really came to the forefront. He had invited me to his suite at the hotel to show me a "big surprise." Herb had an incredible six-room penthouse suite that offered an unbelievable view of Las Vegas. When I got there, Herb had a bandage pressed to his lip, from a wound that he had suffered while wrestling with his buddies in the suite. His surprise—a new UWF championship belt, and a pair of yellow and green ostrich-skin boots that he swore the fans were "going to go nuts over." Well, maybe the fans didn't go nuts, but the wrestlers certainly did, as Mr. Electricity strutted out to the ring with the belt and the ostrich boots. There may have been only a few hundred people in the cavernous arena, but they were Herbie's people, baby, and he was giving them what they came to see.

His announcing that night was truly memorable, as in addition to the fat lip, he was downing cocktails throughout the show and was totally hammered by the time he interviewed Little Tokyo, who had just won the prestigious Midget's World Title. "Congratulations, Little Tokyo," Herb slurred, "maybe you have some sake tonight to celebrate."

Little Tokyo's eyes grew wide and he replied in astonishment, "How do you know sake?" to which Herb offhandedly said with a shrug, "Oh, I was married to a Jap once."

I've got to hand it to Herb, however, as that night in Las Vegas I got to live out a dream when I wrestled the Superfly Jimmy Snuka in a lumberjack match, in which other wrestlers were to stand outside the ring to ensure that the action didn't spill outside. There were a few problems with the match, however, as no one ever assigned any lumberjacks to the match, and we had no idea what Herb wanted out of it. As a result, I began asking wrestlers to be lumberjacks, an invitation that many declined, and as a result had a threatening group of lumberjacks consisting of two male wrestlers, two women, two midgets, and three security guards as we got set to go out. Thankfully, Jack Mulligan took control of the situation, and made wrestlers go out to the ring and help us.

The end of the match posed a problem, as Herb didn't want me to lose, and there was no way I was going to let Jimmy lie down for me. As a result, we did the exact thing that lumberjack matches are supposed to prevent—we fought to a double count-out. The lumberjacks were baffled as we fought outside the ring and into the empty stands. "What are you guys doing," B. Brian Blair yelled to us as he gave chase into the twenty-seventh row.

"It's a double count-out," I yelled as the Fly and I continued to trade punches.

"But you can't do that in a lumberjack match," Blair said, laughing in disbelief.

"Hey, it's Herb's show," I said right back, "we can do anything."

A few months later, I read of Herb's passing in a wrestling newsletter. I called over Colette, who had gotten to know Herb pretty well, and began reading the article, but couldn't get through it without laughing in spite of myself. Like his life, Herb Abrams's death had been way over the top. Apparently someone had alerted the police to a disturbance in a high-rise office in Manhattan, and when they got there, they found women screaming in the hallway, and little Herb running around naked, bathed in baby oil, and swinging a baseball bat, with which he was destroying furniture. He was taken into custody and died shortly after from a massive heart attack.

Colette and I sat down and mourned Herb's death by sharing stories of his life and laughing at what a character he had been. I think Herb would have liked it that way.

In March 1991, I headed to Japan for a one-month tour of Japan for All-Japan Wrestling, which was owned by legendary promoter and wrestler Giant Baba. Baba was one of those great mysteries I have never figured out, in that fans went absolutely nuts over his every move, most of which looked like they couldn't break an egg. Still, Baba had run the successful promotion for decades and I was excited about my trip as I really felt like it might turn into a full-time job. All-Japan ran regular tours throughout the year, and some Americans, like Stan Hansen, worked them all, which added up to twenty-six weeks a year.

I had been a fan of Japanese wrestling for years, ever since seeing my first Tiger Mask–Dynamite Kid match at Brian Hildebrand's house in 1986. I had since amassed a huge library of Japanese tapes, which I studied diligently for hours every day, in the basement apartment in Huntington that Colette and I had moved into a few months earlier.

I opened up a Thomas Harris book called *Red Dragon* as we took off from JFK and was just finished when the plane touched down in Narita Airport. I had trained hard for this match, both mentally and physically, and was ready to take on the Orient.

I did well in All-Japan—so well, in fact, that rumors started circulating about a twenty-week-a-year offer that was going to come my way. This was great. There would be no politics or Ole Anderson to shove me down, and I could feel fulfilled living out my wrestling fantasies 8,000 miles from home.

I ran into trouble at the end of my first week when I broke three ribs in a match with Jumbo Tsuruta, and even more when I broke Johnny Ace's elbow at the end of week number two. I was attempting to suplex Ace (who was Shane Douglas's fellow Dynamic Dude in WCW) backward off the top rope—a move that he intended to counter by turning it into a cross body block that would end up with Johnny on top of me as I bumped backward to the mat. Unfortunately, when I tucked my chin to my chest to protect myself, I also clamped Ace's arm under my chin too, and he was unable to get free in time. When we hit, I heard him groan and I knew he was hurt and I knew I was screwed.

Johnny was Mrs. Baba's favorite wrestler, which suddenly put me out of favor with her. Seeing as how many people felt she actually had more influence on the company than her husband, being out of favor with her was not a good place to be. I called Colette after the match and explained the injury. "That's it, Mick," she yelled enthusiastically, "you show them that they can't push you around." When I explained to her the ramifications of the injury, however, her enthusiasm quickly withered.

I later found out (years later) that I had other things working against me in Japan as well, none of which had to do with the quality of my matches, which had been high. I had come to Japan as a big fan of Bruiser Brody, who had run roughshod over not just the Japanese wrestlers, but their fans as well. The fans loved it; you could see them with huge smiles on their faces as they ran from Brody, as he threw punches at whoever was dumb enough to stick around. They didn't sue over things like that in Japan, they considered it a compliment. I even watched in shock when we got off the bus at Korakuen Hall in Tokyo and saw one of the wrestlers punch a fan who got too close, right in the face. I was even more shocked to see the same fan bow down, while holding his face, and say, "Sank you, sank you very much." This place was crazy, and even though I wasn't into punching fans, I got prepared to play along.

Over the course of my first few weeks—the pre–Ace injury weeks—I had made it a habit of diving into the crowd. I would charge a guy, and he would backdrop me into the fans. I would shoot another guy into the metal guard rail, and he'd reverse it and I'd end up flying backward into the crowd. It was as if all of Japan was my own personal mosh pit.

Unfortunately, however, fans were getting hurt—not just from me landing on them, but in their attempts to get out of the way of my 287 pounds as well. Just as unfortunately, the Japanese wrestling publications had taken to calling me "The American Onita," in honor of a popular hardcore FMW (Frontier Martial Arts Wrestling) wrestler, and had taken to calling my matches "FMW style." Apparently, this didn't sit well with Baba, who considered the Onita-led FMW to be "garbage wrestling" and certainly didn't enjoy the comparison. Eventually referee Joe Aguchi came to me and said sadly, "Jack-san ["san" in Japan is a sign of respect], Mr. Baba ask you please stop hurting fans."

It wasn't the last time that Aguchi came to me with a request from Baba, as a short while later he became the bearer of bad news again. "Jack-san," poor old Joe again sadly began, "Mr. Baba wants you to maybe wear nicer clothes."

"Didn't he get it?" I thought as I looked at my sweats, suede fringe Indian boots, and red flannel. "It's not the clothes, it's me." The rest of the guys, for the most part, wore loose athletic pants and tank tops or sweatshirts. If I was put in those same clothes, I would still look bad. Hell, years later, in the World Wrestling Federation, I wrestled in a tuxedo just because they knew how bad I would look in stylish clothes. In retrospect, I'm glad I didn't figure all this out until later, because I would have had a miserable time. As it was, I wasn't exactly having the time of my life, as I missed Colette terribly, to the point that I was writing her letters daily, which I later burned and buried so that I would never have to risk my children finding out just how lonely a guy their dad had been over in Japan.

At the end of two weeks, the Funk Brothers were flown in for the second part of the tour. Terry and his brother Dory had helped build the entire sport in Japan, and to this day are loved by the fans for their thirty-year history there. I was excited as hell to finally have a match with the Funker, whom I had remained in contact with since we both split from WCW. I loved Terry's style, and during the course of my career have borrowed liberally from it, a fact that the Funker was honored by when I asked his permission to rip him off shamelessly. "Cactus Jack," he had told me just a few months earlier, "you can take anything of mine you want because the old Funker is just about done." Nine years later, at age fifty-four, he is doing somersaults off ten-foot balconies.

No matter what mannerisms I "borrowed," I knew that I would never throw a punch like Terry's, which was truly a thing of beauty. Many people, including me, considered the Funker's big left hand to be the nicest punch in the business. A few minutes into the big match, Terry took me into the corner, and I saw him rear back with the big left. This was going to be great. Here it comes. *Thwack*. I felt like I did when I was eight and my mother came clean about Santa Claus. I had just learned the hidden "secret" of the great Funk left hand. It was so simple—I'd been a fool for not knowing the whole time. Terry Funk had just punched me as hard as he could in the forehead.

"No wonder that punch looks so good," I later whined to Terry. "You hit me as hard as you could."

"Oh, Cactus Jack," Terry mumbled and laughed in his kindly old Uncle Terry way, which made it impossible to be angry with him, "all this time, you thought that I was just really good."

I got to know Stan Hansen well in Japan, and in an odd way, he went on to play a major role in my life. Stan was a true superstar in Japan, and he had been there so long that he was almost a part of the culture. He had been Brody's partner for several years, and I think he kind of liked the little bit of Brody he saw in me. Hansen was known as the stiffest of all the American wrestlers, and his "lariat" or clothesline was a destructive force, partly because of the force he threw it with and partly because he could barely see without his glasses and had no idea where he was hitting guys with it.

Hansen was a legitimately tough guy, but like most tough guys, he didn't feel the need to prove it, and he was actually a true gentleman outside the ring. Sensing that I was not a party guy, Stan kind of took me under his wing and began bringing me out with him so that I wouldn't just sit for hours in my room, as he correctly guessed I would have. He was also a great family man who talked so much about his

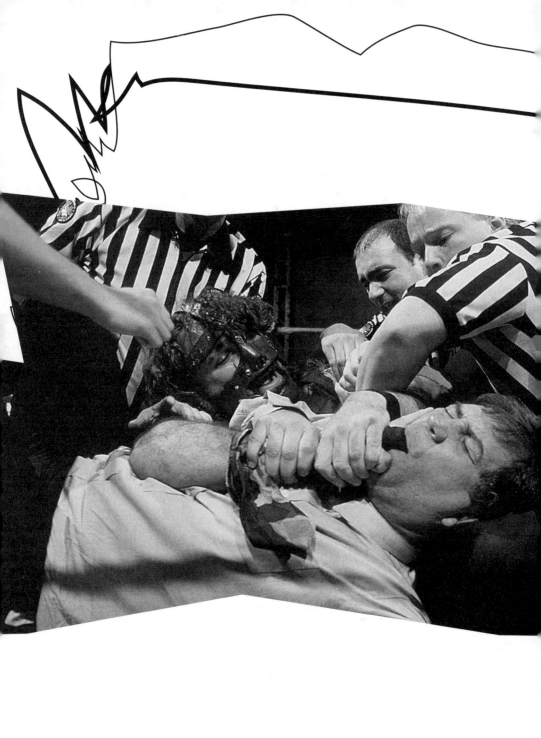

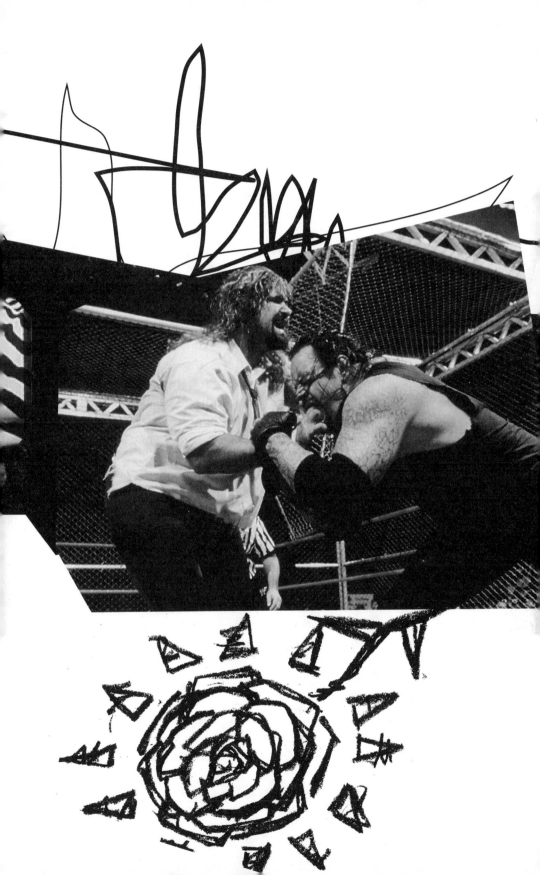

kids that I seriously began to think about having a little one of my own. Colette had talked to me about the idea before, but I had never felt ready for the responsibility. I walked out of Shakey's "all you can eat" pizza restaurant one early afternoon and told Stan that I'd catch up with him later, as I had a phone call I needed to make. As Stan walked away, I dialed the United States, where it was about eleven o'clock at night. "Hello," Colette sleepily answered, "who is it?"

"It's me," I said anxiously followed by, "Would you like to have a baby?"

When I came home, I was exhausted, sore, and at $1,500 a week for four weeks, about six grand richer. My ribs had bothered me for the entire trip, to the point that I had to wear a flak jacket afterward for several months. I had a trip to the Caribbean island of Aruba a few days later and brought Colette with me. It was there, with dedication, hard work, and relentless repetition, that we went about the arduous task of conceiving a child. I had been warned over the years by other wrestlers that I might be risking damage to my reproductive system by the constant pounding I was taking on the cold, hard, concrete floor. Because of the high-impact landings, they feared that I might not be able to have a child. In Aruba, I was determined to prove those experts wrong.

I had some tremendous matches as an independent, but will probably best be remembered during this time for the series of matches I had with Eddie Gilbert for Joel Goodhart in Philadelphia. Goodhart ran the Tri-State Wrestling Association, or TWA, which was the precursor of Extreme Championship Wrestling, or ECW. He believed in a hardcore, bloody style and had his own theory on what made a show successful. "Most groups' first match doesn't mean anything," he was fond of saying, "but our guys are different. We want the first match to go all over the building so people can't wait to see what's next."

Now this might sound like simple logic, but to me, it flies in the face of the scientifically proven "three ring circus" theory of wrestling, in that there is something for everyone. If you didn't like the clowns, you would like the elephants, and so on and so forth. To me Joel's shows were the circus equivalents of seeing a guy get shot out of a cannon thirty times. On small shows, in little high schools, Joel would force-feed this repetitious menu of violence for so long that most people looked like they would never want to attend wresting again upon leaving. ECW is often much the same way, but they have a much better assortment of characters to have some fun with.

As he was my most consistent booker, however, I was very thankful to Joel. His quarterly extravaganzas in the Philadelphia Civic Center were the biggest independent shows in the country. It was in these shows that my matches with Eddie took place. After seeing Eddie and me in action in late 1990, Joel booked us in a "falls count anywhere" match (pinfalls count anywhere in the building) a few months later. I considered that match to be the best of my career for two years, right until my match at *Beach Blast* in June 1992 took over the honors. On the heels of that, Goodhart asked me if I would be interested in doing a barbed wire match with Eddie.

In these days, until Japan raised the bar by taking down the ropes and stringing up wire in its place, barbed wire was simply strung up between the ropes. While it wasn't as dangerous as the conditions I would later wrestle in, it still was no day at the beach, and I knew that considerable risk went along with it. I was very tentative about doing the match, unless it was done under the right conditions, and one of my conditions was that the match seem special by keeping it as the sole gimmick on the card. "I'll do it," I told Joel, "but only if we cut down on the blood in the other matches."

I drove to Philadelphia with Colette, who by this time had already seen enough injury and punishment inflicted on me to be concerned about any match, let alone one with barbed wire involved. I was nervous, yet excited about the match, and I was getting dressed when I saw a preliminary wrestler walk by with a little trickle of blood on his forehead. "That's odd," I thought, but went back to getting ready. A minute later, another wrestler, another trickle. I started to become concerned. Next I saw another wrestler walk in who had not a trickle of the red stuff, but a whole face full of it. Now I was worried. Who was going to watch my gorefest with Eddie if all of Joel's wrestling school guys were bleeding in the first match? I asked one of the guys with the trickle (let's just call him trickle number one) what was going on.

"Oh, we were in the battle royal," he said.

"So, why are you bleeding from a battle royal," I wanted to know.

"It's a last blood battle royal," he quickly replied.

"Last blood?" I asked disbelievingly, even though I really knew the answer to my own question.

"Yeah," trickle number two piped in, "the last guy not bleeding is the winner."

Immediately I ran out and caught the last five minutes of one of the sorriest affairs I'd ever seen. Ten guys, some of whom had never had a match before, were fighting in and around the ring. They were trying to poke, prod, gig, hit, and bust one another and themselves in an attempt to draw blood. So much for cutting down the blood in the other matches.

Eddie and I were forced to turn up the volume in our match even higher than we would have. As a result, the match was actually ruled a no-contest when I became so badly wrapped up in the barbed wire that I couldn't get out. Normally a no-contest ruling would be a reason to riot in Philly, but because of the serious nature of the predicament I was in, the fans were respectful. Actually, they were pretty concerned. Even when Colette came out to check on me, I didn't hear a single catcall, even though compassion was usually a dirty word to Goodhart's fans.

In the ring, meanwhile, Eddie was doing a number on a couple of younger wrestlers, after piledriving the referee. After the match, the strangest occurrence took place as the referee was brought out on a gurney and placed into the ambulance. I was lying in the hall with several holes in me. Eddie had passed out from blood loss and exhaustion, and the referee was rushed to the emergency room for the simple reason that he was afraid to tell the EMT people that he was faking it.

Goodhart was excited about the match and all the media attention that he was receiving because of it. A few weeks after the barbed wire match, he told me of his master plan—a two-of-three-falls match with Gilbert and me, with each match being a gimmick match. Together we came up with the matches—a falls count anywhere, a stretcher match (the loser is the first one unable to get up), and a steel cage match.

To do all of these in one night would certainly be challenging, not to mention exhausting, and I embarked on a rather strenuous training program for the big night. I actually felt like I was in the best shape of my career as I pulled into the Civic Center. What followed were forty minutes of what Eddie Gilbert actually called the best matches in his life. Coming from Eddie that was high praise, as he was one of the most talented and hardest-working guys in the business before his untimely death three years later in Puerto Rico.

When I was given the chance to come back to WCW following the three-way match, Eddie was invited as well. As a matter of fact, we had the same starting date, but Eddie didn't show. Part of the reason,

Eddie explained on the phone, was that he didn't want to tarnish the reputation of what he and I had accomplished. After leaving WCW under less than ideal circumstances a year and a half earlier, Eddie felt that he was going to be punished upon his return, and part of his punishment, as he saw it, was to be placed in situations where he could never live up to our reputation for great matches. How could we? In TWA, we had pulled out all the stops, and had engaged in what would more accurately be called wars, as opposed to matches. WCW would never allow that to happen, and Eddie refused to give anyone Gilbert vs. Cactus unless it was allowed to be done right.

We tried to resurrect our history after I left WCW in 1994, but could never quite get it done. I regret that. I also regret not wrestling on the first Eddie Gilbert Memorial Card right before I went to the World Wrestling Federation because I know it would have meant a lot to his brother Doug and his mom and dad. The best I can do is remember Eddie for what he was to me—a teacher, a mentor, and a friend.

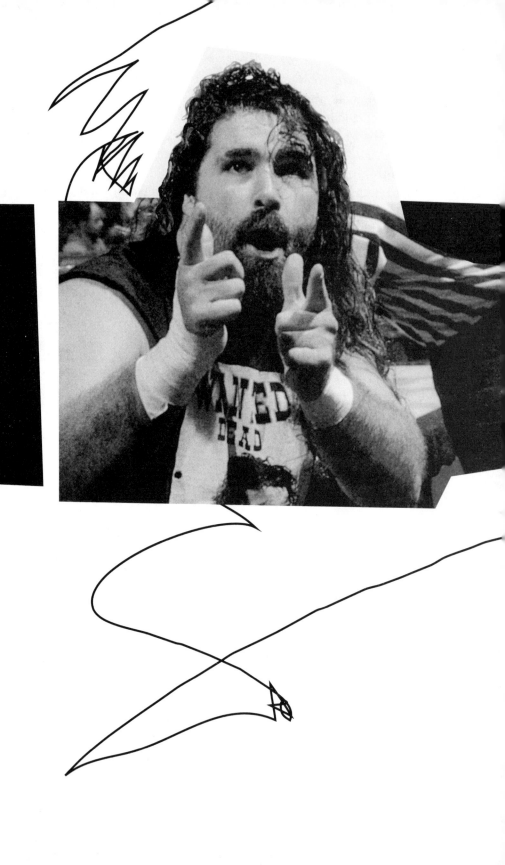

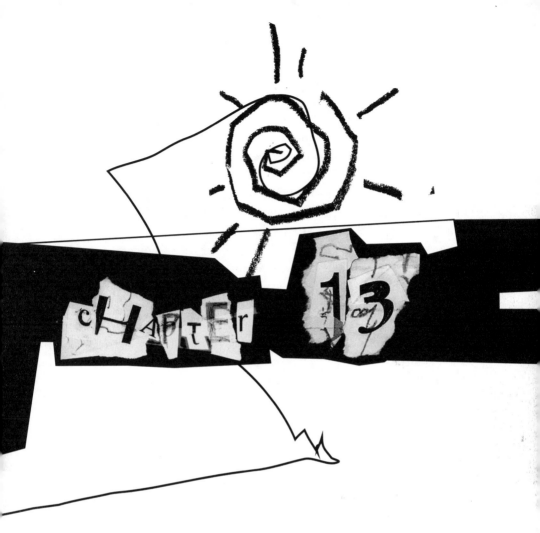

cHAPTEr 13

I had wrestled independently
for the past fourteen months. In that time I had improved tremendously, gained valuable confidence, learned to work the mike, and had a much better idea of who I was in the ring and what I was trying to accomplish. Unfortunately, my bank account had not expanded at the same rate that my wrestling had, and with Colette two months pregnant, I decided to more actively pursue more gainful employment.

At the time, one of the promotions I was working for was Joe Pedecino's Global Wrestling Federation, which was using my old stomping grounds of the Dallas Sportatorium as its base of operations. Supposedly Joe had a backer from Nigeria who had $10 million to invest in the promotion, but I'd been around too long and heard too many rumors and promises to believe anything I heard. So with nothing to lose I boarded a bus from New York to Baltimore to serve as the special guest on a wrestling trip to the *Great American Bash*. This had historically been one of WCW's premier events, but WCW was in a state of disarray. Ric Flair had just left the company and "We want Flair" chants echoed throughout the arena. Both the show in Baltimore and the promotion seemed to lack direction. After the show I made my way backstage and said hello to some of the boys. I introduced myself to Magnum T. A., who was the assistant booker for the company. At one time, Magnum was a main event wrestler, a definite future world champion, whose career had been cut short due to a tragic car accident. Magnum didn't exactly gush all over me—I guess he hadn't been privy to my feud with David Sammartino—but he did offer some encouragement.

Two weeks later, WCW came to the Meadowlands arena in New Jersey. Colette and I decided to go—after all, in this business, as in many others, if you're out of sight, you're out of mind. I almost didn't get into the back until Paul E. Dangerously, who would later play a much larger role in my life as the genius behind ECW, granted us access.

I said hello to some of the guys, including Barry Windham. If you remember the Barry Windham of 1987 to 1991, you would surely recall one of the best wrestlers in the game. Barry was not someone that I was especially close with, but he pulled me aside and told me that the company was desperate for talent, and that if I stuck around, there was a good chance that I could get hired.

Two days later, Magnum called with news that would change my life. I should probably point out that for the previous few weeks I had been in touch with Kevin Sullivan, who had gathered together another band of misfits, and thought that I would be a perfect fit.

Mag: "I've been talking with the Dream [Dusty Rhodes] and we think we've come up with a spot for you."

Me: "Really, is it with Kevin's guys?"

Mag: "No, we'd like to put you into a program right away with Sting."

Sting! Man, that was like hitting the jackpot. Sting was the number one man in WCW, a well-built, charismatic athlete with spiked bleached hair and a painted face. The Stinger was not the greatest interview in the world, but his athletic ability and his enthusiasm usually made up for it. Sadly, Sting's marquee value had dropped slightly over the past several months due to poor opponents and lackluster feuds. That's where I came into the picture.

I later learned that this run with Sting, as well as my stint in WCW, were planned to be short-lived. The office, knowing of Sting's slightly shriveling value, hoped to "feed" him a string of "monster" heels in rapid-fire succession. Jim Ross, who apparently had been trying to sell Dusty on me for quite a while, was able to volunteer me for this limited role. It was thought that a quick conquering of so many monsters in such a short time would boost Sting's image, enabling him to draw more money with a real wrestler. In retrospect, I guess I'm lucky I didn't know of this plan, because I flew to Sioux City, Iowa, without the pressure of that knowledge.

Believe me, I was relieved to see that the Steiners were not on the board against me—instead, my opponent for my return to WCW was the notorious Larry Santo, notorious for both the worst-looking tights and best pained facial expressions of all the "underneath" wrestlers. I was flattered that many of the WCW wrestlers gathered around the monitor to watch the return of Cactus Jack. Apparently, Rick Steiner was my biggest fan in the back, as he encouraged the other wrestlers to "watch this" and "wait till you see this." I didn't disappoint. I felt like this was a big moment and I took advantage of it.

I actually received a nice response from the crowd—the kind of response that said, "We missed you." It's funny, sometimes people perceived as big stars leave for a while and receive no response when they return. I guess I had carved out a reputation with my work ethic, reckless style, and tight, firm buttocks. (What the hell!)

This was a triumphant return for me as I dropped the big elbow on Santo on the concrete, performed the flying upside-down Cactus Jack crack smash (front somersault) off the ring apron, and offered the WCW debut of the Double Arm DDT—a move that I blatantly stole from Kenta Kobashi of All-Japan Wrestling. But hey, what the hell, they've stolen half a dozen moves from me. At one point, Jim Ross added to the drama with one of his classic calls. "My goodness, Larry Santo has a family—and Cactus Jack doesn't care." Over the years, Ross has added so much to so many matches that I'll often visualize moves with his announcing calls in mind.

Later that night, I was given a chance to do a few thirty-second interviews for the company's syndicated television shows. I cut a promo on Sting that ended with the line, "When you feel that lump in your throat, it won't be emotion, it will be your liver!" I also did a promo where I talked about having trouble sleeping and having to count all the ways I would hurt Sting in order to get some shut-eye. "I fell asleep at 789 and I hadn't even gotten to your legs yet!" I squealed. Apparently Diamond Dallas Page—at the time solely a manager and not yet the master of the "Diamond cutter," ran to Dusty and said, "You've really got to take a look at this guy." I think WCW opened their eyes to Cactus Jack in a pretty big hurry.

A few days later, I received another call from Magnum, requesting that I come to Philadelphia. Nikita Koloff had quit the company, and Sting had no opponent for the next few evenings. I drove with Colette to the show, where I had a most interesting conversation with Sting. At this point in time, my match with Larry Santo hadn't aired yet, and I had never been informed as to just exactly what my role was supposed to be. Hey, according to Magnum, I was coming in as a top guy.

"Hey," said Sting, "do you have any ideas?"

"Yeah, actually, I've got a lot of ideas," I said enthusiastically.

"Man, that's great, I'm so tired of working with guys who don't have any."

I proceeded to share my thoughts, some of which were pretty wild. Sting's eyes grew wide. "Hey, I thought you were just coming in here to put me over."

"I know," I replied, "but I don't see any reason why I can't get myself over at the same time."

Sting looked at me as if this were a completely foreign idea, and in many ways it was, because with the exception of Flair, it had been a long time since Sting had wrestled somebody who could accomplish both at the same time. Aware of the attention that we were attracting, Sting asked me to step into the bathroom. He looked somewhat worried, not because he thought I was going to jump him backstage or anything, but because I did have a reputation for being a little bit strange, and maybe he felt like this whole Cactus Jack idea was a mistake.

"Do you really expect Sting, a guy who's been pushed on top for five years, to go fifty-fifty with a guy who hasn't even been on TV?" the stunned Sting asked.

"Yes," I stated simply.

"Why?" he wanted to know.

"Because I feel that with one month of TV exposure and one month of interviews, I can get over, and therefore be in a better position to get you over." This was actually a very lofty goal, but I was so full of confidence that I wouldn't take no for an answer.

"Look," I said getting a little impatient, "let's just set up one thing. If it doesn't get a reaction that you like, we won't do anything else. If it does, we'll work from there."

So that's how we left it—me ready to take on the world and Sting wondering whom he'd pissed off to draw this assignment.

When we did our first series of moves, culminating with me taking a big bump over the guard rail, the crowd went crazy. Sting got a big smile on his face. The rest of the match went off without a hitch— as a matter of fact, it was probably one of Sting's better matches in a while. When we got backstage, Sting was excited—he'd actually found someone he could look forward to wrestling. He shook my hand, and I can honestly say that we never had another problem after that. He's someone I consider one of my favorite all-time opponents, and in the back of my mind, I'd still like to lock up with him one more time before I'm through.

Abdullah the Butcher, my opponent from a year earlier, was another of the wrestlers brought in to "feed" Sting. With the success of Cactus Jack, the "feeding" angle was stopped, and Dusty decided to team me up with Abdullah. Abby was one of the great monsters in the business. In real life, Abby was a sharp business man and an even sharper dresser who now owns and operates Abdullah the Butcher's House of Ribs in Atlanta. He chewed unlit cigars and spoke with a surprisingly high voice and was a man with such class that he once held a fart in for over 200 miles so as not to offend my wife, who was traveling with me. There was a small bit of irony attached to this team. As a freshman in college, I had taped a picture of Abdullah to my wall, and by the end of the year had everyone in Fitzgerald Hall believing that Abdullah the Butcher was my father. Strange, when you consider that Abby was a 400-pound black man, with grooves carved into his head so deep that he used to flip out people in casinos by inserting gambling chips into them.

At the end of August, Magnum asked to speak with me in Richmond, Virginia. He had a contract with him that he wanted me to sign. The contract was for a first year of $78,000 and an option for a second year at $156,000. Now, coming from my $10 days at the Polka High School, this seemed like a lot of money, but I had two things going for me. One, I still believed that Joe Pedecino had a

$10 million backer, and the contract offer of $100,000 he had given me was legitimate. And two, I had a great belief in myself.

"I don't want to seem like a big shot, but I've got an offer of $100,000 in Global that would have me home in my bed four nights a week," I said. (Of course, the $10 million man never did appear.)

"Cactus, that seventy-eight grand is just the dangling carrot. After a year, you'll get 156," Magnum countered.

I thought about it, and speaking from my heart, to a guy who knew what it was like to have his career taken away from him, said, "Magnum, you've seen me wrestle. With my style, there might not be another year for me. I need 156 now."

That logic seemed to hit home with Magnum, as he quietly said, "That might be possible—I'll speak with Jim Herd." Herd, a former Pizza Hut bigwig, was at that time the president of WCW.

In the afternoon of September 4, 1991, Jim Herd approached me in Albany, Georgia, the site of that evening's *Clash of the Champions*. Herd had a reputation as a hard-ass, so I didn't know quite what to expect when he opened his mouth. What followed was the shortest contract negotiation in history. "Cactus, Magnum told me what you wanted, and he said he thinks you're worth it and so do I. I'll have legal draw up the contract." That was it. With those few words I was now making six F'ing figures!

On the *Clash* in Albany, Sting had a match with Johnny B. Badd (Marc Mero), the future husband of Rena Mero (formerly known as Sable). Midway through the match, a large gift-wrapped refrigerator box with a bright red bow on it was wheeled halfway down the wooden ramp that led from the entrance area to the ring. I would, in my three years with WCW, go on to execute many painful moves on this wooden ramp which was used for all the big shows. I was nervous as hell inside that box and kept saying prayers for my son, who was at this point four months in utero. When the time was right, I burst from the box. I blew right past Badd and assaulted Sting. Sting fell to the outside, and while he lay prone on the blue mats, I ascended to the second turnbuckle. The announcers' table from which Jim Ross and Tony Schiavone were calling the match was directly in front of me, so I knew I had to get quite a bit of distance just to clear it. With as much spring as I could muster in my "this white man really can't jump" legs, I took flight, and in a clip that would be shown hundreds of times over the next few years, dropped the most perfect elbow of my career. It looked like it killed Sting, and I'm sure at the time it probably felt like it, but the important thing was it made for great television. Sting was helped to the back and there was a new sheriff in town. His name was Spaceman Frank Hickey. No, I'm sorry, it was Cactus Jack.

Later in the show, I was set to give my first live interview. As they were counting us down—ten, nine, eight, seven, six—Paul E. Dangerously, who was conducting the interview, turned to me and said, "Who would have thought—two homeboys from New York, live on national television." Paul E. handed me the mike, and in my big live debut I . . . sucked. Well, actually it wasn't that bad, but the angle that followed it was tremendous. While I was talking, another gift-wrapped refrigerator box (hey, I don't know where they kept getting them from) was rolled onto the ramp. I assumed it was "my business partner and close personal friend, Abdullah the Butcher. I think I'll give Abdullah a big Cactus Jack hug." (In addition to being a great kisser, I'm also quite a hugger.) "That's a good idea" said Paul E., "give Abdullah a big Cactus Jack hug."

Now when I hugged the box, it wasn't my big, black, butcher buddy who appeared, but a fired-up Sting, who apparently possessed remarkable healing powers because only twenty minutes earlier, his career had been called "over." After a few punches, the Stinger grabbed me and in a shocking move, hip tossed me off the five-foot-high ramp to the cold, hard concrete below. This was a brutal move and was especially shocking in a time period when the cold, hard concrete gimmick was mine, mine, all mine. Try taking a piece of raw liver out of your refrigerator and place it on your kitchen counter. Good. Now push it off the table and listen to it hit the kitchen floor. Good. Did you hear that sound? That's what my 287 pounds sounded like when it hit the cold, hard concrete. But did I stay down? As Steve Austin would say, "Oh, hell no." I got up and hit the Stinger with a garbage can, then emptied the contents on him, before brawling though the curtain. Arn Anderson, after seeing the melee, offered this opinion in his patented style: "I know one thing, if I threw someone off the ramp like that and he got up . . . I'd run."

When we got to the back Sting looked at me and said simply, "You're great." It was definitely a big night for me—I had a six-figure income, and the Stinger thought I was great.

For some reason, WCW kept me off the road for a month after this angle—hey, we wouldn't want to actually draw fans, would we? I couldn't understand it, but I had three grand a week coming in to comfort me.

In the meantime however, Abdullah and I were getting over like a million bucks on TV. Our interviews were becoming a much-anticipated and enjoyed part of the shows. Abby didn't talk, but his mannerisms and facial expressions were tremendous. Dusty loved "bang bang," and encouraged me to use it in every promo. It was his idea to throw a birthday party for Sting, which turned out to be one of my favorite segments of the year. Paul E. hosted the interview in which Abdullah and I emerged with a pink cake that read "Happy Birthday Sting." (And no, believe it or not, it didn't end up in anybody's face.) I began by singing to Sting in my deranged warble.

"Happy birthday to you. Bang bang, happy birthday to you, bang bang . . ." I looked at the crowd, they weren't laughing; some of them actually looked scared. With the song over, Abdullah started eating up the cake, until Paul E. cuts in, "Um that's really nice, but, um, it's not the guy's birthday."

"I know that," I shot back. "Don't you think I know that? But I wasn't at Sting's last birthday; I wish I had been at Sting's last birthday. But it's really important that we celebrate it now," I continued, my voice gathering volume and my eyes locked on Paul E. "Because Sting's last birthday . . . was Sting's *last* birthday. Bang bang! Bang bang!" Somehow we had come into Center Stage theater with a birthday cake and a children's song, and managed to leave it bigger, better, and badder heels.

Abdullah was always an adventure to team up with. Some guys like to plan lots of moves and then perform them, like a dance in the ring. Abdullah was the exact opposite. You didn't plan anything with Abdullah, because (1) he didn't like it that way, and (2) he wouldn't remember, anyway. So for the next several months, for the most part, we wrestled Sting, Steiner, Sting and Steiner, or a three-man team consisting of Sting, Steiner, and someone else. It was like a theater of the bizarre, and sometimes it worked out well, such as at the Omni in Atlanta, where a tag match in a cage had the fans rocking in the aisles. And sometimes it worked out badly, such as in Lakeland, Florida, in December 1991.

Abby and I vs. Sting and Steiner was the evening's main event. I locked up with Steiner and out of the corner of my eye could see Abby fumbling around in his pockets for a foreign object. Abby always came to the ring with an assortment of things to use—a fork being his perennial favorite. He kind of reminded me of the kid in *Old Yeller* emptying his pockets and having a frog jump out of them. Except Abby was about fifty years older than the kid. And 350 pounds heavier. And black. And with huge divots in his head. Anyway, I brought Steiner to our corner, and Abby was still fumbling with his pockets. We went back to the center of the ring. I tried bringing him to our corner a second time, and again, Abby wasn't ready. Suddenly, Steiner darted behind me, and with about as much care as an airport baggage handler throwing a piece of luggage off a plane, launched me high overhead with a belly-to-back suplex. I landed high on the top of my head, to the point where I ended the move lying on my stomach with my feet lying on the bottom rope.

"Why would you do that to the guy?" asked Sting later in the dressing room. "I mean the guy has beaten himself up trying to get me over, and you nearly killed him."

"I thought he was going to try to take something on [take advantage of] me," Steiner replied.

Now I'm not a liberty-taker inside the ring. I'm rough and much of what I do is quite painful to be on the receiving end of, but I have too much respect for my opponents to try to take something on them. And if I ever decide to start, Rick Steiner definitely won't be the guy I do it to. I mean, I'm not that deranged, nor do I really love pain, no matter what you've been told over the last fifteen years.

The next evening, Terry Taylor walked up to me in the dressing room. He probably was spouting one of his Terry Taylorisms, such as: "Two questions: who is your favorite wrestler, and why am I?" Terry was a funny and charming guy, to the point where even my mother-in-law had a tiny crush on him. That evening, however, Terry's humor and charms were falling on deaf ears—literally. A few minutes later, I could barely hear Grizzly Smith, a weathered agent who was also the father of wrestlers Sam Houston and Jake Roberts, speak to me, and I felt as if the conversation was taking place underwater. Grizz looked into my eyes, the pupils of which were about the size of pinpoints, and said more words that I had trouble hearing. "Son, I think you've got yourself a concussion."

We finished our swing in Florida, with the other wrestlers ordered not to hit me in the head. When we got back to Atlanta, I had my first (but definitely not my last) CAT scan, and I'll be damned if the old, wizened Grizzly Smith wasn't right—I had a concussion. I've only had eight documented concussions in my career, with "documented" being the key word, as I've had my bell rung so many times that I'd probably have to rank high on the all-time list of brain-swelling injuries.

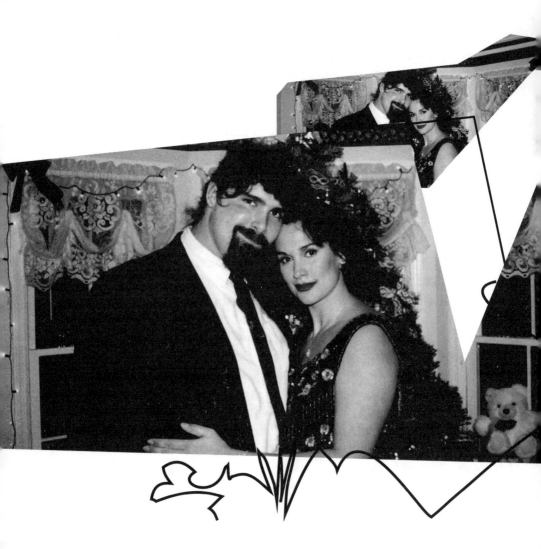

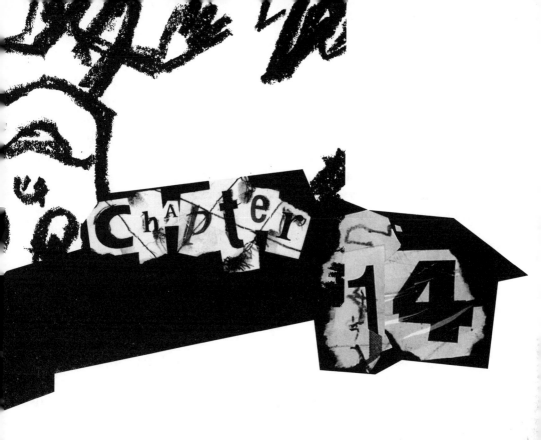

Chapter 14

In addition to all this wrestling success, things were really shaping up for us as a family. We finally had a little financial security, and were able to buy some nice things to welcome our impending newborn into the world. I even bought a new car—a '92 Ford Crown Victoria that I still have today. It's a piece of crap now, but hey, there's a lot of history inside that car. For the Christmas holidays, Colette and I drove back home from Atlanta, where we'd been renting an apartment. Colette ended up staying with my parents for the remainder of her pregnancy, while I hit the road to seek even greater fame and fortune.

In addition to my fame and fortune, something else was growing at the same time. Me. Some husbands put on "sympathy" weight during their wives' pregnancy. Being a sensitive guy, I couldn't bear to make Colette feel bad about herself as her former model waist gave way to a huge basketball underneath her shirt. In addition, I suffered the double whammy of picking up "Abdullah weight" on the road. "Let's get some ice cream, champ" was one of Abby's favorite sayings as we sped onward into 1992 in our rented Cadillac. This was at a time when WCW picked up the tab for our rentals. When that ended, so did the Caddies. Even today as a "World Wrestling Federation Superstar," I am much more likely to be speeding onward in a rented Lumina.

I was gaining a reputation at this time as a guy who could "work with anyone." In addition to being able to have a good match with pros like Bobby Eaton and Ricky Steamboat, I was able to pull out some decent ones from guys that didn't exactly set the world on fire. One of these guys was a big, muscular kid named Van Hammer. Hammer had two things working against him. One, he was given a push well before he was ready for it, and two, he was given the gimmick of a heavy metal guitar player, even though he couldn't play a lick. It reminded me of when I carried a bullwhip out to the ring with me in Memphis. If you don't crack it, people know you don't have a clue. So, if a guy walks to the ring with a guitar and never plays it, well, I think you get the picture.

Hammer was also a natural heat getter with the boys. He didn't mean to, he was actually a nice guy, but he had a tendency to bury himself with his ways. Statements like "I came here to save the company" didn't sit well with guys who'd busted their asses for years and didn't have their own $25,000 music video. The first time I saw Hammer, he came strutting down the ramp, in preparation for his debut on a *Clash of the Champions* (the Albany *Clash*). He was wearing no shirt and was all oiled up to showcase his chiseled physique, and was wearing a pair of tight black bicycle shorts that showcased his . . . well, never mind. Let's just say I could tell what religion he was before ever saying hello.

As a result, most guys didn't care to help him out or even have a decent match with him. I, on the other hand, saw him as a challenge, like a piece of clay that I could mold. Instead of looking at his faults, I chose to look at his strengths, which were: He was an exceptional natural athlete, and he was willing to do whatever I wanted. And I wanted to do a lot.

We had a match in Topeka, Kansas, that people talked about for years—a falls count anywhere inside or outside the building. The outcome of this match was somewhat in jeopardy when I had a short meeting with Dusty. I tried to stroke his ego by telling him that I felt that a falls count anywhere was my specialty match, the same way that the leather strap match had been his. I even added that I potentially thought I could have a hell of a match of this type with his son

Dustin. (Which we later did.) The Dream thought about it for a few seconds and said in his unique Dusty lisp (hey, why are all my bookers lispers?), "That's it, baby, you'll be known as the King of Falls Count Anywhere—you can take it all over the country." I must admit, I doubted his sincerity, but I'll be damned if we got to Topeka, and things hadn't been reconsidered.

Nowadays, these falls count anywhere matches are usually called hardcore matches, and it's commonplace for wrestlers to fight outside the building, and in Al Snow and Bob Holly's case, even into the Mississippi River. But in early 1992, our fight into the rodeo arena outside the Topeka Coliseum was considered unique.

We fought all over the arena, and I even debuted one of the downright dumbest moves of my career—the sunset flip off the second turnbuckle to the concrete floor. In this move, I launch myself off the second turnbuckle, and in mid-air flip upside down while hooking my opponent's waist on the way over. This theoretically leads to a pinning predicament, but with all of my new 300-plus pounds landing squarely on my lower back and butt, almost led to a hospital predicament. "Holy shit," screamed referee Nick Patrick, who as a second-generation wrestler had just about seen it all, "I've never seen anything like that."

We ended up fighting outside the building, and we spilled across the parking lot to the rodeo arena that actually had bulls brought in to add to the spectacle. Out of nowhere, a 400-pound black cowboy appeared and attempted to hit me with a scoop shovel. I instead maneuvered Hammer into the shovel's path, and the shovel made a nice solid bonk off the back of his neck and head. I punched the cowboy, knocking off his hat, and I'll be damned if that 400-pound black cowboy didn't turn out to be Abdullah. I covered Hammer and gained the pinfall right next to a pile of dried-up horse manure.

But the battle wasn't over yet. Abby and I continued the assault in the rodeo arena, where Missy Hyatt was on special hazard duty as an on-the-scene reporter. Earlier in the day, Dusty had pulled me and Abby aside and whispered, "I didn't say this, but I want the girl to end up in the water." And, wouldn't you know it, in the freakiest of freak accidents, Missy Hyatt ended up taking an eighteen-degree bath in a horse trough.

The next day, Kip Frye, who had earlier in the week replaced Jim Herd as president of WCW, awarded Hammer and me a $5,000 bonus to be split between us. This was a Kip Frye policy. He gave $5,000 to the most valuable performer on all the big shows. Out of respect, we also cut Abdullah and Nick Patrick in for a share of the profits.

Kip Frye was almost the exact opposite of Jim Herd. Whereas Herd was gruff, Frye was polite to a fault. Also whereas Herd tended to be tight with a dollar, someone in the Turner organization must have authorized a budget increase, because Frye started throwing around money. It was almost as if Kip was walking around looking for acceptance from the wrestlers, and he decided the best way to do it was by signing them to big contracts. Hell, the Freebirds were given $50,000 raises and then were taken off the road for six months.

Kip was also like a kid when it came to appearing on television. After his first appearance on the tube, he sprinted to the back and picked up the phone. "Did you see me, did you see me?" he inquired anxiously as I wondered just what qualifications were required to run a multimillion-dollar wrestling company.

On the way to the matches one day, Diamond Dallas Page was singing Frye's praises. "The good thing about Kip" said DDP, "is that he's willing to listen to the wrestlers."

Kevin Nash thought about it and countered, "The good thing about Kip is he's sexy in a shy kind of way." Nash was the King of ridiculous observations; at seven feet tall, he may well be the country's tallest standup comic—which in reality is how he finally became a star some years later. He may well have been the worst wrestler in the business at one point (the Nash vs. Kazmaier battles still make me shudder) but he was always willing to learn, and because he was so well liked, the guys were always willing to help out. On one road trip, I talked to Kevin for two straight hours about using his size to be a dominant force, instead of the Vinnie Vegas comedy lounge wrestler that he was being portrayed as. A short time later, he left WCW for the World Wrestling Federation, and I saw him specifically doing some of the things I had talked about. I was very proud.

DDP was a classic. A former nightclub manager and walking cartoon character, he had gotten his start as a manager for Verne Gagne's American Wrestling Association. His main attribute at that time was that he was willing to pay his own airfare to television tapings (along with paying for his two diamond girls) and work for free. He had eventually caught on in his home state of Florida as an announcer, where he hooked up with Dusty Rhodes, and the Dream brought him on board when he took over the book for WCW.

Page was eventually replaced as an announcer—even as one of his best friends, I've got to admit that his bag of play-by-play clichés was about as well received as a set of fingernails on a chalkboard. As a manager, he had been, at best, average. He had been relieved of his duties as manager of the Freebirds, probably because his style was almost a duplicate of Michael Hayes, who was already one of the Birds. So DDP at the tender age of thirty-five decided to step into the ring and become a wrestler, where, against all odds, he became a top name in the business.

It certainly wasn't easy—most people didn't want to see him succeed. Amid all the negativity, I remember one person predicting big things from him. I was riding in the rental car shuttle bus with Abby, when I saw DDP strutting across the parking lot, with one of his tacky outfits and some outrageous pair of shades. "He's going to make it, champ," I heard the Butcher say.

"Dallas?" I asked, with shock in my voice, wondering if years of headshots and cage matches had finally taken their toll on my partner. "Why?"

"He lives his gimmick, champ" was Abby's reply. "He lives his gimmick."

Indeed he did. He used the same tired clichés in real life that he did on TV. "How are you doing?" a lady would ask as we waited for change at her tollbooth.

"Lady," DDP would start, "if I was doing any better, I'd have to be twins just to handle it." I tended to roll my eyes a lot when I traveled with Dallas.

His first match, in Baltimore, sometime in the spring of 1992, was a classic, or at least the circumstances surrounding it were. I watched the whole thing, and to be honest, it wasn't at all bad for a beginner. A few minutes after the match, I saw Dallas, and he was visibly upset. "Hey," I said, putting my arm around him, "it wasn't that bad." I then proceeded to compliment some of his work and helpfully offer hints on how he might improve it.

"Thanks, Jackie," he said (he always called me Jackie). "I appreciate it." I felt like I had helped a little, but even when I left, his eyes were still red from crying.

Later, Steve Austin asked me if I'd heard about Dallas and Chip, who had been one of his opponents that night. As it turned out, Dallas wasn't upset about the match at all—he was upset about the fistfight that had occurred in the dressing room afterward. Apparently Firebreaker Chip (part of the little-missed team of the Patriots) had taken exception to some of the match, and being pumped up, had gotten in DDP's face about it. Now, this may have been Page's first match, but he'd been part of the business for five years, and he wasn't about to back down. Somewhere in the argument, Chip threw a punch, and the fight broke out. The scuffle ended when DDP hooked Chip in a front facelock, a simple but effective submission hold that in real life is a finisher in almost any fight. Dallas had to be pulled off Chip, and then walked outside the dressing room, which is where I consoled him. I don't know, maybe you can't blame Chip (the real-life Curtis Thompson)—after all, the Patriots idea was one of the lowest in a long list of WCW lame ideas. (Does anyone else remember the Ding Dongs?) Maybe if I'd been given the gimmick of a "firebreaker," who walked around giving fire tips, I may have had a little "Chip" on my shoulder, too.

I've got a couple of favorite DDP stories. The first one centered around Dallas's return to his old stamping grounds of Fort Myers, Florida. I was traveling with Page and Scotty Flamingo (later known as Raven) on the loop through Florida, and was forced to endure story after story about how "over" Page was in Fort Myers. Behind his back, we'd dismiss DDP's claims. "Nobody can be as popular as Page claims he is," we'd scoff. When we got to Fort Myers, we began to doubt our thoughts—every paper had a story about DDP. Man, Page was pumped, too. He was going to return to Fort Myers a hero, and, brother, he was going to tear the house down! Well, it didn't work out quite that way.

Dallas's opponent that night was the returning Curtis Hughes. Hughes at 300 pounds was a hell of a performer. On returning, he looked to be about 380 and was now known as Big Cat Curtis Hughes. Now, if I was wrestling a guy in his hometown, I would make extra sure to have my flying shoes on, and would go out of my way to make the guy the look good in front of his friends and family. Unfortunately, too many guys had gotten in Hughes's ear and convinced him that he was "too big to bump," especially for a beginning guy like Page.

What followed was ten of the worst minutes of wrestling I'd ever seen, with Page throwing everything but the kitchen sink at Hughes, and the Big Cat standing still like the rock of Gibraltar. To make matters worse, Kevin Nash was late hitting the ring and failed to break up a pin attempt that would have led to a disqualification. Instead, Page lay on his back, waiting in vain for a save that didn't arrive, while the referee counted one, two . . . three. The legendary Diamond Dallas Page had done the J-O-B in his own hometown.

He was crushed. Almost to the point of tears. He was so upset that he didn't even want to go out to the nightclub he used to run even though he'd set up a deal where the boys could eat and drink all night for free. Eventually we convinced him, and we headed out for a night on the town at Norma Jean's, where, to tell you the truth, Dallas wasn't as popular as he'd claimed. In truth, he was even more popular—he was the MAN! Girls everywhere wanted to talk to him—guys gathered close just to be around him. Dallas even started to smile, and he was returning to his normal state of overbearing stories and worn-out clichés when, out of the corner of his eye, he saw him. As if burying DDP's hopes and dreams in his own hometown wasn't enough, Big Cat Curtis Hughes had showed up to eat Dallas's free food and to drink his free beer.

Hughes later resurfaced a few times in the World Wrestling Federation. On his second run, a short-lived stint in early 1997, he was brought in as Hunter Hearst Helmsley's "butler." After one show, Hughes had to be hospitalized. While he was laid up, Hughes's duties were taken over by Hunter's first choice, a muscular female wrestler named Chyna.

My other favorite DDP story occurred somewhere in the Carolinas in the middle of 1993. I was traveling with DDP and Stunning (not quite Stone Cold yet) Steve Austin, and we were in the second day of a week-long loop. Now, you've got to understand, despite all the cartoonish characteristics, Dallas was a very intense individual, so intense in fact that he used to ask us to videotape his match every night. He'd then study those damn things for hours, looking to improve in any way he could. Often, Steve and I would goof on Page by supplying color commentary during the matches. Dallas jokes now that he could get a fortune for these homemade videos with Stone Cold and Mankind making the calls.

Because of his intensity, Dallas was easy to rile up on a road trip. On the first day of this particular trip, Steve and I made a little bet. "How quick do you think we can crack Page?" I asked, looking forward to this somewhat cruel pleasure.

"Three days," replied Austin, looking forward to the challenge. Three was good, but I had just a little bit more faith. "We can crack him in two days," I stated solemnly, giving Austin my best Jack Lord "Book him, Danno" look. The race was on.

The first day started with a quality shot. Austin fired it. "My wife wanted me to pick up a couple of antiques on this trip," Steve innocently said.

"What did you tell her?" Page responded.

"I told her I'd already picked up DDP at the airport," Austin said, laughing. Man, an age joke, an especially sensitive subject for the man who claimed he'd never had a bad day in his life. The verbal blow was a good one, but the aging Page shrugged it off.

By day two, however, he wasn't shrugging anything off—he was downright cranky. We checked into a hotel after the evening's show, and a still sweaty Dallas was looking forward to a hot shower. He stormed out of the bathroom angered that no towels had been left for us. He called immediately and demanded that housekeeping bring some on the double. The towels arrived while DDP was down the hall, getting ice for his many nagging injuries—the guy strapped so many ice packs to his body that I often suggested he just buy a huge cooler and just lie in it. Steve and I looked at each other—Page was on the verge of cracking—we couldn't let up now. Thinking quickly, Austin hid all the towels except two under a bed. When Page inquired about the status of the towels, I informed him that the towels had indeed come, and that housekeeping had left them in the bathroom. No sooner had Page walked into the john than he came storming out. "This is what they brought us," he screamed, holding aloft one hand towel and a washcloth for Steve and me to see. "Goddammit, I'm going to get them myself."

The moment Page walked out, Steve reached under the bed and pulled out about eight plush bath towels that he placed directly on the TV so that it would be the first thing Page saw upon his reentry to the room. "What a maroon," I said in my best Bugs Bunny impression. "He's just about done."

Dallas finally did take his shower, and he emerged from the bathroom in typical fashion: buck naked except for an ice pack on his shoulder and Saran wrap around his knees (that he claimed kept the joints loose). He then began his presleep ritual that included thumbtacking the blinds to the wall, so as not to allow even the faintest ray of sunshine into the room in the morning. I found the whole nude thing a little uncomfortable, to tell you the truth. Usually the only guys who walked around naked were the midgets, who seemed proud of what some people call "God's practical joke," and guys like Scorpio, who was kind of like a genitalactic freak of nature. DDP was more or less a normal white guy. Hey, I'm no pecker checker, but with Page's protruding peter bouncing around, it was hard not to notice. The guy's penis was everywhere.

Poor Page turned the lights off and settled into his bed for a long comfortable nap. Little did he know that his evening wasn't quite over. Earlier, a fan had given us a whole batch of chocolate chip cookies that she had baked. While Dallas showered, Steve and I had dumped approximately thirty-six soft chewy beauties between the sheets of DDP's bed, and now as he lay there I could tell that those delicious tollhouses were starting to take effect. It started with a little wriggle, and them grew to the point where he knew something was wrong.

"What, what, what's this," Dallas said, to no one in particular. Steve and I remained silent. Suddenly, it hit him.

"There's fucking cookies in my bed," he yelled. "Someone put fucking cookies in my bed."

Silence. Dallas was now screaming at the top of his lungs. "I want to know who put fucking cookies in my bed, right now!"

I soon gave myself away. I was laughing so hard under my covers that I couldn't help myself. By holding in this laugh, my stomach was rising up and down rapidly, and Dallas detected the quick in-and-out breathing from my nostrils.

"You," he yelled and jumped from his bed, turning on the light and throwing back the covers to reveal a plethora of crumbs, chunks, and chips that a helpful fan had hoped would be eaten by three of her favorite sports-entertainers. Instead, in an ironic twist, her baking bid had backfired! Instead of being eaten, these innocent cookies had eaten up the livid Page, who was now hellbent on vengeance. Dallas lunged for me and threw back my sheets—unlike the naked Page, I was attired in Fruit of the Looms. He then gathered as many of the broken pieces as he could carry and threw them on top of me. It wasn't enough; he wanted to make sure the cookies would torture me and ruin my sleep, the way that I had ruined his. He sat on me and began jumping, trying to grind the offending cookies into my body, as I listened to the strange symphony of bouncing bed springs and crackling Saran wrap.

"There," he yelled, "how do you like it, how do you like fucking cookies in your bed!" He waited for my reply.

"Well," I started, "it's not the cookies that I mind, it's the fact that you're rubbing your naked ass all over me."

DDP got up slowly. He was a defeated man. He went back to his bed and swept away the remaining cookie parts. He turned off the light and lay back down. After about a minute, he spoke. Quietly. Sadly. "Guys," he began, "I think I'm going to get my own room tomorrow."

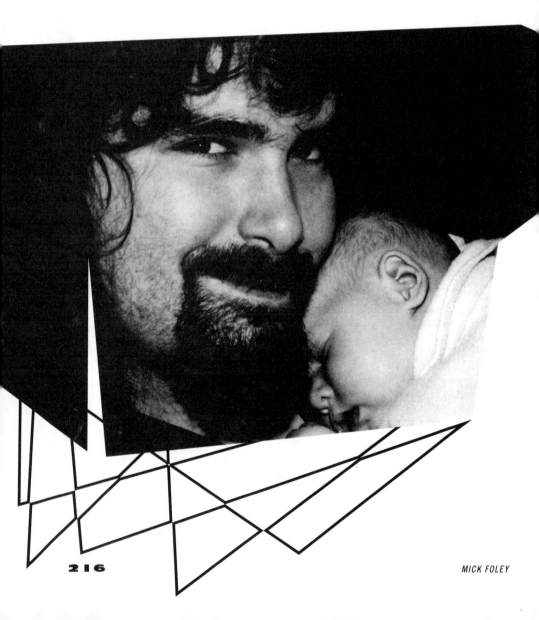

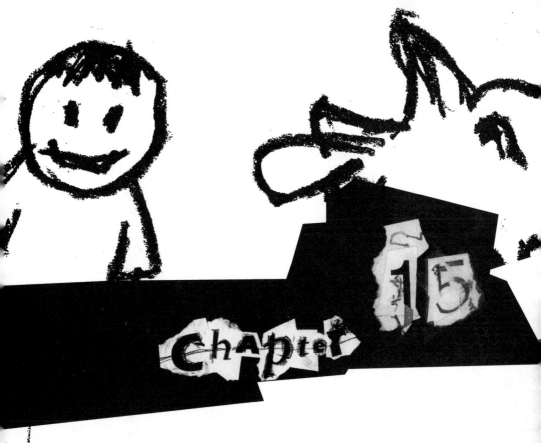

Chapter 15

On February 20, 1992, I became a father. Dewey Francis Foley was born in Massapequa, New York, and after a month of readjusting from his trip through the womb, we packed up our car and two dogs and headed for Atlanta and the house on Lake Lanier that I had just rented. The house turned out to be a real hassle, because as charming as it was to live on the lake, the house was more accurately a cottage. It was musty, without enough room, and you actually had to walk outside to get from our bedroom to the rest of the house. We did have plenty of fun, however, as we would dive off our dock and swim with the dogs, while little Dewey looked on from his infant seat. We had two Shetland sheepdogs, or Shelties: one that Colette had gotten in 1981 named Confusion and another that we'd gotten a year ago as a "practice" baby named Fuzzy. From Confusion to Fuzzy in ten years—my wife had certainly changed. Confusion's not with us anymore, but we've got a big, goofy black lab named Delilah and two guinea pigs named Allen and Ruby to keep us busy.

At about two months of age, Dewey came down with an illness that doctors couldn't detect. Several of them told us there was nothing wrong, but still a persistent cough continued to worry us. One night, when we were in the car returning from a trip, Dewey was coughing so bad that I really thought we were going to lose him. He was whooping and gasping, and we were completely unable to help him. I began speeding for the nearest hospital. It was 2 A.M. and the highway was empty, so I gathered some speed—up to about seventy-five in a sixty-five mph zone. I saw the red lights of a North Carolina State trooper, and I slowed down to explain the dire situation. Can you believe it?—the SON OF A BITCH actually wrote us a ticket. I was so damn mad that I blatantly cursed out an officer of the law. Now I have respect for the law, hell I even carried a photo of *Hawaii Five-O's* Steve McGarrett in my wallet with me for years, but this guy was a disgrace and a prick. I didn't pay the ticket out of principle, and ended up having my license suspended over it. Sometimes, it just doesn't pay to make a stand. Dewey would later be all right, but not before giving the cough to me.

The coughing started affecting my matches. I could wrestle for about a minute before an attack would set in. The coughing would lead to dry heaving and I would have to bail out of the ring to try to regain my composure. One night in Perry, Georgia, the situation got ugly.

I was wrestling Ron Simmons, a true football legend, and one of the great storytellers in the business. Ron, who had grown up in near-by Warner Robins, Georgia, was an intense performer, and he was particularly looking forward to his hometown crowd. A few minutes into the match, Simmons shot me into the ropes and caught me with a move called the spinebuster. This is legitimately a pretty tough move to take, because the impact is so sudden and violent on the back, but it was even rougher when the powerful former Heisman Trophy candidate did it. In spite of the impact, it was a move that I thought I took well. Some guys instinctively put down their hands or elbows to try to block the bump, and others hold on for dear life, and make it look like crap, but I always took it quick and clean. *Bam!* It was an impressive sight. Two months earlier, I had even taken the move from Ron in a Pay-Per-View match on the wooden ramp, prompting another great Jim Ross call. "That is a wooden ramp, folks—please don't sit at home saying, 'Well, he knows how to fall.' "

Something went wrong on that night in Perry. I took the bump and couldn't breathe. I got up, and blood started filling my mouth, spilling up from my insides. Simmons was in the corner, in a three-point stance ready to hit me with football-style tackles aimed at my knees. I tried to tell him I was hurt, but when I opened my mouth, the only thing that came out was blood. Ron charged at me for the tackle. Ordinarily I would cut a flip upon impact, a move that did two things. One, it looked good, and two, lessened the risk of knee injury. Instead, I went down like a wounded deer. Simmons looked confused, but he went to the corner and got down in his stance. Again I tried to speak and again blood oozed out instead. Simmons hit me again, and again I fell like a sack of shit. Mercifully, he pinned me.

I walked back to the dressing room, worried that my career was over. Every four or five steps I stopped to empty my mouth of the red stuff. Over the years, I've bled so damn much that I can't help making a few observations about this liquid that courses through our veins. I've seen it spill out of me like water, and I've seen it so thick that my face looked like a coagulated mask of plasmic Jell-O. I've seen it look like black ink running down my arm, and I had seen my bathtub almost black when I rinsed my blood-soaked clothing in it. My wife used to joke about the "Norman Bates" shower I would take after a match where the "juice" had been flowing. This night in Perry, however, was the brightest red blood I had ever seen. I think internal blood is always brighter for some reason. When I think back to the gob of internal blood that I spat on the floor of the Dallas Sportatorium in '89, it seems that it also was noticeably brighter than its head wound cousins. It was almost fluorescent.

Grizzly Smith was there to size up the situation. "Cactus," he said softly, "I believe we'd better get you to a hospital." Thus began a series of tests and probes and barium swallows that yielded no further insight into what the hell was wrong with me. A couple of nights later, I was wrestling Barry Windham, and after about a minute the coughing and dry heaves began. We finished the match, but upon returning to the dressing room, I was told that Windham said, "That guy shouldn't be in the ring."

This condition did lead to a somewhat humorous situation in Baltimore, however. I was teaming up with Paul E. and Bobby Eaton against the Steiners in a four-and-a-half-man tag bout. I guess Paul was considered half a man. We went about a minute, and Scott threw me around in his usual sensitive style. I started to cough. Then I started to dry-heave. Bobby Eaton may have, other than Gerald Brisco (one of Vince McMahon's famed stooges, along with Pat Patterson), the weakest stomach I've ever seen. Bobby took one look at me and started to heave too. It was a pretty pathetic sight, as these two despicable heels stood in center ring taking turns attempting to throw up.

It was at about this time that Kip Frye stepped down as president of WCW. His replacement was the legendary Bill Watts.

I've written a little bit about Bill Watts before. To do him justice requires a lot more writing. The Cowboy was either loved or hated depending on whom you talked to. Jim Ross loved the guy. So did Scandor Akbar, my old Devastation Incorporated boss. Grizzly Smith rubbed his hands in anticipation upon hearing the news. "The Cowboy" he said, "is going to turn this place around." Watts was revered by many for the success and excitement of his old Mid-South wrestling group. At the time he sold it to Jim Crockett, whose NWA (National Wrestling Alliance) would in turn be sold to Ted Turner to become WCW, Watts's television show (renamed UWF) was the best in the country. His was the forerunner of episodic, cliffhanging wrestling, and his music videos and editing were state-of-the-art. The World Wrestling Federation later went on to perfect these same qualities, making Monday's *Raw Is War* the hottest show on cable TV. Unlike the Federation, though, Watts didn't portray his show as sports-entertainment, or his performers as entertainers. He ran a wrestling show, dammit, and his guys were wrestlers. If you respected the business, like I did, it was easy to see why people loved him.

It was just as easy to see why people hated him. They thought he was a bully and a tyrant, and a dinosaur, and a cheapskate. Let me put the emphasis for now on cheapskate. Almost immediately, Watts began cutting costs. On his first day in, he did away with the catered meals at television tapings. Forget that we were often at the building for ten hours on TV days. Bring your own food or starve! Away went the coffee at all house shows. Take that, all you caffeine addicts! But more important, down went the contracts. Guys who were negotiating with Kip Frye for large raises were screwed. Terry Taylor went from looking at a hundred grand raise to looking for a job. Arn Anderson had his contract cut in half, and several other guys were put on nightly deals. Watts must have loved me, though. Thankfully, he re-signed me at exactly the same money I had made the year before.

Watts even made a special call to my house to see how I was feeling during my coughing illness. The Cowboy concluded his call to me with these thoughtful words—"Goddammit, Jack, take care of yourself. You're a goddamn crazy son of a bitch, and you have no regard for your body, and I gotta tell you, I get off on that." I'm damn near tears now as I write this, thinking about the compassion in his voice.

Once on a *Clash of the Champions*, Scorpio caught me with a kick and I went down. Apparently, Bill didn't think it had looked good, and he let me have it when I got in the dressing room. "Sorry, Bill," I said, "I thought he caught me pretty good."

"Dammit, Jack," Watts shot back as I waited for the verbal assault. It never came. Instead, he put his hand on my shoulder and said, "Dammit, Jack, that's okay, I know you're trying your best." It was almost like I was the teacher's pet.

Now, wait, don't think I'm going to go easy on the Cowboy, just because he wasn't too bad to me. Because I'm not. Bill Watts had some of the most dated, useless ideas and senseless rules that I'd ever heard. In a meeting one day at Center Stage, he let us have it. Within one hour, Bill completely changed not only our professional lives, but our personal lives as well. Let's call them Bill's commandments.

```
Thou shalt not jump off the top rope.
Thou shalt not play cards in the dressing room.
Thou shalt not land on protective mats outside the ring.
Thou shalt not bring your children into the locker room.
Thou shalt not bring wives to the television tapings.
Thou shalt not use sleeperholds.
Heels shalt not travel with babyfaces.
Thou shalt not talk to each other outside of the arena.
Thou shalt not stay in the same hotel together.
Thou shalt not train in the same gym together.
And the biggest commandment of them all . . .
Thou shalt not leave the building until
          the final bell of the final match.
```

The last was the one that angered the boys the most. Nikita Koloff questioned this commandment at a meeting a short time later. Bill addressed the boys and then asked if there were any questions. Koloff raised his hand and when called on, made a plea for sanity.

"Yeah, Bill, I know that it's important for the guys to stay until the end, but sometimes, when we've been away from our families for a few weeks, we might have a chance to catch a night flight home. Do you think in those situations, we might be able to get out a little earlier?"

Bill thought about it for about a second and a half, and then with all the warmth and sensitivity of an IRS auditor, shot forth, "Yeah, it's a tough business on families. Any more questions? Okay, let's go."

This whole staying till the end thing resulted in one really humorous situation. We were wrestling in a minor league baseball stadium in Charlotte, North Carolina, on the last day of a ten-day tour. A lot of the boys still lived in Charlotte, dating back to the days that Jim Crockett ran the NWA out of Charlotte. Most of the boys now lived in Atlanta, which was only a four-hour drive. Either way, everyone was going to get home. But not until the final bell of the final match. I wrestled Ricky Steamboat in the third match of the night, but had to wait until the end. Steamboat lived in Charlotte, and he couldn't go home. And remember, in honor of the fourth commandment, his son wasn't allowed in the dressing room.

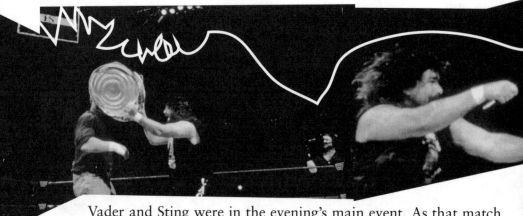

Vader and Sting were in the evening's main event. As that match started, all the wrestlers got into the cars and lined up single file, pointing toward the exit. As the match was winding down, we all started our engines. At the finish, the boys all made their move, and before the referee even finished the three-count, we turned the Charlotte baseball stadium into the Charlotte motor speedway.

I don't know why Bill loved to keep the guys on the road, worn out and miserable. I think he found it romantic.

About this time, my health started to improve. It turned out that both Dewey and I were diagnosed with whooping cough. Pertussis, its technical name, was something that I thought was extinct, but it turned out that we both caught this very rare condition. Dewey improved before I did, and I slowly came around, finally feeling better right before one of the biggest matches of my life—a "falls count anywhere" against Sting at the June 1992 *Beach Blast*. The match took place at the Mobile Civic Center—not what most would call a tropical paradise, and in truth, we were several miles from water. I had trained hard for this match and in doing so, I had lost most of my "Abdullah" weight. (Sadly, Abby had quit the company shortly after Watts arrived.) Also, I had immersed myself in mental visualization for this match—I had seen it in my head a thousand times.

The match turned out even better than I'd hoped. The Stinger was up for it, as it had been a while since we'd wrestled against each other. The timing was on, the pacing was great, and some of the transitions were breathtaking. Even Ross and the new color man Jesse "The Body" Ventura were on top of their game. I lost the match, but didn't

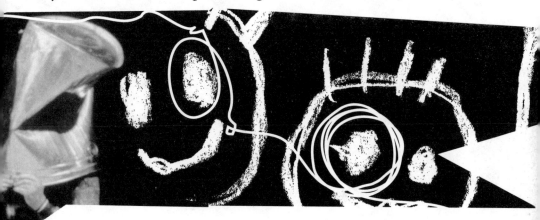

give a damn. As George Costanza might have said, "Baby, I'm back!" Even Watts was happy. "Gentlemen," he told us, "it just doesn't get any better than that."

For years I considered that to be the greatest match of my career. Sting was genuinely flattered to hear me say that, and he'd occasionally ask me after other big matches, "Was mine still your favorite?" I think he was actually saddened when he heard that another one replaced it. It was almost as if he were the queen in Snow White and the magic mirror broke the bad news.

I couldn't stop thinking about that match all the way on the 400-mile drive home. I had the top down on my '84 Chrysler and life was good; my health was good, I'd just torn the roof off the Mobile Civic Center, I had a beautiful wife and son, and I was still making six F'ing figures a year. A month later, we bought our first house—a beautiful little Victorian with a wraparound porch in Acworth, Georgia.

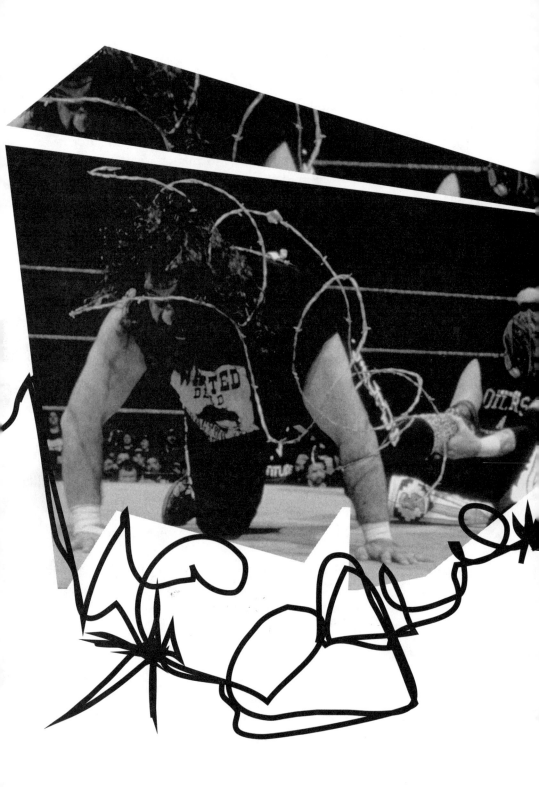

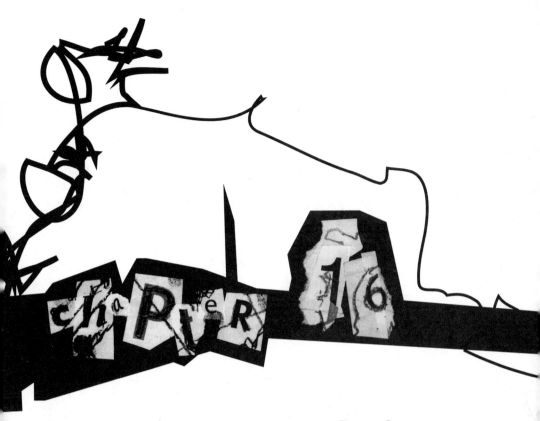

Despite all his faults, Bill did have
a gift for exciting television. There was one taping in particular that
showed me Watts's gift for creating great human drama. Now, Dusty
was still the booker, but Watts was definitely in charge, and one of
Bill's trademarks was creating a black babyface and building the company around him. When the Cowboy saw Ron Simmons, I think he
heard cash registers ring. Ron had all the qualities that Watts loved;
he was big, he was black, he could talk, he had a legitimate sports
background, and he was a legitimate tough guy.

Bill started the ball rolling by doing a great angle with Sting. I honestly can't remember all the details, but it culminated in the return of
Jake "the Snake" Roberts as he appeared from the crowd, and left the
Stinger lying. This left Sting unable to wrestle Vader in the evening's
main event. A lottery was held in the ring instead, with the winner to
face Vader. Simmons won, and later defeated that ear-tearing bastard
to become the new WCW heavyweight champion. People were actually crying in the arena—they were so damn happy. I really thought
the Cowboy had helped the company turn the corner.

I'm often asked about my most painful injury. The answer usually surprises people. They ask about the ear in Germany, the barbed wire in Japan, and the fall off the cage at the 1998 *King of the Ring*. All worthy contenders, but the most painful injury I ever had was a torn abdominal muscle that I suffered against Ron Simmons at the September 1992 *Clash of the Champions* in Atlanta.

I couldn't honestly claim to be the number one heel in the company anymore. Actually, I hadn't been in a long time. Rick Rude had come in about ten months earlier, and he had become a hotter heel than I ever had been. Still, I was a valuable guy to have around, and when Simmons became champion, I drew the assignment of being his first challenger. I was flattered to draw the assignment, but I was puzzled by the promotion of the match. Watts had this idea that it was important to turn the Atlanta Omni into the "Madison Square Garden of the South," and as such, spent an inordinate amount of time promoting that one building. On the Saturday before the *Clash*, Ron Simmons had a live interview, but was instructed by Watts to concentrate on his upcoming Omni match with Rick Rude, which would be seen by a few thousand, instead of his *Clash* match with me, which would be seen by millions. I always felt that this strategy made WCW look like a bush league regional promotion instead of a national powerhouse.

The *Clash* special was actually celebrating the twentieth anniversary of wrestling on TBS. Ted Turner had always stayed loyal to his wrestling shows, because his *Georgia Championship Wrestling* was one of the shows that kept his "Superstation" afloat in the 1970s. Several celebrities were in attendance, and video tributes were paid throughout the night to many of the stars who had wrestled on the station over the years.

Inside Center Stage, I joked that there might very well be a new champion crowned. Arn Anderson overheard me, and put me in my place with a classic Arnism. "Jack, I don't care if that son of a bitch has a heart attack and dies," Arn began. "You will roll him on top of you."

The match had one thing working against it. Watts had brought in my old buddy Ole Anderson to be, of all things, a troubleshooting referee. You would have thought that after all the years he had spent in the business, Ole would have absorbed through osmosis some understanding of what a referee does. He didn't seem to have a clue. He didn't know that a wrestler who rolls back into the ring and out again breaks up the ten-count, his mannerisms were stiff, and he counted pinfalls as if he were trying not to break a fingernail.

Yeah, Ole was hurting our match all right, but we tried to make up for it. Ron was throwing forearms as if he were trying to make his wrist go completely through my jaw bone. I later told Ron that I could take as stiff a forearm as he wanted to give, but that he would have to keep them up over my ears, or else I wouldn't be able to chew for a week. You've got to understand that a world title around your waist puts a great deal of pressure on you. Pressure to perform, pressure to draw, and in this case, pressure to garner television ratings. The pressure took a naturally intense guy like Simmons and made him almost impossible to control. It was like holding a tiger by the tail. I finally stopped big Ron and prepared to dive off the ring apron with the big elbow onto his prone body. Because there were no protective mats, he was on the cold, hard concrete floor. I landed on the concrete, and pain shot through my body, the likes of which I'd never felt before. I swear, I thought I'd broken my pelvis. The pain was so bad, I thought I was going to pass out.

I couldn't understand it—it hadn't even been a real big leap. Maybe six feet. But I'd dropped so many, for so long, that maybe it was just a matter of time before something gave out. Unfortunately, I still had a live nationally televised match to continue. It would have been nice if Ron had beaten me with a simple roll up or small package (painless finishing moves), but that wasn't quite his style. Instead he shot me in the ropes and BOOM! Spinebuster. Not enough. Another Irish whip—another BOOM! Powerslam. One, two, three, thank God it's over.

It wasn't over, however. When I got to the back, Watts asked me to go out and contribute commentary to the next match between the team Barry Windham and Dustin Rhodes, and my new stablemates, the Barbarian and Butch Reed. The videotape showed my face as almost completely white from the pain I was in, even though, to my surprise, I did a good job keeping up with Ross and Ventura on the commentary. At the end of Barb and Reed's victory, the camera showed Jake Roberts nodding his head in approval—as if he were the mastermind of the whole plan. That was the first and last time that our foursome was ever together. Butch Reed was fired a week later for missing a flight, and Jake left the next month.

After the *Clash*, I was taken directly to the hospital, where I was X-rayed and examined and even, for some strange reason, given a rectal probe. When I received the diagnosis, I felt like the world's biggest wimp. No, said the doctor, it wasn't a broken pelvis or any break at all. I had torn a muscle in my lower abdomen. What? How the hell can something like that hurt so bad? I felt humiliated, because I just didn't understand how devastating an injury like that could be. Hell, it was the same injury that forced Bill Goldberg out of football. Still, I got home at two and woke up at seven, confident that I would wrestle that evening. I was wrong. I could barely walk and needed a wheelchair to get around the airport. In the afternoon, I bumped my toe on a crack in the sidewalk and almost cried. I got to the matches, and after taking one look at me, Grizzly Smith told me that I wouldn't be wrestling. I put up a very small protest, but I knew he was right. My streak was over. After eight and a half years in the business, I had missed a match because of injury. The next morning, I got an idea of how seriously I was hurt when I looked down and saw that my entire penis had turned black and blue. Unfortunately, even though my penis was now black, it remained the same size.

While I was hurt, Cowboy Bill made me the Barbarian's manager. I've got to hand it to Bill—he kept me in the mix. The Barbarian was getting a shot at Simmons on the next Pay-Per-View, *Halloween Havoc 1992* from Philadelphia. The main event of that show would be the ill-fated "Spin the Wheel, Make the Deal" match between Jake and Sting. To pump the Pay-Per-View, we shot a series of training clips showing the Barbarian to be impervious to pain—kind of like he is in real life. Jake and Sting shot a tremendous mini-movie that turned the show into a huge success . . . financially (it was WCW's highest-grossing Pay-Per-View for a long time). Artistically, it was a bust, with Jake and Sting being especially hard on the eyes. A couple of days later, Jake was gone.

Jake was and still is one of the unique characters in the business. A strange mixture of a hell of a guy and Satan, Jake is a guy I both genuinely like and am troubled by. As a wrestler, he was one of he best, or at least until the Honky Tonk Man hit him so hard over the head with a guitar that it nearly crippled him. These days, Jeff Jarrett hits a guy with a cheap-ass guitar, the thing explodes upon impact, a cloud of smoke adds to the effect, and nobody gets hurt too bad. Back in 1987, Honky hit Jake with the best guitar money could buy, the only thing that broke were Jake's vertebrae, and he went down in a heap, never to be quite the same man again.

His psychology and interviews were among the best in the sport. Without ever raising his voice, he was able to spellbind the audience, and I was not the only one who felt like I was going to school when I was in his presence. On the other hand, he could be a devious S.O.B. He would often go out of his way to make other people look bad. He was known to take somebody's best shot and stand there daring him for more. Hell, he even did it to Muhammad Ali in the Superdome when Ali was a special guest there. This was back in Watts's old Mid-South territory, and Bill had brought Ali in to be in the corner of one of his big stars. When the time was right, Ali climbed up on the ring apron, and the heels fed "the Greatest" for the big punch. BAM! went Ali, down went a wrestler. BAM! went Ali, and down went another. Now it was Jake's turn. BAM! went Ali, and Jake just stood there. BAM! went Ali again, and Jake once again refused to move, this time doing Ali's own shuffle and saying "C'MON, C'MON," and trying to goad Ali into the ring. I wouldn't have wanted to be in his shoes when Watts got a hold of him, even though Jake's rationale was simple. "Hey, he didn't have to get up and work here the next day—I did."

Actually, it was a performance just like that one that changed the course of Kevin Nash's career. Nash took a look at Jake no-selling some punches, turned to me, and said, "I know one thing, if Jake can get away with doing that with those skinny legs and that pot belly, than I sure as hell can do it too." Nash's improvement was immediate.

I really got to know Jake a lot better when we traveled together in the World Wrestling Federation. Jake had become a born-again Christian and had been preaching around the country. Upon his return to the Federation, Jake used the television exposure to continue preaching the word of God. It was this preaching that led to the most famous slogan and best-selling T-shirt in wrestling history. After defeating Jake at the 1996 *King of the Ring,* Steve Austin was interviewed and said of the Snake, "You come out here and you talk about your Psalms and you talk about your John 3:16—well, Austin 3:16 says I just whooped your ass!" The rest is history.

I enjoyed traveling with Jake because he was funny as hell, had great road stories, had an encyclopedic knowledge of the business, and most important, because I thought I was traveling with a man of God. Jake Roberts made me feel good about myself. Over time, however, chinks started appearing in Jake's religious armor. For one thing, he told his stories about the bad old days with just a little bit too much gusto—as if he wished those days weren't really over for good. Also, some of the things he did appeared to be not exactly divine.

I was on a road trip with Jake, Ron Simmons, and Justin Bradshaw in the winter of '96. Jake was chugging down brews, and felt the need to relieve himself. "Pull over," slurred Jake, who promptly got out of the car and whizzed all over the tire of a parked car.

When he reentered the vehicle, I questioned Jake's urinary decision by saying, "Gee, Jake, do you imagine the Pope pulls over the Popemobile so he can pee on parked cars?"

It was not the only time that Jake's urine would play a part in my life.

Jake opened the door to the Fairfield Inn late one night in Detroit. I don't want to jump to conclusions and say that Jake was drunk, but he was staggering and cursing, and he did smell like a strange mixture of barley, hops, and yeast. Later that night, actually in the wee hours of the morning, I awoke to a strange sound. The sound of water running, or more correctly, the sound of Jake pissing between our beds. "What the hell are you doing?" I yelled at Jake, who simply replied "Uugh" before passing out in his bed.

I lay there for a little while, before the potent potpourri of Jake's farts, piss, and beer breath really started to bother me. I actually went down to the lobby and inquired about getting another room. The lady at the desk told me that if I checked in now I'd have to pay for the whole night, but if I waited until 6 A.M., I would pay only for the day. I looked at the clock—it was 4:20 A.M. For the next hour and forty minutes, I watched reruns of *Kung Fu* and thought about what a great guy Jake was. When I woke up in the morning I headed for the gym. Apparently, the evening news was already out, as Dennis Knight (or Midion) was there to greet me with his dead-on Mankind imitation. "Excuse me, ma'am," he squealed to an imaginary hotel receptionist, "I thought I'd specifically asked for a nonsmoking, non-urine room."

Eventually the chinks in Jake's religious armor became huge dents and finally gaping holes. On a road trip from Boston to Newark, Jake was going into detail about his preaching experience. I was really moved. I asked Jake if he felt he got a lot out of doing this. "Brother"—Jake grinned in his best weathered Sam Elliott voice—"$1,500 a shot, plus gimmicks." Apparently, Jake misinterpreted my meaning of "getting a lot out of it." Many of the guys liked to tease Jake about his religious gimmick. One night in Calgary, Paul Bearer (my manager at the time) tore out a cartoon from *Hustler* magazine and taped it to Jake's locker. The cartoon depicted a Catholic priest walking into an adult store and pointing to a blow-up sex doll dressed as an altar boy, while saying, "I'll take two of those." Paul then wrote Jake's name on the cartoon and waited for Jake to arrive. When Jake did, his reaction was classic: He simply looked up at the sky and in a line right out of Luke 23:24 said, "Forgive them, Father, for they know not what they do." What happened next truly shocked me as Jake healed two lepers, turned water into wine, made a blind man see, and upon leaving the room, walked across the water.

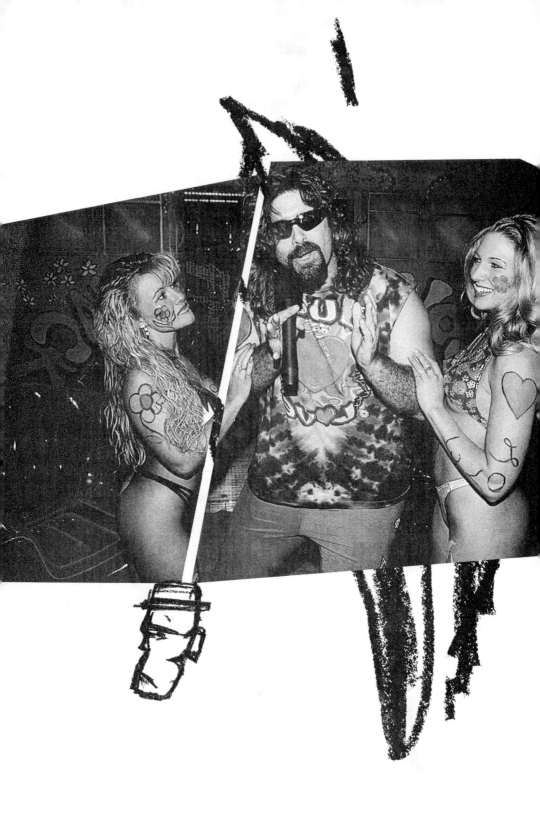

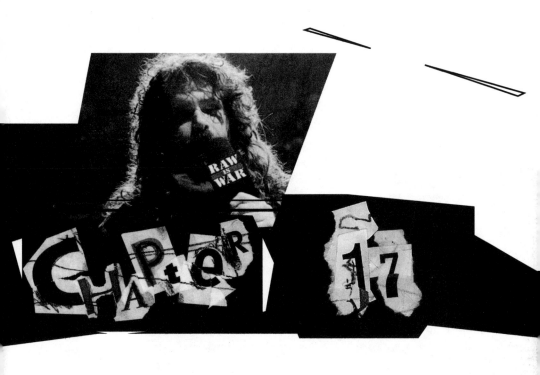

Guess who became a good guy.

I'd been getting cheered quite a bit anyway, and WCW was badly in need of a guy whom fans could actually like. I was told by the company that they were happy with their number one guy, Sting, but that nobody else was even close. I knew I could be that guy—close to Sting in position, if not salary. I'd been with the company for a year and a half and unless the fans were blind or stupid, it was pretty obvious that I'd been going above and beyond the call of duty for a long time.

The idea to turn me was set in motion when Rick Rude became injured, and as a result would be unable to wrestle in the upcoming *Clash's* ten-man steel cage main event. A match was set up in Montgomery, Alabama, between me and Mr. Wonderful (Paul Orndorff). Orndorff had five years earlier been one of the biggest-drawing cards in wrestling. His run with Hulk Hogan had set attendance records throughout the country, but in working such a hectic schedule, at such an intense pace (as was his style), he had come down with a serious nerve injury to his neck. Because the money on top with Hogan was so good, Orndorff never slowed down until he found himself one day unable to lift his arm. He left the sport for a few years, but had been on the independent scene for a while, and with great determination had built himself back up to tremendous physical condition. One arm was noticeably smaller than the other, but his determination was such that the smaller arm actually became the stronger of the two. It was this same determination that Orndorff brought to this match.

Harley Race was the manager at ringside—he would be making the determination of who the tougher man was. Paul and I had a real good match, while Harley yelled encouragement from the outside. Harley's enthusiasm turned to aggression as he tried to roll me back in the ring to continue. I took exception and knocked Harley on his ass, a move that prompted Vader to come out and exact revenge. With my sweatpants halfway down my butt, the Mastodon splashed me twice and left me lying. I guess Paul Orndorff was judged the winner by process of elimination.

In the locker room, I thought about my revenge. I was planning on coming through the crowd to attack Harley's new duo from behind while they cut an interview in the ring. Someone suggested using a shovel as a weapon, and I began practicing half-speed shovel shots on the wall—after all, this wasn't a class that DeNucci had offered. I was scared that I might seriously hurt someone—this wasn't a plastic or even an aluminum shovel, it was solid steel. Harley saw me practicing these wimpy blows and came over to me. He pointed to Vader, and with his weathered, gravelly, thirty-years-in-the-business voice said, "If you don't hit him, I'm going to come back here and hit you." He had put the fear of Harley in me.

Harley was like that. He was an eight-time world champion, who had overcome polio as a kid, and nobody was more respected. He was known both for his classic matches in his prime and his classic Kansas City barbecues in the present. One time in Baltimore, I had split my eyebrow right down to the bone on the guard rail outside the ring. The Maryland State Athletic Commission was required by law to pay for any injury that occurred inside the ring, but was not so required on injuries that occurred outside the ring. Back in the dressing room, Harley called over the doctor and said, "He was split by a headbutt inside the ring."

The doctor disagreed, saying, "Oh, come on now, Harley, I think it happened on the guard rail."

Harley waited about a second and answered back, this time in a much firmer tone, "I said it was a headbutt and it happened inside the ring." I was brought to the hospital immediately. That doctor had the fear of Harley put into him too.

In the backstage area, I could see Vader, Orndorff, and Harley in the ring. I knew this was another big moment in my career, and I was nervous as hell. I kept thinking of my son's tiny blue and green shoes, and repeating, "I love you, my little monster man." It's strange how often in this business I juxtapose beautiful images with brutal acts—and a brutal act was about to take place.

I made my move and came through the crowd with my newfound steel friend. As I hit the ring, I could hear Vader deliver one of his standard lines, "I fear no man, and I feel no pain." I swung for the fences, and Vader sure as hell felt that pain. *Whack*! "Owww!"—in an un-Vader-like high-pitched shriek. Orndorff was next, and I swung for his head, although he helped cushion the blow with his hands. Harley even fed me for one—the tough old bastard. What happened next was spontaneous, because the original plan had fallen through. About five of the underneath guys were going to come out as I continued my assault, but upon seeing how ugly it was getting, they literally ran away. Instead, Kevin Nash, Mark Canterbury, and Dennis Knight hit the ringside area, where by now I was waiting. These guys were my friends, but I was running on adrenaline and fear of Harley, a very powerful fuel. There were six hits; three shovel hits and three guys hitting the floor. When it was over, Vader had a burst bursar sack on his elbow, and Canterbury had a major concussion. I felt bad about it, but hey, I'd suffered a lot over the years, and besides I was a good guy now, a fan favorite—a babyface.

A few days later, Orndorff approached me in the shower area. He said he knew coming in that this was probably his last shot at getting a good run with a major company. He told me that he'd just signed a contract with WCW, and he told me that he thought our match had had a lot to do with him getting an offer. He wanted to say thank you. I thought that it was an incredibly classy thing (and I'm getting goose bumps writing about it now) for a guy of his magnitude to say. Orndorff still works for WCW as a part of their front office staff, and if I really did play a part in getting him there, it makes me very proud.

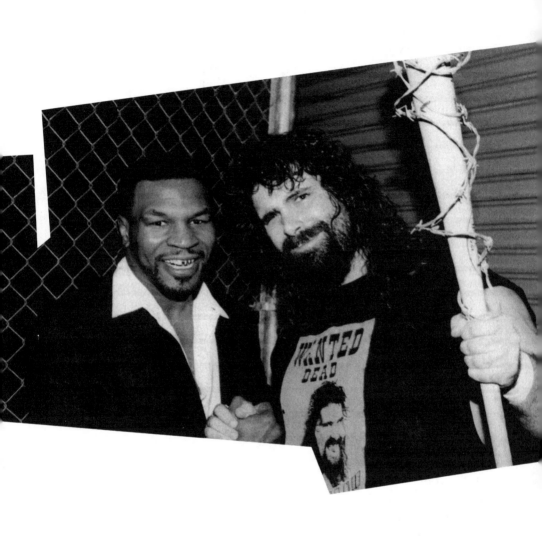

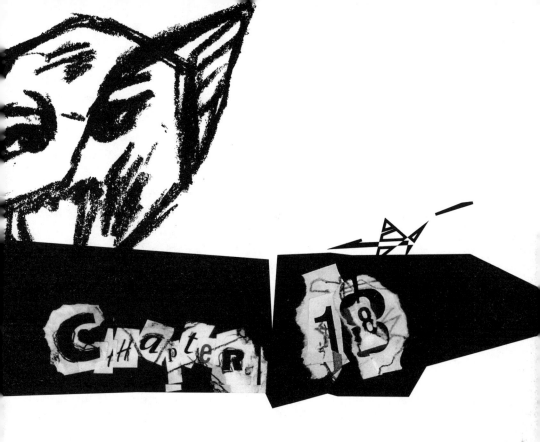

"Ding Dong, the witch is dead" came

the voice over the telephone. It was my old friend DDP, and it was his way of saying that Bill Watts had been let go.

"That's great," I said, not really meaning it, but not wanting to be ostracized as a Bill Watts supporter. "But who's taking his place?"

"Try to guess," said DDP. I tried a half-dozen times but failed. Finally he gave the word that, in all fairness to the guy, would change the face of wrestling—quite a bit. "Bisch." I was stunned.

Bisch was Eric Bischoff, who had been until that time an announcer and not a very good one. What I didn't know was that Bischoff had been impressing the Turner brass with his reasonable ideas and his smooth personality—in a sense he had been impressing them by being everything that Bill Watts was not. The Turner people had been getting real tired of Cowboy Bill. He cursed like a sailor, peed in a garbage can at an office party, and was uncouth in general. He had even punched Shane Douglas in order to get a cut on his head to "swell up for the camera." If Shane had thought about it, he could have staggered up, fallen down the stairs, pooped his pants, and sued to become part owner of WCW. As it turns out, the final straw for

Watts came when some comments that Bill had made to an underground newsletter became public and were brought to the attention of baseball home run king Hank Aaron, who had a front office job with Turner. The comments were construed as racist, which didn't sit well in a politically correct company like Turner's, and the Cowboy was forced to ride out into the sunset.

I may not have always liked what Bill did, and sometimes I didn't even like him, but I can't help feeling proud that I had the chance to work for him and that he respected me. About five years later, I actually had the opportunity to "wrestle" Cowboy Bill in Tulsa. The Undertaker had been hospitalized with a staph infection, and road agent Jack Lanza contacted Bill about coming in and wrestling Mankind. "Mankind, who the hell is that?" Bill asked, before being told that he was the former Cactus Jack. That night, Watts slapped Paul Bearer so hard he drew blood, and backdropped me, threw me into the casket, and slammed the lid—all without losing his cowboy hat.

I actually thought for a while that the whole Bischoff hiring was going to work out well for me. As an announcer, Eric had not exactly been the most respected guy among the wrestlers, and I was one of the few guys who hadn't treated him like a peon. I actually considered the guy a friend, and hey, there are worse things in the world than having a friend for your boss. Unfortunately, something happened that I hadn't counted on; once in power Eric made new friends, and dirty, unkempt Cactus Jack wasn't on the new list. Actually, I can't say Bischoff was ever bad to me, and maybe I wasn't completely off the list, but I had been pushed down it.

A few personnel changes were made that didn't bode well for me. Jim Ross was taken off the air, saw the writing on the wall, and left shortly after. Eric's take on Ross was that he was fat and he was Southern, and didn't play well to mainstream U.S.A. Well, Jim Ross is still fat, and he's still Southern, but he's also the best announcer who's ever called a match, and he's a big reason that *Raw Is War* is the hottest show in the country, which, last time I checked, included mainstream U.S.A. That troubleshooting referee himself, Ole Anderson, was hired to help Dusty with the booking. With Ross, who was one of my biggest supporters, jumping ship, and Anderson, one of my biggest detractors, simultaneously jumping on board, I really didn't know what the future held for me.

As it turned out, the future was a little rough on Cactus Jack. Within a month, I went from working main events to jerking the curtain (being the opening match). I had another problem in that I was having trouble getting the right reaction from the fans. Don't get me wrong, I was getting a great reaction when I came out, and I had very quickly become the number two good guy behind Sting, but it was hard for the heels to get any "heat" on me. Because I had been portrayed for the last year and a half as a guy who not only felt little pain (false), but also seemed to enjoy it (even falser), the fans had little sympathy for me. I mean, why would they feel bad for someone who was doing something he loved? A match with Vader was a different story, though. We had recently had a match in Gainesville, Georgia, and Vader's stuff looked (and was) so devastating that the fans had rallied behind me during the heat. I called Dusty and set up a meeting wanting to stress the point that I was just a flesh-and-blood man who could be (and had been) injured. I thought a series of matches with Vader would help the fans see me in a more sympathetic light.

I laid out a scenario to Dusty—one that culminated in a devastating injury. The Dream thought about it for a few minutes, and then got a look on his face as if he'd just had a major revelation. He started to speak, Dusty-style, in his excited, animated fashion. "That's it, baby, and when Vader hurts you, you'll have amnesia. You'll go home, but you won't even know your family . . ." He continued to speak, but all I could think was how outlandish the whole thing was, and that it would never work. Nobody was going to believe amnesia. This was WCW, dammit—not *Days of Our Lives*. I was just about to speak up when Dusty said the magic words, "We'll take you off the road for four months and we'll pay you."

Let me see—I could get buried and languish in the opening matches, or I could be with my wife and son for four months and come back in a main event feud. The choice wasn't difficult. When he asked me what I thought, I gushed, "I love it, Dream, I really love it."

Vader and I had two matches to set up the injury. I talked a little bit about the first one, but it was so brutal that it really deserves an extra little look. I thought the psychology was pretty simple; I get the living crap beaten out of me, but somehow pulled out a victory. I began talking to Vader about swelling my eye up a little bit, and he seemed to brush it off by offering me another idea. "Maybe I can get a little blood from your nose, too."

"Okay," I said. Harley was there and helpfully offered to bust my eyebrow open.

Busting an eyebrow is the little known and little exercised act of creating a gash over the eyebrow by punching downward with the point of the knuckles. When done correctly, it is as effective at creating realism as anything in the business. When done incorrectly, by stressing force over technique, it does nothing but raise welts. There were only a few people whom I trusted to bust me open, and Harley was one of them. Oddly, even though I have the reputation for being a Hardcore Legend, I was surprisingly inept when it came to eyebrow busting. One night in ECW in 1997, I tried to open up Tommy Dreamer, and I was failing miserably. After I bounced punches off his nose, cheek, and forehead, he looked at me and asked painfully, "Please stop hitting me."

The bell rang and Vader started in. He pushed me into the turnbuckle, pushed my head back, and brought down four forearms in a row, right across the bridge of my nose. BAM, BAM, BAM, BAM! You could actually hear the sick sound of his wrist bone breaking my nose. Vader looked for blood, and when he didn't see it, he became a man obsessed. He forgot all about the eye swelling and continually went after my nose. I wanted to tell the dumb bastard that I'd reconsidered, and that maybe he ought to think about stomping his foot on the mat instead. Finally, about a thimbleful of blood dribbled out, and he remembered our talk about the eye. *Boom, boom*—two punches to the cheek and eyebrow and I went down. I have an unedited version of the tape (WCW refused to show some of it), and those two punches were awesome. I rolled out to the floor, where Harley was waiting anxiously for his big punch. He took one look at me, however, and saw that blood was already streaming from both my eyebrow and cheek, in addition to the little dribble from my broken nose. "Dammit, it's already done," grumbled a disappointed Harley as he rolled me back into the ring.

The fans were completely caught up in the contest, as I think most of them could tell that something a little different was going on. Vader went for a splash against the rail, and caught nothing but steel, as I moved out of harm's way. One Cactus Jack upside-down crack smash later, and I rolled back into the ring, the winner of a count-out victory. The fans reacted as if I'd just won the Super Bowl. It was a rare moment of real emotion, in a promotion that was almost void of it.

Believe it or not, the locker room was like a huge celebration afterward. The other wrestlers were blown away by what they'd just seen. Even Ole Anderson came by and admitted that it had been a hell of a match. Lex Luger jokingly checked Ole's trousers to see if he'd been "aroused" by the beating, as Ole was known to enjoy misery and human suffering. Vader and I hugged and even Harley tried his best to put on a happy face, despite the bitter letdown he'd just endured.

I asked our TV people it they wanted to tape some fired-up backstage interviews. They said they really didn't think they could air my face in its current state. The next day, Eric Bischoff told me that Turner wasn't going to allow the match to air but that he was fighting them on the matter. I hated to think that the whole thing had been for naught. I'd been stitched up above and below my eye, my nose had been broken, causing both my eyes to blacken, and I'd dislocated my jaw. As a guy who had a martial arts background, Bischoff could appreciate what I'd been through. "Cactus," he said, "I've had my ass kicked lots of times, but never that bad, and never by someone I let do it." Little did Bischoff know that the worst ass kickings in his life would occur six years later, in the Monday night ratings wars.

The match did air, and I have to in all sincerity thank Bischoff for taking a stand—but every drop of blood had been taken out. I don't know how many hours they spent trying to homogenize it, but by making liberal use of crowd shots, long shots, and major editing, it paled in comparison to the real deal. Tony Schiavone is actually a pretty good announcer, but his stomach seemed a little weak for it, as he continually said, "Oh my goodness, oh my goodness." Governor Ventura seemed to enjoy it, though. Jim Ross, who was at this time announcing for the World Wrestling Federation, left a message on my machine saying that he'd seen the match, and really wished he'd been the one to call it.

A strange thing happened right after the match aired. A commercial played hyping *Slamboree*, WCW's Pay-Per-View that paid homage to the stars of the past. I'll be damned if every star they showed (the Crusher, Verne Gagne, Blackjack Mulligan) wasn't wearing "the crimson mask." I guess WCW's policy on blood was that they could air it if the footage was twenty years old, but week-old blood—no way!

About a week later, I got a surprising phone call from the people in television production. They wanted to do promos for my return match with Vader that would air on the following Saturday, and they needed me right away. "Oh yeah," they added, before hanging up, "we need you to look the way you did after the match."

"Hey," I thought, "that's just great." I had offered them the opportunity to capitalize on a unique situation, and they'd been too squeamish, and now they'd reconsidered. With the odd taping schedule WCW employed, however, the two matches were taped almost two weeks apart, even though they would air on consecutive Saturdays. By now, my wounds were all but healed. Now, in my book (yes, once again, it is my book), there is nothing quite as good as the real thing, but I was about to receive an A for effort. I must have looked like quite a sight as I barreled down Highway 75 in my '84 convertible, with one hand on the wheel and the other brandishing a skin-removing square of sandpaper. At the stop lights, I threw punches at the rubbed-raw cheekbone area for added emphasis.

The return match was a scary, eerie night that I'll long remember. Before leaving home I wrote a note for Colette. It was essentially a last will and testament instructing her on what to do in case things didn't turn out too well. Thank God she never had to read it. I hope you don't think I'm exaggerating when I say that the ramifications of this match were tremendous and the risk of serious injury was extremely high. As the willing participant of a powerbomb on the concrete floor, I was putting myself in a precarious predicament. I was essentially letting the most dangerous man in the business perform the sport's most dangerous move on a concrete floor. As mentioned earlier, I had seen Vader temporarily paralyze Joe Thurman with the move inside the ring that had some give to it. I had seen that powerbomb literally knock out others, and as mentioned earlier, I had seen some kids quit the company rather than risk the consequences of the powerbomb. The biomechanics of the powerbomb are simple—simply flip your bent-over opponent in the air as high as possible, and bring his back, neck, and head down to the canvas with as much force as possible. It can be scary to watch.

Something seemed wrong when I walked into Center Stage that afternoon. The hallways seemed a little darker and the atmosphere seemed a little heavier. Dusty called me into his office. "Just for the record, Cactus," the Dream started, without his usual animation, "I don't want you to do this." I think by saying this, Dusty was relieving both his conscience and any legal liability that the company might have.

"I appreciate that, Dusty," I said, "but this is important to me."
Vader also tried to talk me out of it, but again I said no.

I had an interview scheduled for the middle of the show. Dusty
wanted to talk to me about it. Again he was uncharacteristically low-
key. "Cactus, when you give this interview, I don't want you to think
beforehand about anything you're going to say. This is an emotional
night—I want the fans to feel your emotion." This was a valuable
piece of advice, and with the knowledge that Dusty Rhodes was one
of the great promo men in the business, I took it to heart. As good as
many of my promos were, I had the habit of walking around backstage before interviews, practicing what I was going to say. That night
from Center Stage, I spoke right from the heart. I honestly can't
remember what I said, but that night, as is true in most cases, it's not
as much what you say that's important, but how it's said. I'll always
be thankful to the Dream for that small piece of advice, advice that
would make my later ECW interviews so memorable.

The match itself was a solid piece of business. Many considered it
to be better than the first, although, obviously, I couldn't absorb the
same shots to the face again. As the match drew to a conclusion, I
attempted another Cactus Jack upside-down crack smash—the same
move that had led me to victory a week before. This time, Harley
jerked Vader out of the way, and I landed hard on the blue protective
mat. As Schiavone and Ventura called the action, Vader threw back
the blue mats, revealing the cold, concrete floor below. I was crossing
myself as Vader picked me up off the floor. As he put my head between
his massive thighs, I was talking out loud. "I love you, Colette, I love
you, my tiny man." Vader crouched down, and with all his might lifted
me into the air. "My God, if he does that, he'll kill him," yelled
Schiavone. A moment later, I hit the concrete. My initial reaction was
strange. "That didn't feel too bad—but I bet it didn't look too good
on TV." Then my right foot and hand went numb.

I lay there for about forty minutes, while we waited for an ambulance. Now, a lot of fans speculated that I wasn't as hurt as I acted,
and to some extent, that was true. I probably could have moved, but
the longer I lay there with the other wrestlers all around me, the more
I thought I really was in trouble. After a few minutes, I became scared
to even try to move my hand and foot. "How are you doing, you sexy
thing?" asked Scorpio, in an attempt to get me to laugh.

"Scorp," I said softly, "I can't move my foot."

"Sorry," replied Too Cold.

The ambulance finally arrived, and I was put on a stretcher. Several people in the audience were crying. I was placed in the ambulance, and of all people, Jesse Ventura came along for the ride. As the ambulance pulled away, with sirens wailing, the show faded to black. It was great drama. Was it staged? Yes, but in many ways it was real nonetheless.

I was wheeled into the hospital, and while strapped to the gurney, I was asked by an especially sensitive fan if I would pose for a picture with her. Upon admission, I was checked out thoroughly, given a battery of tests, including a CAT scan that revealed—you guessed it—a concussion. X-rays were taken and, fortunately, revealed no fractures. The doctor informed me that I had suffered a severe blow to the back of my head, which had likely caused my brain to more or less "short circuit," causing the temporary loss of sensation in my extremities. I was given a list of things to do and not to do, and was released at about 1 A.M. Janie Engle, a WCW front office employee, drove me home. I was groggy, but all things considered, I felt pretty fortunate. In reality, Vader had actually taken care of me pretty well. He had followed through with me, and released me low, to ensure a safer landing. If it had been a typical Vader powerbomb, things might have been a lot worse. "Pull over please," I asked Janie, about a mile or two from my house. I proceeded to bolt out of the car and left remnants of my prematch meal all over Highway 575.

When I got home, Colette met me at the door and gave me a long embrace. I went upstairs and kissed my sleeping little buddy, then went into our bedroom, where against doctor's orders, I fell asleep myself. I awoke to the ringing of the phone. "I just called to check on you," said a weathered, slightly inebriated voice on the phone. It was Handsome Harley.

"Do you think it went okay?" I asked.

Harley paused and softly (for Harley that is) said, "Cactus, it couldn't have gone any better if we'd done it a hundred times." He spoke one more time before he hung up. "You're the new Harley Race, kid." That was the greatest compliment I have ever received.

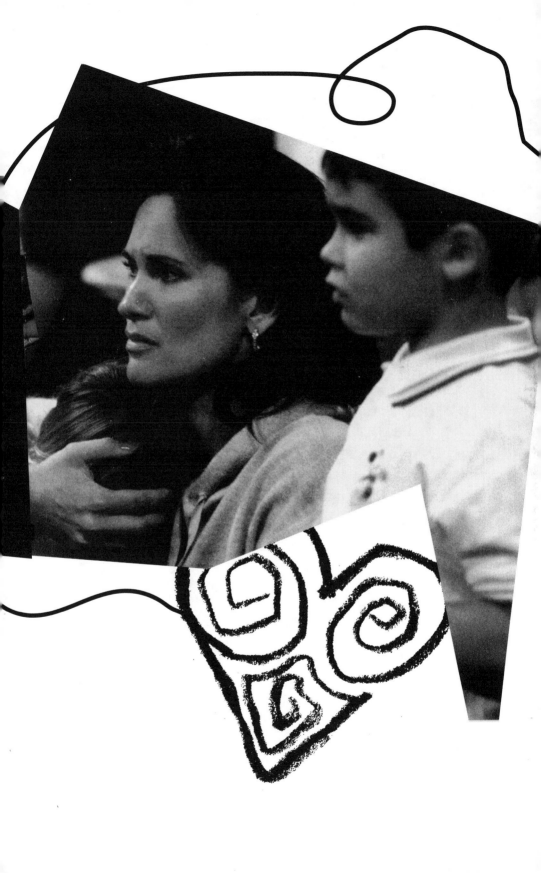

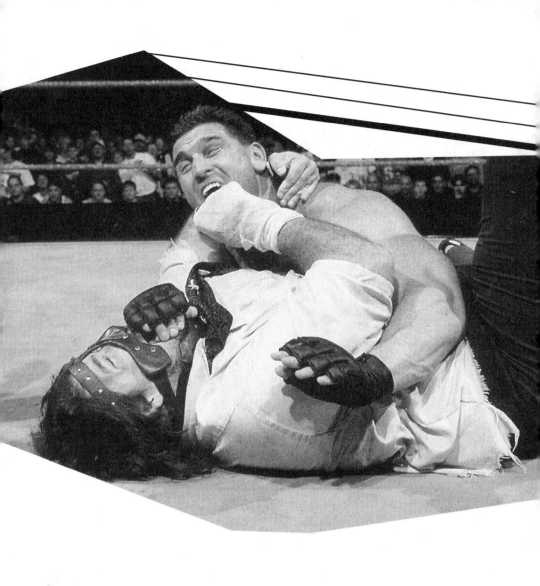

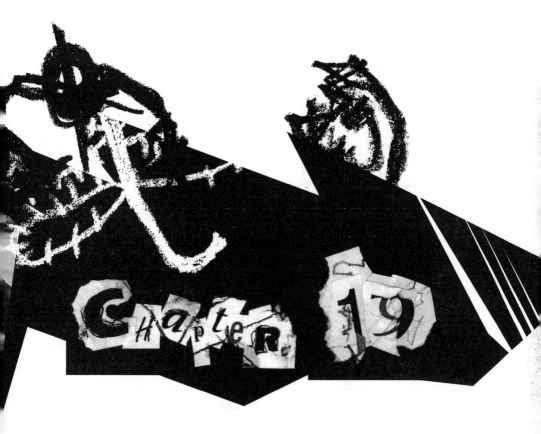

I convalesced at home, while a pair
of writers prepared an elaborate story line that would air throughout my twelve-week absence. Even though I would be off the road for four months, I would be back for television tapings after three. I really felt like I was on top of the world; I could finally spend quality time with my son and wife, who was now one month pregnant with our second child. And I had just come out in one piece from a daring angle, which would no doubt set the box office on fire when I returned. I was confident that when my contract rolled around in four months I would be well compensated for all my sacrifices. Everything was going to be just fine for the Foleys—right? Come on now, this is WCW we're talking about here, a company that could screw up a wet dream. Sacrifice? Dedication? Loyalty? They were seemingly foreign words to my employers. Of course they'd screw it up. One phone call saw to that.

"Hello, Cactus, this is Tony Schiavone calling. How are ya feeling?"

"Not too bad, Tony, what's going on?"

"Well, I wanted to talk to you about your vignettes."

"How are they? I can't wait to see what they come up with."

"Well, one of the things that we've decided is that there's got to be some humor in them."

"Tony, to tell you the truth, I don't see anything funny about the whole situation. I mean, head injuries aren't usually a real comedic thing."

"I understand that, it's just that we feel we can't air twelve weeks of serious vignettes—it will turn people off."

"Tony, the vignettes are only a couple of minutes long each, surely you guys can put some humor somewhere else in the show."

"I'm sorry, Cactus, we talked about it, and we decided that this would be best. Janie will drive by later and give you a script."

After reading the script, I felt as if they had reached out with a steel-toed boot and kicked me, as DeNucci might say, "right in the ball." I saw my career and pay raise fading away before my eyes. In this script, I was to portray Cactus Jack as an escaped mental patient, who, believing himself to be a veteran sailor, leads a group of home-less people to a better sense of purpose and self-respect. Wow! There was even a scene where a reporter attempts in vain to get information from Colette as to my whereabouts, while Dewey causes havoc in the background. Unfortunately, Colette was not even allowed to play her-self, because as Dusty put it, "We don't think your wife ought to be so attractive." So a dumpy woman was brought on to portray my wife, a small piece of casting buffoonery that bothered Colette for months. Even today, when many people think of Mick Foley's wife, they envi-sion the dumpy chick with the bad clothes and the droopy boobs (not that there's anything wrong with that) instead of the white-hot chick who fell so hard for her battle-scarred ring warrior.

I thought that this thing had failure written all over it. I sensed that Eric Bischoff had some reservations about it, even though he had given the go-ahead to three days of filming for the vignettes. I was not needed for the first two vignettes, which consisted of a visit to the mental hospital, and the aforementioned visit with the fictitious Colette. I called director Neil Pruitt, who was a friend of mine, and asked him how it went. Now usually a director, or artist of any kind, is the first person to stand behind his work. I was expecting Neil to say, "Oh man, it's great," or, "Wait till you see this—you'll love it." Instead his stammered answer was slow in coming. "Well," Neil said, "it's got a little more humor in it than I would like."

"Can you show it to me?" I asked, with a knot tightening in my stomach.

"I'll be right over," said Pruitt.

I slipped the tape in the VCR and within two minutes, saw all my aspirations crumble before me like the cookies in Diamond Dallas's bed. I could feel my figurative ball swelling to grapefruit-size proportions from the blow of the steel-toed boot entitled "Lost in Cleveland." In the vignette, a tabloidlike female television reporter seeks clues to find the missing Cactus Jack at the mental hospital he has escaped from. A helpful patient with a blanket folded over his lap, eating Cheez Doodles with a toothpick, and eerily reminiscent of Dustin Hoffman's idiot savant in *Rain Man,* says, "Jack, over there, yeah, Jack's definitely over there." Running over to a man shooting baskets at a tiny basketball hoop, the reporter yells, "Jack, Jack, is that you, Jack," causing a man to turn around and say in a terrible Nicholson impression (hey, I'm not making this stuff up), "How's it going, nursey baby?" Upset at this cruel hand that fate had dealt her, the reporter whines that she'll never find Jack. "Jack?" asks the Hoffman character. "Cleveland, yeah, Jack's in Cleveland, definitely Cleveland."

I lay down and waited for the swelling to dissipate. I wondered how this could have happened. It was as if a bunch of guys had gathered in a board room and said, "Okay, gentlemen, what we've got here is an angle that people believe in, a wrestler who was willing to put his life on the line, and a feud that's going to draw a ton of money. Now tell me, what can we do about this nagging problem? I know, let's make the fans feel like idiots for ever believing in anything we did. That way, they'll be cynical and uncaring the next time we try to do an exciting angle on television. As for that wrestler guy, well, we'll show him. We'll make him curse the day he ever sacrificed his body for this company. Let's make him look like a complete nincompoop. Oh, we'll show him. Head bouncing off the concrete and all that concussion business. We'll make a farce out of him, that's what we'll do. Gentlemen, you have my word that as long as I'm in charge, this company will never, and I do mean NEVER, make a dime. Meeting adjourned."

I couldn't envision this stinker ever finishing its twelve-week run. What I could envision was the plug being pulled after about three weeks, and with WCW doing its "the fans won't know—we'll just pretend it never happened" routine, I'd be in worse career jeopardy than when I'd started this whole angle. Fortunately, I had an ace up my sleeve. Well, not an ace, exactly—it was more like a ligament. It wasn't up my sleeve, either, it was in my knee, and it had been torn some four months earlier during a match with Ricky Steamboat. I figured a ligament replacement operation would give me my four months off, guaranteed.

"Dusty," I said, in a call to the WCW offices. "Oh yeah, man, I love them, Dream," I lied, hoping that the phone wasn't magically connected to a polygraph machine that would have surely been dancing off the charts. "Yeah, while these things are running, I was thinking about having a little knee surgery done. What do you think?" I had my fingers crossed. "I can. Oh great, yeah, don't worry, I'll be able to shoot the vignettes—I've still got two weeks, right? Oh yeah, I saw it. Loved it. Especially the Nicholson imitation. Okay, thanks, Dusty. Bye."

On May 12, 1993, I had my right posterior cruciate ligament replaced with a cadaver's patella tendon. Sure enough, about eight weeks later, Eric Bischoff pulled the plug on "Lost in Cleveland." It was a mercy killing.

Actually, I don't mean to be so hard on Dusty—it wasn't his fault. Like me, Dusty compared a lot of his ideas to movie scenarios, and I think his real career goal was to direct in Hollywood. The idea could have worked, but this was WCW's first attempt at using writers, and they let the writers take the whole thing in a ridiculous direction. Hey, I wanted to believe in the project too, especially when I showed up on the set and saw the elaborate scenery, props, and hordes of extras. Still, all the same, if you do have a copy of these rare sketches, resist the urge to watch them, even if the idea of a clean-shaven, eyebrowless Cactus Jack talking about mizzenmasts and nor'easters does turn you on. Instead, please, if you have any respect for me at all, burn it—now, to preserve the sanctity of my reputation for future generations.

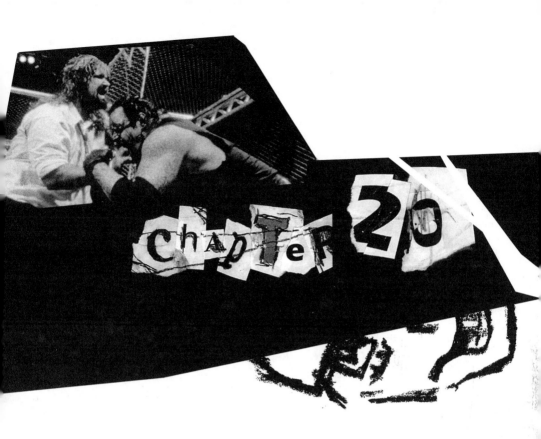

CHAPTER 20

I tried to put the whole Cleveland thing behind me and just enjoy the time at home. I was scheduled to come back at the September *Clash of the Champions*, and in the meantime, I rehabbed my knee with diligence for my showdown in late October with Vader. I know most people don't think of Cactus Jack or Mankind as training hard for anything, but I think they've been misled. The truth is, I usually show up ready to go, and I have had long, fast-paced matches with some really well-conditioned athletes. Now, as far as being not all that impressive when it comes to lifting heavy weights, I'll plead guilty, but with the footnote that over the years, my joints, muscles, and tendons have been through quite an ordeal. Over the years, when guys in the business have had less than stellar physiques, announcers have covered for them by claiming they had great tendon strength. Sometimes, as in the case of Dan Severn, it was true. I'm actually in the process right now of trying to get Jim Ross to sell the fans on the idea that I am one of those guys. Can't you just hear it? "My goodness, look at that tendon strength. Foley is deceptively strong." Actually, it's one of the small comforts in my life to know that on any given day, I can walk into any gym in the country and lift the exact same amount of weight that I did when I was a sixteen-year-old kid.

I started getting the feeling that something wasn't right. This feeling started right after my return at the *Clash*, and grew as my *Halloween Havoc* match with Vader drew closer. I was scheduled to wrestle Yoshi Kwan, a martial artist who was Harley's newest wrestler. He was undefeated over the course of several months, with the idea being that if I beat him at the Pay-Per-View, I could start gunning for Vader. Instead, I watched in disgust as Kwan lost to Johnny B. Badd, who wasn't even booked on the PPV. I asked Dusty about it, and he apologized for the error, but it didn't stop the company from airing the match twice more that weekend.

After defeating the not-quite-as-impressive Kwan, I noticed more small details that didn't seem to be quite right. As one of the better promo men in the company and with a strong reason to seek vengeance, I knew that I could help sell this show on the mike. Instead, in the four weeks leading up to the show, I was given one live interview to build up the main event. In that same amount of time, Dusty gave himself four live interviews to promote the fact that he was going to be in his son's corner for another match. Priorities were definitely screwed up.

Also interesting to me was the fact that I wasn't written into any of the television shows that would air after the *Havoc* show in October of 1993. I asked Dusty what he had in mind for me after *Havoc*, and he admitted he had nothing immediate. It was obvious to me that somebody somewhere didn't want a Pay-Per-View that Cactus Jack was headlining to be a success. It was more or less booked to be a failure. Just like Stallone's Rambo felt when he learned the only reason he had been sent on a dangerous mission was that he was supposed to fail, I too felt expendable.

It was in this atmosphere that I attempted to renegotiate my contract. In the history of wrestling, I don't think anyone has ever done more research or work in attempting to renegotiate. I presented Eric Bischoff with a twenty-page, professionally printed thesis complete with charts, graphs, statistics, and analyses. My research had shown me that I was as valuable as anyone in the company, and as such, I certainly believed I deserved to be paid that way. I didn't expect the $750,000 that guys like Sting were pulling in at the time, but I felt like I deserved something.

"You're preaching to the choir," Bischoff said, simultaneously stroking my ego and letting me know that all my hard work wasn't going to earn an extra nickel. "If it was up to me, I'd be glad to give you more, but my hands are tied here." What could I do? In today's open market, an unsigned wrestler headlining an upcoming Pay-Per-View show would be worth a fortune, even if just to screw up the other company. I wasn't in that position, however; the World Wrestling Federation had made it clear to me that they weren't interested, or at least J. J. Dillon had. J. J. was Vince McMahon's right-hand man, and the guy I got ahold of once a year when my contract came up. Every year, he'd give me about a minute and five seconds of his time. "Sorry, we're not looking for talent right now. You should be happy you're working—a lot of guys aren't, you know? Give us a call next year." That was it. They weren't looking for talent? The World Wrestling Federation was always on the lookout for talent. Excuse my language here, but I'm a little upset thinking about this—I was Cactus Fucking Jack and all I get is one minute with J. J. Fucking Dillon? Whoa, it felt good to get that off my chest. How about one more? Okay. I was Cactus Fucking Jack and all I get is one minute with J. J. Fucking Dillon. Four "F" words in one paragraph—Diamond Dallas would be so proud.

Actually, as it turned out Vince McMahon himself wasn't a big Cactus Jack fan, so maybe every year around the first of September he'd put J. J. on a Cactus Jack alert, with direct orders to "get rid of that fat, psycho, eyebrow-busted-open bastard." Jim Ross had continually pushed for me, but Vince continually dismissed it, saying (I found out years later) that I "didn't look like a star." Yeah, Vince, and I guess Gobbledygooker and Mantaur did. Considering the parade of stiffs who stunk up World Wrestling Federation rings for years, Vince ought to be slapped for insulting the Hardcore Legend like that. Or at least forced to watch an hour of Al Snow matches. No wonder I hit Vince so damn hard when I finally got the chance.

Bischoff actually went down the WCW roster one by one checking off names, either saying yes or no—yes they were making more money than me or no they weren't. I've got to admit, there were a lot of guys on that list who were making less money than I was, but I'd noticed one name that was conspicuous by its absence. "What about Jesse?" I said. Bischoff looked at me as if I'd just disgraced the good name of the Virgin Mary. He actually physically got out of his seat slightly and leaned forward, asking, "Were you in the number one movie in the country last week?" referring to Jesse's role in the Stallone flick *Demolition Man*.

Now Jesse was a good guy, and considering who he is, I should probably be kissing his gubernatorial ass, but the truth is he was paid an exorbitant amount of money to make jokes on the air, and tell stories about the Crusher and Verne Gagne to the boys backstage. "No," I had to admit. "I wasn't."

It was no use. Bischoff wasn't going to budge. I really had no other recourse. I had a family to think of and a child on the way in two months, and to make matters more difficult, Colette was dilating early and was forced to spend the last ten weeks of her pregnancy in bed. I explained this situation to Bischoff and then said in a voice that was pretty near cracking with emotion, "If I take the same money, can I have the next six weeks off to spend helping my wife?"

Knowing he had the upper hand, but really not being as big a prick about it as he could have, Eric said, "Cactus, you just had four months off."

I pointed to our schedule that was behind his desk, and pleaded my case one last time. "Eric, you've got me teaming up with Ice Train (a huge, but green, wrestler) in junior high schools in the backwoods of the Carolinas. How important could that match be?" Maybe a little of what I was saying was getting through. Maybe dedication and a track record of proven performances still meant something.

"If you get the time off, will you sign for 156?" he asked.

"Yes, I will." I left the CNN Center that afternoon, vowing that I would never let myself be put in that position again.

Halloween Havoc was an artistic and athletic victory, but an emotional defeat. Actually, I was lucky to even make it. We had a match in Phoenix on Friday night, followed by a day off and then *Havoc* in New Orleans. I left the house on Friday morning, running a little late. I could never get the roof of the convertible to latch on just right, so as a result, I just drove all the way with the top down. It was cold this late October morning, however, and raining hard. It didn't usually matter, though; as long as I kept up a decent speed, the rain would usually just blow on by. Usually. This time it was raining way too hard, and I was occasionally having to stop for traffic. But I decided to gut it out. By the time I got to Atlanta, I was drenched from head to toe. By the time I got to Phoenix, I was sick as a dog. I went to eat with my old buddy Robert Fuller. I ate a Reuben sandwich and promptly threw it up. (To this day I can't eat a Reuben sandwich, which had been a longtime favorite.) That night I stumbled through a match where I was so bad that I made Al Snow look like Satoro Sayama by comparison. I stopped at a gas station to get some liquids into my body—funny, earlier that day, I had plenty of liquids hitting my body. A bunch of kids recognized me. "Cactus Jack," they yelled as I went to open the door. "Can we have your autograph?" *Vumphoow.* I threw up everywhere, including on one of the kid's shoes. It was almost as bad as a night in Baltimore in which I threw up about eleven strawberry margaritas all over the room I was sharing with Scotty Flamingo. Wow—between the dry-heaves, blood spitting, vomit, and urine, this book is turning out to be a little more scatalogical than I would have imagined.

Actually, as I've said, I'm not much of a drinker at all. Back in the days I'm writing about now, I would go out maybe half a dozen times a year, nowadays maybe twice. I just don't find going out to be all that much fun, and as Stan Hansen once told me, "there's nothing good that can happen to you when you go out." For the sake of my marriage, my pocketbook, and my body's healing process, I'm much better off lying in bed, watching Nick-at-Nite or a movie or reading a book, or once in a great while, getting to know my body a little better. If someone asks me what the best quality a wrestler can have is, I can honestly say it would be the ability to enjoy doing nothing. Which isn't to say I don't do things. I catch movies whenever I pass a multiplex with time to spare, visit historic battlefields or monuments I see, and am the self-professed king of amusement parks. As a matter of fact, Al Snow and I almost had to go to wrestlers' court to face formal charges of stranding Bob Holly at the airport in order to go to a carnival. We were guilty as hell, but we settled out of court to the tune of two nights' free lodging, meals, and rental car, and the reimbursement of $80 that the cranky, curmudgeonly "I don't want to go to a carnival" Bob had to pay for his own car.

I guess you are wondering about how *Halloween Havoc* turned out, unless you want to hear more stories about how the guy you paid twenty-five bucks to read about is a socially inept, amusement park–obsessed loser who has been ostracized by all but a few of his fellow wrestlers. In addition, I have what Steve Austin considers the worst taste in music of any wrestler in the business. If, on the other hand, you're one of those "Foley is God" type of fans, I implore you to give Steve Earle or Emmylou Harris a try.

Havoc was actually a tremendous matchup. Some people feel that it was the best match Vader and I ever had, and some feel it was the most brutal. I don't know about that, but it was definitely a physical affair that left me battered and bleeding from a busted eyebrow. No, Harley still didn't get to do it. The next time I go to Harley's for a barbecue, I'm going to let the poor SOB bust me open, just so I won't have it on my conscience.

When many fans think about *Halloween Havoc* 1993, they may recall a particularly painful move that for my money was the single most gut-busting, suicidal maneuver I've ever tried. In actuality, I really was going to commit suicide: career suicide. I was trying to end my career right there in the Lakefront Center in New Orleans. The plot to end my eight years in the ring began when I placed a sleeper hold on Vader, who was staggering on the wooden ramp. A sleeper hold is a simple move that in theory deprives the brain from receiving oxygen by placing pressure on both carotid arteries—causing a man to go to "sleep." Similar pressure from a different maneuver had helped cost me my ear in Germany. In reality, nobody has won a match with a sleeper in years. It's usually just used to get a cheap pop from the crowd when you run out of things to do. But my sleeper had a purpose. I jumped on Vader's back, still holding the sleeper, causing the Mastodon to stumble like a drunken sailor with a 300-pound weight on his back. Here it comes, I thought, bracing myself for the pain and hoping that it would be severe. With a sudden burst of energy, Vader put my plan into effect. He dropped straight back while kicking his legs up in the air, literally crushing me between the bulk of his 450 pounds and the unforgiving wood of the entrance ramp. Vader rolled to the side, and I instinctively rolled into a fetal position, secure in the knowledge that my career was over.

There was no way that a human body could endure such a blow—not without permanent damage. And permanent damage was what I was looking for. With all that force landing directly on top of me, there was no way I could continue. Bones, vertebrae, discs, nerves—something in there had to be shot. Or at least I hoped so.

A few years prior to this, wrestlers had started purchasing disability insurance policies from the prestigious Lloyds of London company. Agents were more than happy to oblige them—after all, how much risk could a "fake" sport like wrestling carry with it? As it turned out for the Lloyds people, it carried plenty. Most of the policies called for generous payouts for career-ending injuries, based on a percentage of what your previous two years' salary had been. What Lloyds didn't understand, and in reality what few others do as well, is that pro wrestlers regularly perform with injuries that most normal people would consider career-ending. Unlike, say, a bus driver, who takes disability and retires early, a wrestler with the same type of injury would be getting suplexed and thrown around twenty days a month. It's considered part of the price you pay.

The guys were not faking their injuries, they were simply taking advantage of what the medical community had established as being normal by being, in a sense, abnormal. Now, my payout would not have been that large because in comparison to others, my salary wasn't, but I certainly would have received enough money to get by for a few years, until I figured out something else to do with my life. I was tired of wrestling; I was tired of the pain, I was tired of the lies, I was tired of the politics, and I was tired of the bullshit. I wanted out, and this was my ticket.

There was only one problem. Me. My body had become so conditioned to taking punishment that it had somehow managed to take this. So I did the only thing I knew how. I got up. Slowly. And then, as in Germany, I went on as best I could.

There you have it, a shocking revelation that until now, I'd only revealed to Eddie Gilbert in the midst of a three-beer buzz in Puerto Rico. To this day, I don't know if what I was attempting was illegal. I'm pretty sure I can't be arrested for it, even if what I did could be constituted as attempted insurance fraud. As it turns out, Lloyds of London refused to renew my policy. I always imagined that one of the bigwigs from Lloyds was watching TBS one day and heard Jim Ross say, "Look at Cactus Jack, with all the risks he takes, I wouldn't expect him to last much longer." So Lloyds of London, a company that insures against asbestos, theft, fire, floods, and natural disasters (as well as insuring Mary Hart's legs), wouldn't insure Mick Foley, a simple entertainer—I kind of like that.

Shortly after that match, I was asked by a fan on a call-in radio show what the highest moment of my career was. I replied that it was during *Halloween Havoc* right after I had drilled Vader with a foreign object at ringside. I looked up at the crowd and did a slow half-turn, covering about a third of the arena with my eyes. Everywhere I looked, people stood in unison, almost like fans doing the wave. Except they weren't performing a rah-rah choreographer move—they were transfixed by the intensity of the match. It truly was a powerful moment. The same fan than asked what my lowest point was. My answer was simple. "About ten minutes later, when I knew I'd never be that high again." Thankfully, I was wrong.

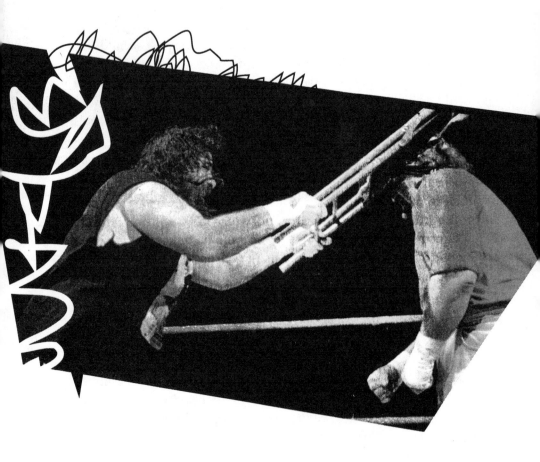

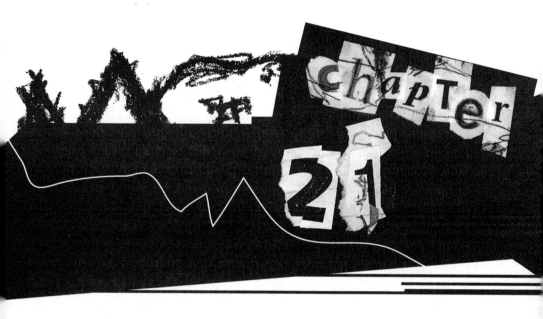

Dusty finally came up with a plan

for me—I was going to form a team with Maxx Payne. Now Maxx was a great guy, and we got along really well, but it was quite a drop from where I had been before. But at a certain point in that company—a point many of their current wrestlers are at right now—you simply stop caring as much and keep collecting a paycheck.

I wasn't the only one getting the shaft at the time. The Hollywood Blonds, Steve Austin and Brian Pillman, were inexplicably broken up. Every once in a while, I'll hear someone talk about Austin, and say, "He wasn't anything until he came to the World Wrestling Federation." The truth is, Austin was always good. He was an excellent television champion, and he and Pillman were probably the hottest team I had seen in years. They were funny, they knew how to wrestle as a team, and the matches they had with Rick Steamboat and Shane Douglas regularly stole the show in '93.

I had known Pillman off and on since late 1989, but had only recently become closer with him. A doctor had told Brian that if he didn't stop drinking, he'd be dead within a few years, and he took the advice to heart. In addition to changing his ways, he made a conscious effort to change some of his acquaintances. Brian began calling me regularly, and offering me his "Pillman's pick of the week," which was usually a saying or bit of psychological advice. I would then try to use his "pick" in an interview. When I left the company, I fell out of touch with him, and when I saw him again, during a short stint with ECW, he seemed like a different person. Sadly, although we shared the same car on the night of his death, it seemed as if I hardly knew him when he passed. As I write this now, it is the eve of the Brian Pillman Memorial Show for which I will wrestle to raise money for the future education of his children. I am hoping that by helping his family after his death, I can make up for the fact that I didn't try to help him while he was alive.

Amid all the setbacks and disappointment, the Foley family welcomed Noelle Margaret into the world on December 15, 1993. I had wrestled that night at the Crystal Chandelier nightclub teaming with Maxx Payne against Tex Slazenger and Shanghai Pierce. Yes, I was now reduced to wrestling in bars. I then went to the airport to pick up my dad for the holidays, went to the wrong terminal, and sat about fifty yards away from him for an hour, while each wondered where the other was. When I returned home, Colette was waiting with her bag. Away we went, and I fell asleep while Colette endured the agony of labor without me. We tried to tape the miracle of birth, but I ended up bumping the camera and getting magnificent footage of the doctor's head. Maybe it's not so bad, though. I had a friend who actually had me watch footage of his wife delivering their baby. I almost asked if they had the tape of DDP and Big Cat Hughes from Fort Myers instead.

Two days after Noelle's birth, the wrestlers all gathered at CNN Center for our first ever meeting with Ted Turner. Now, I respect Ted for his vision and his philanthropy, and he helped make a very good movie about the Battle of Gettysburg, but when it came to his wrestling product, Ted was a little out of touch. It seemed as if the only wrestler in the room that Ted knew was Ric Flair. "I know Ric wrestled there—Ric, how do you feel about that—Ric, Ric, Ric." Eric Bischoff may not have been a great announcer, and his later on-air heel persona may have, at times, made me want to throw a brick through my TV, but hey—he was no fool. He knew where his bread was buttered. Ric Flair became the new booker about eleven seconds after the meeting adjourned.

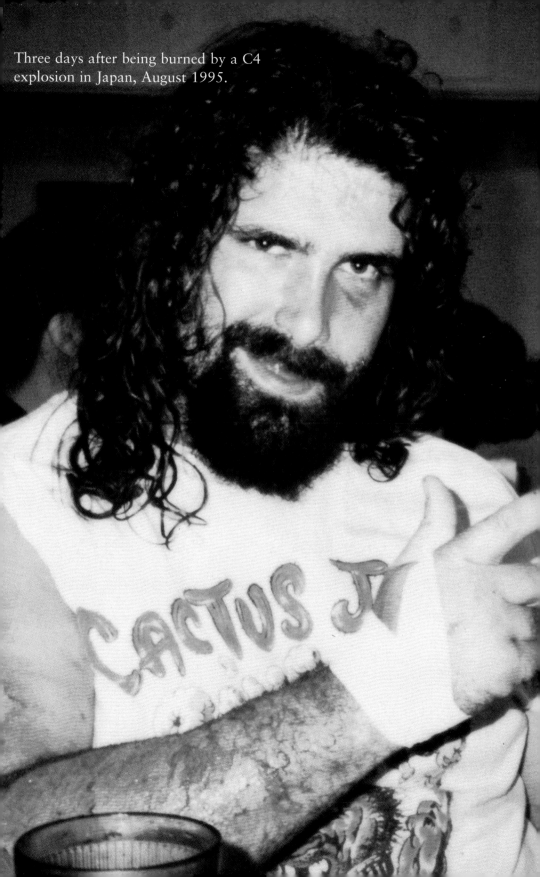

Three days after being burned by a C4 explosion in Japan, August 1995.

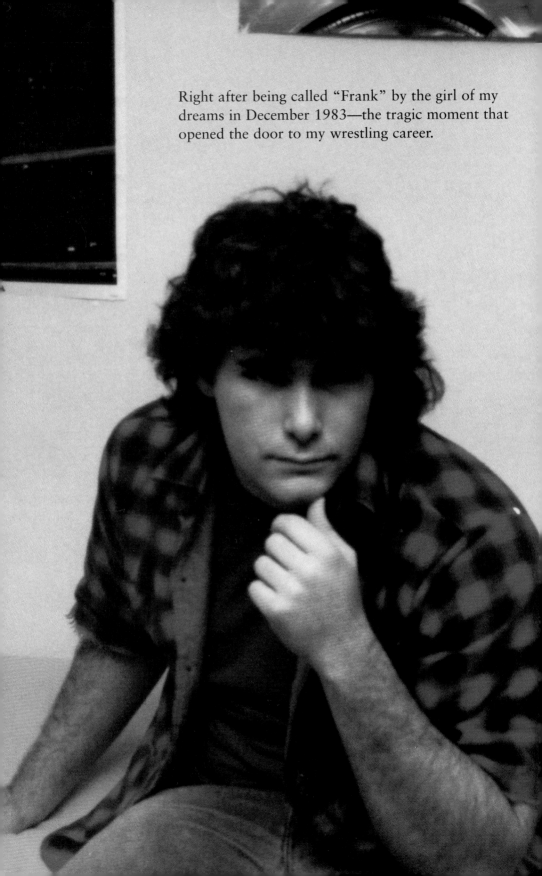

Right after being called "Frank" by the girl of my dreams in December 1983—the tragic moment that opened the door to my wrestling career.

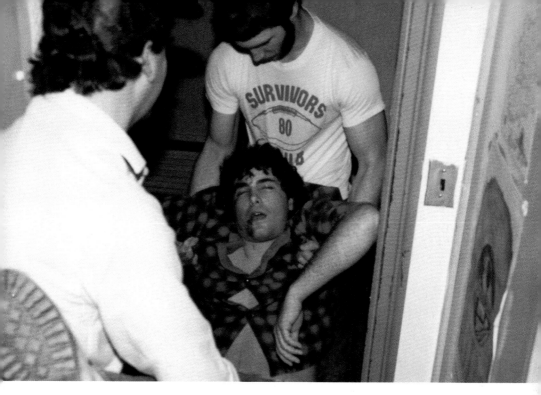

Above: A shot from the photo essay that was a precursor to the Dude Love films, December 1983.

Below: Dude Love goes down for the count during the filming of *The Loved One*, January 1985.

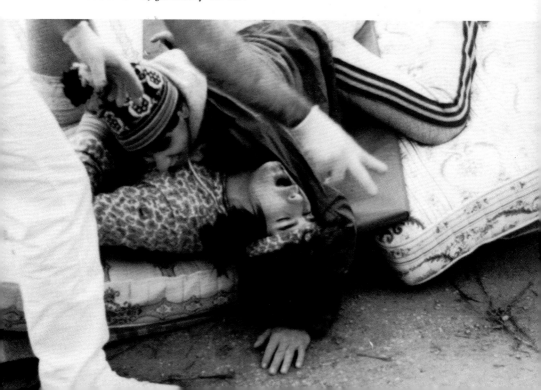

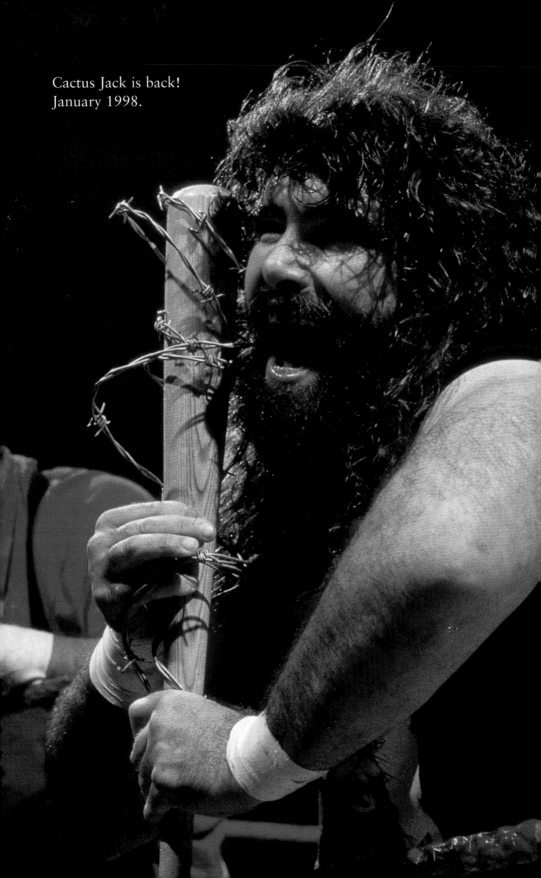

Cactus Jack is back!
January 1998.

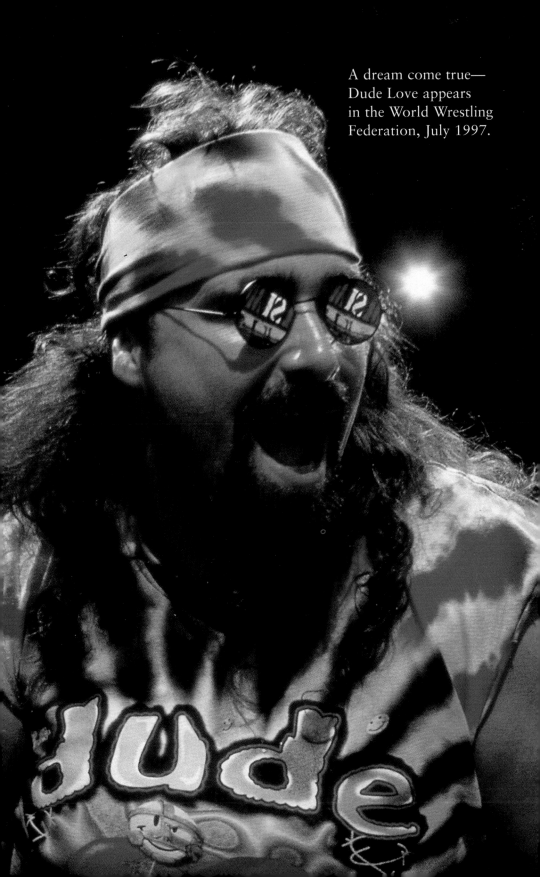

A dream come true—
Dude Love appears
in the World Wrestling
Federation, July 1997.

The Dude does some damage during a classic bout with Stone Cold, May 1998.

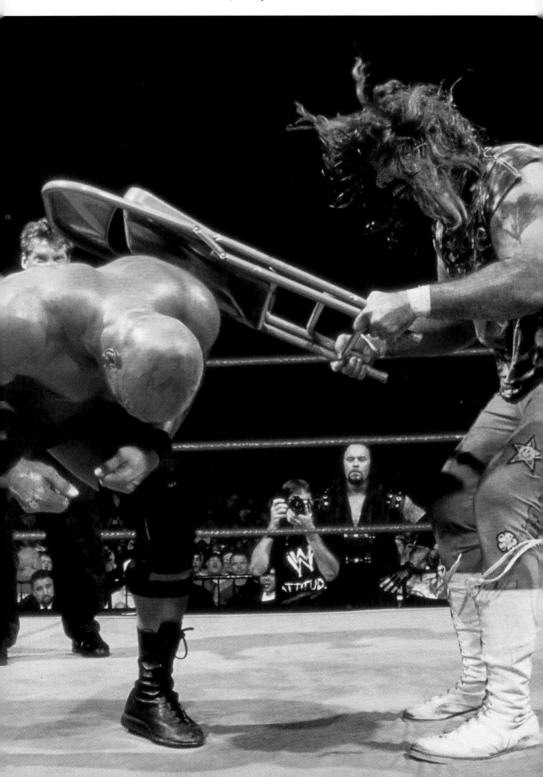

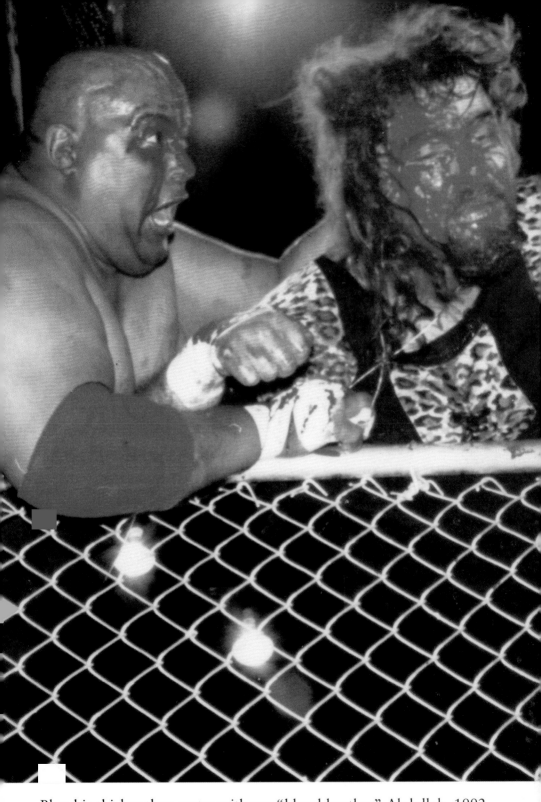

Blood is thicker than water with my "blood brother" Abdullah, 1992.

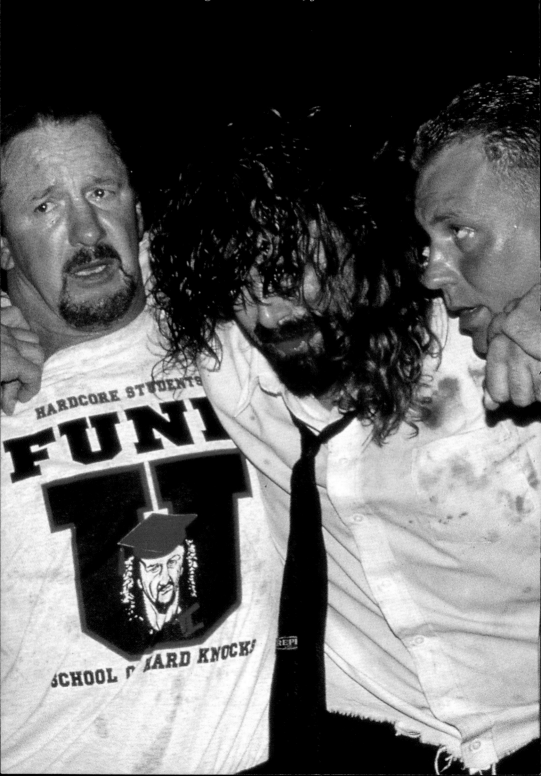

Being helped out of the ring by the Funker
following Hell in a Cell, June 1998.

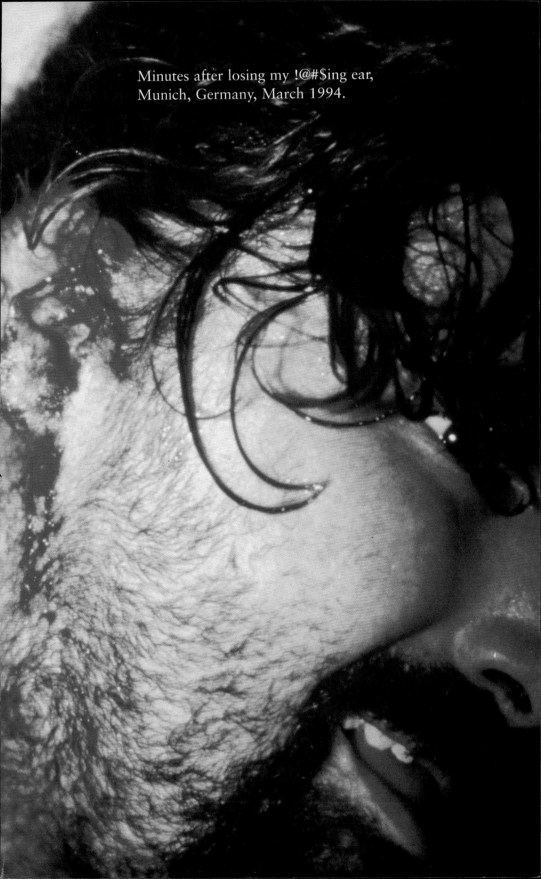

Minutes after losing my !@#$ing ear,
Munich, Germany, March 1994.

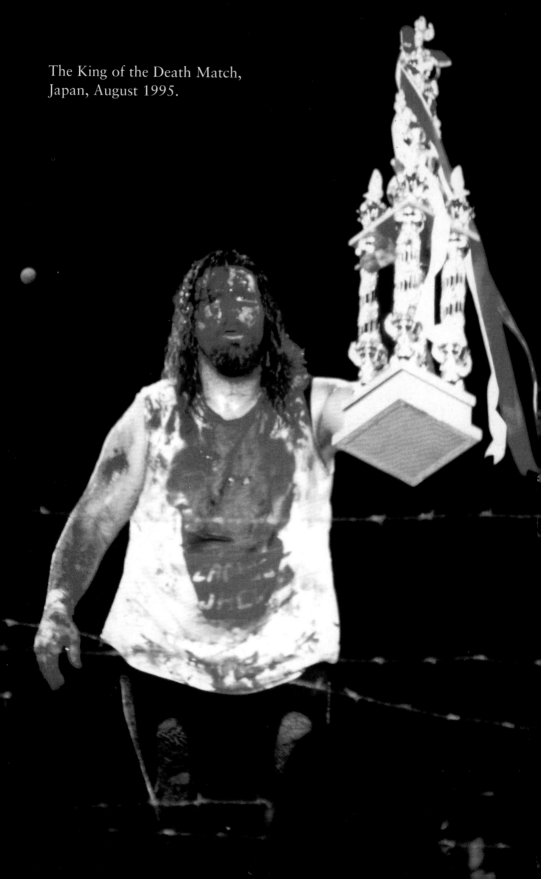

The King of the Death Match,
Japan, August 1995.

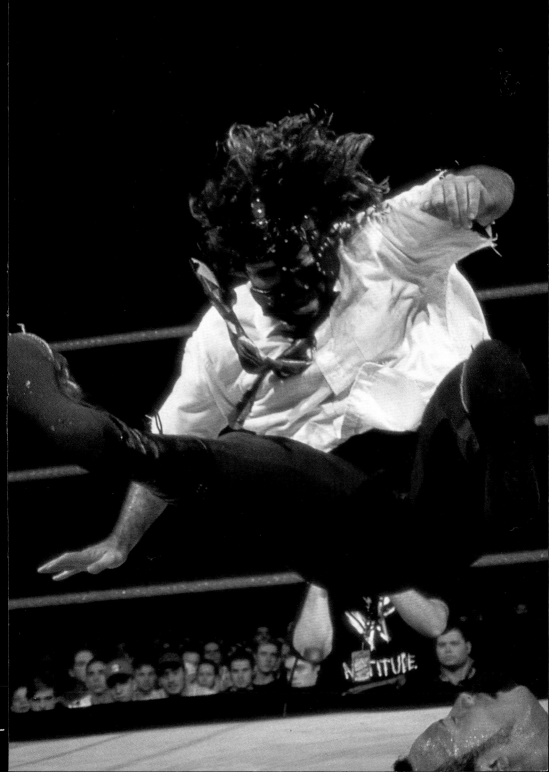

Dropping a leg on The Rock during a classic
title matchup, February 1999.

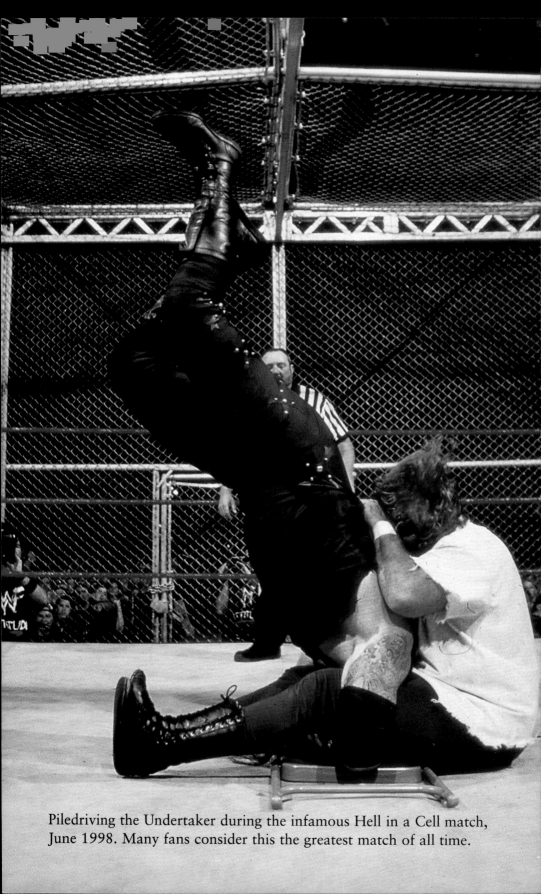

Piledriving the Undertaker during the infamous Hell in a Cell match, June 1998. Many fans consider this the greatest match of all time.

Battling Triple H in 1999.

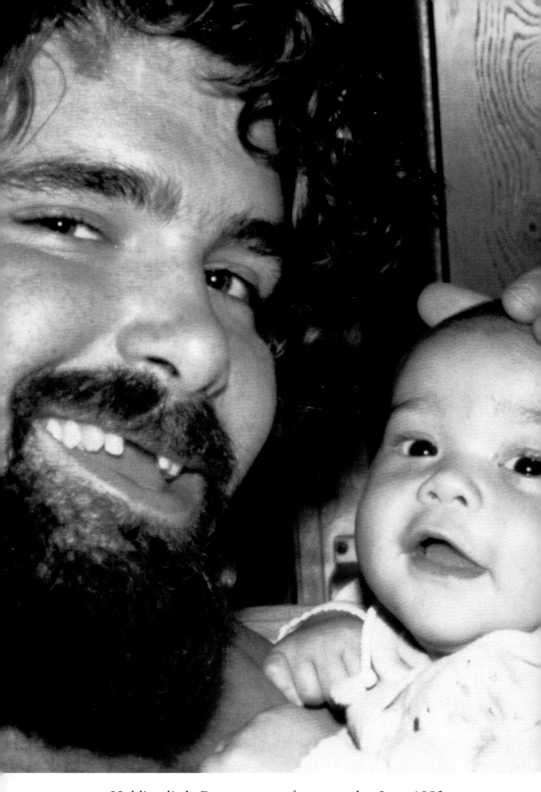

Holding little Dewey at age four months, June 1992.

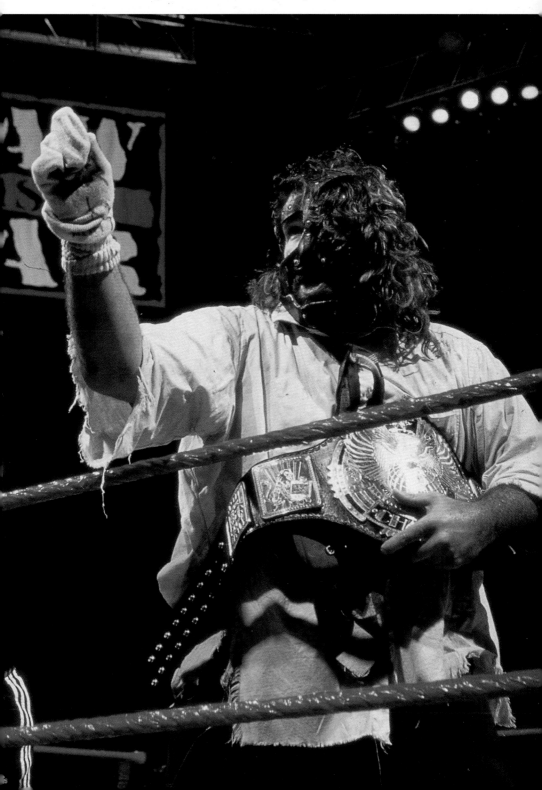

"Yo, Adrian, I did it!" Winning my first World Wrestling Federation title after beating The Rock's candy ass, December 1998.

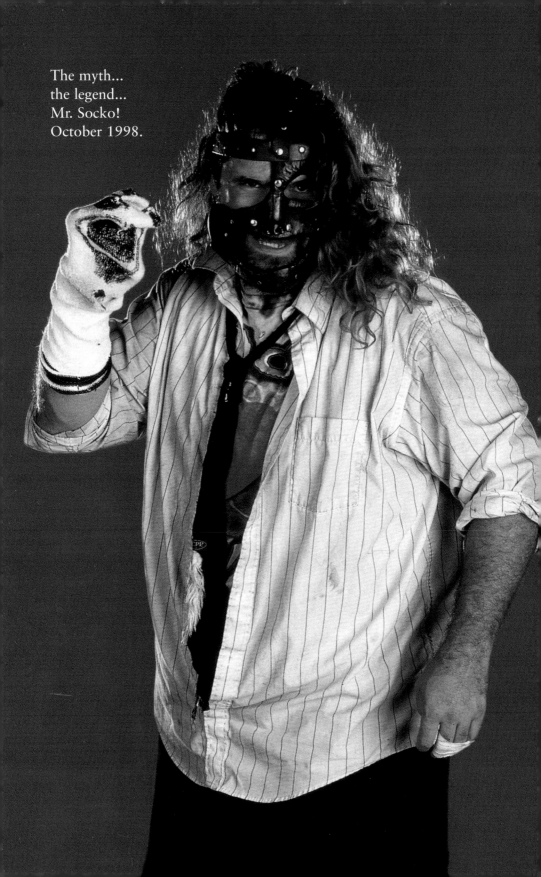

The myth...
the legend...
Mr. Socko!
October 1998.

The next few months were uneventful, as I teamed with Maxx and wondered if I was going to ever get another chance on top. Bischoff had made the decision to curtail most of the road shows, and instead concentrate on the television product. That was fine with me. If I was going to hate the company, I would much rather hate it at home with Colette and the two children.

In March, we headed for Germany and the hangman incident that cost me my ear. I called Colette the next afternoon from Germany, expecting sympathy to be showered on me. I had attempted to call home after my operation, but was told that Eric would take care of it, and to get some rest. "Hi, Colette, how are you?" I said into the receiver, waiting for the sobs that I so richly deserved. Instead, I got: "The damn dog is barking, I think Noelle has an ear infection, and Dewey's being a grouch."

"Did anyone from the office call you?" I asked slowly, already knowing the answer to my question.

"What happened, are you all right?" screamed Colette, apparently deducing from my question that something indeed had gone wrong.

"Well, I've got good news and bad news," I started. "The good news is I'm coming home tomorrow—the bad news is that my right ear isn't coming with me."

The hospital in Munich wanted to keep me for a full week, but when I found out all they were keeping me for was intravenous antibiotics, I convinced them to let me fly home, where I would continue the IV treatment. I checked into the hospital in Atlanta, where they assigned me a registered nurse, and I headed home. Believe it or not, I was actually in high spirits, because I knew, I just knew, that no one could screw this angle up. I guess I should have known better.

I showed up at Center Stage theater the next week, raring to go—wondering what the brainpower in WCW had come up with to take advantage of this unexpected "gift."

To me, this would be a booker's dream. Forget the bogus knee injury angles, this was a certifiable gold mine. I mean, how could anyone not see the money in a Cactus vs. Vader "you tore off my ear, you son of a bitch" grudge match? The match would sell itself. It would be so easy, it would—oops, I forgot we were talking about WCW here. I had one more match with Vader, about a month later in a little theater in Columbia, South Carolina, in front of a thousand fans. Not exactly what I would call making the most of the situation.

I knew also that all of Flair's talk about turning me into a top heel was bullshit, as well. In some ways, I'm fortunate that I lost my ear, because if I'd let Flair have a say in my career for another year, I'd be cleaning pools right now. So when Flair is retired, and the fans are singing his praises (and rightfully so) as one of the greatest of all time, I hope those same fans will remember that as a booker, this is the same guy that let both Mick Foley and Stone Cold Steve Austin walk away.

With depression setting in, and with the knowledge that I had no future in WCW, I scheduled, with Bischoff's approval, an operation that would reconstruct a new ear out of one of my ribs and the cartilage behind my ear. Eric assured me that as the accident occurred inside the ring, I would be fully compensated during my six-month absence. After that, it would be September again—time to call J. J.

I had one more match before the surgery—a Chicago street fight (an anything-goes, falls-count-anywhere match) that would team me and Maxx in a war with the Nasty Boys. I knew it was my last match, but I just couldn't get up for it. I wondered, "How am I going to get through this without stinking the place up?" The answer was simple. Survival. Jerry Saggs broke a pool cue over my head, and Brian Knobbs nearly dented my skull. The Nasties were sloppy as hell, and more than a little dangerous, but they knew how to brawl. About a minute into this thing, I realized that I'd better start fighting or I was going to get killed out there. About three minutes in, I realized we were in the midst of something pretty special. Saggs attempted to piledrive me on a table for the finish. The table buckled under our weight and we crashed to the ramp. As I got up, Saggs pushed me and I fell backward off the five-foot ramp and onto the cold, hard concrete below. I didn't land flat, however, and I knew that my shoulder was injured. But at least I'd earned the right to rest, right? Not quite yet. Saggs hopped down off the ramp, and I winced when I saw Knobbs throw him a scoop shovel. It was plastic, but I knew with this crazy bastard swinging, it would hurt just the same. He raised the shovel high overhead, almost like an axe. I remembered what DeNucci had taught us about protecting our teeth and nose, and I turned my head to the side. Saggs proceeded to hit me about as hard as another human being could, but at least I'd be out of WCW.

Man, you think I would have learned by now, right? I was awakened two days later by the sound of the telephone. It was Kevin Sullivan.

"Brotha, I need a fayva."

"Kevin, hey, what can I do?"

"Brotha, Evad blew out his knee, I don't have a pahtnah—brotha, you might think I'm crazy, but I think if the two of us teamed in Philadelphia, we'd blow the roof off the fuckin' place."

I tried to tell Kevin about my ear operation, but he could be a very hard person to say no to. His wrestling "brother" Evad was so named because his character supposedly had dyslexia and couldn't say "Dave." The two of them were scheduled to take on the Nasties at the next month's Pay-Per-View *Slamboree* in Philadelphia. Without a partner at *Slamboree*, Sullivan's whole stint with WCW might be in jeopardy, I felt, but in retrospect I should have realized that, as Kevin himself had once told me, he was like the phoenix, and eventually would have risen again.

Later, Flair called and said, "I want you to come to TV today." I tried to tell Flair about the operation, but he persuaded me by saying, "We want to go all the way with you and Kevin." For some reason, in a decision I would soon regret, I went to TV.

It would be easy for me to point fingers and blame people for bringing me back. The truth, however, is twofold. First, I felt that by going "all the way" with me and Kevin, my value would be raised and that I would maybe, just maybe, get that elusive pay raise, although probably for me, finding the Ark of the Covenant would be easier. And second, I really felt that wrestling in front of the Philadelphia fans might lift me out of the emotional mire in which I was walking.

I really had become a miserable bastard. I hadn't cut the grass in three weeks. I had a two-year-old son and a four-month-old daughter that I barely had the energy to play with. My vaunted lovemaking skills were now barely adequate. Worst of all, I had rented *Sophie's Choice* and watched it twice . . . in a row. As mesmerizing as Meryl Streep's performance is, it's not exactly the type of film that makes you want to go out and dance a jig. The thought of a big showdown in front of my favorite audience was just the thing I needed.

I went to TV that day with a renewed sense of purpose. Kevin and I revived our old Slaughterhouse chemistry, even though I was no longer "in urgent need of advice." We were on fire—until we went to Orlando.

Orlando was the site of WCW's syndicated television tapings.

Every three months, we would head to Disney MGM Studios to film thirteen episodes of the most boring wrestling shows ever witnessed by human eyes. The wrestling was an "attraction" at the park, and a new theme park audience of about 300 fans was brought in for every new show. The fans would boo or cheer according to a sign that said "boo" or "cheer," so although the studio was noisy as hell, there wasn't an ounce of genuine emotion in the place. Most of the matches stunk, and because it was Disney, nothing that could be construed as violence was allowed. But, because the tapings covered so many weeks of syndication, a wrestler was able to get a decent idea of where his career was going—and mine was going nowhere.

Kevin and I were not on any of the television shows—no interviews, no angles, no run-ins, no matches—no nothing. The second to last nail was hammered when I overheard Paul Orndorff and and his tag team partner Paul Roma giving an interview about how they had defeated Cactus Jack and Kevin Sullivan for the belts. At this point, Kevin and I hadn't even won the belts. This was really not what I considered "going all the way" with us. This meant that even if Kevin and I set the world on fire as champions, it would all be for nothing. I was, once again, being booked to fail. Kevin and I had a meeting with Flair, and even though Naitch and Sullivan had been friends for two decades, I did all our talking.

"Ric, a few weeks ago, you said you were going to go all the way with us, but I've been here [in Orlando] three days, and we haven't been on television for three days."

Flair, who only rarely drops his perfect gentleman manners, honored me by doing so. "Hey, last I heard, you wanted to take six months off for psychological counseling." Flair then tried to draw a comparison between me and Barry Windham, who was at the end of nursing a year-long knee ligament injury. Barry had been paid the entire time, to the tune of eight grand a week. This was a perfect example of office gossip leading to factual errors, and the very rare occasion that the old cliché "When you assume it makes an ass out of you and me" was actually correct.

"Ric," I said, "I think you've got a few things mixed up. I did want six months off, but that was for ear surgery. I canceled that because you asked me to come back. I am seeing a psychologist for post-amputation depression, but even if WCW does pay for it, we're talking about four hundred dollars, not four hundred thousand like Barry. And to insinuate that I'd milk any injury is an insult."

Flair took this all in. "So you want to wrestle?" he asked.

"Yes I do, Ric—until my contract is up, you can book me on every show you run."

The next day, I was booked in a Texas Tornado Match with Vader. Actually, it was a Texas Death Match, but, being in Disney, a few concessions had to be made. In Texas Death Match rules, pinfalls count, but they don't end the match. The wrestler has ten seconds to answer the bell. The match continues until one man can't answer the bell.

Vader and I picked up right where we had left off. We had actually been given a little leeway by WCW to get a little rough, but we took it a few steps further. I had Vader rocking and reeling with punches that were thrown damn near as hard as I could. I gave him a chairshot that had him seeing stars. I went for the elbow off the ring apron, but Harley tripped me and I tumbled to the floor. Vader then threw back the blue protective mats, and exactly one year later, to the day, that my foot and hand had gone numb in Atlanta, powerbombed me on the cold, hard concrete floor.

Vader covered me for the easy pin. But the match wasn't over yet. The referee began his count as I lay prone. One, two, three—no movement. Four, five—I started to move. Six, seven—I was on my knees. Eight, nine—Cactus Jack was on his feet. Then, with the ref's back turned, Harley hit me from behind, and I went down. Ten—I lost the match. The loss, as is usually the case in our sport, didn't really matter, because in this case the real victory was a moral one. I had taken the powerbomb and had gotten up. Nothing could be simpler.

I went to the back feeling like the weight of the world was off my shoulders. It's amazing how a good match can make you feel that way. I talked excitedly with Eric about the story of the match. I told him about the coincidence of the two matches occurring on the same day one year apart. He agreed it was great timing, and assured me that they would play it up when it aired on TV. Even though Jim Ross was working for the competition, I could hear his voice in my head. "The referee is counting, folks, but it's just a formality—this one is over. What we really need is some medical attention down here. But wait, what's this, Cactus Jack is starting to move. My God, he's on his knees! Ladies and gentleman, in twenty-five years, this is the damnedest thing I've ever seen. Cactus Jack is up, Cactus Jack is up!" It didn't matter who was calling the match, however—this was too good to miss. Only a complete idiot could screw this thing up.

I went back to our hotel, the Residence Inn. I couldn't stop sweating and I was lightheaded, but I was on a natural high. Even with a probable concussion, I was in the mood to celebrate. We went to a place called Jungle Jim's and I scarfed down the biggest steak on the menu, while Colette turned her back and breast-fed Noelle. As good as my steak was, I couldn't help but feel a little envious of my daughter.

Kevin and I were raising havoc every night with the Nasty Boys. At a show in Melbourne, Florida, in late April, Kevin and I were taking the fight to the Nasties outside the ring. I was working over Saggs, while Kevin tried to get a fan's beer to throw at Knobbs. The fan resisted, but Kevin physically insisted, and he let a three-quarter-full beer fly. When Knobbs turned around, however, it was obvious that beer was not the liquid that had been inhabiting the cup. Knobbs's pasty white face and a major portion of his bleached blond Mohawk were now brown. Tobacco juice was everywhere. Knobbs reached with his hands and tried to clear it from his eyes. He opened his mouth, and more came spilling out. He snorted and some came from his nostrils as well. "Sorry, brotha," Kevin said, laughing, with a warmth that would have made Bill Watts proud. It may have been the most disgusting thing I've ever seen in wrestling. And that's coming from someone who's seen the Mean Street Posse in action.

The next day, we traveled to Fort Lauderdale. I tripled up in a room with Steve Austin and Steve Regal. These were two of my favorite guys to travel with, and we were looking forward to having a good time. Now, nevermind the fact that these three big-time wrestlers were so cheap that they actually had three guys jammed into a flea-bitten Econolodge. The key thing was that the lodge was right across the street from the beach, and having practically grown up in the Atlantic Ocean as a kid, I was going to be hitting the surf as soon as I could throw my trunks on.

The three of us walked across the street, and I dove in gracefully and headed out to sea, while Austin and Regal soaked up some rays in the beautiful South Florida sun. I floated on my back for a few minutes, several hundred yards from shore, and when I looked to the beach, I saw that both Steves were gone. Then, in the distance, I saw them walking back across the street. A minute later, I could see them sitting by the pool. "That's strange," I thought. "Trading the ocean for the pool." But hey, I wasn't going to let those party poopers ruin my fun. I frolicked some more. After a while, I headed in to shore.

I got to the sand, reached for my towel, and began to dry off. I looked around to see if any hot chicks had been checking me out, but didn't notice any. "Sure are a lot of guys here, though," I thought. I looked some more and saw two guys holding hands. The idea that something was a little odd was starting to sink in. Then I saw two guys kissing, and the sinking process started to accelerate. As did the sprinting process. I don't think David Hasselhoff could have kicked up the sand any faster, as I hightailed it off the beach, across highway A1A, and into the pool area of the Fort Lauderdale Econolodge. Austin and Regal were laughing hysterically. "You pricks," I yelled, even while laughing myself. "You left me on a gay beach!"

After the matches, we returned to the hotel and headed out to get something to eat. The hotel was located on the main strip of the city, where plenty of restaurants were located, so we decided to walk. "Hold on, guys," I said after we'd taken only a few steps. I had just spotted a phone booth, and realized I hadn't called home yet. "You guys go on without me—just sit somewhere outside, so I can see you— I'll catch up in a minute." I began to talk, but within a minute or two, Austin and Regal were back. I was flattered. "Man," I thought, as Colette whispered sweet nothings into my ear. "These guys must really like me." When I got off the phone, I realized that affection had nothing to do with their decision to wait for my company.

"There are fags everywhere," a somewhat rattled Austin yelled.

"Yeah," added Regal in his distinguished British way. "The whole bloomin' street is filled with dinnermashers."

I quickly sized up the situation. Regal, a handsome blond chap, was wearing a casual ensemble of golf shirt, tennis shorts, and flip-flops. Austin, who at this point in his career also had short blond hair, was wearing a Gold's gym tank top, high-tops, and a pair of decidedly non-toughest-SOB-in-wrestling-looking fluorescent pink shorts. As two good-looking, well-toned blond guys walking through what was apparently a gay area of town, they would look like a couple of pinup candidates for *Honcho* magazine. Add a big, hairy, ugly guy like Cactus Jack into the mix, however, and the picture was a little more innocent.

We sat down outside at a little restaurant and ordered from the menu. Austin ordered a grilled chicken dinner and a white wine spritzer. No, just kidding—it was a beer. Regal ordered a hamburger, but asked that the extra grease be patted with a napkin, to make it healthier. I too asked for a burger, but asked that the napkin used on Regal's beef be wrung out and dripped on mine.

"I'm sorry," the waitress said, looking as if she were at the end of a long day. "Our cook is pretty drunk—he can make you a cold sandwich, though."

The three of us thought about it, but opted instead to just order beverages. I looked at the table. There was a big splatter of picante sauce on it that had been bothering me since we sat down. I have been involved in some of the grisliest matches in wrestling history, but for some reason, I hate to look at food that has already been eaten. Especially tomato-based products like picante sauce. "Excuse me, ma'am," I said. "But would you mind cleaning off our table?"

The waitress sprung into action. With one quick movement her hand hit the table, and with only the sound of bare flesh sweeping plastic, the aromatic mixture of tomato, onions, and cilantro spilled to the cold concrete floor below. She then looked at her forefinger, and with an equally quick sucking action, vanquished the remnants. On the turnoff scale, it may not have been on a par with Test vs. Rodney, but it was damn close.

The next morning, we woke up and fumbled through the television stations on the remote control. "Let's keep it there," I requested when the sterile ambiance of *WCW Worldwide* flickered onto the screen. My match with Vader was on. *Boom, boom, boom*—I was really nailing big Leon. I was nervous with anticipation as Vader threw back the mat. They hadn't made reference to the injury of exactly one year ago yet, but now the story would surely unfold. Vader picked me up for the powerbomb and sent me crashing down to the concrete. *Splat.* To tell you the truth, this one actually looked more devastating than the one in '93. I listened for the brilliant call—sometimes the right words can really cement an image in the fans' minds. Here it comes. Bobby Heenan was the first to comment on this historic, career-turning moment. "That'll give you Excedrin headache number nine," said the brain, with about as much raw, naked emotion as Al Gore on sedatives. "Indeed it will," added Schiovanne. Then—nothing. Or nothing that I had suggested, visualized, hoped for, or at least, in a worst-case scenario, would have settled for. No "My God, he's on his knees!" No "This is the damnedest thing I've ever seen!" No "One year ago to this very day . . ." No talk about last year's injury. No moral victory. Just "Excedrin headache number nine." I had said it would take a total idiot to screw it up, and, by golly, they hadn't let me down. This was the final nail. I thought about it for two days, and made my decision to quit World Championship Wrestling.

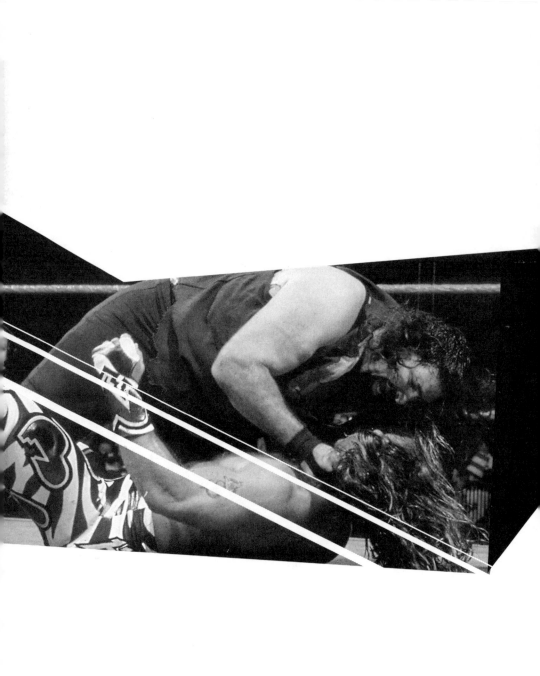

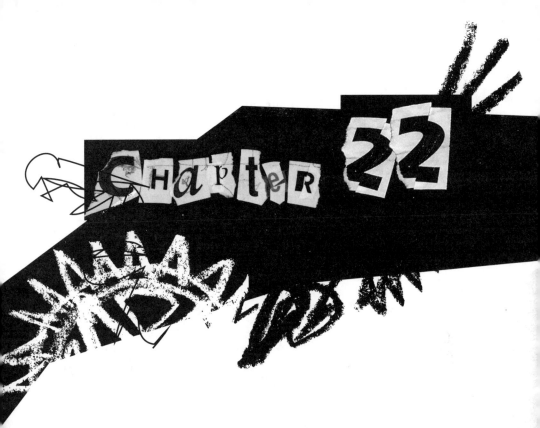

Leaving a six-figure job is not an easy decision to make, especially with the uncertainty of the independent wrestling scene. Bischoff was surprised when I told him the news, but he did not seem all that upset about it. Colette was a different story. "What do you mean, you're leaving—you've got a four-month-old daughter, Mickey," Colette yelled, trying to reason with me.

"We'll be all right," I assured her. "I can work lots of places."

"But you can't make this kind of money anywhere else," she continued.

"Listen, hon, if I stick around, I will be worthless within a year," I fired back. "At least this way, I can buy some time, and maybe come back when things are different."

The wrestlers were surprised as well. Arn Anderson walked up to me shortly after he heard of my decision and asked me about it. "Jack, we aren't even working as much anymore, why would you want to leave?"

Now Arn was a guy I respected, and I wanted him to understand my motivation. "Double A," I began, as I searched for words that wouldn't include blasting Flair, who was a close friend of his. "I've worked too hard for too long to have a joke made out of my career."

I then recounted the "Excedrin headache number nine" example.

"Point well taken," Arn agreed.

Four months is a hell of a long time to give notice for. Usually when a guy is on his way out, the company resorts to burying his career with defeat after defeat on television, or simply phasing him out. A guy could suffer a lot of defeats in four months. Looking back, I probably should have just rescheduled my surgery and taken off after the Philadelphia show. That way, I could have sat back, collected money, left the company on good terms—and with a right ear, no less. For some reason, that's not my style. That would be like me hitting a wiffleball to right field or like my dad hiring a typist to finish his dissertation. The easy way just wasn't in the Foley blood. Instead, I forged on, almost daring them to bury me. In a shocking reversal of company policy, they didn't. As a matter of fact, they pushed the hell out of me, at least for a little while. For the next four months, Cactus Jack was all over the television. Never once, however, did anyone try to persuade me to stay. In the seven months since I had signed my contract, someone must have authorized Bischoff to open up the purse strings, as wrestlers who had never worked a main event match in their lives began cashing bigger checks than I ever had. Not surprisingly, the purse strings were never opened near me.

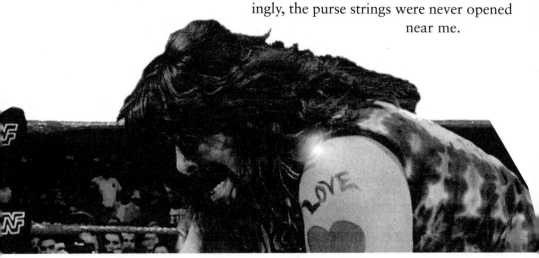

Kevin and I won the tag team titles at *Slamboree* in Philadelphia in a tremendous match. It might have been even better than the one in Chicago. It was especially gratifying to have such a great match with the knowledge that my dad was in the crowd, as were longtime friends John McNulty and John Imbriani. Even Eric Bischoff noticed how excited I was about the bout, saying, "Now that's the Cactus Jack I want to see."

A month later we successfully defended out belts against Saggs and Knobbs. I had a 300-mile drive home, before heading out early the next morning for another match in Philadelphia—this time in the cozy confines of the ECW arena. This match had a little controversy surrounding it and would lead to considerably more in the future.

ECW was a small promotion based out of Philadelphia that prided itself on its rabid fans and hardcore wrestling style. Todd Gordon, who had been the financial backer for Joel Goodhart's TWA, was the owner and was a big fan of mine. Paul E. Dangerously, wrestling's mad scientist, was their booker and had, on a shoestring budget, put together the most exciting wrestling show on television. Kevin, who had worked for ECW before his return to WCW, was a close friend of Todd's, and he hoped to act as a liaison between the two companies. At that point, the two sides were even looking at the idea of doing talent exchanges. As it turned out, WCW worked its way around exchange by offering ECW talent big money, and very nearly sucked it dry. The company today stays afloat due to a few loyal wrestlers and the creativity of Paul E.

Using Kevin's help, Todd wanted to book a "dream match" between Cactus Jack and an ECW wrestler named Sabu. Sabu was fast becoming the biggest name on the independent circuit. As a nephew of the original Sheik (a sixties and seventies wrestling legend), Sabu had grown up wanting to be a star like his uncle. After years of setting up rings and paying his dues, he had finally caught on, first in Japan, where gory death matches had left his body zigzagged with thick bands of scars, and then in the States, where he had become Paul E.'s biggest star. Without uttering a single word, he had captured the ECW fans' imagination with his wide array of suicidal maneuvers. Todd felt that this match would be a gold mine.

I did, too. But I wanted it to be my gold mine. This was a match that promoters around the country were going to want to book, and I was going to give it to them—but only when the time was right. As long as I stayed under contract to WCW, the time wasn't right. I explained my feelings to everyone involved, but in the end, I was outvoted. This was an important match for both companies, and I had to go.

I thought we had a hell of a match. I later saw a tape, and still thought so. Unfortunately, expectations were so high for this match that they were impossible to live up to. There were people in that converted bingo hall who literally thought they were going to see someone die. When I finished the match, my lower back was in a great deal of pain. There was no shower in that little sweatbox arena, and my body started to break out in hives. I wanted nothing more than to have a hot shower and a clean bed, but remembering the importance of the match, I stuck around for three more hours until it was my time to do interviews. In them, I tried my best to put over ECW and Sabu, and explain what it felt like to lose to a better man. To illustrate just how upset I was, I spit on the WCW tag team belt.

I had no idea how much trouble my saliva would cause.

By the time I left the arena, I could barely walk. I ate dinner with Shane Douglas, who was now an ECW mainstay, and a couple of the other guys, and then I walked back to the hotel next door, with shuffling, six-inch steps. By six o'clock that morning, I had hives covering over half my body. I got up for a second shower and had trouble moving at all. I called a fan who brought me to the hospital. An emergency room can't do a whole lot for a back injury, but they diagnosed a strained muscle and sent me home. Now I know the pain of a torn abdominal muscle had been surprising to me. But a strain? Come on. Who did they think they were dealing with?

I had an MRI done on my lower back when I got to Atlanta. Back then, they needed to wait for a few days before getting the results. Nowadays, the results are almost instantaneous. In the interim, I actually started to feel better, and I began wrestling again.

The phone rang as I prepared to head to Center Stage for a match with Orndorff and Roma. Janie Engle was on the line, and she asked me if I'd "hold for Ric."

"Cactus," Flair began accusingly, "did you do an interview where you spit on the WCW tag team belt?" Now someone had told me that Gene Okerland had stooged off my ECW interview to Flair, after seeing it on the Sunshine Network in Florida, so I was prepared.

"Yeah Ric, I did," I said excitedly. "Did you see it?"

Flair seemed taken aback by my tone. "Why would you do an interview where you spit on the championship belt?" he inquired.

"Well, Ric," I explained to my boss, with even more excitement in my voice, "I wanted the fans to understand that as much as I valued that belt, I valued my pride a little more. By spitting on the belt, I felt that I was adding an exclamation point to that fact. I knew how important this match was for WCW, so I wanted to give a little something extra."

With that, Flair said he needed to take another call. I was all fired up. "Fuck him," I silently mouthed, while raising my middle finger in a Stone Cold salute. When Flair got back on the line, he said he had to go, but that he'd talk to me at TV. It would be great to say that I went there and verbally tore Naitch a new asshole, but the truth is that, not wanting to create waves, I apologized for disrespecting the image of the belt. Flair was pleasant enough about the whole thing, as I watched this forty-five-year old man comb back his hair as he looked in the mirror, as if he thought he was the Fonz. Heyyy!

A nurse showed me my MRI results, which revealed two bulging discs and one herniated disc. If you think of the discs in your back as jelly donuts, a bulge occurs if the jelly has started to put pressure on the donut, causing it to bulge, and a herniation is when the jelly actually squirts out. Well, my jelly had actually squirted out. The nurse left and Dr. Rosenrosen (the name has been changed to protect my bank account) walked in a few minutes later. He started in by saying, "Well, Michael, it looks like you've got two bulging discs."

I kept waiting for him to continue, but he didn't. Finally, I continued his diagnosis for him. "What about the herniated disc?" I asked, which startled him.

"Oh, how did you know about that?"

My reply was simple. "I read the report." He was clearly caught off-guard, and began backpedaling with his brain. "Well, it is but it isn't," came his somewhat less than scientific reply. That was all I needed to hear. I took my MRIs and sought a second opinion. Dr. Armstrong was the guy wrestlers went to when they didn't trust Rosenrosen. Armstrong took one look at my MRIs and strongly advised me not to wrestle until I saw a back specialist. He said the MRI detected a portion of the disc that had fragmented and was floating freely in my spinal column. If this fragment lodged in the wrong area, it could be serious trouble. Unfortunately, I had to leave for Florida the next day and didn't have time to see a specialist. Dr. Armstrong wished me luck and sent me off with a note that read, "Do not wrestle. To do so would risk serious and permanent injury including, but not limited to: loss of control of bowel and bladder function, loss of sensation in extremities, and paralysis. Do not wrestle until seen by a specialist."

I called WCW and told them the news, but told them that I would come to Florida anyway. When I got to the Residence Inn, Kevin called me in to his room. "What's going on here?" he asked.

"They don't believe me, do they?" I said sadly, knowing that my question was merely rhetorical.

"Of course they don't," Kevin shot back. "Ric thinks you did this because he yelled at you about spitting on the belt."

I was getting hot. "Where is he?"

I went to a boardroom, where Flair was sitting with several other members of the booking committee. "Cactus," Flair began, the tone of his voice sounding like trouble to me. "Kevin tells me you won't be able to wrestle tomorrow, is that true?"

"Yes, Ric, it is," I answered.

"Are you sure?" he shot back, as if I were on trial.

"Yes, I am, Ric," I answered again.

Now he'd hit a nerve. I pulled out Dr. Armstrong's note, and with more than a little anger in my voice addressed the Nature Boy. "I've got a legitimate medical note from a respected orthopedic surgeon that tells me I would be risking loss of bowel and bladder control and paralysis if I wrestle. I'm actually scared, Ric, and none of you seem to give a damn, and for once in my life I'm going to put myself and my family before this business. I am not going to wrestle."

"Is this true?" he said to someone whose identity escapes me.

"Well," the unknown man told Flair, "the doctor did say he could use some time off."

"But what about tomorrow?" Flair inquired.

"The doctor says that one more match shouldn't make a difference," the unknown man answered.

Now it was my turn to step back in. I explained the "it is, but it isn't" diagnosis, and stressed the second opinion.

"That's true, Ric," unknown said, actually backing me up on this matter. "A lot of the boys don't trust Rosenrosen, so they go to Dr. Armstrong."

"Look," I said, "my note says, 'Don't wrestle until seeing a back specialist'—if you can get me to a specialist who can give me a milogram and a CAT scan, and if that doctor says I can wrestle, then I will." Away I went to the Sand Lake Regional Hospital.

Unfortunately, the hospital was not able to give me those tests on short notice. The doctors echoed Dr. Armstrong's advice before I left. I should have listened, but I didn't. When I got back to the Residence,

I went to the boardroom, opened the door, and said, "I'll wrestle, but I'm not doing anything risky."

"You see how soon they forget." I was on the floor stretching at the Orlando arena when a familiar, gruff voice addressed me. I looked up and saw Harley. There was sadness in his eyes. "Everything you've done for them, and this is how they repay you."

I didn't say anything, but nodded my head. If I'd spoken at all, I very well might have cried.

"Cactus," he continued, "I hope you remember this night for a long time."

"You know something, Harley—I will." I sent Harley a Christmas card that year that said simply, "I wish the office had done half as much for me as you have." Two years later, his wife told me how much it had meant to him.

I did wrestle that night, and I was scared as hell. It was the worst Pay-Per-View match that I have ever been in, and the fans knew it. Now, I've been in some stinkers before, but I always had this feeling inside me that no matter how bad things sucked, I could always somehow pull it out of the gutter. I got that same feeling in Orlando that night as we cluster fucked to a symphony of silence, but I waited on the ring apron until the feeling went away. After twenty-two minutes of a match that was about nineteen minutes too long, we dropped the tag team titles to Orndorff and Roma—just as they had so mysteriously predicted over ten weeks earlier.

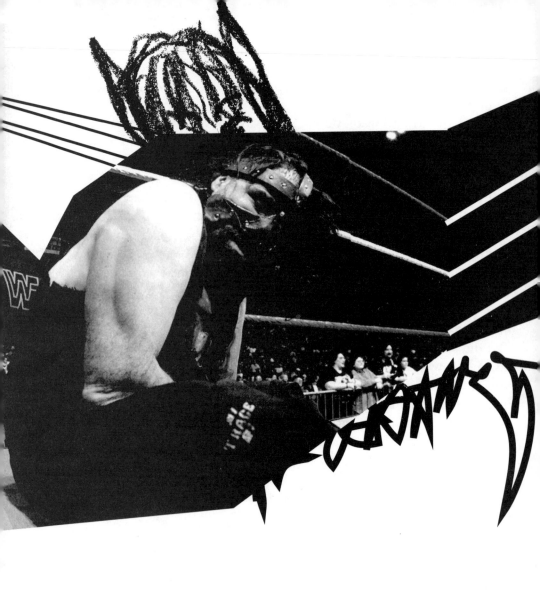

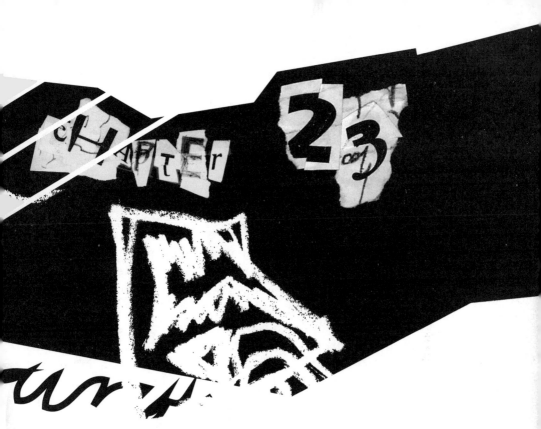

CHAPTER 23

ECW turn

By this point, it was clear that due
to irreconcilable differences, the remaining months of the WCW–Cactus
Jack marriage weren't going to be happy ones. Gary Juster, a company
attorney, told me that they would be willing to let me leave a month
early with full pay, on the condition that I came back at the September
Pay-Per-View and wrestled Kevin Sullivan. That sat fine with me, and
Juster said they'd work on the legal aspects.

I still had one more controversy to handle, however. The phone
rang, and I was dumb enough to answer it. I should have just sat at
home and let the machine pick it up, or better yet, thrown both the
phone and the machine into Lake Alatoona, but I didn't think quick
enough. It was Janie Engle, and she said that Flair had a big angle to
turn me heel on Kevin and he needed me at TV.

"I thought you guys were done with me," I said to Janie.

"I know," she replied, "but baseball went on strike, and Turner's
giving us more hours to fill, and Ric really needs you."

"Damn," I thought as I hung up the phone, "I don't want to be a
heel." It was early August and since I had given my notice three
months earlier, my phone had been ringing steadily with independent
offers. I had already taken several opening dates with ECW and some

other groups as well, and was booked on a two-week tour of Austria. My weight was down to 280, and with my back pain reduced (it'll never be completely gone) I was really in a groove. For merchandising purposes, a must on the independent scene, it was vital that I be considered a "good guy." But what could I do? The wheels of the heel turn were already in motion.

I heard Flair's scenario, and it was exciting, except for the fact that it would cost me a fortune in potential independent merchandise revenue. I was dejected, and I asked veteran wrestler Rip Rogers, the cheapest man in wrestling, for his professional opinion. Despite the fact that Rip was a guy considered too weird even for this sport, I liked him and valued his opinion. Actually, I felt like Rip was probably the most talented guy in the business who never really "made it"— because his reputation preceded him and usually destroyed him. Once Barry Windham lost his keys when they dropped into the toilet and sank to the bottom of his cloudy brown Jack Daniel's diarrhea concoction. Barry thought the keys were lost for good, until Rip rolled up his sleeves and went to work. He emerged a moment later with the keys and a newfound respect/disgust from the boys. Another time, two wrestlers jokingly suggested they were going to have some "jailhouse romance" with Rip. "Go ahead," Rip said, pulling down his pants and spreading his cheeks. It was quite a sight to see Rip running backward down the hall, chasing the two wrestlers, his puckered starfish leading the charge.

"I really wish I could leave this place as a baby," I said, before adding, "This angle's going to change all that."

"No it won't," Rip shot back quickly and assuredly.

"You don't think leaving Kevin lying will turn me heel?" I asked.

"Cac," Rip said, laughing, "Kevin Sullivan is the least sympathetic character in the business, the fans will love you for it."

"What about Dave? He's sympathetic." I countered, waiting to see what the ketchup soup drinker would come back with.

"Yeah he is," Rip had to admit. "But Cac, even the fans can tell he's just a mediocre worker."

It was true. Dave Sullivan was one of the nicest guys in the business. So nice, in fact, that the boys would always mention what a hell of a guy he was before they mentioned what an abysmal worker he was. Sure enough, Rip's words came to fruition. When I dropped Kevin, the cheers were deafening. When I dropped Dave, they intensified further. By the time I finished giving my interview, I was as big a babyface as I'd ever been. I guess I'd be selling T-shirts and eight-by-ten glossies after all.

Later that night, Kevin called me at home. I had bolted out while Kevin was receiving medical attention, and was already on West Peachtree Street, with the night air blowing through my "good guy" hair, by the time he got to the dressing room. "Brotha," said Kevin, "you were the babyface out there tonight."

"I know," I said to Kevin compassionately, "but who would have ever thought it?"

A month later, I called Kevin from Austria, the day before our Pay-Per-View match in Roanoke, Virginia. I told him where I was, and that I'd be cutting it real close with my flight schedule. "Don't worry, though," I assured him, "I'll be there." I left a town in Austria, whose name escapes me right now, and drove three hours to Vienna. From Vienna, I caught a flight to Frankfurt, and after a three-hour layover, continued on to Atlanta. In Atlanta, I ran to barely meet my connecting flight to Roanoke, and once in Roanoke hailed a cab to the Civic Center. Pay-Per-Views usually require the talent to be at the building six hours before bell time. I got there fifteen minutes before the first match went on. Kevin and I were second.

"Brotha," a relieved Kevin said with a sigh, "we were panicking." My final WCW match was billed as a loser-leaves-WCW match. Because I already had three months of independent dates booked, the outcome was in about as much doubt as the night I showed up at the Sportatorium in Dallas with everything I owned stuffed into my '80 Plymouth Arrow.

"Give me a slam off the second turnbuckle to the floor" was all I said as I rushed to the dressing room.

As my Michael Hayes–penned entrance music, "Mr. Bang Bang," began, Kevin called out to me, "Brotha, do I stand on the floor or the apron when I throw you?"

I looked at the five-foot, seven-inch former Games-master and before stepping through the curtain for my final WCW match ever, answered his question. "Kevin, if you stand on the floor . . . you'll never reach me."

With no preparation, and with twenty-three hours of traveling behind me, I charged into Kevin. Guess what? We had a pretty good match. Anyone with an appreciation for spontaneity and give-and-take brawling would have enjoyed it especially. WCW had certain rules pertaining to violence, but we ignored those right off the bat. I mean, what were they going to do—fire me? The announcers were still trying to portray me as the bad guy, but the fans cheered me harder than ever. As for Kevin, well, the writing was on the wall, and out of necessity, he turned on poor "Evad" about a week later, leading to some of the

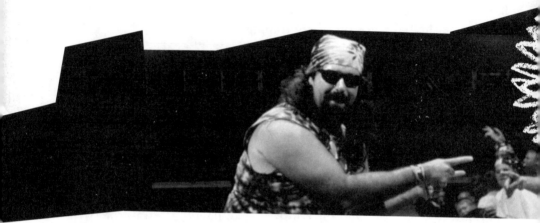

worst matches of all time. Kevin later had a run on top with Hogan and others, and as the man who replaced Flair as booker, was largely responsible for helping the company climb out of its creative hole.

Yeah, I lost the match. Looking at the fans, I made the decision to run into the crowd, where I was mobbed by hundreds of well-wishers, some of whom were genuinely moved. WCW could have shown this special moment, but they cut instead to a sterile, pretaped backstage interview. The thought hit me to disrobe gradually until all my wrestling attire was thrown to the fans, but, thankfully, common sense prevailed. After all, I would much rather be known as the guy who gave it his all, instead of the guy whose ass looked like a piece of Swiss cheese that had backed into a belt sander.

I was in the shower, cleansing not only my body, but three years of memories, when Bischoff approached me. He thanked me for my effort, and told me if I behaved myself, I'd be welcome to come back at a later time. He hugged me, and, while the hot water produced its steamy fog around us, we held each other for a long, long time.

Come on, you didn't really buy that, did you? No, there was no shower, no steam, no hug, and no holding for a long, long time. Actually, he caught up to me as I was walking out the door. He did thank me, did tell me I could come back, and then shook my hand. I then walked out into the cool, autumn breeze—a free man.

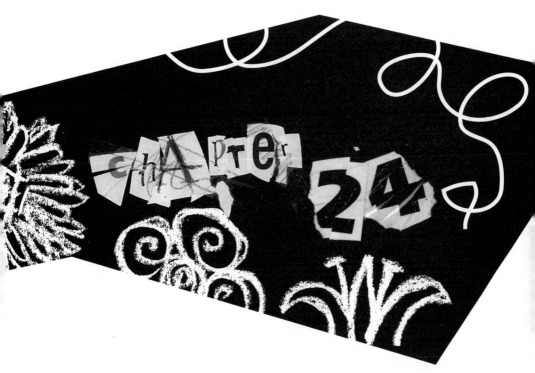

I had walked into WCW in August
1991 with about two grand in the bank and a baby on the way. I left three years later with a house, a car, two children, and some solid financial investments that I could build on. I never made truly big money in WCW; $156,000 might seem like a lot, but after taxes and road expenses, it's not exactly the type of income that sets you up for life after three years. Still, without WCW, Cactus Jack would be a distant memory, and Mankind would have never existed. The coverage I received with WCW made it possible for me to go out on my own and continue to make a decent living. There are a couple of last things I'd like to get off my chest before I slam the door shut on this part of my career. The first centers around a comment I made about Eric Bischoff, shortly after leaving, and the second looks at a lawsuit I filed against the company for the loss of my ear.

Soon after my departure from WCW, I did an interview with an industry newsletter, or dirtsheet, called the *Pro Wrestling Torch*. The *Torch* would always get ahold of wrestlers after they left the big companies, and get them to vent their spleen. As a result, right there on the pages of the *Torch*, guys would bury their careers and burn their bridges by insulting and hurting the feelings of their fellow wrestlers and former bosses. I was no different. When asked if I had ever been asked to tone down my ring style, I answered, "All the time—one night in Chicago, Eric Bischoff was literally pleading with me not to do anything extreme." Now, I know Bischoff read this, and I know that since he was a martial arts tough guy, it had to have hurt. It's not his fault he has perfect cheekbones. In retrospect, the word "pleading" may have been an exaggeration. In truth, Bisch was legitimately concerned about my health, and having known my family personally, was "asking" me to tone it down.

There you have it—an intimate confession. It is my hope now that Eric Bischoff can hate me for the right reasons. Such as, because I'm a guy he let walk away, who is now a major reason he wakes up with boot marks all over his butt cheeks every Tuesday morning. Tuesday morning refers to the Monday night wrestling Nielsen ratings, which aren't available until the next day. So, with the truth now known, I would just like to ask for forgiveness. Please. I'm pleading with you.

There have been several people who felt I was hypocritical in filing a lawsuit against WCW for the loss of my ear, while at the same time, allowing that same lost ear to be exploited by the World Wrestling Federation. Let me address this.

First, understand, I was not filing a ridiculous suit for millions of dollars based on pain and suffering, mental duress, and lots of other mumbo-jumbo. I filed a suit for the exact amount of money that it would cost to have reconstructive surgery done—approximately $42,000—and six months' salary at my old rate of $3,000 a week—the time it would take to heal. This was the same agreement that I had with WCW before I naively agreed to return to the ring.

I explained all of this to my attorney, in addition to giving him a run-down of all the sacrifices I had made on behalf of the company. I also explained the outrageous salaries that were now being paid to WCW wrestlers who had never even headlined a card. He agreed that this was unfortunate, but not applicable, and that our only recourse was to sue for negligence. Now, I've been banged up pretty good over the last fifteen years, and the last thing I want to do is point fingers and blame other people for the career choices and ring risks that I have willingly taken. But I felt I was in the right, even if negligence was not the road I wanted to take. As it turned out, I never got a dime, because of a Georgia law that forbids an employee from suing an employer. But the point I want to make is this: I sued for negligence because there is no law in our legal system that prevents a company from paying Johnny B. Badd twice as much money as they pay Cactus Jack. Maybe not . . . but, by God, there ought to be.

Yes, indeed, I was a free man. Free to choose when, where, why, how, how long, how many times, and with whom I wrestled. Forget the fact that I'd have no more guaranteed income—the important thing is, I was free.

The independent scene is a difficult one. Making your own book-ings, cutting your own deals, and hoping that some of the less reputable promoters won't bail out on a show, are only a few of the hassles involved. Working the indies also requires receiving money up front, so as to guarantee you won't get screwed. Even with a fifty per-cent deposit, the screwing sometimes occurred anyway. One time, I was booked in the westernmost part of West Virginia on a Sunday afternoon. I drove all night from eastern Pennsylvania to arrive on time. I checked into a hotel and called home. "Good," Colette shouted into the receiver. "I'm glad I caught you in time. The promoter called this morning and said that the show was canceled." When I informed Colette that I'd just traveled ten hours, she wasn't so glad after all. I swore to the promoter, who called himself Mad Dog something or other, that I would do whatever I had to do to ensure that he would never be successful in the business. So Mad Dog, if you read this, it's not too late to send me my money, you prick!

Even when I was earning top dollar by industry standards, it was a tough row to hoe on the independent scene. Due to my exposure on Turner's nationally televised shows, and with the reputation I had received as a damn hardworking wrestler, I was able to demand top dollar for the shows: $500 for a weekday or a smaller show, $750 for a larger one. If promoters booked me on several shows, I would cut deals with them. I realized that the chances of making what I had with WCW were next to impossible. But man, I was going to try.

It wasn't long before I was questioning my decision to leave the company. Colette, for her part, had never really stopped questioning the decision. I was determined to prove her wrong. So, on a hot night in late September, I set out for the prestigious confines of the Alpharetta Auction Barn. The barn was only a forty-minute drive from my house, so I was willing to accept a smaller fee of two hun-dred for the night. That was all right, though, because I had packed up plenty of Cactus Jack T-shirts that I bought for a song from the

WCW liquidator, and plenty of glossy eight-by-tens to make up for the smaller payoff. I brought along my sister-in-law Gail as well, to help keep up with what would surely be an insatiable demand.

As we headed for Alpharetta, I could visualize the entire scene. I could literally see it as it played out in my head. There would be a line out the door, filled with people holding intricately detailed and lovingly created Cactus Jack signs. I could even foresee a couple of unscrupulous scalpers, forcing small children to shell out big money to see their hero inside the auction barn.

When I pulled in to what would generously be described as a shit hole, I guessed that the scalpers had decided to stay home. Upon further review, I realized that there was not a real great proliferation of signs, or fans to wield them, for that matter. The place was practically empty. I had flashbacks of Polka High School all over again.

I walked into the oversize closet they called a dressing room, and detected the classic combination of urine and stale beer. I turned to see if Jake had somehow been booked on this same small show. What I saw instead was a group of hungry wrestlers looking at me with reverence in their eyes. "See what happens" began one, with a strong north Georgia accent, but not the slightest hint of sarcasm in his voice. "Ya bring in Cactus Jack, and we double the house." It was true. My star status and international recognition had brought the crowd at the auction barn from twenty-eight to fifty-seven! Apparently there were some people who wanted to watch my "goddamn trampoline act" after all.

I headed out to the gimmick table anyway, where Gail was waiting with my assortment of eight-by-tens and my "Bang Bang" T-shirts. "The crowd may be small," I told Gail, "but I bet every one of these fans is going to want something to bring home with them." I was wrong. After ten minutes and a total gross of $12, I started thinking of a line from an old Ricky Nelson song: "I sang a song about a Honky Tonk, it was time to leave."

It's important not to overstay your welcome when working the gimmick table. Some guys want to work the table right until bell time, hoping for that one last dollar, but the idea for me is to stay only as long as there is a line. Well, there was no line, so I actually started contradicting my own advice—I was looking for that last dollar. After a few minutes, I decided to pack it in, and left with about a half a thimbleful of dignity.

I entered the ring for the night's final match to a smattering of applause and one guy yelling, "You suck, Cactus Jack, you suck!" I was sporting a piece of white athletic tape on my head, which covered a small wound I had suffered two days earlier, in a match with my old partner Abdullah the Butcher. Abby had accidentally punctured my forehead with one of his foreign objects, and as a result, I had a small but deep hole in my head.

I had made up my mind to leave Alpharetta and its auction barn without getting hurt. Like many independent rings, this one was a piece of garbage, and offered a variety of ways to get hurt. Blown knees and ankles were a common consequence of working in a bad ring. I locked up with my opponent and grabbed him in a headlock. As I held him there, taking the chance to show off my seventeen-inch pythons, I felt a drip on my forearm. Then another one. Drip, drip, drip—now it was faster. I looked down at my arm and saw a growing family of blood drops nestling into the hairy area of my forearms. I must have grazed my head as I locked up, and now, in front of fifty-seven fans and my wife's sister, I was busted wide open.

"There goes my little wrestling match," I thought, as I felt the flood of dark red liquid that was now cascading down my head. I let my opponent go and threw him outside. I then went to work on him out there, and encouraged him to do the same to me, in the hope that it would look to the fans as if the injury had come from some type of brawling maneuver, instead of from a harmless lockup.

I picked up a garbage can and hit him with it. You could see the indentation where the devastating Rubbermaid had made contact with human skull. I then picked it up and brought the dark gray container down over his head, so that he was trapped in there. Now, I had been the victim of more trash cans over the head than anybody, and knew just what to do. Stagger around in a large circle, while your foe prepares himself for the big punch, clothesline, dropkick, etc. I had even lain prone in the ring one time in WCW with my upper body and head entombed in the Rubbermaid while Sting splashed me from the top rope. The entire concept is foolproof—there is just an innate desire in people's hearts to see grown men stagger around in circles while wearing a garbage can. It's been that way since well before Biblical times, although I'm not sure that it was ever documented. This guy had his own theory, however. The can hadn't been on him for more than a second when he threw it off—straight into the air. The force of the can paled in comparison, however, next to the force of his projectile vomiting, which continued without interruption for about thirty seconds. I looked down at my Cactus Jack boots, which revealed some new spots that didn't quite fit into the leopard skin motif. I could hear Ricky Nelson's voice singing just a little louder. It was time to leave.

I drove home with some serious doubts about my future. Gail was talking, but I remained more or less silent. Bleeding is a pretty intimate experience, and it was not one that I cared to share with my sister-in-law at that moment. I walked into my home, took a Bates Motel shower, and went to bed, with visions of scalpers and lines out the door dancing in my head.

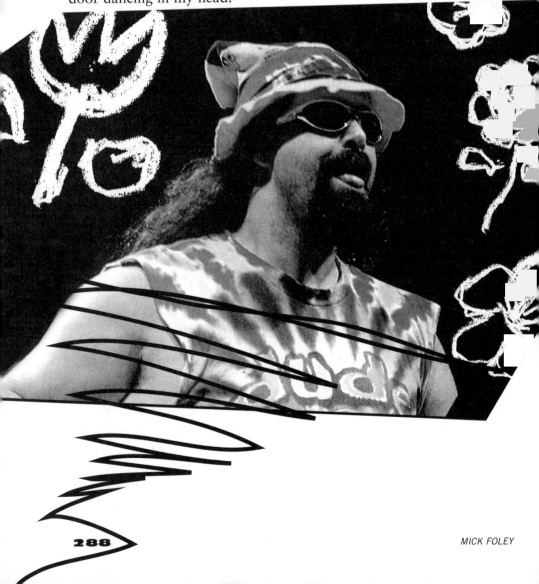

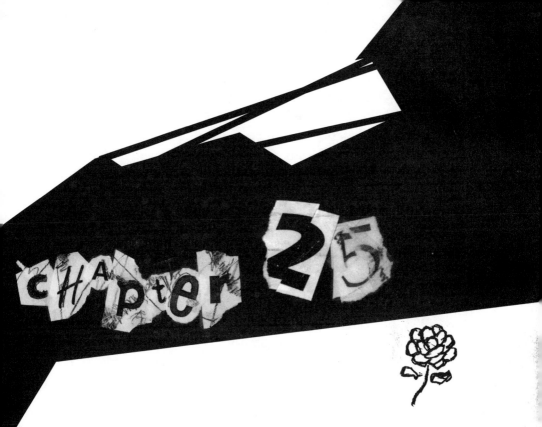

I made my return to the ECW arena
at the end of September. I had no belt to spit on this time, so I assumed
I would avoid any further controversy. I had already agreed with Todd
and Paul E. to make ECW my top priority. At that time, the company
was booking only four shows a month, and I agreed to appear in all
of them. I was excited about the show, because it was to be my first
singles match ever with the Funker, Terry Funk—the same guy who,
four years earlier, jokingly claimed not to have seen "shit" in me.

I had been a friend of Terry's for years, and he was pretty much my hero
in the business. He had seen it all and done it all, but he still had the decency
to respect all the other wrestlers, and he never failed to be polite to the fans.
When the bell rang, however, Terry was a different man. He would become
a wild-eyed madman at every show, no matter how small the crowd. He
could be that out-of-control madman one moment, and kindly old Uncle
Terry the next. Even at the age of fifty, he took a tremendous beating, and
even years later, at fifty-four, took a World Wrestling Federation beating
from me so bad that I apologized to him for days about it. "Cactus, now,
don't give me that shit," he'd say in his soft-spoken mumble-whisper.
"That's part of the business, and I was glad I could do it for you."

Terry was the king of storytellers, and I always listened closely for bits of information I could use. You had to listen closely when the Funker talked—he spoke so damn softly. One time on a propeller plane flight, I sat across the aisle while he talked for two hours. I nodded and laughed the whole time, not wanting to tell the Funker that I couldn't hear a word he said. On this evening in Philadelphia, he had offered some especially prophetic advice. "Cactus, just remember—every match is a great match until it begins."

In addition to the stories Terry told, I loved to hear stories that were about Terry. One of them occurred in Knoxville, where Terry was in town to defend the NWA heavyweight championship in the mid-seventies. In those days, the world champion would defend his belt against all the regional champions. On this occasion, Terry was being interviewed by a newscaster who was grilling Terry about what she called the "pageantry" involved in wrestling. This was during an era when wrestlers didn't consider themselves "entertainers," and the world championship was meant to be taken very seriously. "You wrestlers really crack me up," the reporter said, looking down somewhat on this simple wrestler. "With all the pageantry and such."

Terry laughed and started to speak. For a guy who whispered and mumbled, he was actually one of the best interviews in the business. "What if I came to the ring and a band was playing," Terry said with a laugh. "And what if there were girls in short skirts who danced when I got into the ring. And then, by golly, some cannons would go off—wouldn't that be great?" The reporter agreed; this had affirmed her opinion of pageantry in wrestling. But the Funker wasn't through. "I've just described exactly what happens every time the Dallas Cowboys score a touchdown." Another Funk victory.

One of my favorite Funk interviews, and one that the World Wrestling Federation wrestlers still imitate today, was also one of his worst. So bad that it was good—or maybe it was just good, and no one realized it. Terry was working for Jim Cornette's Smoky Mountain Wrestling promotion in 1994, and was preparing for a match with Bullet Bob Armstrong. Armstrong was a Southern wrestling legend and patriarch of the Armstrong family, which includes current World Wrestling Federation star Road Dogg. Even today, at fifty-five, Bob will walk into the small gym my wife and I own in the Florida Panhandle, sporting an impressive pair of guns. In this interview, Funk was deliberating on how he could anger a southeasterner like Armstrong into finding the guts to fight him.

"I know," Funk began in a very slow, deliberate tone, "Bob Armstrong is a son of a bitch!—no, no, that won't anger a southeasterner, because they have no self-respect. I know, how about this—all of your sons are bastards! There, that oughtta do it. No, no, because no southeasterner really cares about his kids. I know—your wife is a whore! Yeah, that's it. No, no, no—southeasterners don't really care about their wives either. Wait, wait, I've got it—the one thing that would make a gutless son of a bitch like Bob Armstrong mad enough to fight. Here it is—your mistress is a whore!"

The fans were, as in most cases at the ECW arena, extremely excited about the evening's show. Now, I use the term "arena" lightly, as it more closely resembled a larger auction barn. In actuality, when I started with ECW, we often had to clear the building in time for midnight bingo. I could most accurately describe the ambiance as a *Rocky Horror Picture Show* for wrestling. There was a "dollar" store next door to the arena, and they did a brisk preshow business on pots and pans and various other culinary utensils. The fans would then bring their purchases to the arena, where they would generously hand them to their favorite wrestlers. I became so used to swinging these cheap aluminum objects that one time I grabbed one and was in mid-swing by the time I realized I had a cast-iron skillet in my possession. Approximately two weeks later, the recipient of the skillet blow, the Sandman, was able to wrestle again.

I am often asked what the strangest foreign object I ever used was. No doubt about it, the two-man kayak that was once handed to me at the arena tops the list. Or maybe the Leonard Cohen album I used on Mikey Whipwreck.

Terry and I were scheduled to be on last. Like most ECW shows, we would have to try to follow a lot of strange and exciting action. By the time we got out there, we knew, the fans would have seen a variety of chair shots, pan shots, stop sign shots, in-crowd brawling, out-of-the-ring dives, and obscenity-laced ring interviews. It wouldn't be easy, and in retrospect, main eventing in ECW never was.

Keeping in mind Funk's theory, "Every match is a great match until it begins," I grabbed the mike. "Terry," I called, in my Cactus Jack warble, "it's going to hurt me to kick your ass all over the ECW arena—but . . . not as bad as it's going to hurt you!"

I handed Terry the mike. He smiled that lovable old Uncle Terry smile and said, "That's what I've always loved about you, Cactus—

you've always been a dreamer." Terry and I then shook hands and tore into each other. As two veteran hardcore warriors, the Funker and I didn't have to rely on cheap, violent stunts to get a pop out of the crowd—we knew how to work. No, we didn't have to rely on it, but we did anyway—giving the crowd the same variety of chair shots, pan shots, stop sign shots, and out-of-the ring brawling that they had already seen for the past three hours.

We did throw in one added bonus, however. It was actually a combination of two moves we discussed earlier, but paired together for maximum audience enjoyment: a hangman complemented by a busted eyebrow. Terry threw me to the ropes, and I caught my head and neck in perfect textbook form, even if I doubt the existence of just such a textbook. My legs were kicking, but my head was in perfect position. I looked up with my right eye, and saw Terry throwing that big left. BAM—his fist went off like a rifle against my eyebrow bone. The blow helped knock me out of the ropes, and I lay on the cold, concrete floor (no protective mats at ECW), relishing that rare feeling of pain and satisfaction. We had the fans rocking and rolling, when a tag team called the Public Enemy hit the ring. Seeing that the PE had pooped on our party, Terry and I banded together to fight them off. After a minute, they went down, and Terry told me to get him a chair. There were no more within easy reach, so I called to a fan to throw me his. He willingly obliged, and a chair sailed into the ring. Then another one flew in. Then another. Then another, and another, and another. It was literally raining chairs, as the plastic seating devices were coming from all angles. In all my years, it was the damnedest thing I'd ever seen. I stood there in wonderment at this spectacle, until one of the chairs bounced off my head, and I realized it was time to leave. In a scene that would be replayed weekly on ECW television for years, the ring had been bombarded with over 200 chairs—with the Public Enemy literally buried underneath. When they emerged from under the sea of hard plastic, we had next month's main event already booked—Funk and Cactus would be taking on the Public Enemy.

The backstage area of the bingo hall often more closely resembled a triage unit at a hospital. So many guys were trying so hard to impress this unique audience that injuries were inevitable. Guys were practically killing themselves to earn the fans' approval, and the fans in ECW could often be callous about these ring mishaps.

J. T. Smith was a perfect example of an ECW guy who would do anything to get over. I had met him four years earlier, and he had unfortunately taken me on as his role model. He would do Cactus Jack moves, but he didn't have the Cactus Jack ability to absorb them, and as a result, he spent a lot of his time either injured or in agony. On one memorable night, J. T. attempted a springboard dive off the ropes to the floor, and slipped—sending him crashing headfirst to the concrete below. As he lay unconscious, the crowd broke into the chant they used whenever someone visibly messed up a move—"You fucked up, you fucked up." Over the course of time, incidents like these would weigh very heavily on my mind. Ironically, J. T. Smith, the guy who spent years searching for acceptance, finally found it in ECW as a comedy act. As a black man portraying an old-world Italian, J. T. would talk like a paisano and would screw up moves on purpose, and the fans loved him for it. "You fucked up, you fucked up!" became a chant of affection.

I worked a string of independent shows for anyone who met my price, before returning to the ECW arena three weeks later, for the big match with Public Enemy. I worked hard on all these shows, but I'd be less than honest with you if I didn't admit that my main purpose was to sell as many Cactus Jack pictures, shirts, and assorted paraphernalia as I could. In addition to purchasing Cactus Jack shirts through a liquidator, I also bought a host of kids' belts and foam fingers that I hawked shamelessly through these shows. The ECW arena was different, however. If I sold pictures at all, it would only be for a few minutes, as it was important for me to retain my "aura" in that atmosphere. An "aura" could be ruined in a hurry if these ruthless fans caught you saying, "Please buy a picture." Within a month, however, I would unveil a new shirt that would both make me a hell of a lot of money and revolutionize the way ECW looked at merchandising. The "Wanted Dead" T-shirt—a black shirt with a weathered yellow Old West–style wanted poster on it—was so nice that it blew away anything else for sale. For a while, the ECW arena looked like the future Austin 3:16 craze, with a sea of black and yellow to meet me. Unlike the Austin phenomenon, however, the "Wanted" craze was limited to a thousand fans at the ECW arena, and not millions worldwide. Paul E. took note of this small-scale success, however, and went to work. Today, ECW merchandise is a huge seller, nationwide.

When I got to my hotel, I was alerted by Todd Gordon that Terry had missed his flight and wouldn't be making it to the show. Actually, due to reasons of his own, Terry would not set foot in an ECW ring for another six months, paving the road to our future feud overseas. Todd was beside himself—this was a huge match, and the rabid fans at the arena would be hard to appease without it.

"What do we do?" I asked Todd. "Can we use a substitute?"

"It'll never work," Todd stated dismally. "The only guy the fans wouldn't shit on is Big Al," referring to a huge wrestler whose chokeslam had made him a cult favorite in the arena. Al chokeslammed everybody: Santa Claus, midgets, two wrestlers at once, women—even the guy playing the National Anthem. Aside from that one move, however, Al didn't do a whole lot well.

I thought about the situation for a minute before asking, "What about Mikey?"

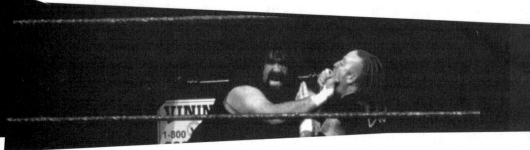

The real-life John Watson was a smallish nineteen-year-old kid who grew up idolizing Cactus Jack and didn't look like he had an athletic bone in his body. He was trained by a guy named Sonny Blaze, whom I myself had trained in Mark Tendler's garage. John was so unimpressive that Sonny refused to charge him money to train, out of guilt, because he assumed the poor kid would never make it. John began setting up the ring at the ECW arena, and was spotted performing moonsaults and various other high-flying maneuvers inside the empty building. Paul E. saw this unassuming kid, and somewhere in his mind, Mikey Whipwreck was born.

Paul cast Mikey as the ultimate loser, a gimmick that had been a cult hit for his Jim Ignitowski–like "wrestling school dropout" several years earlier. The difference was, Mikey had talent. Paul began booking him against the top guys in the company, and every week, he'd take a world-class ass kicking. Dressed in sweatpants with shorts over them and a long-sleeve dragon-printed shirt, and looking all of about eleven years old, Mikey didn't exactly send shivers down spines. Throw in a hometown of Buffalo and the theme music of the Beck song

"Loser," and you've got a pretty good idea of what was going on.

It was months before Mikey even got in an offensive move. When he did, it was major news. "Oh, my God, oh, my God!" announcer Joey Styles yelled. "His first offensive move!" So without any offense, Mikey got beat up—a lot. But he was so good at it that fans actually started taking notice. The ECW fans may have been heartless, but they could recognize good wrestling. Soon Mikey was a cult favorite. One night, several months before my ECW arrival, Mikey won the ECW television title on a fluke, and the place went ballistic.

As a champion, Mikey was finally given a chance to talk. Unlike traditional wrestlers, Mikey didn't exude confidence while talking—on the contrary, he was terrified. He'd get on the microphone and attempt to hand the belt back. He'd claim that his mother didn't want him to wrestle. He'd start to say, "Let me tell you something, Pit Bull number 1," before thinking about it and crying, "I'm gonna get killed!" Then for several weeks straight, Mikey would wrestle, get destroyed, but somehow win by fluke. The guy was winning title matches without getting in a single offensive maneuver. By the time he lost the title, he had been on the receiving end of some brutal beatings, but was also the recipient of tremendous applause.

Without Funk, we knew we needed a gimmick, and I felt like Mikey was it. I went to the ring alone to the sounds of Steppenwolf's "Born to Be Wild." The fans were aware that Funk was not in attendance, but no substitute had been named. When Public Enemy hit the ring, I grabbed the house mike and said I would be returning shortly with my partner. Joey Styles called the action as I disappeared behind the curtain. "Who is Cactus Jack going to find? What tough guy, what tremendous athlete, what former world champion will he return with—it's MIKEY! Oh, my God, it's Mikey!" I came though the curtain dragging Mikey by the arm, as he tried desperately to get away. He looked like a child who doesn't want to sit on Santa's lap, or an adult who is forced to watch an Al Snow match.

I started in with the P.E., and Mikey promptly ran away to the back, leaving poor Cactus Jack defenseless against the ECW tag team champions. After a few minutes of this beating, when all looked lost, Mikey reemerged—and in true ECW fashion, he had a foreign object. But it wasn't a chair or any other normal instrument of destruction—because that wouldn't be Mikey-like. Instead he held a flimsy piece of paneling that looked about as threatening as a gaggle of baby geese.

Flimsy or not, the paneling made a hell of a noise upon impact, and he took turns bringing it down on the heads of the P.E. When the paneling broke, Mikey Whipwreck—the man of no offense—began throwing lefts and rights to the jaws of both men. The roar of the crowd rose with each blow, until he was laid out with a vicious double-team move. As he lay unmoving, Grunge and Flyboy Rocco Rock (P.E. members) began the attack on me.

As we went over the railing, I noticed Mikey still lying there, motionless. Now we were in the crowd, and still no Mikey. For five minutes I took abuse while Mikey lay motionless inside the ring. Finally we returned, and Rocco went to the top rope for what would surely be the *coup de grace*. As the Flyboy stood perched atop the ropes, I got up and stumbled, falling into the ropes, sending the Flyboy testicles-first into the turnbuckle below. He screamed on impact, fell into the ring, and tripped over Mikey, who still hadn't budged. With Rocco prone, and holding his testes for comfort, Mikey found the strength to drape an arm over him. I stopped Grunge from interfering, and the referee made the historic count. One, two, three, and ECW had new tag team champions. There was a whole tour of Japanese wrestling fans sitting ringside at the show, and when I saw them, I hopped the rail and celebrated, as the Japanese media flashed away. I had no idea then just how much I'd see the Japanese fans and their press in the future.

Victor Quinones was a longtime promoter from Puerto Rico, who was booking talent for a small blood-and-guts group in Japan, called IWA. I received a call from him about coming to Japan and competing in their death matches that featured barbed wire and a variety of other torturous devices. I told him that I'd pass. At that time, I was having fun in ECW and was being booked around the country, and I had no desire to have my body torn to shreds. I really had no idea just how shredded I would become.

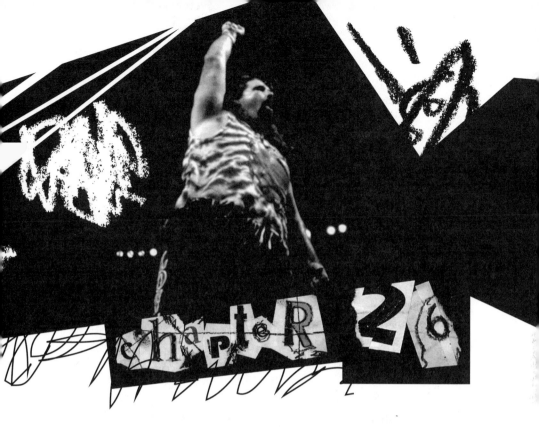

I had a weekend of matches for ECW in November, and decided to bring Dewey along with me. He was two and a half years old, and I figured it would be a great bonding time for father and son. He enjoyed the trip, and even rolled around the ring a little when we got to the small arena in Hamburg, Pennsylvania, that the World Wrestling Federation had used to tape television in before it went big-time. I bailed out of the ring to do a telephone interview, during which I told the interviewer that the two most important philosophies in life were simple ones learned in childhood: "He who smelt it, dealt it," and "Bang bang, you're dead." Actually, I find the whole "He who smelt it" theory to be full of holes, as is its counterpart, "He who denied it, supplied it." In reality, especially in wrestling dressing rooms, the dealer of a gaseous emission is more likely to exit the room, and leave others to enjoy it, or else laugh with pride—thereby shooting the denial theory to pieces.

I was booked in Hamburg with Sabu. The two of us had become a hot ticket around the country, and I certainly was earning my money. We had engaged in more than a few classic battles, including one at the Silver Nugget in Las Vegas that included a foray into the casino area. I piledrove Sabu onto the blackjack table, sending gamblers scurrying and chips flying. Looking back at it, however, it may not have been the wisest decision in the world—if we had been at a bigger casino, with more money at stake, there is the possibility we could have been physically punished for our action.

I pumped myself up mentally for a long time in Hamburg. Dewey was fast asleep in the dressing room on a mattress made out of ring robes and turnbuckle pads. Sabu's music was playing when I heard a faint sound. My son had awakened, and he didn't seem pacified by the shaved heads and wild outfits all around him. He started to cry—softly at first, but with progressively more volume, until it escalated into a full-blown tantrum. "This can't be happening," I said out loud, as I could feel my entire hour of mental preparation sailing away. I tried to comfort the little guy, but he was beside himself, and I could hear "Born to Be Wild" booming from the loudspeakers. I had to go. I kissed my son good-bye, placed him in the arms of the towering wrestler named 911, and walked sadly out the door.

I was not prepared for Sabu, but I knew that many fans would drive hundreds of miles for a Sabu–Cactus Jack showdown. I was always determined not to let them down, and I tried my best to make this match a great one—even with the extenuating circumstances involved. I didn't mention these circumstances to Sabu—for some rea-son, I didn't think the "homicidal, suicidal, maniac," as he was known, would be all that sensitive to my paternal problems.

Instead, we went at it full tilt. I knocked the Indian madman to the ropes, and picked up a wooden ringside chair to crown him with. Sabu moved, and the force of my swing ricocheted off the middle rope and propelled the chair backward into my own waiting head. I stum-bled in my old faithful 360-degree angle—or the watusi as some call it—while Sabu stepped to the second rope on the outside ring. He was ready to attempt a moonsault, and under perfect conditions, would make chest-to-chest contact. Not too difficult, except for the fact that his body would be upside down and in mid-air when the desired con-tact would be made. In this case, however, our chests never connected. Nothing did. I reached my hands up to try in vain to intercept him, as this 210-pound missile flew high overhead. Now, in fifteen years of wrestling, I've heard plenty of sickening sounds—many of them from my own body—but this was among the worst. Sabu's body impaled itself on the steel guard rail, and I grimaced as I heard the one-two combination of ribs breaking on steel, and guttural, animal-like screams welling up from deep inside Sabu's lungs. The crowd sensed in an instant that something was wrong, and actually cleared out of the way to allow him room to breathe.

I stalled for time, but returned shortly to see if he could go on. "Gimme time, gimme time," he yelled, and I commenced to throwing chairs into the ring and using whatever else was available to allow him some recuperation time.

When I came back, he was still gasping for air, but was struggling bravely to get to his feet. We then continued, and actually had a hell of a match. We fought down the aisle to the dressing room, and before heading back to the ring, I reached into a garbage can and pulled out an empty Coors Light bottle. "Use this," I said.

"To do what?" came the reply.

"To hit me with," I insisted. I crawled into the ring, again using the dependable watusi, as I waited for the crashing sound of glass and the oohs and ahhs from the Hamburg crowd that would lead to the end of the match. Well, I got the oohs and ahhs, but not the crashing sound I was anticipating. Instead, there was a loud thunk as the glass bottle literally bounced off my head and spun clumsily on the canvas.

In my beer-bottle-battered haze, I looked at the spinning Coors container, and thought back fondly to Spin the Bottle on our sixth grade camping trip, and how excited I was when the bottle pointed to Sue Cirisano. The memory of Sue running for the door instead of honoring the strict and time-honored tradition of giving me a good one on the smacker finally brought me back to my senses, and I said the only words I could think of—"Hit me again." Again the bottle came down, and again it thunked off my skull. "Again," I said. Another thunk. By this time, even the bloodthirsty ECW fans were starting to feel a little bad about this whole scenario, but dammit, we had a match to finish, and I wasn't about to do a job for the bottle. One more swing and one more thunk. Then another swing, and finally the satisfaction of shattering glass showering around me.

I went to the dressing room, where my recovered son was waiting with a two-and-a-half-year-old hug that only a father can truly appreciate. "Did you win, Daddy?" he asked innocently.

"No, buddy, but it was a good match anyway—would you like to see Grandma and Grandpa now?" So, with five lumps on my head and glass in my hair, we hopped into my rented Lumina, and off to Grandmother's house we went.

It was during this time that I began working for Jim Cornette's Smoky Mountain promotion. Without a doubt, Corny had more energy than anyone I've ever met. Even while working as a manager in the World Wrestling Federation, he somehow found the time to book and star in his own promotion. Smoky and ECW were like night and day. Instead of hardcore, bloodthirsty fans, Smoky had old-time fans. These were fans who still believed in good guys and bad guys, and to whom cheating was still reason to become upset.

As Cactus Jack, I was instantly embraced as a fan favorite, but more importantly, as a guy whose shirts they wanted to buy. I was embroiled in a feud with Chris Candido that was actually a lot of fun, and I was making money courtesy of the generous fans of Kentucky, Tennessee, and North Carolina. Corny gave me free rein over my interviews, which for some reason were laced with double entendres and bad poetry. During one promo I compared my quest to free the simpleminded Boo Bradley from the evil clutches of Chris Candido to that of a missionary. I then stated that I was to going to really enjoy the "missionary position." The feud with Candido also inspired these thoughtful verses.

```
Candido, oh Candido, I'll beat you up,
I'll make you bleed-o
Like Rocky did Apollo Creed-o
Oh Candido
I'll scare you stiff, oh yes indeed-o,
You'll leave a skid inside your Speedo
Oh Candido
```

Pretty serious stuff. I was able to work quite a few shows for Cornette, highlighted by the traditional Thanksgiving and Christmas shows, but I was most happy to be able to spend some time with my old friend Brian Hildebrand.

While I had been busy traveling up and down the roads for the past several years, Brian had been stuck on the independent circuit. While guys without an ounce of his talent had made it big, Brian had continued managing at whatever shows he could find, and would even wrestle as a Ninja Turtle or some other creation that was geared to the kids. When Corny opened up the territory, Brian was among the first guys he called, and when I got there, he was firmly entrenched as not only a referee, but the head of merchandise, and a dozen other jobs as well. "This place would shut down if it weren't for Gerbil," was a common comment from veteran grappler Tracy Smothers, referring to Brian's new nickname.

When Smoky began an interpromotional feud with the USWA, Brian had finally gotten a chance to wrestle, and as a vicious heel referee turned wrestler, was finally able to truly showcase his talents. I feel bad for any wrestler who never gets his big shot, but my heart had gone out for years to Brian, because he was so damn good and no one seemed to notice. I was genuinely glad for him that, by the time I got to Smoky, his skills had been recognized. During my time in the area, I had met his lovely wife, Pam, and had the pleasure of watching more wrestling, eating more pasta, and seeing more mountain views than at any other time of my life.

I saw Brian a few days ago at the Brian Pillman show. Even at ninety-eight pounds (due to a long battle with stomach cancer) he had the determination to referee two matches, and he even looked good doing it. I was also able to read him some of this book, and it was gratifying to see how much he enjoyed it. He later told me that the story of the gay beach in Fort Lauderdale had caused him to laugh harder than he had in months. Hang in there, Brian—you're a credit not only to this business, but to the better angels of our nature. [Editor's note: Brian passed away after the writing of this book on September 8, 1999.]

In late November, I received word that Terry Funk had signed a contract to wrestle for the IWA in Japan. I picked up the phone and called Victor Quinones. It was the only time in my eighteen months as an independent that I asked for work. I was booked to leave on New Year's Eve for a ten-day tour. My body would never be quite the same.

*   *   *

I flew to Tokyo in style. Seat 38E was far enough away from the movie screen as to make viewing difficult, but close enough to both the toilet and the smoking section to ensure a pleasant sensory experience. Northwest Airlines' cold soba noodle breakfast is an especially disagreeable one, and when we landed, I was exhausted, sick to my stomach, and smelled like a 290-pound cigarette. Tracy Smothers was on the flight as well, and we were met at the airport by one of the "young boys," as the beginning Japanese wrestlers were commonly referred to.

I waited at baggage claim for my two travel bags and my twelve dozen "Wanted" shirts to arrive. Before my trip, my old partner Kevin Sullivan had spoken to me and advised me to take shirts to sell. I figured it would be a lot harder for the promotion to say no once I was there, so I never called for permission. As it turned out, I made more money in Japan as a seller of T-shirts than I did as the King of the Death Match.

Tajiri, the young boy who met us, spoke very little English. Apparently, his Japanese left something to be desired as well, as the cab dropped us off six blocks from our hotel—forcing us to walk with all our luggage. "Sorry, sorry" was all Tajiri could say, as I shouldered two huge boxes, and wondered if maybe an apologetic phone call to Eric Bischoff might have been a better move than coming here. "What are we doing here?" I kept whining to Tracy as, even in the winter weather, the sweat began trickling down my brow.

We finally checked into our hotel, where after dinner with a Japanese superfan named Masa—who still remembered me from my trip in 1991—I tried to sleep. As a small promotion, IWA had to cut corners to survive. It flew all the wrestlers on coach, bused us for hours every day, and lodged us in some pretty crummy accommodations. At $300 a day, I was, with the exception of the Funker, the most highly paid *gai-jin* (foreign) wrestler by far. As a true Japanese icon, Terry had a deal that was pretty lucrative, but some of the South American wrestlers were working for seventy-five a day. The next day, we headed for the venerable Japanese venue, Korekeun Hall. Korekeun was a 2,200-seat auditorium on the fifth floor of a Japanese office building, which was used by several different promotions. It was not unusual for three different promoters to use the hall on the same day, and as I walked in the dressing room, a few women wrestlers were still in the process of packing up.

When the doors opened up, I was waiting anxiously with stacks of Cactus shirts in front of me and a jumbo marker in my hand. I was already dressed for my match, which would be a no rope–barbed wire death match, pitting Terry Funk and Japanese daredevil Shoji Nakamaki against me and Tracy Smothers. Interestingly, four years before the invention of Mr. Socko, I was wearing a long tube sock on my right arm, as I was planning on doing the Cactus clothesline over the top of the barbed wire. I knew the possibility was strong of catching my arm on the wire as I went over, a possibility that could do massive amounts of injury to my skin, veins, and tendons as well. The sock, as it would later in my life, would protect me.

The fans streamed in, and actually made a beeline for my table. Apparently, Cactus Jack had become a pretty big name in Japan, due to the Japanese media presence at many American shows. Even with a twenty-five percent cut going to the office, I knew my payoff was expanding rapidly.

I came out during intermission, when the young boys took down the ring ropes and replaced them with spools of barbed wire, which they ran in lines and zigzags to resemble a set of four flesh-eating roman numeral tens. My music was playing as I unloaded my last shirt. I could hear IWA boss Mr. Asano calling my name, but, dammit, I had merchandise to sell. It didn't matter that I was going to get literally torn up out there—shirts came first. I often imagined how ridiculous this would look if applied to a regular sporting event. "Frank, we're waiting for Holyfield's entrance, but he doesn't seem to be ready—wait, I've just got word that he's at the gimmick table pushing his T-shirts. Don't worry, a few more Polaroids and the champ will be on his way."

I came down to the ring and received a tremendous ovation. They were chanting my name in unison, which in reality sounded less like "Cactus, Cactus," and more like "Cock-toos-uh, Cock-toos-uh." It was flattering nonetheless. When Nakamaki and Terry made their way to the ring, they chanted even louder for Terry, which sounded a lot more like "Telly." The hall was sold out, and the fans were primed for mayhem, which I began delivering. Funk and I climbed up the first level of the stands and began going punch for punch in front of the awestruck fans. The Funker picked up a chair and slammed it over my head. Japanese folding chairs were strange in that they were not as heavy as their American cousins, but were put together in such a way that a good shot could pop the seat straight up in the air.

Back in the ring, Tracy was putting the boots to Nakamaki. Tracy was a tremendous wrestler, who could just about do it all, but for some strange reason, he didn't have the inclination to risk life and limb on the dangerous barbs. Nakamaki was a different story. Not talented in the least, Nakamaki was a forty-year-old, non-athletic, former journalist who had cult hero status as a guy willing to do anything. Wait . . . I think I just described myself. But unlike me, Nakamaki was not much of a ring general—he just kind of lay there screaming and bleeding. But his reputation as a daredevil was well earned—he was willing to do anything, and he was dying to try some of it with me. Actually, Nakamaki looked up to me, and although we didn't speak each other's language, we had a verbal exchange that we shared for the next fifteen months. "You danger man," I would say, before a laughing Nakamaki fired back, "No—you danger man!"

I gave Nakamaki a couple of shots and set him up by the wire strands. I backed up and raised my sock-covered arm. The fans stood with anticipation as I charged the Japanese danger man. Even though videotaped evidence later showed me to be moving rather slowly, it was still a dramatic moment, as the two of us flew over the top—my arm dragging the wire down with it. I looked at my left arm, and saw two angry gashes that revealed the white cells underneath. I lay there recovering as a small amount of blood began to well up inside the gash. I don't have a medical degree, but I find it strange how some gashes never bleed, and some small cuts seem to bleed forever. A month later, I would attempt this same move and wouldn't be so lucky. The wire snapped on impact and I went hurtling forward—absorbing the fall on the top of my head. I could hear the Japanese reaction of "uhwahh," but was temporarily unable to do anything but breathe. I eventually got up and won the match, but the move bothered my neck for several months.

The Funker returned to the ring, and we fought to the dressing room, where I had a special prop waiting. A young boy handed me a lighter, while I disposed of Funk. I grabbed the lighter and reached for the chair that had a towel strapped to it that had been soaked in kerosene. I put lighter to chair, and—presto!—the fire chair was born. I walked down the aisle accompanied by the Japanese chorus of "uhwahh," and slid into the ring. I wound up the chair and brought it down across Nakamaki's back. "Uhwahh!" With the help of the fire chair, Cactus Jack was victorious in his return to Japan. Unfortunately, my trusty fire chair would almost cost Terry Funk his life ten months later.

We set out the next day on a long bus trip, and arrived in a country town about four hours south of Tokyo. We were feeling pumped from the previous night's sellout. Sellouts were rare for a small group like IWA—I was about to find out just how rare. We were booked inside a 1,000-seat arena, and like most days in Japan, arrived about five hours before the show. The young boys would spar and do endless free squats, while the *gai-jins* threw a football, did some situps, read a book, or used whatever time killers they could.

I was actually able to see quite a bit of Japan during these five-hour pre-show periods. Because most of the shows took place in smaller cities, we could walk around the towns and appreciate the ancient culture. I much preferred the beautiful mountains of the Japanese countryside to the mass of humanity in Tokyo.

Unfortunately, our attendance reflected that lack of mass humanity as well. For the next week, we were lucky to draw a hundred fans, even with the legendary Funker on the card. In truth, the fans never quite forgave Terry for coming back after his emotional retirement tour in 1980. He was still an icon, but was not as revered as he was in his heyday. IWA had made the mistake of booking arenas in the southern part of the country, under the premise that it would be warmer there. Well, it was slightly warmer, but the buildings weren't heated in the south, and as a result, the *gai-jins* would all huddle around a portable kerosene heater in an attempt to stay warm. When our music played, we'd take off our winter coats and hit the ring to entertain a very small group of fans who made very little noise and were dressed in very warm clothes.

Mr. Asano had liked me right away. Asano was a multimillionaire, whose value ranged from $50 million to $500 million, depending on the Japanese real estate and stock markets. Even with his wealth, he threw around nickels like they were manhole covers. But he was a big "Cock-toos Jack" fan, and he made it clear that he wanted me back on all his tours. Asano also wanted to play up my death match image. He'd been impressed by my barbed wire heroics, and he wanted my name to become synonymous with skin-tearing metal. So, for the rest of the tour, and for months afterward, I wore a barbed wire necklace around my neck. I wrapped the stuff around my leg to drop legs and around my arm to drop elbows. When I talked to the press, I sometimes had it wrapped around my whole body, and no, I'm not talking about the rubber-tipped barbed wire that is currently used in WCW. For a while in the IWA, it truly did look as though I was "born to be wired."

The final match of the tour took place in the city of Guma, where Terry and I were scheduled for another no rope, barbed wire death match. We were booked into another small venue, which again would be void of both heat and human bodies. This match was being filmed for commercial videotape release in Japan, and that fact made a great deal of difference. It was not as if I hadn't been wrestling hard in front of the frozen, minuscule crowds, but video always upped the ante, even if I knew I'd never see a cent of the profits. There is something about commercial video that represents immortality, because I know that when I'm done, commercial videotape will be the greatest representation of what my career stood for.

Pride was another huge factor. I had come over here specifically to wrestle Terry Funk, and now I had my chance. I realized the crowd would be small, but the Japanese media presence would be large, and several hundred thousand fans would read about and see photos of the match. I also had the belief that I could help make this promotion a success. Unlike WCW, the rug would not be pulled out on me, and the ball would not be taken away from me. I knew that when handed the ball, I would be given the chance to run as far as I could. I saw this match as the night I took the handoff. With fewer than 200 fans in attendance, I felt in my heart and in my mind that January 9, 1995, was the most important match of my life.

As the wire went up, I listened to a song called "Winter" by Tori Amos, which is, in my mind, the most beautiful thing I've ever heard. I was all out of T-shirts, and in truth, wouldn't have sold them this night because I was completely focused. As the song played, I became more and more intense. As the beautiful images in her song peaked, so did my ability to see brutal images in my mind. I was practically flying on adrenaline, a claim I can't make for many future matches with audiences one hundred times as large.

The Funker and I tied up, and I took over immediately, pelting him with forearms to the side of the head. I whipped him toward the wire, but he put the brakes on and pointed to his brain, as the crowd applauded politely. I stopped him once more, and again attempted to whip him into the hungry wire, but this time the Texas Bronco slid out underneath the bottom strand and beckoned me to follow. I did so, and we proceeded to tear both the building and ourselves apart.

A few minutes into the action, I threw the Funker through a row of chairs and sought out my special fire chair, which I had hidden under the ring. At this point, the fans, while not many, were standing and in a frenzy, as they realized that something special was going on inside that freezing gym. A young boy handed me a lighter, and a second later, the fire chair lived again. I brought the chair down across the grizzled Funker, and then, in one of the stupider acts of my career, placed it on the gym floor. The gym floor in Guma, like most buildings we worked in, was covered with a rubber tarpaulin. In retrospect,

I was lucky the whole building didn't go up in flames. I followed up my stupid decision with an equally dumb one, as I allowed Terry to hip toss me on the blazing chair. I rolled off the chair, and the young boys doused me with large buckets of water. My shoulder would turn a shade of gray and stay that way for several months.

I rolled into the ring and the Funker followed me, this time with the fire chair in his possession. I put the boots to Terry, and wound up with the weapon one more time. BAM! went the chair, and Terry's back literally smoked from the impact. I placed the flaming chair on the canvas, where it was promptly doused by the young boys. These kids were so nice and dependable that I made it a point to be nice to them. Also, I knew that these kids would be future stars in the sport, and didn't want them to be kicking my ass all over the Orient in the years to come.

Once in the ring, I made a decision that would make my previous two bonehead moves look like Einstein's theory of relativity. "Go ahead, Terry, I'm ready," I said, as Funk launched me toward the wire. Of all the moves I could think of, I was about to try the most dangerous of all—a hangman in the barbed wire! I knew the results could be truly disastrous, but I was determined to give Mr. Asano his $300 worth. I took flight and caught my head and neck between the second and third strands of wire, as the rest of my body sailed over the top. The timing was perfect, but the wire gave way, leaving me sitting on the arena floor, with sharp barbs still lodged deeply in both my pinkies. I gave a firm tug from my seated position and became free, but in doing so, exposed huge chunks of flesh.

Bleeding badly, I lay on the floor, as the Funker retreated to the back before returning with a special present of his own—a flaming branding iron. I got to my feet and Terry made a charge. He brought the iron down toward my face, but I blocked it, creating an artistic standstill where the fire from the iron danced off the reflection of my bloody facial features. A boot to the stomach broke the struggle, and I lay on the ground as the Funker stalked his prey. I had taped gauze to my chest and had soaked my shirt in water, but the iron still hurt like hell as Terry ground it into my chest. I took about two seconds of this—enough time to snap plenty of pictures—before retreating to the relative safety of the ring. Once inside, the action continued, until, at the seventeen-minute mark, Terry covered me for the pin. It was an exhaustive, brutal, and blood-soaked battle, and I was glad it was over.

But it wasn't over quite yet. Terry had rolled outside the ring and collapsed. In a story that Tracy Smothers loves to tell, Terry was moaning my name. "Cactus, Cactus." I was on the other side of the gym by this point, on my hands and knees, when I heard his mournful cry.

"Terry, where are you?" I cried back, and a slow, emotionally moving crawl began. In Japan, pro wrestling has always been considered more of a sport than it is in the U.S., and the fans gathered around to see this culmination of a mutual show of respect.

"Cactus, Cactus."

"Terry, Terry."

"Cactus."

"Terry." We were finally together, and I extended my badly bleeding hand. Terry shook it, and the two of us embraced, as the 200 in attendance applauded wildly. Then yours truly ruined the scene as I forearmed my hero in the head and gave him a quick piledriver on the floor. "Uhwahhh" came the response, as I left a trail of my bloody handprints crawling away from the shaking Funker.

Back in the dressing room, the other *gai-jins* were in a state of disbelief. Tracy Smothers couldn't stop commenting that it was the most brutal bout he'd ever seen. Terry, who dressed with the Japanese boys (all the other Americans dressed with their own group), was met with an equal reaction in his dressing room across the gym. The Japanese media came in and barraged me for photos, as I proceeded to cut one of the best promos of my life for the video—even if no one could understand what I was saying.

I wanted to shower off the blood that seemingly ran from everywhere, and in truth I was cut in over fifty places. My hands were especially a mess, and the chunks of flesh that peeked up at me from my fingertips were grim and painful reminders of the price we pay for doing what we love. A large gash on my forehead continued to pour as I reached for the comfort of a hot shower. No such luck, however, as in addition to the lack of heat in the building, there was—you guessed it—no hot water. I felt like I'd already endured enough pain, and I just didn't feel up to exposing my naked, bloody body to a stream of ice-cold water. Instead, I took a quick "whore's bath," rising my hands and face as best I could, before throwing on a set of clean clothes. I sanitized my forehead gash with liquid New Skin, and wrapped it with gauze, before looking to my hands. Most of the cuts were not that bad—a few were even superficial—but my pinkies were a mess. I surveyed the situation and made my first aid move. I put about five drops of the New Skin into each wound and then packed the meat back into its hole with my fingers. Tracy then wrapped athletic tape around it and we walked out to the waiting bus.

We drove for an hour and then stopped at a rest area to eat. Terry had driven the first leg of the trip with a group of fans known as "Funk's Army." The rest stop menu was real basic when it comes to Western food, and most of the time I just opted for spaghetti. After the meal, Terry rejoined us on the bus. We sat there reminiscing fondly about our match and wondered about marketing the video in the U.S. It was a definite blending of the thrill of victory with the agony of defeat as our tales of the past and ambitions for the future were tempered only by the stale iron stench of our own blood.

*　　*　　*

Owen

May 29, 12:46 A.M.—I was sitting in front of a TV monitor, watching the World Wrestling Federation *Over the Edge* show as I wrote about Japan. I saw a Blue Blazer vignette and had to smile; Owen Hart was one of wrestling's best performers, and his adventures as the Blazer, especially, were favorites of mine. I returned to writing and looked up minutes later, expecting to see the Blazer in action, but I saw a large crowd shot instead. Pat Patterson came into the room and said that Owen had fallen off a catwalk, some sixty feet above the ring, and was being worked on by paramedics as we spoke. As part of his Blazer routine, Owen was scheduled to descend from the catwalk in true Blazer superhero fashion. Apparently he had problems with his rigging apparatus, and he had crashed inside the ring. I said prayers for Owen as I raced down the hallway, and I arrived just as he was being wheeled into the ambulance. The situation looked grave as one EMT stood atop the stretcher, leaning over Owen, and attempted to revive him with cardiopulmonary resuscitation. We learned an hour later that Owen had died.

I will talk about Owen at length later on, for he was truly one of the funniest men in the business, and Owen Hart stories are always a favorite in the dressing room. I traveled with Owen frequently, and I can honestly say that he was one of the nicest people I've had the pleasure of meeting. He was kind, he was honest, he was considerate, but most of all, he loved his family. I never met Owen's wife or his two children, but I felt as if I had. He spoke of them warmly and often, and my heart goes out to the three of them as well as the entire Hart family. He was a special man, and he deserves a special place in heaven. The world knew of Owen Hart as a great wrestler, but he was an even better human being. Good-bye, my friend—you left us way too soon.

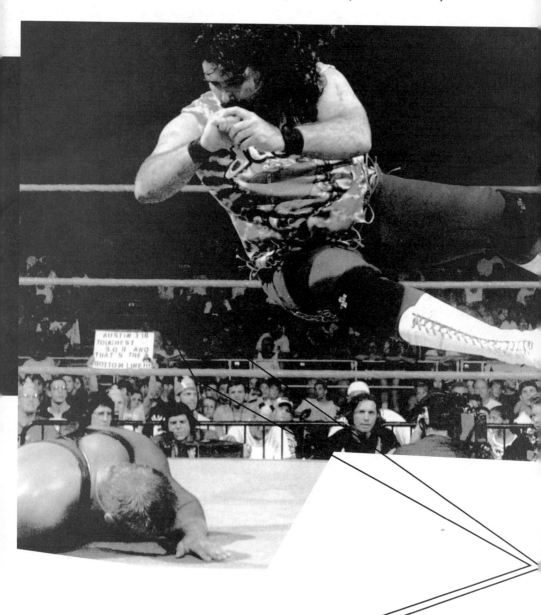

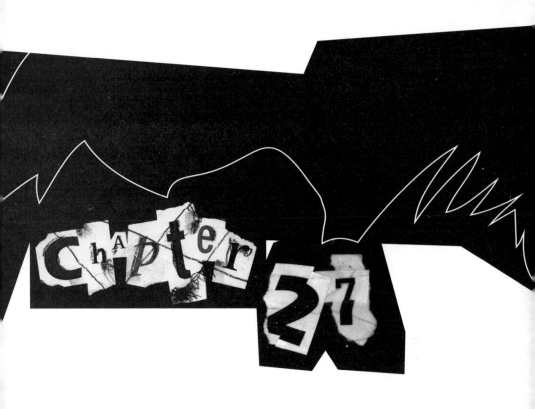

Chapter 27

I returned to the States and
immediately restructured my priorities. My son was really starting to
miss his dad, so I started easing up slightly on my schedule. Between
Japan, where I was now spending ten days every month, and ECW, I
began leaving myself some room to relax. I would simply not book
myself on one weekend a month, and I would then have eleven-day
stretches during which I could heal up and spend quality family time.
At three, my son was at a great age, and I began doing lots of father-
son activities with him that we continue to this day. He went to his
first amusement park and loved it immediately. We ended up getting
passes to a kids' park called American Adventures that gave us especially fond memories. At only one year of age, my Noelle was a little
young for the park, but by the age of two, she was feeling her oats and
would ride just about anything. Now, at five, she has no fear of anything, even Space Mountain, where her only postride comment is "I
want to do it again."

Mikey and I had lost the tag belts to the Public Enemy, and I had
begun a feud with a guy called the Sandman, who is currently
wrestling as Hardcore Hak in WCW. The Sandman character was a

beer-swilling, cigarette-smoking, cane-swinging Philadelphia guy who was loud and abrasive. We did have good chemistry in the ring together, and in addition to having good matches, I was inspired to cut some of my best promos. Unfortunately for Hak, he was on the receiving end of the aforementioned cast-iron skillet, and was sidelined for two weeks. This left me no one to wrestle in March's ECW arena show. Paul E.'s mind went to work, and he came up with a winner.

I was set to wrestle a mystery partner in the main event of the evening. Speculation was running rampant as to who it might be. Abdullah the Butcher, King Kong Bundy, Road Warrior Hawk, and even the estranged Funker were names that were thrown around. One thing was for sure—Paul E. would never let the fans down. I went to the ring first and waited for the mystery opponent. A huge box was rolled to the ring, draped in curtains. Through the curtain and out of the box stepped the legend. The man. The myth. D. C. Drake. Now D. C. Drake was a hell of a nice guy, and a few years earlier had been a mainstay for Joel Goodhart's TWA, but in the three and a half years that had elapsed, he seemed to have lost some of the zing off his fastball. We stunk up the arena, and the ECW faithful were not happy at all with our five-minute extravaganza. Thankfully, the night was not over.

Out of the box stepped the Sandman, whose brains, by this point, were in the final process of unscrambling. He was dressed in his familiar attire of red shirt, white tennis sneakers, and red, white, and blue exercise pants. I was waiting for him, and after ducking a swing with his cane, gave him three shots and threw him right back into the box from which he'd come. The curtain fell down on top of him, but I wasn't quite through. I reached in and pulled him out, curtain and all, and rolled his sorry ass into the ring. I could see him wobbling in his red, white, and blue pants as I prepared to pull the curtain off and inflict more damage. I pulled the curtain off, but to the surprise of everyone, saw not the Sandman, but the legendary Terry Funk in all his glory. The Funker had returned! The response from the crowd was phenomenal, when the fans realized just who it was that stood before them. We went punch for punch, until the Sandman cut me off from behind, and armed with two Singapore canes (better known as the martial arts weapon, the Kendo stick), the two identically clad grapplers commenced to putting a hurting on me. I took a total of forty-six (no, I'm not kidding) cane shots to the head, arms, back, and legs before Shane Douglas interrupted the proceedings.

Shane, the self-coined Franchise, was the ECW champ and the most hated heel in the company. Despite our different roles in the promotion, ECW announcer Joey Styles had, in the past, readily acknowledged our real-life friendship and background at DeNucci's. When Shane stepped slowly into the ring, he motioned for Funk and Sandman to hold me, and readied to level me with his championship belt. Shane started for me, but veered right at the last moment and laid out Funk. He stepped left and laid out the Sandman. The crowd went wild, but more importantly, the Cactus-Funk feud would continue to be big news on both sides of the Pacific. I cut some interviews with Shane, and then rested up for my next tour of Japan.

I flew to Japan for a short trip—just two shows. The importance of the trip cannot be overstated, however, as our first show would be in the sold-out 64,000-seat Tokyo Dome, as part of a thirteen promotion supercard. For a promotion that was used to doing business in small, freezing gyms, this was a huge opportunity. Thirteen offices would contribute one match each to this card, which would set an all-time gate record of somewhere around $6 million. We knew that the other promotions would each try to steal the show, as we were likewise planning on doing our damnedest to achieve. The match we had booked was an eight-man, barbed wire board, barbed wire bat death match that would pit the team of Funk, Leatherface, Nakamaki, and Ono against me, the Headhunters, and someone I can't remember. The barbed wire bat was a standard baseball bat wrapped heavily in barbed wire, and the barbed wire boards were simply plywood boards that had loose bales of barbed wire nailed into them. The concept was a little different, but simple nonetheless. All eight men would line up on the stage area of the massive dome. The announcer would count us down from ten, and at zero, we would all make a mad dash for the ring, which contained the deadly bat. The match would then continue, until one of the team's members was pinned in this anything-goes free-for-all.

I had my doubts about just what the sprint down the sixty-yard Tokyo Dome ramp might look like—I mean we didn't exactly look like a track team backstage. On one side, Funk was over fifty and had knees that looked like a cartoonist had drawn them on his body. They certainly didn't look like human knees. Nakamaki was no athletic wonder, and Leatherface was a 320-pound Canadian who was coming off a severe foot injury. He had tried to catch one of the

Headhunters, two 400-pound identical twins from the Dominican Republic, and the fall had not just broken his foot, but crushed it. I myself had been one of the slowest guys on the Ward Melville lacrosse team—long before the ring injuries took their toll. Well, maybe Ono or the guy I can't remember could run.

We stood in the waiting area while the match before us went on. To put it kindly, the match was godawful, but the crowd was going crazy. The contestants Rhuma Go and his two masked Americans were putting on one of the worst performances I'd ever seen, but the sold-out crowd was eating up every bit of it. These guys made the Test–Rodney match look like Flair–Steamboat. "This is great," I yelled to one of the Headhunters. "If they react to this garbage, wait till they see Terry." The reprehensible match mercifully ended, and four at a time, the two teams took to the stage.

There was a slight bit of applause when our team showed up— very slight. To tell you the truth, I thought my growing recognition would have resulted in a better response than this. I got over it quickly, and waited anxiously for the huge roar that would greet the legendary Funker. The Funker arrived, but unfortunately, the roar didn't. It was polite, and far more than our team had merited, but it was far from deafening. I couldn't figure it out, especially given the reaction to the previous match, and I stood dumbfounded in front of 64,000 fans. What I didn't realize is that Rhuma Go is a big wrestling joke that the whole country is in on. His matches were supposed to be bad, and the fans loved him for it. This was information that I wished I'd had access to, because to tell you the truth, I felt like a big jerk standing out there.

As a matter of fact, we stood there for a long time. Someone had forgotten to tell the announcer about the ten-second countdown, and as a result, we had no way of starting our match. Finally, after what seemed like hours, but was probably a good five minutes, I heard Funk yell over, "I guess someone better run." I took the initiative and took off down the ramp. Because the 64,000-seat dome had all the emotion of the world's largest funeral, I figured I would be able to hear footsteps on the hard wooden ramp. I didn't. Instead, I looked back and saw the danger man a good thirty yards behind me. I slowed to a jog, and then finally a slow walk, while I waited for Nakamaki to catch up. When he finally did, I turned around and followed a boot to his midsection up with a DDT on the ramp. "Uhwahh." It was slight, but I heard it. The rest of the crew still had a lot of catching up to do. I walked into the ring and casually took control of the bat. Seconds later, Terry stepped through the ropes, and I raised the bat over my head to give the impression that I actually intended to use it on him. I was being so deliberate that my body language was literally screaming out to be cut off. I was expecting a boot to the stomach or at worst a wide open back to swing at, but the Funker did neither. Instead he closed one eye and looked up at me with the other. His fists were clenched tightly, and his body was shaking. I could read his body language loud and clear. It was literally screaming, "Hit me."

I brought the bat down hard over Terry's head. I won't pretend it was full speed, but it wasn't half-assed either. I had just taken a three-quarter-speed swing at a defenseless old man with a baseball bat wrapped in barbed wire. "Uhwahh!" I heard the reaction that time. It had hurt me to have to lambaste my own idol, but in fulfillment of my prediction made seven months earlier in the ECW Arena, not as bad as it had hurt him. Rivulets of blood streamed down Terry's face from four different puncture wounds. Terry had dropped to his knees, and was obviously in great pain. This time, when I lifted the bat overhead, he was quick to react. He kicked me in the stomach, and when I dropped the bat, he was there to recover the fumble. I looked at the blood streaming down his face and knew that payback would be hell. I gave him my back, and he took full advantage of it. Four times the bat went up, and four times it came down. Four times I heard the "uhwahh" from the crowd, as they started to gain an understanding of what the IWA was all about.

I separated from Terry and turned my attention elsewhere. Nakamaki and I had a big move lined up, and I figured the time was right. I put the boots to the journalist-turned-wrestler and then placed one of the barbed wire boards in the middle of the ring. I took a bottle of lighter fluid from one of the young boys and proceeded to generously douse the board. I returned the bottle, and was handed a lighter. Believe it or not, that psycho danger man bastard wanted me to suplex him off the top rope onto a board of flaming barbed wire. The crowd that minutes earlier hadn't given a damn about us were now on the edge of their seats. The buzz from the sold-out crowd was giving me a buzz of my own, as I set the lighter to the board. "Uhwahh" went the crowd, but . . . nothing. Another flick of my Bic, but I couldn't get the damn thing to light. The crowd caught on, and

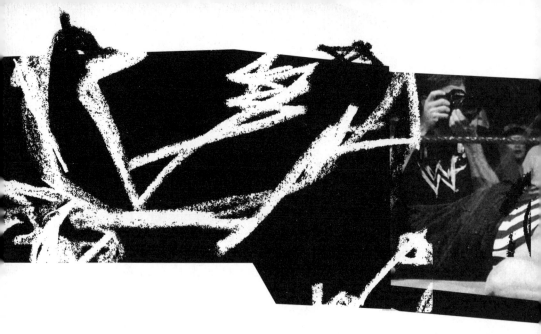

began laughing at us. It was not a great feeling. Finally, after flicking uselessly, I gave up.

I could see the disappointment in Nakamaki's eyes as we quickly came up with a plan B. As plan Bs go, it was pretty good. I slammed Nakamaki on the failed board, and then threw another on top of him. Headhunter B climbed the top rope and completed a perfect moonsault—sandwiching Nakamaki between the boards with his 400-pound frame. "Uhwahh." We had them back.

The match concluded with what one wrestling journalist called "the greatest clusterfuck of incredible moves ever seen in the ring." Bodies were flying all over, and somewhere in the mayhem, I split my left arm open, causing the thick pink scars that have become something of a trademark. I honestly don't remember who won, but we had all worked extremely hard, and the match itself had been a major victory for our little group of dedicated bloodletters. I wrestled the next night with my arm heavily bandaged. It was a decent match, but nothing memorable. I do remember vividly that I never received a dime out of that $6 million house.

On a strange side note, I found out later that the fire marshal would have shut down the entire show if the board had gone up in flames. I would have gone down in wrestling history as the guy who killed the biggest show of all time. Asano was so mad at us that he slapped the referee, even though he was completely innocent. I guess you can get away with that if you have $500 million.

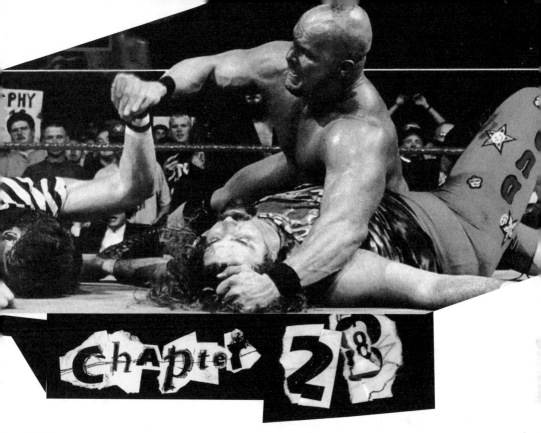

Chapter 28

When I returned home, Colette

had great news. She had been offered a job with Wilhelmina Models in New York, the same company she had done so well with years earlier. Within fifteen months, she had gone from a 180-pound pregnant housewife into something out of the pages of *Muscle and Fitness*. I'd had my doubts when she started doing Jane Fonda aerobics in the living room, but was pleasantly surprised to see her still stepping and jumping weeks later. She was obviously pleased with the results, and with my encouragement, began coming with me to the gym that Sting owned outside Atlanta. Colette started wearing out the cardio equipment, and her achievements were not going unnoticed, as no less an authority than Diamond Dallas Page declared her an "inspiration."

I began talking to Colette about giving modeling another try, as I truly felt that she was more beautiful than I'd ever seen her—modeling photos included. In the years since Colette had left modeling, the industry had changed quite a bit, and girls were no longer "washed up" at twenty-three. She had photos done in Atlanta, and was welcomed back to her old company—albeit in their "mature ladies" division.

We rented out our house in Atlanta and packed up for my old

stomping grounds, Long Island, New York. Colette had some reservations about making us move, but I assured her that the move would also make things easier on me as well. From New York, I could fly nonstop to Tokyo, and could commute to most ECW shows as well. All in all, a move to New York would be easier on me, and allow Colette a second chance to do what she loved. My parents were also thrilled to be close to their grandchildren and loving, Hardcore Legend of a son.

Months later, Colette thanked me for never once making her feel fat or unattractive, even though she herself had felt that way. I kissed her and told her that she'd always been beautiful to me. Still, I was glad to have my gorgeous, slim wife back. Yesss!

The next few months seemed to blend together, professionally. I feuded with Funker in the U.S., and I feuded with Funker overseas. Actually, Terry was not on all the Japanese tours, and sometimes it was just me and Leatherface on the *gai-jin* side of things. The trips were long and the amenities stank, but I was selling my shirts, and getting over with the fans, and the boredom of life so far from home was a price I had to pay. I read a hell of a lot over there, and became better acquainted with my body. I read books of all types ranging from classics like *Moby Dick* to biographies and Civil War history. My personal favorite was a book I found called *Sins*, by Judith Gould, which actually featured my wife on the cover (she'd modeled for the painting). The book was definitely not typical men's fare, but I was fascinated by the idea that my wife was the title character who built her own fashion empire.

Despite the hard work and solitude, I was proud of my efforts in Japan. Tarzan Goto had jumped ship from the rival FMW, and his addition helped fuel an IWA resurgence. IWA had announced plans for a King of the Death Match tournament for the beginning of August in the 40,000-seat Kawasaki Stadium. The idea had seemed ludicrous at first, but with me, Funk, Goto, the Headhunters, and Nakamaki leading the way, the IWA had become the hottest small promotion in Japan.

Colette was working steadily—nothing big yet, but enough to make it worthwhile. Dewey was adjusting well to Dad's long absence, and Noelle's little personality was really starting to bloom. I remember when she was only weeks old, I said to Colette, "I bet she's going to have her own little personality," which was a nice way of saying,

"We really don't have a very good-looking child." We thought that we were going to have a very plain-looking daughter with a very serious personality, for Noelle seldom smiled as a baby. At about that time in Long Island, however, she began to really blossom, and the beauty of her tiny face is now matched only by the beauty of her little ways.

I was able to drive to most of the ECW shows, which was a big help, and I'd often drive my buddy Mikey home with me, where he'd sleep on our bed in the basement, before I'd drop him off in the morning. One day I had Colette and the kids with me as we returned Mikey to his home, and we saw a mother cat frolicking with her kittens.

"Aren't those kitties nice?" I asked my son, who nodded in agreement. "Can you say that, buddy?" I asked, knowing that like most kids, Dewey had trouble with certain letters.

"Nice titties," Dewey yelled out, prompting an unsuspecting Mikey to spit milk all over our dashboard.

My hard work was paying off—I had been gone from WCW for almost a year, and although I hadn't made nearly as much money as I had with the big company, I had actually saved more of it. I didn't need anybody, I could make my own schedule, and I loved it.

I pulled into the ECW arena in August of 1995, a few hours late, as I had become lost on the way to the building. I had been to the damn place over a dozen times, but its whereabouts always seemed to elude me. I had Colette and the kids with me, as we were planning on going to Pennsylvania Dutch country afterward. Paul E. ran up to me in desperation. "Cactus," he gasped, "I've got a big angle, and it will change the course of your career and maybe even your life. You don't have to do it, and you can think about it for a long time."

"What is it, Paul?" The mad scientist was sweating, and was looking older than his thirty years.

"Cactus—I want to turn you heel."

This was indeed a career-altering decision that could very well change the course of my life. I thought about it deeply—for about three seconds. "Okay," I said, "let's do it."

I was scheduled to take part in an eight-man tag team match. On one side would be Raven and three of the Dudley Boys. The Dudley Boys had started out as a takeoff on the Hanson Brothers, who had appeared in the Paul Newman hockey movie *Slapshot*. The movie was dated, but the Hansons were timeless. Their taped-up black eyeglasses, overalls, and long greasy hair lent a comedic look that was countered by an aggressive style. In time, the Dudley clan would grow to include an American Indian, a black guy, and Sign Guy Dudley, who should not be confused with the original sign guy—a strange fan who sat first row ringside, and held up a vast arsenal of original signs. The original sign guy had once held up a sign that said "Cane Dewey," a thought that was supposed to be humorous, but had made Colette sick to her stomach upon hearing of it. Our team consisted of Cactus Jack, Pitbulls 1 and 2, and Tommy Dreamer. Tommy was a personal project of Paul E.'s who was willing to do anything for the acceptance of the fans. He had once been a laughingstock of the company, as no matter what body part he sacrificed, the fans continued to shower him with ridicule. The hardcore ECW fans had despised him partly because he was a good-looking young man, and partly because of his ridiculous ring attire that included green suspenders. Eventually his

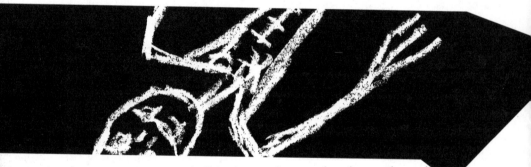

determination, Paul E.'s ingenuity, and other talented wrestlers got him over to the point where he was at least respected if not completely loved. The fans' chants to him of "He's hardcore, he's hardcore," seemed at least partially in jest, but nonetheless he seemed poised on the brink of stardom and needed just a little something extra to push him completely over. I was it.

The match was well received by the 1,000-plus in attendance at the bingo hall. Tommy was in the midst of a nearly year-long feud with Raven that had seen Tommy on the receiving end of unbelievable punishment, but no clean victories. This was the night he finally had his chance. The ring had emptied, and Tommy had planted Raven with a DDT. The referee moved in for the count, but it was broken up at two by a big Cactus Jack cowboy boot to the head. (My gear bag had been stolen months earlier, including my leopard-skin Cactus boots, and I had been too cheap to replace them.) I lifted the baffled Dreamer off the floor, and caught him quickly with a double arm DDT on a chair. I pulled Raven overtop of him, and once again, Dreamer was denied. I left the ring to the open-jawed response of the crowd. Some of the best work of my career was about to begin.

I left the auditorium of the ECW arena for the tranquillity of the Amish farmlands. After a few days of relaxation and shoo fly pie, I flew to Tokyo for a ten-day tour that would culminate in the longest day of my life.

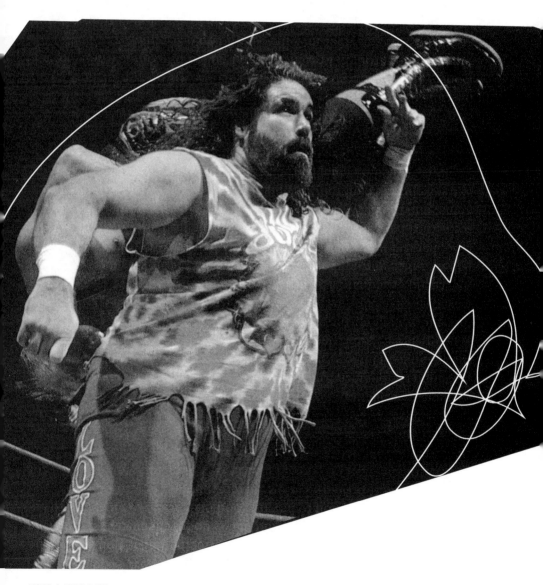

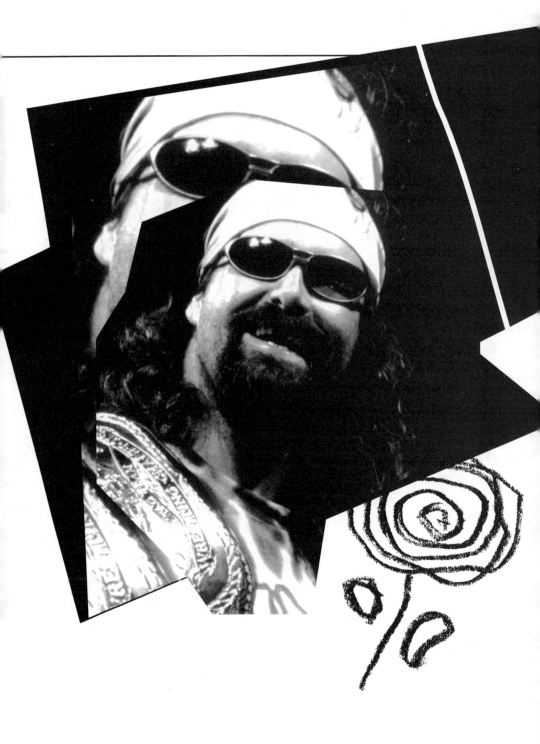

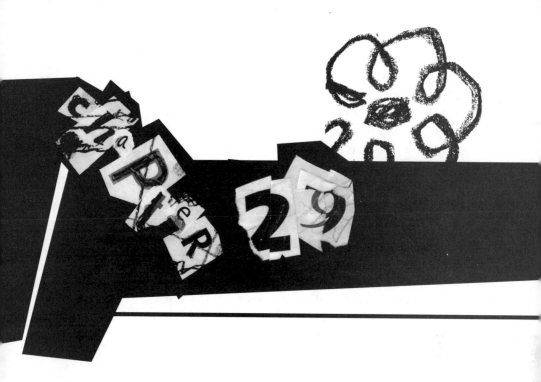

August 18, 1995. We had been on
the road for eight days and had traveled via the Japanese bullet train
into the wee hours of the morning. We were awakened after about five
hours' sleep, and took the two-hour bus trip from the Ikebukuru section of Tokyo into Yokohama. I stepped off the bus in front of the
dilapidated baseball stadium, and knew right away that I was going to
be in trouble. It was only ten in the morning, but the temperature was
already over ninety. The humidity was almost unbearable.

I walked into the stadium, where they had three rings set up in the
infield part of the stadium. The day would be filled with a variety of
inhuman gimmick matches, and the three-ring setup would ensure
speedy transitions between matches. Without them, we would have
been there until September. I looked at the brackets for the King of the
Death Match tournament. I would be facing Terry Gordy in the opening round in a barbed wire bat, 10,000 thumbtack match. The
thumbtacks would be placed in two shallow boxes and the object was
simple—get your opponent in the box, in an attempt to get the pin. If
I were victorious in the opening match (which I had reason to believe I
would be), I would take on the winner of Nakamaki–Ono contest in a
barbed wire board, bed of nails match. Pretty self-explanatory. Then,
on to the grand finale, the coup de grace, the big daddy of them all. The
no rope, barbed wire board, C4 explosive, exploding ring death match.

I don't mind telling you that the concept scared me a little bit. I was okay with everything up until the C4, and then had some questions. The C4 was rigged to four of the barbed wire boards, and would be detonated upon impact. I had seen exploding rings in Japanese videos before, and they were a sight to be seen. At the ten-minute mark of the match, a cannonlike concussion would go off on all four sides of the ring. The concussions were ear-splitting in volume, and threw unbelievable firepower into the sky. I had been told by the Funker, who had survived one of these things, that if you lie on the canvas, you'd be okay, but that it was hotter than hell and hard to breathe for a few minutes, until the smoke cleared.

Victor Quinones summoned me to the outfield, where the demolitions expert was about to give us a C4 demonstration. I stood there looking at the barbed wire board, which had two explosives attached to each end of the six-foot plywood. Funk, Nakamaki, Leatherface, and I gathered around, and the expert flicked a switch. BABOOM! It was the loudest thing I'd ever heard in my life. Scariest too. I was the first to speak up. "No way," I gasped, "that thing will kill us." Nakamaki and Leatherface agreed.

Then the wizened, grizzled Funker spoke up, and with thirty years of experience aiding his judgment, said, "No, no, that looks fine, but I think we need two more right in the middle—then it will be great."

"Terry," I said, with more than a little desperation in my voice, "you've got to be kidding—there will be nowhere to land. How can we land if there will be explosives all over the damn thing?"

Terry thought about it, and smiled his Terry smile. "No, no Cactus—it'll be fine. Trust me!" I did, and later wished I hadn't.

At one o'clock, we hit the gimmick table for a two-hour selling session. I had been coming to Japan only seven months, but in that time the Japanese yen had lost a great deal of its value. I sold my shirts for 2,000 yen, but that amount brought in only $16 U.S., whereas in January, the same shirt yielded $24 U.S. I knew that I was in for a torturous tournament, but dammit, I'm a salesman, not a wrestler. I was positioned with the Headhunters at the table by the rear entrance. While the Japanese boys sat under a veranda by the main entrance, the gai-jins sweated it out in the hot sun. Sales were brisk for this big event, and I left the table at bell time as a hotter, sweatier, but somewhat richer man.

I readied myself for the Gordy match. Terry Gordy had at one time been one of the ten best wrestlers in the world. He had been celebrated as a member of the original Freebirds, and had been a legend in All-Japan wrestling before an accident put him in a coma for several days. When he reemerged, he was never quite the same.

Terry had attempted his comeback a short while later, but it was painful to watch. The vicious, aggressive Gordy was gone, and in his place stood a confused, sluggish man. His punches and kicks, which had at one point been his calling card, now looked particularly weak. One of my saddest memories was of Terry at an independent show in Chattanooga, Tennessee, where at intermission, he took to the ring for Polaroids. Only two or three fans bothered to pose with one of wrestling's true greats, and my heart went out to him. Even sadder, Terry didn't take that as a cue to leave, and instead stood inside the empty ring for several minutes—smiling his sad Muppet smile.

To his credit, however, Terry had trained intensely after his injury. He was actually in better physical condition than he was in his prime, and as the months went by, some of the mental fog seemed to lift. There were brief periods in matches where he looked like the Gordy of old. Unlike the U.S., where a wrestler is seemingly forgotten overnight, the Japanese had a deep sense of tradition, and Terry's name was still valuable. Knowing this, Mr. Asano had hired him for the tournament, the ramifications of which, apparently, Terry was unaware of.

A week earlier, the IWA had held a press conference to hype the tournament, which had gained surprisingly strong fan support. When asked about his first-round match, Terry referred to an excellent bout that we had wrestled for the Global Wrestling Federation in the summer of 1991. "Jack, I dropped you on your head once, and I can do it again."

I was given a chance to respond and yelled, "That was different, Gordy. Tell me what you're going to do when you step into that ring at Kawasaki Stadium and see those 10,000 thumbtacks? I'm going to turn your ass into the world's largest pin cushion."

Terry's eyes seemed to grow as wide as saucers, and after the press conference, he approached me. "Bro," he said in his deep, sad, basset hound voice, "I didn't know anything about no thumbtacks."

I approached this match very seriously for a couple of reasons. I wanted to have a great match to set the tone for the show, but just as importantly, I wanted to honor and preserve Terry's reputation. I was really concerned about the weakness of Terry's punches and told him so. "Terry," I said "I want this match to look good, and I think maybe to play it safe, you should just hit me your hardest out there."

"Are you sure, bro?" he wanted to know.

"Yeah, Terry, I am."

Terry looked at me sadly, and I could tell the words that followed were difficult for him to say. "Bro, just help me out there."

I came out of the dugout to the strains of a song by the band Megadeth. The Japanese had a great knack for picking cool entrance music and this was no different. I could feel the hot sun beating down on me as I looked at the crowd, which was pretty damn impressive. Thirty thousand fans had turned out to see the little company that could. Gordy was then announced, and we lined up on opposite sides of field, about thirty yards from the ring, as the announcer counted us down in English. Ten, nine, eight—I was nervous as hell. Seven, six, five—my heart was pounding, but I knew that I was ready. Four, three, two—Gordy jumped the gun, and by the time my big ass got into the ring, he was waiting with the barbed wire bat. I fed him my back, and he took full advantage. I took two hard hits and bailed out to the floor, where Gordy followed. "Go ahead, Terry, hit me," I yelled. Whatever fears I'd had about his punches disappeared immediately. BAM, I felt the smack of fist against skull. BAM. BAM. BAM. BAM. I finally turned and staggered away. I reached for my head, and felt the sticky warmth of my own blood. Without even meaning to, Terry had busted my eyebrow open. He hadn't let me down. I could almost hear Harley grumbling all the way from Kansas City. As a matter of fact, the cover photo of the *Raw* issue titled "Blood, Guts, and Mick Foley" was taken right after these punches were thrown.

I rolled into the ring, and the Terry Gordy of old followed me in. He whipped me into the turnbuckle, and followed me in with a brutal clothesline. When I ran, I stepped into the shallow box, and the sole of one of my cowboy boots filled with thumbtacks. Another whip, another clothesline, and I went down, next to the box, with my face actually turned to its side on top of the tiny gold tacks. Gordy gave me a stiff boot to the other side of my face, and I could feel the pushpins sinking into my flesh. "Uhwahh." I staggered to my feet and did my best slow, stumbling watusi, so that every fan could take a good look. The response was incredible—like a feeling of disgust and enjoyment at the same time. It seemed kind of like when the great white shark is dragging Quint into its mouth in the movie *Jaws*—painful to watch but fun nonetheless. I guess it was kind of like watching the Mean Street Posse in action, except for the fun part.

A minute later, and Terry picked me up for the powerbomb. The timing was off and Terry didn't get me very high, but he brought me down right in the middle of the tacks, and the crowd went wild. Gordy turned to the fans and did his unique celebratory dance, while I picked up a handful of tacks. When Terry turned to me, I threw the tacks at his face. When he covered up, I gave him a boot to the stomach and a DDT into the box for the win.

It had been a tremendous match, and I was exhausted, but happy. With the exception of his hand, Terry had escaped thumbtack free. In contrast to my press conference prediction, it was actually I who had turned into the world's largest pincushion. After the match, I was interviewed for the *King of the Death Match* commercial video, which would be a huge success around the world, despite the fact that I never received a dime for it. My interview was strong, as I praised Gordy for having taught me a valuable lesson, but it couldn't match Terry's for its verbiage and delivery: "Fuck, I can't believe that fucker beat me. Fuck!"

I retreated to the dressing area, where I was shocked to find that there was no water, soda, juice, or beverages of any kind. I looked around to see if Bill Watts had secretly taken over. I ended up going into the concession area, where a fan was more than happy to buy a sports drink for the bleeding, sweating Cactus Jack.

The danger man, Shoji Nakamaki, had defeated Ono in their match, so a short while later, I looked on with great interest as two huge beds of nails were brought to ringside. I had only seen one other bed of nails match, featuring the team of Nakamaki and Ono against two Leatherfaces, and it had been obscene in its brutality.

Mike Kirschener had been the original Leatherface, for the FMW promotion in Japan. He'd had a short run in the World Wrestling Federation as Corporal Kirschener in the mid-eighties, but their attempt at making him a new Sergeant Slaughter had failed, and he had been drifting in the business for years before catching on in Japan. He was a nice guy, but he had a short fuse, and two years earlier an argument that he had not started ended with him punching a Japanese man in the face. The punch had been so devastating that the man's face had been almost destroyed, and Kirschener spent six months in a Japanese jail as a result.

During his incarceration, Rick Patterson from Canada was suited up for the popular Leatherface gimmick, and had moved to IWA when Victor Quinones jumped ship. Six months later, with Kirschener returning, the tag team of the Leatherfaces was formed. They only lasted one match—the bed of nails. Kirschener was pretty adamant about not losing in his return to the ring, and when he did, he became incensed. "Let's get these bastards," Kirschener yelled in his deep gravelly voice. Kirschener had ripped off a piece of the board (no small feat) and had handed it to Patterson to press down on Ono's neck. Now the secret of the nails, if there is such a thing, is to try to land on as many of the nails as possible. By doing this, no one nail has the chance to do serious damage. Kirschener was about to prove that theory's flipside—fewer nails equals more damage—as he yelled "Hold him there, I'm gonna drop a fuckin' leg on him." Patterson was a kind human being, and he tried to hold the board steady, to minimize the impact. No such luck however, as the former Corporal came down full force, and drove the nails dangerously deep into Ono's neck. It wasn't enough. "Let's give him a fuckin' powerbomb" he ordered. Ono fought the powerbomb, but Kirschener was not to be denied, and he flipped him up, and dropped him down on the brutal, nail-filled board. He was fired immediately.

Now, I'm not a sadist, and I don't take liberties, but this was a big match, and people were expecting big things. Luckily, the Danger Man loved this type of thing. The hot afternoon sun was giving way to a somewhat cooler evening as I took to the ring. Nakamaki stepped in and the bed of nails, barbed wire board match was on. I put the boots to good old Shoji, and then threw him outside. I set up one of the wire boards against the ring and whipped him toward it. He reversed it and I hit the board but bounded right back with a clothesline. The Insane Clown Posse, a rap group that later appeared in the World Wrestling Federation, released a commercial video of the match that contained some unique commentary. "He shoots Cactus Sack [my name in their version—my father was Prickly Balls] into the barbed wire, but look, it doesn't even faze the toothless bastard." Actually not much was fazing me that day—I was "in the zone."

I was putting a beating on Nakamaki, but was taking some punishment as well. I slammed him inside the ring on the barbed wire board, and went for a big elbow. Shoji moved and it was I who now landed on the wire. Years later, even Paul Bearer winced when he saw the tape and saw wire sticking in my shoulder as I tried to get up. I took some Nakamaki headbutts (his big move) but came right back, and dropped him on the wire. It was time to introduce the bed of nails. I slid it into the ring and propped it up in the corner as the crowd began to buzz. I grabbed the bleeding Danger Man and, standing above him, attempted to grind his head into the nails. Bleeding was part of Nakamaki's gimmick. Don't feel bad for him, he would have bled that night even if I'd never touched him. To many in the strange Japanese subculture of "garbage wrestling," scar tissue was seen as a badge of courage, and many young wrestlers set about getting that badge by any means necessary. To be honest, my career had benefited greatly from my scarred arm—it made me "legitimate" in many fans' eyes.

Nakamaki scooted out backward through my legs and delivered a headbutt. I fell into the bed. "Uhwahh," the crowd loved it. Another headbutt, another fall, another "uhwahh." The nails pierced my skin, and pain shot through my body, but it honestly wasn't that bad. I was rocking and reeling, but I stopped him and threw him to the infield grass. We were right by the second bed of nails, and when I picked him up, they stood in unison to see the impact of flesh on pointed steel. Instead, I slammed him somewhat harmlessly on the stadium infield. I could hear the disappointment from the fans. But I had a definite plan, and it didn't include something as mundane as a simple slam on the nails. No, they deserved more. By God, I was getting paid $300 for the day ($100 per match), and I was going to give the fans and Asano every penny's worth. I lifted the board, leaned it over Nakamaki, and then quickly hopped to the ring apron. The crowd was on its feet again. I think they could smell what I was cooking. I raised my arm toward the heavens and took off on my familiar two-step course down the apron. Nakamaki was only eight feet away, but in this case, distance didn't matter—he was under a bed of F'ing nails! I took off and landed hard. I tried to take care of the poor guy, but I'd be lying if I said I cared more about his physical well-being than about the well-being of the video-tape. His pain would go away, eventually—the video wouldn't. And besides, in an attempt to ease my conscience, "This guy loves it."

Actually he didn't look like he was feeling a whole lot of love as he lay there writhing on the ground. My experience with the nails hadn't been too bad, but I couldn't say the same for Nakamaki. The nails had dug in deep in a couple of spots, and he was in considerable pain. "Okay, okay," he assured me, when I asked him how he was.

The ending was less than smooth, as I attempted to superplex him off the top rope onto the boards. Nakamaki was a notorious "sand bagger" who was almost impossible to lift off the ground. Instead I gave him a sloppy-looking, low suplex in the ring, and finished him with a DDT on the barbed wire board. Two down, one to go.

Meanwhile, on the other side of the bracket, Terry Funk had defeated Leatherface in a chain match, and Tiger Jeet Singh in a glass match, when my interference backfired. Tiger was another veteran of

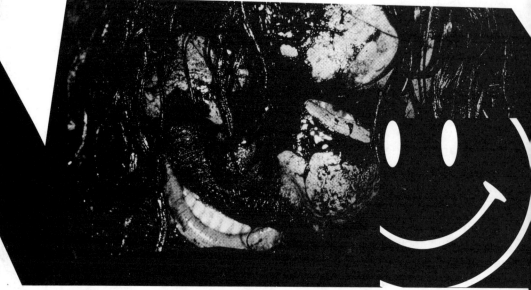

Japan, and in some ways a legend also, but to me, he was the antithesis of Terry Funk. Terry had become an icon through thirty years of blood, sweat, and tears, while Tiger had done it with a few wins over Antonio Inoki, back when Inoki never lost. Terry stayed "over" by constantly giving to other people. He gave of his heart, his wisdom, and his kindness. Tiger stayed "over" by taking.

I had been on the cover of the Japanese wrestling magazine *Baseball* the week of the tournament. Don't ask me why they call it *Baseball*. I don't know. I also don't know why such a technologically advanced country has little porcelain holes in the ground to poop in instead of toilets. The few toilets they did have tended to be luxury models, with heating devices and bidets. I don't know why. I also don't know why their versions of respected news magazines had nude centerfolds. I do know why Tiger stayed over, however—he was smart. He saw me on the cover of *Baseball* magazine and immediately convinced Asano to team the two of us up. As soon as Asano gave the go-ahead, he called a press conference. Even though he was still in his underwear, he had photographers shoot our "training" session, which included "beating up" a couple of young boys in the ring.

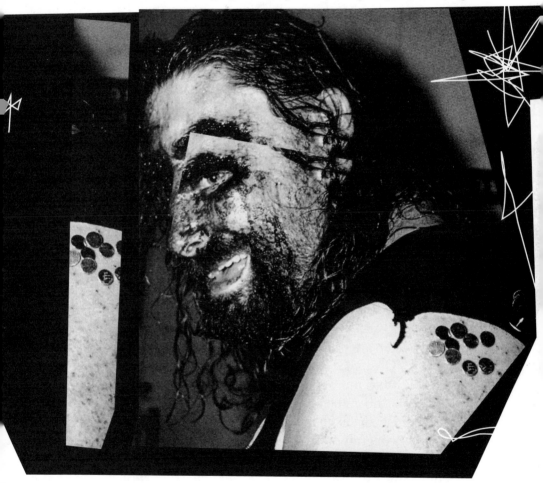

I'm sure the Japanese fans saw it as an example of the wild Tiger on the loose. My wife, however, saw it another way. When I returned home, she took one look at Tiger's picture and said, "Who is the old guy with his balls showing?" Sure enough, upon closer viewing, I could see the great Tiger's wrinkly sack peeking through his BVDs.

Tiger had taken me out to eat with him on the first night of the tour. Twenty years earlier, when wrestling was on primetime TV in Japan, the foreigners who were stars were able to attract "sponsors" who took care of them. The sponsors would wine and dine them, and often give them huge sums of money for the pleasure of their company. It was almost like prostitution, but without the sex. In the current era, sponsors were simply fans who took us out to eat, but a number of old stars like Tiger had held on to their old contacts.

We were picked up in Ikebekuro by a friend of Tiger's in a Cadillac, which was a very rare luxury in Japan. We drove two hours to Kobe and along the way Tiger was giving instructions on how to act in front of the sponsors. "Don't shake hands. Look at me. Do what I do," Tiger kept coaching me on the way to the restaurant. When we got there, I undoubtedly had the best meal of all my tours. The Korean barbecue was unreal, and I ate with gusto, until my belly swelled with satisfaction. Now I wanted to go, but apparently it wasn't time yet.

I sat there while the others talked, and I thought about the Yakuza (Japanese Mafia). The only things I knew were that they sported tattoos over their entire upper bodies (kind of like the World Wrestling Federation dressing room) and had part of their pinky finger cut off as a sign of either loyalty or disloyalty. I looked across the table at my three new buddies, and tried to inconspicuously check out their fingers. I felt like I did when I was trying to look down Irene Farugia's cleavage in tenth grade. There they were—no finger, no finger, no finger. I could hear Ricky Nelson singing again, but I had no way to leave.

Hours later, after hearing no English except for a stunning karaoke version of "Green, Green Grass of Home," it was time to go. I saw Tiger walk up to our sponsors and shake their hands. Hey, I thought that was a no-no. When he did, I heard the unmistakable crumple of paper money being exchanged. Predictably, there were no handshakes or exchanges of crumpled money for the Hardcore Legend. On the way back to Tokyo, I promised myself that I would never do it again. From then on, I stuck to my sponsors—normal fans who would pick up the tab. Most of the time, I drank Met-Rx or paid for myself.

A friend asked me one time how much money I spent during a week in Japan. I asked him to guess, and having heard of outrageous Japanese food prices, he aimed high. "A thousand?" he asked.

"No," I replied, "it's a little lower than that."

"Eight hundred?"

I shook my head. After he'd guessed a couple more figures, I broke the news. "I spend about a hundred a week."

"A hundred," my astonished friend blurted out. "That's only $15 a day."

I smiled and said, "I know, I go to Japan to make money, not to spend it." On this night at the Kawasaki Stadium, however, I was hoping, in addition to money, that I would be bringing as much of myself home as possible.

I looked in the mirror, and saw a weary man looking back. I had a large gash over my right eye, and considerable swelling underneath it. My left arm was slightly cut, and my back was killing me. I really wasn't even going to try to have a good match—I was just going to try to get through it. I could still hear those C4 explosions in my mind, and they still scared the hell out of me, despite the Funker's assurances. I though of Colette, Noelle, and Dewey at home. I missed them terribly and wanted to see them. I was looking forward to my post-tour ritual of a Japanese chocolate bar and ice cream in my bed. I was looking forward to the trip home, even if it would be spent jammed into seat 26B. I sat down on my bench and said a prayer.

I walked into the dugout. It was nightfall, and with the humidity all but gone, it had turned into a beautiful starry evening. The semi-main event was in the ring, Tarzan Goto against ultimate fighting champion Dan "the Beast" Severn. Years later, in Chattanooga, I asked Owen Hart how his match with the Beast had gone. Owen said, "He's a nice guy."

I stopped and called to Owen, who was walking away. "Owen, I didn't ask you what kind of guy he was, I asked how the match went."

Owen smiled and gave his little chuckle, which I will miss hearing very much. The answer came back, "He's a really nice guy."

Dan never really could make the transition from ultimate fighting to sports-entertainment. On this night, however, he and Goto were having a hell of a match, and the crowd was eating it up. I stepped back into my dressing room to make some final mental preparations, but I couldn't help feeling good for Dan. He really was a nice guy.

When I went into the ring I was still scared, but filled with a feeling of power that was not unlike my feeling of being on top of the scaffold in Fort Worth six years earlier. Some of the fans were chanting "Cock-toos-uh," but most of them were physically and mentally worn out from hours of sunshine and bloodshed. The Funker arrived in the ring to his decades-old theme music, and chants of "Telly, Telly." He looked old and worn out. Hell, he was old and worn out. His shirt was spattered with blood from his previous match's tumble into the plate glass. It went without saying that Terry would be the guy taking the bump in the glass—it wasn't Tiger's style. Once again, Terry had given, and Tiger had taken.

The bell rang, and we stalked each other like Rocky and Apollo Creed in the last round of *Rocky*. Terry flicked out a couple of weak jabs that grazed my eye, and opened my gash slightly. It was tough to get a rhythm going. Barbed wire matches were tough enough, even without the added presence of boards laced with explosives in every corner. We tried to use the wire, and we tried to do some moves. We fought outside, and used the nonexplosive boards, and I even hit Terry with a half-used spool of barbed wire. We rolled back into the ring and Terry pulled one of the boards into the middle of the ring. Kawasaki Stadium started to buzz. This is what they came to see.

With the ominous board in the center of the ring, we picked up the pace. Punch for punch we went, and then I took over. *Wham!* A forearm staggered the grizzled veteran. *Wham!* Another one had him reeling. Terry was positioned directly in front of the board and was about to go down. Four more forearms to the head and the Funker finally fell, like a tree, onto the explosives blow. BABOOM! "Uhwahh!" It was just as loud, and just as scary as it had been in the outfield seven hours earlier. Scarier, actually, because my idol was lying in the middle of 30,000 people with his body shaking and his arm badly burned. I knew that we shouldn't have allowed the extra explosives. I also knew that it would be my turn next.

I brought Terry to the wire strands on his hands and knees. I draped him over, and then took two steps back. I came with an elbow, but Terry moved out of the way, and I landed awkwardly on the wire with my back and triceps taking the brunt of the barbs. Terry picked me up and shot me into the wire. As I got closer, I became braver, to the point that I thought, "I'm going to take this whole side out." I'd done this twice at Korakuen Hall, and it was impressive, but injuries were likely. I didn't really care at this point; I was pretty banged up already. As it turned out, the point was moot—the wire was strung so well that my entire body barely even made it sag. Oh, it ripped me up, all right, it just didn't look very good.

The move bought Terry some time, however, and when I got up, another explosive board was in center ring, and Terry was waiting with a hip toss. Baboom! "Uhwahh!" "Wait, what's this?" I thought, "I'm not even really hurt." Apparently I had been rolling with the hip toss, and in the split second between impact and detonation, I had narrowly avoided most of the explosion.

Terry stayed on me and threw me outside. After a brief foray into the fans, he threw me back in the ring, and after a flurry of punches, hooked on the dreaded stepover toehold. Actually, it's only dreaded in Japan; if you tried putting on this ancient, boring maneuver in the States, you might find yourself out of a job. The hold was so over in Japan, however, that people lost their minds. Then, just when things looked their worst, my savior, the Tiger, came to my rescue. He stopped Terry with the butt end of his sword, while I set up another board in the corner. Side by side, like the true teammates we were, we threw Terry to the corner. *Baboom!* "Uhwahh!" Terry was entangled in the wire, and in a bad way at the nine-minute mark. We had one minute until the ring was set to explode. My heart was racing as we faced the moment of truth.

Tiger retreated to the back, as I attempted pinfall after pinfall. Finally when the announcer started his ten-second countdown, I slid underneath the wire to watch this tremendous spectacle from outside the ring. Eight, seven, six—Terry tried to stand, but fell back down. The fans were screaming his name. Five, four, three—no matter what happened, or how long it took, I was going to have Terry kick out of my pin attempt. He would be known forever as the guy who kicked out of the ring explosion. Two, one—I covered my ears. Here it comes. *Pfftt.* The four explosions that went off looked like Roman candles. My old neighbor Marc Forte had put on a better fireworks show in his backyard in '76. The fans didn't just fart on it, they looked as if they'd just smelled a giant fart. I felt the whole match slipping away. Terry just stood up with his arms out to his side, as if to say "Hey, it's not my fault." I tried my best to think of a way to save the match, and came up with only one solution. Terry had the same idea. Injuries were about to pile up.

I stepped inside the ring and Terry was there. I put on a sloppy headlock that was really just a setup, and waited for Terry to counter. He lifted me slowly in the air in classic Funk style, and dropped me backward on the remaining explosive board. *Baboom!* "Uhwahh," and "Owuggha!" The third sound was me screaming. I had landed in such a way that Terry's damn middle explosives had gone off directly underneath my arm. I felt like I'd been shot. I should have stayed down forever, but I was so hurt and scared that I popped right up. Terry stayed down—a portion of the explosion had caught under his right triceps, and he was in considerable pain.

I called to the outside and looked under the ring for something to play with. I saw a toolbox and a stretcher, but pulled out a ladder instead. I rolled into the ring and shouldered the ladder lengthwise. As Terry turned, I charged him, and the impact to his head was so severe that I felt somewhat guilty. I got over it. I set up the ladder to the side of the fallen Funker. He was too close to land on, so I gave him a boot that moved him over. I ascended to the fifth step—about six feet in the air. The blood was really flowing from a cut in my hairline. It was so thick that it resembled more of a solid mask than a liquid. A friend of mine, who had been a photographer for *Baseball* for a decade, later said that even though she didn't like blood, she thought my photos were beautiful in an artistic way. I stepped from the ladder and dropped a perfect elbow on Terry.

Terry was really hurting now. As I rolled off him, I could see the anguish in his eyes. I tried to talk to him, but his mumbling was incoherent. I climbed the ladder again, but as I approached the fifth step, Terry got up and fell into the ladder. I felt like the guy in the old *F-Troop* fort, as I felt the ladder tipping. I had talked with Terry earlier about doing this, but had actually envisioned myself sailing over the sharp wire and crashing down onto the floor. Well, the good news is, I didn't crash onto the floor. The bad news is, I did fall into the barbed wire and the consequences were steep. I opened up an angry gash on my right hand and a huge gash that almost cost me my good ear.

It took me quite a while to get up, and when I did, Terry still wasn't moving. He was still down on his back, and was obviously too hurt to continue. I crawled over and draped my arm over him for a somewhat anticlimatic victory. The audience was confused, but not disappointed. I had wrestled way too long and hard that day for my victory to be questioned. I was the King of the Death Match. Cameras flashed continually for the next several minutes, as the press followed my every move. I tried to shake Terry's hand, in accordance with Mr. Asano's wishes, but he was hustled out by the young boys before I got the chance. I was handed a huge trophy, which I held high overhead

MICK FOLEY

for all of Kawasaki to see. I put the trophy down, and haven't seen it since.

While I celebrated, Terry was placed in an ambulance and rushed to the hospital. It was a truly touching scene as the adoring crowd reached out just to touch him, and chanted his name. Terry had done me a gigantic favor. Terry had only lost a couple of matches in the last decade in Japan, and a victory over the Funker was a huge milestone. Terry Funk, who had spent his entire career giving, had just given me a hell of a gift. I guess after all those years, maybe he really did see "shit" in me after all.

I walked slowly back to the dugout area that led to the dressing rooms. Before entering, I stepped onto one of the alternate rings, and delivered a final "bang bang." I walked to the empty concession area, where I saw Mr. Asano. He was beaming, and rightfully so—this had been a huge success for his little promotion. I was covered in blood from head to toe, and had literally risked my life for his company. I thought he would surely recognize this. "Asano-*san*" I said, adding the san to his name as a sign of respect. "Big house today. Maybe sukoshi bonus?"

Asano smiled his $500 million smile at me as he put a 100 yen coin into the soda machine. "Cock-toos," he began, his hand now reaching for the frosty beverage, "ha ha, here bonus." I don't know where the $300 I earned that day went, but I do know where my bonus went. I brought it unopened, back home, where it now occupies a place of honor in my bathroom closet. I don't want to showcase it too much, but I do want to be able to look at it every now and then as a reminder of my past.

I answered questions for the Japanese media, while they took careful inventory of my injuries. They photographed my ear, my hand, my eye, and my head. Strangely, I hadn't thought much about my arm since the explosion, although it did seem to bother me. When the media left, I was practically alone. I had time to think about just what had gone on in the stadium, and just what the kids would think when they saw their battered "Big Daddy-O" stumble in the front door. After careful reflection, I had the sudden revelation that maybe I too needed some medical attention. When I walked out the door, the screaming fans were gone. The ambulance was history. Only Masa, a faithful Tonto to my Kemosabe, had stayed behind. He explained that everyone had gone, and that he'd make sure I got back to Tokyo. We were in luck also, as the hospital was less than a mile away. So, without a trophy, but with my head held high, the King of the Death Match walked to the hospital with his sidekick Masa.

I was stitched up in the same room as Terry. He took some stitches in his head, and his triceps area was badly burned. I took seven stitches in my hand, nine in my eyebrow, eleven in my head, and fourteen behind my ear. Once again, I failed to acknowledge the injury to my arm, even though it was now throbbing with pain. When I returned to the Ikebekuru section of Tokyo, I phoned home and blatantly lied to Colette by telling her I was fine. "A little banged up, hon, but nothing serious." I then had a small dinner with Masa, and headed to my room to count T-shirt money and eat ice cream in bed.

I arrived at the Tokyo airport the next morning and waited to board. I heard my name called and walked to the boarding desk. "Mr. Foley," a woman explained, "you have been upgraded." I didn't know what to think. I had been upgraded without asking. I thought about it while I sat in my wide, comfortable business-class seat, and concluded that they simply must have felt sorry for me. We took off for JFK, and the woman next to me started to wriggle. She tried not to look at me, and when she did, she was clearly uncomfortable. I tried to put myself in her shoes, and the situation became a little clearer. I had prominent stitches in my eyebrow and head. My right cheek was a deeply swollen purple, and I had my left ear bandaged with gauze. To make matters worse, because of the stitches, I couldn't shower, and my hair was particularly matted with dried blood. The dried blood was flaking and falling in small chips onto my shoulder. And to top it all off, my right arm, which I finally deduced had been burned by the explosion, was now turning brown. The poor lady excused herself to go to the restroom, and oddly, after an hour, had not returned. I looked around, and saw her in the distance, resting comfortably somewhere in the vicinity of 21C. This woman had paid a great deal of extra money to sit in business, but had made a conscious decision to sit in coach rather than be next to me. I kind of like that.

When I landed at JFK, my dad was there to pick me up. I shook his hand, and he guessed correctly that the previous evening had been a rough one. I deliberately kept my right arm, which was now a crusty brown, away from him.

I stepped into our rented house in West Babylon, and I was met by a big reaction of "Daddy, Daddy, Daddy!" Colette gave me a hug and quickly said, "What's burning?" I played dumb, but Colette persisted. "God, Mick, that's bad, was someone smoking next to you on the plane?" By this time, I was twisting into some strange positions to keep my wife, children, and father from seeing my arm. I swear, I hadn't fought so hard to keep my high school Mohawk from being seen. My dad said good-bye, and when he stepped out the door, Colette was on me again. "Can't you smell something burning, Mick? It's awful." I finally answered. "Yes, I do, Colette," I admitted, as I turned my right arm to my wife, "it's me."

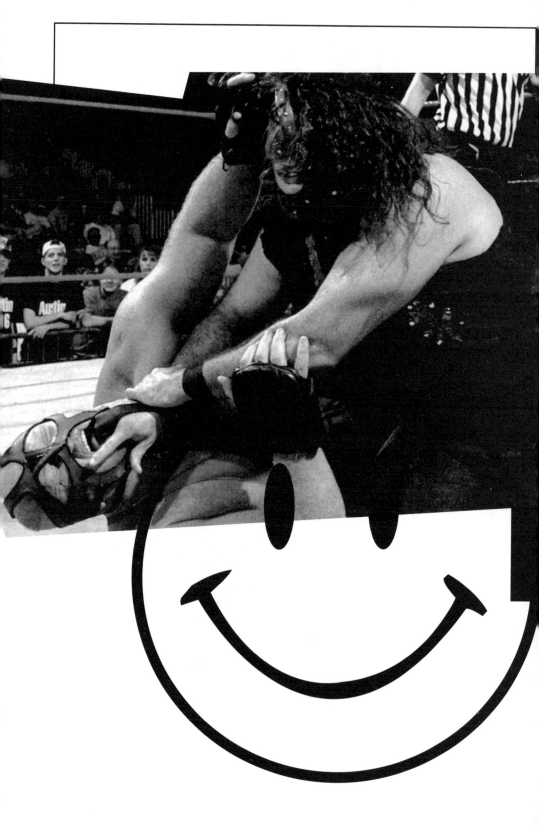

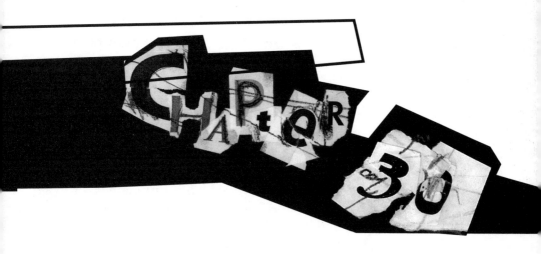

I was home for less than twenty-four
hours before I flew to Las Vegas for an independent match with Sabu.
I wrapped my arm as if I were Boris Karloff in *The Mummy*, but midway through the match, my mummification came undone. As the
gauze unraveled, so did my brown, crusty skin, leaving me with a
bright pink arm from my wrist to my shoulder. At the time, I thought
for sure the scarring would be permanent, but due to proper wrapping
and dressing, the results are barely noticeable.

The next day, I had a match outside Pittsburgh. More unraveling and
more exfoliating. Afterward, I ran into some of the World Wrestling Federation guys in the hotel. They were in town for the next day's *Summerslam*
and actually seemed happy to see me. The next day, there were rumors circulating that Cactus Jack would be doing a run-in at *Summerslam*. On the
plane ride home, a flight attendant looked at my arm and requested that I
put on my sweatshirt "out of respect for the other passengers."

I arrived home and four days later was summoned to ECW headquarters for some interviews. Actually, ECW headquarters was the
basement of the company's cameraman, where amid a run-down toy
train and some hanging laundry, many of the ECW's finest moments

were filmed. Much of the time, Joey Styles "live at the ECW arena" was actually Joey Styles in front of a banner hiding an old washer and dryer. Still, for some reason, I found it an inspiring place, and I needed inspiration to explain my diabolical turn on poor Tommy Dreamer.

Actually, I thought about interviews all the time. Colette would often see me either zoning out or physically shaking, and she would know that I was cutting a promo. We would go to Armitraj gym, and she would catch me standing alone for minutes. While others were lifting and posing, I would be physically shaking as the power of the promo coursed through my veins. "Are you doing interviews?" she would say, and break me from my trance. I didn't get any stronger at the gym, but I sure did think of cool stuff to say.

As Dusty had advised me, I never actually practiced those thoughts—I just kept them in my brain for future reference. The words usually went directly from my heart to my mouth, and the results the past year had been tremendous. But turning heel in a part of the country in which I had been loved for years was a difficult trick to pull off. I remembered what "Freebird" Michael Hayes had told me about being an effective heel. "In his mind, a heel has to feel his actions are justified. It doesn't matter how far out his motives—as long as he feels he's right!"

I had been thinking about psychology and criminal deviance— what makes a warped mind snap. Many of my favorite books were crime dramas, and I especially enjoyed reading about what traumatic event had set the wheels in motion. I liked to refer to Robert De Niro's Max Cady in *Cape Fear* as my favorite heel. In many ways, he wasn't a heel at all; he was a man who had been wronged and went about seeking his own form of vengeance. Max was tough, intense, and filled with testicular fortitude. The babyface of the movie, Nick Nolte, was wishy-washy and weak. My favorite scene in any movie (besides Reed Rothchild asking "How much ya squat?" in *Boogie Nights*) is when Nolte hires three men to rough up Cady and then hides behind a Dumpster to watch his plan unfold. Cady takes a hell of a beating at the hands of a baseball bat, a pipe, and a bicycle chain, but he makes a comeback nonetheless. As the heel stands bloody and battered and delivers the classic line "Come out, come out, wherever you are," the babyface is breathless and cowering. The line between good and bad had never been so thin. I wanted to walk that line with Tommy Dreamer. All I needed was a reason.

I thought about the bloodthirsty ECW fans. I thought of how tough it was to please them and how important it was to Tommy to do so. I remembered a story about Tommy turning down a WCW offer because he wanted to be hardcore, and I wondered if maybe I should have shut my mouth and kept collecting my three grand a week. I looked at my arm, which was still raw, and the scars from my stitches that had just been removed. Then I thought about the months-old sign in the stands, and how it had made my wife's stomach turn. A lightbulb went on in my head. I had found my reason. Colette and the kids came with me to the cameraman's house. I had been through hell and back and was planning on taking a small vacation to relax. Colette dropped me off at the house and took the kids to a nearby park. When she returned an hour later, I was soaked with sweat and in a state of exhaustion. I had also left some pretty heavy thoughts in my wake. I still consider one of them to be among the three best things I've ever done in the business.

August 1995— ECW Television Show Transcript

"I'm going to take you back to a very deciding point in my life— a time when I believed in something. A time when I thought that my face and my name made a difference. Do you remember the night, Tommy Dreamer, because it's embedded in my skull, it's embedded in my heart, and it's embedded in every nightmare that I will ever have. As Terry Funk took a broken bottle and began slicing and dicing Cactus Jack, the pain was so much that, I'll be honest with you, Tommy. The pain was so much that I wanted to say, 'I quit, Terry Funk, I give, I wave the flag, and I'm a coward—just please don't hurt me anymore.' Then I saw my saving grace. You see, Tommy, I looked out in that audience, my adoring crowd, and I saw two simple words that changed my life. 'Cane Dewey.' Somebody had taken the time and the effort and the thought to make a sign that said, 'Cane Dewey.' And I saw other people around, as every moment in my life stopped and focused in on that sign and the pain that shot through my body became a distant memory—replaced by a thought which will be embedded in my skull until my dying day! Cane Dewey. Cane Dewey. Dewey Foley is a three-year-old little boy—you sick sons of bitches. You ripped out my heart, you ripped at my soul, you took everything I believed in, and you flushed it down the damn toilet. You flushed my heart—you flushed my soul—and now it sickens me to see other people making the same mistake. You see, Tommy Dreamer, I have to listen to my little boy say every day, 'Daddy, I miss Georgia,' and I say, 'That's too bad, Son, because your dad traded in the Victorian house for a sweatbox on Long Island. Your dad traded in a hundred-thousand-dollar contract, guaranteed money, insurance, respect, and the name on the dotted line of the greatest man in the world—to work for a scumbag who operates out of a little pissant pawn shop in Philadelphia.' You don't expect me to be bitter? Tommy, when you open up your heart, when you open up your soul, and it gets shit on, it tends to make Jack a very mean boy. And so, I say to you—before I take these aggressions out on you, to look at your future and realize that the hardcore life is a lie, that these letters behind me are a blatant lie, that those fans who sit there and say, 'He's hardcore, he's hardcore, he's hardcore,' wouldn't piss on you if you were on fire, you selfish son of a bitch! But I want you to understand, Tommy, though he's hurt you time and time again, Raven wants you to understand that the hatred I have in here is not for you. No, no—far from it. You see, Tommy, I'm not doing this because I hate you—I love you, man! I only want the best for you—but when I hear that WCW called up your number and you said, 'No thank you'—well, it makes my blood run cold. As cold as that night in the ECW arena. And so I got a moral obligation—you see, Tommy, I'm on the path of righteousness, and righteous men wield a lot of power. So if I've got to drag you by your face to that telephone and dial collect and say, 'Hello, Eric, it's me, Cactus, and though I know I've burned my bridge, and I'll never be taken back with open arms—I've got a wrestler who would gladly trade in his ECW shirt for a pair of green suspenders.' And Tommy, just think of that sound in your ear when Uncle Eric says, 'Welcome home, Tommy Dreamer, welcome home.'"

The response to the interview was overwhelming. Many longtime fans thought it was the best interview of all time. More important, it was accomplishing its goal—to get Tommy over. Tommy was now seen as the underdog standing up for his hardcore beliefs against the evil empire (WCW) and its evil emperor (Bischoff). Bischoff was the perfect heel. ECW fans hated both WCW and the World Wrestling Federation, but at least they respected Vince. Bischoff was reprehensible. To them, Bischoff was nothing but a pretty boy whose goal in life was to lure away ECW talent with promises of big money and better recognition. Come to think of it, he did lure away a lot of ECW talent, and they did get big money and better recognition.

Paul E. loved it. That was part of the beauty of ECW—the freedom led to greater creativity. In my time there, I was free to speak about anything I wanted in any way I chose. I was even free to blast the company and Paul E. himself. Later, Vince McMahon would tolerate and then encourage the same behavior, but at the time, it was unusual.

The only casualty in all this was the poor sign guy. He took it hard and blamed himself. Stevie Richards saw him in the gym and said he was beside himself with guilt. "I thought he knew it was a joke," he moped to Stevie. I eventually mended fences with the guy, but to this day, I don't think he realizes that he actually did me a favor.

I knew I was on to something, and I wanted to keep the ball rolling. I needed more inspiration, and I thought of all the wrestlers who looked to me as their role model and had hurt themselves as a result. Actually, this is still happening, especially with the proliferation of backyard wrestling leagues. I guess because I got my big start by jumping off Danny Zucker's roof, these kids look to me as some sort of guru. As an added bonus, they throw in barbed wire and thumbtacks to honor their hero. I got a letter yesterday from an aspiring wrestler who claimed he was ready to die for the World Wrestling Federation. He was eighteen and said I could recognize him on the videotape he sent me as the "one covered in blood." I'm going to write him a letter back and tell him that I won't even watch his tape until he finishes college.

Maybe I should make something clear to prospective wrestlers—promoters are not impressed by breaking tables, chair shots, and barbed wire. The secret is to learn the basics, develop a character, and work your ass off. Sure, I got my foot in the door by jumping off a roof, but it took me six years before I started outearning the guy who works the Slurpee machine at 7–Eleven. Besides, there are roof jumpers everywhere these days.

Nobody cares about wild moves these days—they care about the guys who do them. Otherwise, Papi Chulo would be on the cover of *TV Guide* instead of Steve Austin. The Undertaker gets more reaction by diving over the top rope twice a year than Taka Michinoku does doing a twisting sukahara every night. I myself get a better reaction by pulling a dirty sweat sock out of my shorts than I ever did by dropping elbows on the concrete. Also, with ultimate fighters, Olympic wrestlers, pro football players, and legitimate bad-asses becoming more and more prominent in the business, you really ought to have some amateur experience. As a general rule, the top guys hate "hardcore" wrestlers. If you show up in the World Wrestling Federation courtesy of a video full of broken tables and barbed wire, a guy like Ken Shamrock will send you back to your backyard with your ball bag in a sling. Trust me—go to college, learn the basics, and break a table after the fans have already started caring about you.

Hey, I didn't mean to go off on a tangent, but I've got to keep my conscience clear.

I decided to keep up the pressure on Tommy—continuing to tell the truth about the ECW fans, apply even more WCW pressure, and up the moral ante. I liked the idea of being on a religious mission—after all, no one likes a zealot. I also wanted to give some historical background on my earlier hardcore ambitions. The interview I cut a few weeks later was right up there with "Cane Dewey." It also showcased how surprisingly sexy I looked in black leather.

September 1995—ECW Television Show Interview

"You know I'd like to apologize for my behavior. I'm embarrassed, certainly I feel a little stupid about the way I acted on this show a few weeks ago. It's just that I get a little emotional when I talk about wrestling, because wrestling's been my livelihood for the past ten years. It's enabled me to live out my childhood dream. So for me to come out on a show such as the ECW television program and badmouth the wrestlers there—well, I'm sorry. But I think that in order to understand what's going around my head, you have to understand where I come from and what my goals were when I got into wrestling.

"See, back in 1985, there was a program called *20/20* that challenged the wrestling industry—which kind of portrayed it in a negative light. Tommy, if you're listening, try to understand that I was about the biggest wrestling fan in the world. And for me to stand in front of that television set and see people running down a business that I loved and held dear—even though I knew very little about it . . . To see my friends laughing at me saying, 'That's what you want to get involved in?' That night I went to bed not with visions of sugarplums dancing through my head, but of broken bones, of battered bodies and bloody corpses, saying to myself, 'If it's the last thing I do, if I have to hold myself up for a human sacrifice—the world will respect professional wrestling.' Oh, and that dream came true—yes, I've sacrificed myself for the past ten years, leaving the better parts of my past lying on concrete floors from Africa, to Asia, to South America, to right in the middle of the ECW arena. And what's it really done? Where have we really come to?

"Lying in a hospital bed in Munich, Germany—seeing my ear being thrown into a garbage can—not being able to take it on the trip back because I didn't know the German word for 'formaldehyde.' And having a nurse walk into my room, looking at that piece of my body that's lying at the bottom of the garbage, and saying, '*Es ist alles schauspiel,*' which means 'It's all a big joke!' Excuse me! I didn't know you opened up the diseased lung of a smoker and said, 'Oh, by golly, I thought smoking was supposed to be good for you!' Do you open up Terry Funk's nonfunctioning liver and say, 'Hey, I didn't know that four decades of heavy drinking took this kind of toll!'? [Not true, but poor Terry got a lot of sympathy for it.] So, if they show that much respect for other patients, what made me any different? Because I was a wrestler. And professional wrestling will never be respected, no matter how many teeth I lose, no matter how many ears I lose, no matter how many brain cells have to die. And so it comes down to the point where it's just not worth it. It's not worth it, and, Tommy Dreamer, you've got to start looking at this realistically.

"Wrestling is a way to make a living—nothing more and nothing less—and as long as it's strictly business, well, you may as well be cuddled in the welcoming arms of World Championship Wrestling. Because ECW fans will be the death of you. You see, they realized, and they were smarter than any of us, that they rule ECW wrestling—not us. What happened, Tommy? You came back from All-Japan wrestling with your trunks and your boots and said, 'By golly, I'm really going to wrestle.' Did Giant Baba hand you a dozen eggs and say, 'Here, crack these on Jumbo Tsuruta's head'? You're a disgrace to the profession, Tommy; you're becoming a damn fool. And I can't sit back and take it, because I've got a moral obligation. Tommy, try to understand I am but a failed experiment in human sociology, and I can accept that. But never in my sickest dreams did I imagine that there would be other wrestlers taking dives onto concrete floors, committing human suicide on my behalf—like I'm the patron saint of all the sick sons of bitches. Is that all I stand for, Tommy? Is that all I stand for, to stand in an arena where J. T. Smith lands head first on the concrete and hears, the fans yell, 'You fucked up, you fucked up?' Well, fuck you. Who the hell do you think you are? We're not a wrestling organization anymore—we're the world's damn biggest puppet show. I'll be damned if I'm going to walk into an arena and let any of you call my match. One, two, three—jump. One, two, three—jump. Well not me, because I'm nobody's stooge, and Tommy Dreamer, if you had a little bit of pride, or a little bit of common sense, you'd understand that those people don't love you—they laugh at you! You took some of the worst beatings the sport's ever seen, and they still laughed in your face. And to think that I stood there with my arm around you and endorsed you, saying, 'He's hardcore, he's hardcore, he's hardcore.' And for that I deserve to die a terrible, painful death, Tommy, because I feel responsible. And I go to bed at night, and I'm not sure where I'm going to spend my eternity. And you, Tommy, are my salvation. Because, by delivering you to a better organization, where you can be appreciated, loved, and held with just the littlest amount of respect in the Turner family, then maybe there's a chance for me, too. Please, Tommy, for my sake, think it over, because a *yes* to Cactus Jack would mean a great deal to me—and a *no*—well, I'd have to take that as your putting a big A-OK stamp of approval on my eternal damnation! I'm counting on you, you selfish little prick. Don't make me hurt you—because I can. Don't make me do it, because if I do, with God as my witness, it won't be in front of those little scumbags at the ECW arena—it'll just be me and you, Tommy, and you won't know when it's coming, and you won't know where. So unless you want to damn me to the depths of hell—answer my call and say, 'Okay, Cactus, you win.' I'll put on the suspenders, I'll groom that mustache, and I'll call Uncle Eric and say, 'Count me in.' Because not only would you be doing yourself a big favor—not only would you be helping your life, you'd be saving mine. You'd be saving . . . mine."

My plan had holes in it, however, because my first series of matches found me on the receiving end of as many cheers as boos. Also, my T-shirts were still selling well despite the fact that I'd verbally torn our fans a new bunghole. I thought real hard about it and realized the factors that I'd failed to consider.

The fans already know they were bloodthirsty, uncaring SOBs and enjoyed the acknowledgment.

I talked about all my hardcore regrets, but then still wrestled in a hardcore style.

I gave great anti-hardcore promos but did them so well that they came off as hardcore. In essence, I was giving hardcore promos about not being hardcore.

A drastic problem like this required a drastic solution. I drew up an emergency three-point plan.

1. Shift WCW praise into overdrive.
2. Don't be quite so angry in interviews.
3. Under *no* circumstances give the fans a match that they could respect.

Number three was the key. Out went the chair shots, elbows, in-crowd fighting, punching, kicking, headbutting, suplexing, slamming, or anything else that could be construed as entertaining. In come the headlocks. Long headlocks. Lots of headlocks. Boring headlocks. Lots of long, boring headlocks. I was going to stink up every gym and arena I came into contact with. And not only that—I was going to brag about it, as well. I would openly claim that I was going to have bad matches, and then . . . I would. I had a match with guy called El Puertoricano (Babu from World Wrestling Federation) that was so bad, it was good. Ten full minutes of headlocks. I turned in other sterling performances as well. For three weeks I did my best to do my worst. My worst was pretty bad indeed.

Todd Gordon and Paul E. started claiming on television that I was stealing money from the company by wrestling so poorly. I shot back with the claim that as a former WCW star, I carried enough weight to do whatever I wanted. This got to Dreamer, who claimed he was going to "beat the hardcore out of me!" To do so, he even brought back my old nemesis, Terry Funk, to be in his corner. After Kawasaki, Terry's body was so worn-out that he needed time to heal and hadn't been to the arena in a while. The match to settle this strange score was set for October 28. What began as a goofy concept very nearly ended in tragedy. ECW calls its annual November show the *November to Remember*. I later joked that this was the October to Forget.

The match opened with Tommy slapping me repeatedly and daring me to retaliate. I wouldn't. He slapped me again. I wouldn't. He slapped me one more time, and finally I couldn't take it. I reared back with my left hand and . . . put on a headlock. The fans were very vocal in their dissatisfaction. Dreamer fought up, but I took him down again. Hey, by this point, I knew my headlocks. He got up and stopped me and threw me to the floor, hoping the change in scenery might spark my hardcore memory. It did. I fired at Dreamer, to the crowd's approval. I had Dreamer reeling, and knowing he was about to fall, I reared back and . . . put on a headlock. This was great stuff.

Finally, Tommy mounted an offense and forced me to retaliate. I did. I threw the blatantly brown-nosing bastard to the concrete and stepped through the ropes to the familiarity of the ring apron. I put up the arm, and the ECW faithful knew just what to expect. The legendary mad-man, Cactus Jack, was about to drop the legendary elbow—except I didn't. Instead, I stopped in midstride and led a WCW cheer by spelling out the letters of the company with my arms—W-C-W, W-C-W, W-C-W. It was more than Dreamer could stand. It made his hardcore blood boil. As the self-billed Innovator of Violence, Tommy had some pretty neat tricks up his sleeve, and he started using them on me in great volume. I was taking a little bit of a beating and decided that in the immortal words of Owen Hart, "Enough is enough—it's time for a change." If Tommy wanted to get hardcore, I was going to show him how it was done. Unfortunately, this was what resulted in the previously mentioned failed eyebrow experiment. With Tommy's face lumpy and red from my errant blows, I reared back for the big one. Actually, this one was only going to look like a "big one." I thought he'd been punched enough already. I threw the haymaker and howled in pain. "Owww!" I yelled, "It's my hand . . . I think I broke my hand." I got on the house mike and addressed this serious health issue. "Ladies and gentlemen, as you can see, I suffered tremendous damage to my hand and, as a result, I just can't go on. The pain is too great. I am truly sorry, but I'm afraid that this match is over. The bout will be ruled a 'no contest.' "

Referee Jim Molano's voice stopped me. "Cactus Jack, this is ECW—there's no such thing as a 'no contest.' "

I thought about that and came up with a solution. "Then do your job and count me out," I countered.

Molano was feeling daring. He got on the mike and said, "Cactus, why are you being such a pussy?"

Whoa! Hold on here, Jim. Pussy is a fighting word—Chuck Cheeseman had proved that in the Chris Anderson altercation back in '77. Still, it wasn't strong enough. I continued my walk to the back.

MICK FOLEY

With Molano's not counting, out came Bill Alfonso—better known as Fonzie. No, not the Fonzie who made up a story about having relatives in Waukesha because he was too proud to accept Richie's invitation to have Christmas dinner with Mr. C. No, not the Fonzie whose crash into the chicken stand outside Arnold's messed up his confidence so bad that he almost never rode his bike again. No, not the Fonzie who had to break it off with Pinky, because he didn't want to go through life as Mr. Tuscadero. This Fonzie was a referee who had earned the hatred of the fans by actually enforcing the rules. Fonzie had only three teeth in his mouth, and they were rotten, but he was a hell of a referee, and he had the Pennsylvania state rule book in his hands. Fonzie got on the mike, and in his high-pitched, whiny, nails-on-a-chalkboard voice, pleaded my case. "Not only is it in the Pennsylvania state rule book, but it is Cactus Jack's constitutional right to be counted out if he so desires." One, two, three, four—the fans were getting hot, as this was shaping up to be the worst ECW main event since Cactus vs. Drake. Five, six, seven—Funk had seen enough.

"If you count one more number," the Funker warned, "then I'm going to knock your goddamned dick in the dirt."

Fonzie looked at the washed-up Texan and spoke his mind. "I'm not afraid of the fans; I'm not afraid of Tommy Dreamer, and I'm certainly not afraid of you, Terry Funk. It is Cactus Jack's CON-STI-TUTIONAL right to be counted out, and I'm going to do it." Fonzie looked contemptuously at Funk and continued his constitutionally allowed count—"Eight." Bam! Down went Fonzie to a stiff left hand.

Funk got on the mike and attempted to lure me into a fight using the same psychology he'd used on Bullet Bob Armstrong, "Cactus Jack," Terry bellowed, "you're a goddamn coward, you son of a bitch." I remained in the back. "Your wife is a whore." Still in the back. "Your mother is a whore." Nothing. "Your children are both whores." That should have done it. But . . . nothing. I could not be broken. The Funker had one more ace up his sleeve. "Bischoff is a homo." That did it! I was out from behind the curtain in a flash to defend my main man's honor. I meant business as I hit the ring, but as I got to the blasphemous Funk, Dreamer stepped in front and started peppering me with big rights. BAM, BAM, BAM, BAM—the crowd was exploding, and I was doing my best to make each one look its most devastating.

Some people didn't seem to get the concept of the match and gave it low marks. I guess if they were looking at it as a standard match, it wasn't that good. But in my view, anytime you can get the ECW crowd oohing and aahing and getting out of their seat in the final match using only punches—you're getting something right.

At this point, Raven made his presence known by using a steel chair on both Funk's and Dreamer's backs. With Funk down, Raven pulled out two foreign objects—a ten-pound weight and a roll of athletic tape. Slowly, I lifted my foot while he taped the weight to the top of my boot. This was great. Unless the Funker was also doubling as Iron Balls McGuinty, he was going to go down. Sure enough, I kicked a field goal with Terry's testicles, and the wounded Texan was helped to the back.

Tommy was all alone now and about to find out what hardcore was all about. Raven and I doubled on him until Funk miraculously returned carrying his flaming branding iron. Raven and I peeled off Dreamer and fed Funk one by one for shots to the back and stomach. The arena was whipped into a frenzy. Our quest for righteousness was not to be denied, however, as referee Bill Alfonso (who had been taken to the back after suffering his one-punch knockout) reemerged with a weapon of his own. It was my old Japanese standby—the fire chair! I was handed the unlit chair and knocked Terry down with a nice shot to the head. Dreamer turned as well and was dropped with a crushing blow to the skull that was lessened only slightly by the kerosene-soaked towel. Raven touched Funk's iron to the towel, and the fire chair lived again in the ECW arena.

I looked at Funk, who was flat on his belly. I raised the chair slowly and could feel the heat on my arms. As I came down with my swing, Dreamer made a dive for Funk and used his body as a shield to spare Terry the blazing consequences. The effect was awesome. Dreamer had seemingly risked his life to save the fallen Funker, and the crowd loved him for it. Everything was going great, when I heard Terry's voice.

"Pick it up again," Terry mumbled in a voice so low that I could barely hear it above the roar of the crowd.

"Are you sure?" I asked.

"Use it again," he reiterated. I picked up the fire chair and slowly raised it again. Terry was getting to his feet, and I stalled to give him more time. When he was fully standing, I slowly charged him with the chair. I could see he was bailing out of the ring, so I started a slow swing that I knew wouldn't come near him. All I wanted was to hit the ropes with the fire chair and give the impression that I was trying for Terry.

Before my shocked eyes, I saw our plan fall to pieces. What appeared to be a giant fireball flew off the chair and instantly ignited Terry, who was bent over by the ring apron. My first thought was to save him. I completely abandoned my character and my story line and dove through the ropes to try to put out Terry. I knew that flames had about three seconds of contact time before they really did their damage. Terry was up to at least two. I took off after Terry, but he was running like a madman. To this day, I try to relive these events in my mind and try to figure out why I couldn't catch him. Was he moving too fast to catch, or was I simply a coward under pressure? The question still haunts me. I do remember thinking, "I've got to catch him," and then wondering, "What do I do once I'm there?" I had no answers. I wish I could point to a burn on my body and say, "This is where I saved my hero, Terry Funk," but all I have to show for it is a heavy conscience.

I remember thinking, "He's gone—Terry's gone" before fate or God or luck lent a hand. The fire seemed to roll off Terry's shoulders as if by magic, and Terry collapsed to the floor. In actuality, a fireball had not flown off the chair, and Terry himself had not become ignited. Instead, the towel that was on fire had flown off the chair and landed on his back. The towel had been burning—not Terry, although I'm sure that was small comfort to Terry as he was helped to the dressing room.

When I got to the back, Terry was on a rampage. His right arm had been severely burned, and he was more than a little annoyed about it. The Funker was throwing furniture, and there were some pretty tough guys cowering in fear of the ticked-off Texan and a host of flying chairs, fans, and tables. As I approached Terry, I could see that his wife, Vicki, was crying. Life is never easy for a wrestler's wife, but for Vicki, who had already seen her husband injured countless times, this night was especially traumatic. I didn't know what to say, and as it turned out, my choice of words was not all that comforting. "Are you all right?" I asked, and was met by a flying chair and a string of obscenities that even my dad would have envied.

"Goddamn motherfucker, there's no excuse for that shit, you son of a bitch!"

Again, my words were not all that soothing. "Sorry, Terry."

He looked at me with rage in his eyes. "You damn well ought to be sorry, you son of a bitch!"

Vicki tried to calm him down, but it was no use, so she tried to

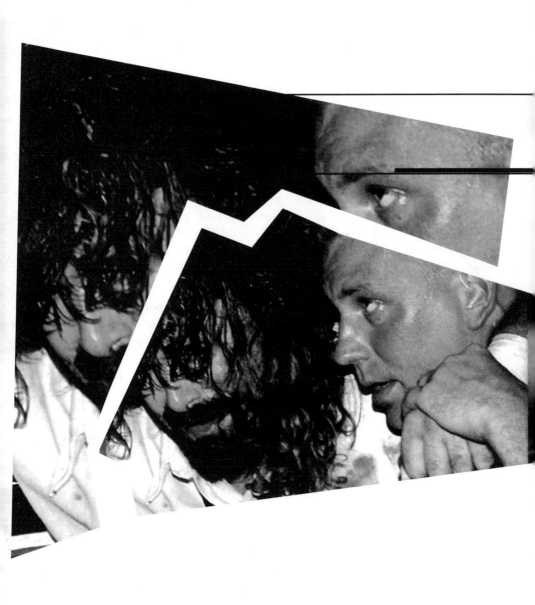
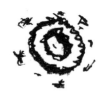

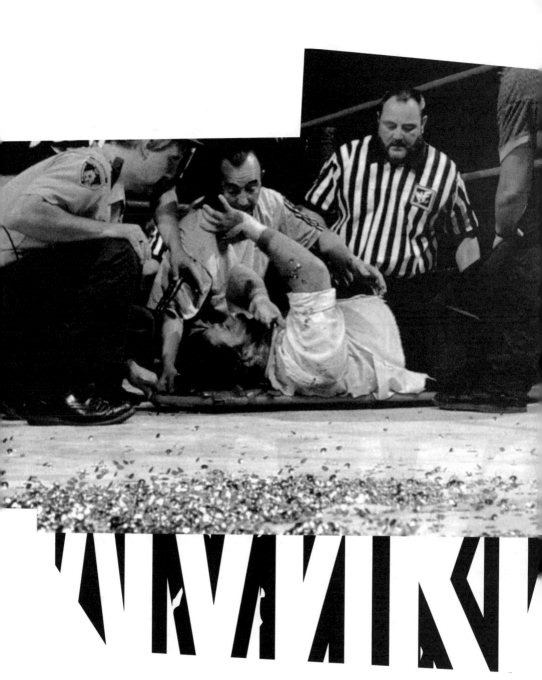

calm me down instead. "Terrance is just upset," she assured me in her west Texas drawl. "Just go home . . . he'll be all right."

I went home, but I was an emotional wreck. I swore to myself that I was going to quit wrestling, but by the time I reached Staten Island, I had decided that I just wouldn't wrestle in this country anymore. By the time I got home, I was thinking that we could probably cut some promos on each other over this. Still, I was very upset when I told Colette about the night's events. Unbeknownst to me, Terry had checked out of the hospital later that night and come back to the arena to cut promos for the next month's match. If I had known, I probably would have slept a little better.

The next morning, I made sure that I called Terry's house. I knew he wouldn't be home, but I wanted to make sure that my voice was the first one he heard when he turned on his answering machine. I went out for the day, and when I came home, he had left a message. I was relieved to hear that he wasn't yelling, but had gone back to the whisper/mumble that I knew so well. "Hello, Cactus. This is Terry Funk, and I just wanted to say that I acted like a damn fool, and I'm sorry. It wasn't your fault, it wasn't my fault, it wasn't anybody's fault—it just happened. But goddamn, huh huh, we sure did give them something to talk about, didn't we? And I'm sure people are going to be talking about this for a long, long time. Good-bye, Cactus Jack, and don't pay any attention to what I said last night—I'm just an old fool."

I liked the message so much that I played it for Colette. I saw her eyes well up with tears as she listened to kindly old Uncle Terry. "He really is a nice man," she said as she handed me the phone. I saved that message for a long time.

We celebrated Halloween two days later. As for most holidays at the Foleys', we made a big deal out of Halloween. When I'm on the road a lot, I try to build up certain events in the kids' minds, as it seems to take the sting out of being gone so long. "Guess where we're going when Daddy gets home," was a familiar battle cry over the telephone. If I didn't have my little perks and special days with the kids to look forward to, I don't think I could last out there.

I had always been a Halloween fanatic. When I was a kid, I used to start plotting my next year's costume as soon as the current Halloween was over. I tried to be creative and flat-out refused to buy one of those cheap, ready-made costumes that other kids wore. It just seemed like you should have to strive a little more for the privilege of eating free candy. My brother didn't share my sense of theatrical importance. As a result, in every picture of us on Halloween, I looked cool, and he looked like a doofus. My mom would never admit it though. "You both look great," she'd say, although photographic evidence certainly seemed to disagree with her.

My kids could not, under any circumstances, look like doofuses on Halloween. I consider myself a pretty lenient parent, but sometimes a dad has to take a stand. Dewey was a huge Batman fan, and exactly as my mom had twenty-five years earlier, I would be summoned into the room to call the action as Adam West and Burt Ward laid the smack down on all the villains' candy asses. "*Bam! Pow! Biff! Kapuff!*" I'd yell as my kids both threw kicks at imaginary bad buys. Dewey wanted to be Batman and Noelle wanted to be Batgirl, which was a dilemma, because I knew that half of West Babylon would be wearing the cowl and cape. I was determined that my kids would have the best of all the costumes, so I special-ordered some outfits from the lady who made my wrestling tights. Sure enough, my kids were the best-looking Batman and Batgirl in town. And they weren't wearing the trendy new black outfit with the built-in muscles either. No, my kids were wearing the classic Adam West blue and gray—the way it was meant to be, dammit!

I may have a reputation for pinching pennies so hard that it makes Abe Lincoln scream—and in some cases, rightfully so—but not when it comes to Halloween. Or Halloween candy. My mother had long ago established a tradition of at least three quality fun-size bars in each little Halloween baggie, along with an assortment of other little goodies. With the exception of the year that I slipped dried cat turds into little Baby Ruth wrappers and gave them to Jacqueline Miller, everybody came out a winner on All Hallow's Eve at the Foleys'. I had been carrying out that tradition for years. Anyone who came to the Victorian house in Georgia walked away a winner, and I was determined to continue that tradition at our "sweatbox on Long Island."

We prepared thirty-six bags and waited for the trickle of innocent toddlers to start coming by. It was more like a flood. The moment school let out, there were kids everywhere. A lot of the teenagers didn't even have costumes, unless they were dressed up as pimply guys with bad haircuts. The candy was gone literally in twenty minutes.

At least we broke even. When we trick-or-treated that night, we went so damn far into the immense neighborhood that by the time we were done, the kids had been asleep in the stroller for an hour. Colette or I would just knock on a door and point to the stroller and accept a single piece of candy on behalf of our sleeping kids.

I will always treasure that Halloween—especially a picture taken the night before, when the kids had worn their costumes to Grandma and Grandpa's house. We had bought Dewey a pair of imitation snake-skin boots at a secondhand store a week earlier, and Dewey thought those boots went with everything. They didn't. I guess that's the reason Adam West never went Western while laying the smack down. Because if he had, he would have looked like my son. Despite all my great intentions, hopes, and ambitions, my son did indeed look like a doofus.

I think my affection for the holidays has played a part in the struggle with my weight. I just seem to associate food with happy memories, and happy memories with food. If I were to play a word association game with special memories, I would almost automatically answer with the food that it reminded me of. Birthday—cake. Christmas—cookies. Halloween—pumpkin pie. Fourth of July—hot dogs. Baseball games with Dad—peanuts. I had such a good time at Hershey Park with the kids a few years ago that I actually started eating Hershey bars with regularity.

We returned to ECW arena for the much-anticipated *November to Remember* show that pitted Cactus and Raven against Funk and Dreamer. After the fire incident, many felt that ECW had finally crossed the line and that there would be a backlash against the promotion. On the other hand, there were many who thought the match was the greatest thing they'd ever seen. There were actually chants of "ECW, ECW!" while Terry was on fire. I ran into some fans a week after the incident who said, "Man, how'd you do that stunt with the fire—that was great." Unfortunately, wrestling has become so good at creating the illusion of disaster that when disaster does hit, it's very difficult to tell the difference. Sadly, when Owen Hart died in the ring during a World Wrestling Federation Pay-Per-View, many initially thought it was just part of the show. I really wish it had been. The fact that the show went on, and that fans still enjoyed themselves—and that I stood two feet from the spot where Owen died—is something that I am having a hard time dealing with.

We made sure that *November to Remember* had some levity to it. The show had actually sold out faster than any other in ECW history, which seemed to rule out the idea of having gone too far. Still, we felt it was important that the brutality be toned down a little bit and that some fun be substituted instead.

My pro-WCW angle was really catching on. In honor of my former employers, I had some special ring attire made up for the showdown. On the surface, it was impossible to tell—but underneath, the "Wanted" shirt hid my secret weapon. Raven and I were having our way with our adversaries—with Funk catching a beating on the outside with Raven, and me putting the boots to Tommy. Tommy's face was a mask of pain as I worked him over. He didn't seem to have a chance. Suddenly, when things were looking bleakest, I pulled off the familiar black-and-gold Cactus shirt. Underneath was the insult to end all insults—at least in the ECW arena. I was now sporting a beautifully airbrushed T-shirt featuring The Shark/John Tenta, Kamala, and The Zodiac/the Butcher/the Booty Man/the Disciple/the Barber/Brutus Beefcake. Collectively, they were known as the Faces of Fear, and although they were all individually nice guys, collectively their respect among the ECW fans was microscopic. In addition to the great art-work on the front, there was a big valentine on the back—it looked like something that a twelve-year-old girl would wear to her first concert.

I stood up and did a meandering circle so that the entire audience could see my horrible shirt. It was a great heat getter. Cheap heat—yes—but heat nonetheless. I went back to Dreamer, who had by this time seen the blasphemous artwork. I kicked him, but it didn't faze him. Another kick, but to no avail. A big punch, and he started shak-ing. Dreamer was now Hulk Hogan and was making a Superman comeback on the Turner-loving turncoat. He let loose with a barrage of punches and sent me down to the canvas with one of his violent innovations. He then ripped the offensive shirt right off my body. I stood up slowly and turned to the crowd. Immediately, they reacted. As I turned in my slow, torturous 360, everyone learned the ugly truth but Tommy. Finally, as I completed my circle, Tommy spotted it, and his eyes grew wide. There it was. Compared to this, the Faces of Fear shirt had been nothing. Compared to this, Kamala, Shark, and Zodiac were hardcore warriors. On my shirt, in front of 1,200 bloodthirsty WCW-hating fanatics, I was sporting a lovingly created, painstakingly detailed image of Eric Bischoff. On the back was this simple wish: "Forgive me, Uncle Eric."

It was almost as if Dreamer was Popeye and Bischoff was his spinach, because Tommy kicked it into overdrive. *Boom, boom,*

boom, boom—Tommy was connecting with solid rights. The crowd was eating it up. A few more punches and Dreamer was ready for the big one. He pulled my shirt up and stretched it over my head so that the WCW Boy Wonder's head completely covered mine. It was almost as if I were wearing a Bischoff mask. I weebled and wobbled inside that shirt, as if it were a Rubbermaid, while Dreamer selected the perfect chair. I could hear the crowd buzzing, and I could see the silhouette of the swinging chair as I waited for impact. Bang! I staggered and stumbled but didn't go down—although, when I lifted my head, it magically appeared as if Bischoff himself had been busted wide open. Was it magic, or was it real—only the people who watched *Secrets of Pro Wrestling* really knew for sure.

I honestly can't remember who won the match that night, although the fact that I can't remember is a pretty good indication that I didn't. As a strange side note, I understand the Bischoff shirt from that show is now worth a huge sum of money.

When I returned home, I received a phone call that was of great interest to me. Jim Ross was on the phone with the news that the World Wrestling Federation wanted to meet with me.

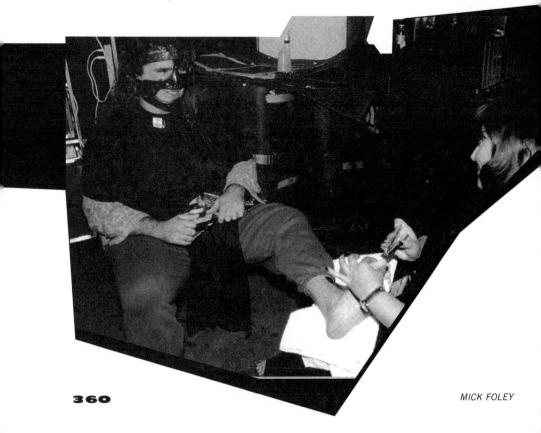

MICK FOLEY

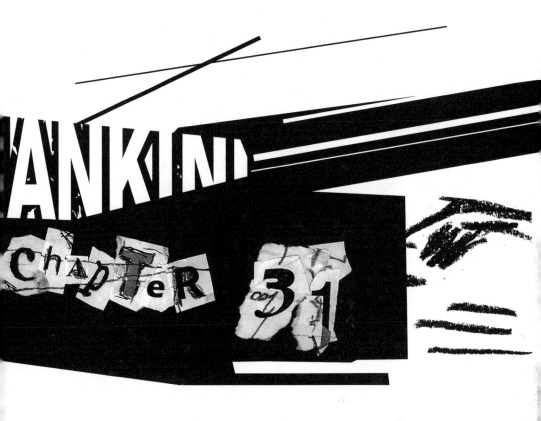

CHAPTER 31

It had been about a year since
I'd spoken to Jim Ross. Jim and I had remained in contact throughout
our different trials and tribulations, but this had been the longest I'd
gone without keeping in touch with him. Despite being the best play-
by-play announcer in the game, Jim had been in and out of the World
Wrestling Federation on several different occasions before finally coming back to stay. Oddly, one of the past differences between Jim and
the Federation centered around his reluctance to don a cowboy hat
and call himself J. R. Coming from a Bill Watts background, Jim did
not see announcers as being "characters" and had fought the idea.
Upon his return, Jim finally donned the Stetson and became J. R. It's
funny . . . because now it's hard for me to imagine him without the
damn hat, and even I refer to him as J. R. Hell, he refers to himself as
J. R. Really, the hat just adds a little flavor and has in no way dimin-

ished his passion for the sport or his unique ability to make a bad match decent and a good match great. J. R. was now Vince's right-hand man, so a call from him was no small deal.

A year earlier, I had informed J. R. that I was working steadily, was having fun, and in no way needed a job. I also let him know that if the right job came about, I would be interested. J. R.'s new call informed me that this might be the right job, and that Vince McMahon had a new idea, and that he would like to set up a meeting. This was a top spot, he informed me, and would hopefully lead to a successful series of matches with the Undertaker.

I had one question before I agreed to a meeting. "Jim," I asked. "You don't tell everyone who comes in that they're being groomed for a top spot, do you—I mean, what did you tell Aldo Montoya when he came in?" (Aldo Montoya was a perennial Federation loser before he went on to stardom in ECW.)

Jim thought about it and came back with an answer. "No, we don't, Cactus. If we say it's a top spot, we mean it. In Aldo's case, he was probably told that it was a good spot, but not a great spot, and that there would be room for advancement if the character caught on."

"All right," I said. "Let's set up a meeting."

There were a lot of considerations to take into account at this time. I was making decent money in Japan, but my goodness, I was getting the hell beaten out of me. The death match tournament was not the last time I came home from Japan in a pretty bad way—not by a long shot. The brutality was taking its toll not only on me but Colette as well, as she was beginning to fear a ringing phone for the bad news it might carry. I had been approached by Mr. Asano about coming back to Japan for seventeen weeks during the next year. I was even offered a raise of five hundred a week—up to $3,500 a week. But seventeen weeks was really 170 days when you include travel—and a hell of a lot more than that when you figure in intangibles like jet lag. Also, without trying to sound like a big shot, I knew that my blood and sweat were worth more to the $500 million man than the fifty-nine grand that he would be paying me.

I would still be able to sell T-shirts, but that gravy train was showing signs of slowing down. I was a popular wrestler with enthusiastic fans, but our fan base was still rather small. Many of the fans who bought the "Wanted" shirt already owned several of them. To stay ahead of the game, I had designed a few new T-shirts, but their designs included tactical errors that I could not have foreseen. One of them featured a silhouette of Cactus Jack against a red sun, with the Japanese writing "King of the Death Match" on the front and "Born to Be Wired" in English on the back. Two problems. One—since the Japanese flag consists of a red sun, a newspaper reporter considered the design to show a lack of respect to the Japanese people. Two—for some reason, Japanese wrestling fans only want slogans that are written in English. Ironically, the ECW fans loved the Japanese writing.

My second shirt was a winner in theory but a flop in practice. O. J. Simpson's murder case was all over the news, and I figured I'd cash in on his international notoriety. I came up with an old-time wrestling card motif that billed a one-time-only death match between Cactus and O. J., who was nattily attired in his Buffalo Bills jersey and a bloody glove, which held a bloody knife. Detective Mark Fuhrman was slated as the special guest referee. I thought the Japanese fans would eat up a shirt featuring these two hardcore icons—with O. J. being a little more extreme than me. I think I sold twelve of them. So, if O. J. wants to sue me for royalties, well, he can have them.

Japanese tradition has prided itself on honor for thousands of years, and going back decades, agreements with U.S. wrestlers were made on a handshake. I even asked Mr. Asano if he wanted to shake hands on the deal or sign a contract. He insisted on a contract—if we'd shaken hands, there is a chance that there would be no Mankind or Mr. Socko in the World Wrestling Federation, as I wouldn't have broken that agreement.

With the exception of the fire incident, I was having a tremendous time in ECW. I got along with everybody, I was free to do whatever I wanted, hell, I was even able to call the owner a "scumbag" and his place of business a "pissant pawnshop." Unfortunately, many of the things I'd said of the ECW fans in interviews were true. They were demanding, bloodthirsty, and insensitive. I was also aware that my presence there, while valuable, was by no means a necessity, as the ECW arena sold out whether I was there or not. By this time, the ECW merchandise machine had started to roll and my "Wanted" shirt was no longer the only quality item on the table. As a matter of fact, there were about eighteen to choose from, and the fans were so passionate about this company that they usually chose an ECW shirt as opposed to that of an individual wrestler.

I also found my stock dropping in other independent organizations. I had been off national television for over a year, and though I hate to admit it, many people had either forgotten about Cactus Jack or didn't care all that much. As a result, I had lowered my price and, once at the show, no longer sold the same quantities of merchandise. Polaroid business was slowing down as well, and while it never got close to the Gordy in Chattanooga level, there were many times when my ego took a little beating.

So I guess my decision to meet with World Wrestling Federation came down to two simple things: physical and financial well-being.

The Federation at that time, however, was far from wrestling utopia. Crowds were down, morale was down, and paychecks were down. I had heard horror stories from the road about Canadian trips where guys hadn't even made enough to meet their road expenses. Wrestlers were at one another's throats, and there were deep divisions among groups of guys in the dressing room. Shane Douglas, who had left ECW months earlier with high hopes for his World Wrestling Federation chances, was now miserable. "Abort mission" was one of Shane's more pleasant messages, as he pleaded with his longtime friend not to follow down the same lamentable path that he had taken. In truth, Shane was at least partly to blame for his Federation woes, as he had let Vince change him from the dynamic, intense Franchise into the monotone, drippy Dean. Now don't get me wrong. A guy with a good vocabulary who thinks he's smarter than anyone can be annoying, but it was not exactly the type of thing that would inspire me to buy a ticket. "Hey, Jimmy, I was watching wrestling, and there was this really smart guy on there—let's go buy a ticket" was not a conversation that I envisioned kids around the country having. No, I wasn't going to fall into the same trap that Shane had—I was too smart for that. Vince was going to get Cactus Jack the way I wanted him—or else, dammit, he wasn't going to get him at all.

I drove to Stamford, Connecticut, that day with lots of questions on my mind. In an uncanny coincidence, I was wearing the same sport coat that I had met Ted Turner in. Actually, maybe the coincidence wasn't quite that eerie, as it was the only sport coat that I owned. The prospect of meeting Vince McMahon was definitely unnerving. This was the same guy that I had been watching since I was a kid, and he was definitely a larger-than-life character. In addition, Vince was the man responsible for starting the wrestling revolution in the mid-eighties. By combining a bold vision with a savvy marketing plan, Vince had gambled everything to turn his father's regional northeast territory into an international powerhouse. His product had infuriated wrestling purists and most old-time promoters, who felt that Vince had turned their beloved sport into a circus. He had taken a low-class, vulgar, and bloody sport and turned it into clean family entertainment. Under those conditions, Cactus Jack was not exactly the old Federation's cup of tea. Now, with business down, and with society rejecting McMahon's dated vision, he was in the beginning stages of spicing up his product. In some ways, just bringing in Cactus Jack for a meeting was evidence of the Federation's new "attitude."

I walked into Titan Towers, an ominous-looking, eight-story structure of glass and steel, and I was shown to Vince's office. This itself was a dubious distinction, as I had been told for years that if Vince really wanted you, he'd have you brought to his house. Still, at least I had a meeting with J. J. F'ing Dillon. I swear, Dorothy had an easier time getting an audience with the Wizard of Oz.

Vince walked into the office looking fit and wealthy. I don't know if that's a proper way to describe a man, but that was the impression that I got. I'd met Vince fleetingly when I did my World Wrestling Federation matches in 1986, but this was over nine years later, and if Vince had remembered our little encounter, he was doing a good job of hiding it.

"Mike, how are you?" boomed the voice—the same voice that I had heard call so many matches from my childhood. Ooh, that wasn't a good sign. I hadn't been called Mike since the early seventies and didn't really enjoy it then. I didn't want to correct him, especially within the first nine seconds of meeting—it would be almost like telling the President he had mustard on his chin. So, instead of speaking up once and correcting the small inaccuracy, I allowed myself to be called the wrong name for two hours.

Actually, other than the "Mike" thing, which we could work around, I hit it off well with Vince. So well, in fact, that we went over to his house, where I borrowed a pair of Vince's trunks and did cannonballs and belly flops into the McMahon pool while Vince flipped hamburgers on the grill. Okay, maybe not that well—maybe there were no burgers, cannonballs, trunks, or home visit—but at least we were cordial.

Vince explained some of the company's past problems to me and how those problems had affected business. A federal steroid trial, in particular, had been especially damaging. Vince was eventually cleared of all charges, but the length of the trial, cost, and energy involved had badly damaged the company and its public perception. Vince told me that the company had actually wanted to change gears and adopt a rougher style much earlier but had found it necessary to maintain a clean image during the aftermath of the trial. Now he was ready to forge ahead, and the timing seemed right to bring in the Hardcore Legend.

I guess I was lucky to have escaped the ECW curse, because it seems that many of the ECW mainstays have floundered and looked out of their league when they jumped to the big two. Much of the time, there is a stigma that surrounds them, and a negative feeling toward them in the dressing room. Vince had sent out feelers, and I found out later had actually gotten positive feedback from some of his bigger stars, like the Undertaker and Kevin Nash. Actually, it was the Undertaker who was most instrumental in my hiring . . . in more ways than one.

I loved the Undertaker's character and had been a fan of it since its debut at the 1990 *Survivor Series*. I had actually known the 'Taker quite well, and rode and roomed with him back in his Mean Mark Callous days. Over the years since, I had run into him on the road a few times and had always been happy to catch up on old times. The Undertaker seemed to have suffered over the past few years, however, due to a lack of decent opponents who could generate interesting feuds. The Giant Gonzalez experiment, in particular, yielded some tough-to-watch matches. At six-foot-nine, and over 300 pounds, Undertaker was one of the largest men in the business, but his last several years had been spent feuding with wrestlers who were either taller or heavier. With the exception of Yokozuna, who 'Taker had done big business with, none of these feuds was able to capture people's imagination.

The idea that Vince had was to match Undertaker up with someone who could get inside his head and could threaten him mentally as well as physically. Vince assured me of his ambitions for this "marriage" by saying that my interviews would really put this thing over. He was so convincing in his accolades for "Mike," as both a wrestler and a human being, that I couldn't wait to become part of the World Wrestling Federation family, even if the money stank and the guys in the dressing room hated one another. Then Vince spoke again.

"We've got a gimmick for you, Mike, and it involves putting you under a hood," Vince said with a big smile, as I felt my heart sink to the bottom of my stomach. A hood was a mask, and outside of Mexico and Japan, a mask was a death knell for a career. Hell, a mask was something the underneath guys wore at Center Stage, when they didn't want their friends and family to know that they were losing on TV. I may have been in awe of Vince, and willing to let him call me the wrong name, but this time I had to speak up.

"Vince, I always felt that my facial expressions were part of my charm—why would you want to cover me up?" It was then that Vince showed me a sketch of a hood that more closely resembled something from *The Man in the Iron Mask*. The mask was actually an idea that was first brought up for the Undertaker after he'd suffered a fracture of his orbital bone and needed a mask to protect his face. Instead of putting the 'Taker in a hockey mask, Vince had requested several ideas for a mask that would add to instead of detract from his image. The drawing I was shown was actually a reject from the Undertaker project that Vince had saved for future reference. Apparently my name had come up some time later, and Vince thought that "Mike" Foley might just have found his niche in the World Wrestling Federation.

I looked at the sketch and picked it up to study it more closely. The mask was actually quite a bit different from the one I would eventually wear. It definitely appeared to be made of metal, with small iron bars caressing my mouth, Hannibal Lecter–style. I could see some possibilities in the sketch, but my heart was still feeling a little low in my gut. "Vince," I asked with confusion in my voice, "why can't I just be Cactus Jack?"

Vince tried to be comforting but failed miserably with his words. "Mike, you've got to understand that the average fan sees wrestling as a glut of performers who seem to blend together. It is hard for our licensees to get behind our products, and hard for us to push your characters if there is no distinction between the competition and us. We feel that with this unique character, we can market Mike, and make Mike a bigger star than he's ever been." His words made sense, and in retrospect the marketing of Mankind has been a great success, but at the time, I was thinking something altogether different. Not only did Vince not want the Cactus Jack I wanted to give him—he didn't want him at all. Poor Mike. He wasn't happy.

Our meeting ended with me holding on to my sketch and trying to hold on to my lunch. I told Vince that I really liked his idea, when actually I was secretly wishing that he had come up with an amnesia angle. J. J. F'ing Dillon walked in and handed me a contract, which I took—but I was sure that I'd never sign. In addition to the lame gimmick I'd been handed, the World Wrestling Federation contract called for no guaranteed money at all—just an opportunity. The opportunity may have seemed enticing back in the days when his wrestlers were on Saturday morning cartoons, but with the knowledge that Federation "superstars" were having trouble paying for their rooms in Red Deer, Canada, I began thinking that Mr. Asano's offer was not that bad after all.

I arrived home and gave the bad news to Colette. Surprisingly, she liked the idea of the new character and began pointing out the possibilities. Colette has a creative mind, and as I mentioned, had been partly responsible for the Cactus Jack transformation from goof to monster back in 1990. She laid out some pretty wild images, and I began to see some possibilities. Then again, these thoughts were coming from a woman who thought Mick Foley was sexy, so how good could her opinion be? I thought about it for quite a while before calling up J. J. F'ing Dillon. I thanked J. J. for having thought of me and told him I had enjoyed my visit to Stamford, but that I didn't think the idea would work and that I would go on living life as Cactus Jack. I've got to admit that part of me felt really good about me telling *him* that I wasn't interested in the World Wrestling Federation.

A few hours later I received a call from Jim Ross, who talked to me for two hours about my decision. He was honest about the plusses and minuses of the Federation and convinced me of Vince's sincerity in pushing the new character. I told him of my semicommitment to Japan and of my desire to continue working in ECW until I actually began on television with the Federation. We worked out a deal where I would start on television after *WrestleMania*, and I would begin a full-time schedule in early May. In the meantime, they would start airing vignettes to introduce their audience to this new character.

I drove to New York City a few days later to be fitted for my mask. The mask maker was a peculiar little Orthodox Jewish guy named Stanley who operated out of his fifth-floor apartment. At first, I was driving around looking for a huge neon sign saying "Masks R Us" or something similar, but I eventually made my way to his strange lair, where I was given hot herbal tea with honey before having plaster poured all over my face to make a mold for my mask. The concept for the mask had changed quite a bit in the last few days. Stanley explained that their sketch would never actually work correctly, so he had modified it with hinges around the mouth. Thankfully, the Hannibal Lecter bars were gone from the mouth, as was the whole metal concept. Instead, it was a light brown rawhide leather mask with a mouth I could actually move. The almost-black color that I now sport is a result of three years of sweating. Needless to say, wearing the mask is not the most pleasant experience in the world.

I left Stanley's and headed several blocks away to the seamstress's office, where an elaborate costume had been made. Afterward, I drove to Stamford for a follow-up meeting with Vince. We talked at length about ideas for the character, and he seemed responsive to most of them. In some ways, I was actually looking forward to changing characters—it would give me a chance to grow and try out some new things.

For one thing, I felt like I needed a new finishing move. The double arm DDT was fine, but I wanted something more sinister. A long time ago, when I was flying onto the concrete and rolling guys into the ring for the pin, I approached Jim Cornette about getting a new finish. "I'm dying, Corny," I told him. "I just can't drop elbows every night. Can you think of something that doesn't hurt me and doesn't require a whole lot of strength?" One of the keys to a good finish is that you should be able to put it on anyone, anywhere, at any time. The tombstone piledriver for example, was a move that the Undertaker had not been able to use in over two years, because all his opponents were up in the 400-pound range. The Stone Cold stunner, on the other hand, can be done all day long on any day to any guy. Cornette was like a wrestling encyclopedia, and if anybody could think of a simple, effective finish, it would be him. "Cactus," he said, smiling, "have you ever heard of the mandible claw?"

I stood with Corny like a student looks to a teacher, as Jimmy laid out not only the biomechanics and philosophy of the hold, but the history behind it as well. "Cactus," Corny began, "in the old Tennessee territory, there was a wrestler named Dr. Sam Shepard. He was the physician that the TV show and movie *The Fugitive* were based on. He was accused of killing his wife, and even though there were really weird circumstances surrounding the case, he was convicted and put in jail. Eventually, his verdict was overturned, but because of his notoriety, the poor guy couldn't work as a physician anymore. He went to work in a small, Southern wrestling circuit, and, using his knowledge of the human anatomy, developed a finishing hold called the mandible claw."

Cornette then proceeded to show me how it worked. "By pressing down with your two middle fingers on the nerves underneath the tongue, and by pressing up with your thumb on the nerves running under the chin, you can damn near kill the guy. You'd have a hell of a finish, and you wouldn't have to kill yourself." I was so excited that I ran right to the Cowboy himself, Bill Watts. I laid it out and waited for his enthusiastic response and maybe even a manly hug. I got nei-

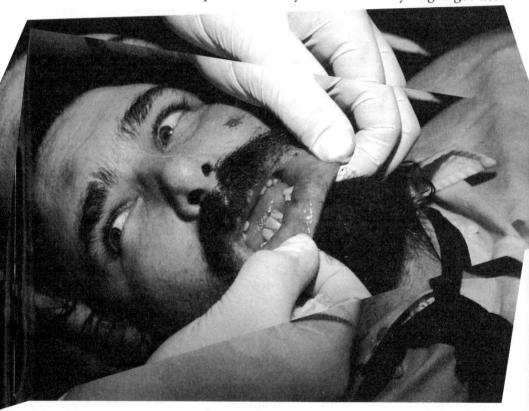

ther. Instead, I got, "Why couldn't I just bite your goddamn fingers off?" I tried to explain the whole nerve idea, but it was no use; Bill had spoken.

I decided to pitch my idea again to a more reasonable man, who wouldn't talk about biting my "goddamn fingers off." I relayed the historical significance and also tried to make him see just how visually exciting the whole thing would look. "Vince, it will be the only move in the business that will allow the camera to get close-ups of both guys at the same time. It will be great."

Vince thought about it for quite a while before answering. "Mick," he began (apparently someone must have alerted him about the name issue) "why wouldn't I just bite your fingers?"

Oh no, I was sunk—or was I? I had to fire back or else the moment would be gone forever. "Because," I began my rebuttal, "it's a nerve hold. No one can bite when the hold is applied. We can have the announcers talk about the element of surprise, and how, once it's on, the match is over."

Vince took it all in and nodded. "Let me think about it" is all he said.

I also had an idea for music. I had loved a particular scene in *The Silence of the Lambs* that had a tremendous juxtaposition of violence and beautiful music. The scene took place in a temporary cell built in the court building of Memphis, Tennessee. As it begins, Hannibal Lecter is listening to a tape of beautiful piano music as he uses the commode. Unknown to the police officers guarding him, Lecter is in possession of a small piece of metal, which he hides between his fingers. The police officers approach the cage with his dinner saying, "Okay, you know the procedure, Doc, grab some floor." Lecter sits with his back to the bars and allows himself to be handcuffed with his hands behind his back. Once he is incapacitated, the officers unlock the cage to lay his dinner on the table. During this food delivery, Lecter is working on the handcuffs with his small piece of metal. When the first officer comes near, Lecter springs into action, snapping

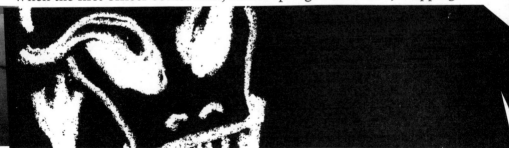

one cuff on one of the officer's wrists, rendering him immobile by snapping the other on one of the cell bars. When the second officer comes for assistance, Lecter bites off a portion of the man's tongue and thoroughly maces his eyes. He then returns to the helpless first officer and, as dramatic music blares, methodically caves in his skull with several blows from the man's own nightstick. The camera then surveys the bloody aftermath as the beautiful piano music gently fades back in. A blood-splattered Lecter is shown to be the picture of serenity as he gently sways to the beautiful sounds.

I explained the scene to Vince. "That's what I want," I told him. "I want separate entrance and exit music—no one's ever done that before. The entrance will be scary, but the exit will be beautiful. I want to be completely at peace with myself after destroying my opponent."

"I see," said Vince. "Let me think about that as well."

I then continued laying out some ideas for the character that I had gotten through reading the crime novels of Jonathan Kellerman. Kellerman was a psychologist turned author, and I was always enthralled by how the plot was usually driven by some obscure mental illness or condition. I proposed some really far-out ways to work these into story lines, none of which ever made it to fruition but probably were good for some raised eyebrows around Titan Towers.

Vince then prepared me for some big news. I could tell he was excited by what he was about to say. "Did anyone tell you your name yet?" he asked me with a smile.

"No," I said. "What is it?"

"Well," Vince continued in his very descriptive way. "In this business, we've had crushers, we've had bruisers, we've had destroyers, but we've never had a mutilator! And that's what you most certainly are—a mutilator!"

Oh, God, I thought. Just when things were going so well. I could hear that dreadful name rolling slowly and painfully across Vince's lips—MEW-TI-LAY-TOR. I wanted to go home. Or to Japan, where it was still Cock-toos-uh Jack, the King of the Death Match.

"What do you think?" Vince boomed.

I struggled for something to say and came out with the three most untruthful words I've ever spoken. "I like it."

Vince wasn't through yet, though. "We'll need a first name, too," he said. "I know you used to use the name Manson."

"I did," I replied, "but I was never really comfortable with it. I didn't like the association with a killer."

Vince smiled. "I was hoping you'd feel that way, because we'd like to call you Mason: Mason the Mutilator." I again pledged my undying support for the name, but inside my head, I was searching desperately for a way out. I had always felt that it was not good enough to shoot something down—it was best to have a solution. I nodded and smiled blankly while mentally trying to dig my career out of the huge hole that Vince had just thrown it in. Suddenly, a light flashed in my head. "Vince, I just had an idea. As much as I like Mason," I lied—hoping that my nose wouldn't start growing right in front of him—"I think I have an even better idea."

"Really," Vince said with sincerity, "I'd like to hear it."

"Well," I asked, "what if you were to call me Mankind the Mutilator?"

Vince seemed puzzled. "I'm not sure I understand," is all he said. I had his interest, but it was important to try to nail it now. If I couldn't sell him on Mankind now, I knew I never would. "You see, Vince, the name would have a double meaning. I could talk about 'the future of mankind' or 'the destruction of mankind' and it would carry two different meanings. I could also blame mankind as a people for creating Mankind as a person. Then, when I talk about Mankind the Mutilator, I could either be talking about myself or be making an indictment of the whole human race."

Vince seemed genuinely impressed. "I like that." He nodded. "Let's go with it."

I don't think you can overestimate the importance of your name in pro wrestling. A good name won't make you, but a bad name sure as hell can break you. When Steve Austin joined the World Wrestling Federation, he was named the Ringmaster, a gimmick that was mediocre at best. Looking for a change in character, Austin suggested a personality that was somewhat cold-blooded. The creative people got a little carried away with the cold temperature as opposed to the cold attitude and sent him three pages of names that included Ice Dagger and Chilly McFreeze. Looking back, even if every other thing in Steve's career had been the same, the names would have killed him deader than poor Kelsey's nuts. Same glass breaking, same music, same stunner, same beer, same middle fingers—it wouldn't have mattered. As soon as he walked down that aisle announced as Baron von Ruthless, you have could stuck a fork in him—he'd have been done.

"There's one more thing we need to know," Vince declared. "I need to know that you're completely comfortable with your gimmick [costume]. You're going to be wearing it for a long time, and I need to know that you're completely happy with it."

I thought about it. I knew I had suggested and asked for a lot of things, and Vince had listened and been more than fair about all of them. I thought maybe I should just stay put with the costume card I had been dealt. Then I thought about my future and how silly I could look in this sort of fake chain metal fabric that made me look like an extra in a Knights of the Round Table film. It was do-or-die time. "Yeah, Vince, I did have one small concern," I managed to squeak out. Vince seemed genuinely amused by my opinions. Most people met with Vince and didn't speak a word against any idea the World Wrestling Federation had because they were just so happy to be there. Surely P. J. Walker knew that his Aldo Montoya gimmick was doomed as soon as he saw the yellow jock strap they wanted him to wear on his head, but he never spoke a word. Surely a veteran like Ron Simmons had second thoughts when Vince showed him the blue helmet that he was supposed to wear, but he walked out of that office looking like a black Spartacus anyway. I was determined not to make the mistake.

"Yeah, Vince, about the gimmick," I continued.

"Yes Mick, what is it?"

"Well . . ." I tried to think how I could delicately phrase this. "I hate it, Vince, I really hate it."

Vince couldn't help but laugh at my exuberance. "Tell me what you hate about it, and we'll try to come up with something else."

I took the gimmick out of the bag and pleaded my case further. "Vince, it's just that I feel like I'm playing dress-up in a movie."

Vince looked and immediately agreed. "This is not what we want," he said and summoned one of the people from Creative Services. "Mick needs a new outfit—he needs something that looks like he made it in his basement—can we work on that?"

Debbie Bonanzio was the woman from Creative Services who immediately began modifying the look until it was simply a ragged brown shirt. It certainly looked like it came from my basement, but now I was dressed in brown from head to toe and was afraid that I would look like a giant turd. I asked about breaking up the monotony of the giant turd by putting a large symbol on the back, and when pressed further, suggested a homemade peace sign. That idea was shot down, but Debbie was told to research it, and a week later a sketch of Mankind's new symbol, an amalgamation of a life sign and a Celtic cross, was approved.

I was happy with the promise of the character and was enthusiastic about making it work. Even the contract, which guaranteed nothing but an opportunity, seemed agreeable that day. I had requested several small changes to the contract, which the company had obliged, and I was sure that the money would take care of itself. Our lease was up in West Babylon, and our renters had moved out in Georgia, so I packed up our belongings and headed south as a proud member of the World Wrestling Federation.

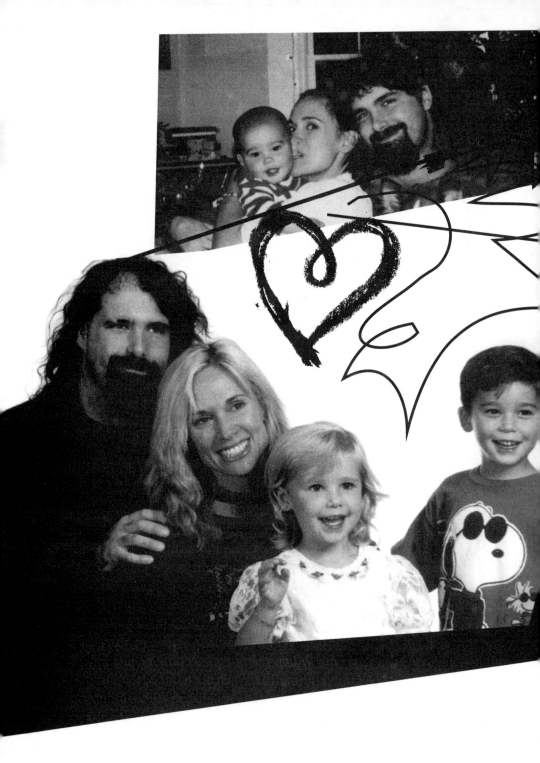

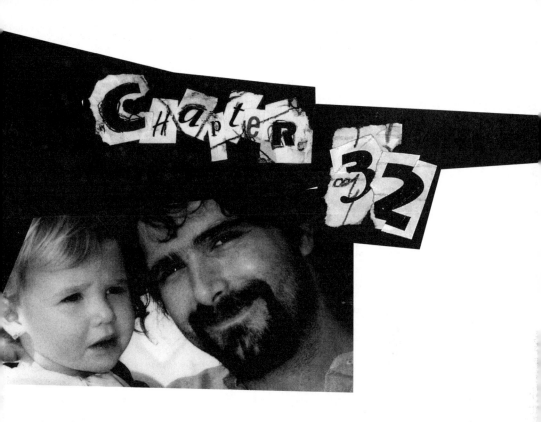

We arrived back in Atlanta, glad

to be home and excited about the holidays. Colette was glad to be home, despite the realization that it signaled the end of her modeling career. Working for Wilhelmina had been exciting, but a real big job hadn't come along yet, and Colette felt that maybe, at age thirty-four, the big jobs were over. To this day, she still does some work, but it's mostly for fun.

I have always loved the Christmas season. I know most people do, but I look forward to it all year long. In addition to my year-round Christmas music selection, I also keep a Christmas Village up in a place of prominence all year long, and some painted ceramic Santas as well. My favorite place in the world as a kid was Santa's Village in New Hampshire, where in the summer of 1996, I made my triumphant return after an absence of twenty-seven years. Now it's my kids' favorite place in the world. "Guess where we're going," I asked my daughter about three months before the trip. "Santa Wiwwage" would come her tiny little two-year-old reply.

It was in the Christmas spirit and in front of the Christmas tree that I cut one of my all-time favorite promos for ECW. My anti-ECW campaign had been a big hit, but I wasn't satisfied—I needed more. I decided that in order for the fans to truly hate me, I had to lose everything about me that they'd ever liked. The look was the first to go. I slicked back my hair real tight into a short, conservative look. Then I shaved my beard and mustache for the first time in years. I put on a sports jacket that I bought especially for the occasion, and threw on a shirt and tie. I'd always hated people who wore loafers with no socks, so I went with those as well.

I also decided to modify my speaking style. Gone was the intensity, the shrieking and the defiance. In came the nerdy phrases, fake laugh, and utter ass kissing. I realized that this was something ECW fans would hate more than anything. I decided I would put over the fans, the product, and the whole ECW mentality, but do it in a way that was incredibly wimpy. In contrast to my earlier promos, which were hardcore anti-hardcore messages, these would be namby-pamby pro-hardcore interviews.

I set the whole interview against the story line of Todd Gordon voting for the most hardcore wrestler of 1995. By brown-nosing both Gordon and the fans, while at the same time adding ridiculous imagery to the hardcore mentality and losing my look and voice, I was sure it would gain me the disdain of the fans. It was also the most fun I ever had in front of a camera. My wife filmed it, and, if I may say so, did a pretty damn good job.

December 1995—ECW TV Show—*A Hardcore Christmas*

Scene—The Foley house. As Burl Ives's "Holly Jolly Christmas" plays in the background, the camera fades in. A sockless loafer is bouncing to the tune of the music as the camera slowly pans out. We see a clean-shaven Cactus Jack sitting in front of a Christmas tree with his two-year-old daughter, Noelle, on his lap. The clean-cut Cactus speaks:

"Ho, ho, ho—Happy Hardcore Holidays, everybody. This is Cactus Jack, along with the rest of the Foleys here to wish you and your family a Happy Holiday Hardcore season. [Noelle laughs.] I took this time out today to try to explain what Christmas means to me, and, by golly, I found out that Christmas can mean a lot of different things. First off, I found out that Christmas can be [yelling] FUN! Ha ha [Noelle laughs]. Why, just the other day there were some Christmas carolers, and I snuck up on their little group and, as the door opened and they began to sing, I started chanting 'ECW, ECW, ECW,' ha ha, and I'll tell you what . . . I would have gotten away with it too, but all the neighbors heard me yelling 'BANG BANG' [Noelle laughs] as I made my way through the neighborhood. But you know, they didn't care. They just thought, 'There goes that nutty Cactus Jack'—but you know what, they realized that it doesn't hurt to have a hardcore person in the neighborhood. Second of all [getting serious], Christmas is for family. Why just the other day, I was taking gingerbread men out of the oven [getting happier], and I'll tell you what, I took one look at that cookie sheet and I was wishing that I could POWEE! Ha ha . . . hit someone over the head with it—right in the kisser. Ha ha, I bet you could get some juice out of that one! BANG BANG!

"Most important, Christmas is for caring [real serious]. Now, I understand that there is a hardcore balloting going on, and that Todd Gordon is in charge of the voting, but more importantly, Todd is in charge of some very prestigious and worthwhile children's charities and I'd like to be the first at this special time of the year to write a generous check. Seeing as I don't know the exact names of the charities, I'm just going to make the check out to Todd Gordon himself, and [winking at camera] I think Todd will know what to do with it. Ha ha. Here, honey, zoom in so they can get a look at all these zeros—ha ha—not too close so they'll see our address and we're liable to have 1,500 hardcore fans on our front lawn chanting, 'He's hardcore, he's hardcore.' Ha ha. I'll tell you what. I love them, and if it were up to me, I'd have them all in for a cup of hot chocolate. Oh, Santa [picking up a plush Santa doll], what's the number one wrestling organization? [Horrible ventriloquist act] ECW ho ho ECW."

Camera fades out, as Noelle cries for "Mama, Mama, Mama."

I left for Japan right after New Year's, but not before doing some ten-second promos to introduce Mankind to the audience. They were just brief sound bites, and because my mask was still undergoing final preparations, the camera really never showed my face, but would instead feature an extreme close-up of my ear or mouth. On that evening in Stamford, "Have a nice day" was born.

I actually came back without a scratch on that tour, although I had a hard time trying to convince Colette of that during my traditional post-tour phone call. Upon my return to the States, I headed to Queens for ECW's debut in the New York area. My beard had grown in a little bit, and despite my different look and ridiculous promos, I still received a hell of a reaction from my hometown fans, as I battled Sabu in a tremendous contest. For some reason, the building was demanding a fifty percent concession fee for any item sold, which I protested immediately. Instead of letting these people whom I'd never met walk away with my money, I had my T-shirt maker hawk them in the parking lot. He came back excited as hell less than twenty minutes later. "We sold them all," he yelled. "Cactus, no matter what, they still love you."

On that same night, Mikey Whipwreck won a strange stipulation match that, although wrestled as a single, allowed him to take possession of both tag team belts. Mikey was then, in theory, allowed to pick his own partner to be tag champs with, but in reality, I immediately ran to the ring, hugged him, and accepted the belt. Mikey and I were now two-time tag team champions, although Mikey would spend the next several weeks wanting out of our partnership.

A week later, my little World Wrestling Federation video spots started airing, and everything changed. When we returned to Queens, I sent my T-shirt guy out onto the street and waited anxiously for all the extra shirt money to jam my pockets. A few minutes later, he returned out of breath with his arms still full of "Wanted" shirts. There were at least four visible loogies on his jacket from where he'd been spit on. "They hate you out there," he cried. "I had to get out of there. I thought they might kill me."

Sure enough, the crowd was hot when I hit the ring with Mikey to defend the belts. I added to the heat by sporting a takeoff on the popular "EC F'N W" shirt that read "W W F'N F." We lost the belts that night, and I turned on poor Mikey, who had just wrestled his heart out—further cementing my new image as a sellout and a scumbag. As a matter of fact, I was showered by chants of "You sold out, you sold out" on my way out of the ring. I stepped back in and addressed the chant. "You know, you people are a lot smarter than I give you credit for," I said. "Because I have a feeling that a year from now, I'm going to have to look in the mirror and admit in my heart that I sold out." The crowd was quiet now, as they took in my impromptu confession. Then I continued with a sarcastic yell. "I sold out the Garden, I sold out the Coliseum, I sold out every damn arena in this country!"

The next day I arrived an hour late at the ECW arena, as I had been at the wedding of my old school buddy Scott Darragh. When I got there, my opponent, Shane Douglas, who was making his return to ECW after a disastrous run in the World Wrestling Federation, was irate. Apparently, Shane's return to the ECW arena had not been warmly received, and he was concerned that he would be booed out of the place against Cactus Jack. "Don't worry," I assured him, "because these people will hate me, and besides, I've got a plan."

I showed up for my match teetering slowly and still dressed in my wedding suit. "I've got some good news and some bad news," I alerted the crowd, which wasn't quite sure where I might be going with this. "The good news is . . . I was at a wedding, and it was beautiful, and I drove back here without any harm to myself or others. The bad news is . . . in all the merriment, I had a little too much to drink, and I don't feel that I can, in good conscience, subject any of you to my drunken, irresponsible ways. Now, how about somebody throwing me a fucking beer!" With that, Shane hit the ring and interrupted my little postnuptial cocktail. We went at it, and a hell of a match ensued.

For a reason that was never quite explained, Brian Hildebrand was our referee, and for a reason that also went unknown, my old friend handcuffed my hands behind my back when I was down. When I got up, Shane had a chair, and began teeing off on my unprotected skull (an idea we would later use in the 1999 *Royal Rumble*). After every shot, he'd grab the mike and try to get me to denounce the World Wrestling Federation. I wouldn't do it. Finally, after I'd taken more punishment than anyone ever ought to, he put the mike in front of my mouth and demanded a denouncement. "Mikey!" was what I screamed. Another chance, another "Mikey!" Shane then hooked on a figure four leg lock, as I screamed in vain for my little buddy.

Finally, Mikey arrived, armed with the chair that I was sure would free me from the figure four. Instead, Mikey faked right and went left and caught me with a brutal shot to the forehead and nose that resulted in a three-count. A match with Mikey was booked for my final ECW appearance in March of 1996 at the ECW arena.

Before I started with the Federation, I had one more tour of Japan to complete. Before I left, I went back to Stamford, where on a snowy afternoon I participated in four vignettes that I was sure were going to propel me to the forefront of the company and Vince's heart. I left the studio that day sure that I'd hit a home run. Everyone there, including Jim Cornette, thought so, too.

The vignettes were filmed in front of a makeshift dungeon and featured me playing with rats and telling stories of piano playing, child abuse, neglect, and disfigurement. I had been reading books like Mary Shelley's *Frankenstein* and was full of antisocial images. "This wasn't as good as Cactus Jack's stuff," I thought as I pulled out of the Federation parking lot. "It's better."

I returned from Japan, and after a few days flew to New York for my final ECW shows. My opponent for the first show in Queens was Chris Jericho. I had met Jericho in Japan and thought he had a hell of a lot of potential—not just as a wrestler, because he was already damn good, but as a personality as well. I had been after Paul E. literally for months about giving him a try, and he had finally given in.

The response to me was brutal, even to the point of hurting my feelings. Even though I'd been doing my best to piss these people off for the last several months, I wanted to feel like they could at least separate fact from fantasy and give me a decent send-off. Instead, they showered me with everything from full beers to deafening chants of "You sold out." That's a chant that has always disturbed me. It reminded me of when the bratty little kid on *One Day at a Time* accuses Schneider, the custodian, of selling out for taking a better job. I didn't buy it then, and I still don't. I mean, it's not as if these fans were taking up collections for ECW wrestlers' retirement funds or taking care of my mortgage.

Even after the match, when I did my "Today, day, I feel like, like the luckiest man, on, the face of the earth, earth" Lou Gehrig speech, the crowd was unforgiving. It was definitely one of those nights when I went to sleep thinking that this whole wrestling thing wasn't worth it. I wondered if my farewell in the ECW arena, where I had sacrificed so much, would be any different. I hoped so, but I doubted it. I had made that particular group of fans a direct target of my wrath and doubted they had forgiven me for it.

I had made up special commemorative T-shirts for my finale. The front was an illustration that a fan had sent me, depicting a somewhat pained-looking Cactus Jack bound by barbed wire to a cactus, as buzzards flew overhead. It did look somewhat Christ-like, but I rationalized it enough to avoid feeling like a total blasphemer. "Well, I was on a cactus, not a cross, and was held there by barbed wire, not nails. Besides, I'm a lot heavier than Jesus ever was." Underneath the illustration were these simple words: "Cactus Jack 1985–1996." The shirts had done well in Japan, and even though I wasn't expecting many to sell in the States, at least they were there for anyone who wanted to commemorate Cactus Jack's last match.

My promos to build up my match had been something of a depar-

MICK FOLEY

ture for me. I had already condemned, criticized, kissed ass, and made fun—now it was time for something different: the completely irrational interviews. I picked out the tiniest detail and lambasted Mikey about it. I blamed him for leaving Doritos in the car by screaming "Good God, man, don't you know I have an eating disorder!" I also criticized his lack of appreciation for the beauty of fall foliage. Last, but not least, I tore into him for replacing my soothing Leonard Cohen tape with "Satanic heavy metal music—for crying out loud, I'm the father of two impressionable children, you sinner!" For his part, Mikey just acted completely flabbergasted.

I was thinking of two reasons for this rather odd take on our feud. One, anyone can get mad about major things, but it takes a dangerous man to get worked up about the changing of the leaves. And two, no matter what I talked about, the building was going to sell out anyway—why not have some fun?

The next night I heard Mikey's music playing, and my mind began to race. I thought about where I'd been and where I was heading. I know that I'd worked my ass off on both sides of the Pacific, but I also knew that I'd been a big fish in a small pond there. The World Wrestling Federation was the great unknown, and I had an eight o'clock flight to Corpus Christi, Texas, the next day to give Mankind a test run in front of the Federation fans. It would not be televised, but instead used as a dress rehearsal before my big debut. I had always hated wearing a mask and doubted that this would be any different. I liked being Cactus Jack, but after tonight, I never would be again. I wanted to make this last match count. *Crash!* I heard the cymbal. Then the familiar guitar riff. John Kay's voice kicked in, and I knew that it was time to go. "Get your motor running, head out on the highway"—I stepped through the curtain.

I was not mentally prepared for the reaction I received. I couldn't have expected it in my wildest dreams. Fans were clapping, and by the time I got to the ring, every last one was on his feet chanting my name in unison. "Cactus Jack, Cactus Jack." It wasn't the loudest reaction I'd ever heard for a wrestler, but it was damn close. What set it apart was that it was so real. It wasn't born out of pandemonium, angles, marketing, or hoopla—it was born out of a genuine respect and appreciation, and it blew me away. I had my head down, because I knew that if I looked up, I'd surely cry. I came real close. But I was moved beyond all description. I was moved when I saw it on tape, and

I'm moved right now while I'm writing it. I could not possibly have asked for a better going-away present. I had launched verbal assaults at these people for over six months, and in the end it turned out that they liked me—they really liked me.

The match was one of my all-time favorites. Poor Mikey took a hell of a beating but kept coming back. I backdropped a charging Mikey and then backsuplexed him into a table I had leaned against the ring post. I worked him over and used a fan named John Owen's crutch to give him a nice shot to the gut. I even premiered the mandible claw, which unfortunately was met with silence.

Somewhere along the way, Mikey took over and used a variety of interesting implements, including the sacred Cohen album I referred to earlier. Actually, I held on to the ancient vinyl disc like Linus holds on to his blanket, while Mikey continued his assault. While holding the album, I staggered through the crowd until Mikey suplexed me at the base of the ramp. While I slowly stood, Mikey ascended to the top of the stage, which was some twelve feet off the floor. With a leap, Mikey became airborne and caught me with a variation of a flying cross body block. I actually lowered my head and caught much of his impact with my head in his chest, which could have been bad news for both of us. Fortunately, we were both okay, and we made our way back through the crowd, at which point Mikey rolled me into the ring.

He followed me in with one of the gray plastic ringside chairs and caught me with three good shots that sent me down for a close two-and-a-half count. Mikey then took to the top rope and attempted a somersault dive, which I avoided. Now it was my turn. I took the chair and turned it around. I always felt that by using the reverse side, and by making contact with the backrest portion, as opposed to the seat itself, the blow was more impressive. It allowed me greater extension and increased force, and the result was more of a loud crack, as opposed to a dull thud. I came down hard across Mikey's back with the first one. *CRACK!* The crowd felt it then. Another one, even harder than the first. *CRACK!* Mikey was wriggling in pain. I then put the chair down and waited for young Mikey to get up. When he arose, I tucked his head between my legs, grabbed the back of his tights, and then pile-drove him on the chair with a quick, stump-pulling motion. One, two, three—and the Cactus Jack era was over.

The crowd rose to their feet and began clapping vigorously. Again, it wasn't pandemonium reigning but a legitimate display of gratitude.

I picked up Mikey and hugged him before raising his hand. Joey Styles made a great call in the television broadcast. "This is the Cactus Jack that we want to remember. This is the Cactus Jack that we love." The crowd's reaction had me close to tears again as I grabbed the house mike. The match had been very memorable, but the post match shenanigans would be just as good.

"This is one screwed-up place" is how I started my farewell speech. "To give me this type of reaction after all the things I've said about you makes it all worth it." I looked down and saw my friend who was always willing to lend his trusty crutch, John Owen. I stepped out of the ring and took off my new Cactus T-shirt. When I handed it to him, he hugged me tight and wouldn't let me go. I tried to pull away, but he had a hell of a grip. I looked at his face, and I could see tears streaming down it—he was embarrassed by his show of emotion. I gently assured him that it was okay and climbed back into the ring. I then continued, "There are two guys that I have to mention here by name because without them there would be no more ECW. One of them is a business visionary, who knew what he wanted and went about creating ECW. The other is a creative genius." I could hear people yelling at Todd Gordon and Paul E. by name. "I want to bring them out for you right now . . . Dancing Stevie Richards, and the Blue Meanie." Meanie and Richards, who were kind of like comedic heels for the company, came running out, pumping their arms in the air and jumping around like little kids. We hugged in midring and the music-only version of "New York, New York" began to play.

To understand the significance of "New York, New York," you have to understand the wrestling industry's habit of referring to every wrestling promotion by its nearest major city. A wrestler going to work in the World Class group would say, "I'm going to Dallas," and a wrestler heading for WCW would say, "I'm going to Atlanta." Even though the World Wrestling Federation was located in Stamford, it had always been known as "New York." The packed house picked up on it right away and actually started singing the words as I did a terrible Rockettes kickline routine with my two cronies. After the music died down, I got on the mike again and said that, as a last request, I wanted to strut out of the ECW arena. So, as Stevie Richards' music kicked in, I did the worst Fargo strut in history—all the way up the aisle and out of the ECW arena. I believe it was the greatest wrestling send-off I'd ever seen.

The next morning I flew to Corpus Christi, Texas, for my first match as Mankind.

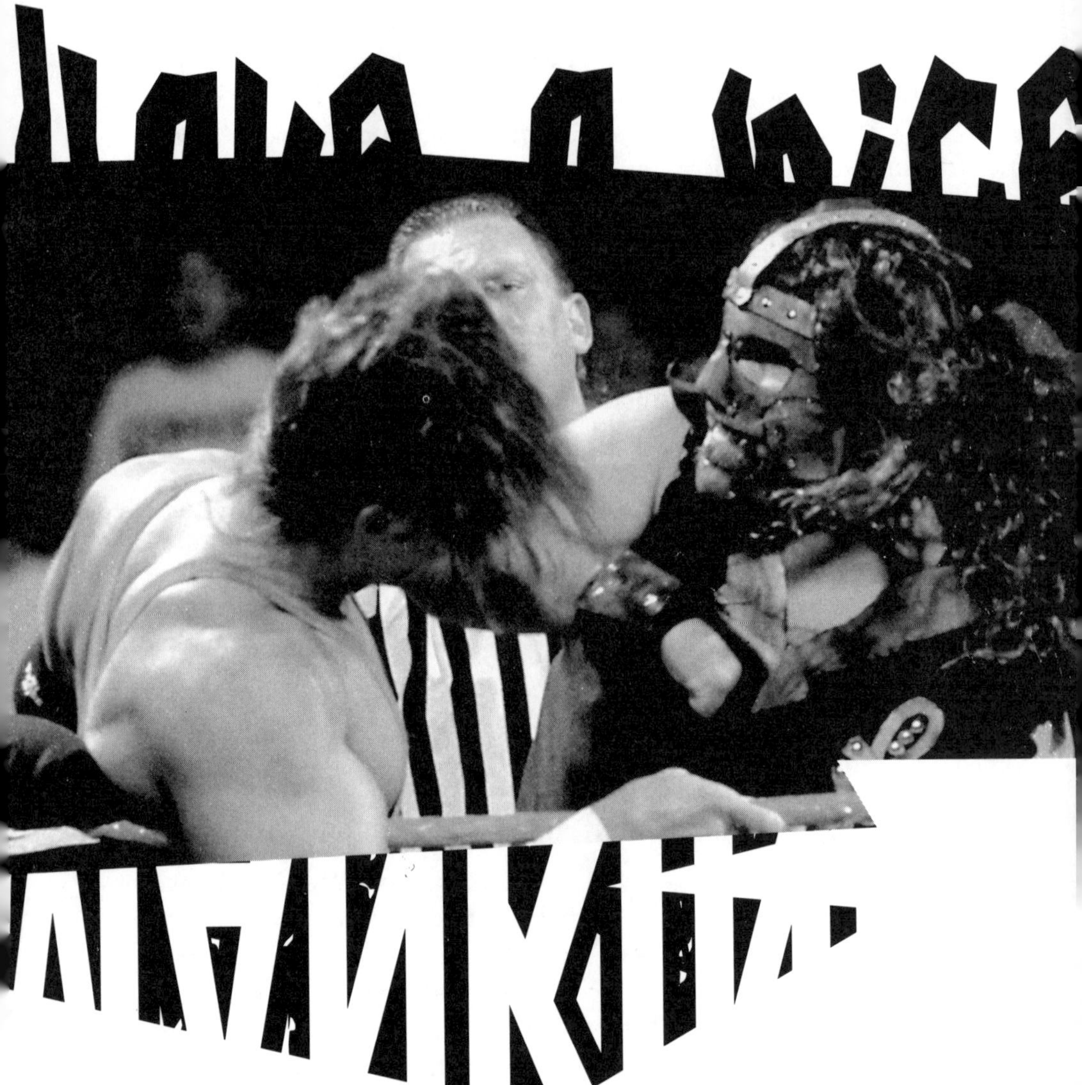

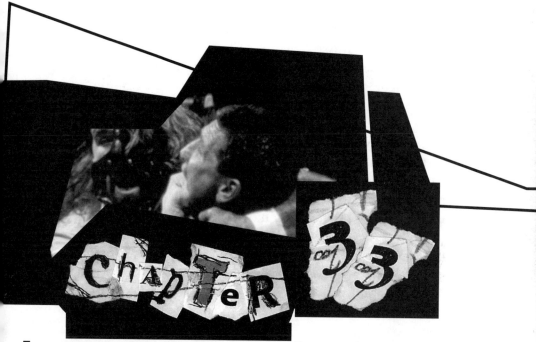

CHAPTER 33

I was nervous and deprived of sleep on my way to Corpus Christi. It just seemed like such a big, scary world in the World Wrestling Federation. Two of their stars had just signed big-money contracts with WCW, which had begun trying to win the wrestling war in earnest. WCW's *Monday Nitro* was heavily promoted on their television stations, and the show had been running neck and neck with the World Wrestling Federation's *Raw*. Nobody knew what type of impact the departures of Kevin Nash and Scott Hall would have, but it had created a poor feeling among the wrestlers. I looked at my booking sheet and realized I knew at least two-thirds of the guys already, but I still had great apprehension about the coming day.

I arrived at the building early and ran into my old WCW teammate, Jake the Snake. Jake was a part of the creative process (he was on the booking committee) in addition to being a wrestler, and we caught up on old times before Jake went back to his hotel and slept through the entire TV taping. As other wrestlers arrived, I met and spoke with people I'd never met and BS'd a little with the guys I did know.

I saw Jim Cornette and ran over to talk about my vignettes, which had already begun airing. "Jimmy," I called, suddenly feeling refreshed at the prospect of the glowing words he would no doubt be sending my way. "What did Vince think?" I asked.

"Well," he started, "everybody from [TV director] Kevin Dunn to [TV writer] Vince Russo loved it. They can't stop talking about it."

That was nice to know, but I was more interested in what the big cheese thought. "What about Vince . . . what did he think?"

Jimmy was thinking, and I knew this was trouble. It was the same feeling I'd had when I talked to Neil Pruitt about my Cleveland vignettes. Jimmy's words did little to assuage me. "I'm not sure Vince understood them," he sadly stated.

I was really confused. Vince had told me he loved my Cactus Jack interviews, and these were not all that different. I told this to Corny, and he had to stop and think some more—not a good sign coming from a man who was one of the greatest speakers in the business. "Cactus, I'm not sure that Vince has ever seen your interviews." Oh man, it was hard to get happy after that. Corny continued his gentle assault on my ego and confidence by saying, "Vince is really too busy to watch matches from Japan and interviews from ECW. The reason he told you your promos were great is that we told him they were." He could see that his words had staggered me and was quick to try to straighten me out. "Look, Cactus, don't let that worry you. Once Vince sees you and gets to know you, he'll be your biggest fan of all!" I left our conversation feeling as if I'd just watched three Al Snow matches.

I actually dozed off a few times during the evening. This was back in the days when they used to tape four one-hour shows in one night, and the tapings had a tendency to burn out an audience. Steve Austin had just become Stone Cold and was featured in every single taping. By the time I made my Mankind debut, most of the fans no longer wanted to be there. I was sent through the curtain to the accompaniment of a somber-sounding dirge, which I later found out was called "Ode to Freud." I listened to Howard Finkel as he made the announcement. "Coming down the aisle, at a weight of 287 pounds—MANKIND." Hey, there was a surprise—not only did they go with "Mankind," they had also shelved "the Mutilator."

To say that my reaction was lukewarm would be generous. As I stumbled to the ring, trying to look like a psychologically abused former piano player, I couldn't help but think about what a difference a day made—from the height of popularity to the depths of apathy—all within twenty-four hours. A few people called out "Cactus Jack"; the

MICK FOLEY

rest just stared. Wrestling audiences can be fickle, and they don't always have a great appreciation for the past. Also, the World Wrestling Federation audience in March 1996 were not the same people who were, by and large, watching WCW in September 1994, when I'd last been featured nationally.

I had an untelevised match with Aldo Montoya that night and got the win when my claw pierced the defenses of his yellow jockstrap mask. As the bell rang, I heard something comforting. It was beautiful piano music, just as I'd asked for in Vince's office. I hadn't wanted to believe too much of what I'd heard, but Vince McMahon was sure proving to be a man of his word, even if he didn't really know much about me.

I called home after my match and was not exactly abuzz over my future as Mankind. My mask especially was a subject that bothered me. It was hot, moved around when I worked, and was tough to breathe in. "Maybe I can just wear it for a few months," I said to Colette. "Maybe then they can do an angle and I can just lose the mask and be myself." Ironically, I'd be given the choice to do just that two and a half years later and would turn it down.

I came back for the next set of TV tapings in California at the end of March. The tapings would take place after *WrestleMania*, which was the biggest show of the year. As was tradition, all the boys arrived a few days early to help promote the show and bask in the hoopla. As a masked wrestler who had not even officially started yet, I was unable to take part in either the promoting or the basking. Instead, for three days I sat in my room at the Hilton (the World Wrestling Federation springs once a year for *WrestleMania* week) and looked out across the parking lot of Disneyland. I could see Matterhorn Mountain beckoning me with its majestic snow-covered peaks, and I grew weaker by the day. Finally, I couldn't take it, and on Saturday, March 30, during the peak of spring break, I took the solitary walk across the street and stepped into the hallowed haven of Disneyland.

The place was packed to capacity, to the point where I didn't even consider getting on a line—but worse than that, I had an unbelievable sense of guilt. I felt like an adulterer, except I was cheating on both my wife and my kids, and I couldn't take it. I called home and confessed my sins and was immediately forgiven. I came back later that night and actually did get to go on a few rides.

I sat through *Mania* the next day and got ready to go to San

Bernardino when Vader, my nose-bleeding, eyebrow-busting friend from my past, yelled, "Hey Cactus! I've got a Caddy and trans is free—I'm just looking for a bit of company. What do you think?" A free Caddy was nothing to sneeze at, so I accepted his offer. I was sitting in the Caddy taking in all the plush amenities that were somewhat lacking in my Lumina, when Leon handed me his hotel bill and his sunglasses. "Hold on to this," he grumbled, as he walked away to grab his luggage. With all but the incidentals such as food and phone paid for, I figured his bill would be somewhat low. I mean, after all, how much can one man eat and talk in three days? My bill was $48. I turned over Vader's bill and glanced at the numbers. I couldn't have been more surprised if I had discovered thirty-two bodies in John Wayne Gacy's crawlspace. The figure was astronomical. Two thousand, five hundred big ones! There were $100 meals and $200 bar bills, $50 tips and $300 sunglasses. I asked him about it, and he seemed nonchalant. "Is that more than you spend?" he asked. I got the feeling right then that this Vader/Mankind union wasn't going to last. You would think that two men who shared the intimate bond of beating the crap out of each other would know each other a little better, wouldn't you?

I was nervous about TV, knowing that this one day could mean the difference between success and failure in the World Wrestling Federation. In my years in the business, I had often seen talented guys screw up once and never get a second chance. I really didn't want to be one of those guys. I was scheduled for a match against Bob Holly— a tough, former racecar driver from Mobile who hadn't had any victories in a while. I know most guys' mentality when it comes to a new guy, and I knew that there was a good chance that Bob wouldn't want an ECW guy to look good at his expense. As it turned out, there was no incident, as Bob did his job and I picked up my victory. I can't claim that the victory was memorable, as I was trying to iron the wrinkles out of a new style, but the episode to follow certainly was.

The Undertaker had a scheduled match against Justin Bradshaw, who would later become one of his "Acolytes," or followers. I watched with anticipation, waiting for a tombstone pile driver. When I saw it happening, I felt my body tense. *Thud!* Undertaker dropped Bradshaw's inverted body on his head. The referee bent to count, but I was already on my way. One, two—I broke up the count with a forearm across the back and sent the Undertaker to the steel steps, which he hit with the upper part of his thighs, sending him spinning over the top. I climbed the ring apron, measured my opponent, and took off. The footage of the diving elbow would be shown countless times, as my feud with the Undertaker had just taken off. I then backed off and waited for the 'Taker to stand before sinking in the mandible claw.

I had performed for less than two minutes, but I was completely exhausted. When I got to the backstage area, I was literally gasping for breath. More important than my nerves was the fact that we had just done some captivating television. A few days later, DDP, my old WCW buddy, called to say, "Bro, I'm tellin' ya—I even told Bisch—that thing's gonna draw!"

Also of interest on this taping was that it was Marc Mero's first taping. Unlike me, Mero had come into the World Wrestling Federation with considerably more than just the promise of an opportunity. This fact would both annoy me and drive me over the next several months. Marc's actually a decent guy, who at one time was a good friend of mine. But business is business, and the fact is that Mero didn't draw. He sure did know how to make money, though.

After the taping, I rode with Vader to San Diego. Vader had broken his eardrum during the evening and asked me to drive. I was happy to, as Vader could quite possibly have been the worst driver in the business. He would look at you while he drove and was quite fond of physically going over his matches in the car. "I'd go *boom, boom, boom, boom,*" he'd say, all the while throwing forearms at me that, although slow, would still connect. He was also the worst car singer I'd ever heard. Everyone sings in the car, but Leon actually thought he was good. He'd close his eyes, lean his head back, and proceed to ruin songs that I had grown up loving. I still can't bring myself to listen to Cat Stevens's "Wild World" to this very day. "Who sings this?" I'd always ask Leon as he started to butcher a popular recording. "The Beatles," he'd reply, or the name of whatever group happened to be singing at the time. "Let's keep it that way," I would admonish him, although my remarks never did stop his lyrical rampage.

My main concern about Vader, however, was financial. That $2,500 tab he'd built up was still fresh in my mind as we headed for San Diego. I was compulsive about saving money in those days, especially because I had no idea how much of it I was going to make. I knew that to save money on the road, I was going to have to split rooms, but I had heard that Vader liked to have his own room at

Marriotts around the country. This flew in the face of everything I had been brought up to believe. Going back to the days when we used to jam eight people in a room to see Springsteen, I had always split rooms. But with Vader, I was starting to have my doubts.

By the time we arrived at the San Diego Marriott, Vader had his shirt off, with potato chip debris all tangled up in his chest hair. He had been drinking and was mumbling his words while alternating gaseous emissions between his mouth and his ass. I had to speak up, money or no money. "Leon, you usually like to get your own room, don't you?" I asked. Leon didn't answer but nodded his head and burped. "Me, too," I said, while thinking of the sanctity of my own private bedroom.

Actually, I've lightened up quite a bit in my money-saving obsession over the years and will often spring for my own hotel and car. With wrestling as popular as it is, it seemed like a pretty good investment in myself to get a good night's sleep. I will not, however, under any circumstances, pay more than $80 for a hotel room. Most of the time, I try to stay in the $50 range. The only time I'll make an exception is when my family travels with me. This sudden transformation didn't happen overnight, as I bounced around with different travel mates for the next three years.

Al Snow and Marty Jannetty were the first guys I hooked up with after my driving divorce from the man they call Vader. Marty had, at one time, been one of the hottest prospects and best young wrestlers in the business, but his love for the night life and a tendency to get himself in trouble had led to various hirings and firings, each of which resulted in a smaller role in the company. Marty's role at this point in 1996 was his smallest ever—as half of the New Rockers tag team, along with Al Snow. At this point, Al had been forced to change his name to Leif Cassidy, a combination of two seventies heartthrobs. At one time, with Shawn Michaels as his partner, Marty had been a part of some of the World Wrestling Federation's greatest matches. Michaels had gone on to be one of the Federation's biggest superstars, while Jannetty seemed to drift aimlessly. His only joy in life, it seemed, was tormenting poor Al. He would ride Al at any opportunity. When Al was in a public toilet, Marty would wad up wet paper towels and throw them at him. When he was in the shower, Marty would throw cold water on him. He would put pitchers of water on top of doors,

MICK FOLEY

and tilt garbage cans in front of them. Life was never dull when Marty was around. He was funny, too. One time, while driving back to Montreal, he had us laughing so hard with Verne Gagne stories that we had to pull the car over to keep from crashing.

Verne Gagne was an old-time wrestler and promoter who, like a lot of old-timers, didn't care for modern-day wrestling. He also promoted the Minneapolis area, which prided itself on its technical wrestling emphasis. By doing a dead-on Verne impression and substituting the word "fuck" for "wrestle," Marty had us on the verge of crying. "Jesus Christ, kid, where'd you learn how to fuck? Not in this territory, because in this territory, fucking comes first! Back in my day, kid, we knew how to fuck. After all, that's what the name on the marquee says—Fucking."

Al is one of my favorites to ride with. I know that I've poked fun at Al several times in this book, but it's not out of any malice toward the Crown Prince of Hardcore, but rather the continuation of a long-standing tradition of insulting each other. The insults actually started out innocently, but soon came to be judged in much the same way a boxing match is. A decent joke was considered a jab, a good quality joke, a straight right, and the big daddy of all insults would result in a knockout. Knockouts were rare, but in all honesty, I scored them much more frequently than Al could ever have hoped to.

Throwing in the (false) accusation of homosexuality was also highly valued in our contest—in fact, for quite a while, it dominated the competition. For example, when I was in the midst of a series of matches with Austin, I would tell Al, "Hey, it's probably unfair that I get all the title shots with Steve, so I'll tell you what . . . tonight I'm going to let you go a couple of rounds with my bald-headed champion." Definite knockout. Part of the rules were that no bodily action or orifice could be referred to by a vulgar or offensive word. It just showed a lack of imagination.

Bob Holly was actually disqualified for his lack of ingenuity. I mean, why use a common word like "cock" when I could tell Al to "go fish for my one-eyed, blue-veined, purple-headed trouser trout" instead? As it turned out, a road trip with Al and me could be pretty overwhelming. After five days in Canada, Too Hot Scott Taylor returned home to his wife, who asked him how he'd enjoyed traveling with us. "It was fine," he told her, "except all they talked about was hammering each other." Scott was not the only one who stopped riding with us after one road trip.

After a while, I was able to use a valuable weapon—the fake laugh. We began to take our feud public, and the fake laugh buried Al. I would tell a joke, and it would be met by howls of fake laughter, while Al's attempts were met with total silence. "I hate you," is all he could manage to say before leaving, a defeated man. When I combined the fake laugh with the growing influence of the Internet, the knockout ratio really started to explode. If I saw the roving camera they used for the World Wrestling Federation Internet show during lunch, Al was as good as done. "What's the difference between me and Jack in the Box?" was the lead-in to just one of my verbal knockouts. "Well," I answered "Jack in the Box serves up a jumbo jack between two buns, and I serve up Cactus Jack between Al Snow's buns."

"Oh, ho, oh, ho, hoooo, ho, ho" (big group laugh). It was a beautiful part of my life, but like many things in life, I took it too far.

Al was a remarkably good sport about all this until I overstepped the boundaries of fair play and took my brutal power and displayed it on national television. First on a pre-*WrestleMania* party, where I told the audience that "in addition to visiting the Liberty Bell and seeing the original Declaration of Independence in Philadelphia, I also went to a very small museum, where up on the third floor, under heavy security, I had found a very rare tape of Al Snow's last good match." A few weeks later, I upped the ante with a knockout so stunning, it made Butterbean–Bart Gunn look like a fifteen-round technical battle. Al felt like he was under pressure to retaliate and nearly ruined his career by launching a five-minute verbal assault on Mankind, while doing guest commentary on the next evening's *Raw*. Besides the fact that it was both unfunny and unimaginative, Vince had personally hated it, and as a result, I felt the need to apologize. "Vince, I'm sorry that I used your show as a forum to push my little rib with Al. It was unprofessional, and I apologize."

Vince then hit me with words I never expected to hear. "Mick, I don't mind when you do it, but Al ruined an entire segment by talking about you." I basically had carte blanche from the boss to ruin Al, to embarrass him and make him suffer. I don't think I will, but it's nice to know I can. Oh, by the way, I invented the whole "head" thing.

Heading into June, Mankind was gaining momentum. The office had pushed me hard, and people were responding. I was getting a chance to cut some pretty decent interviews, and my matches with Undertaker had been stealing the show around the country. I sometimes think about where my life would be if the Undertaker had chosen to be an asshole. I had seen guys put a wrestler in a hole that can be damn tough to dig out of. Shane Douglas had been living proof. He'd come to World Wrestling Federation with huge hopes and had been miserable right off the bat. His lame Dean gimmick didn't help, but neither did opponents who went out of their way to make him look bad. Undertaker had been completely the opposite. His professionalism had been beyond reproach and, as a result, both of our careers had benefited.

I arrived in Milwaukee for the *King of the Ring* Pay-Per-View, not knowing what to expect. I was hoping for a continuation of the quality work we had put out, but beyond that, I really had no idea. Shane Douglas had been real critical of my decision to join the World Wrestling Federation and didn't seem impressed when I told him of my imminent feud with 'Taker. "When push comes to shove, Cactus," he had warned me, "whose shoulders do you think are going to be on the mat?" Well, Shane, in this case, they weren't mine. In what had to be considered a major upset, Mankind cleanly defeated the Undertaker in seventeen minutes of one hell of a match. I think this match was actually a corner turner for the Federation, as it applied liberal use of chairs and outside-the-ring brawling that actually enhanced a rivalry instead of blowing it off. The match also featured the amusing guest commentary of Owen Hart.

*   *   *

I have been trying to think of the best time to speak about Owen. As I write this, it has been eight days since his tragic death in Kansas City. I have been writing every night, usually between the hours of 10:00 P.M. and 4 A.M., and often when I put my pen down, it seems for a few fleeting seconds that the whole thing was a bad dream. Unfortunately, it wasn't, and I usually walk over to a photograph of me, Owen, and Terry Funk and say a prayer for Owen and for his family. I am, as of this writing, on a plane from Calgary, where earlier today I attended Owen's funeral. I told a story on *Raw* a week ago about how my son felt so proud to look like Owen Hart after they had both gotten matching crewcuts three years ago. "Dad, guess what," Dewey had asked me during a long-distance phone call. "I look like Owen Hart."

Colette got on the phone and said, "Your son is so happy to look like Owen." I went on to say that I would be proud if my son could grow up to be a man like Owen.

Several of the Hart family mentioned how touched they were by my words, as they knew they had come from my heart. I had the privilege of meeting Owen's wife, Martha, and she told me how much Owen had thought of me, and how I was one of his favorite people. I will always treasure that brief meeting with Owen's wife and will truly hold her kind words within my heart for the rest of my life.

Owen was an excellent wrestler. He had won an athletic scholarship to the University of Calgary as an amateur wrestler, where he went on to compete in the Canadian national championships. He left after three years to compete for his father Stu's Stampede Wrestling company. Stu himself was a legendary wrestler but was perhaps even better known for training wrestlers in his basement "dungeon," where screams of pain were as much a part of the home as the furniture. Owen was at one point the greatest flyer in North America, and with his added knowledge of amateur wrestling and Stu's dungeon know-how, was one of the best all-around wrestlers in the world. Even after injuries grounded his aerial skills, he went on to be a big star in the World Wrestling Federation, where he was a four-time tag champ, two-time Inter-Continental champ, and European champion as well. I had watched Owen for years before meeting him and had been greatly entertained by many of his classic matches. Little did I know upon meeting him that I would enjoy his bad matches even more.

I had been with the Federation only a few months when we came to Scranton, Pennsylvania. We were working at the Catholic Youth Center, which is a great building for atmosphere but a terrible building for morale, because of the low payoffs that the tiny gym always resulted in. There was a little hallway by the wrestlers' entrance where you could see the action, so I walked out to take a look. Owen was in the middle of a match with Marc Mero and had just shot the Wildman into the ropes. Mero hit Owen with a shoulder tackle, and instead of taking a crisp flat back fall, which is the norm, Owen slowly fell as if he were a tree. "Man, that's terrible," I thought, especially for someone as good as Owen Hart. It got worse. Mero shot Owen into the ropes and prepared for a hip toss. Owen took off across the ring using three giant, slow, high steps and then took a hip toss, which could more accurately have been called an ankle roll. It was horrible. I was in the middle of thinking, "Man, maybe he's having a bad night," when I heard the British Bulldog laughing. "Look at Owen, look at Owen," Bulldog hooted in his thick English accent. "Oh, that's too much. That's too fuckin' much." Now I understood. Owen was definitely stinking up the place, but he was doing it on purpose. I had done that a few times myself, but, unlike me, Owen wasn't doing it as part of a story line or to anger the fans. He was doing it simply to amuse the boys.

There was nothing like a bad Owen Hart match. The strange thing is, most fans didn't pick up on it. He was subtle enough about it that only the other wrestlers knew. Sometimes, however, when I was actually a part of these hideous performances, it seemed like the whole world could tell. In addition to an offense consisting of multiple rakes of the body, kicks in the ass, horrible-looking karate chops that were always preceded by a loud "hi-yah," and cocoa butts (the big, fake-looking version of the popular head butt) so fake that they made Lou Albano look like Karl Gotch, and he was equally terrible on the defensive. For example, a few months later in Kuwait, I was teaming with Owen and Bulldog against the Undertaker, Barry Windham, and Owen's brother, Brett "Hitman" Hart. Barry had Owen in a rear chinlock and was really arching up on it. I didn't think anything of it until I heard Bulldog's familiar cry. "Look at Owen, look at Owen." I did indeed look at Owen and immediately began laughing. While Barry was going through a series of grimaces and growls to accentuate his hold, Owen's face was completely motionless. He wore not the slightest facial expression, and his body moved not a bit until he casually lifted his arm to smoke an imaginary cigarette. "He's too much, he's too fuckin' much," the Bulldog said, laughing. I had to agree.

Later in the match, Brett was tagged in and made a comeback that culminated in his sharpshooter submission hold. The sharpshooter is a legitimately painful hold that places a great deal of stress on the lower back and quadriceps, but if Owen was in pain, he certainly wasn't showing it. As Brett cinched up on the hold, Owen, who had his head facing away from Brett, looked to be in about as much pain as a clam in deep sand. He rubbed his eyes sleepily and checked his wrist for an imaginary watch. Brett cinched up further, and Owen yawned. Finally, Brett rocked back even further, and Owen finally yelled out in pain. But Owen had pleased his biggest admirer. "Oh, that's too fuckin' much," Bulldog repeated.

I was reminded of just how much Davey Boy Smith (Bulldog) had revered Owen when my son rented a video of the 1996 Slammy Awards (the World Wrestling Federation's annual awards show). Owen had won a Slammy the year before and had carried it with him to every match. His tights were adorned with the words "Slammy Award Winner," and he was even introduced for his matches as "The Slammy Award–winning Owen Hart." Now, a year later, Owen was not even nominated, and I felt a little sad to see one of my favorite gimmicks ended. The nominees for Best Bowtie, a prestigious award if ever there was one, were announced, but before a winner could be declared, Owen jumped on stage. "Yes!" he yelled in his overbearing little way. "I did it! I won. I'm a winner—whoo! Bulldog, you might have two titles, but you don't have two Slammys . . . but I do, because I'm a winner—whoo!"

The camera showed Davey Boy, who was literally beaming. He always got the biggest kick out of Owen. Owen continued his little speech threatening Vader and me, who would be facing Owen and Bulldog in the next evening's *WrestleMania*. As he stepped offstage with his new Slammy in hand, he walked toward Vader. A waiter happened to be passing by, and Owen dumped the entire contents of his tray—ten pitchers of iced tea—onto Leon. Vader stood up, not knowing what to do. He was smiling, but he sure as hell wasn't happy. Finally, he ran after the two-time Slammy winner but tripped and fell, and actually missed a few shows due to injury.

I had heard of Owen's reputation as a "ribber" but couldn't appreciate it until I saw him in action. We were in Colorado in July 1996. Business had been up, but this particular crowd was uncharacteristically small. I felt like part of the reason was the show's promoter, a likeable but somewhat goofy-looking cowboy, who seemed content just to hang out with the guys—good house or not. Midway through the card, I looked at Owen and saw him wearing headphones and yelling into the accompanying microphone. "Do it," Owen yelled, "just do it!" I saw Owen listen, and then he yelled some more. "I don't care if there's a match going on . . . I'm the promoter, and I say play the damn music now." This was vintage Owen—attempting to get the sound guy to play the wrong music at inappropriate times. Except not only was this sound guy not cooperating, he was getting hot. But this just made Owen happy. He loved a challenge. "Oh, yeah, well come on down, tough guy—I won't be hard to find. I've got a big cowboy hat and a pair of cowboy boots that I'll stick right up your ass. Oh, yeah, come on down, you bastard, so I can smash my big-ass belt buckle right over your head." I looked over and saw a man who looked exactly like the man that Owen had just described. Same hat, same boots, same big-ass belt buckle. It was the affable promoter, grinning goofily, without a clue that Owen Hart was attempting to arrange an impromptu meeting between him and an angry soundman.

Sometimes Owen's ribs didn't seem so funny at the time. We were in the middle of a ten-day tour in the summer of 1997 and were touching down in St. John's, Newfoundland. Because this was not a usual Federation stop, we were met at the airport baggage claim by a large number of fans. One of them had a camcorder, and I could see on his video screen that he was zooming in on fellow wrestler Chyna's breasts. I went over right away and told the guy that not only was he to stop filming, but he was to rewind his tape and retape over the offensive part. I was hot, and the guy looked like a sheep molester anyway. In a flash, Owen was there to lend a helping hand. "Hey, you two," he said in his phony overexaggerated way. "How about I get some footage of you two together?" I was hot and getting hotter.

"Stop it, Owen," I demanded. "This guy's a little pervert."

"Oh, come on, Jack," Owen cheerily answered back. "Come on, he's a big fan. Let's get some footage. Maybe you can put your arm around him, Jack."

I was still hot, but I knew I was fighting a losing battle. "Owen," I pleaded with him, but it was no use. I'd lost the fight. Now when that little pervert from Newfoundland watches his home videos, he not only has clips of Chyna's breasts, but tape of me with my arm around him as well. He could drive you crazy, and tick you off, but I find myself laughing out loud when I think of Owen now.

He was the undisputed king of the prank phone calls as well. He would drive the guys crazy by calling their rooms, pretending to be an autograph-seeking fan. "What are you . . . too big a star to come down here and sign?" he'd yell into the phone. "Never mind, just give me your room number, and I'll be right up to get them myself." Inevitably, he'd offer to fight them, and many was the time a furious wrestler came running to the lobby . . . only to find a calm Owen saying, "What's wrong, you look upset!"

Owen got me one night in Toledo, Ohio, after I'd bragged to him about what a great rate I'd gotten at the Red Roof Inn. We would always tip each other off as to where the good deals were, because, like me, Owen liked to save his money, but also like me, he'd spare no expense on his family. I was just about to drift off when the phone rang, and a pleasant-sounding man with a soft English accent said, "Hello, Mr. Foley, how are you this evening?" I could literally picture this guy with gray hair and glasses, and a thick wool sweater. The man continued in his pleasant way. "Mr. Foley, I'm afraid that after checking our accounts, we have found that we did not charge you enough money for your room."

I was stunned. I had been in wrestling for over thirteen years at that point and had never heard of raising a rate after checking in. "Sir, I don't think you can do that," I politely stated.

"Oh, young man, I'm afraid I can and . . . wait, wait, wait . . . are you one of the wrestlers?" the old gentleman wanted to know.

"Yes sir, I am" I was glad to tell him.

The old man spoke again. "Wrestling . . . hmmm . . . isn't that all fake?"

I was kind of perplexed, but I wasn't about to lose my rate, and besides, I knew how to handle this. "Well, sir," I pleasantly began, "it's about sixty-seven percent real, one guy got down to sixty-two, and they had to let him go."

But the old man wasn't buying my line. "Oh, Mr. Foley, you're very funny, but just last week, I saw you stomping your foot on the mat instead of really hitting somebody. I used to box, you know."

Now I was starting to become perturbed. "Sir, I really don't think you should be calling up customers and insulting their livelihood."

The old man instantly apologized. "Oh, Mr. Foley, I'm so sorry . . . please forgive me." After I did and assured him everything was fine, he spoke up one more time. "I'm afraid I'm still going to have to raise your rate."

"What?" I yelled, when suddenly I heard laughter on the other end of the line. I knew I'd been had by the best. "Owen," I yelled, "you prick!"

Everything he did seemed to be done with a sense of both innocence and mischief. In a beautiful column that Brett wrote in the *Calgary Sun,* he said, "Owen never stopped looking at the world through the eyes of a child." That trait made every day a new adventure for Owen. Whether he was "accidentally" marking up your hand during an autograph session, writing a sappy "Let's be friends" over where you'd just signed your name, or pulling the emergency brake on poor fan/friend Ronnie Gaffe's truck in the middle of traffic, he truly seemed to love every day.

He had a seriousness to him as well, but far from being a dark side, it may have actually been the part of him I enjoyed most. He didn't drink, disdained drugs, and was the only guy in the company who went out less than I did. He truly loved his wife and kids, Oje and Athena, and his face used to light up when he spoke of them, which was often. He spoke of simple pleasures, like hot chocolate on a porch swing with his wife and planning Disney vacations for his family. His wife said they had not only their next day planned together, but their next month and year, and the next forty years as well. I used to tell my wife that of all the guys, Owen was the most like me. I realize now that it was probably wishful thinking on my part. He was better than me. He was the best of us. He was probably the nicest, funniest, most moral man I have ever met. As I write this, I am reminded of a song titled "Reflections" that was written by Charlie Daniels over twenty years ago, and which I will paraphrase just slightly for Owen:

And Owen, my buddy, above all the rest
I miss you the most, and I love you the best
And now that you're gone, I thank God I was blessed
Just to know you.

I can't interpret every line literally, except for the last one, for there were people who knew Owen longer, loved him better, and will miss him more. But, Owen, I do thank God that I was blessed just to know you. Rest in peace, my aggravating, instigating, wonderful friend— and may God bless your beautiful wife and children.

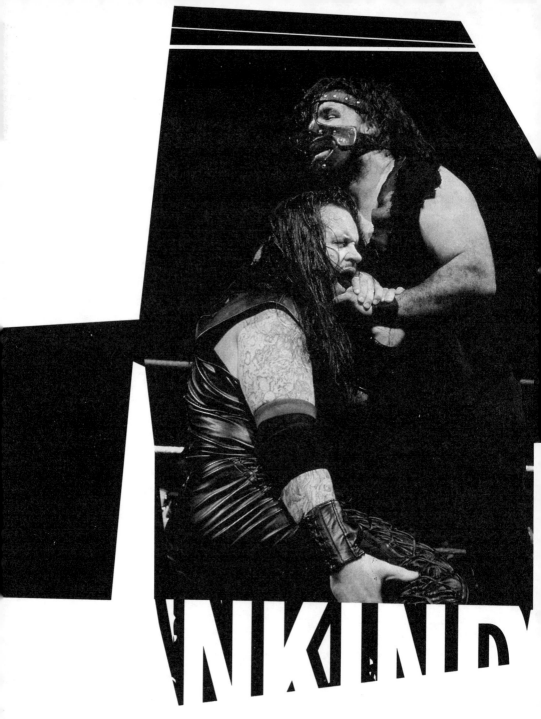

ANKIND

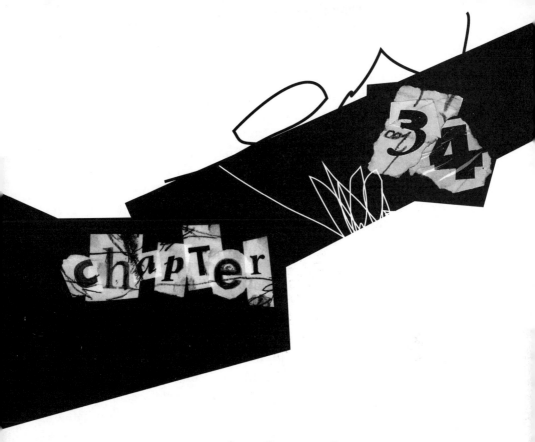

Business was rolling along as we looked toward *Summerslam*, which was traditionally the second biggest show of the year. Shawn Michaels was getting over well as champion and would be facing Vader as half of a double main event. The other half would pit me and Undertaker in a boiler room brawl. The concept of the boiler room brawl was simple but somewhat unusual. The match would start with the two of us inside the boiler room at the Gund Arena in Cleveland and would continue until one of us could leave the room and gain possession of the Undertaker's urn, which Paul Bearer ('Taker's manager) held in midring.

I loved the concept and had actually given similar ideas to WCW, which, not surprisingly, had fallen on deaf ears. By having a match that was unique to television and could not be replicated in arena shows, I felt we had a great ratings draw on our hands. We actually taped the boiler room part of the match the night before the Pay-Per-View and filmed everything else live. Undertaker had been out most of the day in a promotional appearance and was exhausted when he arrived. He then dressed and walked into an empty boiler room.

The match was either a classic or a disaster, depending on whom you talk to—there was really no middle ground. I believed the former and in many ways, the boiler room brawl felt more like an unloved child, whose goodness only I could see. I had read interviews in which actor Billy Crystal felt much the same way about his movie *Mr. Saturday Night*, which was a personal favorite that had met with poor response. I told a mutual friend, Barry Blausteen, who has been working on a wrestling documentary for the past four years, that *Mr. Saturday Night* had been a particular favorite among several wrestlers, including myself, and was told that Billy really appreciated it. So if any fans want to stop me in an airport and heap praise on my unloved child, I would feel much the same way.

I remember Michael Hayes pumping me up before I stepped into the room by saying, "Cactus, this is the match that you'll be showing your grandchildren, and saying, 'This is what Grandpa used to do.'" I stepped in and waited for the 'Taker to arrive. The psychology was that in "the room," I would have the advantage, because since Mankind's Federation debut, he had been filmed inside the room, as if it were his lair. My heart was pounding as he came near. There was no crowd to pump us up, so a great deal of mental preparation had gone into my pre-match ritual. I had to fight the urge to feel stupid inside this big, dark room with only one cameraman as a spectator. Looking back, I honestly feel that there were three things wrong with the match—two of them conceptual and one of them in the execution. For one thing, the entire match was a one-camera shot in dark, murky conditions. The cameraman did a tremendous job, but I later felt that the whole thing had looked like a well-done home movie instead of a Pay-Per-View main event. The second conceptual problem was even more damaging, although the decision itself was born out of a compliment. Vince liked the match so much that he decided not to do commentary over it, even though, as usual, I had visualized much of the match with Vince and J. R. in mind. The third fault, if you can call it that, was that the brawl itself was just too long. Seventeen minutes inside the room itself was an awfully long time, and many people could not see past the silence and length to see the quality and intensity of what we were doing.

One journalist described it as being "like a Hollywood fight scene, except way too long." I think that needs to be rethought a little. A three-minute Hollywood fight scene can take weeks to rehearse and film. We did ours in one take, with one camera. So I think a more accurate critique might read "like a Hollywood fight scene except without rehearsing, choreography, editing, special effects, sound effects, grips, or a best boy." It may have been too long, but damn, we put a lot into it, including a bump that went astray.

Near the end of the match, I had Undertaker down and pulled out a ladder from the darkness. As usual, I could hear the announcer in my head as the match progressed. "He's got a ladder, J. R. . . . I believe he's going to attempt to hit the . . ."

"No Vince, Mankind is setting the ladder up and is ascending its wooden rungs."

"J. R., he must be ten, fifteen, twenty feet in the air—UNBELIEV-ABLE!"

Unfortunately, we got nothing of the sort, even though the live crowd seemed to enjoy watching on the monitors in the arena—especially when Undertaker sat up and dumped me off the ladder. He was able to pull the ladder toward him, and as I started to go, I tried to land in relative safety on a pile of cardboard boxes that were scattered on the floor. Unfortunately, the top of the ladder became caught on the rafters of the boiler room, and I landed violently several feet short of my intended target. My upper body landed somewhat safely, but my lower half (where I actually store nine-tenths of my body weight) landed roughly on the cold, hard concrete below. The botched landing would actually result in the onset of a seven-month sciatic nerve problem that, for a while, I legitimately thought would cause me to retire.

I was actually the first one out of the room, but I was feeling much worse for the wear. We had both beaten on each other pretty good, and I was ready to crash into a comfortable bed after a long, hot shower. Instead, I stood for over an hour inside the building, waiting for one of the TV contract guys to show up in his rented Lincoln and take me to my crummy Days Inn room, across the street from the porno shops, before checking himself into the Marriott.

The next evening, we picked up where we had left off, with me trying to get to the ring, and 'Taker beating on me the whole way there. I kept throwing obstacles in his way, and like Michael Myers from *Halloween*, he kept coming back. I finally got the edge with a somewhat less than my best piledriver, and tried to enter the ring, where Paul Bearer nervously held the sacred urn. The cold, purple-gloved hand of the Dead Man stopped my progress, and we jockeyed for position on the ring apron. 'Taker stopped me for a moment and, using the ropes as a slingshot, hurled my body backward, where it crashed flat-backed on the concrete (which was cold and hard) with a sickening thud. He then dropped to one knee and reached out with his waiting glove for the urn that would signify victory.

There was only one problem for the 'Taker—Paul wouldn't give it to him. He held out his hand again, this time impatiently, while the crowd stood up, and I rolled back into the ring. Undertaker got to his feet, but I was there to cut him off with my mandible claw. Once down, the Undertaker started crawling toward Paul, as I laid in heavy, and I do mean heavy, boots to the head. I can't believe that I kicked someone I actually liked that hard, even if it was a big show. Even with the boots slowing down his progress, he kept crawling to Paul until he was on his knees and looking at his chubby buddy with a "why me" look that made me think of Nancy Kerrigan after the Gillooley/Harding pipe job scandal. Uncle Paul then methodically lifted the magic urn and came down hard with it on the Dead Man's head. He handed me the urn, and we left triumphantly as a team. Undertaker and I had been wrestling each other for five months, but in essence were just getting started.

I left for Puerto Rico three days after the match. Savio Vega was a Puerto Rican wrestler who was running opposition to the long-standing Capital Sports—the company that Bruiser Brody was killed working for. I took the three dates in Puerto Rico as a way to pay for a playset that I was planning on getting the kids. The Undertaker was scheduled to be my opponent for the tour and was still sporting a large gash on his elbow that he had received in the boiler room.

My first night on the island resulted in one of my worst memories. As I heard my music, I made my way to the entrance and was immediately doused with a full cup of liquid from close range that was not just thrown at random, but actually poured down the back of my neck. I'd been hit with beer and sodas for years and had long ago accepted it as part of the job. But this liquid was different. It was, um, well . . . it was warm. I felt the warmth, smelled the foul odor, and knew right away what it was. Someone had poured a full cup of urine on me. Needless to say, I didn't want to wrestle. I really thought maybe the kids would be fine swinging on the $94 Kmart special. I did end up wrestling, and I did buy that playset, even though every time I watched my two peanuts swinging happily or sliding joyfully, I'd automatically think of being doused with bodily fluids. And I'm not talking about the bodily fluid I used to douse Al Snow with either. Yes! Maybe not a knockout, but definitely a stiff jab!

The next day, the Undertaker walked in looking like hell warmed over. This time the Dead Man really did look like a dead man. His face was pale, and he was sweating profusely. Worse yet, his elbow was swollen to twice its normal size. Staph infection was a common casualty of the business, but this was the worst case I had ever seen. A doctor was brought in and lanced the elbow. He then squeezed hard, and I'm not exaggerating when I say that pus shot ten feet across the room. It was nauseating, but somehow the 'Taker made it to the ring and performed the next two nights. After that, in his absence, the old cowboy was called in, resulting in the classic Mankind–Watts showdown I described earlier.

*   *   *

"Genius" is a word often used to describe Vince McMahon. I have been around Vince long enough to feel that it is true, but Vince also has a couple of other attributes that are equally important in the success of his company: common sense and a willingness to admit when he's wrong.

Stone Cold Steve Austin is probably the biggest draw in the history of the sport, but during Labor Day weekend 1996, he was just another guy trying to make a living. And at that time his salary was about half that of Marc Mero.

Labor Day weekend meant the World Wrestling Federation traditional "tent town tour" of New England, where we wrestled in such prestigious venues as the Cape Cod Melody Tent. Actually, the shows were a lot of fun, and promoter Larry Bonhoff was a great guy, but nobody got rich in the tent towns. It was outside one of these tents in the backstage area that I heard one of the most ironic comments of my life.

I was approached backstage by a man named Jimmy Miranda. Now Jimmy has approached a lot of men, but this visit concerned merchandising. He had a list of names on a chart with various marketing ideas listed for them. I could see that Marc Henry, the Olympic weightlifter, figured to be a big part of the World Wrestling Federation's merchandising future. Checked off by his name was everything ranging from foam fingers to red, white, and blue bandannas—at least twenty-five items in all. Also figured in prominently was the Stalker (Barry Windham), who probably had about fifteen potential items. Miranda said that the company wanted to merchandise Mankind and asked what I thought about a Mankind mask for kids. I told him that I was flattered but didn't think that a mask that was supposed to be scary to kids should be able to be worn by kids. I did tell him that I thought a shirt and an action figure would be a good idea, and he checked off both.

At that time, Austin came walking over and said, "Hey, Miranda, when are you gonna come out with some Stone Cold merchandise?" Miranda grew silent and didn't seem to know what to say. Steve again questioned him, jokingly asking, "Come on, Jimmy—how about a shirt for Stone Cold?"

Miranda again seemed at a loss for words and paused at length before slowly breaking the bad news. "I'm sorry, Steve, but the office just doesn't see any interest in your merchandise right now." WOW! And to think, within a year, Austin's merchandise would outsell Marc Henry's two to one. *Two million* to one, that is.

That illustrates the difference between World Wrestling Federation and WCW. In WCW, a guy's spot was his spot. There was, and still is, no room for upward mobility. If WCW had Austin, they wouldn't have done a damn thing with him. Hey, wait a minute, they did have Austin, and if my memory serves me correctly, they didn't do a damn thing with him. Vince, on the other hand, sensed the momentum and went with it, riding the Austin craze to huge levels of popularity and financial gain. In the Federation, merit actually counts. Maybe that's why Tuesday mornings aren't quite as fun for Eric Bischoff anymore.

Bischoff had once been quoted as saying, "I used to really look forward to Tuesday mornings to see the ratings, but lately we've been kicking their ass so bad that it's just not that fun anymore." I guess Eric must have never heard the old proverb about counting your chickens before they hatch. Also, if kicking the other company's ass so bad isn't any fun, I feel real sorry for Vince—he must be miserable.

But, hey . . . let's give Bisch his due—at this point, they were on top and would stay that way for a long time, largely due to the hiring of Nash, Hall, and host of other big names who had jumped ship for some of Turner's guaranteed big money contracts. It got so bad that Vince had to start guaranteeing money as well, in order to keep Titan Sports from sinking like Titanic Sports. The new blood and the hot WCW vs. NWO feud would keep Bischoff on top for most of the next year and a half, but time and greed, and a lack of focus, would eventually send my former company into a tailspin . . . to the point that their audience is now limited mainly to older men and kids whose parents won't let them watch our show. For his part, Vince never panicked and instead focused his shows around his remaining stars and new additions like myself, Austin, and Goldust, who were more than happy to pick up the pieces.

Strangely, in retrospect, losing so much talent may have actually helped the World Wrestling Federation, as well as the competition, and wrestling in general. The loss cleaned out a lot of talent that was stale, made for better morale in the dressing room, ignited the wrestling "war" that spring-loaded the sport's resurgence, and, most important (at least to me), allowed thirty-year-old Mick Foley a chance to have the spotlight.

I had been training diligently for my next Pay-Per-View match, which I had high hopes for. In a period of twenty-four hours, I had gone from trying to figure out what the hell I was going to do on the show with Marc Mero, to being told I would wrestle the champion, Shawn Michaels. Wow, I went from being a curtain jerker to wrestling one of the top guys in the business—with one phone call.

I was excited as hell about working with Michaels, who had a reputation for two things—being a pain in the ass and being a brilliant performer. As far as being a pain in the ass, well, I got along fine with him, even though I couldn't blame others who didn't. As far as being a brilliant performer, he certainly was. He actually looked like the perfect opponent for me, in that he was everything I wasn't. Small, handsome, a great physique, athletic, and a decent dancer too. He was actually a classic babyface wrapped inside a nineties' attitude. I watched hours of tapes of Michaels, hoping to pick up on certain things he did. Instead, I learned that it wasn't necessarily what he did, but how he did it. Literally everything he did looked good. I didn't have to worry about copying anyone else—I would just do it my way, and Shawn Michaels would take care of the rest.

The match, to be held at the Philadelphia CoreStates Center, was on my mind for hours every day. I could visualize every detail and had no doubt that it would be a tremendous match. Going into the match, I was more confident than ever before. I was completely focused, and I knew that I was in shape—a factor that usually haunts me until the moment I step into the ring. That night in Philly I was given interview time to try to turn the fans against me. The World Wrestling Federation crowd was vast in scope compared to the Bingo Hall, but the old Cactus Jack still had his share of fans in the City of Brotherly Love. I don't know if my interview was successful, but there were certainly fewer Mankind fans when I was through. I was also met with scattered shouts of "You sold out," which had been common throughout my Federation tenure. I still don't understand the whole "you sold out" mentality. Selling out suggests going against personal principles and priorities for the sake of money. I guess, in that case, I need to check my personal principles and priorities in wrestling, which are:

I like to wrestle.
I like to do it well, and in front of a large number of people.
I like to be paid well for doing so.

So far, during my four-month run in the Federation, I was wrestling better in front of bigger audiences, and for more money than I ever had before. So even though I usually carry enough guilt with me to start my own religion, in the case of Foley vs. the selfish fans of the world, I was innocent of all charges.

The match itself was even better than I could ever have expected. The pace was tremendous, the timing was perfect, the story was well told, the crowd was hot, and the execution was excellent. We put twenty-seven minutes into what was undoubtedly the finest match of my career. There is no doubt in my mind that it was the best match of the year, and one of the greatest in history. Unfortunately, it often goes overlooked when classic matches are talked about, because it was a matchup with no real history, on a card that was relatively free of hype, and ended with a finish that many didn't like. While it's true that the run-in ending featuring Vader, Psycho Sid, and the Undertaker did tarnish the match a tiny bit, I don't think it should detract from the other twenty-six minutes and forty-five seconds that we worked so hard on. I think it also should be noted that *Mind Games* in Philadelphia in September 1996 was the first time that Shawn Michaels and Mick Foley had ever faced each other in any way, shape, or form. It was truly a special night, and try as I might, I don't think I've ever been quite that good again. This match is also on the short list of the three best things I've ever done in wrestling.

Coming off the heels of *Mind Games*, I was pumped for my next

Pay-Per-View engagement—this time a main event with the Undertaker called *Buried Alive*. The goal was simple—take your opponent from the ring to the graveyard, which was located by the entrance, and "bury" him alive. Now obviously, no one was really going to die, but we had ourselves a hell of a match anyway. I actually lost the match, after being partially buried, but with a little help from Terry Gordy as the Executioner was able to put the Dead Man in the ground. At one point, the office wanted me and Terry to fill the hole by ourselves, but I thought the prospect of filling a six-foot-by-four-foot hole with two guys might be a little unrealistic. As it turned out, my intuition was wise, because not only was I exhausted from wrestling for twenty minutes, but my partner the Executioner was filling the hole in the same manner that a cat covers up poop in a litter box. Thankfully, every bad guy in the company helped out, and even with all that help, we still only got the hole half filled. Then, dramatically, a lightning bolt hurtled through the audience and struck the grave, and the Undertaker's gloved hand broke through the earth as Jim Ross yelled, "He's alive, he's alive," as we went off the air.

When we went off the air, the Undertaker emerged through the dirt, where he was helped to the back. No, I'm sorry, that's not what happened. When we went off the air, the wrestlers dug him out of the grave, and he received emergency medical treatment. No, that wasn't it either. Oh yeah, I remember. When we went off the air, the New Rockers' music played, and Marty Jannetty and Al Snow came running out to wrestle the Bushwhackers in a special "bonus" match.

Once home, I threw a tremendous Halloween party for my kids and their friends. Our new playset was up, and we rented a moonwalk for the driveway, which was a huge success. Following last year's Batman-with-cowboy-boots embarrassment, I gave in and let the kids buy the cheesy costumes I had once sworn they never would. So it was with just a bit of sadness that I watched my children kill off tradition, dressed as Buzz Lightyear and a Banana in Pajamas.

On the heels of *Buried Alive*, I came back again against the Undertaker in November's *Survivor Series* in what was probably the biggest disappointment of my career. In front of the Madison Square Garden fans I was amazingly mediocre. It was a tough one to put behind me, but I vowed to have a strong showing on the following evening's *Raw*.

My opponent the next evening was Steve Austin, in what was the first ever Mankind–Stone Cold match, or the first singles match that Steve Austin and Mick Foley had ever been in . . . period. Steve's character was really catching on, and he'd just had a tremendous *Survivor Series* match with Brett Hart. Steve and I had been talking frequently about the contracts we'd recently been offered that, while not embarrassing, were not nearly on the level of Marc Mero. This filled us both with the potent combination of pride and anger, and we vowed to show Vince the error of his contractual ways. Without even talking about what we'd do, we tore the house down in a match that many called the best *Raw* match in several years. There was nothing fancy about it, just a great give-and-take contest, but the intensity was high, and the chemistry was there, as it would continue to be during our World Wrestling Federation history.

After that night's matches, I met with Vince for a scheduled contract meeting. He acknowledged what a great match I'd had and how large my contributions to the company had been, but he mentioned that he was disappointed that I had not signed my contract yet. I told him that I appreciated the offer but could not, on principle, sign for less money than Marc Mero had. Vince was visibly disappointed. "Mick," he said, "you have to understand from a business perspective that we will be much more likely to get behind somebody who we know we have a long-term investment in."

I did understand that, but the image of *Mind Games* with Michaels, and the house shows with Undertaker, and my match that night with Austin ran through my head. Then I thought of Mero, his poor match that same evening, and a match he had with the Undertaker that was so bad it defied belief. And believe me, it wasn't the Undertaker who was at fault. Then I spoke. "Vince, I can understand that, but you've got to understand that I have to get up every morning and look in the mirror, and it will be hard to do that if I sign for the amount you're talking about."

Vince considered what I'd said before giving his retort. "What we're offering you is just the minimum guarantee. It's a worst-case scenario. It means, even if the bottom drops out of the business, you're going to make at least that amount. But in all likelihood, you're going to make far more than your guarantee."

That was definitely a compelling argument, but unfortunately for the Vin man, I had irrefutable evidence on my side. "Vince," I slowly replied, "I don't want to seem ungrateful, because I've had a great time here, and I'm happy with the way you've used me. Maybe you're not aware of it, but I'm not making a whole hell of a lot more here in the Federation than I was last year in bingo halls and parking lots."

Vince seemed genuinely stunned. "I had no idea," Vince assured me, "but I'll check on that, and, believe me, that's going to change." With that we shook hands and parted ways. Several months would go by before the subject of my contract was brought up again.

The next few months reinforced my opinion of Vince as a true man of his word. Unfortunately, this reinforcement was a good news/bad news proposition for Mick Foley. The good news was that my checks picked up immediately. In some cases, my payoffs doubled in the same arenas I had been to earlier. The bad news was, Vince stuck to his guns about being hesitant to get behind a wrestler who hadn't signed his deal. Don't get me wrong—I wasn't buried or even abused and, in fact, was still often wrestling on the top of the card, but my TV presence was reduced greatly. I even went several months without any interview time on *Raw*. In the meantime, my back was getting progressively worse, to the point where my sciatica was making my life a hard one to live. Sciatica refers to pain that is usually caused by a herniated disc pressing on the sciatic nerve. Although the point of pressure is in the lower back, the pain radiates throughout the entire nerve, which extends down the buttocks all the way past the calf. Many of the everyday things I'd taken for granted became difficult and agonizing to do. Training with weights was next to impossible, cardiovascular work was arduous, and even standing still was physically demanding. Often I would have to sit down after standing only momentarily. I'd be in line at an airport and would have to sit down. Even though done while sitting, a trip to the toilet was no longer fun. Life in general was miserable, and over time I began to overcompensate for the back injury, forcing my body to curl up like the letter "S."

My days off were few and far between, and much of my free time was spent at the chiropractor or with a massage therapist. When I was with Colette and the kids, it was difficult to do anything but lie down and watch TV. Even our yearly trip to Disney World was marred to a great degree by my inability to ride anything but "It's a Small World." Sure, it's a nice, pleasant ride, but after our fifth trip, even three-year-old Noelle was looking at Big Daddy-O as if he were some kind of wimpazoid. Adding to my woes at the Magic Kingdom was the news that my televised match with the Undertaker, which I'd hoped would snap the WCW win streak, had actually been a nonfactor in the ratings, which stayed exactly the same. I had pictured Vince diving to his knees, begging my forgiveness, forever putting me in a different tax bracket from Marc Mero, but unfortunately, as my daughter ran in terror from Minnie Mouse, I realized that it was not meant to be. Later that day, I ran into wrestler Scott Taylor, who may be an even bigger Disney nerd than me. It really is a small world after all—but I wouldn't want to paint it.

After my Disney letdown, I received a phone call at home from Jim Cornette. He was all excited. "Cactus," he said in his high-pitched Louisville lingo, "I know you haven't been in the mix that much, but, dadgum, I think we've got something for you."

Hey, this was great. "What is it, Corny?"

"Well, Cactus, we were thinking of doing a little something where Marc Mero and Rena continue their little spat, and you don't like it, so you deck Marc. You want Rena with your little group, but Uncle Paul doesn't like it . . . so ya deck Paul. Now Paul still doesn't like Rena, but he knows he has to tolerate her for your sake, and the three of you will have your own strange little family."

Now usually Jim Cornette can make anything sound good, but this time I wasn't buying it. I think he would have had an easier time selling me a time-share in Kosovo than convincing me of the career benefits of having a run with Marc Mero. My face must have given me away, because Colette passed me a note reading, "What's wrong?" While Corny rambled, I wrote back, "They want me to wrestle Mero." Colette's face quickly converted into a mask of disdain—as if she'd just smelled a fart or seen an Al Snow match. Jimmy finished his pitch with a big "So whaddya think," and after thinking on it for about a second, I firmly stated, "I hate it, Jimmy . . . I really hate it."

Corny had to laugh. "Jesus Christ, Cactus, why don't you say what you mean? What don't you like about it?"

I got real serious, because I'd been thinking a lot about my future, which didn't look real good at the moment. "Corny," I sadly began, "I've taken a lot of risks, and I've taken a lot of bumps, and most of the time I think I can get through anything. But my back hurts so damn much that I can't take it much longer, and I'm seriously thinking about retiring. And if I'm going to retire, I want to go out on top." Jimmy was temporarily speechless, and when he did speak, it was with uncharacteristic restraint.

"Cactus, I know it's not the best angle in the world, but Vince just wanted to get you involved in something for *WrestleMania*."

I knew Jimmy was telling the truth, and I felt like he deserved the truth in return. "Jimmy," I slowly started while thinking of the right way to verbalize what was going through my mind, "I'm not saying this to sound like a big shot, and I'm not trying to be sarcastic, but please tell Vince that if all this is about getting me in *WrestleMania*, I'd really rather not be on the show."

Corny was stunned. "Wow." He exhaled. "I'll tell him, but goddamn, that's got to be a first." For most of the wrestlers, *WrestleMania* is the biggest moment of their year. For me, a Mankind/Mero matchup with Rena in my corner would not have been the best.

When I got to the next television tapings, I was ribbed by all the office members about my conversation with Corny. To make sure he didn't get secondhand information, I told Mero himself about my feelings. "Marc, just so you know," I explained, "the office proposed a deal with me and you, and I didn't like it, and I told them so." He was actually fine with my decision. Like I've tried to say earlier, I don't dislike Marc Mero, but I can't understate just how much it bothered me that he was bringing in more money than I was. After the taping, Vince was gracious enough to have a meeting with me that included Vince's right-hand man, Bruce Pritchard, Paul Bearer, and future McMahon stooge (and I mean that in a good way) Gerald Brisco. They ribbed with me in a good-natured way about the Mero proposal, and especially the line about missing *WrestleMania*. Then Vince asked in all sincerity if I had a better idea. Remember, I was still honestly considering retirement, and wanted to go out with pride. "What about Vader?" I said. "Vader's kind of been written off, but that's only because his head's been messed around with so much. Let him do what he does best, and I guarantee, I'll show you a match you won't believe." I was passionate about this belief and explained in great detail about our history, my ear, and WCW's refusal to act on what surely would be a big-money matchup.

Vince seemed genuinely impressed, but added some intelligent insight. "I like it, Mick, but let's not go into this thing, which could be huge, based solely on your past history with another company. Let's create our own history, and then we can refer to the past as an additional resource." On that night, the Mankind/Vader team was born, and though it never did lead to a feud of any type, it made for good television with me and Leon always at odds, and even planted a Mankind babyface seed. More important, it gave me a *WrestleMania* matchup with Owen Hart and the Bulldog, and a little bit of pride.

By February, my back was at its absolute worst. At the urging of several wrestlers, I saw a shiatsu massage expert named François Petit, who was also a martial arts world champion and Hollywood fight choreographer. He had worked on wrestlers ranging from Andre the Giant and Ted DiBiase to Steve Austin and Shawn Michaels. The wrestlers swore by him, and I was impressed enough to venture out to Santa Monica, California, for treatment. François has since gone on to work with the wrestlers six days a month and has become a good friend. He tells me now that of all his cases, my back was the strangest and hardest to work on. He said my spine was more like that of a crocodile, as if it had adapted itself to punishment after all the years of abuse. His shiatsu work was not the pristine picture of relaxing therapy, but instead consisted of pressure points and agonizing deep tissue work. If it had been a match, I would have submitted. Some people express doubt about Francois's abilities, but I know for a fact that when I left his house, I could stand straight for the first time in months. Unfortunately, it was short-lived, as being suplexed nightly and sitting in 25B all the way to Germany is probably not the right method of sciatic nerve rehabilitation, but at least for a moment, I had hope.

While I was in Germany, where I actually did get to do PR work, Colette begged me for a vacation. I told her about the great discounts available on last-minute cruises, and she booked us on a three-day trip aboard the Big Red Boat. The ship was set to sail two days after my return to the States, which would give us a chance to go to Jungle Village in Cape Canaveral, a little fun park featuring an arcade, miniature golf, and a maze. It was not unlike hundreds of other small fun parks, but for a few years my kids swore up and down that they liked it better than Disney—no lines, no pushy tour groups, and no six-foot rodent with a head the size of a Maytag washer to run in terror from.

We had fun, but I was literally in agony, and I was forced to do something I'd tried to avoid at all costs. "Hello, Vince," I said over the phone, "this is Mick Foley, and I wanted to talk to you about my back." Vince asked about my condition, and when I gave him the bad news, I added, "Vince, I really hate to do this, but I think I'm going to need some time off to rest my back."

I could hear the sound of pages turning as he rifled through his calendar, before he spoke again in a serious tone. "I see here where I can give you two days off at the end of April."

I couldn't believe it. What kind of an insensitive asshole was I working for? I wanted to chew him out, but I honestly didn't know what to say about it. "Ho, ho, ho, ho"—it had been a joke, and I realized immediately that I had swallowed hook, line, and sinker. Vince then got serious for real. "Mick, please, tell me when, and I will give you as much time off as you need."

I've mentioned before how important it is for me to make all my bookings. To me, it's not only a professional responsibility, but also a matter of personal pride. I don't feel like I have to be on every show—just every show that I'm booked on. Therefore, I rationalized, if I took time off in April, I wouldn't really be missing bookings because the cards hadn't been booked yet. After *WrestleMania*, which was at the end of March, we were scheduled for a Middle East tour to Dubai, or some other country where they wear towels on their heads. In the interim period, I would have a MRI done on my injured back. I asked if I could have time off after that.

I had actually gone for a MRI for my back two months earlier, but had left in shame and hadn't wanted to show my face again. Being in a MRI is kind of like being in a coffin, and you need to lie absolutely still for up to forty-five minutes for the magnetic resonance imaging to take place. Many people get claustrophobic and need to be sedated before going in. I was offered such medication, but calmly told them that when I'd had an MRI done on my knees, I'd been so naturally relaxed that I'd fallen asleep inside. No antianxiety medicine for me, thank you.

I'd forgotten to consider that when a knee is done, the patient's head is left in the open, but that when a back is done, the whole body is enclosed. That was a big consideration to forget. To make matters worse, the damn thing was so small that I had to raise my arms over my head to fit in. After about five minutes, I started to fidget. "Stay still, Mr. Foley," came the voice over my headphones. A few minutes later, my shoulders started hurting from being held still in a strenuous position for so long. I involuntarily kicked my legs. "We're going to have to start over, Mr. Foley," came the voice.

"Great," I sarcastically thought. A few minutes later, I started feeling like the walls were closing in. I felt like my eyeball was in contact with the MRI machine. I'd often felt claustrophobic when I was thrown in the Undertaker's casket after a difficult match, where I tried to breathe coffin air while the audience banged on the damn thing as it rolled down the aisle. This, however, was far worse. I thought deeply about what to do and finally made the only decision that a hardcore King of the Death Match could—I hit the panic button and screamed to be let out.

Determined not to have the same thing happen again, I requested an open MRI, which allows much more room to function in. The feeling is not nearly as intense, but I would still be required to stay still for over forty minutes, and that concerned me. To combat the tendency to twitch, I had Colette read to me from the current book I was working on, *Don't Know Much About the Civil War*, by Kenneth C. Davis. Sadly, Colette doesn't share my passion for history, and as a result, she had about as much enthusiasm as Steve Blackman reading a bedtime story, as she recounted the irony of Thomas Jefferson writing the Declaration of Independence while being a slaveholder himself.

When the MRI was done, I was handed the film that I would take to the doctor with me the following morning. "Can I look at them?" I asked the technician.

"Sure," she replied, "they're yours, but I doubt that you'll be able to see anything on them. You really need a doctor to read them."

Apparently, she didn't know who she was dealing with. I took one look and made my diagnosis. "It looks like a herniation of the disc between L4 and L5, and the pressure on my nerve is what is causing the shooting pain down my leg."

The woman looked impressed. So did Colette. "Look, hon," I told her, while pointing to one of the spiral discs on the film, "this disc is discolored—it's completely white. We'll have to ask the doctor about that."

The next day, I took my MRI results and my expert opinion to the orthopedic surgeon's office. Upon introduction, I asked him to look at the film and then repeated my educated finding. "Looks like a herniation of the disc between L4 and L5, huh, Doc?"

The doctor looked surprised. "It certainly does look that way, Mr. Foley," he affirmed. I shot a smile of pride to Colette.

"Tell him about that disc," she said.

"Oh yes, Doctor," I said, as if we were both part of the same fellowship, "in addition to the herniation of that disc, I am a bit concerned about the severe discoloration of this other disc. As you can tell, it's white instead of the gray color of the other discs."

The doctor smiled and seemed both amused and sad to tell me the news. "Um, Mr. Foley," he knowingly began, "all of your discs are supposed to be white. The gray color indicated a degenerative condition in all of the remaining discs in your back."

"Oh" was all my educated mind could say. I felt as if I were standing in front of him with snakeskin boots and a Batman costume on—a real doofus. A doofus with a pretty screwed-up back.

"We're going to need to do an epidural," he warned me, referring to the practice of injecting long needles directly into the affected disc to reduce the swelling. "Even then," he continued, "it's only a fifty percent chance that you won't have to have surgery."

This wasn't the news I was looking for at all, so I asked one more question, hoping against hope for a favorable reply. "Is there any treatment that doesn't include the epidural shots?"

"No" was his firm reply.

I was scheduled to begin treatment right after *WrestleMania*, but luckily fate intervened, or maybe just dumb luck, because the overseas tour was canceled. The tour was scheduled for eight days, followed by six days off. This gave me two full weeks off—the longest rest we'd had since my arrival in the Federation. I began my conservative treatment of ice and rest in the two days before *WrestleMania*. For those days, I lay in bed all day while applying ice every twenty minutes and eating delicious Chicago-style pizza every two hours. After *Mania*, I continued my rest and ice treatment, combined with stretching, which was absolutely excruciating. Thankfully, and damn near miraculously, it worked. I called Vince up and had him put me back on the booking sheet. I very well could have been George Costanza yelling, "Baby, I'm back!" The doctor seemed almost saddened to hear of my healing powers. I had healed myself and had done it without his needles and surgery. As my daughter would say, "Na-Na-Boo-Boo."

I returned to the ring wars with gusto and was even chosen to be Undertaker's first opponent after winning the World Wrestling Federation title at *WrestleMania*. "Are you sure that people will want to see this match?" I'd asked Vince. Apparently Vince had more faith in me that I did, and the match was signed, and went on to be not only very good, but profitable as well. This was our fifth go-round on Pay-Per-View, and we'd come up big on four of them. I had no way of knowing that we'd come up biggest of all fourteen months later.

The month of May was significant for two odd things that happened. The first took place in Toronto, after the matches, when I BS'd with Bruce Pritchard and Jim Ross while I waited for Stone Cold, who was talking contract with Vinnie Mac. By this point, Austin's career had exploded, and I could no longer reasonably compare my contract desires to his. But I hoped he'd get what he had coming to him anyway. It is a great credit to him that despite his huge success, he has stayed levelheaded and has never stopped being "one of the boys."

Austin had been in conversation behind closed doors with Vince for a while, and the three of us were chatting amicably when Bruce asked me something a little strange. "Do you have any of that footage I heard about when you were Dude Love?"

I had to laugh. "Yeah, I'm sure I have it somewhere, but why?"

Bruce smiled. Maybe as the former Brother Love, he had a deep affection for another Love namesake. "We want to put it on TV," he said.

"Come on," I yelled, disbelieving. "You can't put it on TV, it's terrible."

"It doesn't matter," Bruce assured me, "we'll just put on small clips."

He'd sold me. "Okay, okay," I relented, "but how are you going to use it?"

Bruce looked at J. R. "Don't worry." He smiled. "J. R. has an idea."

The second thing of significance was the first ever matchup between The Rock and Mankind on the May Pay-Per-View from Richmond, Virginia. Unfortunately, at that time, The Rock was Rocky Maivia, and he may have been the most hated wrestler in the company. Which is fine, if that's your job description, but Rocky was supposed to be a good guy. He had all the attributes of a good guy, but unfortunately he had come along twenty years too late, and although he was a good young talent, no one was buying what Rocky had to sell.

I was starting to get a lot of cheers, and since The Rock was getting booed out of every building he appeared in, I was the babyface by process of elimination. Poor Rock. We had a good match, but the fans just hated the guy, and when Rock hit me with a high cross bodyblock off the top, I rolled through with the mandible claw for the victory, and the roar of the crowd was deafening. The next day, one of the guys asked for my impression of Rocky. "Hey, he's a nice guy," I said, "but he just doesn't have it. The office should probably just cut their losses and get rid of the guy." I had no idea that I was talking about the future "People's and Corporate Champion."

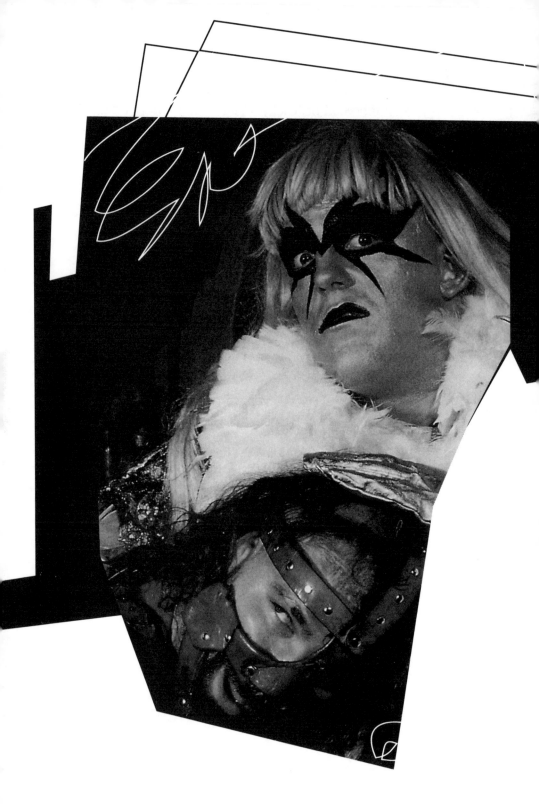

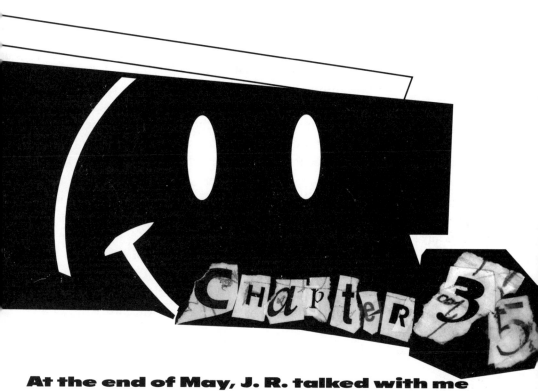

At the end of May, J. R. talked with me
about an idea they were planning. Goldust had just been the subject
of a two-part "up close and personal" interview that had been very
insightful and beneficial to his career. J. R. felt that a similar interview
could yield similar results for me. Vince had heard fragments of my
real history and thought that it was actually more captivating than
any fictional background. We set a date to do the interview and a second day to try to finalize a contract. I had Colette flown in for the
contract talks because she wanted to be there, and also because she
tended to get a better price for my services than I did.

I had been thinking about my interview with J. R. for several days
when I arrived at the television studio for the talk that would change
my career. I was told that Vince might be stopping by to check out the
interview, which was fine with me. Kevin Dunne, who is a director for
the Federation, came up while I was getting dressed, and explained
their concept, which involved appearing without the mask as Mick
Foley. I actually liked the mask by this point, and would wear it for
several hours prior to a match. Now the damn thing smells so bad that
I practically put it on while my entrance music is playing. I believed in

Mankind and didn't want anyone to see the real Mick Foley just yet. So I came up with a game plan. I would tell the real-life Mick Foley stories, and I would give Mick Foley's opinions, but I would do it as Mankind. In actuality, the two weren't that different, as in most cases the most successful gimmicks were simply an amplified extension of a certain part of the real-life personality. I guess in that case, Mankind was the insecure side of my personality; the side that had never quite felt accepted. It was that side that surfaced in the Jim Ross interview, and it surfaced in a way that was both funny and touching, and it changed the way people perceived and felt about Mankind.

People often talk about wrestling being "scripted." Actually, in my case nothing could be further from the truth. Yes, I have a general idea of what I am trying to accomplish, and yes, sometimes I am given specific lines to say that will be beneficial in drawing money, but the truth is, in my three and a half years with the Federation, I have only done two scripted interviews. J. R. and I talked briefly on the phone the night before taping and went over a few ideas, but the entire interview, with the exception of the mandible claw that I caught J. R. with at the end, was completely ad-libbed.

After fifteen minutes of talking, I said something I thought was inappropriate and asked if we could do the question over. It was then that I saw Vince, who had been watching from the wings. "This is absolutely captivating," he said. I had once been told that for Vince to get completely behind someone, he needed to become a fan of his. I believe that night in the studio was when Vince McMahon actually became a fan of mine. I was so completely inside the character that I knew when we were done that something special had just taken place. I consider that interview to be on the list of the three best things I'd ever done.

Mick: I was eight years old at Minnesaukee Elementary School playing a game of "kill the guy with the ball" (it may even be an Olympic sport these days) and in chasing one of the other students, I made a leap for his legs, and the back of his foot kicked me in the lip. And I didn't know what happened; I knew it hurt, Jimmy, I knew it hurt bad, but all of a sudden people started looking at me in a different way like there was something wrong with me. I looked down at my Chicago Bears sweatshirt, back in the days when they were two and twelve, in the waning days of Dick Butkus, and my Chicago Bears white sweatshirt had suddenly turned red and children were running from me, scared, ah, I was bleeding, I was in pain, and I was loving it! Because I felt like I'd finally found something in my life that I could do better than everybody else. Handle pain. Someone said, "Oh, that's just vampire blood," and then saw the open wound from which the blood was flowing. I've still got that shirt, Jimmy, and I remember thinking wouldn't it be nice if I could do something in my life where I could do this all the time? Get that attention every night. Stockbrokers can't do it. Teachers can't do it. The President of the United States can't bleed for a living! But pro wrestlers can. It's the first time that I realized that I had a calling in my life, and I followed it right down the line. That's all I wanted to do. My brother and I watched them all—Chief Jay Strongbow, Bruno Sammartino, the Valiant Brothers, that's what we wanted to be. Then I broke his nose by backdropping him into his bedroom wall and Mom said no more wrestling, but she didn't say no more dreaming.

J. R.: Well, Mick Foley continued to pursue his dream, but he paid a heavy price, the emotional scars of his strange childhood are still evident.

Mick: You know, I want to tell my son, when he gets to be fifteen, not to be the guy that eats strange things. I never exactly brought it upon myself; other people in their cliques, for lack of a better word, they would gang up on me because I was different, because I acted different, looked different. They were throwing worms at me, Jimmy, little wiggly worms; they were throwing them at me. Bending down in athletic class, doing my hurdler's stretch, and there was a bombardment of worms being thrown at me. So what do you do to retaliate? You throw the worm back? At seven or eight people? It's not the fact they were hurting me, they were wounding my pride. They were looking at me like I was garbage. So I picked up the largest specimen, Jimmy, and I sucked it down! To show them that their attempts to hurt my pride would not be successful. I thought, Jimmy, that I'd shown them, but then sure enough the story became exaggerated as everything in life does and it no longer became "Well Mickey Foley ate one worm because some kids were picking on him" it became "Mickey Foley eats a plate full of worms every day." Do you think I got many dates after that, Jimmy?

J. R.: Probably not.

Mick: Do you think girls wanted to kiss a boy who had worms on his breath? I'm a good kisser! But I never got the chance to show it! What am I gonna do, practice on myself, Jimmy? I never had the chance to show the world that I could love and could be loved, because they ruled me out because I had a strange appetite for strange things. I'm not going to say I didn't accept money to eat other strange things, but the fact is that damage had been done and I went through my entire high school days without date number one. You don't think that scarred my soul? Well maybe you're not looking deep enough.

J. R. voice-over: Mickey Foley was searching for a place to belong.

Mick: It was 1983. And upstate New York with its endless rolling fields might be a nice place for a lot of boys, but not when Jimmy Snuka and Don Muraco were in a cage in October in Madison Square Garden—that's where I wanted to be! I didn't want to ride horses along a field, I didn't want to fish for trout in a stream, I wanted to be where the blood and guts were, Jimmy. So I put out my thumb, Jimmy, and it took sixteen or seventeen hours, but I made my way to the Garden. It took just about all the money I had in the world, but I got a front row seat, and I saw the move that would change my life, when Jimmy Snuka came off the top of the cage. And I saw people stand up, and I saw people cheer, and I know I wasn't the only person whose life was changed in that arena. And I realized, Jimmy, that I wanted to do the same thing. I wanted to hear people cheer for me because of some act of bravery that I committed. I wanted to hear, see people's emotions; I wanted to see children cry out of love for me and the things I could do inside a ring.

I made a movie when I was eighteen about myself, maybe as a type of escape where I was a wrestler and it's strange, the first time I ever met Shawn Michaels—you know him.

J. R.: Oh yeah, very well.

Mick: He looked at my scarred and battered body. He didn't know me, but he knew the legend of who I was before, and he said, "Is this the way you always envisioned yourself?" Looking somewhat down on me. And I said, "No, you know the strange thing is I always imagined myself being you." And he said, "You mean the champ?" And I said, "No, I mean the girls." Jewelry, the tattoos, the love. So in my movie I was not Mick Foley. I sure as hell wasn't Mankind. I was Dude Love.

Dude Love tape, November 1983: We are gonna tear this rotten apple right down to its stinking New York core, and while we're here, we're here for only one reason, one reason only: fame, honor, fortune, glory, to destruct, destroy, and to take that that World Wrestling Federation Championship Belt . . .

Mick: And during the course of the movie, dating back to my experience at Madison Square Garden, I decided I was going to do something heroic, I was going to do something to make people cheer for me, so I ascended up onto my friend's roof, and I dove off.

J. R. voice-over: Ironically, *The Loved One* gave Mick Foley his first break; it became an underground hit and somehow wound up in the hands of wrestling great Dominic DeNucci. DeNucci admired Mick's guts more than his skill and took him under his wing. Every weekend for the next two years Mick traveled 800 miles round-trip eating and sleeping in the backseat of his '79 Ford Fairmont still hoping to realize his dream.

Mick: I knew I wasn't ready to be Dude Love yet, I never wanted to be Cactus Jack. I figured here is a horrible name for a horrible wrestler, and by golly as soon as I get the ability that I'll get that heart-shaped tattoo on my chest, I'll put those earrings in, and I'm gonna get the girls. And it never really worked out that way, did it, Jimmy?

J. R.: Not quite.

Mick: I guess nature didn't cooperate with me. Cactus Jack was supposed to be around for three months. He stayed for eleven years. What made Cactus Jack different was that he just wanted it a little bit more. He was willing to go the extra length. He was willing to sleep in a filthy car in order to achieve his dreams. He was willing to forgo romantic relationships to be the best. He was somebody in an era of bodybuilder physiques who carved out his own niche, who said I'm gonna make it on my own style, who said, "No one else is gonna tell me what to do, I'm not going to dye my hair. I'm going to be exactly who I am, and I'm going to do it my way."

J. R.: Don't you think that it's about time in your life where you looked squarely in the mirror and accepted the personal responsibility for who you are? Don't you believe that you yourself have caused and brought on all these problems?

Mick: I think it's time for you to maybe start doing your damn job. I think it's time for you to end this façade of journalistic integrity. You know what you tell the people week in and week out? You say "Look at Mankind, I don't even know if he feels pain, or maybe he likes pain." You see you're a powerful man, Jimmy, you have got the ability to reach a lot of people, to spread the truth, and you neglect to do it. Let me ask you a couple of questions. What is it about pain that I love? You see, I feel just like every other person, you see that? [ripping his hair out violently] It hurts! Is it when I can't get up when my little boy says, "Daddy, I want to play ball" and I can't do it? Is that where the fun starts? Is it where a doctor injects a 12-inch needle into the discs in my spine so I can wrestle one more day? Whoopee! Let the party begin! I can't believe you sit here and ask me those questions. Do I bring it on to myself? I haven't done a damn thing to you. All you've done to people is mislead them and let them think I'm having the time of my goddamned life when I'm in pain! Don't you look at me with that smug look. You make me sick. A man of integrity; I ought to smack you . . .

(Mankind attacks with the mandible claw)

Off-screen voice: Jimmy? Jimmy? Jimmy? Can we get some help . . . ? He's gonna need some help. . . .

The response to the interview was overwhelming. It was shown in four segments, and each week I could feel the momentum growing. The interviews were never intended to make me a "good guy," but the pieces came off so well that I started being cheered. Every week, the reaction grew, to the point where I soon was one of the most loved wrestlers in the company.

I should point out now that it wasn't simply the interview that made the piece so successful—it was the presentation as well. Chris Chambers produced the specials and did a phenomenal job of weaving childhood photos, the infamous Dude Love video, and even Japanese death match footage into the story. Dave Sahadi and Doug Lebow are two other extremely talented producers that the World Wrestling Federation is lucky to have. As a former television production student, I am well aware of their importance to what we do, as without them we might very well look like fat guys in their underwear, pretending to fight.

Perhaps the biggest star of the entire interview series was my fantasy creation of Dude Love. I began receiving letters from fans about my Dude dream that had inspired them to follow theirs, and there was even a small contingent of Dude Love signs in the arenas. I was surprised one evening to hear Bruce Pritchard say, "You know, we're going to make a Dude Love shirt," and I was literally shocked when

Vince later proposed a radical idea. "Mick, for one night only, somewhere in the future, we're going to have a Dude Love match on Pay-Per-View." I could not believe it. Dude Love in the World Wrestling Federation—oh, have mercy!

My contract negotiation had also gone well. It didn't make me rich, but it certainly provided security for my family, and if invested wisely, the money could make me wealthy over time. I was able to have several advantageous conditions worked in, and my final deal was considerably more lucrative than the one offered a year earlier. With the contract talks behind me, I was now able to lie down at night secure in the knowledge that I was making only slightly less than a second-string shortstop hitting .187 for the Mariners. True to his word, however, Vince started putting the company's promotional power behind Mankind, and he seemed to explode in the summer of 1997—the Summer of Love.

Coming off a tremendous final match at the *King of the Ring,* my feud with Hunter Hearst Helmsley was met with great enthusiasm around the country. Helmsley, better known now as Triple H, was a talented wrestler whose star was just starting to rise, and our battles throughout the summer were highlights of my career. I remember one specific match in Nassau Coliseum where I had both Hunter and Chyna (his bodyguard) caught in the dreaded double mandible. The crowd was going crazy, and I couldn't control my emotions. "This is great!" I yelled, with an enthusiasm more befitting a thirteen-year-old touching his first female breast. To further the emotional high, I saw Colette and the kids sitting in the stands as I started to exit through the curtain. I went back, picked up Noelle, and spun her in the air as the usually tough Nassau crowd softened up. I put her down and reached for Dewey, who screamed and ran as if I were a Disney character.

Dewey was funny that way. He loves wrestling more than anything in the world, but for years was terrified of going to the matches. During my first year with the Federation, he had gone into such hysteria in Savannah, Georgia, that I had to dress in the kitchen. Later that summer, in Bangor, Maine, with author Stephen King in attendance, he had actually watched the matches but covered his ears the entire time to drown out the noise. Stone Cold had spotted the little guy in the stands and smiled. "Has he been covering his ears the entire time?" he asked.

"Well, all except during your match," I answered back. "Then he covered his nose."

Now it's a different story, as Dewey surveys the action and expertly offers theories and predictions on all the mat action. And most of the time, his theories and predictions are right on the money.

Mankind merchandise was starting to move as well. I had worn the yellow Mankind happy face T-shirt on my Jim Ross interviews, and they immediately became a big hit. As a matter of fact, they trailed only "Austin 3:16" as the company's best-selling shirt—but by a substantial margin. The Austin shirt was fast on its way to becoming the biggest selling piece of merchandise in wrestling history, so I didn't feel too bad about trailing him. At first, I'd look out and estimate the margin to be two to one, then three to one, four to one, and so on, until the entire arena landscape was full of those things.

The shirt was showing up everywhere—on football players, on rock stars—you name it. Austin 3:16 had become mainstream. I used to sit and wonder if any big stars might wear my shirt. That would be a big thrill. One day, I was looking through some underground thrash metal magazine that a fan had given me. All of a sudden, there it was. A musician was on stage with a "Wanted Dead" Cactus Jack T-shirt. Man, it felt good. It didn't matter that I didn't know the guy's name or wasn't a fan of his type of music—what mattered was that he had thought enough of me to wear my likeness in front of his crowd. I was damn proud, because it seemed to be an affirmation of everything I'd ever worked so hard to achieve. Then I looked closer. The musician had his penis pulled out and was stroking it onstage. My pride shriveled like George Costanza's member after a dip in a cold pool. I haven't seen one of my shirts in a photograph since, and to tell you the truth, I don't want to. I'm afraid.

At this point, Brett Hart and Shawn Michaels had been building up to a rematch of the 1996 *WrestleMania* that was expected to draw a huge audience. In July of 1997, they had their first fight. It didn't do a big Pay-Per-View rate or TV rating because, in fact, it wasn't a televised event. Strangely, it didn't have a big audience either; in fact, it was seen by only a few people. After sixteen months of anticipation, the big match between Shawn and Brett was a real-life fight in the dressing room. The two, who didn't care for each other to begin with, had been doing a series of "shoot" interviews, where they revealed their true feelings about one another. In these, they verbally tore each other apart, and as a result, genuine aggression had developed. Shawn lost his interest as a result of the backstage beating, leaving a huge void in the Federation's plans. Not only was the potentially lucrative Hart–Michaels match ruined, but the tag team scene was in a shambles as well. Michaels and Stone Cold had been tag team champs, and now General Vince and his lieutenants had to think up another battle plan. I was their secret weapon.

Mankind began petitioning Steve to be his partner, while Steve started a campaign of his own to keep the one-eared weirdo away from him. I began wearing a big sign reading "Pick Me Steve" and taking unbelievable punishment to impress the "Texas Rattlesnake." Finally, after I saved him from a "Hart Foundation" beating, Steve seemed to lighten up. He called me into the ring and extended the hand of friendship, which I gladly accepted. Steve then grabbed the mike and, in a departure from his bad-ass persona, let his sensitive side shine forth. "Mankind, a handshake just ain't good enough." Then, the bald bastard held out his arms for a Mankind hug. Hell, I'm a good hugger, so I embraced the "toughest SOB in the World Wrestling Federation." Then, in an act of treachery so great it had Benedict Arnold and Judas Iscariot shaking their heads in disbelief, Austin turned on me. He booted me in the stomach, hit me with the Stone Cold Stunner, and even gave me double middle fingers as I lay there in my anger and my shame. This was the kind of thing that could send Mankind over the edge.

A few days later, I received a surprise phone call from Vince. His booming voice wasted no time in making its point. "Hey pal, how would you like to be Dude Love?"

I didn't know what to say, as his question had caught me completely off-guard. "Do you mean for the next Pay-Per-View?" I finally managed to squeak out, after remembering Vince's previous idea.

"No," Vince boomed back. "I'm talking about from now on."

I gulped and actually felt my body going weak at the prospect of the Dude gracing the sacred World Wrestling Federation ring. "Vince, are you sure? I mean, Mankind's going so well."

Vince was adamant, but his voice was softer now, actually soothing. "Mick, I'm not saying we can't ever go back to Mankind, but I just love the whole Dude Love story—and I know our fans will love it too. It's such a great PR story—Regis and Kathie Lee would love something like this."

Vince had made me see his vision. I was smiling brightly as I said, "You really think so?" Which was kind of like saying, "Put me over just a little more." Vince was happy to oblige.

"Mick, the way I see it, Dude Love is going to be huge. Children will love him. The fans who already love Mankind will love him. And guys won't be afraid to bring their girlfriends to the matches, because the Dude won't threaten them—he'll be a safe sex symbol."

I was sold now but just wanted a little more information. Vince was quick to please. "We will play it up huge. Girls. Pyro. We're even going to team you up with Steve."

The Summer of Love was about to begin.

I walked into the Freeman Coliseum in San Antonio, Texas, in July of 1997 and heard an unusual retro-disco beat booming over the loud-speakers. Vince was right there. "Congratulations, Dude, this is your new music." I had to admit I liked it. I even learned the emotionally touching lyrics and began singing them throughout the day. Hell, I even caught that old softy Jim "the Anvil" Neidhardt singing them one time also.

Dude Love, Dude Love
Dude Love, Dude Love
Dude Love, Dude Love Baby
Dude Love, Dude Love

Believe it or not, I have a platinum album in the closet for "Dude Love" on the *World Wrestling Federation—The Music, Volume III* CD, even though I didn't sing it, write it, or play it.

Next, Vince actually tried to teach me how to walk with rhythm. I had been doing the Mankind stagger, the Cactus Jack stumble, and the Mick Foley limp for so long that I really didn't know how to strut like the hip cat that the Dude was. After several tries, we finally pre-taped some footage of just the Dude's white boots "strutting" across the floor.

The evening's *Raw* main event was to feature tag champs Bulldog and Owen against Austin and a mystery partner. Austin had been taped saying, "I don't need no damn partner," and was attempting to go it alone. Stone Cold was holding his own for the first few minutes, but the champs then took over as the show started to go to commercial break. "Wait," Vince yelled over his play-by-play mike. "We've just been informed that Stone Cold Steve Austin's partner has just arrived." A drum track blared over the loudspeakers as the pretaped footage of the Dude's strutting shoes played to the crowd.

Once back from the break, the beating continued until a strange figure suddenly appeared on the huge "Titantron" video screen. "Oww! Steve-O," the figure yelled, "looks like you could use a little help, like maybe a tag team partner." At this point the action in the ring stopped, and all the men stared in disbelief at this guy on the screen. He was dressed in a tie-dyed shirt and bandanna and looked to be the figure of "cool," even if his mirrored shades were slipping due to the lack of an ear to support them. The cool guy continued his mesmerizing jive talk by yelling, "Now Steve-O, I don't blame you for not wanting to team with that scraggy-looking Mankind, but you never said nothin' about teaming up with the hippest cat in the land. Yo, Steve-O, it's me—Dude Love, and I'm coming to save the day. Oww. Have mercy!"

The crowd roared at the mention of the Dude and roared even louder when the Dude came strutting down the ramp. All three guys in the ring were great at expressing their shock, with Austin in particular looking like he was looking at the "biggest dork in the land." Before the Dude could get to the ring, however, the champions jumped Austin, and the Dude had to wait anxiously in the neutral corner. Finally, the champs screwed up just enough to allow Austin to tag the Dude. The Loved One was a house on fire as he tore into his adversaries with hokey chops and a variety of weak-looking offensive maneuvers. Finally, the Dude saw his opening and caught Davey Boy with the tie-dyed mandible claw, which would briefly be known as the Love Handle. After this match, it was decided to leave the claw to Mankind in order to accentuate the disparity of the two characters. Davey struggled until Owen came off the top rope with a dropkick that floored the Dude. While the ref was putting Owen out, Steve-O reentered the fracas and caught Bulldog with a mighty Stone Cold Stunner—his patented finishing move. Davey went down, and the referee turned around just in time to see the Dude making the cover. One, two, three—we had new champions. The place erupted as the strain of "Dude Love, Dude Love Baby" had the crowd dancing in the aisles. Two paid models, oops, I mean two Dude Love groupies, couldn't take it anymore and hopped the guard rail so that they could get down and boogie with this "safe sex symbol." Austin barged in and began

dancing with us, showing his fellow Texans some intricate break dancing moves not seen since that particular form of entertainment
disappeared ten years earlier. No, he didn't, but he did hand the Dude
a tag team belt and shake his hand before leaving the happy threesome
to dance the show off the air.

I was elated backstage. Vince had single-handedly made this
dream come true. It didn't matter that the Dude couldn't dance a lick
or that his trunks were falling down to the point where he almost
looked like the "hippest plumber in the land." The Dude was a breath
of fresh air. As Vince himself put it a week later, after surveying fan's
opinions, the Dude makes people "feel good about themselves."

For a while that summer, I led a dual existence as Mankind and
Dude Love—even to the point of appearing on the same show as both
guys at different times. In a few matches with Triple H, I started the
match as the Dude, only to be beaten all the way up the aisle. While
Helmsley celebrated, Mankind would suddenly emerge and continue
the battle. Ironically, it was during a Mankind match with Helmsley
that Dude Love would have his finest moments.

Summerslam took place in the Continental Meadowlands Arena
on July 24, 1997. Mankind was scheduled to take on HHH in a steel
cage match to settle their lingering feud. I had just returned from
Santa's Village in New Hampshire and as usual found that the combination of White Mountains Christmas memories and harrowing trips
down the Yule log flume had me ready for action. As a general rule, I
tend to suck big-time inside a cage, but this match was memorable.

We went at it at a good pace for several minutes, before Triple H
took over. At one point, he rammed my head ten unanswered times into
the blue steel bars. Even though I tried to absorb the impact with my
shoulder and chest, I could feel my noggin bounce against the steel about
half of the time and woke up the next morning with the lumps to prove
it. Unfortunately, that would be far from my worst pain of the night.

As things looked their worst for Mankind, Chyna hurled a steel
chair over the top of the cage and then climbed partway up the
bars to shout encouragement. Hunter went for his patented "pedigree," which, if successful, would have planted my head firmly on
the steel chair. In reality, the "pedigree" was a great-looking move
that did carry quite a bit of risk with it. I was able to sweep his legs to
counter the move and then, using my knees as a type of fulcrum on his
ass, was able to drop backward and slingshot him into the bars where

Chyna was standing. The treacherous twosome collided, and the pop was monumental, to the point of being almost Road Warrior–ish, as Chyna flew to the floor below.

Victory was within my grasp. All I had to do was get through the door and touch the floor to be the winner. In this type of cage match, the winner is the first man to climb over the top or through the door and touch the ground. I began crawling for the door but was well aware of what was waiting for me when I got there. At two hundred muscled pounds, Joanie Lauer was as strong as many of the men in the Federation, and actually stronger than the guy whose book you're reading. When she came to the company, many of the men had been hesitant to let a woman show them up—or as former intercontinental champion Ahmed Johnson had so eloquently put it, "Ain't gonna let no bitch hit me." Apparently, I was a little more secure in my manhood and as a result had been power-slammed, punched, kicked, suplexed, and ball-shot by the "ninth wonder of the world." None of that, however, could have prepared me for the pain that I was about to feel.

As I stuck my head through the bars, Chyna made her move. If anyone was at fault for what happened next, I was, because I made my head such a wide-open target. Chyna was merely swinging the door as hard as she could, which is how she knew I insisted on things being done. Maybe I should have tried what many believe is the whole idea behind wrestling anyway—faking it. Because the pain that I felt when Chyna slammed the heavy steel bar door on my head was unbearable. I know that I mentioned earlier my torn abdominal muscle as my most painful injury, but this one was close. It hurt so bad that I didn't even hold my head—I held my shoulder. Pain was shooting all the way down my arm, and I lay still for several moments. At first I thought there was no way I could continue, but then I sadly realized that this was *Summerslam,* and I had one big move still left in me. Somehow, as Triple H made his move, I was able to duck and catch him with a DDT on the steel chair. It was time for the past to look me directly in the eye.

I got up and started to scale the cage. When I reached the apex, Hunter still had not moved. The match was all but over. As I began to climb down to certain victory, the pop was deafening. So loud was it that I temporarily looked around to see if Hegstrand was there. I was literally three feet from victory when I was overcome by a memory, a memory of Madison Square Garden and Jimmy Snuka and the leap that had changed my life. All of a sudden my next move was clear— I too was going to fly off the top of the cage. I stopped my downward descent and looked up. It seemed as if the crowd could read my mind. I took off my Mankind mask and threw it into the ring. I didn't need it anymore because I wasn't Mankind anymore that night: I was Dude Love, and the Continental Arena had suddenly become Danny Zucker's backyard. With each step up the blue bars, the noise grew in volume. When I got to the top, the sound was louder than anything I'd been a part of. I tore open my shirt to reveal my old Dude Love red heart tattoo, flashed the Jimmy Snuka "I love you" sign, and sailed majestically into the New Jersey arena air. *Wham!* I landed hard on

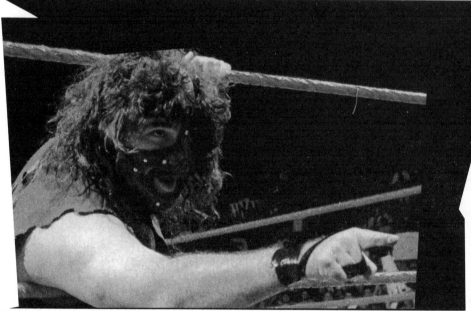

Hunter with an impact that jolted both of our bodies. It was, at that point, the greatest single moment in my career.

I still had a match to win, though. After a few moments of basking in the adulation of the crowd, I crawled to the bars and started to climb. Sensing defeat, Chyna climbed in to help her man. As I climbed, she helped, and as she helped, I climbed, until it was a near dead heat to see who would reach the floor first—Hunter being dragged through the door, or the Dude over the top. Just as things looked their worst, the Dude snatched victory out of the jaws of defeat by dropping the last five feet to the floor. Hunter touched down a split second later, but the results were already in. The Dude had won it. The match, however, had taken its toll on both men, and we lay momentarily motionless. Until the music played.

Upon hearing the beat and the faux Bee Gees groove, it seemed as if the Dude's boots had a life of their own. In a scene taken right from *The Jerk*, where Steve Martin's Navin Johnson learns he has rhythm, the Dude's toes started tapping. The melody must have been infectious, because soon his whole body was moving. Even though badly wounded from Chyna's cranium-crushing cage concussion, the Dude somehow summoned the guts, the pride, and the testicular fortitude to strut out of the Continental Arena. I described it as my "mangled, twisted strut," Hunter later said it looked pretty much like my everyday walk.

I've got to admit to taking some creative liberties with the story I have just written. In truth, the tattoo was almost invisible, as it became smudged during the match, and I also was so afraid of falling when I got to the top that I actually flew from the bar one below the top. The rest of the description is the truth, the whole truth, and nothing but the truth—so help me Dude.

Unfortunately, later that same evening, Steve Austin was badly injured as a result of a ring accident with Owen Hart. The move, an inverted piledriver, saw Austin land squarely on his head and left him unable to move for the next few minutes. It was a truly scary moment that put Austin out of action for several months, but that ironically helped his career reach even greater heights. My own injury from the cage door would affect my neck for several months, but obviously not to the extent that Austin's injury affected him.

The next evening, the Dude squared off with Owen for a match that was memorable mainly for the arrival of the Dudettes to congratulate their man on a hard-fought victory. Actually, the Dudettes in this case were our seamstress, Julie, and a hot chick named Colette, who also happens to be my lovely wife. Given her moment in the spotlight, things very nearly got X-rated, as my wife clearly appeared to be attacking her somewhat embarrassed man on national television. But hey, what the hell, after being alone with the kids 250 days a year, she deserved a little release.

Also, I need to correct a misconception. After the airing of the match, a story circulated that I was actively trying to secure a role for my wife with the company. Actually, the truth is a little tamer. She and the kids had been traveling with me since our Santa's Village vacation. She was asked by one of the agents if she wanted to be on television that night, and she said sure. We both had fun, and I thought my wife looked truly beautiful on the screen.

With Austin out, the Dude embarked on a brutal tour of revenge with Owen Hart. Actually, it may have been brutal, but that was mostly on the fans who had to watch them. I myself was able to heal my body, and had a great time taking part in some of Owen Hart's classic "bad" matches.

As already mentioned, the "Love Handle" was taken away from the Dude to clearly set him apart from Mankind. I began to think about what other lengths I could go to to establish this character. I decided to make the Dude somewhat less imposing than Mankind. Gone was the aggression and tenacity, to be replaced instead by some of the worst-looking offense this side of Baron Sikluna. Weak chops replaced stiff forearms, and on the speaking side of things, Mankind's deranged philosophical shriekings yielded to worn-out seventies clichés. In many ways, I just ripped off Diamond Dallas Page, if not in word, then at least in spirit. I also took a look at the World Wrestling Federation roster and saw that it was filled with legitimate tough guys. The Dude, I decided, needed to be the antithesis of tough. He had the market cornered on "goofy" and took full advantage. In everything the Dude took part in—from his "so bad it was good" entrance video to developing the worst finish in the history of the business, the Dude embodied nerdyness and nincompoopery. The fans loved it.

In the bitter feud with the two-time Slammy Award–winning Hart, the Dude was not afraid to get in touch with his cowardly side either. Unlike other wrestlers, especially Mankind, who were stoic and heroic when it came to absorbing punishment, the Dude was not shy in admitting how little he cared for even the slightest bit of bodily harm. A match in Washington, D.C., at the end of August stood out as special for a few reasons. First, it was the advent of the microphone "sell spot." I was on the house mike shucking and jiving with the capital city fans when the devious Hart jumped me from behind, with absolutely no provocation. With microphone in hand, I strayed from the standard wrestling protocol of macho grunts and groans and replaced them with cries of terror and pleas for mercy. "Oh! God! No, please! Oh, it hurts! Oh, the pain, the pain, please stop! Oh, God, you're killing me!" The Dude was really wimping out, but Owen made the mistake of turning his back and addressing his fans, or "Love children," as I liked to call them. When he turned around, the Dude had somehow found the will to continue. He went at Owen as Owen went "Ooh, ah, ooh, ah" into the microphone. The Dude then wrapped the microphone cable around his adversary's trachea and reared back on these deadly reins. All of a sudden, I heard a voice over the public address system. It was Owen at his hokiest. "I, huh, huh, can't, huh, huh, breathe." I had to cover my face to keep from laughing.

After several more dreadful minutes that would have had Bill Watts turning blue, Owen slipped up, and the Dude took full advantage. Dude went to a corner and à la Shawn Michaels, began stomping his foot. This stomp usually signaled that Michaels's trademark finish "sweet chin music" was on tap. Sweet chin music was a devastating sidekick to the jaw that had helped Shawn become one of the most popular players in the game. The crowd knew, however, that what the Dude had on tap was even more devastating. As Owen turned, the Dude stopped stomping and instead swooped in for the kill like a toothless, one-eared 300-pound bird of prey. The kick was devastating not so much for its power but for its precision, as the point of contact was made exactly three and three-eighths inches above the anklebone. "Sweet shin music" had just rocked the D.C. crowd. Owen gamely hobbled around, but it was too late—the Dude double underhooked him for the DDT and the one, two, three.

As was the custom, the Dude did not celebrate a match without a young lady at his side. The young Dudette who walked down the aisle certainly was a picture of loveliness in her flowered dress and pink bonnet that she had just bought in the Pennsylvania Dutch country. When she was helped into the ring, her eyes were as wide as if she were Cindy Brady when the red light turned on during the quiz show episode. "It's okay, peanut," I calmly assured my daughter as "Dude Love, Dude Love Baby" played to the crowd. "Just do what Daddy does." She then proceeded to imitate my every move, but in a way that was far more graceful than anything I could ever do. When I picked her up and carried her out of the ring and up the aisle, the crowd was applauding warmly. Every face I saw had a smile on it. The Dude may have stunk in the ring, but Vince had been right about one thing—he did make people feel good about themselves.

The Owen classics continued for the next few weeks, but with the added bonus of the still-injured Austin being in Dude's corner for the match. With Stone Cold at ringside, Owen and I had only one objective—to make Austin break character. If he laughed, our match was successful; if he did not, it wasn't. There was no other factor to determine victory. We especially knew that we hit pay dirt if we saw him with his head buried in his arm and his body shaking.

One night, in San Jose, we were mildly concerned about our little stinkathon of a match. Dave Meltzer, who wrote the *Wrestling Observer* newsletter, was in the crowd, and we knew he'd severely blister our effort whether Austin laughed or not. Fun was one thing, but getting ripped to shreds in the underground sheets was another. I approached Owen with my concern. "Do you think maybe we should be a little more serious, seeing as Meltzer's out there?" I asked.

Owen considered it and gave in. "Sure, Jack, we'll just have a regular match."

I went to my dressing room and immediately felt weak in the stomach. Something was definitely wrong. After a few minutes of pondering and soul-searching, I realized what it was. I felt as if a whole choir of ECW fans were shouting in my ear, "You sold out, you sold out."

"Dammit," I thought, "I'm the Dude—I'm supposed to suck." Not only was it expected and gladly accepted, but as Bill Alfonso might have said, "It's his constitutional right to stink up the building if he so desires."

I immediately sought out Owen and confessed my sin to him. Just admitting it seemed to help us both. Without a word, we went our separate ways, to search out ludicrous and completely harmless foreign objects to litter the ring with. When I returned, I had a whole mini-Dumpster full of stuff that even my son would have had a hard time selling. There was only one borderline dangerous weapon, and out of respect for my opponent, I brought up the sensitive subject matter. "Owen," I began, not quite sure how to feel him out for this, "would you mind if I hit you with a bag of popcorn?" With my hands, I pantomimed a circle about the size of a basketball.

He didn't even pause to think of his own well-being before answering, "Sure, Jack, just not too hard."

After a few minutes of action so lame it would be hard for the written word to do justice to it, I dug deep into the inner confines of the Dumpster for my secret weapon. I pulled out my supply of the popped kernels, and it was soon apparent that I'd taken advantage of my opponent's trust in me. For in my hands was a bag of popcorn that was somewhat larger than a basketball—in fact, it was a Hefty Cinch Sack filled to the brim with the dangerous snack. I'm sure that in Owen's eyes, I must have looked like a tie-dyed Grinch on the top of Mount Krumpett. Up went the bag, and down it came with so much force that I resembled a pimply-faced fifteen-year-old trying to ring a bell with his hammer, so he could impress his skanky girlfriend with a cheap-ass stuffed animal at the local carnival. The impact buckled Owen's knees, but he gamely continued until the blows wore him down and he collapsed in a pile of the salty snack food.

I should have stayed on him, but I couldn't resist the urge to show-boat, so I stuffed a handful of the corn into my mouth and turned to give the San Jose faithful a glimpse of the Dude's "twenty-three skidoo" knock-kneed Love dance. When I returned, Owen was ready, and caught me with a boot and a series of weak chops and kicks to my buttocks area that sent me down in the middle of the corn, which by now was strewn about the ring. As he put the boots to me, I lay on my stomach and simultaneously waved my arms overhead and kicked my feet from side to side. When I got up, there was a huge "popcorn angel" in the ring where I had lain. I looked at Austin. He was trying to cover his face, but I could see his stomach shaking and tears rolling down his face. "You two are the shits," was all he could manage to say. That analysis from the Texas Rattlesnake was worth more than any number of stars the *Wrestling Observer* could have possibly given us.

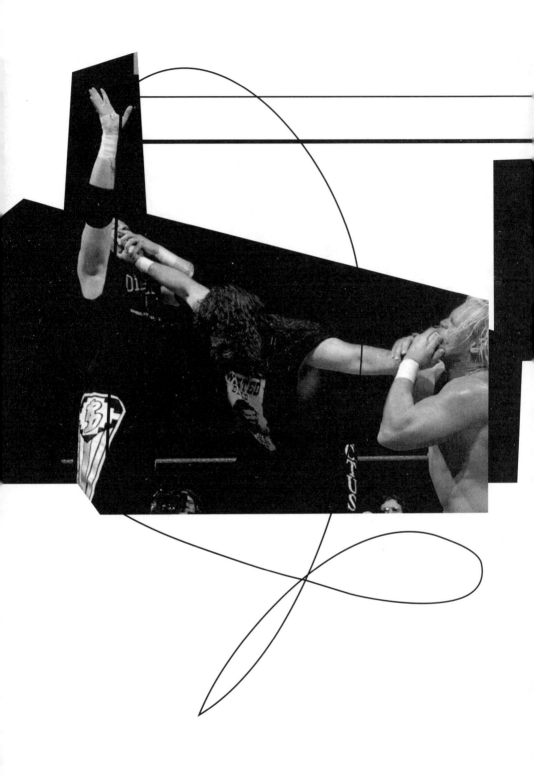

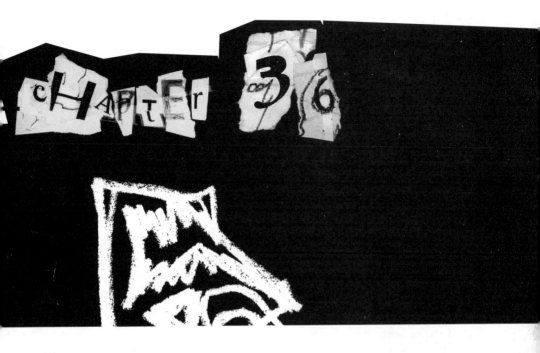

CHAPTER 36

I picked up the ringing phone

on an early September morning in 1997. We had moved three weeks earlier to the Florida Panhandle, but our house was not quite ready to move into and as a result, boxes were strewn everywhere in our small apartment. "Hello," I sleepily answered.

The voice on the other end was anything but sleepy, due to the fact that the man it belonged to had probably downed a half-dozen cups of coffee in the first two hours of the workday. "Mick, this is Vince, and I want to run something by you for this Monday. We would like you to be Cactus Jack in Madison Square Garden," he told me.

A big smile broke out over my face. "Are you sure?" I asked, with my mind going back to those annual thirty-second phone calls with J. J. F'ing Dillon.

Vince was right there to answer my question, "Mick, this is going to be huge," he said before adding, "I've got to admit, pal, I never thought I'd see Cactus Jack in the World Wrestling Federation."

"Neither did I, Vince," I echoed. "Neither did I."

I arrived in Stamford, Connecticut, on Sunday evening and had dinner at the home of Joey Styles, the ECW play-by-play man. We reminisced about the old days, and he even asked me if I thought

Cactus Jack would ever have a shot in the World Wrestling Federation. "I don't know, Joey," I lied right through my missing teeth, "but I doubt it." I hated to lie to a friend, but I wanted the whole Cactus Jack return to be a mystery. When I returned to my hotel, I slept restlessly for a few hours, before being awakened for my short ride to the Titan TV studios. Chris Chambers was there to guide me through eight hours of special effects, technical innovations, and if you don't mind my saying so, tour de force performances on the part of Dude Love, Mankind, and, in a cameo, Cactus Jack, that resulted in all three characters appearing on the Titantron at once. The creative lead-in had really set the stage for the return of the Hardcore Legend.

I was nervous as hell while the piece played, because I honestly didn't know what kind of reaction Cactus Jack would get in New York City. It had been a year and half since Cactus had existed and three since he had been on national television. Wrestling fans have notoriously short memories, and I wondered if the MSG fans would even have seen my WCW exploits.

My doubts were all assuaged, however, when the on-screen Mankind yelled "Cactus Jack is back!" The response of the crowd was shocking in its sheer volume. I had been hoping for a nice reaction, but this had surpassed anything I could have hoped for. When I emerged through the curtain, it was the loudest reaction I'd ever been a part of. My ECW send-off was more emotional and more heartfelt, but this audience was almost twenty times larger, and for that one evening, they were mine, mine, all mine!

The match itself may have been my best outing of 1997, and by the time I piledrove Triple H on a table at the top of the ring, it was as if a new/old star had been born/reborn. I've often wondered what would have happened if I had continued from that point as Cactus Jack. It might have been huge, or it might have died out. Who knows for sure? Also, a full-time Cactus Jack would have nullified the strange events of the next year that resulted in Mankind's sudden ascent in 1998.

Fans often ask about that night and wonder what I was thinking on my way down the ramp. The truth is, my mind was full of mixed emotions when I heard the reaction at MSG. On one hand, I was basking in the adulation and felt like I was on top of the world. On the other hand, I was thinking about my thirty-second calls with

J. J. F'ing Dillon and his assertion that I was lucky to have a job. I had watched Mr. F'ing Dillon for years and always wondered how his interviews as the manager of the Four Horsemen, which were delivered with all the flash and sizzle of a UPS truck, had kept him working at all. Yes, Mr. F'ing Dillon, you may have been half-right during our half-minute conversations—one of us was lucky to have a job.

I had just found out a few months earlier about Vince's contention from years gone by that Cactus Jack "doesn't look like a star." I hope that even someone as wise as Vince truly is learned a lesson about judging a book by its cover.

Actually, I believe it was Vince's admission in October that he wasn't always right that allowed the World Wrestling Federation to truly excel. Brian Pillman had tragically been found dead in a Minneapolis motel room a day earlier. Vince called a meeting of all the guys to address Brian's death but informed us that maybe time had passed him by and that some of the old formulas that had been successful for so long were simply outdated. He was a big enough man to shift responsibility to the wrestlers for much of their character development. That was really the meeting that did away with ridiculous gimmicks and ushered in a new era of realistic human beings that people could actually relate to. This was more or less the birth of the Federation's "attitude" campaign.

Almost immediately old gimmicks were switched, and guys became, to some extent, themselves. Gone was the stodgy, rich persona of Hunter Hearst Helmsley, to be replaced by a wise-ass, double-entendre-spouting Triple H. The Real Double J was taken off Titan death row and was given new life as the Road Dogg. Rockabilly took off his Bedazzler Kmart special jacket, dyed his hair to its natural state, and became Bad Ass Billy Gunn. Rocky Maivia deep-sixed his Chia Pet hairstyle and stereotyped ass-kissing persona to become The Rock. Even Howard Finkel developed a bit of 'tude. For some of the guys, it was too late. If Vader had come in right off the get-go as a killer, he would have drawn big money. Instead, the cowardly Vader never really found his niche. I actually had a very difficult time adjusting to the new Federation "attitude," even though it would take several months for the business to pass me by. Catching back up would be one of the biggest challenges of my career.

*   *   *

No one will ever forget the *Survivor Series* of November 1997. It was without a doubt the most controversial night in the history of the business, the ramifications of which are still being felt today. It was also a night in which my World Wrestling Federation career nearly ended.

I still do not know all the details that set the wheels of the *Survivor Series* controversy in motion, so I will be somewhat brief in outlining its history. Problems seemed to arise when Brett Hart resigned from the Federation, after being wooed by WCW. Brett had been and still was a huge star for Vince McMahon, and had held all the company's major titles, including the world belt on several occasions. In the midst of the ratings war with Turner, Vince felt that the loss of Brett would be devastating to his company and so pulled strings that had previously been unheard of to keep his star. Vince was unable to match the yearly salary that WCW was offering and so, in a sense, offered Brett a lifetime contract that would offer him more over a greater length of time. Brett, it should be mentioned, had a great sense of loyalty to the Federation and took the lifetime contract.

Almost immediately, problems arose, not the least of which was Shawn Michaels pulling out of *WrestleMania* with a knee injury. Brett saw this as a slap in the face from a man he already did not personally care for. The locker room incident had not done a whole lot to pacify the tension.

It should be noted also that Brett was not at all comfortable with the new Federation "attitude," which seemed to push actual wrestling to the rear in favor of story lines and liberal doses of mature content.

Worse yet, with his company in certain financial straits, Vince had gone to Brett and asked to restructure his salary. Brett had balked, and at the time Vince allowed Brett to reopen negotiations with WCW, which would let him work with the Federation until December 5. There was only one problem: Brett was still the World Wrestling Federation champion, and no one seemed to quite know how to get the belt off of him. Brett offered several scenarios, but there was one story line that he was dead set against—he would not lose his title to Shawn Michaels. If Brett had gotten his way, Stone Cold or I would have had the damn belt, and none of the bizarre series of events would have unfolded.

In the midst of all of this, I had a problem: I had not brought my passport to Canada for the Montreal Pay-Per-View. I was very afraid of being detained at the Montreal airport by Canadian police, which was a fairly common occurrence at the Canadian borders. Many wrestlers would have their bags and even their shoes cut open or destroyed by overzealous border cops trying to look like big shots. I had rented a car, which I had planned to drive from Friday's show in Detroit to Saturday's show in Toronto, before driving the 400 miles to Montreal. In Detroit, Owen's buddy Ronnie Gaffe offered to put me up at his home in Hamilton and drive me the rest of the loop. I knew Ronnie looked forward to these road trips for months, so I agreed to tag along. Also, the prospect of driving all night before my big matchup with Kane was a prospect that I was not looking forward to. So I headed off for a trip with the Gaffer, unaware that the absence of my car would have a greater effect than I could imagine.

I was very proud of my match with Kane, who was in the beginning of a huge push as an unstoppable monster. A chokeslam he had given me outside the ring had actually dented the steel ramp structure, something that mightily impressed our road technicians. I thought I had been successful in adding both to Kane's aura of a monster and my aura of never backing down. I was sore but satisfied as I settled down in front of the monitor for the main event.

Brett had reached an agreement to wrestle Shawn for the good of the company, but only with the understanding that the belt would not change hands in Montreal. He walked to the ring that night with the understanding that the match would be disqualified due to interference from the Hart Foundation, which consisted of brother Owen and brothers-in-law Davey Boy Smith and Jim Neidhardt. What actually happened was far more interesting.

As I've said before, people can say what they want about Shawn, and a lot of it might be true, but no one questions his in-ring abilities. With two of the top stars of this generation at their peak, the bout was shaping up as a match-of-the-year contender. The Montreal fans were solidly behind Brett, who was something of a national hero in his native country. Then in a moment, everything seemed to fall apart. The match had for the most part been a one-sided affair, as Shawn was receiving punishment from the Hitman both in and out of the ring. Shawn had momentarily stopped Brett and placed him in the Hitman's own sharpshooter submission. This was interesting, but not all that strange until I saw referee Earl Hebner calling for the bell. The bell rang, and Hebner quickly sprinted from the ring and into a waiting automobile that whisked him away from the arena. Brett and Shawn both seemed dumbfounded. Shawn was handed the belt and was ordered by Vince McMahon to "get the hell out of here." Brett later labeled Shawn as a co-conspirator in the title change, but if true, he did a good job of hiding it as he reached the backstage area. "There is no way I'm accepting his fucking belt like this," the Heartbreak Kid yelled. "This is bullshit."

Back in the ring, Brett started to sense that he'd been swerved out of his title. Confusion turned to anger when that realization sunk in and the Hitman spotted Vince at ringside. Not knowing what else to do, he launched a wad of spit that hit Vince high on the right side of his face. The crowd was still in a state of disbelief when the Hart Foundation joined Brett in the ring and gave support to the man who had given fourteen years of his career to the World Wrestling Federation, only to have the organization screw him over.

The backstage area was also in a state of disbelief. Actually, a state of shock might be a more accurate description. I was really upset by what I had just seen. "You don't do that to a guy like Brett Hart," is all I could say for minutes, as I repeated it over and over. I began to get angrier as time went by. "How can they expect me to work here after this?" I said to Pat Patterson, who was visibly upset by what had just transpired.

"I know, I know," said Pat, with tears welling up in his eyes. "I can't believe it myself." I wasn't mad at Pat, but gave him a message to give to my boss, who, at that specific time, I detested. "Tell Vince that I'm not coming to work tomorrow." Several other wrestlers also echoed my sentiments about not wanting to work for the company. I saw Vince Russo, our head writer, who also looked greatly stressed. "You ought to be ashamed of yourself," I said to Russo, without knowing that he'd been innocent of the deception. Russo later told me that those words hurt him worse than anything he'd ever experienced.

I stormed out of the arena with Ronnie Gaffe in tow. We got in the car, and I was not shy about letting my feelings be known. "I'm not working for this damn company anymore," I spat out emotionally. Ronnie, for his part, was devastated, not only because he'd seen his hero's brother get screwed, but because he could sense his long-anticipated wrestling road trip "vacation" falling apart. "Cactus, please," he begged me, "think about what you are saying."

"I have thought about it, Ronnie," I shot back, "and I'm not going to work." When I got to my hotel, I placed a series of phone calls.

I called Jim Ross first, and left a message that said, "Tell Vince I'm not coming to work. I'm sick to my stomach, and don't feel like I can work here anymore. If you have any questions, you can call me at the Quality Inn."

Next I dialed Brett, who was staying in another hotel. He wasn't in, but I left a message repeating sentiments I'd explained to Ross, and giving him my support. I then tried Owen's room and was relieved to find him in. "What happened?" I asked.

"Well," Owen said matter-of-factly. "Vince walked into Brett's dressing room while Brett was getting changed. He apologized to Brett, but Brett told him, 'Vince, I am going to take a shower. If you are still here when I get out, I'm going to punch you right in the fucking mouth!'"

"Well, did Vince leave?" I asked.

"No," Owen replied, "he stayed there the whole time Brett was in the shower."

"Well, what happened when he got out?" I wanted to know.

"Brett walked up and punched Vince right in the mouth," he calmly told me. "Vince went down, and Shane [Vince's son] tried to help him get his wits, and then they left."

I wanted Owen to know that his family had my support. "Owen, I'm not going to the show tomorrow, and a lot of other guys aren't either. Vince is going to at least have to apologize tomorrow or else he won't have much of a company."

By this time, Kane had walked in (we were splitting a room), and had heard much of what was said. He was also upset, but as a seven-year veteran who had finally found a bankable gimmick, he was not in a position to walk out. I assured him that I understood his position completely, before noticing that my message light was on. I called the operator and was told that Jim Ross had returned my call.

I talked to J. R. for quite a while, and while not condoning what had just happened, he did try to explain the extenuating circumstances that surrounded it. "Mick, you've got to understand that Vince only did what he thinks is necessary for this company's survival," Ross told me.

I listened to everything he said, and a lot of it made sense, but nonetheless, my mind was made up. "Tell Vince that I'm not showing up," was how I finished the conversation.

Next, I had the dubious distinction of informing my wife for the second time in a little over three years that I was walking out on a six-figure salary. By this point, my figure was about double my WCW income, which made my distinction about twice as dubious. I told Colette of my plans and she seemed bewildered. "Are you sure, Mick? Things were going so well," she said.

"It doesn't matter, Colette," I said. "I can't work for people who would do this type of thing."

She was sensitive to how I felt, but realistic as well. "Mick, what will we do for money?" she rightfully wanted to know.

"We don't have to do anything," I assured her. "We have enough money to live on for a long, long time. I can be at home and actually get to spend time with the kids, and I guarantee you when my contract expires in four years, there will still be a place in the business for a guy like me."

Colette was sad, but she knew that my mind was made up, and that I believed in my cause. "Well, I guess I'm behind you then," she said, before saying our good-byes for the evening.

When I hung up, I noticed that the message light was on again. I called the operator and asked for my messages. "Mr. Foley, a Mr. McMahon called and wants you to call him back."

"Oh, God," I said to Kane. "Vince called. I'm sorry, but I just don't think I could handle talking to him right now." I lay awake for a long time that night thinking about the events of the evening. I couldn't help but think that Vince, who had just been punched in the face, had thought enough of Mick Foley to call him when he heard of my decision.

At this point, I was cursing myself for having ridden with Ronnie. Without him, I would have caught the last flight out of Montreal to anywhere and been gone. Because of him, my rental car was in a garage that I couldn't find and I was completely dependent on him to bring me back to my car in Hamilton. Ronnie was intent on traveling to the next two shows, even though from a Hart family perspective, the tour was over. So, while the rest of the crew left for television in Ottawa, I stayed behind in my hotel in Montreal.

I didn't have much to do that day but think, and so I thought a lot.

I still couldn't quite believe what had happened the night before, but hoped that somehow things would work out. When Vince saw his depleted crew, he would be forced to fix things, and then I would be happy to rejoin the Federation. I began thinking about my decision to leave and realized that quitting the company amounted to a breach of my contract and that I would forfeit any moneys that were due to me. I didn't mind sitting out for a year, but I sure didn't want to lose money that I had already worked for. If I left with no notice, I would be out three months of Pay-Per-Views, six months of royalties, and one month of arena shows. That gave me cause to think about giving a three months' notice, so at least I could get what was rightfully mine. Still, an apology or a rectification of the situation by Vince would make things a whole lot easier for me.

I watched *Raw* with great anticipation that night, but was devastated to see that instead of admitting their mistake, the World Wrestling Federation was actually playing it up. They were mocking Brett, and I was disgusted. One by one, I saw wrestlers appear on the screen who told me only one night earlier that they wouldn't be working anymore. I realized that I had absolutely no pull—it was the difference between robbing a store with a real gun and robbing a store with a water pistol. My show of rebellion just wasn't going to work. Surprisingly, the telecast had nothing but positive comments about Mankind.

Later that night, I received a call from Jim Cornette, and we talked for close to two hours. He made me see that even if none of us approved of what Vince had done, we had to understand that he did what he felt was best for the company. WCW was hell-bent on destroying Vince by any means necessary, and when it came to Vince McMahon, Ted Turner did indeed have very deep pockets. I had seen the World Wrestling Federation Women's champion show up on *Nitro* with her belt, and throw it in the garbage. It wouldn't be beneath the WCW to offer Brett a couple of hundred extra grand to do it as well. The Federation had always been able to make its world title mean something—without it, the company would be in a gigantic hole.

Finally, my decision came down to money. I respected Brett and I liked him a great deal personally, but I had to feel that he was going to be all right. He would have about two million a year to fall back on while I would have nothing. I just kept thinking of those figures.

Two million to zero. Zero to two million. With great reservation, I showed up at TV tapings the following afternoon.

I was welcomed back with open arms, and my walkout was never brought up again. As a matter of fact, I received an unusually large payoff for Ottawa—larger still, when you remember that I wasn't even there.

Apparently, Brett had really appreciated the gesture of respect that I had made, and made mention of it in several interviews I read. WCW had a gold mine waiting in Brett but, not surprisingly, failed to take advantage of it. Within months, due to office politics and creative differences, Brett was just another one of the guys. They literally wasted one of the greatest performers in the business. The Federation, on the other hand, used the strange event as a catalyst for greater ideas and ratings. The real-life screwing of Brett Hart was used as a springboard for Vince McMahon's evil Mr. McMahon persona—a persona that helped propel the company to greater success than was once thought possible. The renegade Stone Cold Steve Austin persona now had the perfect foil to play off in the corporate scumbag Mr. McMahon, and house show attendance took off immediately.

Personally, I felt as if my career was at a crossroads. I knew that Vince was a big fan of both Mankind and the Dude, but I felt personally that Cactus Jack could draw the most interest and money. With a return of Cactus Jack in mind, I proposed a somewhat bizarre series of matches with my old friend and nemesis Terry Funk, which would culminate in a coup de grace of barbarity at *WrestleMania*.

I had been talking with Victor Quinones of my IWA Japan past, and he asked if I thought death matches would ever go over in the States. Now it's just my personal opinion, but I find bloodletting and savagery between two friends to be less offensive than heavy sexual content. At least when it's done well. I would never propose putting this type of match on *Raw*, but if it were on Pay-Per-View with a disclaimer, then I wouldn't see anything wrong with it.

I came up with the idea of the best of seven death match tournament. Magnum TA and Nikita Koloff had enjoyed incredible success with this concept in the mid-eighties featuring regular matches, and I figured the added allure of danger would complement their concept nicely. I imagined a press conference where Terry and I would pull these ridiculous matches out of a fish bowl. "Mr. Funk has just chosen a bed of nails match," the announcer would say. After six matches were picked, the fans would be allowed to choose the stipulations for the final showdown. Now, I'll admit, I was going to tamper with the votes just a bit, so that the finale would be a rematch of our Kawasaki Stadium classic—a no rope, barbed wire, barbed wire board, C4 explosive, exploding ring death match. I pictured it airing on *WrestleMania* via satellite live from Terry's Double Cross Ranch near Amarillo, Texas.

I thought I had a winner on my hands and I wanted badly to propose it, but first I had to make sure that I had an opponent to propose. I gave the Funker a call. Less than a year earlier, Terry had been brought in for a couple of shows and the Federation had vowed never to use him again. He had, on the air, called an announcer a "Yankee bastard," and had referred to Vince as a "goddamn son of a bitch!" The company had been somewhat less than thrilled with him, but hell, looking back, Terry's verbal rampage had been a precursor of sorts for the current *Raw* show. The words he had been reprimanded for were pretty common utterances for the new Federation "attitude" and I thought that maybe they'd give the "goddamn Texas bastard" another try. I called Terry up and ran my idea by him. His answer was simple. "Cactus, I would love to work with you again."

Now came the hard part—pitching the idea to Vince. I requested a meeting with him, and we met along with Bruce Pritchard and Jim Ross after television tapings in a dressing room in Columbus, Ohio. I tried to stress the human drama aspect over the blood and guts, although I freely admitted there would be plenty of that also. I also wanted him to know that the quality of matches would be what counted, and I personally gave him my guarantee that they would be top-notch. I proposed that the series of matches would cover the January, February, and March Pay-Per-Views, with March being the *WrestleMania* blow-out. The other four tournament matches could take place after television tapings, with cameras still rolling so that the highlights of the ring atrocities could be aired. I also speculated that a home video of the death match tournament would bring in big money.

Vince seemed intrigued, especially with the notion of a ring exploding at Terry's ranch. "We might possibly be able to do this," the evil McMahon stated.

A few days later, Jim Cornette called me up. "Cactus, Vince loves the idea, but we're going to change it up a little bit," Corny told me. "We want you and Terry to start off as a team at the *Royal Rumble* in January. Somehow, you two have a falling out, and Terry challenges you to a Texas death match right there in Houston, for the February Pay-Per-View. And then you'll have the damnedest fight they've ever seen at *WrestleMania*."

That sounded great, but there was one problem. Vince was planning a huge surprise, which would turn out to be Mike Tyson, and he was expecting a lot of mainstream media to be covering the event. He didn't think that having two human beings blow each other up would be the best way to expose our product to this new audience. In retrospect, he was probably right. They still wanted the Funker, but they wanted him as my tag team partner.

Hell, that didn't sound too bad. After all, Terry and I had probably done enough damage to each other. Maybe it was time that we were on the same side for a while. Now all we had to do was come up with a way to introduce Terry to an audience that, unfortunately, hadn't been privy to the Funker's exploits over the last thirty years.

We put the ball in motion by having Dude Love wrestle Billy Gunn, while his teammate, the Road Dogg, did humorous commentary. The Dude pulled out the match (squeaked out a victory), but was jumped from behind by the Dogg. We fought up the ramp to the top, where a referee tried to break up the melee. Gunn grabbed me and sent me sailing off the seven-and-a-half-foot stage. I once heard the stage referred to as being fifteen feet high, but that would make me about thirteen feet and ten inches tall. Still, the distance seemed large as I hurtled earthward, toward the table that I knew would break my fall. Oops! I missed the table—grazed it, to be accurate—and one of its legs bent as I sailed past it and crashed in a heap on the cold, hard Durham, New Hampshire, concrete.

Gunn and Dogg, collectively known as the New Age Outlaws, reacted with great remorse to my injury. Together, they climbed down the stage and rushed to my aid. As soon as they saw that I was helpless, they immediately began putting the boots to me in one of the funnier examples of poor sportsmanship that I have ever seen. It didn't seem funny at the time, however, as the fall had legitimately shaken me up and would bother me for several weeks.

A holiday season pilgrimage to Santa's Village seemed to revitalize me the next day, as I was allowed to walk around the snow-covered Christmas Wonderland at my leisure. My wife thought I was crazy when I wrote to the owners of my desire to walk around an empty kids' park and even joked that my photo would be on the wall as if in a post office mug shot. Instead, the owners were delighted to hear of my fondness/obsession with their little park. There's just something about that place, I guess, that makes me feel like a kid. To me, there's just nothing like being on a Ferris wheel with my daughter, with the sun setting on a beautiful summer's day, with a gorgeous view of the White Mountains surrounding me. Even if, in the back of my mind, I'm thinking of busting someone open with a steel chair.

I went home for the holidays and enjoyed the feeling of sixteen hours of Christmas music bombarding my senses. Unfortunately, I think I overloaded on Christmas spirit by force-feeding carols and Christmas videos to my kids. "What do you mean, you don't want to watch Frosty," I actually yelled at my kids. "Don't you have any respect for Christmas?" Adding to my Yuletide woes was the fact that I'd been staying awake for hours every night transferring our camcorder family memories onto standard VHS videos. By the time Christmas morning rolled around, I was shot. I tried to be at my Christmas best, but a parade of stinky gifts that Colette had bought me had me about ready to snap. Finally, I opened the gift that broke the camel's back. I opened up Colette's expertly wrapped box to find, of all things, a Tommy Hilfiger T-shirt that was red, white, and blue, with a big, bold TOMMY on the front. You think that I would know better, having seen my mother pretend to like gifts that I knew she'd never use. I remember hearing my dad swear up and down that he "loved" the flowered button-down shirt I'd gotten him when I was nine, only to discover it in his drawer, still in the wrapper, ten years later. Proper gift etiquette eluded me, however, as I searched for the words to describe how I felt. "I hate this thing, Colette," probably wasn't the right choice, but it's the one that I made. Minutes later, I stumbled into my room for a long winter's nap before returning to apologize to all. The next day, I headed for the Nassau Coliseum to introduce the world to the Funker.

I went to the TV studio early in the morning to shoot another unique introduction with Chris Chambers, which would feature the

Dude "morphing" into Cactus Jack. It was there that I learned that Terry Funk wouldn't be my partner but that Chainsaw Charlie would. For reasons that I still don't quite understand, Terry was, at his own request, turned into Chainsaw Charlie, and the result wasn't quite what I was looking for. Cactus Jack stuck around for three months this time, but in truth his impact was not all that great. It might have been a lack of interview time, or it might have been the somewhat anticlimactic debut of Terry chainsawing his way out of a wooden box with a pair of baby-powdered pantyhose on his head, but for some reason, our team didn't quite take off as we had planned.

Don't get me wrong—the team wasn't a failure, but it did fail to live up to what I thought it could be. I thought we could usher in a new era of danger and dynamic promos into the world of sports entertainment. Instead, we were just a couple of popular wrestlers who were miles apart from Steve Austin on the food chain.

At one particular six-man tag in Louisville, Kentucky, my value became very clear to me. Originally, Terry was contracted to do all of five shows with the Federation. When he became my partner, he went on the road full-time. As a concession to the fact that he was fifty-four years old and still working as hard in the ring as ever, the office would occasionally give Terry a few days off. As a result, on this night, I was teamed with Owen Hart and Stone Cold against the Outlaws and The Rock. The crowd was chanting the familiar "Rocky sucks, Rocky sucks," when Road Dogg got on the mike to disagree. "No, he doesn't," said the Dogg. "His timing's good. He looks great, plus he's a pretty good guy."

The match started, and Owen and I got nice responses to our respective moves. Then I tagged in Austin, and the place went crazy. "Did you ever get the feeling that he's the main course and we're just a couple of side dishes?" Owen jokingly asked me. Austin threw some punches, and the crowd went wild.

"Kind of like a baked potato," I said to Owen. Austin flipped off Gunn and the roar got even louder.

"Jack, let's face it, you're like a three-bean salad that no one even wants," Owen countered. Austin hit the Lou Thesz press, a move so silly it could actually be called "the dick to the mouth," and the Louisville Gardens erupted.

"Owen, let's face it, you and I are just little sprigs of parsley that will just be thrown out after dinner," I only half-jokingly answered back.

"Yeah, you're right," Owen agreed. "That's exactly what we are."

As I've mentioned, Steve Austin is a great guy, but I'd be lying if I said that the attention he was receiving in comparison to me didn't hurt me just a little bit. Sometimes more than a little.

The Austin phenomenon notwithstanding, Terry and I did have several great moments together. Our *Royal Rumble* appearance, where Terry and I willingly traded headshots before teaming up to kick The Rock's "rooty poo, candy ass," was a definite highlight. I actually appeared as all three "faces of Foley" in the contest, but I will always best remember the *Rumble* for the reaction of Terry when he realized I had him dead to rights with a steel chair. He rolled up his pantyhose so I could clearly see his face, nodded his head up and down to give me the okay and waited like a man for the chair shot that nearly leveled him. Terry recoiled from the blow by staggering around and throwing two or three Fred Sanford jabs into the air. I presented Terry the same chair, which he accepted as if it were a cherished family heirloom. I then gave Funk the go-ahead, and he clobbered me three times. It was a truly warm moment between friends.

We also had a famous ride in a Dumpster, courtesy of the Outlaws. I had a match with Terry just for the hell of it, which culminated in my flying elbow onto the fallen Funker from the side of the Titantron into a Dumpster. With both of us incapacitated, the Outlaws shut the lid and wheeled us off the ramp, leading to a crash landing on the cold, hard concrete below. It should have, could have, and would have been a truly great image, but the details were all wrong. For one thing, my dive off the Titantron should have been a highlight to match the later Hell in a Cell fall for sheer drama. I had told Vince that I would climb only about eight feet up the massive screen, but I had every intention of going up to about fifteen when we were live. During the course of our brawl, the Dumpster had rolled too close, and when I started climbing, I realized that a higher fall would send me way past the outer limit of the Dumpster. Rather than get down and roll it to the proper distance, I just took off, which would have been impressive enough, if not for the cloud of packing peanuts that poofed up in the air upon impact. When we were helped out of the Dumpster, there were peanuts everywhere. I swear the china I had shipped for Christmas from England didn't look as snuggly as we did when we were helped out of the trash bin.

Finally, we probably overexaggerated our condition, which didn't help our credibility when we came running down the aisle to end the show. Within an hour and a half, we went from being unconscious in an ambulance to hitting the bad guys with our IV stands. Terry was even wearing a hospital gown, although, mercifully, his wrinkled ass never made the air.

Also, we did have a tremendous Dumpster Match with the Outlaws at *Mania*, which saw us capture the belts and helped set the stage for the next part of my career. With the help of a forklift, we were able to dump both Gunn and Dogg into a back-stage Dumpster for the tag team championship. How were we to know that we would be the victims of the little-known "wrong Dumpster rule," which would lead to the stripping of the belts and a rematch inside a steel cage the next evening on *Raw*? Unfortunately, Terry had suffered a bad injury to his lower back when, at fifty-four years of age, he was powerbombed off the ring apron into the Dumpster below. Within minutes of the fall, his back was visibly bruised, and within hours, had filled with liquid. He somehow was able to get through the next night at *Raw*, but it would be the last time that Funk and Cactus would team.

I don't mean to demean what Terry and I did, because, in truth, we had some excellent matches. With all wrestling considerations aside, I will always fondly remember my three-month union with Chainsaw, for it gave me the chance to ride the road with my hero and mentor and to get inside his "middle-aged and crazy" mind. Terry Funk is simply everything that is right about this business. I think my fellow Florida Panhandle neighbor, the Road Dogg Jesse James, put it best when Terry walked past one day and he said, "I don't care what the announcers tell everybody—that's the real toughest son of a bitch in the World Wrestling Federation."

I don't know if people can fully appreciate how difficult it is to continually get up for big matches. I know the general public just sees us as a silly spectacle filled with "make-believe" fighting, but I doubt that even real fans know what it's like to try to get up for big matches again and again—even when the mind and the body are exhausted. We were all battered and bruised after *WrestleMania*, with Funk needing hospitalization, but somehow we all needed to suck it up one more time for the cage match that would change my fortunes.

I had received a surprise phone call from Vince Russo about a week earlier that had changed my outlook on the business. Until the phone call, I was looking at a post-*WrestleMania* program with Marc Mero, who by this point was Marvelous Marc Mero and was having big problems with his valet/wife, Rena (a.k.a. Sable). Of course, the problems with his wife were fictional, but the new "Marvelous" image had given fans a whole new persona. Since recovering from knee surgery, Mero had altered his wrestling style, abandoning high flying for a more conservative ground game.

I actually came up with a good idea for me and Mero that I thought would be entertaining and I had a little bit of hope for the match.

Russo's phone call changed all that. "Vince, how are you," I said into the phone, as I walked around the small gym that Colette and I had just opened.

"Cactus, I got some good news for you," said Russo, with a voice that was pure Brooklyn even though he'd grown up only five miles from me in the middle of Long Island.

"What is it?" I said, with great anticipation running through my mind. "You didn't reconsider that Mero thing, did you?"

"It's better than that," Russo quickly replied. "We want you to wrestle Austin at the next Pay-Per-View."

I loved it, but I knew better than to get excited. "Are you sure it's okay with Steve?" I asked.

Russo quickly relieved my fears. "Are you kidding?" he said. "It was Steve's idea."

I knew that a program with Steve could be a big success, but as Michael Hayes had reminded me years earlier, I would need a reason. The night after *WrestleMania* gave it to me.

Terry and I had a short but brutal fight with the Outlaws and a host of others inside the cage. He could hardly move due to the "Dumpster bomb." I guess because of that, Terry was handcuffed to the cage as the Outlaws worked me over. Showing the intestinal fortitude that was my trademark, I battled back against the odds and was climbing the cage en route to victory. When I got there and hung my body over the cage, the returning X-Pac (who had just jumped ship from WCW) was there to meet me with a chair over the head that sent me back inside. I was beaten up some before being pile-driven onto the same chair for the crushing defeat. (In this cage match, a pinfall could also signal victory.) With the match over, X-Pac entered the ring to resume the assault and was joined by Triple H and Chyna. This was the birth of the new D-Generation X (or DX), and a pretty good birth it was. They took turns beating on me, with X-Pac giving me the "bronco ride" in the corner, Hunter giving me a pedigree on the chair, and the Outlaws giving me a couple of extra chair shots for good measure. The combination of X-Pac's balls bouncing up and down in my face and the repetitive feeling of steel against my skull had me feeling both pissed off and pained as I lay on the canvas.

DX left the ring, and several fans started to leave, thinking the show was over. In an attempt to keep them in their seats, Howard Finkel's voice cut through the Albany, New York, air. "Ladies and gentlemen, remember, coming up soon will be . . . Stone Cold Steve Austin." The place went wild and started chanting his name. "Austin, Austin, Austin," came the noise as I slowly got to my feet. I looked at Terry and the very real pain that was etched on his face. I thought of myself, and the years of painful mornings I'd had to endure. Two of the hardest-working SOBs in the history of the business, and all we were to Albany was sprigs of parsley on a plate. Well, I may have been a sprig, but I was a sprig with feelings, and they'd just been hurt. That was definitely a negative. There was also a positive. I had a reason, and it was a good one.

The next night in Syracuse, New York, I walked out to the ring with a neck brace and a heavy heart. I spoke to the fans, and made my feelings clear:

"I have always taken a lot of chances in the ring, and some very bad things have happened to me over the years. What I've always had is the comfort of knowing that when I looked at my career, my dreams, the things I'd accomplished and the things I'd set my heart on, that it was always worth the pain. So people ask, 'Cactus, how's your neck?' I'd say that I'll be damned if I'm gonna let a group of scum like DX put Cactus Jack away.

"Oh, I guess you see that Terry Funk's not here, and I haven't talked to Terry, but I left a message on his answering machine, and I'm not saying this to sound tough, but Cactus Jack and Terry Funk do not miss wrestling matches. So I have to guess if the Funker was hurt enough to fly home, than it's probably pretty bad.

"I really wish that people could know Terry a little bit more than just what they see in the ring, because people will always debate on who the greatest wrestler of all time is, but I guarantee you, you ask every damn last bunch of people in the dressing room, they'll say that Terry Funk is the gutsiest old bastard they've ever seen in their lives. Now, I guess you've probably seen Terry's back and I hope you saw *WrestleMania,* because it was a tremendous match, and I'm very proud of it. And Terry was lying there on the bed with his belt and he said, 'Cactus, it's all been worth it. But we don't have those belts now, do we?'

"And I'm not gonna get into the reason why, but I will say that when Cactus Jack was lying there, and I was conscious, and I could barely move, it was very hard to move, and I was not very far from being unconscious. And when I looked at Terry Funk, I heard something in my ears and, to tell you the truth, it kind of made me sick.

"That's . . . there was an announcement being made thanking the fans for coming to the World Wrestling Federation, and they said something about Stone Cold Steve Austin, and people started chanting his name. And it's funny, because when I came here two years ago I was Mankind, and there were always people saying, 'Why don't you just be Cactus Jack?' Then I came out in tie-dye and some white boots and they said, 'Why don't you just be Cactus Jack?'

"Well, I gave you Cactus Jack. I gave you every goddamn bit of energy I had, and when I was lying there helpless, you chanted someone else's name. This is not a knock on Stone Cold Steve Austin; hey, I'm happy he's the champion, and he may not admit it, but we've known each other a long time and he's been my friend; but what you did to me and Terry Funk laying there in the middle of the ring was not only distasteful and disrespectful, it was disgusting.

"Well, I can finally say for the first time after thirteen years of blood, sweat, and tears that it's not worth it anymore. It's gonna be a long time before you see Cactus Jack in the ring again."

The next week's *Raw* was remarkable for two reasons—it ended WCW's year and a half run on top of the ratings, and it ushered in the return of Dude Love.

Actually, the show was classic Federation storytelling, with Austin challenging Vince to a match and Vince training for the big showdown throughout the two-hour show. The program was both captivating and entertaining and was a good example of why *Raw* is the hottest television show in the country. One of my favorite segments was when Pat Patterson and Gerald Brisco, known collectively as the Stooges, were giving Vince wrestling pointers in the dressing room. "Now, Vince, you know that Austin always sets up the stunner with a boot to the stomach," advised Brisco, a former collegiate and professional star wrestling from Oklahoma. "When he does that, you hook him here [under the knee]. Once you do that, Vince, you own him. You OWN him."

Vince nodded his head knowingly while Patterson chimed in, "Boy, is he in for a surprise."

Patterson and Briscoe are a shining example of the difference between the Federation and WCW. WCW was not able to make Brett Hart a star—a guy who'd already been one for over a dozen years. Vince, on the other hand, was able to take two out-of-shape retired wrestlers and make them bigger names than they'd been in their heyday. Vince's son Shane, who is now a top performer with the company, once asked me what I would like to do when I was finished wrestling. "I would like to be one of the Stooges," I said.

"I don't know," Shane retorted. "The Stooges get beat up a lot."

"Shane," I shot back, "I'm good at that!"

The show was primed for a crescendo until Dude's music played and the tie-dyed hippie throwback proceeded to ruin the festivities.

"The Dude wants to know, can't we all just get along? I got to level with ya, Philadelphia. The Dude does not feel a whole lot of love out here tonight.

"But, Steve-O, as you know, there's only one cat who can bring peace to the Warzone, and that's Dude Love. Now, Stone Cold, I know you got your heart set on putting some heavy-duty booty to Uncle Vinny, but the Dude has got to put the veto on this one. Oh, we are tight, Steve-O, about as tight as two cats can be. But you got to understand, Steve-O, Vince McMahon writes the checks that let the Dude live the kind of life that the Dude likes to live. So I guess you could say, Uncle Vinny, you are my main man.

"And I want you to remember one thing and remember it good. When you look at Stone Cold Steve Austin, you've got your eyes set on the world's toughest SOB, and he can put you down on your A double S just like . . ."

A furious Vince shoved Dude on his ample butt, and Dude started to stalk the pumped-up owner of the company. Somehow, in all of this, Dude turned on a frustrated Austin, and the show went off the air with Austin feeling the Loved One's wrath. The numbers on the show were phenomenal, even if the Dude's performance did serve to piss off the same people we had just entertained so well. The next week, WCW countered by premiering Hollywood Hogan vs. Bill Goldberg, and once again pulled ahead in the ratings. By doing so, WCW had actually shot itself in the foot. Hogan and Goldberg would have been a surefire Pay-Per-View main event. By throwing the match away for free, WCW had actually lost millions in potential revenue. For the next several months, the ratings would teeter back and forth.

For the next few weeks, a conspiracy theory played out and it was obvious that the Dude was in McMahon's pocket. Dude was even given his own "Love Shack" interview segment, which featured a pink shag rug, love beads, lava lamps, and new Dudettes. The Dudettes seemed to be a different breed now. Gone was the innocence of old—replaced by the skimpiest of thong bikinis. Under those guidelines, my wife graciously declined the company's invitation to resume her role from the previous summer.

The Pay-Per-View match was a tremendous success, both artistically and financially. I actually had a great deal of doubt leading up to this match as I wasn't quite sure how to keep the Dude in character while at the same time making him seem like a threat to the Federation champion. I even dyed my hair a little to try to alter the Dude's persona. I later found out that even the office had reservations about this matchup.

As it turned out, all our fears were quickly relieved, and Austin and I tore the house down. Vince was simply hilarious in his role as the crooked boss who was looking for any opportunity to screw the "Rattlesnake" out of the gold. His facial expressions, with the exception of the bobbing Adam's apple during time of fear, are the best in the business.

At the end of the match, Dude was down and out, as the concerned McMahon tried in vain to lift his 300 pounds off the ground.

Austin wielded a chair, which was supposedly meant for Dude, but strayed by about two feet and caught the evil Vince square in the head. Vince went down, to the delight of the fans, but the bell was rung immediately, signaling the disqualification of the champion. Dude had won! Dude had won! In the words of Owen Hart, "I did it! Yes! I am a winner! Woo!" Unfortunately, the belt cannot change hands on a DQ, so Austin remained the champ.

"Hardcore" is a word that's thrown around often, but its definition is kind of vague. I hope you know by now that I use the term "Hardcore Legend" as a joke, simply because I like the way it sounds and because I get a kick out of referring to myself as a "legend." A legend is an honor that others can bestow upon me, if they so desire. If they mean it, I'm flattered, but the continual Hardcore Legend reference is simply something I do to amuse myself. No less an authority than Terry Funk described who he believed to be truly hardcore. "Vince McMahon is hardcore; you know why, Cactus?" asked the grizzled Funker. "Because he's a millionaire who doesn't need to be getting hit in the head with chairs, but he does it anyway because he loves it." So, as the ECW fans might say, "He's hardcore. He's hardcore."

The next two *Raw*s were big ones, as WCW was preempted for two weeks for the NBA playoffs. This, we felt, would be a chance to expose our superior product to the fans who were getting fed up with the staleness of Turner's product. The first week witnessed Vince giving a title shot to Goldust, a fact that did not sit well with the Dude. Dude came out of character, lamenting the fact that he had worn the tie-dye like Vince wanted; he'd beaten Austin like Vince wanted, and now he was giving my shot to a freak with a bustier like Goldust. This set the stage for the next week's show in Richmond, Virginia.

The show in Richmond may have been one of my finest hours. I came out onstage to start the show and immediately apologized for all my corporate misdeeds of the preceding few weeks. Before I left, I vowed that there were three things that I would never again do— "suck up to a lowlife like Vince McMahon, have my children watch their dad bump and grind with a couple of second-rate strippers, and above all else, I will never, ever let you make me wear this tie-dyed crap again." The crowd roared its approval at Mick Foley's new attitude, until Vince came down and cut one of his all-time best promos. Even though I'd just vowed my independence, it seemed that I couldn't quite shake Vince's hold over me, as I stood mesmerized by Vince's tales of loyalty and sacrifice.

"You want a title shot, Mick?" he yelled into my nodding face. "Then you go out and earn it. Tonight you're going to have a match with Terry Funk, and I don't want you to just beat him. I want you to destroy him. I want you to tear his heart out, so that the blood drips down your arm. Then you'll get your title shot." I was completely under Vince's spell, until the sound of glass breaking and the roar of 18,000 fans signaled the arrival of Stone Cold, who proceeded to tear down the "Love Shack." It was like a strange battle for Mick Foley's soul, with Vince as the Devil and Austin as something of a beer-swilling, foulmouthed Angel. Who would win out in this modern-day morality tale? We would soon find out.

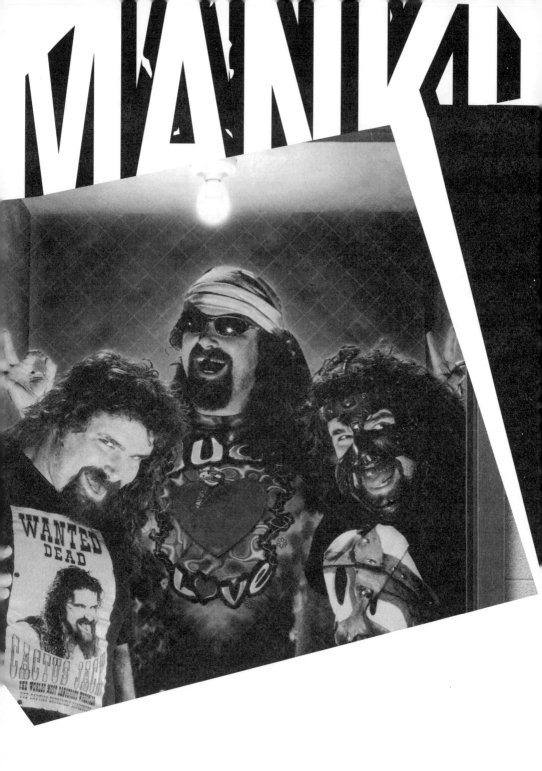

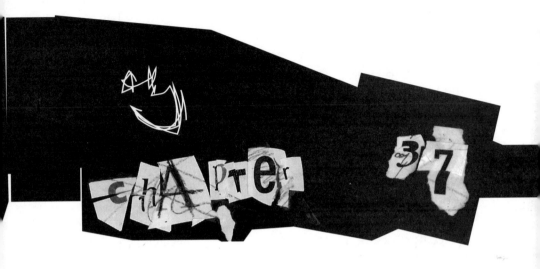

Terry and I had a classic no-holds-
barred contest. Before the match, we spoke very little, but we both
had the clear understanding that this was a very important match.
"Cactus, let's go out there and give it to them," I remember Terry saying before leaving me alone for the next hour to prepare for the
contest.

Many who saw it considered my match with Terry to be the best
Raw match of the year. I felt that it was on a par with my match with
Austin, if not slightly better. For the record, it was the only match I
have ever wrestled as "Mick Foley." These days, it seems that hardcore matches have become an excuse to go all over the building and
hit each other with cool stuff. That may be entertaining, and I'm not
saying it's not painful, but in my mind, it takes away from what these
things should really be about—intensity. Terry and I wrestled with
intensity that night. Lots of it.

I came out the winner and then challenged Austin, who'd been
doing color commentary, to step into the ring. He threw his ever-
present beer in my face, and the temporary loss of vision caused me to
mistakenly clamp the mandible claw onto corporate stooge Pat Patterson.
As my vision cleared, I saw Austin flipping me off, but rolled out of

the ring to avoid further incident. Suddenly, Vince appeared with the two second-rate strippers and my tie-dyed Dude outfit in his arms. As my music kicked in, I walked up the ramp, and to the strains of "Dude Love, Dude Love Baby," I proceeded to do everything I swore I never would. I sucked up to Vince by giving him a big, sloppy hug. I not only took back the Dude outfit but cradled the tie-dyed ensemble with a tenderness usually reserved for old, scratchy Leonard Cohen albums. And yes, the Dude certainly did bump and grind with the strippers for my children and the whole world to see. Not only that, but I did it with a hell of a lot of gusto for a guy who had just been through a war and had a head wound that would require twenty-seven stitches to close. Vince even joined in and in a classic *Raw* moment, the four of us gleefully boogied our way off the air, as Austin shook his head with disgust. Stone Cold had lost out, and the wicked Vince had my soul.

Afterward, I did what I always do after suffering an injury—I looked for a camera. "Vince, let's do an interview," I yelled, and we prepared to capture this touching moment on film. The Dudettes were nice enough to return to their state of near undress, and the cameras rolled. "Hey, Vince, you want a little bit of this action?" I laughed in my Dude way, as I pointed to my two Love chicks.

"Ho, ho, Dude, I'm a married man." Vince laughed with all the conviction of a sleazy used car salesman. "Besides, I think you're going to need all the love you can get. Looks like you've got a little scratch up there," he continued as the camera zoomed in on a three-inch gulley high on the left side of my skull. "We'll probably need a little Band-Aid to patch that up."

The show did a phenomenal 5.4 rating in the Nielsens. As I'd hoped, many of the new viewers stayed tuned to our show, and we started to defeat our southern adversaries with greater and greater frequency. A year later, our show set an all-time record with an 8.1 rating—up a full 50 percent in a year. The basketball game on TNT, stocked with spoiled multimillionaires, did a 1.3.

In the remaining three weeks leading up to the May *Over the Edge* Pay-Per-View, I decided to tweak Dude's image. If Dude was going to be Vince's hand-picked corporate champion, then I felt I needed to look like it. In a move that was very reminiscent of the psychology behind the ECW *Hardcore Christmas*, I once again strove to eliminate anything that the fans had found admirable about me. The hair was slicked back into a neat ponytail, and I borrowed one of Vince's dapper sports jackets and a tie. I probably should have cut the hair and shaved, but I did come forth with a quality prop—a dental flipper of my two front teeth. I hadn't worn these false teeth in so many years that I had difficulty speaking with them, but when I did, it was pure heat. Front teeth? Now that's selling out. Sporting a pair of eyeglasses that were slightly slipping down my amputated auditory appendage and clutching a folded copy of the *Wall Street Journal*, the "new corporate kiss-ass" Dude made his debut in Baltimore. Sounding like a dull college professor or Dean Douglas, the Dude addressed the crowd.

"It seems that as of late, I have been having trouble with my identity. But now with the gracious help of Vince McMahon, I have found out who I am. I am a speaker of four languages. I am a student of American history and a reader of Greek tragedy. I am a leader of men and a lover of women, as well as the toughest SOB in the World Wrestling Federation. As I'm Dude Love—your next World Wrestling Federation champion."

Vince beamed with pride as he announced the special guests for the upcoming Pay-Per-View. First, Pat Patterson was announced as the special guest ring announcer. Next, the esteemed Gerald Brisco was brought out as the special guest timekeeper. Finally, Vince gave a huge buildup for the guest referee, ending with "Here he comes right now." To Vince's embarrassment, there was no referee forthcoming. The crowd started to laugh. Vince tried once again, with a second "Here he comes." Again, no referee. Again, audience laughter. Things weren't looking too good for the corporate team. "Well, I guess I'll have to drag him out myself," Vince yelled before storming up the ramp.

I small-talked in midring with the Stooges, before Pat Patterson picked up the mike and, in his eloquent style, introduced the world to the special referee. "Ladies and gentlemen, he's the best there is, the best there was, and the best there ever will be—Vince McMahon." With that, Vince came bounding down the ramp, sporting a referee's shirt that must have been eight sizes too small. In an attempt to show off his impressive physique, Vince was wearing a shirt so small that my son Dewey would have had trouble squeezing into it. The deck was clearly stacked against Austin, and the time seemed ripe for a new champion. A corporate champion. A kiss-ass champion. I was ready.

I've mentioned before that I consider *Mind Games,* against Shawn

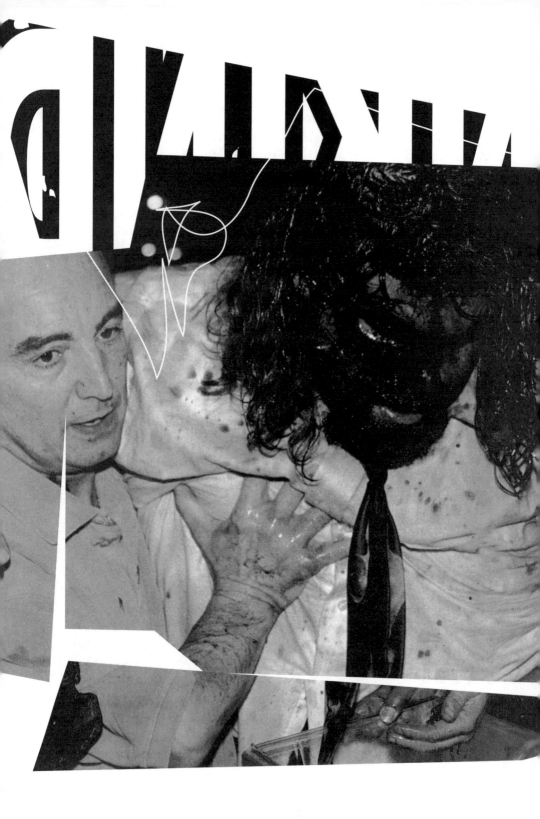

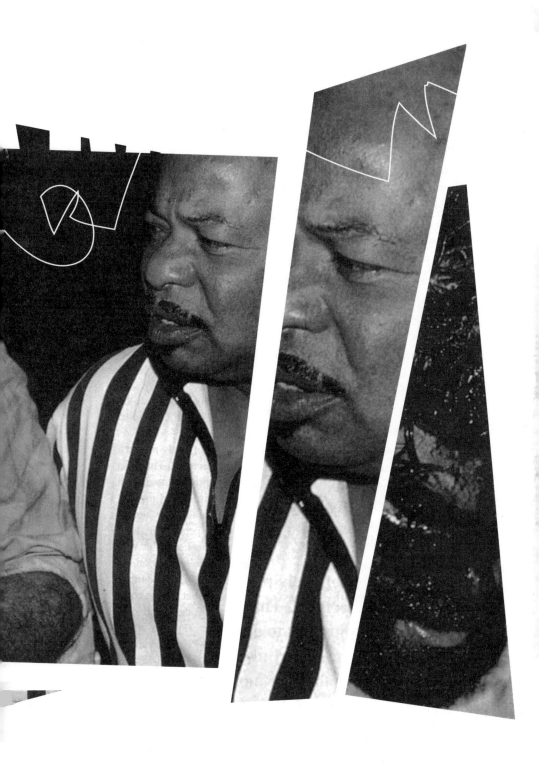

Michaels, to be my best match. The future *King of the Ring* was probably the most emotional. *Over the Edge,* with Austin, however, was undoubtedly the most fun to watch. Don't get me wrong, I got the hell beaten out of me and I was so blown up (out of breath) that I must have been running on something other than oxygen for the last ten minutes. But I have never before or since seen such a reaction from the boys as they watched the replay the following day. Smiles and laughter for twenty minutes as they watched our elaborate twenty-minute epic drama unfold. Thinking about it now, it's a small miracle that things went as well as they did.

In the World Wrestling Federation, we are often allowed to do third-party bookings, which means, basically, that we are allowed to work on our own time for other promoters. In the past year, that has usually meant signing autographs at memorabilia shops, malls, department stores, and car lots. But until promoters learned that wrestlers were nicer, cheaper, and more popular than overpriced "real" athletes, third-party bookings usually consisted of wrestling at small venues for large payoffs.

I had four days off before my showdown with Austin. Resting up probably would have been the wisest thing, but I just had trouble turning down ten weeks' worth of "Memphis payoffs" for one night in a sweaty high school gym. Hey, it might not have been glamorous, but at least it was profitable. So instead of concentrating on my big match and resting up for a cardio machine like Stone Cold, I wrestled in four shows in three days in the boonies of Ohio, and then drove 500 miles to Milwaukee. I was exhausted and questioning my intelligence when I showed up. Somehow, we pulled off a classic.

Pat Patterson came out first as my announcer and proceeded to read off a long, scripted, ridiculous series of introductions. I came out to the Dude Love theme, nattily attired in sports coat and flowered blue pastel tights. I was dancing just a little but not enough to ruin my corporate image. I had never understood why a retro hippie would go out to a faux Bee Gees disco number, but now when I threw in the corporate image, it was completely confusing. I guess the Dude was a disco-dancing corporate hippie. Nonetheless, Patterson continued, announcing my opponent.

The bell rang, and we started the match with a little bit of "believe it or not" scientific wrestling. Don't worry, not too much. Just a couple of reversals that led to a cover and a quick one-count by Vince.

The fast count earned Vince the ire of the Undertaker, who had been brought down by Austin to watch his back. For the rest of the match, Vince played it straight, but by virtue of his mannerisms, made it clear who he was pulling for. I even saw the Adam's apple bob up and down a couple of times when the Dude kicked out of two close pinfall attempts.

A few minutes into the match, I took the advantage on Austin. I was choking him outside the ring when Vince suddenly got wide-eyed and ran over to Patterson. "This is just a reminder," boomed Pat's voice, which still carried a French Canadian accent even after over thirty years in the States, "that this match is a no-disqualification match."

"That's not fair," Jim Ross informed the home viewers. "This match doesn't have any stipulations." Austin eventually took over, but the Dude used a diabolical ballshot to send the champ to the outside. As I was putting the boots to Austin halfway up the entrance aisle, Vince got that wide-eyed look again and sprinted down the aisle, and around the ring to Patterson. A moment later, Pat was on the mike.

"Just a reminder, in this match, falls count anywhere in the building."

"Oh, that's great," said a sarcastic J. R., "I guess they're just making up the rules as they go along."

The impromptu falls count anywhere provision gave us the excuse to work our way over to where a series of parked cars made up the *Over the Edge* set. We spent the next few minutes liberally destroying the already destroyed vehicles, including a Dude Love backdrop that saw Austin smash a front windshield. At one point, with Austin prone in the aisle, the Dude ascended two cars, which were stacked precariously on top of one another. I dove off the hood looking for the elbow, but when Austin moved, I uncharacteristically cheesed out and landed partly on my feet instead of on my hip. The fight continued into the ring, until Austin finally gained the upper hand and caught me with a vicious chair to the face. At that point, the match should have been over, but Vince refused to make the count. Realizing that a screwing was at hand, Stone Cold got in Vince's face, while I came to my senses and picked up a steel chair that Patterson slid me. I came charging and brought the chair down hard, but Austin moved, and my boss took a shot so hard that it literally knocked the caps on his teeth off. I caught Austin with the claw, and before he even went down, Patterson slid in as an apparent substitute ref and attempted to count Austin out. Before he could get to three, however, the Undertaker slid him outside and promptly chokeslammed him. Now it was Gerald Brisco's turn to slide in, attempt a ludicrous three count, and get pulled out and chokeslammed through a table. I got up and turned into Austin's stunner, and Steve made the count himself with Vince's very hand.

The next night, I came out on *Raw* with an eye that was visibly swollen and discolored from my chair to the face the previous night. What followed was a memorable verbal interaction with Mr. McMahon, which left the Dude without his pride and without his job.

Dude Love had been fired, Cactus Jack had retired, leaving only one persona who was still eligible for a paycheck. That's right, the return of Mankind, who had last been seen almost six months earlier. I'd like to say that Mankind's return was an instant success, but in reality, it was met with the type of apathy usually reserved for Al Snow matches (yes!).

Running a weekly two-hour wrestling program head to head against well-financed competition is exciting and often makes for remarkable television, but the speed with which issues are rushed sometimes leaves creative casualties behind. Unfortunately, Mankind was one of those casualties. I had just completed a very emotional interview with Vince McMahon. I'm not saying I was really fired, but I thought it was a good representation of reality. Not everyone can hit his boss when he wants to. Usually, the boss holds the ball and the employee has to play by the rules. I had been embarrassed by my boss on national television, and it felt like there was a part of everyone that could feel for me. When I came running out just an hour later as Mankind, it was almost as if I were wearing a hospital gown and pulling an IV stand behind me. Mankind has gone on to incredible heights since that poorly received run in, but at the time the rapid character changes led to credibility problems that would be tough to overcome.

I had been tentatively scheduled to face Stone Cold at the June *King of the Ring* Pay-Per-View in a special Hell in a Cell match. Hell in a Cell was a match that was devised eight months earlier as a special attraction for the Shawn Michaels–Undertaker feud. The cell referred to an ominous-looking sixteen-foot-high steel mesh structure with a matching ceiling. The cell was so large that, unlike other cages, it literally surrounded the ring. The first cell match had been outstanding—probably the best match of 1997—and the feeling was that a sequel would do big business. Unfortunately, as I learned with the aid of a phone call, the feeling was that Foley vs. Austin III wouldn't.

Vince Russo broke the news, and as he did, I could feel my heart sink. I knew that Mankind wasn't over, but I was hoping that the office wouldn't catch on to the current apathy for a while. Russo's comments made me realize they had. "Cactus, we are just concerned that the audience won't buy another match with you and Steve."

How could I disagree? At this point I didn't think they would buy a match with me against anyone. Who knows—maybe a Mankind vs. Al Snow match with a loser must wrestle Pete Gas for a year stipulation wasn't far away. I decided to verify my intuition by asking Russo, "So, I'm definitely out of the cell match," I said with a whole lot of sadness in my voice.

"No, no," an excited Russo corrected me, "you're still in the cell, it's just that you'll be in there with the Undertaker. Austin will wrestle Kane for the title."

I was overjoyed, but minutes after hanging up, I was plagued with feelings of certain failure in the cell. "I'm screwed," I thought. "I suck inside a cage. Undertaker has a broken foot. No one cares about me, and besides, was the world really calling out for a sixth Mankind–Undertaker Pay-Per-View encounter?" At that point, I had no idea that it would be the most talked-about match of my career.

A couple of weeks before the show, I made the tactical error of stopping by the World Wrestling Federation corporate offices in Stamford, Connecticut. It wasn't stopping there that was the error, it was whom I brought with me, the legendary bastion of common sense, Terry Funk. We were on our way to Providence from a show in Connecticut, and we decided to stop by the office for a workout. Titan Towers probably has the most well-equipped gym of any office building in the country. After I finished punishing my pectorals and bombing my biceps, I called and asked the home video department if I could take a look at *Bad Blood*, the Pay-Per-View during which last year's Hell in a Cell had taken place. I sat in a little office with the Funker as we watched Hell in a Cell unfold. "Damn," I was thinking as I sat there watching Michaels and the Undertaker tear down the house, "there's no way we're going to live up to this."

There was one part in particular that had been impressive. It consisted of a frantic Michaels climbing outside of the cell to get away from the unstoppable 'Taker. He got to the top, but there was nowhere to go, and 'Taker had wreaked havoc all over the top of the cell. Michaels had actually been backdropped and slammed on the ceiling, and I winced at the sight of the 200-pound Heartbreak Kid's body bouncing off the steel mesh. Finally, Michaels was dangling precariously off the side of the cage and ended up dropping onto the table from about the eight-foot mark in a scene that would live on for the next year via video highlights.

Terry and I just sat there for a few minutes, without saying a word. Finally, Terry spoke up. "Cactus," he mumbled, "that one is going to be difficult to beat."

"I know," I agreed. "Plus I'm a hundred pounds heavier than Shawn—I just can't do some of the things in that cage that he can." Once again, we sat in silence for a couple of minutes. I was the one to break the silence. "What do you think I should do?" I asked my mentor, friend, and hero.

His answer would help make me professionally and damn near break me physically. "I think you ought to start the match on top of the cage." You'd think I would know better than to listen to Terry Funk.

We continued to talk on the way to the show, but it was mostly joking around. "Goddamn, Cac," the Funker said, laughing, "maybe you should let him throw you off the top of the cage."

"Yeah," I shot back, "then I could climb back up—and he could throw me off again." Man, that was a good one, and we were having a good time thinking of completely ludicrous things to do inside, outside, and on top of the cage. After a while I got serious and said quietly to Terry, "I think I can do it."

It took quite a while for me to remember the events surrounding Hell in a Cell. Which should give you some indication as to how it turned out. It took several weeks and repeated viewings of the match itself, to piece the whole scene together. I felt kind of like a private eye trying to put together the mystery of my own life. Now, almost a year later, I've got a good handle on the biggest and most memorable night of my fifteen-year career.

I had told the Undertaker a week before the match that I was planning on starting the match on top of the cage. He hadn't seemed real positive about it. Let's face it, I had to tell him. Otherwise, if he walked out, saw me standing up on the top and decided not to follow, I would look like a big dummy climbing back down. Every day I would ask him, and every day he would shoot it down.

MICK FOLEY

The day before the match, I asked him again. He shook his head and asked me a question—not as the deep and dark Undertaker, but as a guy who had known me for eight years and who had, over the course of some titanic battles, developed a bond with me. We'd beaten each other half to death it seemed and then looked out for each other when we were hurt. We hadn't ridden together or shared a room since we first hooked up under different names, but we nonetheless shared a deep and mutual respect. "Jack," he said, "why are you so intent on killing yourself up there?"

"Because," I answered seriously, "I'm afraid this match is going to stink. You can't walk, and, let's face it, I don't have any heat. We've got a heck of a legacy to live up to, and I don't want this match to ruin it. If we can start it out hot enough, we can make people think we had a hell of a match even if we didn't."

Taker thought it over and I thought I could see him cracking. "I'll think about it," he said before we parted ways.

My music played and I walked down the aisle with my trusty steel chair. I got to the cage and threw the chair onto the top, as I planned to make use of it later. I put my fingers in the mesh and started to climb. I slipped. I tried to climb again, but my toes wouldn't fit into the mesh to get a foothold. I cursed my half-thimbleful of natural athletic ability. For a minute, I didn't think I'd ever be able to climb the damn thing. I did, but it sure as hell wasn't pretty, and when I got to the top, I had no feeling in my right index finger from pulling so hard on the fence. It would actually take a week for all the feeling to come back.

I stood up there in nervous anticipation and the scene recalled the memory of my scaffold match in Fort Worth. I enjoyed the feeling of power, but at the same time feared the results of what was about to go down. I had a sick feeling in my stomach, and my legs felt as if they could barely keep me up. A loud *bong* signaled the imminent arrival of the Undertaker, and the Pittsburgh Civic Arena rose in unison in anticipation of his eerie entrance. I had seen that entrance at least a hundred times, but it still often gave me the chills. I remembered the way I felt when his music played in the Market Square Arena in Indianapolis as we got ready to be "buried alive." Paul Bearer had looked at me that night and showed me his arm, which was lined with goose bumps. I had smiled and shown him mine, which was equally bumped. This was different, though. I was confident then. Quite frankly, I was scared as hell now.

A blue spotlight shone, and the Pittsburgh fans held up lighters as was the custom when the Phenom was about to walk the aisle. Theatrical smoke filled the entranceway, and then he was there, walking through the smoke like a six-foot, ten-inch John Wayne. "Damn, I wish I had an entrance like that," I thought as I took the opportunity to look down at the Spanish announcing team, who had the most hazardous jobs in the business. The height was incredible—sixteen feet down, but over twenty-two feet from my vantage point. I had been scared before, but it had always been a "good" scared. This was not good at all. I saw no chance for a happy ending. I walked back to face the aisle, and the 'Taker was about to ascend. "This is it," I thought. "Showtime!"

'Taker climbed the mesh and even with a broken foot, he did it a hell of a lot quicker than I did. He peeked his head up and I gave him a shot, which left him hanging by a hand. Another one had him dangling again, but he blocked a third and came firing back. This gave him time to get up, but when he did, I was there to meet with a chair across the back. *Thwack!* It was a good one. Thwack! again. Another solid shot. I took the 'Taker and started to walk with him. The crowd gasped as the cage sagged and almost gave way. We took another step, and the cage sagged even more beneath our 600 pounds. I attempted to suplex him on my chair, but he cut me off and had me headed toward the edge of the cell structure. He grabbed me by my shirt and trunks, and suddenly I was airborne—sixteen feet high and falling fast, as the Spanish announcers dove for cover. It was the scariest moment of my life, but almost a relief when I landed on the announcer table and felt it crumple beneath my weight. I had missed the monitors, which was my biggest concern, and landed about as perfectly as one could hope for, but the impact had spun me halfway underneath the security railing so that my legs were in the audience. My upper body, meanwhile, was covered with the debris of the table. "Good God almighty," J. R. had yelled upon the impact. "With God as my witness, he's been broken in half."

Actually, I felt surprisingly all right as I lay there among the wreckage. My shoulder was hurting, as it had become dislocated from the fall, and I felt a dull pain in my kidney area. Other than that, I felt okay. I actually had a feeling of inner peace about me as I was tended to by officials, Terry, and even Vince, who had broken character by being legitimately concerned. "At least," I mistakenly thought as I enjoyed the attention, "the worst is over." I was about as wrong in that assessment as a human being can possibly be.

The reaction of the crowd was phenomenal. I have never experienced or seen a reaction like it before, and I doubt I ever will again. For several days after the fact I would watch the video, and I never ceased to be amazed by the reaction. It was like a chain reaction as every single person in the place stood up, even though there was nothing left to see but a prone human body lying underneath what used to be a table. "Good God, he's been—" I'd hear, and I would rewind the tape. "Good God, he's—" Rewind. "Good God—" Rewind. The reaction lasted for minutes—changing from yells of disbelief to rhythmic hockey chants of "Un-Der-Tay-Ker," clap, clap, clap.

'Taker looked almost mythical as he stood perched atop the cage, especially when the cage began to ascend to make room for the stretcher, which was accompanied by a crew of emergency medical technicians. The technicians placed me on the gurney, and J. R. apologized for the short duration of the match. "How can you apologize for that?" countered Jerry "the King" Lawler, as I was rolled up the aisle. The Undertaker was already down the cage and on the floor when I rolled off the gurney and got to my feet. "Can you believe this?" said J. R. in disbelief as I attempted once again to scale the cage. "And he's got a smile on his face."

Climbing the cell with a dislocated shoulder was no easy task, but this time I wasn't scared or hesitant—I was running on adrenaline. I was literally flying in my heart, as the Undertaker and I both raced to the top. The crowd reaction was unbelievable. They had sworn the match was over. They had just seen the damnedest thing in the history of the business, and now we were going to give them more.

If I could change one thing about the match, it would be my next effort. A dynamic exchange of punches atop the sixteen-foot structure would have sent the crowd into a frenzy, but instead I stood there, sluglike, as the Undertaker battered me without any retaliation. He clubbed me once across my back with the chair and then unceremoniously dropped it on the cage. I really wish he would have put it somewhere else. Then he grabbed me around the neck for the "goozle," or chokeslam.

I didn't remember a thing about the next two minutes as I watched the tape in great pain the next day. It was the only time in fifteen years that I have been knocked out cold. I had been knocked goofy countless times. I'd seen stars and rainbows and black patches as a way of life for a long time, but this was the first time that a period of time elapsed and I wasn't aware of it. Like I said earlier, however, video and time have helped me to not only see but remember almost everything. Everything except what I was feeling as I broke through the mesh and crashed to the canvas.

Looking back on it now, it was both the worst chokeslam and the best chokeslam that I'd ever taken. The worst because it was the only time in my association with the Undertaker that I haven't gone high for the goozle. As matter of fact, one of my feet never left the cage. The best, because if I'd taken it correctly, I very well might have been dead. As it was, I landed hard on my back, my neck, and the back of my head. If I'd gone higher, I would have landed directly on my head and I probably wouldn't be here—at least not in control of my limbs. It was indeed a violent, brutal fall, made worse by the fact that I landed in one of the "old" Federation rings, which have little give. The new Federation rings obviously have some give to them—actually, too much give for my taste. But the old rings were torturous in their stiffness, and guys were getting hurt too often and careers were ending early. As a concession, new rings were made, and yes, they bounce—but to tell you the truth, the fans don't seem to care.

To make matters worse, the chair that was placed on the cage followed my body down and smashed into my face from a height of twelve and a half feet. The blow to my face would result in one and a half teeth being knocked out, a dislocated jaw, and a hole beneath my lip that I could stick my tongue through.

"Enough is enough! Would somebody stop the damn match!" J. R. yelled as the ring filled up immediately with medical personnel, office personnel, and Terry Funk. I get goose bumps thinking about it even now, as Ross's call was not part of a wrestling match, but a legitimate cry for my well-being. It was probably the most dramatic call I have ever heard in any sport. Purists can have "The Giants win the pennant, the Giants win the pennant," but I'll take "Would somebody stop the damn match!" any day.

François Petit and the EMTs tried to help me as I lay on my back with my arms outstretched and my legs sickly twisted to one side. I later asked the Undertaker what he thought when he looked down at me from atop the cell. His answer was chilling in its simplicity: "I thought you were dead."

480

I actually rolled over at one point, and when I regained consciousness, I saw a pair of sneakers in the ring. "That's strange," I thought as I tried to gain my bearings. What happened while I was out was actually a marvel of impromptu ingenuity and a credit to the business. As I mentioned in the first chapter, in a real sport, the action would surely stop if a player was knocked out. But no, we are not a real sport, and no, the action doesn't stop. Instead, all the guys tried to buy me some time in hopes that I would come to, in time.

The Undertaker held on to the cage, but free-fell several feet, and you could see him visibly wince and hobble from the pain in his broken foot. Unlike gymnast Kerri Strug, who vaulted to fame on the basis of one landing on a sprained ankle, there would be no White House visits for the Undertaker—only the recognition from the people who know what a tough bastard he really is. Terry Funk was there to meet him and willingly took a chokeslam to give me more time. TV showed multiple replays of my fall through the cage, and when they came back, I was on my feet, but just barely. "I don't believe it," said a stunned J. R. "He's either crazy or he's the toughest SOB I've ever seen."

"How is he still standing?" inquired the King, to which J. R. quickly answered, "I don't have a damn clue."

The Undertaker threw a punch, and I went down—slowly. It may have been the saddest bump ever taken, because there was no strength left in my body. I don't want to sound dramatic or pat myself on the back, but I really had been standing on sheer will alone. Now, as I lay in a heap, it seemed that even my will was gone. "Jack, let's go home," the 'Taker quietly said to me.

"No, no. I'm okay," I replied in a statement that had to be right up there with telling Vince I liked "Mason the Mutilator" as the biggest whopper I ever told.

He took hold of my hand and, in a trademark 'Taker move, ascended to the top rope. Usually, this move results in a massive flying forearm across the chest, but this was no usual match, and I forced the Dead Man off his perch, so that he crotched himself on the top rope. In reality, he was trying to buy me more time, as it was still readily apparent that while the lights might have been on, there was nobody home. Students of the wrestling game have talked about this match for the last year, and most of the accolades have been in my direction, as if Undertaker was just some innocent bystander who happened to be in this historic match. The truth is, without the Undertaker's poise and experience, the match would have been over right after the chokeslam through the cage. The Hell in a Cell is actually the closest example I've ever seen of one wrestler "bottle feeding" another, until I was able to take my first baby steps.

With the Undertaker temporarily incapacitated, the camera zoomed in on me to discover two rather odd findings. One, I appeared to be smiling, and two, there was something white sticking out of my nose. Actually, I wasn't smiling, but was trying to let the camera get a look at me sticking my tongue through the hole under my lip. Unfortunately, with all the blood and facial hair in the way, the audience didn't get to share that special moment. As far as the white thing sticking out of my nose, it was not, as first thought, a piece of table or even a white booger. It was actually half of a tooth. How it got there has been the subject of a great deal of speculation. The tooth almost seemed like the magic bullet in the JFK assassination. Did it go through the mouth and out the sinus cavity as some felt, or was it more likely to have just moved the two inches from mouth to nose, as I have come to believe? To add intrigue to the plot—just who picked up the whole tooth that was lying on the mat and had it sitting in a glass of milk when I returned from the ring?

The match continued for several minutes, and as the fog in my brain lifted, I realized that my right kidney area was in tremendous pain. A look at the videotape reveals that the kidney is where the initial contact with the table was made. As I mounted an offense, I followed up a piledriver on a chair with a leg drop that was given with that same chair placed over the 'Taker's face. When I landed, I was aware of the incredible pain. That kidney would actually hurt me for the next eight weeks.

After the leg drop, I stuck my opponent with a double arm DDT and bailed out of the ring to search for the "special surprise" that I had promised the fans. I returned with a large canvas bag. I reached into my special bag and withdrew it to reveal about a hundred silver tacks that sparkled in the light of the Pittsburgh Civic Arena (The Igloo). I scattered the tacks on the ground, and as the crowd stood in anticipation, I dumped the contents of the entire bag, revealing about 6,000 tacks in all. Since I introduced thumbtacks into the world of sports-entertainment three years earlier, they had begun making their presence in small independent shows, but this was the first national exposure that the pushpins had garnered.

The crowd was truly caught up in the scene as I hammered away at the Phenom, and he seemed primed to fall when I hit the ropes for the final blow. Instead he caught me around the neck in preparation for the goozle, but a knee to his midsection got me free. I hit the ropes again, but this time was met with a big foot to the face. I didn't go down, but bounced off the ropes again, only to be hoisted onto my opponent's shoulder for his "tombstone" piledriver. I slid down his back and hooked on my finishing hold. "Mandible claw, mandible claw," Jim Ross yelled. "No one holds more victories over the Undertaker than Mankind, and a good many of them came from that very hold."

The Undertaker went down to his knees, and I slid behind him while still employing the claw. In an instant, though, 'Taker had me on his back, in the exact same fashion that Vader had at *Halloween Havoc* in 1993. In this case, however, I wasn't looking for my career to end—just the match, in what I hoped would be a dramatic fashion. The crowd was buzzing in expectation of the only logical conclusion to this predicament. BAM. There it was. The audience groaned as I writhed in pain among the tacks. I was up slowly with several hundred tacks sticking into my flesh and clothes. I was hit with a chokeslam that sent me right back into the shiny, metallic resting place from which I'd just risen. "My God, what else can be done? What else will the Undertaker do to Mankind?" yelled J. R., and the question was answered immediately as a tombstone spelled the end of what countless fans have told me was the greatest match they ever saw.

"Mercifully, this is over," Lawler commented as the fans cheered in appreciation of the spectacle they had just seen.

For the next several minutes, highlights of the match were replayed as J. R. tried to sum up just what had taken place. "In twenty-five years, I have never witnessed anything even closely resembling this," he stated. "These two gave you everything in their bodies. They gave you their souls here tonight," and "This has been, perhaps, the most ungodly match that I think we will ever see."

I lay there for a few minutes, as Francois, the Funker, and the referees checked on my condition. The EMTs brought a stretcher into the ring, and as they loaded me on, the camera showed me whispering to referee Mike Chioda. "Was I already on a stretcher once tonight?" I asked Chioda, in a conversation I had no recollection of—even after he reminded me the next day.

"Yes, Jack, you were," was Chioda's reply.

"Then can you help me up, Mike. I don't want to be on a stretcher twice in one night."

With the assistance of Chioda and Terry Funk, I was then helped to the back, as a chorus of "Foley, Foley" made its way to my one and a half ears. J. R. then summed it up as I staggered through the curtain by saying, "How anyone could not admire the effort of this man, Mankind, Mick Foley, is beyond me."

When I walked through the curtain, I was met by a sound of applause from the remaining wrestlers and a hug from Vince McMahon. Despite recent media portrayals of Vince, he was genuinely concerned with my well-being. I responded by talking way too much, way too fast, and way too intelligently for a guy who'd just been through hell. He had to have known that I was messed up. It was almost like a drunk driver who tries so hard to act sober that he gives himself away.

My in-ring conversation with Mike Chioda was not the only one I failed to recollect. Several days after the match, I asked the Undertaker if I had spoken to him afterward. He laughed as he recalled our discussion. "Did I use thumbtacks out there?" is apparently what I had come out with.

He looked at me still covered with the damn things and said, "Yes, you did, Jack, yes you did."

"Oh, good," I reportedly said, and walked away.

My evening wasn't quite over yet, though. Francois put my shoulder back in its socket, helped me gain my bearings, and I limped out to play a part in the finish of the Kane vs. Austin match. When I came back through the curtain, I was led to a spare room by Dr. Frank Romascavage who, without the aid of a local anesthetic, put fourteen stitches below my lip. Vince observed the whole process while a Federation cameraman caught the magic moment on film. Afterward, Vince walked with me to my dressing room. "Mick, I want you to know how much we appreciate everything you've done for this company," he said sincerely, as I nodded blankly. "But please, promise me that I'll never see you do anything like it ever again."

It was now an hour after the conclusion of the saga, and I had forgotten one very important detail—my traditional post-match call to

Colette. Even if I had remembered, it would have been impossible to call, as I had neglected to pay my phone bill and our line had been disconnected. She had actually packed up the kids, who had cried themselves to sleep, and taken them to our gym to await some word of my condition. I was just about to be taken to the hospital when Dave Hebner stopped me. "Cactus, your wife beeped me, and I just got off the phone with her. She's very upset and she wants you to call her at the gym." I was not quite ready for our conversation.

"You can't do this to us, Mickey," she cried—and when I say cried, I do mean cried. "Your children love you and you can't do this to them. I love you and you can't do this to me. Please. Promise me you won't do this anymore." I hadn't apologized so much since I took Noelle on the *Back to the Future* ride at Universal Studios and she thought the dinosaur had really swallowed us. For a long time, the trauma that this match caused my wife had me on the brink of retiring, and Hell in a Cell is still a sensitive subject at home. I watched the match today in preparation for writing about it, and it still, a year after the fact, made Colette cry. My children, however, now think the match is "cool."

For a long time, however, Dewey and Noelle were haunted by the match—especially Noelle. Historically, many wrestlers have not "smartened up" their kids and have led them to believe that Dad is fighting for his life every night. From what I have seen of such cases, such psychology leads to nothing but problems, as children are petrified for their dad, only to later learn that he was a "liar" and a "phony." In a few extreme examples, such deceit has led to long-term estrangement of father and children.

I approached the situation from an entirely different perspective. I told my kids that I never got hurt and that Daddy was simply "playing." Hell in a Cell was the night that my kids learned that Big Daddy-O was a big liar, and as a result, they thought I was getting hurt all the time. For months I would talk to my daughter on the phone and she would say, "Good luck, don't get hurt," to which I would soothingly say, "Don't worry, honey, I won't."

Inevitably, I would hear her little voice a moment later as it sadly said, "I know you're going to get hurt."

I went to the hospital after my phone call with my tooth in its cup of milk. This is done to keep the tooth vital. I have no idea how. After four hours, I emerged with my missing tooth shoved back into its hole and a plethora of dental wires to support it. I hadn't even been aware enough to ask about several of the other body parts that hurt, in particular my kidney, which was throbbing with each step. I stumbled into the Red Roof Inn about 3 A.M. and Al Snow was sensitive enough to inquire about my condition without once using the word "hammer" or any imaginative way of describing his penis. Hell, he probably did, but I was just too out of it to notice.

I generally pride myself on how much punishment I can take without the aid of pain medication. For example, I was given a whole bottle of pain pills following my knee surgery and only took one pill in four days. I will admit, however, to taking so much medication after Hell in a Cell that I was in a stupor for the next two days. I looked like a cross between Popeye Doyle when he was strung out on smack in *The French Connection II*, and an audience after sitting through an Al Snow match.

When I got to the television taping the next day, Francois worked on my poor body for hours while I continually asked female wrestler Luna Vachon to check on the Pay-Per-View replay in the cafeteria. I stumbled into the cafeteria and took a seat. As I mentioned earlier, much of what I was seeing was new to me, and I was shaking with emotion while I watched it, despite my chemically induced condition. When the match ended, I was surprised to see the entire cafeteria, which was filled with the boys, give me a standing ovation. I have never before or since seen a videotape get a standing ovation. It felt very good.

Many people point to *King of the Ring* as the match that catapulted my career to the top. Actually, I found this not to be the case. To me the match with the Undertaker is kind of like the famous Willie Mays catch in the World Series over thirty years ago, in that it has grown in legend. A review of the cell match shows my entrance receiving almost no reaction, and even the chants of "Foley, Foley" in Pittsburgh were depressingly slight. In reality, I found my career to be somewhat sluggish after the famous showdown, with three specific moments sticking out as low points in my career.

Two weeks after the cell match, I was given interview time to hype an Undertaker rematch on the Federation's new *Sunday Night Heat* television show on the USA network. I went out with mike in hand, and in my old ECW fashion tried to make the fans feel what it was like to have my career nearly end. Within forty-eight hours, I had gone from my daughter kissing me on the cheek at Santa's Village "because you're a good man," to having my tooth sticking out of my nose. What I got from the crowd was apathy and disrespect. As I poured out my heart, fans were yelling obscenities and filling the ring with garbage. It was the first time that I clearly felt that the new Federation "attitude" era had passed me by. Cool guys were in—Mick Foley was out. Catchphrases were in—interviews that required an audience to think were out.

I came back to the dressing room, and I was livid. Paul Bearer was the first one to come in after me, and as such, he caught the brunt of my anger. "Damnit, Paul, I don't know why I'm doing this anymore. These people don't give a fuck unless it's a catchy phrase or a set of tits."

Uncle Paul tried to calm me down. "Mommy," he said (Paul had been calling me Mommy ever since a short-lived teaming when I was hooked up with Goldust as a Mommy figure), "it's not you. It's the end of a long night, and they're tired."

I wasn't buying it. "They're not tired. They're assholes, Purse. And you know what—I'm an asshole, too, for even giving a damn." A long time passed before I felt good about performing again.

About a week after the interview incident, I suffered an even greater indignity, this time at the hands of Rena Mero. We were both brought in to Fall River, Massachusetts, for a fund-raiser, and set up at separate tables for autographs. I guess a blind man can see where this one is heading. After a thirty-minute rush of autograph seekers, I sat in silence, while a parade of horny teenagers paraded past me and plopped down their ten bucks for Rena's autograph and a peek at her cleavage. I was literally sick to my stomach. My body still ached from the Hell in a Cell, which the Fall River fans were acknowledging as the greatest match they had ever seen, while they walked past with the Rena photos in hand. I guess to add to my previous list, big boobs were in and dedication, sacrifice, and fourteen years of blood, sweat, and tears were out.

My third low point reared its ugly head right after our July Pay-Per-View, in which Austin and the Undertaker had teamed to defeat Kane and me. It hadn't been a great match, but it was certainly very good. Afterward, I was scheduled to do an autograph session with Owen Hart at the hotel across the street from the San Jose arena. I arrived at the hotel and was greeted by a line about 400 people long.

When the session started, I went right to work. I knew I couldn't personalize the pictures or even talk to the fans much, as we would be hard-pressed to satisfy the voracious appetite of the fans. Ten minutes later, the line did more than just slow down, it stopped. "What's going on?" I asked Owen. "There's still hundreds of people in line."

Owen laughed, as he was privy to information that was unknown to me. "Jack, they're here to see Austin and Shamrock at eleven. Our line is done."

I felt my heart drop down to somewhere in the vicinity of my left ball. "You mean we have to wait here until then?" Owen seemed to take cruel pleasure in seeing my feelings shattered as he chuckled, "I hope you brought a book."

These were the longest two hours of my life. Every once in a while, a straggler would give in and get a picture, and in contrast to the quick Mankind signature the earlier fans had gotten, these lucky few were able to get my life story on their photo. "Dear Johnny," a typical one would start, "it matters not how narrow the gate, nor how charged with punishment the scroll, I am the captain of my fate and the master of my soul. Have a nice day. Your friend, Mankind. Two-time Tag Team Champion."

I really had doubts about my future. I had always been able to adapt to changing elements, but the wrestling phenomenon had gotten so big, so fast, that a guy like me had gotten trampled in the dust. In the same way that most kids would rather scarf down a couple of greasy fast food burgers instead of enjoying an aged and seasoned filet mignon, the new breed of fan wanted satisfaction and wanted it now. Our show was tearing up the Nielsens to the point that a great deal of our audience was completely new to the world of sports entertainment. They had no knowledge of my feuds with Abdullah the Butcher or Eddie Gilbert, and in truth, only half of them had even seen my interviews with Jim Ross. Actually, only a year had passed since those interviews, but I doubted that our new fans would even have the patience to sit through those, unless of course I showed a little cleavage. I decided to take a gamble.

As I mentioned earlier, the best gimmicks in wrestling are actually extensions of a real-life personality. I was feeling a lot like a battered and beaten man that time had left behind and was confused because of it. I decided to portray myself as a battered and beaten man that time had left behind and was confused because of it. I knew for a fact that many of our fans were not actually "cool." I gambled that they would get into a character that likewise was not. I had already begun wearing a torn-up collared shirt and tie to the ring, and now I had my reason. The shirt and tie would represent my last remaining connection to the corporate world that had shunned me. In a sense, the outfit was my connection to Vince McMahon, who was the company's hottest heel, and was the perfect guy to play off of.

I went into *Summerslam* in Madison Square Garden as a co-holder of the tag team belts with Kane. We were the bad guys going up against the now beloved New Age Outlaws, but I was starting to get little lines and sight gags in, and the fans were slowly but surely starting to catch on. The Kane–Mankind team was falling apart as well. It had been revealed through an intricate story line that Kane and the Undertaker were actually in cahoots. With the memory of *King of the Ring* still fresh in my mind, the cahoots thing hadn't sat too well with me, and Kane and I had started a feud of our own, even though we held the tag belts. As a result, Kane never showed up for the match, leaving me to valiantly take on the Outlaws, until Kane popped out of the Dumpster and "smashed" my skull with a sledgehammer. Two weeks later, I showed up with a bruised face, a heavily wrapped hand, and an announcement that "I'd been lucky for two reasons. One, I was able to block the blow with my hand, and two, I really didn't look all that good to begin with."

September 13, 1998, was a fateful day in my career. I did something on that day that a few years (or even one year earlier) I would have thought impossible. I politely turned down a chance to return full-time as Cactus Jack, and pleaded with Vince Russo to leave me as Mankind. "Why?" Russo wanted to know. "I thought we were doing you a favor."

"I know, I know, and I appreciate it," I answered back. This was a big moment, and I knew it, so I didn't want to regret anything later. "It's just that I think I can do everything you have planned for Cactus as Mankind, and I really feel that Mankind is just getting rolling."

Russo laughed. "Well, Vince will be happy," he said. "He's always liked Mankind best; he just thought you'd be happier as Cactus."

"You know, up until a week ago, I would have agreed," I responded. "But I'm starting to get a little soft spot in my heart for Mankind. By the way, I had an idea."

"What is it?" Russo wanted to know.

"Well, you know how all the babyfaces hate Vince?" Russo nodded his head in agreement. "Well, what if I were the one guy who liked Vince, and it drove him crazy? I think it would be great."

Russo smiled a genuine smile and told me, "I'll run it by Vince. I think he'll like it."

As it turned out, Vince did indeed like it, and thus began our strange, pseudo father–son relationship that some felt was meant to mock Brett Hart, but in reality was just meant to be fun. At the TV tapings in San Jose, the short-lived team of Mankind, The Rock, and Ken Shamrock was wreaking havoc on Vince's corporation until Vince pulled the gullible Mankind aside to talk some sense into him. "Mick, I don't want your new friends to get hurt, and I know you don't either," Vince gently told me with his arm around my shoulder. "So maybe the best thing you can do is take Shamrock and The Rock and just convince them to leave. Okay, Mick. Now, go ahead. Get your friends and just leave."

I thought over Vince's proposition, but saw one small problem with it. "Okay, Vince," I replied. "But I don't drive, and I need a ride."

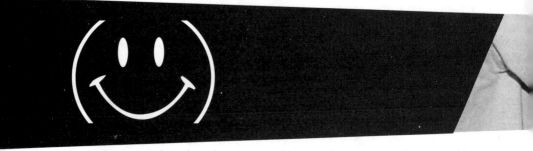

Vince started to laugh. "I'm sorry, Mick, you caught me offguard with that." He smiled as the cameras stopped rolling.

"Sorry, Vince," I apologized "It just came out."

Vince disregarded my apology. "No, no, that's great. As a matter of fact, don't tell me what you're going to say anymore. I'll just react to it."

That set the tone for the entire Mankind–McMahon sequence of events, with Mankind and Vince ad-libbing their way through their unique love/hate relationship. Mankind loved Vince and Vince hated Mankind.

At the next set of tapings, which would turn out to be my biggest merchandising coup, Vince Russo came running up to me in the dressing room of the Joe Louis Arena in Detroit. "Vince just hurt his ankle. They're putting him on a stretcher now." He was practically hyperventilating. "He wants you to be there, and he doesn't want to know what you are going to do. Surprise him." Hell, I didn't even know what to do, as I ran as fast as my concrete-battered body would carry me. Along the way, I picked up a few props.

When I got to Vince, he was just about to be loaded into the ambulance. His gang of stooges were all around him. Amid the concern and the corporate brown-nosing, a hairy arm came into view, cradling a

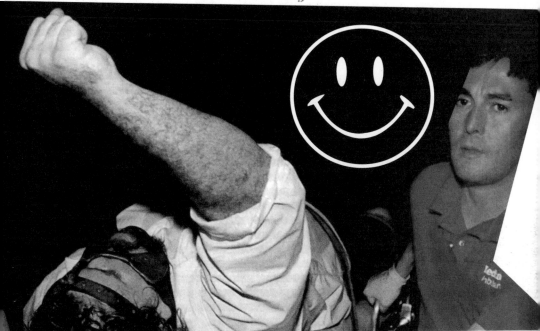

7–Eleven Big Gulp. I pushed the massive cup toward Vince's face, and his expression was priceless. The Gulp disappeared, but then reappeared a moment later, as I diligently tried to get some frosty refreshment into Mr. McMahon's gullet. "Would you get him out of here!" McMahon screamed, and momentarily Mankind was gone. A moment later, that same hairy arm was back, this time holding small pieces of candy. As Vince was being loaded into the ambulance, the arm kept trying to slip the candies into Vince's pocket. Again his face was classic. Vince has a face that somehow lets him convey multiple emotions at once. In this case, it was disgust, pain, and even a little bit of pity. It seemed that I had found a formula that worked. I would kill him with kindness.

The next day in East Lansing, Michigan, Russo informed me that I would go visit Vince in the hospital. He wanted me to "cheer" him up, but again, I was told that Vince didn't want to know the specifics.

Within an hour, I had lined up a veritable smorgasbord of hokey gifts and entertainment. I was loaded to the hilt with "Get Well Soon" balloons, an inflated rubber glove, a cheesy heart-shaped box of chocolates, and a clown named Yurple with floppy purple shoes who specialized in balloon animals. Even with all the top-flight entertainment, I sensed that something was missing. I needed just one more special trick to really brighten Vince's day. In a decision that would both help and haunt me, I grabbed Al Snow.

"Al, I've got a problem," I said. "I'm going to visit Vince in the hospital, and I've got a bunch of great gimmicks I'm bringing with me, but I feel like I need maybe one more. What's something really stupid that I can bring with me that Vince will hate?" Al thought it over inside that pea-size brain of his and quickly replied, "How about a sock puppet?"

Happy now, Al? Are you? Happy, happy, happy? Well, I certainly hope so. Man, it hurts to admit it, but yes, Al Snow did think of Mr. Socko. Well, I guess we're even now, aren't we Al, seeing as how I invented your whole "head" gimmick? The only difference is, without Mr. Socko, I'd still be a fairly popular wrestler—without my "head" idea, Al would be doing my yardwork. "Would you like me to finish planting those seeds, Mr. Foley?" "No, no, that's all right Al, but I have some special seed of my own that I'll be planting in a minute." Ho, ho, ho. Oh, ho, ho, ho. Oh boy, oh that's good. (Fake laugh works every time.)

The scenario was simple—Mr. McMahon was at an undisclosed hospital and was terrified that Stone Cold Steve Austin was going to find him. Although only the recipient of a bruised ankle bone, Vince was nonetheless bedridden with a heart monitor and an oxygen tube hooked up to him. He was being the ultimate cranky patient.

"Mr. McMahon, you've got a visitor," a cheery nurse informed the miserable millionaire.

Immediately, Vince's heart rate monitor started beeping faster. "Him," yelled Vince. "It's him. Why did you let him in here?"

The nurse remained rosy as she informed him, "He was awful big, and he was real insistent on seeing you, and he threatened to beat up the orderlies if we didn't let him in."

The door opened, and Vince prepared himself for the worst. Instead, an inflated surgical glove peeked its way inside the door with a big happy face on it. "Turn that frown upside down," I said in my best goofy voice before bursting through the door. Vince's expressive face now showed both anger and relief as I approached him bearing gifts. I handed him the balloons, which were met with disinterest, and then presented him with the delicious chocolate morsels as I kidded my old, grouchy boss, "Come on, I know Vinnie's got a sweet tooth."

Vince actually opened the heart-shaped box and reacted with revulsion when he saw the contents. "These chocolates are half-eaten," he mumbled in disbelief.

"I know, I know, I got a little bored on the way over here," I replied. "But wait till you see what I've got for you next. A little female entertainment, and I think you know what I mean. Vince, she does a trick with a dog that you won't believe." Vince's face actually cracked a tiny little smile in anticipation of the hot act he was about to witness, when I announced my special guest. "Ladies and gentlemen, say hello to . . . Yurple." Then I followed up the intro with the same weak verbal rendition of the Johnny Carson theme that my wife hates so much. "Rin din di di di di, di, diddly, di dah."

With that, Yurple entered the room and with her clown feet, purple hair, whiteface, and balloon animals, was threatening to steal the show. This woman was a professional, and years of children's birthday parties had honed her stage presence to the point that she was on the verge of stealing all my Monday night glory. I had heard a rumor that Burt Ward used to steal Adam West's glory on the old *Batman* series in much the same way. "Damnit," I thought, as if I were George Clooney on *ER*, "I'm losing him!"

Quickly, while Yurple was in the midst of a complex canine creation, I saw that the cameraman's back was to me, and I made my move. In a flash I pulled out Mr. Socko, got down on my belly, and combat-crawled underneath the bed like a valiant Marine in *The Sands of Iwo Jima*. "What the hell was that?" Vince shouted as he felt the rustling beneath him. "What, what the—"

All of a sudden, my hand and wrist were in the air, with a dirty sweat sock over them. The face was hand drawn and was either beautiful in its simplicity or simply ugly, depending on how you look at it. The camera clearly showed my face, but that didn't stop me from beginning the worst high-pitched ventriloquist act in the history of sports entertainment. "Hi, I'm Mr. Socko, and I've come to save the day. I hear you have a boo-boo, and Mr. Socko is going to kiss it and make it feel better."

"No, no," Vince interjected, "don't kiss the boo-boo!" This was great. I had a world-famous millionaire genius for a boss, and thus far I had both hit him so hard with a chair that his dental work had flown off and gotten him to say, "No, no, don't kiss the boo-boo" on national television.

Unfortunately for Vince, I overextended my reach and ended up lying on him, and as a result, instead of kissing the boo-boo, I had inadvertently hurt the boo-boo. Mr. McMahon had seen enough. "Please," he implored us, "please just take your things and go." When we were a little slow in leaving, he tried a more direct approach instead. "Dammit! Leave! Leave!" he bellowed, and sent us on our way amid a flurry of balloons and chocolate wrappers. After we left, the camera zoomed in on the beleaguered and outraged McMahon as he sarcastically repeated the two magic words, "Mr. Socko."

The next day, many of the wrestlers were ribbing me about Mr. Socko, but I really did not think too much about it. I thought it had been funny, but not any funnier than some of the other things we'd been doing. Actually, Austin was Mr. Socko's biggest fan. He had seen the hospital shenanigans on a television monitor while preparing for a later bedside attack in which he shocked Vince with a cardiac fibrillator, and "violated" him with an enema tube. He thought it was great. I wasn't so willing to accept his adulation because I truly believed he was joking around with me. But throughout the day, he kept mentioning Mr. Socko, so I finally asked him if he was serious. "Jack, I'm not bullshitting you," he replied with typical Austin subtlety. "That was one of the funniest damn things I've ever seen."

Later, Russo came running over. It seems that the poor guy is always running. It's just my theory, but I don't think that Russo was ever the same after the Sachem–Ward Melville bleacher clearing basketball brawl back in 1979. "Did you bring Mr. Socko," he gasped, with an urgency that was reminiscent of Mike Brady searching for the missing blueprints during the King's Island episode.

"Yeah," I calmly answered, "but why?"

"Cactus, I'm not kidding ya," he began in his out-of-breath Brooklynese/Long Island–ese, "there must be at least a hundred Mr. Socko signs!"

Sure enough, Mr. Sockomania was running wild. Not only were there signs hailing the new cotton hero, but when I got ready to square off with Mark Henry, a loud "Socko, Socko" chant echoed in the arena. Henry (this was before he was known as "Sexual Chocolate") began working on my left ankle, as the "Socko" chant grew louder. Out of nowhere, I dazed the world's strongest man and started to untie my shoe to "reduce the swelling" as the announcers speculated. But no, it was not medical attention, but my trusty sidekick that I was seeking. As Henry stumbled to his feet, I put the filthy sock on my right hand. Mr. Socko seemed almost to be smiling. Henry turned around and I jammed the offensive athletic apparel into his mouth. "Ding, ding, ding." We had a winner. It was the birth of the "Socko claw," but more importantly, the birth of a star. "Mr. F'ing Socko."

September and October were great months for me. I had gotten past my creative slump, and my fears of wrestling passing me by no longer seemed valid. I had been in a great three-way cage match with Shamrock and The Rock in September, and had followed it up with a pretty good October Pay-Per-View with Shamrock. I was personally proud of it because it involved more wrestling and working on an individual body part than I had done in a long time. I had also continued to wreak havoc on Mr. McMahon's mind with my caring ways, including a story line where I kept Vince company while a heavily armed and recently unemployed Austin stalked him.

"Why don't you just rehire him?" I asked my wheelchair-bound boss. "The fans love him. He's got lots of fire and pizzazz, and he makes for some exciting television."

Vince would not be deterred. "You don't understand, Mick, it's not that simple. This is about principle."

"Vince, I'll be honest with you," I addressed the boss. "I really admire your moral fortitude. Come on, let's play some games!"

The show broke for a commercial and when it came back, the fans were treated to an opening shot of my big ass filling their television screen. As the camera panned back, I was revealed to be engaged in a game of solitary Twister, which despite my encouragement, I couldn't get Vince to join in on. Finally, I succumbed to the intensity of the game, and toppled over onto the curmudgeonly Vince. "Get out, dammit! Get out!" he bellowed, even though my ouster would eliminate his only line of defense from Austin.

"Hey man, stop being a party pooper," I snarled, in typical tough-guy rhetoric.

Most of all, as October came to a close, I had Mr. Socko. With him, a bad match was good, and a good match was great. I had taken to tucking him inside my tights, and making an elaborate ritual of pantomime before actually pulling him out. In some ways, pulling the floppy cotton sock out of my tights was not all that new. To tell the truth, I had been pulling a limp, white object out of my pants for years—I'd just never gotten cheered for it.

November 1 was a historic night in Houston, and not just because we were in the same building that Ahmed Johnson had refused to put Kurrgan over in. No, this was the building in which my kindness and understanding finally won Vince over. Vince had just gone through an on-air "falling out" with his son Shane, and was no doubt feeling a little melancholy about life. Maybe he was thinking about the hospital or Twister, or maybe he was just sensitive, but whatever the case, he summoned me into his office. In the office, he bestowed upon me a sacred gift, which in actuality was a broken, glued-together old belt. "Mick, this is yours." He smiled. "You've earned it; this is the new hardcore championship belt."

I was overcome with emotion. "I'll be honest with you, Vince," I tearfully said. "I love it."

Vince looked at me and it was obvious that he had something on his mind. "You know, Mick," he began, with about as much sincerity as the Grinch addressing Cindy Lou Who, who was no more than two, "I lost a son tonight, but in some ways, I think I've gained one too." Vince smiled at me as the stooges wheeled him away.

Just as he was about to exit the room, I responded to his touching claim with an equally touching "Gee, thanks . . . DAD." At the sound of "Dad," Vince's face literally looked as if he'd just swigged down a glass of sour milk. I even got the Adam's apple to bob, as if he were actually having trouble swallowing what I'd just told him.

The next night, I was officially welcomed upon my entrance by Vince's stooges, and became Vince's "boy." *The Survivor Series* was coming up at the end of November and all indicators pointed to the possibility that Vince was hand-picking me to be his "corporate champion" and tear right through the *Survivor* championship tournament. First, however, I had to look the part. Borrowing more than slightly from the *Hardcore Christmas* Cactus and the Kiss-Ass Dude, I was given a complete makeover. My hair was shortened by seven inches, I was completely shaved (I still wore the mask), I was given a manicure and pedicure, and I began wrestling in a tuxedo.

In that very tuxedo, I engaged Ken Shamrock in an excellent battle for my Hardcore Championship belt. The belt actually went on to become a coveted possession, to the point that I believe it means more than any strap in the company, save the big one—the World Wrestling Federation Championship. Our match spilled up onto the ramp where "Dad" was watching with the stooges and the corporate bodyguard, the Big Boss Man. Behind my back, the Boss Man helped me gain the win, and I was elated to learn of my victory when Patterson and Brisco handed me the belt. I looked for Vince, and ad-libbed a big hug. When I got back to the dressing room, Al Snow informed me, "You should have seen Vince's face when you hugged him. It was hilarious." Sure enough, when I saw the tape of it, I had to laugh, Vince was great. Within three seconds of the hug, Vince's face had run a gamut of emotions from disgust, to acceptance, to fake happiness, to indifference. Though he was supposed to be like a father to him, "Dad" didn't seem to care for Mankind all that much. Heading into the *Survivor Series*, the fish were smelling just a little bit in Denmark.

To win the title, I would have to wrestle and win four matches. Despite promising myself that I would come into this tournament in top shape, I was uneasy about my conditioning for such a big Pay-Per-View. My first-round opponent was a "mystery opponent" that many in attendance thought would be Shawn Michaels. Shawn had retired from active competition eight months earlier and had only sparingly been heard from since. I was brought out to the ring first, and while inside the squared circle I heard Vince read off an incredible introduction before announcing "the man, the myth," Duane Gill. Out came Gill, who would later have a small but fun run as "Gillberg." Gill acted overjoyed at just seeing his visage on the overhead screen as he lost match after match to former Federation stars, and was startled by his own pyro. The match was over in twenty seconds, and I prepared for my next matchup. Obviously, Vince was going to make everything as simple as possible for his "corporate champ."

Al Snow was next, and he did the J-O-B on the PPV. Vince had masterminded a plot that included stealing Mr. Socko and placing him around Al Snow's "head." Now usually I'm a big fan of the Federation story lines, but this one was a little weak. For one thing, Mr. Socko was actually several different Sockos, as I usually threw my Socko to the crowd after a match. Apparently this sock was special, as I mourned its loss. For his part, Al looked like a complete moron for parading around with a Mr. Socko headband stapled to his "head." When I saw the missing Socko, I went ballistic and, as usual, Al played Winger to my Hulka, as I scored the victory.

My semifinal opponent was Stone Cold, and we picked up right where we left off and tore the Kiel Center in St. Louis apart. A referee went down, and as Austin hit me with the stunner, babyface referee Shane McMahon slid in to make the count. One, two, and nothing. Steve looked at Shane and the younger McMahon flipped him off, revealing himself to be a no-good SOB just like his dad. At this point, I was waiting for the Big Boss Man to make his presence felt, but he was nowhere to be found. He reminded me of the reindeer in the story my mom used to read me, who fell asleep in a snow bank and missed out on the "Happiest Christmas of All." Trust me, though, there was nothing happy about the finish of this match, even if I did emerge the victor. My means of victory was so weak that it never aired in any form on World Wrestling Federation programming. Actually, compared to this, my "Lost in Cleveland" vignettes didn't look too bad.

The final match of the tournament, with the Federation title hanging in the balance, pitted me against The Rock. By virtue of his charisma, good looks, endless stream of catch phrases, and two big moves, The Rock was riding a huge wave of momentum and popularity into the finals. One of the two moves, the "people's elbow," was the most ludicrous thing I'd ever seen in any form of entertainment, but its effect on a crowd was phenomenal. Momentum and popularity aside, I had to be considered the heavy favorite going in, due to my close relationship with Dad.

I had only one problem. I really had no clue what I was going to do in this huge main event. I was physically exhausted and mentally drained. For a wrestler with only two years' experience, The Rock had incredible poise in the ring, but he too looked worn and confused. We locked up, and I drew a blank. Another lockup and another blank. I was worried as hell. Within a minute, I had The Rock on the mat with a rear chinlock—a sure sign that the match was sailing down the tubes. Our match was literally dying, and as the senior member in the ring, I would be held to blame.

Somehow, we turned it around. The momentum began to grow and we turned up the volume to the point that it was a very good match. The Rock was making a comeback and had things going his way until I caught him charging at me and backdropped him over the ropes. As The Rock struggled to his feet, I climbed to the second turnbuckle outside the ring, as I had done many times before. This time, however, there was nobody home, and I crashed hard into the Spanish announcer team table with my right knee absorbing the impact. Because I had hit the edge, the table didn't break like it normally did. Instead, it put up a hell of a fight before crumpling to the ground. I lay on the ground and tried to will myself back into the ring. The pain was intense, as I had dislocated my kneecap and torn my medial meniscus. The injury would eventually put me on the operating table six months later. Regardless of the pain, I had a match to finish. I rolled into the ring, and saw The Rock waiting for a big clothesline. I ducked it, and instead delivered my double arm DDT. I went for the cover. One, two, and . . . ooh, The Rock just kicked out, but it was real close. I lifted up my button-down shirt that I'd bought at Kmart for $12.50, but would later sell for $200. The fans knew what was coming next, and despite the fact that they disliked Vince's new stooge, let out a mighty roar. The Rock turned around and I clamped on the hold. He struggled mightily, but managed to counter with his second big move, the Rock Bottom. The Rock was groggy, but placed an arm over my chest. The referee dove down. One, two, and . . . I just kicked out, about as close as a count could get. The Rock stood up. He glared at the St. Louis crowd, and the place just erupted. The Rock threw off the elbow pad, signaled for the move, and then went about completing the single worst move ever created in sports-entertainment. *Boom.* People's elbow. The place exploded. This had to be it. One, two, . . . I just barely kicked out, and a big "ooh" echoed throughout the arena.

It was about time for things to get screwy. The Rock looked at Vince and gave him the "people's eyebrow," the same facial gesture that Lee Majors had used so well throughout his career. Vince nodded and shot his version of the arched brow back. The Rock then calmly stepped between my legs, and crossed them with my right foot hooked between his biceps and armpit. He turned me over, and Vince frantically called for the bell. I had not been in the sharpshooter for more than two seconds and the match was over.

Vince hugged The Rock, and proclaimed him the new "corporate champion." In a complete reworking of Brett Hart's *Survivor Series* screw-job ending, I had now been "screwed." Somehow, Vince had managed to take last year's real-life situation and turn it into the most creative finish of the year.

Immediately, The Rock became the most hated man in the company and my popularity took off. I was entering into the territory that only Austin had previously had access to. I was about to get my hands on the McMahons. Over the course of the next several weeks, I wreaked havoc on Vince, Shane, and the corporate stooges. I beat up Vince in a parking lot and destroyed Patterson and Brisco in a boiler room. I had the honor of giving Shane a beating in his first professional match, which was very good for what it was. With Shane in trouble, the stooges ran in for the save, but I was able to cut them off and caught Brisco with the Socko claw. Patterson came running as well, and I had a claw waiting for him too. No, it was not a mandible claw, but instead the dreaded ball claw that I had once had used against me in the famous "backyard match" at Danny Zucker's house. My parents were visiting for the holidays, and my dad thought the claw and Patterson's subsequent selling of it was the funniest thing he'd ever seen. "Play that back again," he howled, and as a result, we got to see poor Pat tap dancing in terror as I traumatized his two testes half a dozen times. "Show it again, Dad, show it again," my kids kept saying, as we laughed as a family at the gonadal goings-on. It was a perfect example of wrestling bringing a family together.

The next morning, I was awakened by the sounds of my children laughing. They were watching that same tape over and over again. I thought so much of it that I even addressed it the following Monday in Albany, New York. "Last week was a big week for me," I informed the raucous *Raw* contingent. "It was the first time that I'd ever touched another man's testicles, and I've got to admit that, in a rugged, manly type of way, I kind of enjoyed it." Fortunately, footage of the previous week's scrotal assault was aired while I was speaking in order to clue fans in on what the hell I was talking about. Otherwise, they might have thought that I was referring to a secret camping trip or something.

The stage was set for Worcester, Massachusetts, the next evening. We had been defeating WCW in impressive fashion, but they had been promoting a huge title match for their Georgia Dome *Nitro*, with which *Raw* would be competing. We decided to give them a title match of our own.

The Royal Rumble was set to be our next Pay-Per-View at the end of January. Triple H and I were set to wrestle in a *Rumble* qualifying match, with Shane McMahon as the special guest referee. The match was forgettable except for Shane's ridiculously fast count that spelled defeat for Mankind. Helmsley said that he hated to win like that, but with a spot in the *Rumble* at stake, he'd take a win any way he could get it. "Here's a late Christmas present, Mick," he muttered as he booted the junior McMahon and proceeded to pedigree him into mat.

Now I had a tremendous task in front of me. I needed to put a painful submission hold on Shane, but it needed to be visually exciting. A choke old or front facelock wouldn't do. To add pressure to the situation, I also needed to perform this painful hold while talking into a microphone, so I needed one hand free. In a flash I remembered my amateur career, and my propensity for leg wrestling that was unusual for a big man. I remembered the hold that used to make my friend Allen Bloomberg cry and even made future *King of Queens* star Kevin James suffer in the hot basement wrestling room at Ward Melville High. (Yes, he really was on the team with me.) Seconds later, I had Shane hooked in a pretty impressive guillotine body ride, which is more or less a lying abdominal stretch. "This is a move that Jim McGonigle taught me at Ward Melville," I sneered over the mike while Shane whimpered beneath me. It turned out that Coach McGonigle, who had beaten leukemia when I was in grade school and had coached both me and my brother in high school, became more well known from that one comment than he had from twenty years of diligent coaching.

With Shane at my mercy, I called out, "Vince, I want a title shot, and I want it tonight," while Shane moaned in displeasure. "Give it to me, or I'll break his goddamn shoulder."

I then put the mike to Shane's face so that he could say a few words. "Oww, oww, oww," was all he could manage. With his own flesh and blood in peril, Vince almost immediately gave The Rock up, and agreed to the big showdown. The Rock was displeased, but the crowd was not, as they prepped for an epic battle.

I almost didn't make the epic. I decided to take off through the people as I'd seen so many wrestlers do before. I almost didn't get out in one piece. I had neglected to tell security of my grand exit scheme, and as a result, there was no one to block the fans from reaching out and touching me. And slapping me. And tearing off my clothes. For anyone who wondered why I showed up for battle with a shredded garment, now you know. What scared me is that these people liked me and they nearly killed me. If they hadn't, I might have had to no-show my date with destiny.

I got back to the dressing room with almost no time to prepare. I knew Vince's Corporation and DX, who had kind of taken me in as their "little buddy," would be surrounding the ring. I wanted to make sure they didn't fight until the time was right. I had seen way too many similar situations end up in disaster because of overzealous ringside onlookers and I wanted to make sure that momentous occasion didn't suffer a similar fate. I barely had even a chance to wish The Rock luck when his music played. Although the situations were completely different, I felt just like I had before my *King of the Death Match* finale in Japan. I just wanted to get through it.

Fortunately, we did much more than that. We had engaged in a better bouts before, and we would engage in better in the future, but this night was special. Too many wrestlers think the secret of a great match is to line up as many great moves as possible, and run them off from A to Z. That may be great for them, but it takes out the factors that make the match turn into magic—emotion and spontaneity. Our title match may have been lacking in choreography, but it was filled with emotion and spontaneity, and as a result, felt magical as it unfolded.

I was "Rock Bottomed" on a table, which was a first, and as a result, was on the defensive as The Rock began kicking my "rooty poo, candy ass" all over the Worcester Centrum. Time and again, the "great one" fired away, but I waited for a mistake, and with my white shirt in tatters, mounted a small offensive. I stunned The Rock with a suplex and then slowly got to my feet. As the Corporate Champion gained his bearings, I took off for the ropes, but was unable to spring off due to the Big Boss Man's interference. I pulled Boss Man up to the ring apron and fired a punch, which set off a chain reaction of Corporation and DX fisticuffs. With the referee's attention on the ringside melee, young Shane, who was still nursing his sore shoulder, slid the championship belt in to The Rock. I turned around, and *WHAM*, The Rock caught me on the head with a shot so hard that you could hear the heavy belt dong off my skull. The referee turned around to see the "great one" going for the cover. In the closest of counts, I kicked out on two and twenty-seven twenty-eighths for a huge "ooh" from the frantic fans.

The Rock was irate, but he readied himself quickly for a second belt shot that would surely allow him to walk out of Worcester still wearing ten pounds of gold. He swung mightily, but just like Casey of Mudville fame, struck out, and I was there to benefit from his mistake. One boot to the stomach and a double arm DDT later, and both of us were lying on the ground in a weakened state. The DX–Corporation battle was really picking up outside, and the referee headed out to restore order. Amazingly, none of the combatants heard the gigantic sound of glass breaking or the thunderous ovation that came with it as Stone Cold made his way to the ring, brandishing a steel chair.

Austin had not been heard from since a December 13 injury, and the absence had served only to make the fans' hearts grow fonder. As The Rock was recovering, Stone Cold slid into the ring and caught the rising champion with a nice chair shot to the top of the People's Skull. *Klong!* The champ wasn't rising anymore. The referee looked up to see me just barely covering The Rock and slid in to make the count that would list my name forever in the annals of sports-entertainment history. One, two, three. The bell rang, and it was one of the sweetest sounds I'd ever heard.

For years, I had never believed this could happen. I had been respected by my peers and even idolized by certain fans, as witnessed by the "Foley Is God" signs that were gracing the Centrum in Worcester. I had shed blood on five different continents and had taken part in what were arguably some of the finest matches ever seen. Still, I had wrestled for fifteen years with the knowledge that I didn't look like a star, let alone a champion. I had learned to accept and even love my role as the lovable loser who somehow never wins the big one, and I can honestly say that before that day of December 29, 1998, I never believed that it would happen. But it had happened, and the reaction was heartwarming.

The Worcester fans were on their feet, and I was on the shoulders of D-Generation X as they paraded me around the ring. Several pictures later showed the members of DX smiling broadly, and I know that the smiles were too bright to not be real. Much like the early Dude, Mankind—or more accurately, Mick Foley—had made the people feel good about themselves. A chant of "Foley, Foley," began, but unlike my traumatic night at *King of the Ring*, these chants were loud and growing louder. I was let down from the shoulders of the DX and grabbed the house mike. I first addressed Vince, who was yelling and fussing his way off stage, although secretly I suspect he was beaming. I then got down on my knees and spoke from my heart.

"At the risk of not sounding cool," I began, "I want to dedicate this belt to my two little people at home, Dewey and Noelle—Daddy-O did it!"

I lost the belt at the *Royal Rumble* in an emotional and brutal bout only twenty-six days later. But if you want to read about that, you can buy The Rock's damn book.

The End

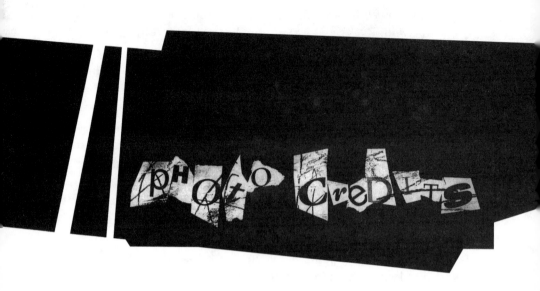

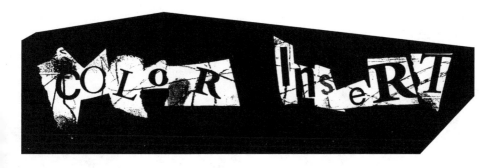

*   *   *   *   *

The ECW Transcripts "August 1995–ECW Television Show Transcript" on page 343, "September 1995–ECW Television Show Interview" on page 346, and "December 1995–ECW TV Show–*A Hardcore Christmas*" on page 378 are furnished courtesy of ECW and are used by permission.

MANKIND

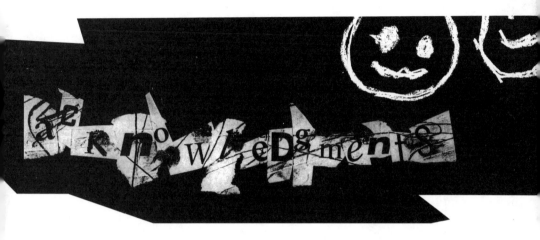

ACKNOWLEDGMENTS

Special thanks to God for all the blessings in my life. Thanks to my wife, Colette, and my kids, Dewey and Noelle, for their love, support, and understanding.

I'd like to acknowledge Jim Bell for trusting me to write the book myself, and Scott Amann, Jim Byrne, Ed Kaufman, Florence Louisgrand, Robert Mayo, Marissa McMahon, Derek Phillips, Jennifer Russell, Stanley Shenker, Phil Speer, Jason Walker, Susan Warner, and Noah Wilker for their invaluable assistance.

Thanks also to Judith Regan for having faith; my publicists, Jennifer Suitor and Paul Olsewski; Robin Arzt, Paul Brown, Dan Cuddy, Claudia Gabel, Cassie Jones, Susan Kosko, and Kyle Kushner for turning 760 pages of handwritten notebook paper into a book; and last but not least, my editor, Jeremie Ruby-Strauss, who can now finally get some sleep.